THE LOEB CLASSICAL LIBRARY

FOUNDED BY JAMES LOEB

EDITED BY

G. P. GOOLD

PREVIOUS EDITORS

T. E. PAGE   E. CAPPS

W. H. D. ROUSE   L. A. POST

E. H. WARMINGTON

JOSEPHUS

III

LCL 210

JOSEPHUS

THE JEWISH WAR

BOOKS IV–VII

WITH AN ENGLISH TRANSLATION BY

H. ST. J. THACKERAY

HARVARD UNIVERSITY PRESS

CAMBRIDGE, MASSACHUSETTS
LONDON, ENGLAND

WINGATE UNIVERSITY LIBRARY

First published 1928
Reprinted 1957, 1961, 1968, 1979, 1990

ISBN 0-674-99232-6

Printed in Great Britain by St Edmundsbury Press Ltd,
Bury St. Edmunds, Suffolk, on wood-free paper.
Bound by Hunter & Foulis Ltd, Edinburgh, Scotland.

CONTENTS

For maps see Volume II of
Josephus: *The Jewish War*, Books I–III

Editorial Note (1979): Readers of this volume should note that the theory of the late Robert Eisler, that the Slavonic version of the *Jewish War* preserves in some places a genuine tradition overlaid in our Greek manuscripts by Christian interpolation, has failed to win any authoritative support. Neverthethe Appendix has been retained for its intrinsic interest. See also the notes and appendix on the *Testimonium Flavianum* in Volume IX (pp. 48 ff. and 573 ff.) of the Loeb Josephus. Comprehensive bibliographies are given in Volumes VI, VII, VIII, and IX, to which may be added R. J. H. Shutt, *Studies in Josephus* (1961).

G. P. G.

THE JEWISH WAR

ΙΣΤΟΡΙΑ ΙΟΥΔΑΪΚΟΥ ΠΟΛΕΜΟΥ ΠΡΟΣ ΡΩΜΑΙΟΥΣ

ΒΙΒΛΙΟΝ Δ΄

1 (i. 1) Ὅσοι δὲ μετὰ τὴν Ἰωταπάτων ἅλωσιν Γαλιλαῖοι Ῥωμαίων ἀφεστήκεσαν, οὗτοι τῶν ἐν Ταριχαίαις ἡττηθέντων προσεχώρουν, καὶ παρέλαβον πάντα Ῥωμαῖοι τὰ φρούρια καὶ τὰς πόλεις πλὴν Γισχάλων καὶ τῶν τὸ Ἰταβύριον ὄρος 2 κατειληφότων. συνέστη δὲ τούτοις καὶ Γάμαλα πόλις Ταριχαιῶν ἄντικρυς ὑπὲρ τὴν λίμνην κειμένη. τῆς δ᾽ Ἀγρίππα λήξεως αὕτη τε ἦν καὶ Σωγάνη καὶ Σελεύκεια, καὶ αἱ μὲν ἐκ τῆς Γαυλανίτιδος ἀμφότεραι· τοῦ γὰρ ἄνω καλουμένου Γαυλανᾶ μέρος ἦν ἡ Σωγάνη, τοῦ κάτω δ᾽ ἡ Γάμαλα· 3 Σελεύκεια δὲ πρὸς τῇ Σεμεχωνιτῶν λίμνῃ. ταύτῃ τριάκοντα μὲν εὖρος, ἑξήκοντα δὲ μῆκος στάδιοι·

ᵃ Usually identified with *Kul̯at el Ḥoṣn*, close to the E. side of the lake, opposite Tiberias ; by others with *Dschamle*, a day's journey E. of the lake, Schürer, *G.J.V.*³ i. 615 f. At the opening of the war it kept its allegiance to Rome, under the influence of Agrippa's officer Philip, *Vita* 46-61 ; afterwards it joined the insurgents.

2

HISTORY OF THE JEWISH WAR
AGAINST THE ROMANS

BOOK IV

(i. 1) SUCH Galilaeans as after the fall of Jotapata Most of still remained in revolt from Rome now, on the reduc- Galilee
surrenders: tion of Tarichaeae, surrendered; and the Romans places still
in revolt. received the submission of all the fortresses and towns except Gischala and the force which had occupied Mount Tabor. Gamala *a* was also in league with these rebels, a city situated on the other side of the lake, opposite Tarichaeae. Gamala formed part of the territory allotted to Agrippa, like Sogane and Seleucia *b*; Gamala and Sogane were both in Gaulanitis, the latter belonging to what is known as Upper, the former to Lower, Gaulan; Seleucia was near the lake Semechonitis.*c* That lake is thirty furlongs in breadth and sixty in length; but its

---

b Sogane (in Gaulan, unidentified; distinct from S. in Galilee) and Seleucia (*Selukiyeh*, N.E. of Bethsaida Julias) are mentioned together in *Vita* 187, *B.* ii. 574, as places fortified by Josephus.

c *Baheiret el Huleh*, the little lake N. of Gennesaret; *B.* iii. 515. Its length as here given (60 " stades "=nearly 7 miles) must include part of the northern marshes; the dimensions on the modern map are 4 miles by 3 (at its broadest part).

διατείνει δ' αὐτῆς τὰ ἕλη μέχρι Δάφνης[1] χωρίου
τά τε ἄλλα τρυφεροῦ καὶ πηγὰς ἔχοντος, αἱ
τρέφουσαι τὸν μικρὸν καλούμενον Ἰόρδανον[2] ὑπὸ
τὸν τῆς χρυσῆς βοὸς νεὼν προπέμπουσι τῷ μεγάλῳ.
4 τοὺς μὲν οὖν ἐπὶ Σωγάνης καὶ Σελευκείας[3] ὑπὸ[4]
τὴν ἀρχὴν τῆς ἀποστάσεως δεξιαῖς Ἀγρίππας
προσηγάγετο, Γάμαλα δ' οὐ προσεχώρει πεποιθυῖα
5 τῇ δυσχωρίᾳ πλέον τῶν Ἰωταπάτων. τραχὺς
γὰρ αὐχὴν ἀφ' ὑψηλοῦ κατατείνων ὄρους μέσον
ἐπαίρει τένοντα, μηκύνεται δ' ἐκ τῆς ὑπεροχῆς
εἰς τοὔμπροσθεν ἐκκλίνων ὅσον κατόπιν, ὡς
εἰκάζεσθαι καμήλῳ τὸ σχῆμα, παρ' ἣν ὠνόμασται,
τὸ τρανὸν τῆς κλήσεως οὐκ ἐξακριβούντων τῶν
6 ἐπιχωρίων. κατὰ πλευρὰ[5] μὲν δὴ καὶ πρόσωπον
εἰς φάραγγας ἀβάτους περισχίζεται, τὸ κατ'
οὐρὰν δ' ὀλίγον ἀναφεύγει τὰς[6] δυσχωρίας, ὅθεν
ἀπήρτηται τοῦ ὄρους· καὶ τοῦτο δ' ἐπικαρσίᾳ
παρακόψαντες τάφρῳ δύσβατον οἱ ἐπιχώριοι κατ-
7 εσκεύασαν. πρὸς ὀρθίῳ δὲ τῇ λαγόνι δεδομη-
μέναι πεπύκνωντο δεινῶς ἐπ' ἀλλήλαις αἱ οἰκίαι,
κρημνιζομένη τε ἡ πόλις ἐοικυῖα κατέτρεχεν εἰς
8 ἑαυτὴν ἀπὸ τῆς ὀξύτητος. καὶ πρὸς μεσημβρίαν
μὲν ἔκλινεν, ὁ νότιος δ' αὐτῆς ὄχθος εἰς ἄπειρον
ὕψος ἀνατείνων ἄκρα τῆς πόλεως ἦν, ἀτείχιστος

---

[1] Δάνης Reland; cf. A. viii. 226.
[2] PA (as in A. vii. 210 +): Ἰορδάνην the rest.
[3] Niese: ἐπὶ Σωγάνην κ. Σελεύκειαν mss.
[4] L: ἐπὶ PA: παρὰ the rest.
[5] A Lat.: πλευρὰν the rest.
[6] Niese: τῆς mss.

---

[a] Probably *Khurbet Dufna*, a little S. of Dan (Laish), the
source of one tributary of the Jordan.

4

marshes extend as far as Daphne,[a] a delightful spot with springs which feed the so-called little Jordan, beneath the temple of the golden cow,[b] and speed it on its way to the greater river.[c] Now Sogane and Seleucia had quite early in the revolt been induced by Agrippa to come to terms; but Gamala refused to surrender, relying even more confidently than Jotapata upon the natural difficulties of its position. From a lofty mountain there descends a rugged spur rising in the middle to a hump, the declivity from the summit of which is of the same length before as behind, so that in form the ridge resembles a camel; whence it derives its name, the natives pronouncing the sharp sound of that word inaccurately.[d] Its sides and face are cleft all round by inaccessible ravines, but at the tail end, where it hangs on to the mountain, it is somewhat easier of approach; but this quarter also the inhabitants, by cutting a trench across it, had rendered difficult of access. The houses were built against the steep mountain flank and astonishingly huddled together, one on top of the other, and this perpendicular site gave the city the appearance of being suspended in air and falling headlong upon itself. It faced south, and its southern eminence, rising to an immense height, formed the citadel;

[b] One of the two golden calves erected by Jeroboam at Dan and Bethel respectively (1 Kings xii. 29, Jos. *A.* viii. 226).

[c] The eastern stream descending from Caesarea Philippi, *Banias.*

[d] *i.e.* they slurred the sharp (lit. "clear") K into Γ, calling it Gamala, not Kamala. The remark is made purely from the *Greek* point of view; "camel" both in Hebrew (*Gāmāl*) and in Aramaic (*Gamlā'*) has initial G.

5

[ὁ][1] δὲ ὑπ᾽[2] αὐτῆς[3] κρημνὸς εἰς τὴν βαθυτάτην κατατείνων φάραγγα· πηγὴ δ᾽ ἐντὸς τοῦ τείχους, ἐφ᾽ ἣν τὸ ἄστυ κατέληγεν.

9 (2) Οὕτως οὖσαν φύσει δυσμήχανον[4] τὴν πόλιν τειχίζων ὁ Ἰώσηπος ἐποίησεν ὀχυρωτέραν ὑπο-
10 νόμοις τε καὶ διώρυξιν. οἱ δ᾽ ἐν αὐτῇ φύσει μὲν τοῦ χωρίου θαρραλεώτεροι τῶν κατὰ τὴν Ἰωτα- πάτην ἦσαν, πολὺ δ᾽ ἐλάττους μάχιμοι, καὶ τῷ τόπῳ πεποιθότες οὐδὲ πλείονας ὑπελάμβανον· πεπλήρωτο γὰρ ἡ πόλις διὰ τὴν ὀχυρότητα συμφυγόντων· παρὸ καὶ τοῖς ὑπ᾽ Ἀγρίππα προ- πεμφθεῖσιν ἐπὶ τὴν πολιορκίαν ἀντεῖχεν ἐπὶ μῆνας ἑπτά.

11 (3) Οὐεσπασιανὸς δ᾽ ἄρας ἀπὸ τῆς Ἀμμαθοῦς, ἔνθα πρὸ τῆς Τιβεριάδος ἐστρατοπεδεύκει· μεθ- ερμηνευομένη δ᾽ Ἀμμαθοῦς θερμὰ λέγοιτ᾽ ἄν, ἔστι γὰρ ἐν αὐτῇ πηγὴ θερμῶν ὑδάτων πρὸς ἄκεσιν ἐπιτηδείων· ἀφικνεῖται πρὸς τὴν Γάμαλαν.
12 καὶ πᾶσαν μὲν κυκλώσασθαι φυλακῇ τὴν πόλιν οὐχ οἷός τε ἦν οὕτως διακειμένην, πρὸς δὲ τοῖς δυνατοῖς φρουροὺς καθίστησι καὶ τὸ ὑπερκείμενον
13 ὄρος καταλαμβάνεται. τειχισαμένων δὲ ὥσπερ ἔθος τῶν ταγμάτων ὑπὲρ αὐτοῦ στρατόπεδα χωμάτων ἤρχετο κατ᾽ οὐράν, καὶ τὸ μὲν κατ᾽ ἀνατολὰς αὐτῷ μέρος, ᾗπερ ὁ ἀνωτάτω τῆς πόλεως πύργος ἦν, ἔχου[5] τὸ πέμπτον καὶ δέκατον τάγμα, τὸ πέμπτον δὲ ⟨τὰ⟩ κατὰ μέσην ἐξειργά-

---

[1] ins. PAL.
[2] Niese: ὑπὲρ mss., περὶ Destinon perhaps rightly (cf. § 74).
[3] αὐτὴν L.
[4] δύσμαχον C and perhaps Lat.
[5] Destinon: ἐφ᾽ οὗ mss. The text of the next line is uncertain : I follow Niese, who inserts the bracketed τὰ.

6

below this an unwalled precipice descended to the deepest of the ravines. There was a spring within the walls at the confines of the town.

(2) This city, which nature had rendered so impregnable, Josephus had fortified with walls [a] and secured still further by mines and trenches. Its occupants felt greater confidence in the nature of their site than did those of Jotapata, though far inferior to them in the number of combatants; indeed such trust had they in their position that they would admit no more. For the city was packed with fugitives owing to the strength of its defences, which had enabled it to hold out for seven months against the force [b] previously sent by Agrippa to besiege it.

(3) Vespasian now broke up the camp which he had pitched in front of Tiberias at Ammathus [c] (this name may be interpreted as " warm baths," being derived from a spring of warm water within the city possessing curative properties) and proceeded to Gamala. Finding the complete investment of a city in such a situation impossible, he posted sentries wherever this was practicable and occupied the mountain that overhung it. The legions having, according to custom, fortified their camps on these heights, Vespasian commenced the erection of earthworks at the tail end; those on the east of the ridge, over against the point where stood the highest tower in the town, were raised by the fifteenth legion, those opposite the centre of the city were undertaken by

Vespasian besieges Gamala.

[a] *B.* ii. 574.
[b] Under Aequus Modius, *Vita* 114.
[c] *Hammam*, between Tiberias (N.) and Taricheae (S.); *cf. B.* iii. 462, and for the warm baths *A.* xviii. 36.

ζετο τὴν πόλιν, τὰς δὲ διώρυγας ἀνεπλήρου καὶ
14 τὰς φάραγγας τὸ δέκατον. κἂν τούτῳ προσελθόντα
τοῖς τείχεσιν Ἀγρίππαν τὸν βασιλέα καὶ περὶ
παραδόσεως τοῖς ἐφεστῶσι πειρώμενον διαλέγεσθαι
βάλλει τις τῶν σφενδονητῶν κατὰ τὸν δεξιὸν
15 ἀγκῶνα λίθῳ. καὶ ὁ μὲν ὑπὸ τῶν οἰκείων θᾶττον
περιεσχέθη, Ῥωμαίους δ' ἐπήγειρεν εἰς τὴν
πολιορκίαν ὀργή τε περὶ τοῦ βασιλέως καὶ περὶ
16 σφῶν αὐτῶν δέος· οὐ γὰρ ἀπολείψειν ὠμότητος
ὑπερβολὴν κατ' ἀλλοφύλων καὶ πολεμίων τοὺς
πρὸς ὁμόφυλον καὶ τῶν συμφερόντων αὐτοῖς
σύμβουλον οὕτως ἀγριωθέντας.
17   (4) Συντελεσθέντων οὖν τῶν χωμάτων θᾶττον
πλήθει χειρῶν καὶ τῶν πραττομένων ἔθει προσῆγον
18 τὰς μηχανάς. οἱ δὲ περὶ τὸν Χάρητα καὶ Ἰώσηπον,[1] οὗτοι γὰρ ἦσαν τῶν κατὰ τὴν πόλιν
δυνατώτατοι, καίπερ καταπεπληγότας τοὺς ὁ-
πλίτας τάττουσιν, ἐπειδὴ μέχρι πολλοῦ πρὸς τὴν
πολιορκίαν ἀνθέξειν οὐχ ὑπελάμβανον, ὕδατι καὶ
19 τοῖς ἄλλοις ἐπιτηδείοις μὴ διαρκούμενοι. παρα-
κροτήσαντες δ' ὅμως ἐξήγαγον ἐπὶ τὸ τεῖχος,
καὶ πρὸς ὀλίγον μὲν ἀπημύναντο τοὺς προσάγοντας
τὰς μηχανάς, βαλλόμενοι δὲ τοῖς καταπελτικοῖς
καὶ τοῖς πετροβόλοις ἀνεχώρουν εἰς τὴν πόλιν.
20 καὶ προσαγαγόντες[2] οἱ Ῥωμαῖοι τριχόθεν τοὺς
κριοὺς διασείουσι μὲν τὸ τεῖχος, ὑπὲρ δὲ τῶν
ἐρειφθέντων εἰσχεόμενοι μετὰ πολλοῦ σαλπίγγων
ἤχου καὶ κτύπου τῶν ὅπλων αὐτοί τ' ἐπαλαλάζοντες
21 συνερρήγνυντο τοῖς κατὰ τὴν πόλιν. οἱ δὲ τέως
μὲν κατὰ τὰς πρώτας εἰσόδους ἐνιστάμενοι
προσωτέρω χωρεῖν ἐκώλυον καὶ καρτερῶς τοὺς

---

[1] Ἰώσην L[1]; cf. § 66.   [2] Μ: προσάγοντες the rest.

the fifth, while the tenth legion was employed in filling up the trenches *a* and ravines. During these operations King Agrippa, who had approached the ramparts and was endeavouring to parley with the defenders about capitulation, was struck on the right elbow with a stone by one of the slingers. He was at once surrounded by his troops, but the Romans were thus stimulated to press the siege alike by resentment on the king's behalf and by concern for themselves, convinced that men who could so savagely attack a fellow-countryman, while advising them for their welfare, would shrink from no excess of cruelty towards aliens and enemies. *Agrippa wounded.*

(4) With such a multitude of hands accustomed to the task, the earthworks were rapidly completed and the engines brought into position. Chares and Joseph, the most prominent leaders in the town, drew up their troops, though the men were dispirited by the thought that they could not long withstand a siege owing to a deficiency of water and other necessaries. Their generals, however, encouraged them and led them out to the ramparts, where for a while they kept at bay those who were bringing up the engines, but the fire of the catapults and stone-projectors drove them back into the town. The Romans then applying the battering-rams at three different quarters broke through the wall, and pouring through the breach with loud trumpet-blasts, clash of arms, and the soldiers' battle-cries, engaged the defenders of the town. The latter, when the first Romans entered, for a time held their ground, arrested their further advance and stubbornly re- *Romans enter Gamala with disastrous results.*

• Previously dug by Josephus, § 9.

22 Ῥωμαίους ἀνεῖργον· βιαζόμενοι δὲ ὑπὸ πολλῶν
καὶ πάντοθεν τρέπονται πρὸς τὰ ὑψηλὰ τῆς
πόλεως καὶ προσκειμένοις τοῖς πολεμίοις ἐξ
ὑποστροφῆς ἐπιπεσόντες συνώθουν εἰς τὸ κάταντες
καὶ τῇ στενότητι καὶ δυσχωρίᾳ θλιβομένους ἀν-
23 ῄρουν. οἱ δὲ μήτε τοὺς κατὰ κορυφὴν ἀμύνασθαι
δυνάμενοι μήτε διεκπαίειν τῶν σφετέρων πρόσω
βιαζομένων ἐπὶ τὰς οἰκίας τῶν πολεμίων, πρόσ-
24 γειοι γὰρ ἦσαν, ἀνέφευγον. αἱ δὲ ταχέως κατηρεί-
ποντο πληρούμεναι καὶ τὸ βάρος μὴ στέγουσαι,
κατέσειε δὲ πολλὰς μία τῶν ὑπ' αὐτῆς[1] πεσοῦσα
25 καὶ πάλιν ἐκεῖναι τὰς ὑπ' αὐτάς. τοῦτο πλείστους
διέφθειρε τῶν Ῥωμαίων· ὑπὸ γὰρ ἀμηχανίας
καίτοι συνιζανούσας ὁρῶντες ἐπεπήδων ταῖς
στέγαις, καὶ πολλοὶ μὲν κατεχώννυντο τοῖς
ἐρειπίοις, πολλοὶ δ' ὑποφεύγοντες μέρη[2] τοῦ
σώματος κατελαμβάνοντο, πλείστους δ' ὁ κονιορτὸς
26 ἄγχων ἀνῄρει. συνεργίαν θεοῦ τοῦτο Γαμαλεῖς
ὑπελάμβανον καὶ τῆς κατὰ σφᾶς ἀμελοῦντες
βλάβης ἐπέκειντο, πρός τε τὰ τέγη τοὺς πολεμίους
ἀνωθοῦντες [καί τοι][3] κατολισθάνοντας ἐν ὀξέσι
τοῖς στενωποῖς καὶ ἀεὶ τοὺς πίπτοντας ὕπερθεν
27 βάλλοντες ἔκτεινον. καὶ τὰ μὲν ἐρείπια χερμάδων
πλέα ἦν[4] αὐτοῖς, σίδηρον δὲ παρεῖχον οἱ τῶν
πολεμίων νεκροί· παρασπῶντες γὰρ τὰ τῶν
πεσόντων ξίφη κατὰ τῶν δυσθανατώντων[5] ἐχρῶντο.
28 πολλοὶ δ' ἀπὸ πιπτόντων ἤδη τῶν δωμάτων σφᾶς

---

[1] V[2]: the other mss. have αὐτήν, αὐτοῖς, or αὐτῶν.
[2] μέρει Dindorf with one ms.
[3] Bracketed by Niese: the text is doubtful and the Lat. suggests that some words have fallen out.
[4] πλέα ἦν] πλῆθος L Lat.
[5] δυσθανατούντων PA.

pulsed them ; then, overpowered by numbers pouring in on all sides, they fled to the upper parts of the town, where, rounding upon the pursuing enemy, they thrust them down the slopes and slew them while impeded by the narrowness and difficulties of the ground. The Romans, unable either to repel the enemy above them or to force their way back through their comrades pressing forward behind, took refuge on the roofs of the enemy's houses, which came close to the ground.[a] These, being crowded with soldiers and unequal to the weight, soon fell in ; one house in its fall brought down several others beneath it and these again carried away those lower down. This disaster was the ruin of multitudes of Romans ; for, having nowhere to turn, although they saw the houses subsiding, they continued to leap on to the roofs. Many were buried by the ruins, many in trying to escape from under them were pinned down by some portion of their persons, and still more died of suffocation from the dust. Seeing in this the interposition of divine providence, the men of Gamala pressed their attack regardless of their own casualties; they forced the enemy, stumbling in the steep alleys, up on to the roofs and with a continual fire from above slew any who fell. The debris supplied them with boulders in abundance and the enemy's dead with blades ; for they wrested the swords from the fallen and used them to dispatch any still struggling in death. Many flung themselves from the houses when in the act of collapsing and died from the fall.

---

[a] The " perpendicular " nature of the site (such as that of Clovelly or Rocca di Papa) has to be remembered, § 7; the roof at the end higher up the slope would be πρόσγειος, while its other end would be well above the ground.

JOSEPHUS

29 αὐτοὺς βάλλοντες ἔθνησκον. ἦν δ᾽ οὐδὲ τραπέντων
ἡ φυγὴ ῥᾴδιος· κατὰ γὰρ ἄγνοιαν τῶν ὁδῶν καὶ
παχύτητα τοῦ κονιορτοῦ μηδὲ ἀλλήλους ἐπι-
γινώσκοντες ἀνειλοῦντο καὶ περὶ σφᾶς ἔπιπτον.
30 (5) Οἱ μὲν οὖν μόλις εὑρίσκοντες τὰς ἐξόδους
31 ἀνεχώρησαν ἐκ τῆς πόλεως· Οὐεσπασιανὸς δ᾽
ἀεὶ προσμένων τοῖς πονουμένοις, δεινὸν γάρ τι
πάθος αὐτὸν εἰσῄει κατερειπομένην ὁρῶντα περὶ
τῷ στρατῷ τὴν πόλιν, ἐν λήθῃ τοῦ καθ᾽ αὑτὸν
ἀσφαλοῦς γενόμενος λανθάνει κατὰ μικρὸν ἀνωτάτω τῆς πόλεως προελθών, ἔνθα μέσοις ἐγκατα-
λείπεται τοῖς κινδύνοις μετ᾽ ὀλίγων παντελῶς·
32 οὐδὲ γὰρ ὁ παῖς αὐτῷ Τίτος τότε συμπαρῆν,
τηνικαῦτα πρὸς Μουκιανὸν εἰς Συρίαν ἀπεσταλ-
33 μένος. τραπῆναι μὲν οὖν οὐκέτ᾽[1] ἀσφαλὲς οὔτε
πρέπον ἡγήσατο, μνησθεὶς δὲ τῶν ἀπὸ νεότητος
αὐτῷ πεπονημένων καὶ τῆς ἰδίας ἀρετῆς, ὥσπερ
ἔνθους γενόμενος, συνασπίζει μὲν τοὺς ἅμ᾽ αὐτῷ
34 τά τε σώματα καὶ τὰς πανοπλίας, ἐνυφίσταται
δὲ κατὰ κορυφὴν ἐπιρρέοντα τὸν πόλεμον καὶ
οὔτε ἀνδρῶν πλῆθος οὔτε βελῶν ὑποπτήξας
ἐπέμενε, μέχρι δαιμόνιον τὸ παράστημα τῆς
ψυχῆς συννοήσαντες οἱ πολέμιοι ταῖς ὁρμαῖς
35 ἐνέδοσαν. ἀτονώτερον δὲ προσκειμένων αὐτὸς
ὑπὸ πόδα ἀνεχώρει, νῶτα μὴ δεικνὺς ἕως ἔξω
36 τοῦ τείχους ἐγένετο. πλεῖστοι μὲν οὖν Ῥωμαίων
κατὰ ταύτην ἔπεσον τὴν μάχην, ἐν οἷς ὁ δεκαδ-
άρχης Αἰβούτιος, ἀνὴρ οὐ μόνον ἐφ᾽ ἧς ἔπεσε
παρατάξεως, ἀλλὰ πανταχοῦ καὶ πρότερον γεν-
ναιότατος φανεὶς καὶ πλεῖστα κακὰ Ἰουδαίους

---

[1] PAL: οὔτε the rest.

12

Even those who fled found flight no easy matter ; since through their ignorance of the roads and the dense clouds of dust they failed to recognize their comrades and in their bewilderment fell foul of each other.

(5) Thus, with difficulty discovering the outlets, these fugitives beat a retreat from the town. Meanwhile Vespasian, always keeping close to his distressed troops, being deeply affected by the sight of the city falling in ruins about his army, had, forgetful of his own safety, gradually and unconsciously advanced to the highest quarters of the town. Here he found himself left in the thick of danger with a mere handful of followers : even his son Titus was not with him on this occasion, having been just sent off to Syria to Mucianus.[a] Thinking it now neither safe nor honourable to turn, and mindful of the hardships which he had borne from his youth and his innate valour, he, like one inspired, linked his comrades together, with shields enveloping both body and armour, and stemmed the tide of war that streamed upon him from above ; and so, undaunted by the multitude either of men or missiles, he stood his ground, until the enemy, impressed by such supernatural intrepidity, relaxed their ardour. Being now less hard pressed, he retreated step by step, not turning his back until he was outside the walls. In this engagement multitudes of Romans fell, including the decurion Aebutius, a man who had shown the utmost gallantry and inflicted the severest losses on the Jews, not only in the action in which he perished,

Vespasian's perilous position.

[a] Governor (*legatus*) of Syria, and subsequently one of the strongest supporters of Vespasian's claims to the empire.

37 ἐργασάμενος. ἑκατοντάρχης δέ τις, Γάλλος ὀνόματι, μετὰ στρατιωτῶν δέκα περισχεθεὶς ἐν τῇ
38 ταραχῇ κατέδυ μὲν εἰς τινος οἰκίαν, τῶν δ᾽ ἐν αὐτῇ
   διαλαλούντων παρὰ δεῖπνον ὅσα κατὰ τῶν Ῥωμαίων ἢ περὶ σφῶν ὁ δῆμος ἐβουλεύετο κατ-
   ακροασάμενος, ἦν δ᾽ αὐτός τε καὶ οἱ σὺν αὐτῷ
   Σύροι, νύκτωρ ἐπανίσταται καὶ πάντας ἀποσφάξας
   μετὰ τῶν στρατιωτῶν εἰς τοὺς Ῥωμαίους διασώζεται.
39 (6) Οὐεσπασιανὸς δ᾽ ἀθυμοῦσαν τὴν στρατιὰν
   ἀγνοίᾳ[1] πταισμάτων καὶ διότι τέως οὐδαμοῦ
   τηλικαύτῃ συμφορᾷ κέχρηντο, τό γε μὴν πλέον
   αἰδουμένους ἐπὶ τῷ τὸν στρατηγὸν μόνον τοῖς
40 κινδύνοις ἐγκαταλιπεῖν, παρεμυθεῖτο, περὶ μὲν
   τοῦ καθ᾽ αὑτὸν ὑποστελλόμενος, ὡς μηδὲ τὴν
   ἀρχὴν μέμφεσθαι δοκοίη, δεῖν δὲ τὰ κοινὰ
   λέγων ἀνδρείως φέρειν, τὴν τοῦ πολέμου φύσιν
   ἐννοοῦντας, ὡς οὐδαμοῦ τὸ νικᾶν ἀναιμωτὶ
   περιγίνεται, παλίμπους δ᾽ ἡ τύχη παρίσταται.[2]
41 τοσαύτας μέντοι μυριάδας Ἰουδαίων ἀνελόντας
   αὐτοὺς ὀλίγην τῷ δαίμονι δεδωκέναι συμβολήν.
42 εἶναι δ᾽ ὥσπερ ἀπειροκάλων τὸ λίαν ἐπαίρεσθαι
   ταῖς εὐπραγίαις, οὕτως ἀνάνδρων τὸ καταπτήσσειν
   ἐν τοῖς πταίσμασιν· 'ὀξεῖα γὰρ ἐν ἀμφοτέροις
   ἡ μεταβολή, κἀκεῖνος ἄριστος ὁ κἂν τοῖς εὐτυχή-
   μασιν νήφων, ἵνα μένῃ καὶ δι᾽ εὐθυμίας ἀνα-

[1] Destinon : ἀνοίᾳ mss. (cf. Vita 167 for similar confusion):
ἐννοίᾳ, "at the thought of," Bos.

[2] παλίμπους κτλ. Niese (and so apparently the first hand
of L): δαπανᾷ δ᾽ ἡ τύχη τι καὶ παρίσταται PAM[1]: ἡ γὰρ
παλίμπους τύχη περιίσταται VRCM[2].

---

[a] Aebutius had skirmishes with Josephus in Galilee early
in the war, Vita 115-120, and as " a man of marked energy

but on all previous occasions.[a] One centurion, named Gallus, being cut off with ten of his men in the fray, crept into a private house, where he—a Syrian like his companions—overheard the inmates discussing at supper the citizens' plans of attack on the Romans and of self-defence ; during the night he arose and fell upon them, slew them all, and with his men made his way safely back to the Roman camp.

(6) Vespasian, seeing his army despondent owing to their ignorance of reverses and because they had nowhere so far met with such a disaster, and still more ashamed of themselves for leaving their general to face danger alone, proceeded to console them. Refraining from any mention of himself, for fear of appearing to cast the slightest reflection upon them, he said that they ought manfully to bear misfortunes which were common to all, reflecting on the nature of war, which never grants a bloodless victory, and how Fortune flits back again to one's side.[b] "After all," he continued, " you have slain myriads of Jews, but yourselves have paid but a trifling contribution to the deity.[c] As it is a mark of vulgarity to be over-elated by success, so is it unmanly to be downcast in adversity ; for the transition from one to the other is rapid, and the best soldier is he who meets good fortune with sobriety, to the end that he may still remain cheerful when

Vespasian
consoles
his troops.

and ability " was selected for special duty at the outset of the siege of Jotapata, *B.* iii. 144.

[b] The rare word παλίμπους ("with returning foot" or " retrograde ") occurs, together with another word, δυσύποιστος, only attested elsewhere in Jos. *A.* xv. 208, in an epigram of Meleager of Gadara (*Anth. Pal.* v. 163), from which Josephus or his συνεργός not improbably borrowed it.

[c] *i.e.* the god of war (or Fortune), who demands blood.

43 παλαίων τὰ σφάλματα. τὰ μέντοι συμβεβηκότα
νῦν οὔτε μαλακισθέντων ἡμῶν[1] οὔτε παρὰ τὴν
τῶν Ἰουδαίων ἀρετὴν γέγονεν, ἀλλὰ κἀκείνοις τοῦ
πλεονεκτῆσαι καὶ τοῦ διαμαρτεῖν ἡμῖν αἴτιον ἡ
44 δυσχωρία. καθ᾽ ἣν ἄν[2] τις ὑμῶν μέμψαιτο τῆς
ὁρμῆς τὸ ἀταμίευτον· ἀναφυγόντων γὰρ ἐπὶ τὰ
ὑψηλὰ τῶν πολεμίων αὐτοὺς ὑποστέλλειν ἐχρῆν,
καὶ μὴ κατὰ κορυφὴν ἱσταμένοις τοῖς κινδύνοις
ἕπεσθαι, κρατοῦντας δὲ τῆς κάτω πόλεως κατ᾽
ὀλίγον προκαλεῖσθαι τοὺς ἀναφεύγοντας εἰς ἀσφαλῆ
καὶ ἑδραίαν μάχην. νυνὶ δὲ ἀκρατῶς ἐπὶ τὴν
45 νίκην ἐπειγόμενοι τῆς ἀσφαλείας ἠμελήσατε. τὸ δ᾽
ἀπερίσκεπτον ἐν πολέμῳ καὶ τῆς ὁρμῆς μανιῶδες
οὐ πρὸς Ῥωμαίων, οἳ πάντα ἐμπειρίᾳ καὶ τάξει
κατορθοῦμεν, ἀλλὰ βαρβαρικόν, καὶ ᾧ μάλιστα
46 Ἰουδαῖοι κρατοῦνται. χρὴ τοίνυν ἐπὶ τὴν αὐτῶν
ἀρετὴν ἀναδραμεῖν καὶ θυμοῦσθαι μᾶλλον ἢ
47 προσαθυμεῖν τῷ παρ᾽ ἀξίαν πταίσματι. τὴν δ᾽
ἀρίστην ἕκαστος ἐκ τῆς ἰδίας χειρὸς ἐπιζητείτω
παραμυθίαν· οὕτω γὰρ τοῖς τε ἀπολωλόσι τι-
48 μωρήσεσθε καὶ τοὺς ἀνελόντας ἀμυνεῖσθε. πειρά-
σομαι δ᾽ ἐγώ, καθάπερ νῦν, ἐπὶ πάσης μάχης
προάγειν τε ὑμῶν εἰς τοὺς πολεμίους καὶ τελευταῖος ἀποχωρεῖν."
49 (7) Ὁ μὲν οὖν τοιαῦτα λέγων τὴν στρατιὰν
ἀνελάμβανεν, τοῖς δὲ Γαμαλεῦσιν πρὸς ὀλίγον
μὲν θαρρῆσαι τῷ κατορθώματι παρέστη παρα-
50 λόγως τε συμβάντι καὶ μεγάλως, λογιζόμενοι δ᾽
ὕστερον ἀφῃρῆσθαι σφᾶς αὐτοὺς καὶ δεξιᾶς
ἐλπίδας, τό τε μὴ δύνασθαι διαφεύγειν ἐννοοῦντες,

[1] L Lat.: ὑμῶν the rest.
[2] L: ἄγαν the rest: γ᾽ ἂν Destinon.

16

contending with reverses. What has now happened, to be sure, is attributable neither to any weakness on our part nor to the valour of the Jews ; the one cause of their superiority and of our failure was the difficulty of the ground. In view of that, fault might be found with your inordinate ardour ; for when the enemy fled to the higher ground, you should have restrained yourselves and not by pursuit exposed yourselves to the perils impending over your heads. Instead, having mastered the lower town, you should gradually have lured the fugitives to a safe combat on firm ground ; whereas, through your intemperate eagerness for victory, you neglected your own safety. But incautiousness in war and mad impetuosity are alien to us Romans, who owe all our success to skill and discipline : they are a barbarian fault and one to which the Jews mainly owe their defeats. It behoves us therefore to fall back upon our native valour and to be moved rather to wrath than to despondency by this unworthy reverse. But the best consolation should be sought by each man in his own right hand : for so you will avenge the dead and punish those who slew them. For my part, it shall be my endeavour, as in this so in every engagement, to face the enemy at your head and to be the last to retire."

(7) By such words as these he reanimated his troops. The people of Gamala, on their side, derived a momentary confidence from their unlooked for and signal success ; but when they subsequently reflected that they had deprived themselves of all hope of terms, and thought of the impossibility of escape (for

17

ἤδη γὰρ ἐπέλιπε τἀπιτήδεια, δεινῶς ἠθύμουν καὶ
51 ταῖς ψυχαῖς ἀναπεπτώκεσαν. οὐ μὴν εἰς τὸ
δυνατὸν ἠμέλουν σωτηρίας, ἀλλὰ καὶ τὰ παρ-
αρρηχθέντα[1] τοῦ τείχους οἱ γενναιότατοι καὶ τὰ
μένοντα περισχόντες ἐφύλασσον οἱ λοιποί. τῶν δὲ
52 Ῥωμαίων ἐπιρρωννύντων[2] τὰ χώματα καὶ πάλιν
πειρωμένων προσβολῆς οἱ πολλοὶ διεδίδρασκον
ἐκ τῆς πόλεως κατά τε δυσβάτων φαράγγων,
ᾗπερ οὐκ ἔκειντο φυλακαί, καὶ διὰ τῶν ὑπονόμων.
53 ὅσοι γε μὴν δέει τοῦ ληφθῆναι παρέμενον, [ἐν]
ἐνδείᾳ διεφθείροντο· πανταχόθεν γὰρ τροφὴ τοῖς
μάχεσθαι δυναμένοις συνηθροίζετο.
54   (8) Καὶ οἱ μὲν ἐν τοιούτοις πάθεσι διεκαρτέρουν,
Οὐεσπασιανὸς δὲ πάρεργον ἐποιεῖτο τῆς πολιορκίας
τοὺς τὸ Ἰταβύριον κατειληφότας ὄρος, ὅ ἐστι
55 τοῦ μεγάλου πεδίου καὶ Σκυθοπόλεως μέσον· οὗ
τὸ μὲν ὕψος ἐπὶ τριάκοντα σταδίους ἀνίσχει,
μόλις προσβατὸν κατὰ τὸ προσάρκτιον κλίμα,
πεδίον δ᾽ ἐστὶν ἡ κορυφὴ σταδίων ἓξ καὶ εἴκοσι,
56 πᾶν τετειχισμένον. ἤγειρε δὲ τοσοῦτον ὄντα τὸν
περίβολον ὁ Ἰώσηπος ἐν τεσσαράκοντα ἡμέραις
τῇ τε ἄλλῃ χορηγούμενος ὕλῃ κάτωθεν καὶ
ὕδατι· καὶ γὰρ τοῖς ἐποίκοις μόνον ἦν ὄμβριον.
57 πολλοῦ οὖν πλήθους ἐπὶ τούτου συνειλεγμένου[3]

---

[1] Herwerden: περιρρηχθέντα mss.
[2] ἐπιχωννύντων MVRC.
[3] πολλῆς οὖν πληθύος ἐπὶ τοῦ τόπου συνειλεγμένης Niese,
avoiding the double hiatus.

---

[a] § 9.
[b] If " the Great Plain " means here, as usual, the plain of
Esdraelon, the description above is inaccurate, as Mt. Tabor
lies well to the N. of a line drawn through that plain, and its

their supplies had already failed them), they became
sorely dejected and lost heart. Nevertheless, they
did not neglect to take what precautions they could
to protect themselves : the bravest guarded the
breaches, the rest manned what still remained of the
wall. But when the Romans proceeded to strengthen
their earthworks and to attempt a fresh assault, the
people began to run from the town, down trackless
ravines, where no sentries were posted, or through
the underground passages [a] ; while all who stayed
behind from fear of being caught were perishing
from hunger, as every quarter had been ransacked
for provisions for those capable of bearing arms.

(8) While the people of Gamala under such straits
were still holding out, Vespasian undertook, as a
minor diversion from the siege, the reduction of the
occupants of Mount Tabor. This lies midway between the Great Plain and Scythopolis,[b] and rises to
a height of thirty furlongs,[c] being almost inaccessible
on its northern face ; the summit is a table-land
twenty-six furlongs [c] long, entirely surrounded by a
wall. This extensive rampart was erected in forty
days by Josephus,[d] who was supplied from below
with all materials, including water, the inhabitants
depending solely on rain. To this spot, on which a
vast multitude had assembled, Vespasian dispatched

Diversion
against
Mt. Tabor;
success of
Placidus.

continuation, the valley of Jezreel, to Scythopolis. If the
plain of Asochis (described as " the great plain in which my
quarters lay " in *Vita* 207) is meant, the description is
approximately correct.

  [c] These figures are absurdly inaccurate ; the summit is
only 1843 feet above the Plain of Esdraelon (1312 ft. from
the base), the platform on the summit is 3000 ft. long and
1300 ft. at its greatest breadth (*Encycl. Bibl. s.v.*).

  [d] Tabor is mentioned in a list of places fortified by him in
Vita 188.

JOSEPHUS

Οὐεσπασιανὸς Πλάκιδον σὺν ἱππεῦσιν ἑξακοσίοις
58 πέμπει. τούτῳ τὸ μὲν προσβαίνειν ἀμήχανον ἦν,
ἐλπίδι δὲ δεξιῶν καὶ παρακλήσει¹ πρὸς εἰρήνην
59 τοὺς πολλοὺς προεκαλεῖτο.² κατῄεσαν δὲ ἀντ-
επιβουλεύοντες· ὅ τε γὰρ Πλάκιδος ὡμίλει πρᾳό-
τερον σπουδάζων αὐτοὺς ἐν τῷ πεδίῳ λαβεῖν,
κἀκεῖνοι κατῄεσαν ὡς πειθόμενοι δῆθεν, ἵν'
60 ἀφυλάκτῳ προσπέσωσιν. ἐνίκα μέντοι τὸ Πλα-
κίδου πανοῦργον· ἀρξαμένων γὰρ τῶν Ἰουδαίων
μάχης φυγὴν ὑποκρίνεται καὶ διώκοντας ἑλκύσας
ἐπὶ πολὺ τοῦ πεδίου τοὺς ἱππεῖς ἐπιστρέφει,
τρεψάμενος δὲ πλείστους μὲν αὐτῶν ἀναιρεῖ,
τὸ δὲ λοιπὸν πλῆθος ὑποτεμόμενος εἴργει τῆς
61 ἀνόδου. καὶ οἱ μὲν τὸ Ἰταβύριον καταλιπόντες
ἐπὶ Ἱεροσολύμων ἔφευγον, οἱ δ' ἐπιχώριοι πίστεις
λαβόντες, ἐπιλελοίπει δ' αὐτοὺς ὕδωρ, τό τε ὄρος
καὶ σφᾶς αὐτοὺς Πλακίδῳ παρέδοσαν.
62 (9) Τῶν δ' ἐπὶ τῆς Γαμάλας οἱ παραβολώτεροι
μὲν φεύγοντες διελάνθανον, οἱ δ' ἀσθενεῖς διεφθεί-
63 ροντο λιμῷ· τὸ μάχιμον δ' ἀντεῖχεν τῇ πολιορκίᾳ,
μέχρι δευτέρᾳ καὶ εἰκάδι μηνὸς Ὑπερβερεταίου
τρεῖς τῶν ἀπὸ τοῦ πέμπτου καὶ δεκάτου τάγματος
στρατιῶται περὶ τὴν ἑωθινὴν φυλακὴν ὑπο-
δύντες τὸν προύχοντα κατὰ τούτους πύργον ὑπ-
64 ορύσσουσιν ἡσυχῇ. τοῖς δ' ὑπὲρ αὐτοῦ φύλαξιν
οὔτε προσιόντων αἴσθησις, νὺξ γὰρ ἦν, οὔτε προσ-
ελθόντων ἐγένετο. οἱ δὲ στρατιῶται φειδόμενοι

¹ L: παρακλήσεως the rest.
² Destinon: προσεκαλεῖτο mss.

ᵃ The tribune who had seen service in Galilee before
Vespasian's arrival (*Vita* 213) and after (*ib.* 411, *B.* iii. 59,
20

Placidus *a* with six hundred horse. That officer, finding the ascent of the mountain impracticable, made peaceable overtures to the crowd, holding out hopes of terms and exhorting them to avail themselves of the offer. They descended accordingly, but with counter-designs of their own; for while the object of Placidus with his mild address was to capture them in the plain, they came down ostensibly in compliance with his proposal, but with the real intention of attacking him while off his guard. The craft of Placidus, however, won the day; for when the Jews opened hostilities he feigned flight and, having drawn his pursuers far into the plain, suddenly wheeled his cavalry round and routed them. Masses of them were slain; the remainder he intercepted and prevented from reascending the mountain. These fugitives abandoning Mount Tabor made off to Jerusalem; the natives, under promise of protection, and pressed by the failure of their water-supply, surrendered the mountain and themselves to Placidus.

(9) At Gamala, while the more adventurous were stealthily escaping and the feebler folk dying of famine,[b] the effective combatants continued to sustain the siege until the twenty-second of the month Hyperberetaeus, when three soldiers of the fifteenth legion, about the time of the morning watch, crept up to the base of a projecting tower opposite to them and began secretly undermining it; the sentries on guard above failing, in the darkness, to detect them either when approaching or after they had reached it. These soldiers, with as little noise as

Overthrow of a tower at Gamala

c. 9 November A.D. 67

110, etc.), and who subsequently subdued Peraea (*B.* iv. 419 ff.).

[b] Resuming and partly repeating the narrative in §§ 52 f.

τοῦ ψόφου [καὶ] πέντε τοὺς κραταιοτάτους ἐκ-
65 κυλίσαντες λίθους ὑποπηδῶσι. κατερείπεται[1] δ'
ὁ πύργος ἐξαίφνης μετὰ μεγίστου ψόφου, καὶ
συγκατακρημνίζονται μὲν οἱ φύλακες αὐτῷ, θορυ-
βηθέντες δὲ οἱ κατὰ τὰς ἄλλας φυλακὰς ἔφευγον·
66 καὶ πολλοὺς διεκπαίειν τολμῶντας οἱ Ῥωμαῖοι
διέφθειραν, ἐν οἷς καὶ Ἰώσηπόν[2] τις ὑπὲρ τὸ
παρερρηγμένον τοῦ τείχους ἐκδιδράσκοντα βαλὼν
67 ἀναιρεῖ. τῶν δ' ἀνὰ τὴν πόλιν διασεισθέντων
ὑπὸ τοῦ ψόφου διαδρομή τε ἦν καὶ πτόα πολλή,
καθάπερ εἰσπεπαικότων πάντων τῶν πολεμίων.
68 ἔνθα καὶ Χάρης κατακείμενος καὶ νοσηλευόμενος
ἐκλείπει, πολλὰ τοῦ[3] δέους συνεργήσαντος εἰς
69 θάνατον τῇ νόσῳ. Ῥωμαῖοί γε μὴν μεμνημένοι
τοῦ προτέρου πταίσματος οὐκ εἰσέβαλλον ἕως
70 τρίτῃ καὶ εἰκάδι τοῦ προειρημένου μηνὸς (10)
Τίτος,[4] ἤδη γὰρ παρῆν, ὀργῇ τῆς πληγῆς ἦν
παρ' αὐτὸν ἐπλήγησαν ἀπόντα Ῥωμαῖοι, τῶν
ἱππέων ἐπιλέξας διακοσίους, πρὸς οἷς πεζούς,[5] εἰσ-
71 έρχεται τὴν πόλιν ἡσυχῆ. καὶ παρελθόντος οἱ
μὲν φύλακες αἰσθόμενοι μετὰ βοῆς ἐχώρουν ἐπὶ
τὰ ὅπλα, δήλης δὲ τῆς εἰσβολῆς ταχέως καὶ τοῖς
εἴσω γενομένης, οἱ μὲν ἁρπάζοντες τὰ τέκνα καὶ
γυναῖκας ἐπισυρόμενοι πρὸς τὴν ἄκραν ἀνέφευγον
μετὰ κωκυτοῦ καὶ βοῆς, οἱ δὲ τὸν Τίτον ὑπ-
72 αντιάζοντες ἀδιαλείπτως ἔπιπτον· ὅσοι δὲ ἀπ-
εκωλύθησαν ἐπὶ τὴν κορυφὴν ἀναδραμεῖν ὑπ'
ἀμηχανίας εἰς τὰς τῶν Ῥωμαίων φρουρὰς ἐξ-
έπιπτον. ἄπειρος δ' ἦν πανταχοῦ φονευομένων ὁ

---

[1] Niese: κατηρείπετο or καταρρίπτεται mss.
[2] Ἰώσην L[1] Lat.; cf. § 18.
[3] πολλὰ τοῦ Niese: πολλοῦ mss.

possible, succeeded in rolling away the five chief stones and then leapt back ; whereupon the tower suddenly collapsed with a tremendous crash, carrying the sentries headlong with it. The guards at the other posts fled in alarm ; many who essayed to cut their way out were killed by the Romans, and among them Joseph, who was struck dead while making his escape across the breach. The people throughout the town, confounded by the crash, ran hither and thither in great trepidation, believing that the whole of the enemy had burst in. At that same moment Chares, who was bedridden and in the hands of physicians, expired, terror largely contributing to the fatal termination of his illness. The Romans, however, with the memory of their former disaster, deferred their entry until the twenty-third of the month.

(10) On that day Titus, who had now returned,[a] indignant at the reverse which the Romans had sustained in his absence, selected two hundred cavalry and a body of infantry, and quietly entered the town. The guards, apprised of his entry, flew with shouts to arms. News of the incursion rapidly spreading to the interior of the town, some, snatching up their children and dragging their wives after them, fled with their wailing and weeping families up to the citadel ; those who faced Titus were incessantly dropping ; while any who were debarred from escape to the heights fell in their bewilderment into the hands of the Roman sentries. On all sides was heard the never ending moan of the dying, and

leads to the capture of the town.

---

[a] From his visit to Mucianus in Syria, § 32.

4 + δὲ mss. : omit Destinon and Niese (ed. min.).
5 A numeral has perhaps dropped out.

στόνος, καὶ τὸ αἷμα πᾶσαν ἐπέκλυζε τὴν πόλιν
73 κατὰ πρανοῦς χεόμενον. πρὸς δὲ τοὺς ἀναφεύγοντας εἰς τὴν ἄκραν ἐπεβοήθει Οὐεσπασιανὸς
74 πᾶσαν εἰσαγαγὼν τὴν δύναμιν. ἦν δ' ἥ τε κορυφὴ
πάντοθεν πετρώδης καὶ δύσβατος, εἰς ἄπειρον
ὕψος ἐπηρμένη, καὶ πανταχόθεν τοῦ † βάθους[1]
κατέγεμεν περιειλημμένη κρημνοῖς [κατέτεμνόν
75 τε]. ἐνταῦθα τοὺς προσβαίνοντας οἱ Ἰουδαῖοι
τοῖς τε ἄλλοις βέλεσι καὶ πέτρας κατακυλινδοῦντες
ἐκάκουν· αὐτοὶ δὲ δι' ὕψος ἦσαν δυσέφικτοι βέλει.
76 γίνεται δὲ πρὸς ἀπώλειαν αὐτῶν ἄντικρυς θύελλα
δαιμόνιος, ἣ τὰ μὲν Ῥωμαίων ἔφερεν εἰς αὐτοὺς
βέλη, τὰ δ' αὐτῶν ἀνέστρεφεν καὶ πλάγια παρ-
77 έσυρεν. οὔτε δὲ τοῖς ὑποκρήμνοις ἐφίστασθαι διὰ
τὴν βίαν ἐδύναντο τοῦ πνεύματος, μηδὲν ἑδραῖον
78 ἔχοντες, οὔτε τοὺς προσβαίνοντας καθορᾶν. ἐπανα-
βαίνουσι δὲ Ῥωμαῖοι, καὶ περισχόντες οὓς μὲν
ἀμυνομένους ἔφθανον, οὓς δὲ χεῖρας προΐσχοντας·
ἐτόνου δὲ τὸν θυμὸν αὐτοῖς ἐπὶ πάντας ἡ μνήμη
τῶν ἐπὶ τῆς πρώτης εἰσβολῆς ἀπολωλότων.
79 ἀπογινώσκοντες δὲ τὴν σωτηρίαν πανταχόθεν οἱ
πολλοὶ περισχόμενοι τέκνα καὶ γυναῖκας αὐτούς
τε κατεκρήμνιζον εἰς τὴν φάραγγα· βαθυτάτη δ'
80 αὕτη κατὰ τὴν ἄκραν ὑπώρυκτο. συνέβη δὲ τὴν
Ῥωμαίων ὀργὴν τῆς εἰς ἑαυτοὺς ἀπονοίας τῶν
ἁλόντων πραοτέραν φανῆναι· τετρακισχίλιοι μέν γε
ὑπὸ τούτων ἐσφάγησαν, οἱ δὲ ῥίψαντες ἑαυτοὺς
81 ὑπὲρ πεντακισχιλίους εὑρέθησαν. διεσώθη δὲ πλὴν
δύο γυναικῶν οὐδείς· τῆς Φιλίππου δ' ἦσαν

---

[1] πλήθους LP²M², "crowded with people": text doubtful:
? read πάθους, "fraught with tragedy." The words in
brackets appear to be a doublet of κατέγεμεν.

24

the whole city was deluged with blood pouring down
the slopes. To aid the attack on the fugitives in
the citadel Vespasian now brought up his entire
force. The summit, all rock-strewn, difficult of access,
towering to an immense height, and surrounded with
precipices, everywhere yawned to depths below.[a]
Here the Jews worked havoc among the advancing
enemy with missiles of all kinds and rocks which
they rolled down upon them, being themselves from
their elevated position no easy mark for an arrow.
However, to seal their ruin, a storm miraculously
arose which, blowing full in their faces, carried
against them the arrows of the Romans and checked
and deflected their own. Owing to the force of the
gale they could neither stand on the edge of the
precipices, having no firm foothold, nor see the
approaching enemy. The Romans mounted the crest
and quickly surrounded and slew them, some offering
resistance, others holding out their hands for quarter ;
but the recollection of those who fell in the first
assault whetted their fury against all. Despairing
of their lives and hemmed in on every side, multitudes plunged headlong with their wives and children
into the ravine which had been excavated [b] to a vast
depth beneath the citadel. Indeed, the rage of the
Romans was thus made to appear milder than the
frantic self-immolation of the vanquished, four thousand only being slain by the former, while those who
flung themselves over the cliff were found to exceed
five thousand. Not a soul escaped save two women ;

---

[a] Literally " was full of depth " : see critical note.
[b] See § 9.

ἀδελφῆς θυγατέρες αὗται, αὐτὸς δ᾽ ὁ Φίλιππος
᾽Ιακίμου τινὸς ἀνδρὸς ἐπισήμου, στραταρχήσαντος[1]
82 ᾽Αγρίππᾳ τῷ βασιλεῖ. διεσώθησαν δὲ τὰς παρὰ
τὴν ἅλωσιν ὀργὰς ῾Ρωμαίων λαθοῦσαι· τότε γὰρ
οὐδὲ νηπίων ἐφείδοντο, πολλὰ δ᾽ ἑκάστοτε ἁρπά-
83 ζοντες ἐσφενδόνων ἀπὸ τῆς ἄκρας. Γάμαλα μὲν
[οὖν][2] οὕτως ἑάλω τρίτῃ καὶ εἰκάδι μηνὸς ῾Υπερ-
βερεταίου, τῆς ἀποστάσεως ἀρξαμένης Γορπιαίου
μηνὸς τετάρτῃ καὶ εἰκάδι.

84 (ii. 1) Μόνη δὲ Γίσχαλα πολίχνη τῆς Γαλιλαίας
ἀχείρωτος κατελείπετο, τοῦ μὲν πλήθους εἰρηνικὰ
φρονοῦντος, καὶ γὰρ ἦσαν τὸ πλέον γεωργοὶ καὶ
ταῖς ἀπὸ τῶν καρπῶν ἐλπίσιν ἀεὶ προσανέχοντες,
παρεισεφθαρμένου δ᾽ αὐτοῖς οὐκ ὀλίγου λῃστρικοῦ
τάγματος, ᾧ τινες καὶ τοῦ πολιτικοῦ συνενόσουν.
85 ἐνῆγε δὲ τούτους εἰς τὴν ἀπόστασιν καὶ συν-
εκρότει Λήΐου τινὸς υἱὸς ᾽Ιωάννης, γόης ἀνὴρ καὶ
ποικιλώτατος τὸ ἦθος, πρόχειρος μὲν ἐλπίσαι
μεγάλα, δεινὸς δὲ τῶν ἐλπισθέντων περιγενέσθαι,
παντί τε ὢν δῆλος ἀγαπᾶν τὸν πόλεμον εἰς
86 δυναστείας ἐπίθεσιν. ὑπὸ τούτῳ τὸ στασιῶδες
ἐν τοῖς Γισχάλοις ἐτέτακτο, δι᾽ οὓς τάχ᾽ ἂν[3] καὶ
πρεσβευσάμενον περὶ παραδόσεως τὸ δημοτικὸν
ἐν πολεμίου[4] μοίρᾳ τὴν ῾Ρωμαίων ἔφοδον ἐξεδέχετο.
87 Οὐεσπασιανὸς δὲ ἐπὶ μὲν τούτους Τίτον ἐκπέμπει

---

[1] τετραρχήσαντος PAL Lat.
[2] om. PA Lat.
[3] τάχα ἂν L: τυχὸν the rest.
[4] conj.: πολέμου mss. For the phrase ἐν πολεμίου μοίρᾳ
cf. Demosthenes 639.

---

^a *Vita* 46, etc., *B.* ii. 421, 556, with note a on § 2 above.
^b *El-Jish*, in the north of Galilee.

these were nieces, on the mother's side, of Philip,
son of Jacimus, a distinguished man who had been
commander-in-chief to King Agrippa.[a] They owed
their escape to their having concealed themselves at
the time of the capture of the town ; for at that
moment the rage of the Romans was such that they
spared not even infants, but time after time snatched
up numbers of them and slung them from the citadel.
Thus on the twenty-third of the month Hyperbere- *c. 10 Nov.*
taeus was Gamala taken, after a revolt which began
on the twenty-fourth of Gorpiaeus. *c. 12 Oct.*

(ii. 1) Only Gischala,[b] a small town in Galilee, GISCHALA
now remained unsubdued. The inhabitants were incited to
revolt by
inclined to peace, being mainly agricultural labourers, John.
whose whole attention was devoted to the prospects
of the crops ; but they had been afflicted by the
invasion of a numerous gang of brigands, from whom
some members of the community had caught the
contagion. These had been incited to rebel and
organized for the purpose by John, son of Levi, a
charlatan of an extremely subtle character, always
ready to indulge great expectations and an adept in
realizing them ; all knew that he had set his heart
on war in order to attain supreme power.[c] Under
him the malcontents of Gischala had ranged themselves and it was through their influence that the
townsfolk, who would otherwise probably have sent
deputies offering to surrender, now awaited the
Roman onset in an attitude of defiance. To meet Titus, sent
these rebels Vespasian dispatched Titus with a against
Gischala,

---

[a] *Cf.* the character sketch of John in ii. 585 ff., with the
parallel there quoted from Sallust's description of Catiline ;
here ποικιλώτατος recalls " varius " of Sallust, and with the
last clause *cf.* " hunc . . . lubido maxuma invaserat rei
publicae capiundae " (*De Cat. conj.* 5).

σὺν χιλίοις ἱππεῦσιν, τὸ δέκατον δὲ τάγμα ἀπαίρει
88 εἰς Σκυθόπολιν. αὐτὸς δὲ σὺν δυσὶ τοῖς λοιποῖς
ἐπανῆλθεν εἰς Καισάρειαν, τοῦ τε συνεχοῦς καμάτου
διδοὺς ἀνάπαυσιν αὐτοῖς καὶ δι᾽ εὐθηνίαν τῶν
πόλεων τά τε σώματα καὶ τὸ πρόθυμον ὑποθρέψειν
89 οἰόμενος ἐπὶ τοὺς μέλλοντας ἀγῶνας· οὐ γὰρ ὀλίγον αὐτῷ πόνον ἑώρα περὶ τοῖς Ἱεροσολύμοις
λειπόμενον, ἅτε δὴ βασιλείου μὲν οὔσης τῆς
πόλεως καὶ προανεχούσης ὅλου τοῦ ἔθνους, συρ-
ρεόντων δὲ εἰς αὐτὴν τῶν ἐκ τοῦ πολέμου δια-
90 διδρασκόντων. τό γε μὴν φύσει <τε>[1] ὀχυρὸν
αὐτῆς καὶ διὰ κατασκευὴν τειχῶν ἀγωνίαν οὐ
τὴν τυχοῦσαν ἐνεποίει· τὰ δὲ φρονήματα τῶν
ἀνδρῶν καὶ τὰς τόλμας δυσμεταχειρίστους καὶ
91 δίχα τειχῶν ὑπελάμβανεν. διὸ δὴ τοὺς στρατιώτας καθάπερ ἀθλητὰς προήσκει τῶν ἀγώνων.
92 (2) Τίτῳ δὲ προσιππασαμένῳ τοῖς Γισχάλοις
εὐπετὲς μὲν ἦν ἐξ ἐφόδου τὴν πόλιν ἑλεῖν, εἰδὼς
δέ, εἰ βίᾳ ληφθείη, διαφθαρησόμενον ὑπὸ τῶν
στρατιωτῶν ἀνέδην τὸ πλῆθος, ἦν δ᾽ αὐτῷ κόρος
ἤδη φόνων καὶ δι᾽ οἴκτου τὸ πλέον ἀκρίτως
συναπολλύμενον τοῖς αἰτίοις,[2] ἐβούλετο μᾶλλον
93 ὁμολογίαις παραστήσασθαι τὴν πόλιν. καὶ δὴ τοῦ
τείχους ἀνδρῶν καταγέμοντος, οἳ τὸ πλέον ἦσαν
ἐκ τοῦ διεφθαρμένου τάγματος, θαυμάζειν ἔφη
πρὸς αὐτούς, τίνι πεποιθότες πάσης ἑαλωκυίας
πόλεως μόνοι τὰ Ῥωμαίων ὅπλα μένουσιν,
94 ἑωρακότες μὲν ὀχυρωτέρας πολλῷ πόλεις ὑπὸ
μίαν προσβολὴν κατεστραμμένας, ἐν ἀσφαλείᾳ δὲ
τῶν ἰδίων κτημάτων ἀπολαύοντας ὅσοι ταῖς
Ῥωμαίων δεξιαῖς ἐπίστευσαν, ἃς καὶ νῦν προ-

[1] ins. Bekker.   [2] + τὸ μὴ αἴτιον M.

thousand horse ; the tenth legion he dismissed to
Scythopolis. He himself with the two remaining
legions returned to Caesarea, to recruit them after
their incessant toil, and with the idea that the
abundance of city life would invigorate their bodies
and impart fresh alacrity for coming struggles. For
he foresaw that no light toil was in store for him
under the walls of Jerusalem, seeing that it was
not only the royal city and the capital of the whole
nation, but the rendezvous to which all fugitives had
flocked from the seat of war. The strength of its
defences, both natural and artificial, caused him
serious solicitude ; and he conjectured that the spirit
and daring of its defenders would, even without
walls, render their reduction a difficult task. He
accordingly trained his soldiers, like athletes, for the
fray.

(2) Titus, on riding up to Gischala, saw that the urges the inhabitants to surrender.
town might easily be carried by assault. But he
knew that were it taken by storm a general massacre
of the population by his troops would ensue ; he was
already satiated with slaughter and pitied the masses
doomed along with the guilty to indiscriminate
destruction ; he therefore preferred to induce the
town to capitulate. Finding the ramparts crowded
with men, mainly of the corrupted gang, he told
them that he wondered on what they were relying
that, when every other city had fallen, they alone
stood out to face the Roman arms. They had seen
cities far stronger than their own overthrown at the
first assault, but beheld in the secure enjoyment of
their possessions all who had trusted the pledges
proffered by Roman hands—hands which he now

τείνειν αὐτοῖς μηδὲν μνησικακῶν τῆς αὐθαδείας.
95 εἶναι γὰρ συγγνωστὸν ἐλευθερίας ἐλπίδα, μηκέτι
96 μέντοι τὴν ἐν τοῖς ἀδυνάτοις ἐπιμονήν· εἰ γὰρ οὐ
πεισθήσονται λόγοις φιλανθρώποις καὶ δεξιαῖς
πίστεως, πειράσειν αὐτοὺς ἀφειδῆ τὰ ὅπλα, καὶ
ὅσον οὐδέπω γνώσεσθαι[1] παιζόμενον[2] τοῖς Ῥωμαίων μηχανήμασιν τὸ τεῖχος, ᾧ πεποιθότες
ἐπιδείκνυνται μόνοι Γαλιλαίων, ὅτι εἰσὶν αὐθάδεις
αἰχμάλωτοι.
97 (3) Πρὸς ταῦτα τῶν μὲν δημοτικῶν οὐ μόνον
οὐκ ἀποκρίνεσθαί τινι μετῆν, ἀλλ' οὐδ' ἐπὶ τὸ
τεῖχος ἀναβῆναι· προδιείληπτο γὰρ ἅπαν τοῖς
λῃστρικοῖς, καὶ φύλακες τῶν πυλῶν ἦσαν, ὡς μή
τινες ἢ προέλθοιεν ἐπὶ τὰς σπονδὰς ἢ δέξαιντό
98 τινας τῶν ἱππέων εἰς τὴν πόλιν. ὁ δ' Ἰωάννης
αὐτός τε ἀγαπᾶν ἔφη τὰς προκλήσεις καὶ τοὺς
99 ἀπιστοῦντας[3] ἢ πείσειν ἢ συναναγκάσειν· δεῖν
μέντοι τὴν ἡμέραν αὐτὸν ἐκείνην, ἑβδομὰς γὰρ
ἦν, χαρίσασθαι τῷ[4] Ἰουδαίων νόμῳ, καθ' ἣν
ὥσπερ ὅπλα κινεῖν αὐτοῖς, οὕτω καὶ τὸ συν-
100 τίθεσθαι περὶ εἰρήνης ἀθέμιτον. οὐκ ἀγνοεῖν δὲ
οὐδὲ Ῥωμαίους, ὡς ἀργὴ πάντων αὐτοῖς ἐστιν
ἡ τῆς ἑβδομάδος περίοδος, ἔν τε τῷ παραβαίνειν
αὐτὴν οὐχ ἧττον ἀσεβεῖν τῶν βιασθέντων τὸν
101 βιασάμενον. φέρειν δ' ἐκείνῳ μὲν οὐδεμίαν βλάβην
τὰ τῆς ὑπερθέσεως, τί γὰρ ἄν τις ἐν νυκτὶ βου-
λεύσαιτο δρασμοῦ πλέον, ἐξὸν περιστρατοπεδεύ-
102 σαντα παραφυλάξαι; μέγα δὲ κέρδος αὐτοῖς τὸ

---

[1] AM : γνωσθήσεσθαι the rest.
[2] L[1], cf. Lat. ludum fore : πιεζόμενον the rest.
[3] ἀπειθοῦντας P.
[4] + τῶν L.

extended to them without a thought of vindictiveness for their obstinacy. If hopes of liberty were pardonable, there was no excuse for holding out under impossible conditions. For, should they decline his humane proposals and pledges of good faith, they would experience the relentlessness of his arms and learn all too soon that their walls were a mere plaything for the Roman engines—those walls on the strength of which they alone of the Galilaeans were displaying the obstinacy of prisoners.

(3) To this speech not one of the townsfolk had an opportunity of replying, not being allowed even to mount the wall; for it had all been already occupied by the brigands, while sentries had been posted at the gates to prevent either the exit of any anxious to make terms or the admission of any of the cavalry into the town. It was John who replied, saying that for his part he acquiesced in the proposals and would either persuade or coerce refractory opponents. Titus must, however (he said), in deference to the Jewish law, allow them that day, being the seventh, on which they were forbidden alike to have resort to arms and to conclude a treaty of peace. Even the Romans must be aware that the recurrence of the seventh day brought them repose from all labour; and one who compelled them to transgress that law was no less impious than those who so acted under compulsion. To Titus the delay could cause no injury; for what plot could be laid in a single night, except for flight, and that he could guard against by camping round the city? To

John of Gischala imposes upon Titus.

31

μηδὲν παραβῆναι τῶν πατρίων ἐθῶν. πρέπει[1]
δὲ τῷ παρὰ προσδοκίαν εἰρήνην χαριζομένῳ τοῖς
103 σωζομένοις τηρεῖν καὶ τοὺς νόμους. τοιούτοις
ἐσοφίζετο τὸν Τίτον, οὐ τοσοῦτον τῆς ἑβδομάδος
στοχαζόμενος, ὅσον τῆς ἑαυτοῦ σωτηρίας· ἐδε-
δοίκει δὲ ἐγκαταληφθῆναι[2] παραχρῆμα τῆς πόλεως
ἁλούσης, ἐν νυκτὶ καὶ φυγῇ τὰς ἐλπίδας ἔχων τοῦ
104 βίου. θεοῦ δ᾽ ἦν ἔργον ἄρα τοῦ σώζοντος τὸν
Ἰωάννην ἐπὶ τὸν τῶν Ἱεροσολυμιτῶν[3] ὄλεθροι
τὸ μὴ μόνον πεισθῆναι Τίτον τῇ σκήψει τῆς
ὑπερθέσεως, ἀλλὰ καὶ τῆς πόλεως πορρωτέρω
105 στρατοπεδεύσασθαι πρὸς Κυδασοῖς· μεσόγειος δ᾽
ἐστὶ Τυρίων κώμη καρτερά, διὰ μίσους ἀεὶ καὶ
πολέμου Γαλιλαίοις, ἔχουσα πλῆθός τε οἰκητόρων
καὶ τὴν ὀχυρότητα τῆς πρὸς τὸ ἔθνος διαφορᾶς
ἐφόδια.

106   (4) Νυκτὸς δ᾽ ὁ Ἰωάννης ὡς οὐδεμίαν περὶ τῇ
πόλει Ῥωμαίων ἑώρα φυλακήν, τὸν καιρὸν ἁρ-
πασάμενος, οὐ μόνον τοὺς περὶ αὐτὸν ὁπλίτας
ἀλλὰ καὶ τῶν ἀργοτέρων συχνοὺς ἅμα ταῖς
107 γενεαῖς ἀναλαβὼν ἐπὶ Ἱεροσολύμων ἔφευγε. μέχρι
μὲν οὖν εἴκοσι σταδίων οἷόν τε ἦν συνεξαγαγεῖν
γυναικῶν καὶ παιδίων ὄχλον ἀνθρώπῳ κατα-
σπερχομένῳ τοῖς ὑπὲρ αἰχμαλωσίας καὶ τοῦ ζῆν
φόβοις, περαιτέρω δὲ προκόπτοντος ἀπελείποντο,
108 καὶ δειναὶ τῶν ἐωμένων ἦσαν ὀλοφύρσεις· ὅσον
γὰρ ἕκαστος τῶν οἰκείων ἐγίνετο πορρωτέρω,
τοσοῦτον ἐγγὺς ὑπελάμβανεν εἶναι τῶν πολεμίων,
παρεῖναί τε ἤδη τοὺς αἰχμαλωτισομένους δοκοῦντες

---

[1] πρέπειν Dindorf with Lat. decere ; but speeches tend
to drift into *oratio recta* at the close.
[2] ἐγκαταλειφθῆναι, " deserted," PA[1]LV[2] Lat.

them there would be great gain in being spared any transgression of their national customs. Moreover, it would be becoming in the gracious bestower of an unexpected peace to preserve the laws as well as the lives of his beneficiaries. By such language John imposed on Titus; for he was concerned not so much for the seventh day as for his own safety, and, fearing that he would be caught the instant the city was taken, rested his hopes of life on darkness and flight. But after all it was by the act of God, who was preserving John to bring ruin upon Jerusalem, that Titus was not only influenced by this pretext for delay, but even pitched his camp farther from the city, at Cydasa.[a] This is a strong inland village of the Tyrians, always at feud and strife with the Galilaeans, having its large population and stout defences as resources behind it in its quarrel with the nation.

(4) At nightfall John, seeing no Roman guard about the town, seized his opportunity and, accompanied not only by his armed followers but by a multitude of non-combatants with their families, fled for Jerusalem. For the first twenty furlongs he succeeded in dragging with him this mob of women and children, goaded though he was by terror of captivity and of his life; but after that point as he pushed on they were left behind, and dreadful were their lamentations when thus deserted. For, the farther each was removed from his friends, the nearer did he fancy himself to his foes; and believing that their captors were already upon them they were

John's flight to Jerusalem.

[a] Probably Kedesh-Naphtali = Kedasa (Kad-) in ii. 459.

---

[3] P²AM : Ἱεροσολύμων the rest.

ἐπτόηντο, καὶ πρὸς τὸν ἀλλήλων ἐκ τοῦ δρόμου
ψόφον ἐπεστρέφοντο καθάπερ ἤδη παρόντων οὓς
109 ἔφευγον· ἀνοδίαις τ' ἐνέπιπτον οἱ πολλοί, καὶ περὶ
τὴν λεωφόρον ἡ τῶν φθανόντων ἔρις συνέτριβεν
110 τοὺς πολλούς. οἰκτρὸς δὲ γυναικῶν καὶ παιδίων
ὄλεθρος ἦν, καί ' τινες πρὸς ἀνακλήσεις ἀνδρῶν
τε καὶ συγγενῶν ἐθάρσησαν μετὰ κωκυτῶν ἱκε-
111 τεύουσαι περιμένειν. ἀλλ' ἑνίκα τὸ Ἰωάννου
παρακέλευσμα σώζειν ἑαυτοὺς ἐμβοῶντος καὶ
καταφεύγειν ἔνθα καὶ περὶ τῶν ἀπολειπομένων
ἀμυνοῦνται Ῥωμαίους ἂν ἁρπαγῶσι. τὸ μὲν
οὖν τῶν διαδιδρασκόντων πλῆθος ὡς ἕκαστος
ἰσχύος εἶχεν ἢ τάχους ἐσκέδαστο.

112 (5) Τίτος δὲ μεθ' ἡμέραν ἐπὶ τὰς συνθήκας πρὸς
113 τὸ τεῖχος παρῆν. ἀνοίγει δ' αὐτῷ τὰς πύλας ὁ
δῆμος, καὶ μετὰ τῶν γενεῶν προελθόντες[1] ἀνευ-
φήμουν ὡς εὐεργέτην καὶ φρουρᾶς ἐλευθερώσαντα
114 τὴν πόλιν· ἐδήλουν γὰρ ἅμα τὴν τοῦ Ἰωάννου
φυγὴν καὶ παρεκάλουν φείσασθαί τε αὐτῶν καὶ
παρελθόντα τοὺς ὑπολειπομένους τῶν νεωτερι-
115 ζόντων κολάσαι. ὁ δὲ τὰς τοῦ δήμου δεήσεις
ἐν δευτέρῳ θέμενος μοῖραν ἔπεμπε τῶν ἱππέων
Ἰωάννην διώξουσαν, οἳ τὸν μὲν οὐ καταλαμ-
βάνουσιν, ἔφθη γὰρ εἰς Ἱεροσόλυμα διαφυγών,
τῶν δὲ συναπαράντων ἀποκτείνουσι μὲν εἰς
ἑξακισχιλίους, γύναια δὲ καὶ παιδία τρισχιλίων
116 ὀλίγον ἀποδέοντα περιελάσαντες ἀνήγαγον. ὁ δὲ
Τίτος ἤχθετο μὲν ἐπὶ τῷ μὴ παραχρῆμα τιμωρή-
σασθαι τὸν Ἰωάννην τῆς ἀπάτης, ἱκανὸν δὲ
ἀστοχήσαντι τῷ θυμῷ παραμύθιον ἔχων τὸ
πλῆθος τῶν αἰχμαλώτων καὶ τοὺς διεφθαρμένους,
117 εἰσῄει τε ἀνευφημούμενος εἰς τὴν πόλιν, καὶ τοῖς

panic-stricken and turned at every sound made by
their comrades in flight, under the impression that
their pursuers had overtaken them. Many strayed
off the track, and on the highway many were crushed
in the struggle to keep ahead. Piteous was the fate
of the women and children, some making bold to
call back their husbands or relatives and imploring
them with shrieks to wait for them. But John's
orders prevailed : " Save yourselves," he cried, " and
flee where you can have your revenge on the Romans
for any left behind, if they are caught." So this
crowd of fugitives straggled away, each putting out
the best strength and speed he had.

(5) Early next day Titus appeared before the Titus enters
walls to conclude the treaty. The gates were opened Gischala.
to him by the people, who came out with their
wives and children and hailed him as benefactor
and the liberator of their town from bondage ; for
they proceeded to tell him of John's flight and
besought him to spare them, and to enter the town
and punish the insurgents who remained. Titus,
regarding the citizens' petition as of secondary
importance, at once dispatched a squadron of cavalry
in pursuit of John. These failed to overtake him,
the fugitive making good his escape to Jerusalem,
but of his companions in flight they killed some six
thousand and rounded up and brought back nearly
three thousand women and children. Titus was
mortified at failing to visit John's trickery with
instant chastisement, but, with this host of prisoners
and the slain as a sufficient solace to his disappointed
resentment, he now entered the city amidst general

---

¹ Niese : προσελθόντες MSS.

στρατιώταις ὀλίγον τοῦ τείχους παρασπάσαι κελεύσας νόμῳ καταλήψεως, ἀπειλαῖς μᾶλλον ἢ
κολάσει τοὺς ταράσσοντας τὴν πόλιν ἀνέστελλε·
118 πολλοὺς γὰρ ἂν καὶ διὰ τὰ οἰκεῖα μίση καὶ δια-
φορὰς ἰδίας ἐνδείξασθαι τοὺς ἀναιτίους, εἰ δια-
κρίνοι τοὺς τιμωρίας ἀξίους· ἄμεινον δ' εἶναι
μετέωρον ἐν φόβῳ τὸν αἴτιον καταλιπεῖν ἤ τινα
119 τῶν οὐκ ἀξίων αὐτῷ συναπολεῖν· τὸν μὲν γὰρ ἴσως
κἂν[1] σωφρονῆσαι δέει κολάσεως, τὴν ἐπὶ τοῖς
παρῳχηκόσι συγγνώμην αἰδούμενον, ἀδιόρθωτον
δὲ τὴν ἐπὶ τοῖς παραναλωθεῖσι τιμωρίαν εἶναι.
120 φρουρᾷ μέντοι τὴν πόλιν ἠσφαλίσατο, δι' ἧς τούς
τε νεωτερίζοντας ἐφέξειν καὶ τοὺς εἰρηνικὰ
φρονοῦντας θαρραλεωτέρους καταλείψειν ἔμελλεν.
Γαλιλαία μὲν [οὖν][2] οὕτως ἑάλω πᾶσα, πολλοῖς
ἱδρῶσι προγυμνάσασα Ῥωμαίους ἐπὶ τὰ Ἱεροσόλυμα.

121 (iii. 1) Πρὸς δὲ τὴν εἴσοδον τοῦ Ἰωάννου ὁ πᾶς
δῆμος ἐξεκέχυτο, καὶ περὶ ἕκαστον τῶν συμ-
πεφευγότων μυρίος ὅμιλος συνηθροισμένοι τὰς
122 ἔξωθεν συμφορὰς ἀνεπυνθάνοντο. τῶν δὲ τὸ μὲν
ἆσθμα θερμὸν ἔτι κοπτόμενον ἐδήλου τὴν ἀνάγκην,
ἠλαζονεύοντο δὲ κἂν κακοῖς, οὐ πεφευγέναι
Ῥωμαίους φάσκοντες, ἀλλ' ἥκειν πολεμήσοντες
123 αὐτοὺς ἐξ ἀσφαλοῦς· ἀλογίστων γὰρ εἶναι καὶ
ἀχρήστων παραβόλως προκινδυνεύειν περὶ Γίσχαλα
καὶ πολίχνας ἀσθενεῖς, δέον τὰ ὅπλα καὶ τὰς
ἀκμὰς ταμιεύεσθαι τῇ μητροπόλει καὶ συμφυλάσ-
124 σειν. ἔνθα δὴ παρεδήλουν τὴν ἅλωσιν τῶν
Γισχάλων, καὶ τὴν λεγομένην εὐσχημόνως ὑπο-

---

[1] Bekker: καὶ mss.   [2] P: om. the rest.

acclamations ; and, after directing his troops to pull
down a small portion of the wall in token of capture,
he proceeded to repress the disturbers of the city's
peace rather by threats than by punishment. For
he feared that, should he attempt to pick out the
offenders who deserved chastisement, many from
private animosity and personal quarrels would accuse
the guiltless, and he thought it better to leave the
guilty in suspense and alarm than to involve any
innocent persons in their destruction ; since the
sinner might perhaps learn wisdom through fear of
punishment and respect for the pardon granted him
for past offences, whereas the death penalty unjustly
inflicted was irremediable. He secured the town,
however, by a garrison, calculated to check the rebels
and to give confidence to the peaceable citizens on
his departure. Galilee was thus now wholly subdued, All Galilee
after affording the Romans a strenuous training for subdued.
the impending Jerusalem campaign.

(iii. 1) When John entered the capital, the whole JERUSALEM:
population poured forth and each of the fugitives John of
was surrounded by a vast crowd, eagerly asking Gischala.
what had befallen outside. The newcomers, though
their breath, still hot and gasping, betrayed their
recent stress, nevertheless blustered under their
misfortunes, declaring that they had not fled from
the Romans, but had come to fight them on safe
ground. "It would have been stupid and useless,"
they said, "recklessly to risk our lives for Gischala
and such defenceless little towns, when we ought
to husband our arms and energies for the metropolis
and combine to defend it." Then they casually
mentioned the fall of Gischala and their own

125 χώρησιν αὐτῶν οἱ πολλοὶ δρασμὸν ἐνενόουν. ὡς
μέντοι τὰ περὶ τοὺς αἰχμαλωτισθέντας ἠκούσθη,
σύγχυσις οὐ μετρία κατέσχε τὸν δῆμον, καὶ
μεγάλα τῆς ἑαυτῶν ἁλώσεως συνελογίζοντο τὰ
126 τεκμήρια. Ἰωάννης δ' ἐπὶ μὲν τοῖς καταλει-
φθεῖσιν[1] ἧττον ἠρυθρία, περιιὼν δ' ἑκάστους ἐπὶ τὸν
πόλεμον ἐνῆγεν ταῖς ἐλπίσιν, τὰ μὲν Ῥωμαίων
ἀσθενῆ κατασκευάζων, τὴν δ' οἰκείαν δύναμιν
127 ἐξαίρων, καὶ κατειρωνευόμενος τῆς τῶν ἀπείρων
ἀγνοίας, ὡς οὐδ' ἂν πτερὰ λαβόντες ὑπερβαῖέν
ποτε Ῥωμαῖοι τὸ Ἱεροσολύμων τεῖχος οἱ περὶ
ταῖς Γαλιλαίων κώμαις κακοπαθοῦντες καὶ πρὸς
τοῖς ἐκεῖ τείχεσι κατατρίψαντες τὰς μηχανάς.
128 (2) Τούτοις τὸ πολὺ μὲν τῶν νέων προσδι-
εφθείρετο καὶ πρὸς[2] τὸν πόλεμον ἦρτο, τῶν δὲ
σωφρονούντων καὶ γηραιῶν οὐκ ἦν ὅστις οὐ τὰ
μέλλοντα προορώμενος ὡς ἤδη τῆς πόλεως
129 οἰχομένης ἐπένθει. ὁ μὲν οὖν δῆμος ἦν ἐν τοιαύτῃ
συγχύσει, προδιέστη δὲ τὸ κατὰ τὴν χώραν
130 πλῆθος τῆς ἐν Ἱεροσολύμοις στάσεως. ὁ μὲν γὰρ
Τίτος ἀπὸ Γισχάλων εἰς Καισάρειαν, Οὐεσπασιανὸς δὲ ἀπὸ Καισαρείας εἰς Ἰάμνειαν καὶ
Ἄζωτον ἀφικόμενος παρίσταταί τε αὐτὰς[3] καὶ
φρουροὺς ἐγκαταστήσας ὑπέστρεψε, πολὺ πλῆθος
ἐπαγόμενος τῶν ἐπὶ δεξιᾷ προσκεχωρηκότων.
131 ἐκινεῖτο δ' ἐν ἑκάστῃ πόλει ταραχὴ καὶ πόλεμος
ἐμφύλιος, ὅσον τε ἀπὸ Ῥωμαίων ἀνέπνεον εἰς

---

[1] A[1]L[1] Lat.: καταληφθεῖσιν the rest.
[2] + μὲν MSS.   [3] C: αὐταῖς the rest.

---

[a] § 130, describing the movements of Titus and Vespasian,
comes in rather awkwardly, breaking the close connexion
between §§ 129 and 131.

" retreat," as they decently called it, though most of their hearers understood them to mean flight. When, however, the story of the prisoners came out, profound consternation took possession of the people, who drew therefrom plain indications of their own impending capture. But John, little abashed at the desertion of his friends, went round the several groups, instigating them to war by the hopes he raised, making out the Romans to be weak, extolling their own power, and ridiculing the ignorance of the inexperienced; even had they wings, he remarked, the Romans would never surmount the walls of Jerusalem, after having found such difficulty with the villages of Galilee and worn out their engines against their walls.

John as leader of war-party in Jerusalem.

(2) By these harangues most of the youth were seduced into his service and incited to war ; but of the sober and elder men there was not one who did not foresee the future and mourn for the city as if it had already met its doom. Such was the confusion prevailing among the citizens, but even before sedition appeared in Jerusalem, party strife had broken out in the country. For when Titus moved from Gischala to Caesarea, Vespasian proceeded from Caesarea to Jamnia and Azotus, and, having reduced those towns and garrisoned them, returned with a large multitude who had surrendered under treaty.[a] Every city [b] was now agitated by tumult and civil war, and the moment they had a respite from the Romans they turned their hands against

Sedition and party strife in Judaea.

[b] In this picture of the effects of sedition the historian probably has in mind, as elsewhere, the famous reflections of Thucydides (iii. 81-84) on revolution.

39

ἀλλήλους τὰς χεῖρας ἐπέστρεφον. ἦν δὲ τῶν
ἐρώντων τοῦ πολέμου πρὸς τοὺς ἐπιθυμοῦντας
132 εἰρήνης ἔρις χαλεπή. καὶ πρῶτον μὲν ἐν οἰκίαις
ἥπτετο τῶν ὁμονοούντων πάλαι τὸ φιλόνεικον,
ἔπειτα ἀφηνιάζοντες ἀλλήλων οἱ φίλτατοι[1] καὶ
συνιὼν ἕκαστος πρὸς τοὺς τὰ αὐτὰ προαιρου-
133 μένους ἤδη κατὰ πλῆθος ἀντετάσσοντο. καὶ
στάσις μὲν ἦν πανταχοῦ, τὸ νεωτερίζον δὲ καὶ τῶν
ὅπλων ἐπιθυμοῦν ἐπεκράτει νεότητι καὶ τόλμῃ
134 γηραιῶν καὶ σωφρόνων. ἐτράποντο δὲ πρῶτον
μὲν εἰς ἁρπαγὰς ἕκαστοι τῶν ἐπιχωρίων, ἔπειτα
συντασσόμενοι κατὰ λόχους ἐπὶ λῃστείαν τῶν
κατὰ τὴν χώραν, ὡς ὠμότητος καὶ παρανομίας
ἕνεκεν αὑτοῖς μηδὲν Ῥωμαίων τοὺς ὁμοφύλους
διαφέρειν καὶ πολὺ τοῖς πορθουμένοις κουφο-
τέραν δοκεῖν τὴν ὑπὸ Ῥωμαίοις ἅλωσιν.

135 (3) Οἱ φρουροὶ δὲ τῶν πόλεων τὰ μὲν ὄκνῳ τοῦ
κακοπαθεῖν, τὰ δὲ μίσει τοῦ ἔθνους, οὐδὲν ἢ μικρὰ
προσήμυνον τοῖς κακουμένοις, μέχρι κόρῳ τῶν
κατὰ τὴν χώραν ἁρπαγῶν ἀθροισθέντες οἱ τῶν
πανταχοῦ συνταγμάτων ἀρχιλῃσταὶ καὶ γενόμενοι
πονηρίας στῖφος εἰς τὰ Ἱεροσόλυμα παρεισ-
136 φθείρονται, πόλιν ἀστρατήγητον καὶ πατρίῳ μὲν
ἔθει πᾶν ἀπαρατηρήτως δεχομένην τὸ ὁμόφυλον,
τότε δ' οἰομένων ἁπάντων τοὺς ἐπιχεομένους[2]
137 πάντας ἀπ' εὐνοίας ἥκειν συμμάχους. ὃ δὴ καὶ
δίχα τῆς στάσεως ὕστερον ἐβάπτισεν τὴν πόλιν·
πλήθει γὰρ ἀχρήστῳ καὶ ἀργῷ προεξαναλώθη
τὰ τοῖς μαχίμοις διαρκεῖν δυνάμενα, καὶ πρὸς

---

[1] + λαοὶ mss. : expunged in A.
[2] ἐπεισχεομένους MC (similar variant in § 307).

each other. Between the enthusiasts for war and the friends of peace contention raged fiercely. Beginning in the home this party rivalry first attacked those who had long been bosom friends ; then the nearest relations severed their connexions and joining those who shared their respective views ranged themselves henceforth in opposite camps. Faction reigned everywhere ; and the revolutionary and militant party overpowered by their youth and recklessness the old and prudent. The various cliques began by pillaging their neighbours, then banding together in companies they carried their depredations throughout the country ; insomuch that in cruelty and lawlessness the sufferers found no difference between compatriots and Romans, indeed to be captured by the latter seemed to the unfortunate victims far the lighter fate.

(3) The garrisons of the towns, partly from reluctance to take risks, partly from their hatred of the nation, afforded little or no protection to the distressed. In the end, satiated with their pillage of the country, the brigand chiefs of all these scattered bands joined forces and, now merged into one pack of villainy, stole into poor Jerusalem— a city under no commanding officer and one which, according to hereditary custom, unguardedly admitted all of Jewish blood, and the more readily at that moment when it was universally believed that all who were pouring into it came out of goodwill as its allies. Yet it was just this circumstance which, irrespectively of the sedition, eventually wrecked the city ; for supplies which might have sufficed for the combatants were squandered upon a useless and idle mob, who brought upon themselves, *Irruption of the brigands (Zealots) into Jerusalem.*

41

τῷ πολέμῳ στάσιν τε ἑαυτοῖς καὶ λιμὸν ἐπικατ-
εσκεύασαν.

138 (4) Ἄλλοι τε ἀπὸ τῆς χώρας λῃσταὶ παρελθόντες εἰς τὴν πόλιν καὶ τοὺς ἔνδον προσλαβόντες
χαλεπωτέρους οὐδὲν ἔτι τῶν δεινῶν παρίεσαν·

139 οἵ γε οὐ μόνον[1] ἁρπαγαῖς καὶ λωποδυσίαις τὴν
τόλμαν ἐμέτρουν, ἀλλὰ καὶ μέχρι φόνων ἐχώρουν,
οὐ νυκτὸς ἢ λαθραίως ἢ ἐπὶ τοὺς τυχόντας, ἀλλὰ
φανερῶς καὶ μεθ' ἡμέραν καὶ τῶν ἐπισημοτάτων

140 καταρχόμενοι. πρῶτον μὲν γὰρ Ἀντίπαν, ἄνδρα
τοῦ βασιλικοῦ γένους καὶ τῶν κατὰ τὴν πόλιν
δυνατωτάτων, ὡς καὶ τοὺς δημοσίους θησαυροὺς

141 πεπιστεῦσθαι, συλλαβόντες εἷρξαν· ἐπὶ τούτῳ
Ληουίαν τινὰ τῶν ἐπισήμων καὶ Συφὰν υἱὸν
Ἀρεγέτου,[2] βασιλικὸν δ' ἦν καὶ τούτων τὸ γένος,
πρὸς δὲ τοὺς κατὰ τὴν χώραν προύχειν δοκοῦντας.

142 δεινὴ δὲ κατάπληξις εἶχε τὸν δῆμον, καὶ καθάπερ
κατειλημμένης τῆς πόλεως πολέμῳ τὴν καθ'
αὑτὸν ἕκαστος σωτηρίαν ἠγάπα.

143 (5) Τοῖς δ' οὐκ ἀπέχρη τὰ δεσμὰ τῶν συνειλημμένων, οὐδὲ ἀσφαλὲς ᾤοντο τὸ μέχρι πολλοῦ

144 δυνατοὺς ἄνδρας οὕτω φυλάσσειν· ἱκανοὺς μὲν γὰρ
εἶναι καὶ τοὺς οἴκους αὐτῶν πρὸς ἄμυναν οὐκ
ὀλιγάνδρους ὄντας, οὐ μὴν ἀλλὰ καὶ τὸν δῆμον
ἐπαναστήσεσθαι τάχα κινηθέντα πρὸς τὴν παρα-

145 νομίαν. δόξαν οὖν ἀναιρεῖν αὐτούς, Ἰωάννην τινὰ
πέμπουσιν τὸν ἐξ αὐτῶν εἰς φόνους προχειρότατον·

---

[1] ? read μόναις.
[2] PA, cf. Ῥεγέτου L, Rageti Lat.: Ραγ(Ρεγ-)ώλου, Ραγουήλου
the rest.

---

[a] He, with two other relatives of Agrippa II, Saul and
Costobar, had sought through the king's influence to nip

in addition to the war, the miseries of sedition and famine.

(4) Fresh brigands from the country entering the city and joining the yet more formidable gang within, abstained henceforth from no enormities. For, not restricting their audacity to raids and highway robberies, they now proceeded to murders, committed not under cover of night or clandestinely or on ordinary folk, but openly, in broad daylight, and with the most eminent citizens for their earliest victims. The first was Antipas,[a] one of the royal family and he carried such weight in the city that he was entrusted with the charge of the public treasury. Him they arrested and imprisoned, and after him Levias, one of the nobles, and Syphas, son of Aregetes—both also of royal blood—besides other persons of high reputation throughout the country. Dire panic now seized the people, and as if the city had been captured by the enemy none cherished any thought but that of his personal security. They arrest and murder eminent citizens.

(5) The brigands, however, were not satisfied with having put their captives in irons, and considered it unsafe thus to keep for long in custody influential persons, with numerous families quite capable of avenging them; they feared, moreover, that the people might be moved by their outrageous action to rise against them. They accordingly decided to kill their victims and commissioned for this purpose the most handy assassin among them, one John,

the Jewish revolt in the bud (ii. 418); later, he remained in Jerusalem when the others fled (ii. 557).

43

Δορκάδος οὗτος ἐκαλεῖτο παῖς κατὰ τὴν ἐπιχώριον
γλῶσσαν· ᾧ δέκα συνελθόντες εἰς τὴν εἱρκτὴν
ξιφήρεις ἀποσφάττουσιν τοὺς συνειλημμένους.[1]
146 παρανομήματι δ' ἐν[2] τηλικούτῳ μεγάλως ἐπεψεύ-
δοντο[3] καὶ πρόφασιν[4]· διαλεχθῆναι γὰρ αὐτοὺς
Ῥωμαίοις περὶ παραδόσεως τῶν Ἱεροσολύμων,
καὶ προδότας ἀνῃρηκέναι τῆς κοινῆς ἐλευθερίας
ἔφασκον, καθόλου τ' ἐπηλαζονεύοντο τοῖς τολμήμασιν ὡς εὐεργέται καὶ σωτῆρες τῆς πόλεως
γεγενημένοι.
147 (6) Συνέβη δὲ εἰς τοσοῦτον τὸν μὲν δῆμον
ταπεινότητος καὶ δέους, ἐκείνους δ' ἀπονοίας
προελθεῖν, ὡς ἐπ' αὐτοῖς εἶναι καὶ τὰς χειροτονίας
148 τῶν ἀρχιερέων. ἄκυρα γοῦν τὰ γένη ποιήσαντες,
ἐξ ὧν κατὰ διαδοχὰς οἱ ἀρχιερεῖς ἀπεδείκνυντο,
καθίστασαν ἀσήμους καὶ ἀγενεῖς, ἵν' ἔχοιεν
149 συνεργοὺς τῶν ἀσεβημάτων· τοῖς γὰρ παρ' ἀξίαν
ἐπιτυχοῦσι τῆς ἀνωτάτω τιμῆς ὑπακούειν ἦν
150 ἀνάγκη τοῖς παρασχοῦσι. συνέκρουον δὲ καὶ
τοὺς ἐν τέλει ποικίλαις ἐπινοίαις καὶ λογοποιίαις,
καιρὸν ἑαυτοῖς ἐν ταῖς πρὸς ἀλλήλους τῶν κωλυόν-
των φιλονεικίαις ποιούμενοι, μέχρι τῶν εἰς ἀνθρώπους ὑπερεμπλησθέντες ἀδικημάτων ἐπὶ τὸ θεῖον
μετήνεγκαν τὴν ὕβριν καὶ μεμιασμένοις τοῖς ποσὶ
παρῄεσαν εἰς τὸ ἅγιον.
151 (7) Ἐπανισταμένου τε αὐτοῖς ἤδη τοῦ πλήθους,

---

[1] εἰργμένους LC Exc. and margin of PAM.
[2] ἐπὶ CA[marg.]: Niese (ed. min.) omits.
[3] Dindorf: ἀπεψεύδοντο mss.
[4] προφάσεις ἀνέπλαττον PAM.

---

[a] *i.e.* " Gazelle," in Aramaic Bar Tabitha (*cf.* Acts ix. 36) ;
Dorcas was used also by Greeks as a woman's name (Wetstein).

known in their native tongue as son of Dorcas *a* ; he with ten others entered the gaol with drawn swords and butchered the prisoners. For such a monstrous crime they invented as monstrous an excuse, declaring that their victims had conferred with the Romans concerning the surrender of Jerusalem and had been slain as traitors to the liberty of the state. In short, they boasted of their audacious acts as though they had been the benefactors and saviours of the city.

(6) In the end, to such abject prostration and terror were the people reduced and to such heights of madness rose these brigands, that they actually took upon themselves the election to the high priesthood. Abrogating the claims of those families from which in turn the high priests had always been drawn,*b* they appointed to that office ignoble and low born individuals, in order to gain accomplices in their impious crimes ; for persons who had undeservedly attained to the highest dignity were bound to obey those who had conferred it. Moreover, by various devices and libellous statements, they brought the official authorities into collision with each other, finding their own opportunity in the bickerings of those who should have kept them in check ; until, glutted with the wrongs which they had done to men, they transferred their insolence to the Deity and with polluted feet invaded the sanctuary.

(7) An insurrection of the populace was at length

b For this limitation of the high priesthood to a few privileged families see Schürer, *G.J.V.* (ed. 3) ii. 222. The contents of this section are partly repeated in that which follows ; a duplication perhaps indicating imperfect editorial revision.

ἐνῆγε γὰρ ὁ γεραίτατος[1] τῶν ἀρχιερέων Ἄνανος,
ἀνὴρ σωφρονέστατος καὶ τάχα ἂν διασώσας τὴν
πόλιν, εἰ τὰς τῶν ἐπιβούλων χεῖρας ἐξέφυγεν, οἱ
δὲ τὸν νεὼν τοῦ θεοῦ φρούριον αὑτοῖς καὶ τῶν
ἀπὸ τοῦ δήμου ταραχῶν ποιοῦνται καταφυγήν,
152 καὶ τυραννεῖον ἦν αὐτοῖς τὸ ἅγιον. παρεκίρνατο
δὲ τοῖς δεινοῖς εἰρωνεία, τὸ τῶν ἐνεργουμένων
153 ἀλγεινότερον· ἀποπειρώμενοι γὰρ τῆς τοῦ δήμου
καταπλήξεως καὶ τὴν αὑτῶν δοκιμάζοντες ἰσχὺν
κληρωτοὺς ἐπεχείρησαν ποιεῖν τοὺς ἀρχιερεῖς
οὔσης, ὡς ἔφαμεν, κατὰ γένος αὐτῶν τῆς διαδοχῆς.
154 ἦν δὲ πρόσχημα μὲν τῆς ἐπιβολῆς[2] ἔθος ἀρχαῖον,
ἐπειδὴ καὶ πάλαι κληρωτὴν ἔφασαν εἶναι τὴν
ἀρχιερωσύνην, τὸ δ' ἀληθὲς τοῦ βεβαιοτέρου[3]
κατάλυσις καὶ τέχνη πρὸς δυναστείαν τὰς ἀρχὰς
δι' αὑτῶν καθισταμένοις.

155 (8) Καὶ δὴ μεταπεμψάμενοι μίαν τῶν ἀρχ-
ιερατικῶν φυλήν, Ἐνιάχιν καλεῖται, διεκλήρουν
ἀρχιερέα, λαγχάνει δ' ἀπὸ τύχης ὁ μάλιστα
διαδείξας αὐτῶν τὴν παρανομίαν, Φαννί τις ὄνομα,
υἱὸς Σαμουήλου κώμης Ἀφθίας, ἀνὴρ οὐ μόνον
οὐκ ἐξ ἀρχιερέων, ἀλλ' οὐδ' ἐπιστάμενος σαφῶς
156 τί ποτ' ἦν ἀρχιερωσύνη δι' ἀγροικίαν. ἀπὸ γοῦν
τῆς χώρας αὐτὸν ἄκοντα σύραντες ὥσπερ ἐπὶ
σκηνῆς ἀλλοτρίῳ κατεκόσμουν προσωπείῳ, τήν

---

[1] γεραίτερος PAM.
[2] Niese: ἐπιβουλῆς MSS.
[3] L[1]: + νόμου the rest.

---

[a] For his murder and an encomium on his character see
§§ 316-325.   [b] Or " by families "; see § 148.
[c] The φυλή (" clan ") is a subdivision of the πατρία or
ἐφημερίς (" course ").   Josephus himself belonged to the

46

pending, instigated by Ananus, the senior of the Insurrection
against
Zealots
headed by
Ananus. chief priests, a man of profound sanity, who might possibly have saved the city, had he escaped the conspirators' hands.*a* At this threat these wretches converted the temple of God into their fortress and The Zealots
occupy the
temple refuge from any outbreak of popular violence, and made the Holy Place the headquarters of their tyranny. To these horrors was added a spice of and select
a high-priest
by lot. mockery more galling than their actions. For, to test the abject submission of the populace and make trial of their own strength, they essayed to appoint the high priests by lot, although, as we have stated, the succession was hereditary.*b* As pretext for this scheme they adduced ancient custom, asserting that in old days the high priesthood had been determined by lot; but in reality their action was the abrogation of established practice and a trick to make themselves supreme by getting these appointments into their own hands.

(8) They accordingly summoned one of the high-priestly clans,*c* called Eniachin, and cast lots for a high priest. By chance the lot fell to one who proved a signal illustration of their depravity; he was an individual named Phanni, son of Samuel, of the village of Aphthia,*d* a man who not only was not descended from high priests, but was such a clown that he scarcely knew what the high priesthood meant. At any rate they dragged their reluctant victim out of the country and, dressing him up for his assumed part, as on the stage, put the sacred

first of the twenty-four priestly courses, and to the most eminent of its constituent clans, *Vita* 2. The clan Eniachin is mentioned here only; the suggestion of Lowth to read ἡ ʼΙακίμ for ʼΕνιάχιν (ʼΕνιακείμ), comparing 1 Chron. xxiv. 12 (the *course* Jakim), is uncalled for. *d* Site unknown.

47

τ' ἐσθῆτα περιτιθέντες τὴν ἱερὰν καὶ τὸ τί δεῖ
157 ποιεῖν ἐπὶ καιροῦ διδάσκοντες. χλεύη δ' ἦν
ἐκείνοις καὶ παιδιὰ τὸ τηλικοῦτον ἀσέβημα, τοῖς
δ' ἄλλοις ἱερεῦσιν ἐπιθεωμένοις πόρρωθεν παιζόμενον τὸν νόμον δακρύειν ἐπῄει καὶ κατέστενον
τὴν τῶν ἱερῶν τιμῶν κατάλυσιν.

158 (9) Ταύτην τὴν τόλμαν αὐτῶν οὐκ ἤνεγκεν ὁ
δῆμος, ἀλλ' ὥσπερ ἐπὶ τυραννίδος κατάλυσιν
159 ὥρμηντο πάντες· καὶ γὰρ οἱ προύχειν αὐτῶν
δοκοῦντες, Γωρίων τε υἱὸς Ἰωσήπου καὶ ὁ
Γαμαλιήλου Συμεών, παρεκρότουν ἔν τε ταῖς
ἐκκλησίαις ἀθρόους καὶ κατ' ἰδίαν περιιόντες
ἕκαστον ἤδη ποτὲ τίσασθαι τοὺς λυμεῶνας τῆς
ἐλευθερίας καὶ καθᾶραι τῶν μιαιφόνων τὸ ἅγιον,
160 οἵ τε δοκιμώτατοι τῶν ἀρχιερέων, Γαμάλα μὲν
υἱὸς Ἰησοῦς Ἀνάνου δὲ Ἄνανος, πολλὰ τὸν
δῆμον εἰς νωθείαν κατονειδίζοντες ἐν ταῖς συνόδοις
161 ἐπήγειρον τοῖς ζηλωταῖς· τοῦτο γὰρ αὐτοὺς
ἐκάλεσαν ὡς ἐπ' ἀγαθοῖς ἐπιτηδεύμασιν, ἀλλ'
οὐχὶ¹ ζηλώσαντες τὰ κάκιστα τῶν ἔργων [καὶ]²
ὑπερβαλλόμενοι.

162 (10) Καὶ δὴ συνελθόντος τοῦ πλήθους εἰς
ἐκκλησίαν καὶ πάντων ἀγανακτούντων μὲν ἐπὶ
τῇ καταλήψει τῶν ἁγίων ταῖς τε ἁρπαγαῖς καὶ
τοῖς πεφονευμένοις, οὔπω δὲ πρὸς τὴν ἄμυναν
ὡρμημένων τῷ δυσεπιχειρήτους, ὅπερ ἦν, τοὺς
ζηλωτὰς ὑπολαμβάνειν, καταστὰς ἐν μέσοις ὁ

¹ ἀλλ' οὐχὶ L Lat.: ἄλλους the rest.   ² om. PA Lat.

ᵃ Probably the Joseph, son of Gorion, who, along with
Ananus, was given supreme control in Jerusalem at the outbreak of war, ii. 563 ; the younger Gorion here mentioned
bears his grandfather's name.

vestments upon him and instructed him how to act in keeping with the occasion. To them this monstrous impiety was a subject for jesting and sport, but the other priests, beholding from a distance this mockery of their law, could not restrain their tears and bemoaned the degradation of the sacred honours.

(9) This latest outrage was more than the people could stand, and as if for the overthrow of a despotism one and all were now roused. For their leaders of outstanding reputation, such as Gorion, son of Joseph,[a] and Symeon,[b] son of Gamaliel, by public addresses to the whole assembly and by private visits to individuals, urged them to delay no longer to punish these wreckers of liberty and purge the sanctuary of its bloodstained polluters. Their efforts were supported by the most eminent of the high priests, Jesus,[c] son of Gamalas, and Ananus, son of Ananus, who at their meetings vehemently upbraided the people for their apathy and incited them against the Zealots ; for so these miscreants called themselves, as though they were zealous in the cause of virtue and not for vice in its basest and most extravagant form.

(10) And now, the populace being convened to a general assembly, when indignation was universally expressed at the occupation of the sanctuary, at the raids and murders, but no attempt at resistance had yet been made, owing to a belief, not unfounded, that the Zealots would prove difficult to dislodge,

Popular indignation roused.

General Assembly and speech of Ananus.

[b] Probably identical with Simon, son of Gamaliel, of whom, notwithstanding his opposition to Josephus, the historian, writes in the highest terms in *Vita* 190 ff.

[c] Befriended Josephus, *Vita* 193, 204 ; for his death and the historian's encomium upon him see §§ 316 ff.

49

Ἄνανος καὶ πολλάκις εἰς τὸν ναὸν ἀπιδὼν ἐμ-
163 πλήσας τε τοὺς ὀφθαλμοὺς δακρύων " ἦ καλόν
γ'," εἶπεν, " ἦν ἐμοὶ τεθνάναι πρὶν ἐπιδεῖν τὸν
οἶκον τοῦ θεοῦ τοσούτοις ἄγεσι καταγέμοντα καὶ
τὰς ἀβάτους καὶ ἀγίας χώρας ποσὶ μιαιφόνων
164 στενοχωρουμένας. ἀλλὰ περικείμενος τὴν ἀρχιερα-
τικὴν ἐσθῆτα καὶ τὸ τιμιώτατον καλούμενος τῶν
σεβασμίων ὀνομάτων, ζῶ καὶ φιλοψυχῶ, μηδ'¹
ὑπὲρ τοὐμοῦ γήρως ὑπομένων εὐκλεῆ θάνατον·
†εἰ δὲ δεῖ² μόνος εἰμι³ καὶ καθάπερ ἐν ἐρημίᾳ τὴν
ἐμαυτοῦ ψυχὴν ἐπιδώσω μόνην ὑπὲρ τοῦ θεοῦ.
165 τί γὰρ καὶ δεῖ ζῆν ἐν δήμῳ συμφορῶν ἀναισ-
θητοῦντι καὶ παρ' οἷς ἀπόλωλεν ἡ τῶν ἐν χερσὶ
παθῶν ἀντίληψις; ἁρπαζόμενοι γοῦν ἀνέχεσθε
καὶ τυπτόμενοι σιωπᾶτε, καὶ τοῖς φονευομένοις
166 οὐδ' ἐπιστένει τις ἀναφανδόν. ὦ τῆς πικρᾶς
τυραννίδος. τί [δὲ] μέμφομαι τοὺς τυράννους;
μὴ γὰρ οὐκ ἐτράφησαν ὑφ' ὑμῶν καὶ τῆς ὑμετέρας
167 ἀνεξικακίας; μὴ γὰρ οὐχ ὑμεῖς περιιδόντες τοὺς
πρώτους συνισταμένους, ἔτι δ' ἦσαν ὀλίγοι,
πλείους ἐποιήσατε τῇ σιωπῇ καὶ καθοπλιζομένων
ἠρεμοῦντες καθ' ἑαυτῶν ἐπεστρέψατε τὰ ὅπλα,
168 δέον τὰς πρώτας αὐτῶν ἐπικόπτειν ὁρμάς, ὅτε
λοιδορίαις καθήπτοντο τῶν εὐγενῶν,⁴ ·ὑμεῖς δ'
ἀμελήσαντες ἐφ' ἁρπαγὰς παρωξύνατε τοὺς ἀλιτηρίους, καὶ πορθουμένων οἴκων λόγος ἦν οὐδείς·
τοιγαροῦν αὐτοὺς ἥρπαζον τοὺς δεσπότας, καὶ
συρομένοις διὰ μέσης τῆς πόλεως οὐδεὶς ἐπήμυνεν.

¹ Destinon (Lat. nec . . quidem): μήθ' PAML: μηκέτι
the rest.
² εἰ δὲ δεῖ conj.: εἰ δεῖ μή PA: εἰ δὴ μή L: εἰ δὲ δὴ
the rest.

Ananus arose in the midst and, often gazing on the
Temple with eyes filled with tears, spoke as follows :
" Truly well had it been for me to have died ere
I had seen the house of God laden with such abom-
inations and its unapproachable and hallowed places
crowded with the feet of murderers ! And yet I
who wear the high priest's vestments, who bear that
most honoured of venerated names, am alive and
clinging to life, instead of braving a death which
would shed lustre on my old age. If it must be
then, alone will I go and, as in utter desolation,
devote this single life of mine in the cause of
God. Why, indeed, should I live amongst a people
insensible to calamities, who have lost the will to
grapple with the troubles on their hands ? When
plundered you submit, when beaten you are silent,
nay over the murdered none dares audibly to groan !
What bitter tyranny ! Yes, but why blame I the
tyrants ? For have they not been fostered by you
and your forbearance ? Was it not you who by
allowing those first recruits to combine, when they
were yet but few, swelled their numbers by your
silence, and by your inaction when they were arming
drew those arms upon yourselves ? You should have
cut short their opening attacks when they were
assailing the nobles with abuse ; instead, by your
negligence you incited the miscreants to rapine.
Then, when houses were pillaged, not a word was
said—consequently they laid hands on their owners
as well ; and when these were dragged through the
midst of the city, none rose in their defence. They

---

3 Destinon with Lat.: εἰμί MSS.
4 Destinon: συγγενῶν MSS.

169 οἱ δὲ καὶ δεσμοῖς ἠκίσαντο τοὺς ὑφ' ὑμῶν προ-
δοθέντας, ἐῶ λέγειν πόσους καὶ ποδαπούς· ἀλλ'
ἀκαταιτιάτοις ἀκρίτοις οὐδεὶς ἐβοήθησε τοῖς δεδε-
170 μένοις. ἀκόλουθον ἦν ἐπιδεῖν τοὺς αὐτοὺς φο-
νευομένους. ἐπείδομεν καὶ τοῦτο, καθάπερ ἐξ
ἀγέλης ζῴων ἀλόγων ἑλκομένου τοῦ κρατι-
στεύοντος ἀεὶ θύματος, οὐδὲ φωνήν τις ἀφῆκεν,
171 οὐχ ὅπως ἐκίνησε τὴν δεξιάν. φέρετε δὴ τοίνυν,
φέρετε πατούμενα βλέποντες [καὶ][1] τὰ ἅγια καὶ
πάντας ὑποθέντες αὐτοὶ τοῖς ἀνοσίοις τοὺς τῶν
τολμημάτων βαθμοὺς μὴ βαρύνεσθε τὴν ὑπεροχήν·
καὶ γὰρ νῦν πάντως ἂν ἐπὶ μεῖζον προύκοψαν,
172 εἴ τι τῶν ἁγίων καταλῦσαι μεῖζον εἶχον. κεκράτη-
ται μὲν οὖν τὸ ὀχυρώτατον τῆς πόλεως· λεγέσθω
γὰρ νῦν τὸ ἱερὸν ὡς ἄκρα τις ἢ φρούριον· ἔχοντες
δ' ἐπιτετειχισμένην τυραννίδα τοσαύτην καὶ τοὺς
ἐχθροὺς ὑπὲρ κορυφὴν βλέποντες, τί βουλεύεσθε
173 καὶ τίσι τὰς γνώμας προσθάλπετε; Ῥωμαίους
ἄρα περιμενεῖτε, ἵν' ἡμῶν βοηθήσωσι τοῖς ἁγίοις;
ἔχει μὲν οὕτως τὰ πράγματα τῇ πόλει, καὶ πρὸς
τοσοῦτον ἥκομεν συμφορῶν, ἵν' ἡμᾶς ἐλεήσωσι
174 καὶ πολέμιοι;[2] οὐκ ἐξαναστήσεσθε, ὦ τλημονέ-
στατοι, καὶ πρὸς τὰς πληγὰς ἐπιστραφέντες, ὃ
κἀπὶ τῶν θηρίων ἔστιν ἰδεῖν, τοὺς τύπτοντας
ἀμυνεῖσθε; οὐκ ἀναμνήσεσθε τῶν ἰδίων ἕκαστος
συμφορῶν, οὐδ' ἃ πεπόνθατε πρὸ ὀφθαλμῶν
θέμενοι τὰς ψυχὰς ἐπ' αὐτοὺς θήξετε πρὸς τὴν

---

[1] ins. L[1] Lat.: om. the rest.
[2] Mark of interrogation substituted for full stop in MSS.

---

[a] ἐπιτετειχισμένην τυραννίδα; the phrase comes from
τυραννίδα . . . ἐπετείχισεν ὑμῖν in the fourth Philippic attributed to Demosthenes (133).

52

next proceeded to inflict the indignity of bonds upon
those whom you had betrayed. The number and
nature of these I forbear to state, but though they were
unimpeached, uncondemned, not a man assisted them
in their bondage. The natural sequel was to watch
these same men massacred; that spectacle also we
have witnessed, when as from a herd of dumb cattle
one prize victim after another was dragged to the
slaughter; yet not a voice, much less a hand, was
raised. Bear then, yes bear, I say, this further sight
of the trampling of your sanctuary; and, after yourselves laying each step of the ladder for the audacity
of these profane wretches to mount, do not grudge
them the attainment of the climax! Indeed by
now they would assuredly have proceeded to greater
heights, had aught greater than the sanctuary remained for them to overthrow.

" Well, they have mastered the strongest point in
the city—for henceforth the Temple must be spoken
of as a mere citadel or fortress—; but with such a
tyrants' stronghold entrenched in your midst,[a] with
the spectacle of your foes above your heads, what
plans have you, what further cherished hopes console
your minds? Will you wait for the Romans to
succour our holy places? Has the city come to such
a pass, are we reduced to such misery, that even
enemies must pity us? Will you never rise, most
long-suffering of men, and turning to meet the lash,
as even the beast may be seen to turn, retaliate on
them that smite you? Will you not call to mind
each one of you his personal calamities and, holding
before your eyes all that you have undergone, whet

53

175 ἄμυναν; ἀπόλωλεν ἄρα παρ' ὑμῖν τὸ τιμιώτατον
τῶν παθῶν καὶ φυσικώτατον, ἐλευθερίας ἐπιθυμία,
φιλόδουλοι δὲ καὶ φιλοδέσποτοι γεγόναμεν, ὥσπερ
ἐκ προγόνων τὸ ὑποτάσσεσθαι παραλαβόντες.
176 ἀλλ' ἐκεῖνοί γε πολλοὺς καὶ μεγάλους ὑπὲρ τῆς
αὐτονομίας πολέμους διήνεγκαν καὶ οὔτε τῆς
Αἰγυπτίων οὔτε τῆς Μήδων δυναστείας ἡττήθησαν
177 ὑπὲρ τοῦ μὴ ποιεῖν τὸ κελευόμενον. καὶ τί δεῖ
τὰ τῶν προγόνων λέγειν; ἀλλ' ὁ νῦν πρὸς Ῥωμαίους πόλεμος, ἐῶ διελέγχειν πότερον λυσιτελὴς
ὢν καὶ σύμφορος ἢ τοὐναντίον, τίνα δ' οὖν ἔχει
178 πρόφασιν; οὐ τὴν ἐλευθερίαν; εἶτα τοὺς τῆς
οἰκουμένης δεσπότας μὴ φέροντες τῶν ὁμοφύλων
179 τυράννων ἀνεξόμεθα; καίτοι τὸ μὲν τοῖς ἔξωθεν
ὑπακούειν ἀνενέγκαι τις ἂν εἰς τὴν ἅπαξ ἡττή-
σασαν τύχην, τὸ δὲ τοῖς οἰκείοις εἴκειν πονηροῖς
180 ἀγεννῶν ἐστι καὶ προαιρουμένων. ἐπειδὴ δὲ
ἅπαξ ἐμνήσθην Ῥωμαίων, οὐκ ἀποκρύψομαι
πρὸς ὑμᾶς εἰπεῖν ὃ μεταξὺ τῶν λόγων ἐμπεσὸν
ἐπέστρεψε τὴν διάνοιαν, ὅτι κἂν ἁλῶμεν ὑπ'
ἐκείνοις, ἀπείη δὲ ἡ πεῖρα τοῦ λόγου, χαλεπώτερον
οὐδὲν παθεῖν ἔχομεν ὧν ἡμᾶς διατεθείκασιν οὗτοι.
181 πῶς δ' οὐ δακρύων ἄξιον ἐκείνων μὲν ἐν τῷ ἱερῷ
καὶ ἀναθήματα βλέπειν, τῶν δὲ ὁμοφύλων τὰ
σκῦλα σεσυληκότων καὶ ἀνελόντων τὴν τῆς
μητροπόλεως εὐγένειαν, καὶ πεφονευμένους ἄνδρας
182 ὧν ἀπέσχοντο ἂν κἀκεῖνοι κρατήσαντες; καὶ
Ῥωμαίους μὲν μηδέποτε ὑπερβῆναι τὸν ὅρον τῶν

your souls for revenge upon them ? Have you then lost that most honourable, that most instinctive, of passions—the desire for liberty ? Have we fallen in love with slavery, in love with our masters, as though submission were a heritage from our forefathers ? Nay, they sustained many a mighty struggle for independence and yielded neither to Egyptian nor to Median domination, in their determination to refuse obedience to a conqueror's behests. But why need I speak of the deeds of our forefathers ? We are now at war with Rome ; I forbear to inquire whether such war is profitable and expedient or the reverse, but what is its pretext ? Is it not liberty ? If, then, we refuse to bow to the lords of the inhabited world, are we to tolerate domestic tyrants ? Yet subservience to the foreigner might be attributed to fortune having once for all proved too strong for us ; whereas to surrender to villains of one's own country argues a base and deliberate servility.

" Now that I have mentioned the Romans, I will not conceal from you the thought which struck me while I was speaking and turned my mind to them : I mean that even should we fall beneath their arms —God forbid that those words should ever be our lot !—we can suffer no greater cruelty than what these men have already inflicted upon us. Is it not enough to bring tears to the eyes to see on the one hand in our Temple courts the very votive offerings of the Romans, on the other the spoils of our fellow-countrymen who have plundered and slain the nobility of the metropolis, massacring men whom even the Romans, if victorious, would have spared ? Is it not lamentable, that, while the Romans never

βεβήλων μηδὲ παραβῆναί τι τῶν ἱερῶν ἐθῶν,
πεφρικέναι δὲ πόρρωθεν ὁρῶντας τοὺς τῶν ἁγίων
183 περιβόλους, γεννηθέντας¹ δέ τινας ἐν τῇδε τῇ
χώρᾳ καὶ τραφέντας ὑπὸ τοῖς ἡμετέροις ἔθεσι
καὶ Ἰουδαίους καλουμένους ἐμπεριπατεῖν μέσοις
τοῖς ἁγίοις, θερμὰς ἔτι τὰς χεῖρας ἐξ ὁμοφύλων
184 ἔχοντας φόνων; εἶτά τις δέδοικεν τὸν ἔξωθεν
πόλεμον καὶ τοὺς ἐν συγκρίσει πολλῷ τῶν οἰκείων
ἡμῖν μετριωτέρους; καὶ γὰρ ἄν,² εἰ ἐτύμους δεῖ
τοῖς πράγμασι τὰς κλήσεις ἐφαρμόζειν, τάχα ἂν
εὕροι τις Ῥωμαίους μὲν ἡμῖν βεβαιωτὰς τῶν
185 νόμων, πολεμίους δὲ τοὺς ἔνδον. ἀλλ' ὅτι μὲν
ἐξώλεις οἱ ἐπίβουλοι τῆς ἐλευθερίας, καὶ πρὸς
ἃ δεδράκασιν οὐκ ἄν τις ἐπινοήσειεν δίκην ἀξίαν
κατ' αὐτῶν, οἶμαι πάντας ἥκειν πεπεισμένους
οἴκοθεν καὶ πρὸ τῶν ἐμῶν λόγων παρωξύνθαι
186 τοῖς ἔργοις ἐπ' αὐτούς, ἃ πεπόνθατε. καταπλήσ-
σονται δ' ἴσως οἱ πολλοὶ τό τε πλῆθος αὐτῶν καὶ
τὴν τόλμαν, ἔτι δὲ καὶ τὴν ἐκ τοῦ τόπου πλεονεξίαν.
187 ταῦτα δ' ὥσπερ συνέστη διὰ τὴν ὑμετέραν ἀμέ-
λειαν, καὶ νῦν αὐξηθήσεται πλέον ὑπερθεμένων·
καὶ γὰρ τὸ πλῆθος αὐτοῖς ἐπιτρέφεται καθ'
ἡμέραν, παντὸς πονηροῦ πρὸς τοὺς ὁμοίους αὐτο-
188 μολοῦντος, καὶ τὴν τόλμαν ἐξάπτει μέχρι νῦν
μηδὲν ἐμπόδιον, τῷ τε τόπῳ καθύπερθεν ὄντες
χρήσαιντ' ἂν³ καὶ μετὰ παρασκευῆς, ἂν ἡμεῖς

---

¹ natos Lat.: γεννηθέντας Niese.
² om. ἄν L.
³ Niese: χρήσαιντο MSS.

ᵃ Or, if τῶν βεβήλων is neuter, " the limit of the unhallowed
(permitted) ground." The reference is to the stone balustrade
(δρύφακτος) separating the inner temple from the outer
court, with its warning inscriptions in Greek and Latin,

overstepped the limit fixed for the profane,[a] never violated one of our sacred usages, but beheld with awe from afar the walls that enclose our sanctuary, persons born in this very country, nurtured under our institutions and calling themselves Jews should freely perambulate our holy places, with hands yet hot with the blood of their countrymen ? After that, can any still dread the war with the foreigner and foes who by comparison are far more lenient to us than our own people ? Indeed, if one must nicely fit the phrase to the fact, it is the Romans who may well be found to have been the upholders of our laws, while their enemies were within the walls.

" However, of the abandoned character of these conspirators against liberty and that it would be impossible to conceive any adequate punishment for what they have done, I feel sure that you were all convinced when you left your homes, and that before this address of mine you were already driven to exasperation against them by those misdeeds from which you have suffered. Perhaps, however, most of you are overawed by their numbers, their audacity, and the further advantage which they derive from their position. But, as these arose through your supineness, so will they now be increased, the longer you delay. Indeed, their numbers are growing daily, as every villain deserts to his like ; their audacity is fired by meeting so far with no obstruction ; and they will doubtless avail themselves of their superior position, with the added benefit of

forbidding foreigners to pass under pain of death, v. 193 f. While the ordinary Roman scrupulously observed the rule, (ii. 341 Neapolitanus pays his devotions " from the permitted area "), conquerors such as Pompey, and even Titus himself, penetrated to the Holy Place (*Ap.* ii. 82, *B.* i. 152, vi. 260).

189 χρόνον δῶμεν. πιστεύσατε δ' ὡς, ἐὰν προσ-
βαίνωμεν ἐπ' αὐτούς, ἔσονται τῇ συνειδήσει
ταπεινότεροι, καὶ τὸ πλεονέκτημα τοῦ ὕψους ὁ
190 λογισμὸς ἀπολεῖ. τάχα τὸ θεῖον ὑβρισμένον ἀνα-
στρέψει κατ' αὐτῶν τὰ βαλλόμενα, καὶ τοῖς σφετέροις διαφθαρήσονται βέλεσιν οἱ δυσσεβεῖς. μόνον
191 ὀφθῶμεν αὐτοῖς, καὶ καταλέλυνται. καλὸν δέ,
κἂν προσῇ τις κίνδυνος, ἀποθνῄσκειν πρὸς τοῖς
ἱεροῖς πυλῶσι κἂν τὴν ψυχήν, εἰ καὶ μὴ πρὸ
παίδων ἢ γυναικῶν, ἀλλ' ὑπὲρ τοῦ θεοῦ καὶ τῶν
192 ἁγίων προέσθαι. προστήσομαι δ' ἐγὼ γνώμῃ
τε καὶ χειρί, καὶ οὔτ' ἐπίνοιά τις ὑμῖν λείψει πρὸς
ἀσφάλειαν ἐξ ἡμῶν οὔτε τοῦ σώματος ὄψεσθε
φειδόμενον.''

193 (11) Τούτοις ὁ ῎Ανανος παρακροτεῖ τὸ πλῆθος
ἐπὶ τοὺς ζηλωτάς, οὐκ ἀγνοῶν μὲν ὡς εἶεν ἤδη
δυσκατάλυτοι πλήθει τε καὶ νεότητι καὶ παραστήματι ψυχῆς, τὸ πλέον δὲ συνειδήσει τῶν εἰρ-
γασμένων· οὐ γὰρ ἐνδώσειν αὐτοὺς εἰς ἔσχατον[1]
194 συγγνώμην ἐφ' οἷς ἔδρασαν ἀπελπίσαντας[2]· ὅμως
δὲ πᾶν ὁτιοῦν παθεῖν προῃρεῖτο μᾶλλον ἢ περιιδεῖν
195 ἐν τοιαύτῃ τὰ πράγματα συγχύσει. τὸ δὲ πλῆθος
ἄγειν αὐτοὺς ἐβόα καθ' ὧν παρεκάλει, καὶ προκινδυνεύειν ἕκαστος ἦν ἑτοιμότατος.

196 (12) ᾿Εν ὅσῳ δὲ ὁ ῎Ανανος κατέλεγέ τε καὶ
συνέτασσε τοὺς ἐπιτηδείους πρὸς μάχην, οἱ
ζηλωταὶ πυνθανόμενοι τὴν ἐπιχείρησιν, παρῆσαν
γὰρ οἱ ἀγγέλλοντες αὐτοῖς πάντα τὰ παρὰ τοῦ
δήμου, παροξύνονται κἀκ τοῦ ἱεροῦ προπηδῶντες
ἀθρόοι τε καὶ κατὰ λόχους οὐδενὸς ἐφείδοντο τῶν

---

[1] Hudson with one ms.: ἐσχάτην the rest.

preparation, if we give them time. But, believe me, if we mount to the attack, conscience will humble them and the advantage of superior height will be neutralized by reflection. Maybe, the Deity, whom they have outraged, will turn their missiles back upon them,[a] and their own weapons will bring destruction upon the impious wretches. Only let us face them and their doom is sealed. And, if the venture has its attendant risks, it were a noble end to die at the sacred portals and to sacrifice our lives if not for wives and children, yet for God and for the sanctuary. But I will support you both with head and hand : there shall be no lack on my part of thought to ensure your safety, nor shall you see me spare my person."

(11) Thus did Ananus incite the populace against the Zealots. He knew full well how difficult their extermination had already become through their numbers, vigour, and intrepidity, but above all through their consciousness of their deeds ; since, in despair of obtaining pardon for all they had done, they would never give in to the end. Nevertheless, he preferred to undergo any suffering rather than allow affairs to remain in such confusion. The people too now clamoured for him to lead them against the foe whom he urged them to attack, each man fully ready to brave the first danger.

(12) But while Ananus was enlisting and marshalling efficient recruits, the Zealots hearing of the projected attack—for word was brought to them of all the people's proceedings—were furious, and dashed out of the Temple, in regiments and smaller units,

Ananus and the citizens prepare to attack the Zealots.

Fierce fighting.

---

[a] As at Gamala, § 76.

[a] Destinon (*cf.* v. 354): ἐλπίσαντας (or -ες) MSS.

JOSEPHUS

197 προστυγχανόντων. ἀθροίζεται δ' ὑπ' Ἀνάνου ταχέως τὸ δημοτικόν, πλήθει μὲν ὑπερέχον, ὅπλοις
δὲ καὶ τῷ μὴ συγκεκροτῆσθαι λειπόμενον τῶν
198 ζηλωτῶν. τὸ πρόθυμον δὲ παρ' ἑκατέροις ἀνεπλήρου τὰ λείποντα, τῶν μὲν ἀπὸ τῆς πόλεως
ἀνειληφότων ὀργὴν ἰσχυροτέραν τῶν ὅπλων, τῶν
δ' ἀπὸ τοῦ ἱεροῦ τόλμαν παντὸς πλήθους ὑπερ-
199 έχουσαν· καὶ οἱ μὲν ἀοίκητον ὑπολαμβάνοντες
αὑτοῖς τὴν πόλιν εἰ μὴ τοὺς λῃστὰς ἐκκόψειαν
αὐτῆς, οἱ ζηλωταὶ δ' εἰ μὴ κρατοῖεν οὐκ ἔστιν
ἧστινος ὑστερήσειν τιμωρίας, συνερρήγνυντο[1] στρα-
200 τηγούμενοι τοῖς πάθεσι, τὸ μὲν πρῶτον κατὰ τὴν
πόλιν καὶ πρὸ τοῦ ἱεροῦ λίθοις βάλλοντες ἀλλήλους
καὶ πόρρωθεν διακοντιζόμενοι, κατὰ δὲ τὰς
τροπὰς οἱ κρατοῦντες ἐχρῶντο τοῖς ξίφεσι· καὶ
πολὺς ἦν ἑκατέρων φόνος, τραυματίαι τε ἐγίνοντο
201 συχνοί. καὶ τοὺς μὲν ἀπὸ τοῦ δήμου διεκόμιζον
εἰς τὰς οἰκίας οἱ προσήκοντες, ὁ δὲ βληθεὶς τῶν
ζηλωτῶν εἰς τὸ ἱερὸν ἀνήει καθαιμάσσων τὸ θεῖον
ἔδαφος· καὶ μόνον ἄν τις εἴποι τὸ ἐκείνων αἷμα
202 μιᾶναι τὰ ἅγια. κατὰ μὲν οὖν τὰς συμβολὰς
ἐκτρέχοντες ἀεὶ περιῆσαν οἱ λῃστρικοί, τεθυμω-
μένοι δ' οἱ δημοτικοὶ καὶ πλείους ἀεὶ γινόμενοι,
κακίζοντες τοὺς ἐνδιδόντας καὶ μὴ διδόντες τοῖς
τρεπομένοις ἀναχώρησιν οἱ κατόπιν βιαζόμενοι,
πᾶν μὲν ἐπιστρέφουσι τὸ σφέτερον εἰς τοὺς
203 ὑπεναντίους· κἀκείνων μηκέτ' ἀντεχόντων τῇ βίᾳ,
κατὰ μικρὸν δ' ἀναχωρούντων εἰς τὸ ἱερὸν συν-
204 εισπίπτουσιν οἱ περὶ τὸν Ἄνανον. τοῖς δὲ κατάπληξις ἐμπίπτει στερομένοις τοῦ πρώτου περιβόλου, καὶ καταφυγόντες εἰς τὸ ἐνδοτέρω ταχέως

[1] A²: + δὲ the rest.

and spared none who fell in their way. Ananus
promptly collected his citizen force, which, though
superior in numbers, in arms and through lack of
training was no match for the Zealots. Ardour,
however, supplied either party's deficiencies, those
from the city being armed with a fury more powerful
than weapons, those from the Temple with a recklessness outweighing all numerical superiority ; the
former persuaded that the city would be uninhabit-
able by them unless the brigands were eradicated,
the Zealots that unless they were victorious no form
of punishment would be spared them. Thus, swayed
by their passions, they met in conflict. This opened
with a mutual discharge of stones from all parts of
the city and from the front of the Temple and a
long range javelin combat ; but, when either party
gave way, the victors employed their swords, and
there was great slaughter on both sides and multitudes were wounded. The injured civilians were
carried into the houses by their relatives, while any
Zealot who was struck climbed up into the Temple,
staining with his blood the sacred pavement ; and
it might be said that no blood but theirs defiled the
sanctuary. In these engagements the sallies of the
brigands proved invariably successful ; but the
populace, roused to fury and continually growing
in numbers, upbraiding those who gave way, while
those pressing forward in rear refused passage to
the fugitives, finally turned their whole force upon
their opponents. The latter no longer able to withstand this pressure gradually withdrew into the
Temple, Ananus and his men rushing in along with Ananus masters the outer court
them. Dismayed by the loss of the outer court, the
Zealots fled into the inner and instantly barred the

205 ἀποκλείουσι τὰς πύλας. τῷ δ' Ἀνάνῳ προσ-
βαλεῖν μὲν οὐκ ἐδόκει τοῖς ἱεροῖς πυλῶσιν,
ἄλλως τε κἀκείνων βαλλόντων ἄνωθεν, ἀθέμιτον
δ' ἡγεῖτο, κἂν κρατήσῃ, μὴ προηγνευκὸς εἰσ-
206 αγαγεῖν τὸ πλῆθος· διακληρώσας δ' ἐκ πάντων εἰς
ἑξακισχιλίους ὁπλίτας καθίστησιν ἐπὶ ταῖς στοαῖς
207 φρουρούς· διεδέχοντο δ' ἄλλοι τούτους, καὶ παντὶ
μὲν ἀνάγκη παρεῖναι πρὸς τὴν φυλακὴν ἐκ περιόδου,
πολλοὶ δὲ τῶν ἐν ἀξιώμασιν ἐφεθέντες ὑπὸ τῶν
ἄρχειν δοκούντων μισθούμενοι πενιχροτέρους ἀνθ'
ἑαυτῶν ἐπὶ τὴν φρουρὰν ἔπεμπον.
208 (13) Γίνεται δὲ τούτοις πᾶσιν ὀλέθρου παραίτιος
Ἰωάννης, ὃν ἔφαμεν ἀπὸ Γισχάλων διαδρᾶναι,
δολιώτατος ἀνὴρ καὶ δεινὸν ἔρωτα τυραννίδος ἐν
τῇ ψυχῇ περιφέρων, ὃς πόρρωθεν ἐπεβούλευε τοῖς
209 πράγμασιν. καὶ δὴ τότε τὰ τοῦ δήμου φρονεῖν
ὑποκρινόμενος συμπεριῄει μὲν τῷ Ἀνάνῳ βου-
λευομένῳ¹ σὺν τοῖς δυνατοῖς μεθ' ἡμέραν καὶ
νύκτωρ ἐπιόντι τὰς φυλακάς, διήγγελλε δὲ τὰ
ἀπόρρητα τοῖς ζηλωταῖς, καὶ πᾶν σκέμμα τοῦ
δήμου πρὶν καλῶς βουλευθῆναι παρὰ τοῖς ἐχθροῖς
210 ἐγινώσκετο δι' αὐτοῦ. μηχανώμενος δὲ τὸ μὴ
δι' ὑποψίας ἐλθεῖν ἀμέτροις ἐχρῆτο ταῖς θεραπείαις εἰς τόν τε Ἄνανον καὶ τοὺς τοῦ δήμου
211 προεστῶτας. ἐχώρει δ' εἰς τοὐναντίον αὐτῷ τὸ
φιλότιμον· διὰ γὰρ τὰς ἀλόγους κολακείας μᾶλλον
ὑπωπτεύετο, καὶ τὸ πανταχοῦ παρεῖναι μὴ καλούμενον ἔμφασιν προδοσίας τῶν ἀπορρήτων παρεῖχε.

¹ + μὲν PAVR : + τε Destinon.

ᵃ §§ 106 ff.
ᵇ Cf. § 85 with note. This passage again recalls Sallust's

62

gates. Ananus did not think fit to assail the sacred
portals, especially under the enemy's hail of missiles
from above, but considered it unlawful, even were
he victorious, to introduce these crowds without
previous purification ; instead, he selected by lot
from the whole number six thousand armed men, and
whom he posted to guard the porticoes. These were the Zealots
to be relieved by others, and every man was bound in the
to fall in for sentry duty in rotation ; but many temple.
persons of rank, with the permission of their superior
officers, hired some of the lower classes and sent
them to mount guard in their stead.

(13) The subsequent destruction of this entire John of
party was largely due to John, whose escape from Gischala,
Gischala we have related.[a] He was a man of extreme to Ananus,
cunning who carried in his breast a dire passion for
despotic power and had long been plotting against
the state.[b] At this juncture, feigning to side with
the people, he would accompany Ananus on his
rounds, whether holding consultations with the
leaders by day or visiting the sentries by night, and
then divulge his secrets to the Zealots ; so that every
idea proposed by the people, even before it had been
thoroughly considered, was through his agency
known to their opponents. Seeking to escape
suspicion, he displayed unbounded servility to
Ananus and the heads of the popular party, but this
obsequiousness had the reverse effect ; for his
extravagant flatteries only brought more suspicion
upon him, and his ubiquitous and uninvited presence
produced the impression that he was betraying

portrait of Catiline : " animus audax, subdolus (parallel to
δολιώτατος here) . . hunc . . lubido maxuma invaserat rei
publicae capiundae."

212 συνεώρων μὲν γὰρ αἰσθανομένους ἅπαντα τοὺς
ἐχθροὺς τῶν παρ' αὑτοῖς βουλευμάτων, πιθανώ-
τερος δ' οὐδεὶς ἦν Ἰωάννου πρὸς ὑποψίας τοῦ
213 διαγγέλλειν. ἀποσκευάσασθαι μὲν οὖν αὐτὸν οὐκ
ἦν ῥᾴδιον, ὄντα <τε>[1] δυνατὸν ἐκ πονηρίας καὶ
ἄλλως οὐ τῶν ἀσήμων, ὑπεζωσμένον τε πολλοὺς
τῶν συνεδρευόντων τοῖς ὅλοις,[2] ἐδόκει δ' αὐτὸν
214 ὅρκοις πιστώσασθαι πρὸς εὔνοιαν. ὤμνυε δ' ὁ
Ἰωάννης ἑτοίμως εὐνοήσειν τε τῷ δήμῳ καὶ μήτε
βουλήν τινα μήτε πρᾶξιν προδώσειν τοῖς ἐχθροῖς,
συγκαταλύσειν δὲ τοὺς ἐπιτιθεμένους καὶ χειρὶ
215 καὶ γνώμῃ. οἱ δὲ περὶ τὸν Ἄνανον πιστεύσαντες
τοῖς ὅρκοις ἤδη χωρὶς ὑπονοίας εἰς τὰς συμ-
βουλίας αὐτὸν παρελάμβανον, καὶ δὴ καὶ πρεσβευτὴν εἰσπέμπουσι πρὸς τοὺς ζηλωτὰς περὶ
διαλύσεων· ἦν γὰρ αὐτοῖς σπουδὴ τὸ παρ' αὐτοῖς
μὴ μιᾶναι τὸ ἱερὸν μηδέ τινα τῶν ὁμοφύλων ἐν
αὐτῷ πεσεῖν.

216 (14) Ὁ δ' ὥσπερ τοῖς ζηλωταῖς ὑπὲρ εὐνοίας
ὀμόσας καὶ οὐ κατ' αὐτῶν, παρελθὼν εἴσω καὶ
καταστὰς εἰς μέσους πολλάκις μὲν ἔφη κινδυνεῦσαι
δι' αὐτούς, ἵνα μηδὲν ἀγνοήσωσι τῶν ἀπορρήτων,
ὅσα κατ' αὐτῶν οἱ περὶ τὸν Ἄνανον ἐβουλεύσαντο·
217 νῦν δὲ τὸν μέγιστον ἀναρριπτεῖν κίνδυνον σὺν
πᾶσιν αὐτοῖς, εἰ μή τις προσγένοιτο βοήθεια
218 δαιμόνιος. οὐ γὰρ ἔτι μέλλειν Ἄνανον, ἀλλὰ
πείσαντα μὲν τὸν δῆμον πεπομφέναι πρέσβεις
πρὸς Οὐεσπασιανόν, ἵν' ἐλθὼν κατὰ τάχος παρα-

----

[1] ὄντα τε Dindorf: ὄντα most mss.: οὔτε VR.
[2] ὅπλοις PAL[2].

----

[a] Literally "girt about (or 'under') him many," cf. ii.
275 ἴδιον στῖφος ὑπεζωσμένος " with his own band of followers

secrets. For it was observed that their enemies were aware of all their plans, and there was no one more open to the suspicion of disclosing them than John. It was, however, no easy matter to shake off one who had gained such influence through his villainy, who was in any case a man of mark, and who had won many followers[a] among those who met in council on the general weal; it was therefore decided to bind him over to loyalty by oath. John promptly swore that he would be true to the people, that he would betray neither counsel nor act to their foes, and would assist both with his arm and his advice in putting down their assailants. Relying on these oaths, Ananus and his party now admitted him without suspicion to their deliberations, and even went so far as to send him as their delegate to the Zealots to arrange a treaty; for they were anxious on their side to preserve the Temple from pollution and that none of their countrymen should fall within its walls. *is bound over to loyalty* *and sent as delegate to the Zealots.*

(14) But John, as though he had given his oath of allegiance to the Zealots instead of against them, went in and, standing in their midst, addressed them as follows. "Often have I risked my life on your behalf, to keep you fully informed of all the secret schemes devised against you by Ananus and his followers; but now I am exposing myself to the greatest of perils, in which you will all be involved, unless some providential aid intervene to avert it. For Ananus, impatient of delay, has prevailed on the people to send an embassy to Vespasian, inviting *John incites the Zealots to seek aid from outside against Ananus.*

grouped around him"; a metaphorical use of the verb unattested elsewhere.

λάβῃ τὴν πόλιν, ἁγνείαν δὲ παρηγγελκέναι κατ'
αὐτῶν εἰς τὴν ἑξῆς ἡμέραν, ἵν' ἢ κατὰ θρησκείαν
εἰσελθόντες ἢ καὶ βιασάμενοι συμμίξωσιν αὐτοῖς.
219 οὐχ ὁρᾶν δὲ μέχρι τίνος ἢ τὴν φρουρὰν οἴσουσιν
ἢ παρατάξονται πρὸς τοσούτους. προσετίθει δ'
ὡς αὐτὸς εἰσπεμφθείη κατὰ θεοῦ πρόνοιαν ὡς
πρεσβευτὴς ὑπὲρ¹ διαλύσεων· τὸν γὰρ Ἄνανον
ταύτας αὐτοῖς προτείνειν, ὅπως ἀνυποπτοτέροις²
220 ἐπέλθῃ. δεῖν οὖν ἢ τῷ λόγῳ τοῦ ζῆν τοὺς φρου-
ροῦντας ἱκετεύειν ἢ πορίζεσθαί τινα παρὰ τῶν
221 ἔξωθεν ἐπικουρίαν· τοὺς δὲ θαλπομένους ἐλπίδι
συγγνώμης εἰ κρατηθεῖεν, ἐπιλελῆσθαι τῶν ἰδίων
τολμημάτων ἢ νομίζειν ἅμα τῷ μετανοεῖν τοὺς
δεδρακότας εὐθέως ὀφείλειν διηλλάχθαι καὶ τοὺς
222 παθόντας. ἀλλὰ τῶν μὲν ἀδικησάντων διὰ μίσους
πολλάκις γίνεσθαι καὶ τὴν μεταμέλειαν, τοῖς
ἀδικηθεῖσι δὲ τὰς ὀργὰς ἐπ' ἐξουσίας χαλεπωτέρας·
223 ἐφεδρεύειν δέ γε ἐκείνοις φίλους καὶ συγγενεῖς
τῶν ἀπολωλότων καὶ δῆμον τοσοῦτον ὑπὲρ καταλύσεως νόμων καὶ δικαστηρίων τεθυμωμένον,
ὅπου κἂν ᾖ τι μέρος τὸ ἐλεοῦν, ὑπὸ πλείονος ἂν
αὐτὸ τοῦ διαγανακτοῦντος ἀφανισθῆναι.
224 (iv. 1) Τοιαῦτα μὲν ἐποίκιλλεν ἀθρόως δεδισσόμενος, καὶ τὴν ἔξωθεν βοήθειαν ἀναφανδὸν μὲν
οὐκ ἐθάρρει λέγειν, ᾐνίσσετο δὲ τοὺς Ἰδουμαίους·
ἵνα δὲ καὶ τοὺς ἡγεμόνας τῶν ζηλωτῶν ἰδίᾳ

¹ περὶ P.
² L¹ (Lat. nihil suspicantes): ἀνοπλοτέροις PAL²: ἀ(ν)όπλοις
the rest.

___

ᵃ A specious statement, in view of his known reluctance to
allow his followers to enter the Temple without previous
purification (§ 205).
ᵇ In the collocation of " laws and law-courts " we seem

66

him to come at once and take possession of the city. To your further injury, he has announced a purification service [a] for to-morrow, in order that his followers may obtain admission here, either on the plea of worship or by force of arms, and attack you hand to hand. Nor do I see how you can long sustain either the present siege or a contest with such a host of opponents." He added that it was by the providence of God that he had himself been deputed to negotiate a treaty, as Ananus was offering them terms, only to fall upon them when off their guard. "It behoves you, therefore," he continued, "if you care for your lives, either to sue for mercy from your besiegers, or to procure some external aid. But any who cherish hopes of being pardoned in the event of defeat must either have forgotten their own daring deeds, or suppose that the penitence of the perpetrators should be followed by the instant reconciliation of the victims. On the contrary, the very repentance of wrongdoers is often detested and the resentment of the wronged is embittered by power. Watching their opportunity to retaliate are the friends and relatives of the slain and a whole host of people infuriated at the dissolution of their laws and law-courts.[b] In such a crowd, even if some few were moved to compassion, they would be crushed by an indignant majority."

(iv. 1) Such was the embroidered tale he told to create a general scare; what "external aid" was intended he did not venture to say outright, but he was hinting at the Idumaeans. But in order to incense the personal feelings of the Zealots' leaders

The Zealots invoke the aid of the Idumaeans.

to hear the historian's Greek assistant speaking; cf. § 258 and Vol. II. Introd. p. xiii.

παροξύνῃ, τὸν Ἄνανον εἴς τε ὠμότητα διέβαλλε
225 καὶ ἀπειλεῖν ἐκείνοις ἐξαιρέτως ἔλεγεν. ἦσαν δὲ
Ἐλεάζαρος μὲν υἱὸς Γίωνος,[1] ὃς δὴ καὶ πιθανώ-
τατος ἐδόκει τῶν ἐν αὐτοῖς νοῆσαί τε τὰ δέοντα
καὶ τὰ νοηθέντα πρᾶξαι, Ζαχαρίας δέ τις υἱὸς
226 Ἀμφικάλλει,[2] γένος ἐκ τῶν ἱερέων ἑκάτερος. οὗτοι
πρὸς ταῖς κοιναῖς τὰς ἰδίας καθ' ἑαυτῶν ἀπειλὰς
ἀκούσαντες, ἔτι δ' ὡς οἱ περὶ τὸν Ἄνανον δυναστείαν αὐτοῖς περιποιούμενοι Ῥωμαίους ἐπι-
καλοῖντο, καὶ γὰρ τοῦτο Ἰωάννης προσεψεύσατο,
μέχρι πολλοῦ μὲν ἠποροῦντο, τί χρὴ πράττειν εἰς
227 ὀξὺν οὕτως καιρὸν συνεωσμένους· παρεσκευάσθαι
μὲν γὰρ τὸν δῆμον ἐπιχειρεῖν αὐτοῖς οὐκ εἰς
μακράν, αὐτῶν δὲ τὸ σύντομον[3] τῆς ἐπιβολῆς[6]
ὑποτετμῆσθαι τὰς ἔξωθεν ἐπικουρίας· πάντα γὰρ
ἂν φθῆναι παθεῖν πρὶν καὶ πυθέσθαι τινὰ τῶν συμ-
228 μάχων. ἔδοξε δ' ὅμως ἐπικαλεῖσθαι τοὺς Ἰδουμαίους, καὶ γράψαντες ἐπιστολὴν σύντομον, ὡς
Ἄνανος μὲν προδιδοίη Ῥωμαίοις τὴν μητρόπολιν
ἐξαπατήσας τὸν δῆμον, αὐτοὶ δ' ὑπὲρ τῆς ἐλευ-
229 θερίας ἀποστάντες ἐν τῷ ἱερῷ φρουροῖντο, ὀλίγος
δ' ἔτι χρόνος αὐτοῖς βραβεύοι τὴν σωτηρίαν, εἰ
δὲ μὴ βοηθήσουσιν ἐκεῖνοι κατὰ τάχος, αὐτοὶ μὲν
ὑπ' Ἀνάνῳ τε καὶ τοῖς ἐχθροῖς, ἡ πόλις δ' ὑπὸ
Ῥωμαίοις[5] φθάσει γενομένη. τὰ δὲ πολλὰ τοῖς
ἀγγέλοις ἐνετέλλοντο πρὸς τοὺς ἄρχοντας τῶν
230 Ἰδουμαίων διαλέγεσθαι. προεβλήθησαν δ' ἐπὶ τὴν
ἀγγελίαν δύο τῶν δραστηρίων ἀνδρῶν, εἰπεῖν τε

[3] PAL Lat.: Σίμωνος the rest.
[2] Φαλέκου CM²V².
[3] PAL Lat.: σύντονον the rest.
[6] Niese: ἐπιβουλῆς mss.   [5] Ῥωμαίους PL¹.

as well, he accused Ananus of brutality, asserting
that his special threats were directed at them.
These leaders were Eleazar, son of Gion,[a] the most
influential man of the party, from his ability both
in conceiving appropriate measures and in carrying
them into effect, and a certain Zacharias,[b] son of
Amphicalleus, both being of priestly descent. They,
on hearing first the menaces against the whole
party and then those specially levelled at themselves,
and, moreover, how Ananus and his friends were
summoning the Romans in order to secure supreme
power for themselves—this was another of John's
libels—were long in doubt what action they should
take, being so hard pressed for time; since the
people were prepared to attack them ere long, and
the suddenness of the scheme cut short their chances
of aid from without, as all would be over before any
of their allies even heard of their situation. They
decided, nevertheless, to summon the Idumaeans,
and drafted a letter concisely stating that Ananus
had imposed on the people and was proposing to
betray the capital to the Romans; that they themselves having revolted in the cause of freedom were
imprisoned in the Temple; that a few hours would
now decide their fate, and that unless the Idumaeans
sent prompt relief, they would soon have succumbed
to Ananus and their foes, and the city be in possession of the Romans. The messengers were instructed
to communicate further details to the Idumaean
chiefs by word of mouth. Those selected for this
errand were two active individuals, eloquent and

---

[a] Or, with the other reading, E. son of Simon, who plays
an important part elsewhere, ii. 564 f., v. 5 ff.
[b] Not mentioned again.

ἱκανοὶ καὶ πεῖσαι περὶ πραγμάτων, τὸ δὲ τούτων
231 χρησιμώτερον, ὠκύτητι ποδῶν διαφέροντες· τοὺς
μὲν γὰρ Ἰδουμαίους αὐτόθεν ᾔδεισαν πεισθησο-
μένους, ἅτε θορυβῶδες καὶ ἄτακτον ἔθνος αἰεί τε
μετέωρον πρὸς τὰ κινήματα καὶ μεταβολαῖς χαῖρον,
πρὸς ὀλίγην τε κολακείαν τῶν δεομένων τὰ ὅπλα
κινοῦν καὶ καθάπερ εἰς ἑορτὴν εἰς τὰς παρατάξεις
232 ἐπειγόμενον. ἔδει δὲ τάχους εἰς τὴν ἀγγελίαν·
εἰς ὃ μηδὲν ἐλλείποντες προθυμίας οἱ πεμφθέντες,
ἐκαλεῖτο δ' αὐτῶν Ἀνανίας ἑκάτερος, καὶ δὴ πρὸς
τοὺς ἄρχοντας τῶν Ἰδουμαίων παρῆσαν.

233 (2) Οἱ δὲ πρὸς τὴν ἐπιστολὴν καὶ τὰ ῥηθέντα
παρὰ τῶν ἀφιγμένων ἐκπλαγέντες, ὥσπερ ἐμμανεῖς
περιέθεόν τε τὸ ἔθνος καὶ διεκήρυσσον τὴν στρα-
234 τείαν. ἤθροιστο δ' ἡ πληθὺς τάχιον τοῦ παραγγέλματος, καὶ πάντες ὡς ἐπ' ἐλευθερίᾳ τῆς
235 μητροπόλεως ἥρπαζον τὰ ὅπλα. συνταχθέντες δ'
εἰς δύο μυριάδας παραγίνονται πρὸς τὰ Ἱεροσόλυμα, χρώμενοι τέσσαρσιν ἡγεμόσιν, Ἰωάννῃ
τε καὶ Ἰακώβῳ παιδὶ[1] Σωσᾶ, πρὸς δὲ τούτοις·ἦν
Σίμων υἱὸς Θακίου[2] καὶ Φινέας Κλουσώθ.

236 (3) Τὸν δὲ Ἄνανον ἡ μὲν ἔξοδος τῶν ἀγγέλων
ὥσπερ καὶ τοὺς φρουροὺς ἔλαθεν, ἡ δ' ἔφοδος
τῶν Ἰδουμαίων οὐκέτι· προγνοὺς γὰρ ἀποκλείει
τε[3] τὰς πύλας αὐτοῖς καὶ διὰ φυλακῆς εἶχε τὰ
237 τείχη. καθάπαν γε μὴν αὐτοὺς ἐκπολεμεῖν οὐκ
ἔδοξεν, ἀλλὰ λόγοις πείθειν πρὸ τῶν ὅπλων.
238 στὰς οὖν ἐπὶ τὸν ἀντικρὺς αὐτῶν πύργον ὁ μετὰ

---

[1] Perhaps παισὶ should be read (Niese).
[2] Κλαθᾶ or Καθλᾶ the inferior mss.; cf. 271, v. 249, vi. 148.
[3] ἀποκλείει τε Destinon: ἀποκλείεται or ἀποκλείει mss.

---

[a] Or perhaps "John and James, sons of S." John was

persuasive speakers on public affairs, and, what was still more useful, remarkably fleet of foot. For the Zealots knew that the Idumaeans would comply forthwith, as they were a turbulent and disorderly people, ever on the alert for commotion and delighting in revolutionary changes, and only needed a little flattery from their suitors to seize their arms and rush into battle as to a feast. Speed was essential to the errand; in this no want of alacrity was shown by the delegates, each named Ananias, and they were soon in the presence of the Idumaean chiefs.

(2) The leaders, astounded by the letter and the statements of their visitors, raced round the nation like madmen, making proclamation of the campaign. The mustering of the clan outstripped the orders, and all snatched up their arms to defend the freedom of the capital. No less than twenty thousand joined the ranks and marched to Jerusalem, under the command of four generals: John, James son of Sosas,[a] Simon son of Thaceas, and Phineas son of Clusoth.

(3) Though the departure of the messengers had eluded the vigilance alike of Ananus and of the sentries, not so the approach of the Idumaeans. Forewarned of this, he shut the gates against them and posted guards upon the walls. Unwilling, however, to make complete enemies of them, he determined to try persuasion before having recourse to arms. Accordingly Jesus, the chief priest next in

The Idumaeans march to Jerusalem.

subsequently slain by an Arab archer in the Roman army, v. 290; James appears often in the sequel, iv. 521, v. 249, vi. 92, 148, 380. Simon is the orator of the party, iv. 271, and wins special distinction in the field, v. 249, vi. 148. Phineas is not heard of again.

Ἄνανον γεραίτατος τῶν ἀρχιερέων Ἰησοῦς, πολλῶν ἔφη καὶ ποικίλων τὴν πόλιν κατεσχηκότων
θορύβων ἐν οὐδενὶ θαυμάσαι τὴν τύχην· οὕτως,
ὡς τῷ συμπράττειν τοῖς πονηροῖς καὶ τὰ παρά-
239 δοξα· παρεῖναι γοῦν ὑμᾶς ἀνθρώποις ἐξωλε-
στάτοις μετὰ τοσαύτης προθυμίας ἐπαμυνοῦντας
καθ' ἡμῶν, μεθ' ὅσης εἰκὸς ἦν ἐλθεῖν οὐδὲ τῆς
240 μητροπόλεως καλούσης ἐπὶ βαρβάρους. "καὶ εἰ
μὲν ἑώρων τὴν σύνταξιν ὑμῶν ἐξ ὁμοίων τοῖς
καλέσασιν ἀνδρῶν, οὐκ ἂν ἄλογον τὴν ὁρμὴν
ὑπελάμβανον· οὐδὲν γὰρ οὕτως συνίστησι τὰς
εὐνοίας ὡς τρόπων συγγένεια· νῦν δ', εἰ μέν τις
αὐτοὺς ἐξετάζοι καθ' ἕνα, μυρίων ἕκαστος εὑρε-
241 θήσεται θανάτων ἄξιος. τὰ γὰρ λύματα[1] καὶ
καθάρματα τῆς χώρας[2] ὅλης, κατασωτευσάμενα
τὰς ἰδίας οὐσίας καὶ προγυμνάσαντα τὴν ἀπόνοιαν
ἐν ταῖς πέριξ κώμαις τε καὶ πόλεσι, τελευταῖα
λεληθότως παρεισέρρευσαν εἰς τὴν ἱερὰν πόλιν,
242 λῃσταὶ δι' ὑπερβολὴν ἀσεβημάτων μιαίνοντες καὶ
τὸ ἀβέβηλον ἔδαφος, οὓς ὁρᾶν ἔστι νῦν ἀδεεῖς
ἐμμεθυσκομένους τοῖς ἁγίοις καὶ τὰ σκῦλα τῶν
πεφονευμένων καταναλίσκοντας εἰς τὰς ἀπλήστους
243 γαστέρας. τὸ δ' ὑμέτερον πλῆθος καὶ τὸν κόσμον
τῶν ὅπλων ὁρᾶν ἔστιν οἷος ἔπρεπεν καλούσης μὲν
τῆς μητροπόλεως κοινῷ βουλευτηρίῳ, συμμάχους
δὲ κατ' ἀλλοφύλων. τί ἂν οὖν εἴποι τοῦτό τις ἢ
τύχης ἐπήρειαν, ὅταν λογάσι πονηροῖς αὐτανδρον
244 ἔθνος ὁρᾷ συνασπίζον; μέχρι πολλοῦ μὲν ἀπορῶ,

---

[1] Lowth: θύματα mss.: ludibria Lat., whence ἀθύρματα
Hudson.
[2] πόλεως PAL.
[3] + αὐτοῖς mss.: συνασπίζοντας (Destinon) or, with altered

72

seniority to Ananus, mounted the tower opposite to the Idumaeans and addressed them as follows :

"Among the many and manifold disorders which this city has witnessed, nothing has astonished me more than the decree of fortune by which even the most unexpected things co-operate to aid the wicked. Here, for instance, are you, come to assist these most abandoned of men against us, with such alacrity as was hardly to be looked for even had the mother city summoned you to meet a barbarian invasion. Had I seen your ranks composed of men like those who invited you, I should not have thought such ardour unreasonable ; for nothing so unites men's affections as congeniality of character. But as it is, were one to review these friends of yours one by one, each would be found deserving of a myriad deaths. The scum and offscourings of the whole country, after squandering their own means and exercising their madness first upon the surrounding villages and towns, these pests have ended by stealthily streaming into the holy city : brigands of such rank impiety as to pollute even that hallowed ground, they may be seen now recklessly intoxicating themselves in the sanctuary and expending the spoils of their slaughtered victims upon their insatiable bellies. You, on the other hand, in your numbers and shining armour present an appearance such as would become you had the capital in public council summoned you to its aid against the foreigner. What, then, can this be called but a spiteful freak of fortune, when one sees a nation armed to a man on behalf of notorious scoundrels ?

Jesus the chief priest addresses the Idumaeans from the walls. The paradox of a nation in arms on behalf of scoundrels.

---

punctuation, συνάσπιζον : αὐτὸς (Bekker) should perhaps be read.

τί δή ποτε καὶ τὸ κινῆσαν ὑμᾶς οὕτω ταχέως
ἐγένετο· μὴ γὰρ ἂν δίχα μεγάλης αἰτίας ἀναλαβεῖν
τὰς πανοπλίας ὑπὲρ λῃστῶν καὶ κατὰ δήμου
245 συγγενοῦς. ἐπεὶ δὲ ἠκούσαμεν Ῥωμαίους καὶ
προδοσίαν, ταῦτα γὰρ ὑμῶν ἐθορύβουν τινὲς ἀρτίως,
καὶ τῆς μητροπόλεως ἐπ’ ἐλευθερώσει παρεῖναι,
πλέον τῶν ἄλλων τολμημάτων ἐθαυμάσαμεν τοὺς
246 ἀλιτηρίους τῆς περὶ τοῦτο ψευδοῦς ἐπινοίας· ἄνδρας
γὰρ φύσει φιλελευθέρους καὶ διὰ τοῦτο μάλιστα
τοῖς ἔξωθεν πολεμίοις μάχεσθαι παρεσκευασμέ-
νους οὐκ ἐνῆν ἄλλως ἐξαγριῶσαι καθ’ ἡμῶν ἢ
λογοποιήσαντας προδοσίαν τῆς ποθουμένης[1] ἐλευ-
247 θερίας. ἀλλ’ ὑμᾶς γε χρὴ σκέπτεσθαι τούς τε
διαβάλλοντας καὶ καθ’ ὧν, συνάγειν τε τὴν
ἀλήθειαν οὐκ ἐκ τῶν ἐπιπλάστων λόγων ἀλλ’ ἐκ τῶν
248 κοινῶν πραγμάτων. τί γὰρ δὴ καὶ παθόντες ἂν
ἡμεῖς Ῥωμαίοις προσπωλοῖμεν[2] ἑαυτοὺς νῦν. παρὸν
ἢ μηδὲ ἀποστῆναι τὸ πρῶτον ἢ προσχωρῆσαι
ταχέως ἀποστάντας, ὄντων ἔτι τῶν πέριξ ἀπορ-
249 θήτων; νῦν μὲν γὰρ οὐδὲ βουλομένοις διαλύσα-
σθαι ῥάδιον, ὅτε Ῥωμαίους μὲν ὑπερόπτας πε-
ποίηκεν ὑποχείριος ἡ Γαλιλαία, φέρει δ’ αἰσχύνην
ἡμῖν θανάτου χαλεπωτέραν τὸ θεραπεύειν αὐτοὺς
250 ὄντας ἤδη πλησίον. κἀγὼ καθ’ ἑαυτὸν μὲν ἂν
εἰρήνην προτιμήσαιμι θανάτου, πολεμούμενος δ’
ἅπαξ καὶ συμβαλὼν θάνατον εὐκλεᾶ τοῦ ζῆν
251 αἰχμάλωτος. πότερον δέ φασιν ἡμᾶς τοὺς τοῦ
δήμου προεστῶτας πέμψαι κρύφα πρὸς Ῥωμαίους
252 ἢ καὶ τὸν δῆμον κοινῇ ψηφισάμενον; εἰ μὲν

---

[1] πορθουμένης PMV¹R Lat.

[2] Havercamp with one ms.: προσπωλοῦμεν the majority.

[a] *i.e.* like yourselves.

" I have long been wondering what motive could The charge
have brought you so promptly ; for never, without of treachery
is
grave cause, would you have armed yourselves from ridiculous.
head to foot for the sake of brigands, and against a
kindred people. But now that we have heard the
words ' Romans ' and ' treason '—for that was what
some of you were clamouring just now, and how
they were here to protect the freedom of the
metropolis—no other audacity of these wretches has
amazed us more than this ingenious lie. For indeed
men with an inborn passion for liberty,[a] and for it
above all ready to fight a foreign foe, could by no
other means be infuriated against us than by the
fabrication of a charge that we were betraying their
darling liberty. You, however, ought to reflect who
are the authors of this calumny and at whom it is
aimed, and to form your opinion of the truth not
from fictitious tales but from public events. For
what could induce us to sell ourselves to the Romans
now ? It was open to us either to refrain from
revolt in the first instance or, having revolted,
promptly to return to our allegiance, while the surrounding country was still undevastated. But now,
even if we desired it, a reconciliation would be no
easy matter, when their conquest of Galilee has
made the Romans contemptuous, and to court them,
now that they are at our doors, would bring upon
us a disgrace even worse than death. For my own
part, though I should prefer peace to death, yet
having once declared war and entered the lists, I
would rather die nobly than live a captive.

" Do they say, however, that we, the leaders of
the people, communicated secretly with the Romans,
or that the people themselves so decided by public

75

ἡμᾶς, εἰπάτωσαν τοὺς πεμφθέντας φίλους, τοὺς
διακονήσαντας τὴν προδοσίαν οἰκέτας. ἐφωράθη
τις ἀπιών; ἀνακομιζόμενος ἑάλω; γραμμάτων
253 γεγόνασιν ἐγκρατεῖς; πῶς δὲ τοὺς μὲν τοσούτους
πολίτας ἐλάθομεν, οἷς κατὰ πᾶσαν ὥραν συνανα-
στρεφόμεθα, τοῖς δὲ ὀλίγοις καὶ φρουρουμένοις καὶ
μηδ᾽ εἰς τὴν πόλιν ἐκ τοῦ ἱεροῦ προελθεῖν δυναμένοις ἐγνώσθη τὰ κατὰ τὴν χώραν λαθραίως
254 ἐνεργούμενα; νῦν δ᾽ ἔγνωσαν, ὅτε[1] δεῖ δοῦναι
δίκας τῶν τετολμημένων, ἕως δ᾽ ἦσαν ἀδεεῖς
255 αὐτοί, προδότης ἡμῶν οὐδεὶς ὑπωπτεύετο; εἰ δ᾽
ἐπὶ τὸν δῆμον ἀναφέρουσι τὴν αἰτίαν, ἐν φανερῷ
δήπουθεν ἐβουλεύσαντο, οὐδεὶς ἀπεστάτει τῆς
ἐκκλησίας, ὥστε τάχιον ἂν τῆς μηνύσεως ἔσπευσεν
256 ἡ φήμη πρὸς ὑμᾶς φανερωτέρα. τί δέ; οὐχὶ καὶ
πρέσβεις ἔδει πέμπειν ψηφισαμένους[2] τὰς δια-
λύσεις; καὶ τίς ὁ χειροτονηθείς; εἰπάτωσαν.
257 ἀλλὰ τοῦτο μὲν δυσθανατούντων καὶ πλησίον
οὔσας τὰς τιμωρίας διακρουομένων σκῆψίς ἐστιν·
εἰ γὰρ δὴ καὶ προδοθῆναι τὴν πόλιν εἵμαρτο,
μόνους ἂν τολμῆσαι καὶ τοῦτο τοὺς διαβάλλοντας,
ὧν τοῖς τολμήμασιν ἓν μόνον [κακὸν] λείπει, προ-
258 δοσία. χρὴ δὲ ὑμᾶς, ἐπειδήπερ ἅπαξ πάρεστε
μετὰ τῶν ὅπλων, τὸ μὲν δικαιότατον, ἀμύνειν τῇ
μητροπόλει καὶ συνεξαιρεῖν τοὺς τὰ δικαστήρια
καταλύσαντας τυράννους, οἳ πατήσαντες τοὺς
νόμους ἐπὶ τοῖς αὐτῶν ξίφεσι πεποίηνται τὰς
259 κρίσεις. ἄνδρας γοῦν ἀκαταιτιάτους τῶν ἐπι-

---

[1] Bekker with Lat.: ὅτι mss.
[2] L: ψηφισομένους the rest.

decree ? If they accuse us, let them name the friends whom we sent, the underlings who negotiated the betrayal. Was anyone detected leaving on his errand, or caught on his return ? Have any letters fallen into their hands ? How could we have concealed our action from all our numerous fellow-citizens, with whom we are hourly associating, while their small and beleaguered party, unable to advance one step into the city from the Temple, were, it seems, acquainted with these underhand proceedings in the country ? Have they heard of them only now, when they must pay the penalty for their crimes, and, so long as they felt themselves secure, was none of us suspected of treason ? If, on the other hand, it is the people whom they incriminate, the matter presumably was openly discussed and none was absent from the assembly ; in which case rumour would have brought you speedier and more open intelligence than your private informer. Again, must they not have followed up their vote for capitulation by sending ambassadors ? Who was elected to that office ? Let them tell us. No, this is a mere pretext of die-hards who are struggling to avert impending punishment. For had this city been indeed fated to be betrayed, none would have ventured on the deed save our present accusers, to complete whose tale of crimes one only is lacking—that of treason.

" But now that you are actually here in arms, the duty which has the highest claims upon you is to defend the metropolis and to join us in extirpating these tyrants, who have annulled our tribunals, trampled on our laws, and passed sentence with the sword. Have they not haled men of eminence and

Three courses are now open to you.

77

JOSEPHUS

φανῶν ἐκ μέσης τῆς ἀγορᾶς ἁρπάσαντες δεσμοῖς
τε προηκίσαντο καὶ μηδὲ φωνῆς μηδ' ἱκεσίας
260 ἀνασχόμενοι διέφθειραν. ἔξεστιν δ' ὑμῖν παρελθοῦσιν εἴσω μὴ πολέμου νόμῳ θεάσασθαι τὰ
τεκμήρια τῶν λεγομένων, οἴκους ἠρημωμένους
ταῖς ἐκείνων ἁρπαγαῖς καὶ γύναια καὶ γενεὰς
τῶν ἀπεσφαγμένων μελανειμονούσας, κωκυτὸν δὲ
καὶ θρῆνον ἀνὰ τὴν πόλιν ὅλην· οὐδεὶς γάρ ἐστιν,
261 ὃς οὐ γέγευται τῆς τῶν ἀνοσίων καταδρομῆς· οἵ
γε ἐπὶ τοσοῦτον ἐξώκειλαν ἀπονοίας, ὥστε μὴ
μόνον ἐκ τῆς χώρας καὶ τῶν ἔξωθεν πόλεων ἐπὶ
τὸ πρόσωπον καὶ τὴν κεφαλὴν ὅλου τοῦ ἔθνους
μετενεγκεῖν τὴν ληστρικὴν τόλμαν, ἀλλὰ καὶ ἀπὸ
262 τῆς πόλεως ἐπὶ τὸ ἱερόν. ὁρμητήριον γοῦν αὐτοῖς
τοῦτο καὶ καταφυγὴ ταμιεῖόν τε τῶν ἐφ' ἡμᾶς
παρασκευῶν γέγονεν, ὁ δ' ὑπὸ τῆς οἰκουμένης
προσκυνούμενος χῶρος καὶ τοῖς ἀπὸ περάτων γῆς
ἀλλοφύλοις ἀκοῇ τετιμημένος παρὰ τῶν γεννη-
263 θέντων ἐνθάδε θηρίων καταπατεῖται· νεανιεύονταί
τε ἐν ταῖς ἀπογνώσεσιν ἤδη δήμους τε δήμοις καὶ
πόλεσι πόλεις συγκρούειν καὶ κατὰ τῶν σπλάγχνων
264 τῶν ἰδίων τὸ ἔθνος στρατολογεῖν. ἀνθ' ὧν τὸ μὲν
κάλλιστον καὶ πρέπον, ὡς ἔφην, ὑμῖν συνεξαιρεῖν
τοὺς ἀλιτηρίους καὶ ὑπὲρ αὐτῆς τῆς ἀπάτης
ἀμυνομένους, ὅτι συμμάχους ἐτόλμησαν καλεῖν
265 οὓς ἔδει τιμωροὺς δεδιέναι· εἰ δ' αἰδεῖσθε τὰς
τῶν τοιούτων ἐπικλήσεις, ἀλλά τοι πάρεστι
θεμένοις τὰ ὅπλα καὶ παρελθοῦσιν εἰς τὴν πόλιν
σχήματι συγγενῶν ἀναλαβεῖν τὸ μέσον συμμάχων
τε καὶ πολεμίων ὄνομα, δικαστὰς γενομένους.

78

unimpeached from the open market-place, ignomin-
ously placed them in irons and then, refusing to
listen to expostulation or entreaty, put them to
death ? You are at liberty to enter, though not by
right of war, and behold the proofs of these statements : houses desolated by their rapine, poor widows
and orphans of the murdered in black attire, wailing
and lamentation throughout the city ; for there is not
one who has not felt the raids of these impious
wretches. To such extremes of insanity have they
run as not only to transfer their brigands' exploits
from the country and outlying towns to this front
and head of the whole nation, but actually from the
city to the Temple. That has now become their
base and refuge, the magazine for their armament
against us ; and the spot which is revered by the
world and honoured by aliens from the ends of the
earth who have heard its fame, is trampled on by
these monsters engendered in this very place. And
now in desperation they wantonly proceed to set at
variance township against township, city against city,
and to enlist the nation to prey upon its own vitals.
Wherefore,[a] as I said before, the most honourable
and becoming course for you is to assist in extirpating
these reprobates, and to chastise them for this deceit
which they have practised on yourselves in daring
to summon as allies those whom they should have
dreaded as avengers.

" If, however, you still respect the appeals made
to you by men such as these, it is surely open to
you to lay down your arms and, entering the city in
the guise of kinsmen, to assume a neutral rôle by

[a] Or perhaps " On the contrary " or " Instead of aiding
such a cause " (Traill).

JOSEPHUS

266 καίτοι λογίσασθε, πόσον κερδήσουσιν ἐφ᾽ ὁμο-
λογουμένοις καὶ τηλικούτοις κρινόμενοι παρ᾽ ὑμῖν
οἱ τοῖς ἀκαταιτιάτοις μηδὲ λόγου μεταδόντες·
λαμβανέτωσαν δ᾽ οὖν ταύτην ἐκ τῆς ὑμετέρας
267 ἀφίξεως τὴν χάριν. εἰ δ᾽ οὔτε συναγανακτεῖν
ἡμῖν οὔτε κρίνεσθαι δεῖ,[1] τρίτον ἐστὶ καταλιπεῖν
ἑκατέρους καὶ μήτε ταῖς ἡμετέραις ἐπεμβαίνειν[2]
συμφοραῖς μήτε τοῖς ἐπιβούλοις τῆς μητροπόλεως
268 συνέρχεσθαι. εἰ γὰρ καὶ τὰ μάλιστα Ῥωμαίοις
ὑποπτεύετε διειλέχθαι τινάς, παρατηρεῖν ἔξεστι
τὰς ἐφόδους, κἄν τι τῶν διαβεβλημένων ἔργῳ
διακαλύπτηται, τότε φρουρεῖν τὴν μητρόπολιν
ἐλθόντας, κολάζειν τε τοὺς αἰτίους πεφωραμένους·
οὐ γὰρ ἂν ὑμᾶς φθάσειαν οἱ πολέμιοι τῇ πόλει
269 προσῳκημένους.[3] εἰ δ᾽ οὐδὲν ὑμῖν τούτων εὔ-
γνωμον ἢ μέτριον δοκεῖ, μὴ θαυμάζετε τὰ κλεῖθρα
τῶν πυλῶν, ἕως ἂν φέρητε τὰ ὅπλα.''

270 (4) Τοιαῦτα μὲν ὁ Ἰησοῦς ἔλεγε· τῶν δὲ
Ἰδουμαίων οὐδὲν[4] τὸ πλῆθος προσεῖχεν, ἀλλὰ
τεθύμωτο μὴ τυχὸν ἑτοίμης τῆς εἰσόδου, καὶ
διηγανάκτουν οἱ στρατηγοὶ πρὸς ἀπόθεσιν τῶν
ὅπλων, αἰχμαλωσίαν ἡγούμενοι τὸ κελευόντων
271 τινῶν αὐτὰ ῥῖψαι. Σίμων δὲ υἱὸς Κααθὰ[5] τῶν
ἡγεμόνων εἷς, μόλις τῶν οἰκείων καταστείλας τὸν
θόρυβον καὶ στὰς εἰς ἐπήκοον τοῖς ἀρχιερεῦσιν,
272 οὐκέτι θαυμάζειν ἔφη φρουρουμένων ἐν τῷ ἱερῷ
τῶν προμάχων τῆς ἐλευθερίας, εἴ γε καὶ τῷ
273 ἔθνει κλείουσί τινες ἤδη τὴν κοινὴν πόλιν, καὶ

[1] δοκεῖ Hudson with one ms.
[2] MVC: ἐπιβαίνειν the rest.
[3] L: προσῳκισμένους the rest.
[4] PAML (Lat. ?): οὔτε the rest.
[5] Κλαθᾶ M: Καθλᾶ VRC Lat.; cf. § 235.

80

becoming arbitrators. Consider, too, what they will gain by being tried by you for such undeniable and flagrant offences, whereas they would not suffer unimpeached persons to speak a word in their defence ; however, let them derive this benefit from your coming. But if you will neither share our indignation nor act as umpires, a third course remains, namely to leave both parties to themselves and neither to insult us in our calamities nor join with these conspirators against the mother city. For, however strongly you suspect some of us of having communicated with the Romans, you are in a position to watch the approaches, and if any of these calumnies is actually discovered to be true, you can then come to the protection of the metropolis and punish the detected culprits ; for the enemy could never take you by surprise while you are quartered here hard by the city. If, however, none of these proposals appears to you reasonable or fair, do not wonder that these gates are barred, so long as you remain in arms."

(4) Such was the speech of Jesus. But the Idumaean troops paid no heed to it, infuriated at not obtaining instant admission ; while their generals were indignant at the thought of laying down their arms, accounting it captivity to fling them away at any man's bidding. Thereupon Simon, son of Caathas, one of the officers, having with difficulty quelled the uproar among his men and taken his stand within hearing of the chief priests, thus replied : Abusive reply of Simon, the Idumaean chief.

" I am no longer surprised that the champions of liberty are imprisoned in the Temple, now that I find that there are men who close against this nation the city common to us all ; men who, while

Ῥωμαίους μὲν εἰσδέχεσθαι παρασκευάζονται, τάχα
καὶ στεφανώσαντες τὰς πύλας, Ἰδουμαίοις δὲ ἀπὸ
τῶν πύργων διαλέγονται καὶ τὰ ὑπὲρ τῆς ἐλευ-
274 θερίας ὅπλα κελεύουσι ῥῖψαι, μὴ πιστεύοντες δὲ
τοῖς συγγενέσι τὴν τῆς μητροπόλεως φυλακὴν τοὺς
αὐτοὺς δικαστὰς ποιοῦνται τῶν διαφόρων, καὶ κατ-
ηγοροῦντές τινων ὡς ἀποκτείνειαν ἀκρίτους,
αὐτοὶ καταδικάζοιεν ὅλου τοῦ ἔθνους ἀτιμίαν·
275 τὴν γοῦν ἅπασι τοῖς ἀλλοφύλοις ἀναπεπταμένην
εἰς θρησκείαν πόλιν τοῖς οἰκείοις νῦν ἀπο-
276 τετειχίσθαι.[1] '' πάνυ γὰρ ἐπὶ σφαγὰς ἐσπεύ-
δομεν καὶ τὸν κατὰ τῶν ὁμοφύλων πόλεμον
οἱ διὰ τοῦτο ταχύναντες, ἵν' ὑμᾶς τηρήσωμεν
277 ἐλευθέρους. τοιαῦτα μέντοι καὶ πρὸς τῶν φρουρουμένων ἠδίκησθε, καὶ πιθανὰς οὕτως ὑποψίας οἶμαι
278 κατ' ἐκείνων συνελέξατε. ἔπειτα τῶν ἔνδον φρουρᾷ
κρατοῦντες ὅσοι κήδονται τῶν κοινῶν πραγμάτων, καὶ τοῖς συγγενεστάτοις ἔθνεσιν ἀθρόοις
ἀποκλείσαντες μὲν τὴν πόλιν ὑβριστικὰ δ' οὕτως
προστάγματα κελεύοντες, τυραννεῖσθαι λέγετε καὶ
τὸ τῆς δυναστείας ὄνομα τοῖς ὑφ' ὑμῶν τυραννου-
279 μένοις περιάπτετε. τίς ἂν ἐνέγκαι τὴν εἰρωνείαν
τῶν λόγων ἀφορῶν εἰς τὴν ἐναντιότητα τῶν
πραγμάτων; εἰ μὴ καὶ νῦν ὑμᾶς[2] ἀποκλείουσιν
Ἰδουμαῖοι[3] τῆς μητροπόλεως, οὓς αὐτοὶ τῶν
280 πατρίων ἱερῶν εἴργετε. μέμψαιτ' ἂν εἰκότως τις
τοὺς ἐν τῷ ἱερῷ πολιορκουμένους, ὅτι θαρσήσαντες
τοὺς προδότας κολάζειν, οὓς ὑμεῖς ἄνδρας ἐπιση-
μους καὶ ἀκαταιτιάτους λέγετε διὰ τὴν κοινωνίαν,

---

[1] ἀποτετείχισθε A, making the drift into *oratio recta* begin
earlier.
[2] ἡμᾶς PAL.   [3] Ἰδουμαίους PAL Lat.

preparing to admit the Romans, maybe crowning
the gates with garlands, parley with Idumaeans
from their towers and bid them fling down the arms
which they took up in defence of liberty ; men who,
refusing to entrust to their kinsmen the protection
of the mother city, would make them arbitrators in
their disputes, and, while accusing certain individuals
of putting others to death without trial, would themselves condemn the whole nation to dishonour. At
any rate, this city, which flung wide its gates to
every foreigner for worship, is now barricaded by
you against your own people. And why ? Because
forsooth, we were hurrying hither to slaughter and
make war on our fellow-countrymen—we whose sole
reason for haste was to keep you free ! Such doubtless was the nature of your grievance against your
prisoners,[a] and equally credible, I imagine, is your
list of insinuations against them. And then, while
detaining in custody all within the walls who care
for the public welfare, after closing your gates against
a whole body of people who are your nearest kinsmen and issuing to them such insulting orders, you
profess to be tyrant-ridden and attach the stigma
of despotism to the victims of your own tyranny!
Who can tolerate such ironical language, which he
sees to be flatly contrary to the facts, unless indeed
it is the Idumaeans who are now excluding you from
the metropolis, and not you who are debarring them
from the national sacred rites ? One complaint
might fairly be made against the men blockaded in
the Temple, that, while they had the courage to
punish those traitors whom you, as their partners
in guilt, describe as distinguished persons and un-

---

[a] Viz. that they wished to keep you free.

οὐκ ἀφ' ὑμῶν ἤρξαντο καὶ τὰ καιριώτατα τῆς
281 προδοσίας μέρη προαπέκοψαν. ἀλλ' εἰ κἀκεῖνοι
τῆς χρείας ἐγένοντο μαλακώτεροι, τηρήσομεν[1]
Ἰδουμαῖοι τὸν οἶκον τοῦ θεοῦ καὶ τῆς κοινῆς
πατρίδος προπολεμήσομεν,[1] ἅμα τούς τε ἔξωθεν
ἐπιόντας καὶ τοὺς ἔνδον προδιδόντας ἀμυνόμενοι
282 πολεμίους. ἐνθάδε πρὸ τῶν τειχῶν μενοῦμεν ἐν
τοῖς ὅπλοις, ἕως ἂν Ῥωμαῖοι κάμωσι προσέχοντες
ὑμῖν[2] ἢ ὑμεῖς ἐλεύθερα φρονήσαντες μεταβάλησθε.''
283 (5) Τούτοις τὸ μὲν τῶν Ἰδουμαίων ἐπεβόα
πλῆθος, ὁ δὲ Ἰησοῦς ἀθυμῶν ἀνεχώρει τοὺς μὲν
Ἰδουμαίους μηδὲν φρονοῦντας ὁρῶν μέτριον,
284 διχόθεν δὲ τὴν πόλιν πολεμουμένην. ἦν δ' οὐδὲ
τοῖς Ἰδουμαίοις ἐν ἠρεμίᾳ τὰ φρονήματα· καὶ
γὰρ τεθύμωντο πρὸς τὴν ὕβριν εἰρχθέντες τῆς
πόλεως καὶ τὰ τῶν ζηλωτῶν ἰσχυρὰ δοκοῦντες,
ὡς οὐδὲν ἐπαμύνοντας ἑώρων, ἠποροῦντο καὶ
285 μετενόουν πολλοὶ τὴν ἄφιξιν. ἡ δὲ αἰδὼς τοῦ
τέλεον ἀπράκτους ὑποστρέφειν ἐνίκα τὴν μεταμέλειαν, ὥστε μένειν[3] αὐτόθι πρὸ τοῦ τείχους
286 κακῶς αὐλιζομένους· διὰ γὰρ τῆς νυκτὸς ἀμήχανος
ἐκρήγνυται χειμὼν ἄνεμοί τε βίαιοι σὺν ὄμβροις
λαβροτάτοις καὶ συνεχεῖς ἀστραπαὶ βρονταί τε
φρικώδεις καὶ μυκήματα σειομένης τῆς γῆς
287 ἐξαίσια. πρόδηλον δ' ἦν ἐπ' ἀνθρώπων ὀλέθρῳ
τὸ κατάστημα τῶν ὅλων συγκεχυμένον, καὶ οὐχὶ
μικροῦ τις ἂν εἰκάσαι συμπτώματος τὰ τέρατα.
288 (6) Μία δὲ τοῖς Ἰδουμαίοις καὶ τοῖς ἐν τῇ
πόλει παρέστη δόξα, τοῖς μὲν ὀργίζεσθαι τὸν
θεὸν ἐπὶ τῇ στρατείᾳ καὶ οὐκ ἂν διαφυγεῖν ἐπενεγ-

---

[1] Many mss. have τηρήσωμεν . . . προπολεμήσωμεν.
[2] Hudson : ἡμῖν mss.   [3] ἐμμένειν PAM.

impeached, they did not begin with you and cut off
at the outset the most vital members of this treasonable conspiracy. But if they were more lenient
than they should have been, we Idumaeans will
preserve God's house and fight to defend our common
country from both her foes, the invaders from without and the traitors within. Here before these walls
will we remain in arms, until the Romans are tired
of listening to you or you become converts to the
cause of liberty."

(5) This speech being loudly applauded by the
Idumaeans, Jesus withdrew despondent, finding them
opposed to all moderate counsels and the city
exposed to war from two quarters. Nor indeed were
the minds of the Idumaeans at ease : infuriated at
the insult offered them in being excluded from the
city and seeing no aid forthcoming from the Zealots
whom they believed to be in considerable strength,
they were sorely perplexed, and many repented of
having come. But the shame of returning, having
accomplished absolutely nothing, so far overcame
their regrets that they kept their ground, bivouacking
before the walls under miserable conditions. For
in the course of the night a terrific storm broke out :
the winds blew a hurricane, rain fell in torrents,
lightning was continuous, accompanied by fearful
thunder-claps and extraordinary rumblings of earth-
quake. Such a convulsion of the very fabric of the
universe clearly foretokened destruction for mankind,
and the conjecture was natural that these were
portents of no trifling calamity.

(6) In this the Idumaeans and the city folk were
of one mind : the former being persuaded that God
was wroth at their expedition and that they were

*The
Idumaeans
encamp
before the
walls in a
thunder-
storm.*

*Concern of
the Zealots
for their
Idumaean
allies*

85

κόντας ὅπλα τῇ μητροπόλει, τοῖς δὲ περὶ τὸν
Ἄνανον νενικηκέναι χωρὶς παρατάξεως καὶ τὸν
289 θεὸν ὑπὲρ αὐτῶν στρατηγεῖν. κακοὶ δ᾽ ἦσαν ἄρα
τῶν μελλόντων στοχασταὶ καὶ κατεμαντεύοντο
290 τῶν ἐχθρῶν ἃ τοῖς ἰδίοις αὐτῶν ἐπῄει παθεῖν· οἱ
μὲν γὰρ Ἰδουμαῖοι συσπειραθέντες τοῖς σώμασιν
ἀλλήλους ἀντέθαλπον καὶ τοὺς θυρεοὺς ὑπὲρ
κεφαλῆς συμφράξαντες ἧττον ἐκακοῦντο τοῖς
291 ὑετοῖς, οἱ δὲ ζηλωταὶ μᾶλλον τοῦ καθ᾽ αὑτοὺς
κινδύνου ὑπὲρ ἐκείνων ἐβασανίζοντο καὶ συνελθόντες ἐσκόπουν, εἴ τινα μηχανὴν αὑτοῖς ἀμύνης
292 ἐπινοήσειαν. τοῖς μὲν οὖν θερμοτέροις ἐδόκει
μετὰ τῶν ὅπλων βιάζεσθαι τοὺς παραφυλάσσοντας,
ἔπειτα δ᾽ εἰσπεσόντας εἰς μέσον τῆς πόλεως
ἀναφανδὸν ἀνοίγειν τοῖς συμμάχοις τὰς πύλας·
293 τούς τε γὰρ φύλακας εἴξειν πρὸς τὸ ἀδόκητον
αὐτῶν τεταραγμένους, ἄλλως τε καὶ τοὺς πλείονας[1]
ὄντας ἀνόπλους καὶ πολέμων ἀπείρους, καὶ τῶν
κατὰ τὴν πόλιν δυσσύνακτον ἔσεσθαι τὸ πλῆθος
κατειλημένον[2] ὑπὸ τοῦ χειμῶνος εἰς τὰς οἰκίας.
294 εἰ δὲ καί τις γένοιτο κίνδυνος, πρέπειν αὐτοῖς πᾶν
ὁτιοῦν παθεῖν ἢ περιιδεῖν τοσοῦτον πλῆθος δι᾽
295 αὐτοὺς αἰσχρῶς ἀπολλύμενον. οἱ δὲ συνετώτεροι
βιάζεσθαι μὲν ἀπεγίνωσκον, ὁρῶντες οὐ μόνον τὴν
αὐτῶν φρουρὰν πληθύουσαν ἀλλὰ καὶ τὸ τῆς
πόλεως τεῖχος διὰ τοὺς Ἰδουμαίους ἐπιμελῶς
296 φυλασσόμενον, ᾤοντό τε πανταχοῦ τὸν Ἄνανον
παρεῖναι καὶ κατὰ πᾶσαν ὥραν ἐπισκέπτεσθαι
297 τὰς φυλακάς· ὃ δὴ ταῖς μὲν ἄλλαις νυξὶν οὕτως
εἶχεν, ἀνείθη δὲ κατ᾽ ἐκείνην, οὔτι κατὰ τὴν

---

[1] L: + αὐτῶν the rest.   [2] Bekker: κατειλημμένον MSS.

not to escape retribution for bearing arms against
the metropolis, Ananus and his party believing that
they had won the day without a contest and that
God was directing the battle on their behalf. But
they proved mistaken in their divination of the future,
and the fate which they predicted for their foes was
destined to befall their friends. For the Idumaeans,
huddling together, kept each other warm, and by
making a penthouse of bucklers above their heads
were not seriously affected by the torrents of rain ;
while the Zealots, more concerned for their allies
than for their own danger, met to consider whether
any means could be devised for their relief. The
more ardent advocated forcing a way through the
sentries at the point of the sword, and then plunging
boldly into the heart of the city and opening the
gates to their allies : the guards, disconcerted by
their unexpected assault, would give way, especially
as the majority were unarmed and had never been
in action, while the citizens could not easily be
collected in force, being confined to their houses by
the storm ; even if this involved hazard, it was only
right that they should suffer anything rather than
leave such a vast host disgracefully to perish on
their account. The more prudent, however, dis-
approved of these violent measures, seeing that not
only was the guard surrounding them in full strength,
but the city wall carefully watched on account of
the Idumaeans ; they imagined, moreover, that
Ananus would be everywhere, inspecting the sentries
at all hours. Such, indeed, had been his practice on
other nights, but on this one it was omitted ; not

JOSEPHUS

Ἀνάνου ῥαθυμίαν, ἀλλ' ὡς αὐτός ⟨τε⟩[1] ἐκεῖνος
ἀπόλοιτο καὶ τὸ πλῆθος τῶν φυλάκων στρατη-
298 γούσης τῆς εἱμαρμένης. ἢ δὴ καὶ τότε τῆς νυκτὸς
προκοπτούσης καὶ τοῦ χειμῶνος ἐπακμάζοντος
κοιμίζει μὲν τοὺς ἐπὶ τῇ στοᾷ φρουρούς, τοῖς δὲ
ζηλωταῖς ἐπίνοιαν ἐμβάλλει τῶν ἱερῶν αἴροντας
πριόνων ἐκτεμεῖν τοὺς μοχλοὺς τῶν πυλῶν.
299 συνήργησε δ' αὐτοῖς πρὸς τὸ μὴ κατακουσθῆναι
τὸν ψόφον ὅ τε τῶν ἀνέμων ἦχος καὶ τὸ τῶν
βροντῶν ἐπάλληλον.

300   (7) Διαλαθόντες δ' ἐκ τοῦ ἱεροῦ παραγίνονται
πρὸς τὸ τεῖχος καὶ τοῖς αὐτοῖς πρίοσι χρώμενοι
τὴν κατὰ τοὺς Ἰδουμαίους ἀνοίγουσι πύλην.
301 τοῖς δὲ τὸ μὲν πρῶτον ἐμπίπτει ταραχὴ τοὺς
περὶ τὸν Ἄνανον ἐπιχειρεῖν οἰηθεῖσι, καὶ πᾶς ἐπὶ
τοῦ ξίφους ἔσχε τὴν δεξιὰν ὡς ἀμυνόμενος[2]·
ταχέως δὲ γνωρίζοντες τοὺς ἥκοντας εἰσῄεσαν.
302 εἰ μὲν οὖν ἐτράποντο περὶ τὴν πόλιν, οὐδὲν
ἐκώλυσεν ἂν ἀπολωλέναι τὸν δῆμον αὔτανδρον,
οὕτως εἶχον ὀργῆς· νῦν δὲ πρώτους τοὺς ζηλωτὰς
ἔσπευδον[3] τῆς φρουρᾶς ἐξελέσθαι, δεομένων πολλὰ
καὶ τῶν εἰσδεξαμένων μὴ περιιδεῖν δι' οὓς ἦλθον
ἐν μέσοις τοῖς δεινοῖς μηδ' αὐτοῖς χαλεπώτερον
303 ἐπισεῖσαι τὸν κίνδυνον· τῶν μὲν γὰρ φρουρῶν
ἁλόντων ῥᾴδιον αὐτοῖς εἶναι χωρεῖν ἐπὶ τὴν πόλιν,
εἰ δ' ἅπαξ ταύτην προκινήσειαν, οὐκ ἂν ἔτ'
304 ἐκείνων κρατῆσαι· πρὸς γὰρ τὴν αἴσθησιν συν-
τάξεσθαι[4] αὐτοὺς καὶ τὰς ἀνόδους ἀποφράξειν.

---

[1] ins. Herwerden: the τε appears to have been misplaced
in most mss., which read ὥστε for ὡς.
[2] ἀμυνούμενος R.   [3] C: σπεύδοντες the rest.
[4] Bekker: συντάξασθαι mss.

through any remissness on his part, but by the over-
ruling decree of Destiny that he and all his guards
should perish. She it was who as that night advanced
and the storm approached its climax lulled to sleep
the sentinels posted at the colonnade, and suggested
to the Zealots the thought of taking some of the
temple saws and severing the bars of the gates.
They were aided by the blustering wind and the
successive peals of thunder, which prevented the
noise from being heard.[a]

A party of Zealots sally from the temple

(7) Escaping unperceived from the Temple, they [b]
reached the walls and, employing their saws once
more, opened the gate nearest to the Idumaeans.
They, supposing themselves attacked by the troops
of Ananus, were at first seized with alarm, and every
man's hand was on his sword to defend himself, but,
quickly recognizing their visitors, they entered the
city. Had they then turned upon it in all directions,
such was their fury that nothing could have saved
the inhabitants from wholesale destruction ; but, as
it was, they first hastened to liberate the Zealots
from custody, at the earnest entreaty of the men
who had let them in. " Do not," these urged,
" leave those for whose sake you have come in the
thick of peril, nor expose us to graver risks. Overpower the guards and you can then easily march
upon the city, but once begin by rousing the city,
and you will never master the guards ; for at the
first intimation the citizens will fall into line and
block every ascent."

and open the city gates to the Idumaeans.

[a] Reminiscent of Thucydides' account of the escape from
Plataea : ψόφῳ δὲ . . . ἀντιπαταγοῦντος τοῦ ἀνέμου οὐ κατ-
ακουσάντων (iii. 22).
[b] *i.e.* a small party of the Zealots, as the sequel shows.

305 (v. 1) Συνεδόκει ταῦτα τοῖς Ἰδουμαίοις, καὶ
διὰ τῆς πόλεως ἀνέβαινον πρὸς τὸ ἱερόν, μετέωροί
τε οἱ ζηλωταὶ τὴν ἄφιξιν αὐτῶν ἐκαραδόκουν καὶ
παριόντων εἴσω καὶ αὐτοὶ θαρροῦντες προῄεσαν ἐκ
306 τοῦ ἐνδοτέρου ἱεροῦ. μιγέντες δὲ τοῖς Ἰδουμαίοις προσέβαλλον ταῖς φυλακαῖς, καὶ τινὰς μὲν
τῶν προκοιτούντων ἀπέσφαξαν κοιμωμένους, πρὸς
δὲ τὴν τῶν ἐγρηγορότων βοὴν διανέστη πᾶν τὸ
πλῆθος καὶ μετ' ἐκπλήξεως ἁρπάζοντες τὰ ὅπλα
307 πρὸς τὴν ἄμυναν ἐχώρουν. ἕως μὲν οὖν μόνους
τοὺς ζηλωτὰς ἐπιχειρεῖν ὑπελάμβανον, ἐθάρρουν
ὡς τῷ πλήθει περιεσόμενοι, κατιδόντες δ' ἔξωθεν
ἐπεισχεομένους[1] ἄλλους ᾔσθοντο τὴν εἰσβολὴν τῶν
308 Ἰδουμαίων, καὶ τὸ μὲν πλέον αὐτῶν ἅμα ταῖς
ψυχαῖς κατέβαλλε τὰ ὅπλα καὶ πρὸς οἰμωγαῖς
ἦν, φραξάμενοι δὲ ὀλίγοι τῶν νέων γενναίως
ἐδέχοντο τοὺς Ἰδουμαίους καὶ μέχρι πολλοῦ τὴν
309 ἀργοτέραν πληθὺν ἔσκεπον. οἱ δὲ κραυγῇ δι-
εσήμαινον τοῖς κατὰ τὴν πόλιν τὰς συμφοράς,
κἀκείνων ἀμῦναι μὲν οὐδεὶς ἐτόλμησεν, ὡς
ἔμαθον εἰσπεπαικότας τοὺς Ἰδουμαίους, ἀργὰ δ'
ἀντεβόων καὶ ἀντωλοφύροντο, καὶ πολὺς κωκυτὸς
γυναικῶν ἠγείρετο κινδυνεύοντος ἑκάστη τινὸς
310 τῶν φυλάκων. οἱ δὲ ζηλωταὶ τοῖς Ἰδουμαίοις
συνεπηλάλαζον καὶ τὴν ἐκ πάντων βοὴν ὁ χειμὼν
ἐποίει φοβερωτέραν. ἐφείδοντό τε οὐδενὸς Ἰδουμαῖοι, φύσει τε ὠμότατοι φονεύειν ὄντες καὶ τῷ
χειμῶνι κεκακωμένοι κατὰ τῶν ἀποκλεισάντων

---

[1] ἐπιχεομένους PA.

(v. 1) Yielding to these representations, the Idumaeans marched up through the city to the Temple. The Zealots, who were anxiously awaiting their arrival, on their entering the building boldly advanced from the inner court, joined the Idumaeans and fell upon the guards. Some of the outlying sentries they slew in their sleep, till, roused by the cries of those who were awake, the whole force in consternation snatched up their arms and advanced to the defence. So long as they believed the Zealots to be their only assailants, they did not lose heart, hoping to overpower them by numbers ; but the sight of others pouring in from outside brought home to them the irruption of the Idumaeans. Thereupon, the greater number of them flung courage and armour away together and abandoned themselves to lamentation ; a few of the younger men, however, fencing themselves in, gallantly received the Idumaeans and for a good while protected the feebler crowd. The cries of the latter signified their distress to their friends in the city, but not one of these ventured to their assistance, when they learnt that the Idumaeans had broken in ; instead they responded with futile shouts and lamentations on their side, while a great wail went up from the women, each having some relative in the guards whose life was at stake. The Zealots joined in the war-whoop of the Idumaeans, and the din from all quarters was rendered more terrific by the howling of the storm.[a] The Idumaeans spared none. Naturally of a most savage and murderous disposition, they had been buffeted by the storm and wreaked their

Wholesale slaughter of the guards of Ananus.

----

[a] *Cf.* iii. 247 ff. (Jotapata : the din of battle heightened by the echo from the mountains), vi. 272 ff. (Jerusalem : similar).

311 ἐχρῶντο τοῖς θυμοῖς[1]· ἦσαν δ' ὅμοιοι τοῖς ἱκε-
τεύουσι καὶ τοῖς ἀμυνομένοις καὶ πολλοὺς τήν
τε συγγένειαν ἀναμιμνήσκοντας καὶ δεομένους
τοῦ κοινοῦ ἱεροῦ λαβεῖν αἰδῶ διήλαυνον τοῖς
312 ξίφεσιν. ἦν δὲ φυγῆς μὲν οὐδεὶς τόπος οὐδὲ
σωτηρίας ἐλπίς, συνωθούμενοι δὲ περὶ ἀλλήλους
κατεκόπτοντο, καὶ τὸ πλέον ἐκβιαζόμενοι, ὡς
οὐκέτ' ἦν ὑποχωρήσεως τόπος ἐπήεσαν δ' οἱ
φονεύοντες, ὑπ' ἀμηχανίας κατεκρήμνιζον ἑαυτοὺς
εἰς τὴν πόλιν, οἰκτρότερον ἔμοιγε δοκεῖν[2] οὗ
διέφευγον ὀλέθρου τὸν αὐθαίρετον ὑπομένοντες.
313 ἐπεκλύσθη δὲ τὸ ἔξωθεν ἱερὸν πᾶν αἵματι, καὶ
νεκροὺς ὀκτακισχιλίους πεντακοσίους ἡ ἡμέρα
κατελάμβανεν.

314 (2) Οὐκ ἐκορέσθησαν δὲ τούτοις οἱ θυμοὶ τῶν
Ἰδουμαίων, ἀλλ' ἐπὶ τὴν πόλιν τραπόμενοι πᾶσαν
μὲν οἰκίαν διήρπαζον, ἔκτεινον δὲ τὸν περιτυχόντα.
315 καὶ τὸ μὲν ἄλλο πλῆθος αὐτοῖς ἐδόκει παρανάλωμα,
τοὺς δ' ἀρχιερεῖς ἀνεζήτουν, καὶ κατ' ἐκείνων ἦν
316 τοῖς πλείστοις ἡ φορά. ταχέως δ' ἁλόντες διεφθείροντο, καὶ τοῖς νεκροῖς αὐτῶν ἐπιστάντες τὸν
μὲν Ἄνανον τῆς πρὸς τὸν δῆμον εὐνοίας, τὸν δὲ
Ἰησοῦν τῶν ἀπὸ τοῦ τείχους λόγων ἐπέσκωπτον.
317 προῆλθον δὲ εἰς τοσοῦτον ἀσεβείας, ὥστε καὶ
ἀτάφους ῥῖψαι, καίτοι τοσαύτην Ἰουδαίων περὶ
τὰς ταφὰς πρόνοιαν ποιουμένων, ὥστε καὶ τοὺς
ἐκ καταδίκης ἀνεσταυρωμένους πρὸ δύντος ἡλίου
318 καθελεῖν τε καὶ θάπτειν. οὐκ ἂν ἁμάρτοιμι δ'

---

[1] VM²: ὅπλοις or ἐχθροῖς the rest.
[2] Dindorf: δοκεῖ mss.

ª At the outset of the blockade the guards on duty at

rage on those who had shut them out ; suppliants
and combatants were treated alike, and many while
reminding them of their kinship and imploring them
to respect their common Temple were transfixed by
their swords. No room for flight, no hope of escape
remained ; crushed together upon each other they
were cut down, and the greater part, finding themselves forced back until further retreat was impossible,
with their murderers closing upon them, in their
helplessness flung themselves headlong into the
city, devoting themselves to a fate more piteous in
my opinion than that from which they fled. The
whole outer court of the Temple was deluged with
blood, and day dawned upon eight thousand five
hundred [a] dead.

(2) The fury of the Idumaeans being still un-
satiated, they now turned to the city, looting every
house and killing all who fell in their way. But,
thinking their energies wasted on the common people,
they went in search of the chief priests ; it was for
them that the main rush was made, and they were
soon captured and slain. Then, standing over their
dead bodies, they scoffed at Ananus for his patronage
of the people and at Jesus for the address which he
had delivered from the wall.[b] They actually went
so far in their impiety as to cast out the corpses
without burial, although the Jews are so careful
about funeral rites that even malefactors who have
been sentenced to crucifixion are taken down and
buried before sunset.[c] I should not be wrong in

The
Idumaeans
murder
Ananus
and Jesus.

one time numbered not more than 6000 (εἰς ἑξακισχιλίους
§ 206). That number was apparently afterwards increased.
We are told that on this night they were " in full strength "
or " above strength " (πληθύουσαν § 295).

   [b] §§ 238 ff.   [c] Cf. Deut. xxi. 22 f. ; John xix. 31.

εἰπὼν ἁλώσεως ἄρξαι τῇ πόλει τὸν Ἀνάνου
θάνατον, καὶ ἀπ' ἐκείνης τῆς ἡμέρας ἀνατραπῆναι
τὸ τεῖχος καὶ διαφθαρῆναι τὰ πράγματα Ἰουδαίοις, ἐν ᾗ τὸν ἀρχιερέα καὶ ἡγεμόνα τῆς ἰδίας
σωτηρίας αὐτῶν ἐπὶ μέσης τῆς πόλεως εἶδον
319 ἀπεσφαγμένον. ἦν γὰρ δὴ τά τε ἄλλα σεμνὸς
ἀνὴρ καὶ δικαιότατος, καὶ παρὰ τὸν ὄγκον τῆς
τε εὐγενείας καὶ τῆς ἀξίας καὶ ἧς εἶχε τιμῆς
ἠγαπηκὼς τὸ ἰσότιμον καὶ πρὸς τοὺς ταπεινοτά-
320 τους, φιλελεύθερός τε ἐκτόπως καὶ δημοκρατίας
ἐραστής, πρό τε τῶν ἰδίων λυσιτελῶν τὸ κοινῇ
συμφέρον ἀεὶ τιθέμενος καὶ περὶ παντὸς ποιούμενος τὴν εἰρήνην· ἄμαχα γὰρ ᾔδει τὰ Ῥωμαίων·
προσκοπούμενος δ' ὑπ' ἀνάγκης καὶ τὰ κατὰ τὸν
πόλεμον, ὅπως, εἰ μὴ διαλύσαιντο Ἰουδαῖοι,
321 δεξιῶς διαφέροιντο. καθόλου δ' εἰπεῖν, ζῶντος
Ἀνάνου πάντως ἂν ⟨ἢ⟩[1] διελύθησαν· δεινὸς γὰρ
ἦν εἰπεῖν τε καὶ πεῖσαι τὸν δῆμον, ἤδη δὲ ἐχειροῦτο
καὶ τοὺς ἐμποδίζοντας· ἢ πολεμοῦντες[2] πλείστην
ἂν τριβὴν Ῥωμαίοις παρέσχον ὑπὸ τοιούτῳ
322 στρατηγῷ. παρέζευκτο δ' αὐτῷ καὶ ὁ Ἰησοῦς,
αὐτοῦ μὲν λειπόμενος κατὰ σύγκρισιν, προύχων
323 δὲ τῶν ἄλλων. ἀλλ' οἶμαι κατακρίνας ὁ θεὸς ὡς
μεμιασμένης τῆς πόλεως ἀπώλειαν καὶ πυρὶ
βουλόμενος ἐκκαθαρθῆναι τὰ ἅγια τοὺς ἀντεχο-
μένους αὐτῶν καὶ φιλοστοργοῦντας περιέκοπτεν.
324 οἱ δὲ πρὸ ὀλίγου τὴν ἱερὰν ἐσθῆτα περικείμενοι

[1] ins. Niese.
[2] Destinon : πολεμοῦντας MSS.

---

[a] Ananus is here almost the counterpart of Pericles ; the

saying that the capture of the city began with the death of Ananus ; and that the overthrow of the walls and the downfall of the Jewish state dated from the day on which the Jews beheld their high priest, the captain of their salvation, butchered in the heart of Jerusalem. A man on every ground revered and of the highest integrity, Ananus,[a] with all the distinction of his birth, his rank and the honours to which he had attained, yet delighted to treat the very humblest as his equals. Unique in his love of liberty and an enthusiast for democracy, he on all occasions put the public welfare above his private interests. To maintain peace was his supreme object. He knew that the Roman power was irresistible, but, when driven to provide for a state of war, he endeavoured to secure that, if the Jews would not come to terms, the struggle should at least be skilfully conducted. In a word, had Ananus lived, they would undoubtedly either have arranged terms —for he was an effective speaker, whose words carried weight with the people, and was already gaining control even over those who thwarted him—or else, had hostilities continued, they would have greatly retarded the victory of the Romans under such a general. With him was linked Jesus, who, though not comparable with Ananus, stood far above the rest. But it was, I suppose, because God had, for its pollutions, condemned the city to destruction and desired to purge the sanctuary by fire, that He thus cut off those who clung to them with such tender affection. So they who but lately had worn the

encomium on the latter in Thuc. ii. 65 is doubtless in our historian's mind.

καὶ τῆς κοσμικῆς θρησκείας κατάρχοντες προσ-
κυνούμενοί τε τοῖς ἐκ τῆς οἰκουμένης παρα-
βάλλουσιν εἰς τὴν πόλιν, ἐρριμμένοι γυμνοὶ βορὰ
325 κυνῶν καὶ θηρίων ἐβλέποντο. αὐτὴν ἐπ' ἐκείνοις
στενάξαι τοῖς ἀνδράσι δοκῶ τὴν ἀρετήν, ὀλο-
φυρομένην ὅτι τοσοῦτον ἥττητο τῆς κακίας. ἀλλὰ
γὰρ τὸ μὲν Ἀνάνου καὶ Ἰησοῦ τέλος τοιοῦτον
ἀπέβη.

326 (3) Μετὰ δ' ἐκείνους οἵ τε ζηλωταὶ καὶ τῶν
Ἰδουμαίων τὸ πλῆθος τὸν λαὸν ὥσπερ ἀνοσίων
327 ζώων ἀγέλην ἐπιόντες ἔσφαζον. καὶ τὸ μὲν
εἰκαῖον ἐφ' οὗ καταληφθείη τόπου διεφθείρετο,
τοὺς δὲ εὐγενεῖς καὶ νέους συλλαμβάνοντες εἰς
εἱρκτὴν κατέκλειον δεδεμένους, κατ' ἐλπίδα τοῦ
προσθήσεσθαί τινας αὐτοῖς τὴν ἀναίρεσιν ὑπερ-
328 τιθέμενοι. προσέσχε δ' οὐδείς, ἀλλὰ πάντες τοῦ
τάξασθαι μετὰ τῶν πονηρῶν κατὰ τῆς πατρίδος
329 προείλοντο τὸν θάνατον. δεινὰς δὲ τῆς ἀρνήσεως
αἰκίας ὑπέμενον μαστιγούμενοί τε καὶ στρεβλούμενοι, μετὰ δὲ τὸ μηκέτ' ἀρκεῖν τὸ σῶμα
330 ταῖς βασάνοις μόλις ἠξιοῦντο τοῦ ξίφους. οἱ
συλληφθέντες δὲ μεθ' ἡμέραν ἀνηροῦντο[1] νύκτωρ,
καὶ τοὺς νεκροὺς ἐκφοροῦντες ἔρριπτον, ὡς ἑτέροις
331 εἴη δεσμώταις τόπος. ἦν δὲ τοσαύτη τοῦ δήμου
κατάπληξις, ὡς μηδένα τολμῆσαι μήτε κλαίειν
φανερῶς τὸν προσήκοντα νεκρὸν μήτε θάπτειν,
ἀλλὰ λαθραῖα μὲν ἦν αὐτῶν κατακεκλεισμένων τὰ
δάκρυα καὶ μετὰ περισκέψεως, μή τις ἐπακούσῃ
332 τῶν ἐχθρῶν, ἔστενον· ἴσα γὰρ τοῖς πενθουμένοις ὁ

---

[1] ἀνήγοντο L Lat.

[a] Literally "cosmical," meaning either "open to the
whole world" or perhaps "emblematic of the mundane

sacred vestments, led those ceremonies of world-wide[a]
significance and been reverenced by visitors to the
city from every quarter of the earth, were now seen
cast out naked, to be devoured by dogs and beasts
of prey. Virtue herself, I think, groaned for these
men's fate, bewailing such utter defeat at the hands
of vice. Such, however, was the end of Ananus and
Jesus.

(3) Having disposed of them, the Zealots and the
Idumaean hordes fell upon and butchered the people
as though they had been a herd of unclean animals.
Ordinary folk were slain on the spot where they
were caught ; but the young nobles [b] they arrested
and threw into prison in irons, postponing their
execution in the hope that some would come over
to their party. Not one, however, listened to their
overtures, all preferring to die rather than side with
these criminals against their country, notwithstanding the fearful agonies which they underwent for
their refusal : they were scourged and racked, and
only when their bodies could no longer sustain these
tortures were they grudgingly consigned to the
sword. Those arrested by day were dispatched at
night and their bodies cast forth to make room for
fresh prisoners. To such consternation were the
people reduced that none dared openly weep for or
bury a deceased relative ; but in secret and behind
closed doors were their tears shed and their groans
uttered with circumspection, for fear of being overheard by any of their foes. For the mourner in-

The Zealots
and
Idumaeans
torture and
kill the
nobility.

system " (Traill) ; cf. Ant. iii. 123, 180 ff. (the Tabernacle a
symbol of the universe), with Westcott's note on Heb. ix. 1
(τὸ ἅγιον κοσμικόν).

[b] τοὺς εὐγενεῖς καὶ νέους parallel with τῶν εὐγενῶν νέων
below (§ 333).

πενθήσας εὐθὺς ἔπασχε· νύκτωρ δὲ κόνιν αἴροντες
χεροῖν ὀλίγην ἐπερρίπτουν τοῖς σώμασι, καὶ μεθ᾽
333 ἡμέραν εἴ τις παράβολος. μύριοι καὶ δισχίλιοι
τῶν εὐγενῶν νέων οὕτως διεφθάρησαν.

334 (4) Οἱ δὲ ἤδη διαμεμισηκότες τὸ φονεύειν ἀνέδην
335 εἰρωνεύοντο δικαστήρια καὶ κρίσεις. καὶ δή τινα
τῶν ἐπιφανεστάτων ἀποκτείνειν προθέμενοι Ζαχαρίαν υἱὸν Βάρεις¹· παρώξυνε δ᾽ αὐτοὺς τὸ λίαν
τἀνδρὸς μισοπόνηρον καὶ φιλελεύθερον, ἦν δὲ καὶ
πλούσιος, ὥστε μὴ μόνον ἐλπίζειν τὴν ἁρπαγὴν
τῆς οὐσίας, ἀλλὰ καὶ προσαποσκευάσεσθαι² δυνα-
336 τὸν ἄνθρωπον εἰς τὴν ἑαυτῶν κατάλυσιν· συγ-
καλοῦσι μὲν ἐξ ἐπιτάγματος ἑβδομήκοντα τῶν ἐν
τέλει δημοτῶν εἰς τὸ ἱερόν, περιθέντες δ᾽ αὐτοῖς
ὥσπερ ἐπὶ σκηνῆς σχῆμα δικαστῶν ἔρημον
ἐξουσίας τοῦ Ζαχαρίου κατηγόρουν, ὡς ἐνδιδοίη
τὰ πράγματα Ῥωμαίοις καὶ περὶ προδοσίας δια-
337 πέμψαιτο πρὸς Οὐεσπασιανόν. ἦν δὲ οὔτ᾽ ἔλεγχός
τις τῶν κατηγορουμένων οὔτε τεκμήριον, ἀλλ᾽
αὐτοὶ πεπεῖσθαι καλῶς ἔφασαν καὶ τοῦτ᾽ εἶναι
338 πίστιν τῆς ἀληθείας ἠξίουν. ὅ γε μὴν Ζαχαρίας
συνιδὼν μηδεμίαν αὐτῷ καταλειπομένην σωτηρίας
ἐλπίδα, κεκλῆσθαι γὰρ κατ᾽ ἐνέδραν εἰς εἱρκτήν,
οὐκ ἐπὶ δικαστήριον, ἐποιήσατο τὴν τοῦ ζῆν ἀπόγνωσιν οὐκ ἀπαρρησίαστον, ἀλλὰ καταστὰς τὸ

---

¹ PAVR Lat. : Βαρούχου M¹C : Βαρισκαίου LM².
² ed. pr. and Lat. : προσαποσκευάζεσθαι mss.

ᵃ This incident has gained an interest for N.T. students
from an old suggestion revived by Wellhausen (*Einleitung
in die drei ersten Evangelien*, ed. 2, 1911, pp. 118 ff.) to identify
this Zacharias son of Baris (or Bariscaeus : the reading
Baruch is negligible) with the "Zachariah, son of Barachiah,"
whose death in the temple is referred to by Christ in Matt.

stantly suffered the same fate as the mourned. Only by night would they take a little dust in both hands and strew it on the bodies, though some venturous persons did this by day. Twelve thousand of the youthful nobility thus perished.

(4) Having now come to loathe indiscriminate massacre, the Zealots instituted mock trials and courts of justice. They had determined to put to death Zacharias, son of Baris,[a] one of the most eminent of the citizens. The man exasperated them by his pronounced hatred of wrong and love of liberty, and, as he was also rich, they had the double prospect of plundering his property and of getting rid of a powerful and dangerous opponent. So they issued a peremptory summons to seventy of the leading citizens to appear in the Temple, assigning to them, as in a play, the rôle, without the authority, of judges ; they then accused Zacharias of betraying the state to the Romans and of holding treasonable communications with Vespasian. They adduced no evidence or proof in support of these charges, but declared that they were fully convinced of his guilt themselves and claimed this as sufficiently establishing the fact. Zacharias, aware that no hope of escape was left him, as he had been treacherously summoned to a prison rather than a court of justice, did not allow despair of life to rob him of liberty of speech. He rose and ridiculed the probability of

Mock trial and murder of Zacharias.

xxiii. 35, as the last of a series of Jewish murders beginning with that of Abel. The theory, which rests on a rather remote resemblance of names, is on many grounds untenable. The author of the first Gospel refers to the murder of Z. ben Jehoiada (2 Chron. xxiv. 19 ff.) whom, like some Jewish Rabbis, he confused with Z. ben Berechiah, the prophet of the Restoration (Zech. i. 1).

99

μὲν πιθανὸν τῶν κατηγορημένων διεχλεύασε καὶ
διὰ βραχέων ἀπελύσατο τὰς ἐπιφερομένας αἰτίας.
339 ἔπειτα δὲ τὸν λόγον εἰς τοὺς κατηγόρους ἀπο-
στρέψας ἑξῆς πάσας αὐτῶν διεξῄει τὰς παρανομίας
καὶ πολλὰ περὶ τῆς συγχύσεως κατωλοφύρατο
340 τῶν πραγμάτων. οἱ ζηλωταὶ δ' ἐθορύβουν καὶ
μόλις τῶν ξιφῶν ἀπεκράτουν, τὸ σχῆμα καὶ τὴν
εἰρωνείαν τοῦ δικαστηρίου μέχρι τέλους παῖξαι
προαιρούμενοι, καὶ ἄλλως πειράσαι θέλοντες τοὺς
δικαστάς, εἰ παρὰ τὸν αὐτῶν κίνδυνον μνησθή-
341 σονται τοῦ δικαίου. φέρουσι δ' οἱ ἑβδομήκοντα
τῷ κρινομένῳ τὰς ψήφους ἅπαντες καὶ σὺν αὐτῷ
προείλοντο τεθνάναι μᾶλλον ἢ τῆς ἀναιρέσεως
342 αὐτοῦ λαβεῖν τὴν ἐπιγραφήν. ἤρθη δὲ βοὴ τῶν
ζηλωτῶν πρὸς τὴν ἀπόλυσιν, καὶ πάντων μὲν ἦν
ἀγανάκτησις ἐπὶ τοῖς δικασταῖς ὡς μὴ συνιεῖσι
343 τὴν εἰρωνείαν τῆς δοθείσης αὐτοῖς ἐξουσίας, δύο
δὲ τῶν τολμηροτάτων προσπεσόντες ἐν μέσῳ τῷ
ἱερῷ διαφθείρουσι τὸν Ζαχαρίαν καὶ πεσόντι
ἐπιχλευάσαντες ἔφασαν "καὶ παρ' ἡμῶν τὴν
ψῆφον ἔχεις καὶ βεβαιοτέραν ἀπόλυσιν," ῥίπτουσί
τε αὐτὸν εὐθέως ἀπὸ τοῦ ἱεροῦ κατὰ τῆς ὑπο-
344 κειμένης φάραγγος. τοὺς δὲ δικαστὰς πρὸς ὕβριν
ἀπεστραμμένοις τοῖς ξίφεσι τύπτοντες ἐξέωσαν τοῦ
περιβόλου, δι' ἓν τοῦτο φεισάμενοι τῆς σφαγῆς
αὐτῶν, ἵνα σκεδασθέντες ἀνὰ τὴν πόλιν ἄγγελοι
πᾶσι τῆς δουλείας γένωνται.
345 (5) Τοῖς δ' Ἰδουμαίοις ἤδη τῆς παρουσίας
346 μετέμελε καὶ προσίστατο τὰ πραττόμενα. συναγαγὼν δὲ αὐτούς τις ἀπὸ τῶν ζηλωτῶν κατ'
ἰδίαν ἐλθὼν ἐνεδείκνυτο τὰ συμπαρανομηθέντα
τοῖς καλέσασι καὶ τὸ κατὰ τῆς μητροπόλεως

the accusation, and in few words quashed the charges laid against him. Then, rounding upon his accusers, he went over all their enormities in order, and bitterly lamented the confusion of public affairs. The Zealots were in an uproar and could scarce refrain from drawing their swords, although they were anxious to play out their part and this farce of a trial to the close, and desired, moreover, to test whether the judges would put considerations of justice above their own peril. The seventy, however, brought in a unanimous verdict for the defendant, preferring to die with him rather than be held answerable for his destruction. The Zealots raised an outcry at his acquittal, and were all indignant with the judges for not understanding that the authority entrusted to them was a mere pretence. Two of the most daring of them then set upon Zacharias and slew him in the midst of the Temple, and exclaiming in jest over his prostrate body " Now you have our verdict also and a more certain release,[a] " forthwith cast him out of the Temple into the ravine below. Then they insolently struck the judges with the backs of their swords and drove them from the precincts ; sparing their lives for the sole reason that they might disperse through the city and proclaim to all the servitude to which they were reduced.

(5) The Idumaeans now began to regret that they had come, taking offence at these proceedings. In this mood they were called together by one of the Zealots, who came to them privately and showed up the crimes which they had committed in conjunction with those who had summoned them, and gave a

A Zealot secretly denounces the crimes of his party to the Idumaeans and urges them to depart.

---

[a] The Greek word ἀπόλυσις means both " acquittal " and " decease."

101

347 διεξήει· παρατάσσεσθαι μὲν γὰρ ὡς ὑπὸ τῶν
ἀρχιερέων προδιδομένης Ῥωμαίοις τῆς μητροπόλεως, εὑρηκέναι δὲ προδοσίας μὲν τεκμήριον
οὐδέν, τοὺς δ' ἐκείνην ὑποκρινομένους φυλάτ-
τεσθαι καὶ πολέμου καὶ τυραννίδος ἔργα τολμῶν-
348 τας. προσήκειν μὲν οὖν αὐτοῖς διακωλύειν ἀπ'
ἀρχῆς· ἐπειδὴ δ' ἅπαξ εἰς κοινωνίαν ἐμφυλίου
φόνου προέπεσον,[1] ὅρον γοῦν ἐπιθεῖναι τοῖς ἁμαρτή-
μασι καὶ μὴ παραμένειν χορηγοῦντας ἰσχὺν τοῖς
349 καταλύουσι τὰ πάτρια. καὶ γὰρ εἴ τινες χαλε-
παίνουσι τῷ[2] κλεισθῆναι τὰς πύλας καὶ μὴ δοθῆναι
μετὰ τῶν ὅπλων αὐτοῖς ἑτοίμην τὴν εἴσοδον,
ἀλλὰ τοὺς εἴρξαντας τετιμωρῆσθαι· καὶ τεθνάναι
μὲν Ἄνανον, διεφθάρθαι δ' ἐπὶ μιᾶς νυκτὸς
350 ὀλίγου δεῖν πάντα τὸν δῆμον. ἐφ' οἷς τῶν μὲν
οἰκείων πολλοὺς αἰσθάνεσθαι μετανοοῦντας, τῶν
ἐπικαλεσαμένων δὲ ὁρᾶν ἄμετρον τὴν ὠμότητα
351 μηδὲ δι' οὓς ἐσώθησαν αἰδουμένων· ἐν ὄμμασι
γοῦν τῶν συμμάχων τὰ αἴσχιστα τολμᾶν, καὶ τὰς
ἐκείνων παρανομίας Ἰδουμαίοις προσάπτεσθαι,
μέχρις ἂν μήτε κωλύῃ τις μήτε χωρίζηται τῶν
352 δρωμένων. δεῖν οὖν, ἐπειδὴ διαβολὴ μὲν πέφηνε
τὰ τῆς προδοσίας, ἔφοδος δὲ Ῥωμαίων οὐδεμία
προσδοκᾶται, δυναστεία δ' ἐπιτετείχισται τῇ
πόλει δυσκατάλυτος, αὐτοὺς ἀναχωρεῖν ἐπ' οἴκου
καὶ τῷ μὴ κοινωνεῖν τοῖς φαύλοις ἁπάντων
ἀπολογήσασθαι πέρι, ὧν φενακισθέντες μετά-
σχοιεν.
353 (vi. 1) Τούτοις πεισθέντες οἱ Ἰδουμαῖοι πρώ-

---

[1] R : προσέπεσον most mss. : μετέπεσον L.
[2] Dindorf : τὸ mss.

detailed account of the situation in the capital.
They had enlisted, he reminded them, in the belief
that the chief priests were betraying the metropolis
to the Romans ; but they had discovered no evidence
of treason, whereas its professed defenders were the
daring perpetrators of acts of war and despotism.
These proceedings, he said, the Idumaeans should
have checked at the outset ; but having once become
their partners and plunged into civil war, they ought
now at least to put a limit to their sins and no longer
continue to lend support to men who were subverting
the institutions of their forefathers.   Even were there
any still indignant at the closure of the gates and the
refusal of prompt admission to them while bearing
arms, well, those who had excluded them had now
been punished : Ananus was dead and in one night
almost the whole population had been destroyed.
Such actions, he could perceive, had produced repentance in many of their own party, but among
those who had invited them he saw nothing but
unmeasured brutality, without the slightest respect
for their deliverers : under the very eyes of their
allies they dared to commit the foulest atrocities,
and their iniquities would be ascribed to the Idumaeans, so long as no one vetoed or dissociated himself
from these proceedings.   Since, then, the charge of
treason had been shown to be a calumny and no
invasion of the Romans was expected, while the city
had had planted upon it a despotism not easily to be
overthrown, their duty (he said) was to return home
and by severing their connexion with these scoundrels
to make some amends for all the crimes in which
they had been duped into taking a part.

(vi. 1) Acting on this advice, the Idumaeans first

τον μὲν λύουσι τοὺς ἐν τοῖς δεσμωτηρίοις περὶ
δισχιλίους δημότας, οἳ παραχρῆμα φυγόντες ἐκ
τῆς πόλεως ἀφικνοῦνται πρὸς Σίμωνα, περὶ οὗ
μικρὸν ὕστερον ἐροῦμεν· ἔπειτα ἐκ τῶν Ἱερο-
354 σολύμων ἀνεχώρησαν ἐπ' οἴκου. καὶ συνέβη τὸν
χωρισμὸν αὐτῶν γενέσθαι παράδοξον ἀμφοτέροις·
ὅ τε γὰρ δῆμος ἀγνοῶν τὴν μετάνοιαν ἀνεθάρσησε
355 πρὸς ὀλίγον ὡς ἐχθρῶν κεκουφισμένος, οἵ τε
ζηλωταὶ μᾶλλον ἐπανέστησαν, οὐχ ὡς ὑπὸ συμμάχων καταλειφθέντες, ἀλλ' ἀπηλλαγμένοι τῶν
δυσωπούντων καὶ διατρεπόντων παρανομεῖν.
356 οὐκέτι γοῦν μέλλησις ἢ σκέψις ἦν τῶν ἀδικημάτων,
ἀλλ' ὀξυτάταις μὲν ἐχρῶντο ταῖς ἐπινοίαις εἰς
ἕκαστα, τὰ δοχθέντα δὲ τάχιον καὶ τῆς ἐπινοίας
357 ἐνήργουν. μάλιστα δ' ἐπ' ἀνδρείαν τε καὶ εὐγένειαν ἐφόνουν, τὴν μὲν φθόνῳ λυμαινόμενοι, τὸ
δὲ γενναῖον δέει· μόνην γὰρ αὐτῶν[1] ἀσφάλειαν
ὑπελάμβανον τὸ μηδένα τῶν δυνατῶν καταλιπεῖν.
358 ἀνῃρέθη γοῦν σὺν πολλοῖς ἑτέροις καὶ Γουρίων,
ἀξιώματι μὲν καὶ γένει προύχων, δημοκρατικὸς
δὲ καὶ φρονήματος ἐλευθερίου μεστός, εἰ καί τις
ἕτερος Ἰουδαίων· ἀπώλεσε δ' αὐτὸν ἡ παρρησία
359 μάλιστα πρὸς τοῖς ἄλλοις πλεονεκτήμασιν. οὐδ'
ὁ Περαΐτης Νίγερ αὐτῶν τὰς χεῖρας διέφυγεν,
ἀνὴρ ἄριστος ἐν τοῖς πρὸς Ῥωμαίους πολέμοις
γενόμενος· ὃς καὶ βοῶν πολλάκις τάς τε ὠτειλὰς
360 ἐπιδεικνὺς διὰ μέσης ἐσύρετο τῆς πόλεως. ἐπεὶ

[1] αὐτῶν mss. (as often).

---

[a] §§ 503 ff.

[b] Probably identical with Gorion ben Joseph, § 159.

[c] " Teeming "; cf. Plato, Rep. 563 D μεστὰ ἐλευθερίας,
" ready to burst with liberty " (Jowett).

liberated the citizens confined in the prisons, numbering about two thousand (these immediately fled from
the city and joined Simon, of whom we shall speak
presently *a*); they then left Jerusalem and returned
home. Their departure produced an unlooked-for
effect on both parties : the citizens, unaware of their
repentance, recovered momentary confidence, as if
relieved of an enemy ; the Zealots, on the other
hand, grew yet more insolent, not as though they
had been abandoned by allies, but as quit of critics
who discountenanced and sought to deter them from
their lawlessness. No longer now was there any
delay or deliberation about their crimes ; they devised their plans with lightning rapidity, and in each
case put their decisions into effect even more swiftly
than they devised them. They thirsted above all for
the blood of the brave and the nobility, massacring
the latter out of envy, the former from fear ; for
they imagined that their own safety depended solely
on their leaving no person of authority alive. Thus,
to take one instance among many, they murdered
Gurion,*b* a person of exalted rank and birth, and
yet a democrat and filled *c* with liberal principles,
if ever Jew was ; his outspokenness, added to the
privileges of his position, was the main cause of his
ruin. Nor did even Niger the Peraean *d* escape
their hands, a man who had shown exceptional
gallantry in his battles with the Romans : vehemently
protesting and pointing to his scars, this veteran
was dragged through the midst of the city. When

The
departure
of the
Idumaeans
in disgust

leads the
Zealots to
greater
atrocities.

Further
victims :
Gurion

and Niger.

d He distinguished himself in the opening battle with
Cestius, *B.* ii. 520 ; was at one time governor of Idumaea, ii.
566 ; and led two unsuccessful attacks on the Roman
garrison at Ascalon, when he again won distinction and had a
miraculous escape, iii. 11-28.

δ' ἔξω τῶν πυλῶν ἦκτο, τὴν σωτηρίαν ἀπογνοὺς
περὶ ταφῆς ἱκέτευεν· οἱ δὲ προαπειλήσαντες ἧς
ἐπεθύμει μάλιστα γῆς μὴ μεταδώσειν αὐτῷ, τὸν
361 φόνον ἐνήργουν. ἀναιρούμενος δὲ ὁ Νίγερ τιμωροὺς Ῥωμαίους αὐτοῖς ἐπηράσατο, λιμόν τε καὶ
λοιμὸν ἐπὶ τῷ πολέμῳ καὶ πρὸς ἅπασι τὰς ἀλλήλων
362 χεῖρας· ἃ δὴ πάντα· κατὰ τῶν ἀσεβῶν ἐκύρωσεν
ὁ θεός, καὶ τὸ δικαιότατον, ὅτι γεύσασθαι τῆς
ἀλλήλων ἀπονοίας ἔμελλον οὐκ εἰς μακρὰν στασιά-
363 σαντες. Νίγερ μὲν οὖν ἀνῃρημένος τοὺς περὶ
τῆς καταλύσεως αὐτῶν φόβους ἐπεκούφισε, τοῦ
λαοῦ δὲ μέρος οὐδὲν ἦν, ᾧ μὴ πρὸς ἀπώλειαν
364 ἐπενοεῖτο πρόφασις. τὸ μὲν γὰρ αὐτῶν διενεχθέν
τινι πάλαι διέφθαρτο, τὸ δὲ μὴ προσκροῦσαν κατ'
εἰρήνην ἐπικαίρους ἐλάμβανε τὰς αἰτίας· καὶ ὁ
μὲν μηδ' ὅλως αὐτοῖς προσιὼν ὡς ὑπερήφανος,
ὁ προσιὼν δὲ μετὰ παρρησίας ὡς καταφρονῶν, ὁ
365 θεραπεύων δ' ὡς ἐπίβουλος ὑπωπτεύετο. μία
δὲ ἦν τῶν τε μεγίστων καὶ μετριωτάτων ἐγκλημάτων τιμωρία θάνατος, καὶ διέφυγεν οὐδείς,
εἰ μὴ σφόδρα τις ἦν ταπεινὸς [ἢ]¹ δι' ἀγένειαν ἢ
διὰ τύχην.
366   (2) Ῥωμαίων δὲ οἱ μὲν ἄλλοι πάντες ἡγεμόνες
ἕρμαιον ἡγούμενοι τὴν στάσιν τῶν πολεμίων
ὥρμηντο πρὸς τὴν πόλιν καὶ τὸν Οὐεσπασιανὸν
ἤπειγον ὡς ἂν ὄντα κύριον τῶν ὅλων, φάμενοι
πρόνοιαν θεοῦ σύμμαχον σφίσι τῷ τετράφθαι

¹ om. ἢ L.

ᵃ Or "... had quarrels having long since been":
πάλαι in the central position may be intended as adverb to
both verbs.
   ᵇ In the manner of Thucydides in his reflections on civil
dissensions (στάσεις), iii. 82.

brought without the gates, he, despairing of his life, besought them to give him burial ; but they fiercely declared that they would not grant him the one desire of his heart—a grave—and then proceeded to murder him. In his dying moments Niger imprecated upon their heads the vengeance of the Romans, famine and pestilence to add to the horrors of war, and, to crown all, internecine strife ; all which curses upon the wretches were ratified by God, including that most righteous fate, by which they were doomed ere long to taste in party conflict the effects of their comrades' frenzy. Niger's removal anyhow relieved their fear of being deposed from power ; but there was no section of the people for whose destruction some pretext was not devised. Those with whom any had ancient quarrels having been[a] put to death, against those who had given them no umbrage in peace-time accusations suitable to the occasion were invented : the man who never approached them was suspected of pride ; he who approached them with freedom, of treating them with contempt ; he who courted them, of conspiracy.[b] The one penalty for charges of the gravest or the most trifling nature was death ; and none escaped save those whose humble birth put them utterly beneath notice, unless by accident.[c]

(2) The Roman generals, regarding the dissension in the enemy's ranks as a godsend, were all eager to march against the capital, and urged Vespasian, as commander-in-chief, to take this course. " Divine providence," they said, " has come to our aid by

Vespasian deliberates with his generals about attacking Jerusalem.

---

[c] I omit the first ἢ with L. The natural rendering " those whose humble birth or fortune " etc. gives τύχη a sense which appears unwarranted.

367 τοὺς ἐχθροὺς κατ' ἀλλήλων· εἶναι μέντοι τὴν
ῥοπὴν ὀξεῖαν, καὶ ταχέως Ἰουδαίους ὁμονοήσειν¹
ἢ κοπιάσαντας ἐν τοῖς ἐμφυλίοις κακοῖς ἢ μετα-
368 νοήσαντας. Οὐεσπασιανὸς δὲ πλεῖστον αὐτοὺς ἔφη
τοῦ δέοντος ἁμαρτάνειν, ὥσπερ ἐν θεάτρῳ χειρῶν
τε καὶ ὅπλων ἐπίδειξιν ποιήσασθαι γλιχομένους
οὐκ ἀκίνδυνον, ἀλλὰ μὴ τὸ συμφέρον καὶ τἀσφαλὲς
369 σκοποῦντας. εἰ μὲν γὰρ εὐθέως ὁρμήσειεν ἐπὶ
τὴν πόλιν, αἴτιος ὁμονοίας ἔσεσθαι τοῖς πολεμίοις
καὶ τὴν ἰσχὺν αὐτῶν ἀκμάζουσαν ἐφ' ἑαυτὸν
ἐπιστρέψειν²· εἰ δὲ περιμείνειεν, ὀλιγωτέροις χρή-
370 σεσθαι δαπανηθεῖσιν ἐν τῇ στάσει. στρατηγεῖν
μὲν γὰρ ἄμεινον αὐτοῦ τὸν θεόν, ἀπονητὶ³ Ῥωμαίοις παραδιδόντα Ἰουδαίους καὶ τὴν νίκην ἀκιν
371 δύνως τῇ στρατηγίᾳ⁴ χαριζόμενον· ὥστε χρῆναι,
διαφθειρομένων χερσὶν οἰκείαις τῶν ἐχθρῶν καὶ
τῷ μεγίστῳ κακῷ στάσει χρωμένων, θεατὰς
μᾶλλον αὐτοὺς ἀποκαθῆσθαι τῶν κινδύνων ἢ
θανατῶσιν ἀνθρώποις καὶ λελυσσηκόσιν κατ'
372 ἀλλήλων χεῖρα μίσγειν. "εἰ δέ τις οἴεται τὴν
δόξαν τῆς νίκης ἑωλοτέραν ἔσεσθαι δίχα μάχης,
γνώτω τοῦ διὰ τῶν ὅπλων σφαλεροῦ τὸ μεθ'
373 ἡσυχίας κατόρθωμα λυσιτελέστερον ⟨ὄν⟩⁵· καὶ γὰρ
οὐχ ἧττον εὐκλεεῖς οἴεσθαι χρὴ τῶν κατὰ χεῖρα
λαμπρῶν τοὺς ἐγκρατείᾳ καὶ συνέσει τὰ ἴσα
πράξαντας." ἅμα μέντοι μειουμένων τῶν πολεμίων καὶ τὴν αὐτοῦ στρατιάν, ἀναληφθεῖσαν ἐκ
374 τῶν συνεχῶν πόνων, ἐρρωμενεστέραν ἕξειν. ἄλλως

¹ ed. pr. with Lat. : + ἡμῖν MSS.
² Bekker with Lat. : ἐπιστρέφειν MSS.
³ ἀκονιτὶ VRC (ἀκοντὶ L).   ⁴ στρατιᾷ LVC.
⁵ ins. Herwerden with Cobet.

turning our adversaries against each other; but changes come rapidly and the Jews will quickly return to unanimity through weariness or repentance of civil strife." To this Vespasian replied that they were gravely mistaken as to the right policy, and were anxious to make a theatrical, though hazardous, display of their gallantry and arms, without regard to expediency and safety. For, were he immediately to attack the city, the effect would be merely to reunite their opponents and to turn their forces in fullest strength against himself; whereas by waiting he would find fewer enemies, when they had wasted their numbers in sedition. God was a better general than he, and was delivering the Jews to the Romans without any exertion on their part and bestowing victory upon them without risk to Roman generalship. Consequently, while their adversaries were perishing by their own hands and suffering from that worst of calamities, civil strife, their part was rather to sit as distant spectators[a] of their perils, than to contend with men who courted death and were raving against each other. "But," he continued, "if anyone thinks that the glory of victory will lose its zest without a fight, let him learn that success obtained by sitting still is more fruitful than when won by the uncertainty of arms; indeed those who attain the same ends by self-restraint and sagacity should be deemed no less famous than those who distinguish themselves in action." Moreover, while the enemy's numbers were diminishing, his own army would have recruited their strength after their continuous labours and be at his service reinvigorated.

"Our strength is to sit still."

As at gladiatorial shows.

τε καὶ τῶν στοχαζομένων τῆς περὶ τὴν νίκην
375 λαμπρότητος οὐ τοῦτον εἶναι τὸν καιρόν· οὐ γὰρ
περὶ κατασκευὴν ὅπλων ἢ τειχῶν οὐδὲ περὶ
συλλογὴν ἐπικούρων Ἰουδαίους ἀσχολεῖσθαι καὶ[1]
τὴν ὑπέρθεσιν ἔσεσθαι κατὰ τῶν διδόντων, ἀλλ'
ἐμφυλίῳ πολέμῳ καὶ διχονοίᾳ τραχηλιζομένους
καθ' ἡμέραν οἰκτρότερα πάσχειν ὧν ἂν ἐπελθόντες
376 αὐτοὶ διαθεῖεν αὐτοὺς ἁλόντας. εἴτ' οὖν τἀσφαλές
τις σκοποίη, χρῆναι τοὺς ὑφ' ἑαυτῶν ἀναλισκο-
μένους ἐᾶν, εἴτε τὸ εὐκλεέστερον τοῦ κατορθώματος, οὐ δεῖν τοῖς οἴκοι νοσοῦσιν ἐπιχειρεῖν·
ῥηθήσεσθαι γὰρ εὐλόγως οὐκ αὐτῶν τὴν νίκην
ἀλλὰ τῆς στάσεως.

377 (3) Ταῦτα Οὐεσπασιανῷ λέγοντι συνήνουν οἱ
ἡγεμόνες, καὶ παραχρῆμα τὸ στρατηγικὸν τῆς
γνώμης ἀνεφαίνετο· πολλοὶ γοῦν[2] καθ' ἡμέραν
378 ηὐτομόλουν τοὺς ζηλωτὰς διαδιδράσκοντες. χαλεπὴ δ' ἦν ἡ φυγὴ φρουραῖς διειληφότων τὰς
διεξόδους πάσας καὶ τὸν ὁπωσοῦν ἐν αὐταῖς
ἁλισκόμενον ὡς πρὸς Ῥωμαίους ἀπιόντα δια-
379 χρωμένων. ὅ γε μὴν χρήματα δοὺς ἐξηφίετο
καὶ μόνος ἦν ὁ μὴ διδοὺς προδότης, ὥστε κατελείπετο τῶν εὐπόρων τὴν φυγὴν ὠνουμένων μόνους
380 ἐναποσφάττεσθαι τοὺς πένητας. νεκροὶ δὲ κατὰ
τὰς λεωφόρους πάσας ἐσωρεύοντο παμπληθεῖς,
καὶ πολλοὶ τῶν ὁρμωμένων αὐτομολεῖν πάλιν τὴν
ἔνδον ἀπώλειαν ᾑροῦντο· τὸν γὰρ ἐπὶ τῆς πατρίδος
θάνατον ἐλπὶς ταφῆς ἐποίει δοκεῖν μετριώτερον.
381 οἱ δ' εἰς τοσοῦτον ὠμότητος ἐξώκειλαν, ὡς μήτε

---

[1] ὡς Destinon : atque ideo Lat.   Text doubtful.
[2] L : δὲ the rest.

Above all, this was not the occasion for aspiring to the honours of a brilliant victory; for the Jews were not busily engaged in forging arms, erecting fortifications or levying auxiliaries, in which case delay would be prejudicial to those who granted it, but were risking their necks in civil war and dissension and daily enduring greater miseries than they themselves would inflict on them after defeat, if they advanced to the assault. Whether, therefore, they looked to the path of safety, these Jews should be left to continue their own destruction; or whether they considered the success which would bring the greater renown, they ought not to attack patients suffering from their own domestic disorders; for it would be said, with reason, that they owed their victory not to themselves but to sedition.

(3) In these observations of Vespasian the officers concurred, and the soundness of the general's judgement was soon made evident by the numbers who daily deserted, eluding the Zealots. But flight was difficult, because guards were posted at all the outlets and anyone caught there, on whatever business, was slain, on the assumption that he was going off to the Romans. If, however, he paid the price, he was allowed to go, and only he who offered nothing was a traitor; the result being that the wealthy purchased their escape and the poor alone were slaughtered. Along all the highways the dead were piled in heaps; and many starting [a] to desert changed their minds and chose to die within the walls, since the hope of burial made death in their native city appear more tolerable. The Zealots, however, carried barbarity so far as to grant interment to none,

Many Jews desert to the Romans.

---

[a] Or "who had been eager."

τοῖς ἔνδον ἀναιρουμένοις μήτε τοῖς ἀνὰ τὰς
382 ὁδοὺς μεταδοῦναι γῆς, ἀλλὰ καθάπερ συνθήκας
πεποιημένοι τοῖς τῆς πατρίδος συγκαταλῦσαι καὶ
τοὺς τῆς φύσεως νόμους ἅμα τε τοῖς εἰς ἀνθρώ-
383 πους ἀδικήμασιν συμμιᾶναι καὶ τὸ θεῖον, ὑφ' ἡλίῳ
τοὺς νεκροὺς μυδῶντας ἀπέλειπον. τοῖς δὲ θάπ-
τουσί τινα τῶν προσηκόντων, ὃ καὶ τοῖς αὐτομολοῦσιν, ἐπιτίμιον θάνατος ἦν, καὶ δεῖσθαι
παραχρῆμα ταφῆς ἔδει τὸν ἑτέρῳ χαριζόμενον.
384 καθόλου τε εἰπεῖν, οὐδὲν οὕτως ἀπολώλει χρηστὸν
πάθος ἐν ταῖς τότε συμφοραῖς ὡς ἔλεος· ἃ γὰρ
ἐχρῆν οἰκτείρειν, ταῦτα παρώξυνε τοὺς ἀλιτηρίους,
καὶ ἀπὸ μὲν τῶν ζώντων ἐπὶ τοὺς ἀνῃρημένους,
ἀπὸ δὲ τῶν νεκρῶν ἐπὶ τοὺς ζῶντας τὰς ὀργὰς
385 μετέφερον· καὶ δι' ὑπερβολὴν δέους ὁ περιὼν
τοὺς προληφθέντας ὡς ἀναπαυσαμένους ἐμακά-
ριζεν, οἵ τε ἐν τοῖς δεσμωτηρίοις αἰκιζόμενοι
κατὰ σύγκρισιν καὶ τοὺς ἀτάφους ἀπέφαινον
386 εὐδαίμονας. κατεπατεῖτο μὲν οὖν πᾶς αὐτοῖς
θεσμὸς ἀνθρώπων, ἐγελᾶτο δὲ τὰ θεῖα, καὶ τοὺς
τῶν προφητῶν χρησμοὺς[1] ὥσπερ ἀγυρτικὰς λογο-
387 ποιίας ἐχλεύαζον. πολλὰ δ' οὗτοι περὶ ἀρετῆς
καὶ κακίας προεθέσπισαν, ἃ παραβάντες οἱ
ζηλωταὶ καὶ τὴν κατὰ τῆς πατρίδος προφητείαν
388 τέλους ἠξίωσαν. ἦν γὰρ δή τις παλαιὸς λόγος
ἀνδρῶν ἐνθέων[2] τότε τὴν πόλιν ἁλώσεσθαι καὶ
καταφλέξεσθαι τὸ ἁγιώτατον νόμῳ πολέμου,
στάσις ἐὰν κατασκήψῃ καὶ χεῖρες οἰκεῖαι προ-

---

[1] L Exc. : θεσμοὺς the rest (from previous line).

whether slain within the city or on the roads ; but, Barbarity of Zealots to dead and living. as though they had covenanted to annul the laws of nature along with those of their country, and to their outrages upon humanity to add pollution of Heaven [a] itself, they left the dead putrefying in the sun. For burying a relative, as for desertion, the penalty was death, and one who granted this boon to another instantly stood in need of it himself. In short, none of the nobler emotions was so utterly lost amid the miseries of those days, as pity : what should have roused their compassion, only exasperated these miscreants, whose fury shifted alternately from the living to the slain and from the dead to the living. Such terror prevailed that the survivors deemed blessed the lot of the earlier victims, now at rest, while the tortured wretches in the prisons pronounced even the unburied happy in comparison with themselves. Every human ordinance was They fulfil the predictions of ancient prophecy. trampled under foot, every dictate of religion ridiculed by these men, who scoffed at the oracles of the prophets as impostors' fables. Yet those predictions of theirs contained much concerning virtue and vice, by the transgression of which the Zealots brought upon their country the fulfilment of the prophecies directed against it. For there was an ancient saying of inspired men that the city would be taken and the sanctuary burnt to the ground by right of war, whensoever it should be visited by sedition and native hands should be the first

[a] Literally "the deity"; cf. ii. 148 of the scrupulous care of the Essenes "not to offend the rays of the deity," i.e. the sun.

---

[2] Holwerda: ἔνθεον MS. quoted by Havercamp: ἔνθα the rest.

μιάνωσι τὸ τοῦ θεοῦ τέμενος· οἷς οὐκ ἀπιστήσαντες
οἱ ζηλωταὶ διακόνους αὐτοὺς ἐπέδοσαν.

389 (vii. 1). Ἤδη δὲ Ἰωάννῃ τυραννιῶντι τὸ πρὸς
τοὺς ὁμοίους ἰσότιμον ἠδοξεῖτο, καὶ κατ᾽ ὀλίγους
προσποιούμενος τῶν πονηροτέρων ἀφηνίαζε[1] τοῦ
390 συντάγματος. ἀεὶ δὲ τοῖς μὲν τῶν ἄλλων δόγ-
μασιν ἀπειθῶν, τὰ δὲ αὐτοῦ προστάσσων δεσπο-
τικώτερον, δῆλος ἦν μοναρχίας ἀντιποιούμενος.
391 εἶκον δ᾽ αὐτῷ τινὲς μὲν δέει, τινὲς δὲ κατ᾽ εὔνοιαν,
δεινὸς γὰρ ἦν ἀπάτῃ καὶ λόγῳ προσαγαγέσθαι,
πολλοὶ δὲ πρὸς ἀσφαλείας ἡγούμενοι τῆς αὐτῶν
τὰς αἰτίας ἤδη τῶν τολμωμένων ἐφ᾽ ἕνα καὶ
392 μὴ πολλοὺς ἀναφέρεσθαι. τό γε μὴν δραστήριον
αὐτοῦ κατά τε χεῖρα καὶ κατὰ γνώμην δορυφόρους
393 εἶχεν οὐκ ὀλίγους. πολλὴ δὲ μοῖρα τῶν ἀντι-
καθισταμένων[2] ἀπελείπετο, παρ᾽ οἷς ἴσχυε μὲν
καὶ φθόνος, δεινὸν ἡγουμένων ὑποτετάχθαι τὸ[3]
πρὶν ἰσοτίμῳ, τὸ πλέον δ᾽ εὐλάβεια τῆς μοναρχίας
394 ἀπέτρεπεν· οὔτε γὰρ καταλύσειν ῥᾳδίως ἤλπιζον
αὐτὸν ἅπαξ κρατήσαντα, καὶ καθ᾽ αὑτῶν πρόφασιν
ἕξειν τὸ τὴν ἀρχὴν ἀντιπρᾶξαι· προῃρεῖτο δ᾽ οὖν
πολεμῶν ἕκαστος ὁτιοῦν παθεῖν ἢ δουλεύσας
ἑκουσίως ἐν ἀνδραπόδου μοίρᾳ παραπολέσθαι.

---

[1] ἀφηνιάζετο L Exc.
[2] PC: ἀντικαθημένων the rest.
[3] PAC: τῷ the rest.

---

[a] I can quote no " ancient " authority for the saying.
The following *vaticinium post eventum* occurs in a work
written c. A.D. 80 : ἡνίκα δ᾽ ἀφροσύνῃσι πεποιθότες εὐσεβίην
τε | ῥίψουσιν στυγερούς τε τελοῦσι φόνους περὶ νηῶν, | καὶ τότ᾽
. . [reference follows to flight of Nero and the Roman civil

to defile God's sacred precincts.[a] This saying the Zealots did not disbelieve ; yet they lent themselves as instruments of its accomplishment.

(vii. 1) But now John, aspiring to despotic power, began to disdain the position of mere equality in honours with his peers, and, gradually gathering round him a group of the more depraved, broke away from the coalition. Invariably disregarding the decisions of the rest, and issuing imperious orders of his own, he was evidently laying claim to absolute sovereignty. Some yielded to him through fear, others from devotion (for he was an expert in gaining supporters by fraud and rhetoric) ; a large number thought that it would conduce to their own safety that the blame for their daring crimes should henceforth rest upon one individual rather than upon many ; while his energy both of body and mind procured him not a few retainers. On the other hand, he was abandoned by a large section of antagonists, partly influenced by envy—they scorned subjection to a former equal—but mainly deterred by dread of monarchical rule ; for they could not expect easily to depose him when once in power, and thought that they would have an excuse for themselves if they opposed him at the outset.[b] Anyhow, each man preferred war, whatever sufferings it might entail, to voluntary servitude and being killed off like slaves.

Split in the Zealot party : John assumes despotic power.

war] ἐκ Συρίης δ' ἥξει Ῥώμης πρόμος ὃς πυρὶ νηὸν | συμφλέξας Σολύμων κτλ., *Orac. Sibyll.* iv. 117 ff.

[b] Meaning doubtful. τὴν ἀρχὴν (which is certainly adverbial, not a noun as in Whiston's rendering, " that they had opposed *his having power* ") usually has a negative ; possibly we should read τὸ ⟨μὴ⟩ τὴν ἀρχὴν ἀντιπρᾶξαι, *i.e.* " that he would have a pretext against them if they did not oppose him at the outset."

395 διαιρεῖται μὲν οὖν ἡ στάσις ἐκ τούτων, καὶ τοῖς
396 ἐναντιωθεῖσιν Ἰωάννης ἀντεβασίλευσεν. ἀλλὰ τὰ
μὲν πρὸς ἀλλήλους αὐτοῖς διὰ φυλακῆς ἦν, καὶ
οὐδὲν ἢ μικρὸν εἴ ποτε διηκροβολίζοντο τοῖς
ὅπλοις, ἤριζον δὲ κατὰ τοῦ δήμου καὶ πότεροι
397 πλείονα λείαν ἄξουσιν[1] ἀντεφιλονείκουν. ἐπεὶ δὲ
ἡ πόλις τρισὶ τοῖς μεγίστοις κακοῖς ἐχειμάζετο,
πολέμῳ καὶ τυραννίδι καὶ στάσει, κατὰ σύγκρισιν
μετριώτερον ἦν τοῖς δημοτικοῖς ὁ πόλεμος·
ἀμέλει διαδιδράσκοντες ἐκ τῶν οἰκείων ἔφευγον
πρὸς τοὺς ἀλλοφύλους καὶ παρὰ Ῥωμαίοις ἧς
ἀπήλπισαν ἐν τοῖς ἰδίοις σωτηρίας ἠξιοῦντο.
398   (2) Τέταρτον δὲ ἄλλο κακὸν ἐκινεῖτο πρὸς τὴν
399 τοῦ ἔθνους κατάλυσιν. φρούριον ἦν οὐ πόρρω
Ἱεροσολύμων καρτερώτατον, ὑπὸ τῶν ἀρχαίων
βασιλέων εἴς τε ὑπέκθεσιν κτήσεως ἐν πολέμου
ῥοπαῖς καὶ σωμάτων ἀσφάλειαν κατεσκευασμέ-
400 νον, ὃ ἐκαλεῖτο Μασάδα. τοῦτο κατειληφότες
οἱ προσαγορευόμενοι σικάριοι τέως μὲν τὰς
πλησίον χώρας κατέτρεχον οὐδὲν πλέον τῶν ἐπιτηδείων ποριζόμενοι· δέει γὰρ ἀνεστέλλοντο
401 τῆς πλείονος ἁρπαγῆς· ὡς δὲ[2] τὴν Ῥωμαίων μὲν
στρατιὰν ἠρεμοῦσαν, στάσει δὲ καὶ τυραννίδι
ἰδίᾳ τοὺς ἐν Ἱεροσολύμοις Ἰουδαίους ἐπύθοντο
διῃρημένους, ἁδροτέρων ἥπτοντο τολμημάτων.
402 καὶ κατὰ τὴν ἑορτὴν τῶν ἀζύμων, ἣν ἄγουσιν
Ἰουδαῖοι[3] σωτήρια ἐξ οὗ τῆς ὑπ᾽ Αἰγυπτίοις

---

[1] PA : ἀνάξουσιν the rest.
[2] ὡς δὲ] ὡς PA¹ Lat.: εἶθ᾽ ὡς Niese with A².
[3] Ἑβραῖοι L Lat.

---

[a] *Sebbeh*, above the W. coast of the Dead Sea, near its

Such, then, was the origin of the split in the party, and John confronted his adversaries as a rival sovereign. However, their attitude to each other was purely defensive, and there were seldom if ever any skirmishes in arms between them ; but they were rival oppressors of the people and vied with each other in carrying off the larger spoils. While the ship of state was thus labouring under the three greatest of calamities—war, tyranny, and faction— to the populace the war was comparatively the mildest ; in fact they fled from their countrymen to take refuge with aliens and obtained at Roman hands the security which they despaired of finding among their own people.

(2) But yet a fourth misfortune was on foot to consummate the nation's ruin. Not far from Jerusalem was a fortress of redoubtable strength, built by the kings of old as a repository for their property and a refuge for their persons during the vicissitudes of war ; it was called Masada.[a] Of this the so-called Sicarii had taken possession. So far they had confined themselves to raids upon the neighbouring districts, merely with the object of procuring supplies, fear restraining them from further ravages ; but now when they learnt that the Roman army was inactive and that in Jerusalem the Jews were distracted by sedition and domestic tyranny, they embarked on more ambitious enterprises. Thus, during the feast of unleavened bread—a feast which has been kept by the Jews in thanksgiving for deliverance ever since their return to their native land on their

The Sicarii occupy Masada and make raids on the country.

lower end. Its capture by the insurgents is mentioned in *B.* ii. 408 ; a detailed description of the fortress and of its final capture by the Romans is given in vii. 280 ff.

δουλείας ἀνεθέντες εἰς τὴν πάτριον γῆν κατῆλθον,
νύκτωρ τοὺς ἐμποδὼν ὄντας διαλαθόντες πολίχνην τινὰ κατατρέχουσιν καλουμένην Ἐνγαδδί,
403 ἐν ᾗ τὸ μὲν ἀμύνεσθαι δυνάμενον, πρὶν ὅπλων
ἅψασθαι καὶ συνελθεῖν, φθάσαντες ἐσκέδασαν[1] καὶ
τῆς πόλεως ἐξέβαλον, τὸ δὲ φυγεῖν ἧττον ὄν,
γύναιά τε καὶ παῖδας, ὑπὲρ ἑπτακοσίους ἀναι-
404 ροῦσιν. ἔπειτα τούς τε οἴκους ἐξεσκευασμένοι
καὶ τῶν καρπῶν τοὺς ἀκμαιοτάτους[2] ἁρπάσαντες
405 ἀνήνεγκαν εἰς τὴν Μασάδαν. καὶ οἱ μὲν ἐλή-
ζοντο πάσας τὰς περὶ τὸ φρούριον κώμας καὶ
τὴν χώραν ἐπόρθουν ἅπασαν, προσδιαφθειρομένων
αὐτοῖς καθ' ἡμέραν ἑκασταχόθεν οὐκ ὀλίγων·
406 ἐκινεῖτο δὲ καὶ κατὰ τἆλλα τῆς Ἰουδαίας κλίματα
τὸ τέως ἠρεμοῦν τὸ ληστρικόν, καθάπερ δὲ ἐν
σώματι τοῦ κυριωτάτου φλεγμαίνοντος πάντα τὰ
407 μέλη συνενόσει· διὰ γοῦν τὴν ἐν τῇ μητροπόλει
στάσιν καὶ ταραχὴν ἄδειαν ἔσχον οἱ κατὰ τὴν
χώραν πονηροὶ τῶν ἁρπαγῶν καὶ τὰς οἰκείας
ἕκαστοι[3] κώμας ἁρπάζοντες ἔπειτα εἰς τὴν ἐρη-
408 μίαν ἀφίσταντο. συναθροιζόμενοί τε καὶ συν-
ομνύμενοι κατὰ λόχους, στρατιᾶς μὲν ὀλιγώτεροι
πλείους δὲ ληστηρίου, προσέπιπτον ἱεροῖς καὶ
409 πόλεσιν, καὶ κακοῦσθαι μὲν συνέβαινεν ἐφ' οὓς
ὁρμήσειαν ὡς ἐν πολέμῳ καταληφθέντας, φθάνε-
σθαι δὲ τὰς ἀμύνας ὡς ληστῶν ἅμα ταῖς ἁρπαγαῖς

---

[1] ἐκόλασαν P[1]A[1]VR.
[2] PAM: ἀκμαίους the rest.　　　[3] L: ἕκαστος the rest.

---

[a] And when, consequently, the bulk of the population
would be absent at Jerusalem.

[b] Engedi, 'Ain Jidy, on the W. coast of the Dead Sea,
some 10 miles N. of Masada.

118

release from bondage in Egypt [a]—these assassins, eluding under cover of night those who might have obstructed them, made a raiding descent upon a small town called Engaddi.[b] Those of the inhabitants who were capable of resistance were, before they could seize their arms and assemble, dispersed and driven out of the town ; those unable to fly, women and children numbering upwards of seven hundred, were massacred. They then rifled the houses, seized the ripest of the crops, and carried off their spoil to Masada. They made similar raids on all the villages around the fortress, and laid waste the whole district, being joined daily by numerous dissolute recruits from every quarter. Throughout the other parts of Judaea, moreover, the predatory bands, hitherto quiescent, now began to bestir themselves. And as in the body when inflammation attacks the principal member all the members catch the infection,[c] so the sedition and disorder in the capital gave the scoundrels in the country free licence to plunder ; and each gang after pillaging their own village made off into the wilderness. Then joining forces and swearing mutual allegiance, they would proceed by companies—smaller than an army but larger than a mere band of robbers—to fall upon temples [d] and cities. The unfortunate victims of their attacks suffered the miseries of captives of war, but were deprived of the chance of retaliation, because their foes in robber fashion at once decamped

Similar brigandage throughout Judaea.

[c] Cf. 1 Cor. xii. 26 εἴτε πάσχει ἓν μέλος, συνπάσχει πάντα τὰ μέλη, and for the same simile B. i. 507.
[d] Apparently synagogues or " prayer-houses " are meant ; these were often built outside the towns near rivers or sea coast for purification purposes. Judaea had but the one " temple " at Jerusalem.

119

ἀποδιδρασκόντων. οὐδὲν δὲ μέρος ἦν τῆς Ἰουδαίας, ὃ μὴ τῇ προανεχούσῃ πόλει συναπώλλυτο.

410 (3) Ταῦτα Οὐεσπασιανῷ παρὰ τῶν αὐτομόλων
διηγγέλλετο· καίπερ γὰρ φρουρούντων τὰς ἐξόδους τῶν στασιαστῶν ἁπάσας καὶ διαφθειρόντων
τοὺς ὁπωσοῦν προσιόντας, ὅμως ἦσαν οἱ διελάνθανον καὶ καταφεύγοντες εἰς τοὺς Ῥωμαίους
τὸν στρατηγὸν ἐνῆγον ἀμῦναι τῇ πόλει καὶ τὰ
411 τοῦ δήμου περισῶσαι λείψανα· διὰ γὰρ τὴν πρὸς
Ῥωμαίους εὔνοιαν ἀνῃρῆσθαί τε τοὺς πολλοὺς
412 καὶ κινδυνεύειν τοὺς περιόντας. ὁ δὲ οἰκτείρων
ἤδη τὰς συμφορὰς αὐτῶν τὸ¹ μὲν δοκεῖν ἐκ-
πολιορκήσων ἀφίσταται² τὰ Ἱεροσόλυμα, τὸ δ'
413 ἀληθὲς ἀπαλλάξων πολιορκίας. ἔδει μέντοι³ προ-
καταστρέψασθαι τὰ λειπόμενα καὶ μηδὲν ἔξωθεν
ἐμπόδιον τῇ πολιορκίᾳ καταλιπεῖν· ἐλθὼν οὖν ἐπὶ
τὰ Γάδαρα μητρόπολιν τῆς Περαίας καρτερὰν
τετράδι Δύστρου μηνὸς εἴσεισιν εἰς τὴν πόλιν.
414 καὶ γὰρ ἔτυχον οἱ δυνατοὶ λάθρα τῶν στασιωδῶν
πρεσβευσάμενοι πρὸς αὐτὸν περὶ παραδόσεως
πόθῳ τε εἰρήνης καὶ διὰ τὰς οὐσίας· πολλοὶ δὲ
415 τὰ Γάδαρα κατῴκουν πλούσιοι. τούτων τὴν

---

¹ PC: τῷ the rest.
² Niese (ed. min.): ἐφίσταται PAML (which should perhaps
stand=propius accedit Lat.): ἀνίσταται the rest.
³ Destinon: μὲν τοῦ L: μὲν PA: δὲ the rest.

ᵃ § 378.
ᵇ Gadara is here identified by all commentators with the
important place of that name S.E. of the Sea of Galilee,
modern *Umm Keis* or *Mukes*, a principal city of Decapolis,
and a seat of Greek culture, being the home, among other
writers, of Meleager the epigrammatist and Philodemus the
Epicurean. This identification, though favoured by the
reference to its "many wealthy residents," is open to serious

with their prey. There was, in fact, no portion of
Judaea which did not share in the ruin of the capital.

(3) Of these proceedings Vespasian was informed Vespasian, instigated
by deserters. For, although the insurgents guarded by deserters,
all the exits and slew any who for whatever reason prepares to advance on
approached them,[a] there were notwithstanding some Jerusalem
who evaded them and, fleeing to the Romans, urged
the general to protect the city and rescue the remnant
of its inhabitants, assuring him that it was owing to
their loyalty to the Romans that so many had been
slain and the survivors were in peril. Vespasian,
who already pitied their misfortunes, broke up his
camp, with the apparent purpose of taking Jerusalem
by siege, but in reality to deliver it from siege. It
was, however, first necessary to reduce any places
still outstanding, so as to leave no external impediment to hinder his operations. He accordingly
marched on Gádara,[b] the capital of Peraea and a and occupies
city of some strength, and entered it on the fourth GADARA (in Peraea)
of the month Dystrus. For the leading men had, c. 21 March
unbeknown to the rebels, sent an embassy to him A.D. 68.
offering to capitulate, alike from a desire for peace
and from concern for their property, for Gadara had
many wealthy residents. Of the leaders' deputation

---

objections. (1) *Mukes* was in Decapolis, whereas the
Gadara here mentioned is called the capital or metropolis of
Peraea, of which district Pella, some 15 miles S. of *Mukes*,
was the northern boundary (*B.* iii. 46 f.) ; (2) Gadora
(Gadara ?) *es Salt*, is actually in Peraea and satisfies the other
data, for (3) it is not far from the village to which the
Gadarene fugitives fled (§ 420 note) ; (4) that village was on
the direct line to Jericho, for which they were making
(§ 431), an unnatural refuge for fugitives from the northern
Gadara ; (5) Vespasian was marching southwards from
Caesarea upon Jerusalem (§ 412), not northwards towards
Galilee, which was already subdued.

πρεσβείαν ἠγνοήκεσαν οἱ διάφοροι, πλησίον δὲ
ἤδη ὄντος Οὐεσπασιανοῦ διεπύθοντο, καὶ κατασχεῖν μὲν αὐτοὶ τὴν πόλιν ἀπέγνωσαν δύνασθαι,
τῶν τε ἔνδον ἐχθρῶν πλήθει λειπόμενοι καὶ
Ῥωμαίους ὁρῶντες οὐ μακρὰν τῆς πόλεως,
φεύγειν δὲ κρίνοντες[1] ἠδόξουν ἀναιμωτὶ καὶ
μηδεμίαν παρὰ τῶν αἰτίων εἰσπραξάμενοι τι-
416 μωρίαν. συλλαβόντες δὴ τὸν Δόλεσον, οὗτος γὰρ
ἦν οὐ μόνον ἀξιώματι καὶ γένει τῆς πόλεως
πρῶτος, ἀλλ᾽ ἐδόκει καὶ τῆς πρεσβείας αἴτιος,
κτείνουσί τε αὐτὸν καὶ δι᾽ ὑπερβολὴν ὀργῆς
νεκρὸν αἰκισάμενοι διέδρασαν ἐκ τῆς πόλεως.
417 ἐπιούσης δὲ ἤδη τῆς Ῥωμαϊκῆς δυνάμεως ὅ τε
δῆμος τῶν Γαδαρέων μετ᾽ εὐφημίας τὸν Οὐεσπασιανὸν εἰσδεξάμενοι δεξιὰς παρ᾽ αὐτοῦ πίστεως
ἔλαβον καὶ φρουρὰν ἱππέων τε καὶ πεζῶν πρὸς
418 τὰς τῶν φυγάδων καταδρομάς· τὸ γὰρ τεῖχος
αὐτοὶ πρὶν ἀξιῶσαι Ῥωμαίους καθεῖλον, ὅπως
εἴη πίστις αὐτοῖς τοῦ τὴν εἰρήνην ἀγαπᾶν τὸ μηδὲ
βουληθέντας δύνασθαι[2] πολεμεῖν.
419 (4) Οὐεσπασιανὸς δ᾽ ἐπὶ μὲν τοὺς διαδράντας ἐκ
τῶν Γαδάρων Πλάκιδον σὺν ἱππεῦσιν πεντακοσίοις
καὶ πεζοῖς τρισχιλίοις πέμπει, αὐτὸς δὲ μετὰ τῆς
420 ἄλλης στρατιᾶς ὑπέστρεψεν εἰς Καισάρειαν. οἱ
δὲ φυγάδες ὡς αἰφνίδιον τοὺς διώκοντας ἱππεῖς
ἐθεάσαντο, πρὶν εἰς χεῖρας ἐλθεῖν εἴς τινα κώμην
421 συνειλοῦνται Βηθενναβρὶν προσαγορευομένην· ἐν
ᾗ νέων[3] πλῆθος οὐκ ὀλίγον εὑρόντες καὶ τοὺς μὲν
ἑκόντας τοὺς δὲ βίᾳ καθοπλίσαντες εἰκαίως,

---

[1] κρίναντες MVRC.
[2] δύνασθαι A² Lat. : om. the rest.
[3] VRC Lat. Heg. : Ἰουδαίων the rest.

their adversaries were ignorant and only discovered it on the approach of Vespasian. Despairing of their ability to hold the city themselves, in view of their inferiority in numbers to their opponents within the walls and the proximity of the Romans, visible not far without, they determined to flee, but scorned to do so without shedding blood and exacting punishment from those responsible for their situation. So they seized Dolesus, who was not only by rank and family the first man in the town, but was also regarded as the originator of the embassy ; having slain him and in their furious rage mangled his body, they fled from the city. The Roman army now appearing, the Gadarenes admitted Vespasian with acclamation and received from him pledges of security together with a garrison of horse and foot to protect them against invasions of the fugitives ; for they had pulled down their walls of their own accord without requisition from the Romans, in order that their powerlessness to make war, even if they wished, might testify to their love of peace.

(4) Vespasian sent Placidus *a* with 500 horse and 3000 foot to pursue those who had fled from Gadara, while he himself with the remainder of his army returned to Caesarea. The fugitives, on suddenly catching sight of the pursuing cavalry, before any engagement took place swarmed into a village called Bethennabris *b* ; finding here a considerable number of young men, they armed these with any available weapons, some consenting, others by force, and

Placidus defeats the Gadarene fugitives.

---

a § 57 n.
b Doubtless Beth-Nimrah, *Tell Nimrin*, some 12 miles S.W. of the Peraean Gadara, and on the direct line for Jericho, which lay nearly opposite it on the other side of the Jordan.

422 προπηδῶσιν ἐπὶ τοὺς περὶ τὸν Πλάκιδον. οἱ δὲ
πρὸς μὲν τὴν πρώτην ἐμβολὴν ὀλίγον εἶξαν, ἅμα
καὶ προκαλέσασθαι τεχνιτεύοντες αὐτοὺς ἀπὸ
423 τοῦ τείχους πορρωτέρω, λαβόντες δ' εἰς ἐπιτήδειον περιήλαυνόν τε καὶ κατηκόντιζον, καὶ
τὰς μὲν φυγὰς¹ αὐτῶν οἱ ἱππεῖς ὑπετέμνοντο, τὰς
424 συμπλοκὰς δὲ τὸ πεζὸν εὐτόνως διέφθειρον.² οὐ
μέντοι πλέον τι τόλμης ἐπιδεικνύμενοι οἱ Ἰουδαῖοι
διεφθείροντο· πεπυκνωμένοις γὰρ τοῖς Ῥωμαίοις
προσπίπτοντες καὶ ταῖς πανοπλίαις ὥσπερ τε-
τειχισμένοις, αὐτοὶ μὲν οὐχ εὕρισκον βέλους
παράδυσιν οὐδ' ηὐτόνουν ῥῆξαι τὴν φάλαγγα,
425 περιεπείροντο δὲ τοῖς ἐκείνων βέλεσι καὶ τοῖς
ἀγριωτάτοις παραπλήσιοι θηρίοις ὥρμων ἐπὶ
τὸν σίδηρον, διεφθείροντο δ' οἱ μὲν κατὰ στόμα
παιόμενοι τοῖς ξίφεσιν, οἱ δὲ ὑπὸ τῶν ἱππέων
σκεδαννύμενοι.

426 (5) Σπουδὴ γὰρ ἦν τῷ Πλακίδῳ τὰς ἐπὶ τὴν
427 κώμην ὁρμὰς αὐτῶν διακλείειν, καὶ συνεχῶς
παρελαύνων κατ' ἐκεῖνο τὸ μέρος, ἔπειτα ἐπι-
στρέφων ἅμα καὶ τοῖς βέλεσι χρώμενος εὐστόχως
ἀνήρει τοὺς πλησιάζοντας καὶ δέει τοὺς πόρρωθεν
ἀνέστρεφεν, μέχρι βίᾳ διεκπεσόντες οἱ γενναιό-
428 τατοι πρὸς τὸ τεῖχος διέφευγον. ἀπορία δ' εἶχε
τοὺς φύλακας· οὔτε γὰρ ἀποκλεῖσαι τοὺς ἀπὸ
τῶν Γαδάρων ὑπέμενον διὰ τοὺς σφετέρους καὶ
429 δεξάμενοι συναπολεῖσθαι προσεδόκων. ὃ δὴ καὶ
συνέβη· συνωσθέντων γὰρ αὐτῶν εἰς τὸ τεῖχος
παρ' ὀλίγον μὲν οἱ τῶν Ῥωμαίων ἱππεῖς συνεισ-
έπεσον, οὐ μὴν ἀλλὰ καὶ φθασάντων ἀποκλεῖσαι
τὰς πύλας προσβαλὼν ὁ Πλάκιδος καὶ μέχρι

¹ τὰς μὲν φυγὰς Destinon: τοὺς μὲν φυγάδας mss.

dashed out upon the troops of Placidus. The Romans
at their first onset fell back a little, manœuvring to
entice them further from the walls, and then, having
drawn them to a suitable spot, rode round them and
with their javelins shot them down; the cavalry
intercepting their flight, while the infantry vigorously
broke up their entangled masses. The Jews, in fact,
were cut to pieces after a display of mere audacity;
for, flinging themselves upon the serried Roman
ranks, walled in, as it were, by their armour, they
found no loophole for their missiles and were powerless to break the line, whilst their own men were
transfixed by their enemy's javelins and rushed, like
the most savage of beasts, upon the blade. So they
perished, some struck down by the sword facing the
foe, others in disorderly flight before the cavalry.

(5) For Placidus, anxious to intercept their rushes
for the village, kept riding his cavalry past them in
that direction, and then, wheeling round, with one
and the same well-aimed volley of missiles killed
those who were nearing it and intimidated and beat
back those further off; but in the end the most
courageous cut their way through and fled for the
ramparts. Here the sentries were in doubt what
they should do: they could not bring themselves to
exclude the Gadarenes because of their own men,[a]
whereas if they admitted them they expected to
perish with them. That was in fact what happened;
for in the crush of fugitives at the wall, the Roman
cavalry very nearly burst in with them, and, although
the guards succeeded in shutting the gates, Placidus

---

[a] The recruits obtained from the village, § 421.

[2] διέφερον of Destinon is needless; cf. διαφθείρειν τὴν
συνουσίαν, " break up the party," Plato, *Prot.* 338 D.

δείλης γενναίως ἀγωνισάμενος τοῦ τείχους καὶ
430 τῶν ἐν τῇ κώμῃ κρατεῖ.¹ τὰ μὲν οὖν ἀργὰ πλήθη
διεφθείρετο, φυγὴ δ' ἦν τῶν δυνατωτέρων, τὰς δ'
οἰκίας οἱ στρατιῶται διήρπασαν καὶ τὴν κώμην
431 ἐνέπρησαν. οἱ δὲ διαδράντες ἐξ αὐτῆς τοὺς
κατὰ τὴν χώραν συνανέστησαν, καὶ τὰς μὲν
αὐτῶν συμφορὰς ἐξαίροντες ἐπὶ μεῖζον, τῶν δὲ
Ῥωμαίων τὴν στρατιὰν πᾶσαν ἐπιέναι λέγοντες
πάντας πανταχόθεν ἐξέσεισαν τῷ δέει, γενόμενοί
432 τε παμπληθεῖς ἔφευγον ἐπὶ Ἱεριχοῦντος· αὕτη
γὰρ ἔτι μόνη τὰς ἐλπίδας αὐτῶν ἔθαλπε τῆς σω-
433 τηρίας καρτερὰ πλήθει γε οἰκητόρων. Πλάκιδος
δὲ τοῖς ἱππεῦσι καὶ ταῖς προαγούσαις εὐπραγίαις
τεθαρρηκὼς εἵπετο, καὶ μέχρι μὲν Ἰορδάνου τοὺς
ἀεὶ καταλαμβανομένους ἀνήρει, συνελάσας δὲ
πρὸς τὸν ποταμὸν πᾶν τὸ πλῆθος εἰργομένοις²
ὑπὸ τοῦ ῥεύματος, τραφὲν γὰρ ὑπ' ὄμβρων ἄβατον
434 ἦν, ἀντικρὺ παρετάσσετο. παρώξυνε δ' ἡ ἀνάγκη
πρὸς μάχην τοὺς φυγῆς τόπον οὐκ ἔχοντας, καὶ
ταῖς ὄχθαις ἐπὶ μήκιστον παρεκτείναντες σφᾶς
αὐτοὺς ἐδέχοντο τὰ βέλη καὶ τὰς τῶν ἱππέων
ἐμβολάς, οἳ πολλοὺς αὐτῶν παίοντες εἰς τὸ ῥεῦμα
435 κατέβαλον. καὶ τὸ μὲν ἐν χερσὶν αὐτῶν δια-
φθαρὲν μύριοι πεντακισχίλιοι, τὸ δὲ βιασθὲν
ἐμπηδῆσαι εἰς τὸν Ἰορδάνην πλῆθος ἑκουσίως³
436 ἄπειρον ἦν. ἑάλωσαν δὲ περὶ δισχιλίους καὶ διακοσίους, λεία τε παμπληθὴς ὄνων τε καὶ προ-
βάτων καὶ καμήλων καὶ βοῶν.
437 (6) Ἰουδαίοις μὲν οὖν οὐδενὸς⁴ ἐλάττων ἥδε ἡ
πληγὴ προσπεσοῦσα καὶ μείζων ἔδοξεν ἑαυτῆς

---

¹ Niese: δὲ κρατεῖ L: ἐκράτει the rest.
² εἰργομένους PM.   ³ ἀκουσίως L.   ⁴ οὐδὲν MSS.

led an assault and by a gallant struggle prolonged until evening became master of the wall and of the occupants of the village. The helpless were slaughtered wholesale, the more able-bodied fled, and the soldiers rifled the houses and then set the village alight. The fugitives, meanwhile, roused the country-side, and by exaggerating their own calamities and stating that the entire Roman army was upon them drove all from their homes in universal panic, and with the whole population fled for Jericho ; that being the one remaining city strong enough, at least in virtue of its numerous inhabitants, to encourage hopes of salvation. Placidus, relying on his cavalry and emboldened by his previous success, pursued them, killing all whom he overtook, as far as the Jordan. Having driven the whole multitude up to the river, where they were blocked by the stream, which being swollen by the rain was unfordable, he drew up his troops in line opposite them. Necessity goaded them to battle, flight being impossible, and deploying their forces as far as possible along the bank [a] they met the missiles and the charges of the cavalry, who wounded and drove many down into the stream. Fifteen thousand perished by the enemy's hands, while the number of those who were driven to fling themselves of their own accord into the Jordan was incalculable ; about two thousand two hundred were captured, together with vast spoils of asses, sheep, camels, and oxen.

(6) This blow was the greatest that had befallen the Jews, and appeared even greater than it was ;

General flight of Peraeans for Jericho.

They are defeated with great slaughter at the Jordan.

---

[a] The plural can only refer to the one (left) bank, or rather perhaps to the terraces, one above the other, on that bank of the stream.

διὰ τὸ μὴ μόνον τὴν χώραν ἅπασαν δι' ἧς ἔφευγον
πληρωθῆναι φόνου, μηδὲ νεκροῖς διαβατὸν γενέσθαι τὸν Ἰορδάνην, ἐμπλησθῆναι δὲ τῶν σωμάτων
καὶ τὴν Ἀσφαλτῖτιν¹ λίμνην, εἰς ἣν παμπληθεῖς
438 ὑπὸ τοῦ ποταμοῦ κατεσύρησαν. Πλάκιδος δὲ
δεξιᾷ τύχῃ χρώμενος ὥρμησεν ἐπὶ τὰς πέριξ
πολίχνας τε καὶ κώμας, καταλαμβανόμενός² τε
Ἄβιλα καὶ Ἰουλιάδα καὶ Βησιμώθ³ τάς τε μέχρι
τῆς Ἀσφαλτίτιδος πάσας ἐγκαθίστησιν ἑκάστῃ
439 τοὺς ἐπιτηδείους τῶν αὐτομόλων. ἔπειτα σκά-
φεσιν ἐπιβήσας τοὺς στρατιώτας αἱρεῖ τοὺς εἰς
τὴν λίμνην καταφεύγοντας. καὶ τὰ μὲν κατὰ τὴν
Περαίαν προσεχώρησεν ἢ ἑάλω πάντα μέχρι
Μαχαιροῦντος.
440 (viii. 1) Ἐν δὲ τούτῳ τὸ περὶ τὴν Γαλατίαν⁴
ἀγγέλλεται κίνημα καὶ Οὐίνδιξ ἅμα τοῖς δυνατοῖς
τῶν ἐπιχωρίων ἀφεστὼς Νέρωνος, περὶ ὧν ἐν
441 ἀκριβεστέροις ἀναγέγραπται. Οὐεσπασιανὸν δ' ἐπήγειρεν εἰς τὴν ὁρμὴν τοῦ πολέμου τὰ ἠγγελ-
μένα, προορώμενον ἤδη τοὺς μέλλοντας ἐμφυλίους
πολέμους καὶ τὸν ὅλης κίνδυνον τῆς ἡγεμονίας,
ἐν ᾧ προειρηνεύσας τὰ κατὰ τὴν ἀνατολὴν ἐπι-
κουφίσειν ᾤετο τοὺς κατὰ τὴν Ἰταλίαν φόβους.

---

¹ Ἀσφαλτικὴν PA.
² καταλαβόμενός ML.   ³ Βησιμὼ PA.
⁴ C: τῆς Γαλατίας the rest.

ᵃ The Bituminous Lake=the Dead Sea.
ᵇ Probably Abel-Shittim (*Khurbet el-Keffrein*),some 5 miles
due S. of Beth-Nimrah : mentioned in conjunction with
Julias, *B.* ii. 252.
ᶜ Julias or Livias, formerly Beth-Haram (Betharamatha),

for not only was the whole countryside through which their flight had lain one scene of carnage, and the Jordan choked with dead, but even the Lake Asphaltitis *a* was filled with bodies, masses of which were carried down into it by the river. Placidus, following up his good fortune, hastened to attack the small towns and villages in the neighbourhood, and taking Abila,*b* Julias,*c* Besimoth,*d* and all as far as the Lake Asphaltitis, posted in each a garrison of such deserters as he thought fit ; then embarking his soldiers on shipboard he captured those who had taken refuge on the lake. Thus the whole of Peraea as far as Machaerus *e* either surrendered or was subdued.

All Peraea subdued.

(viii. 1) Meanwhile tidings arrived of the rising in Gaul and that Vindex *f* with the chiefs of that country had revolted from Nero, of which events fuller accounts have been given elsewhere. Vespasian was stimulated by the news to prosecute the war more vigorously, for he already foresaw the impending civil dissensions and the peril to the empire at large, and thought that, in the circumstances, by an early pacification of the east he would allay the anxiety of Italy. Accordingly, while the

Vespasian learns of Gallic revolt from Nero: winter of A.D. 67-68.

modern *Tell Rameh*, 2 miles S. of Abel-Shittim, opposite Jericho : *B.* ii. 59 n., 168 n.

d Beth-Jeshimoth, *Sueimeh*, S. of Julias.

e E. of the upper region of the Dead Sea.

f C. Julius Vindex, prefect of Gallia Celtica, headed a Gallic revolt against Nero ; and Virginius Rufus was sent with the legions of Lower Germany to oppose him. At Vesontio, where the armies met, Vindex and Virginius secretly agreed to conspire together, but the armies coming to no similar understanding, the troops of Vindex were cut to pieces and Vindex committed suicide. Dion Cass. lxiii. 22 ff., Plut. *Galba,* 4 ff., etc.

442 ἕως μὲν οὖν ἐπεῖχεν ὁ χειμὼν τὰς ὑπηγμένας
διησφαλίζετο κώμας τε καὶ πολίχνας φρουραῖς,
δεκαδάρχας μὲν κώμαις ἐγκαθιστάς, ἑκατοντάρχας
δὲ πόλεσι· πολλὰ δὲ ἀνῴκιζε καὶ τῶν πεπορ-
443 θημένων. ὑπὸ δὲ τὴν ἀρχὴν τοῦ ἔαρος ἀναλαβὼν
τὸ πλέον τῆς δυνάμεως ἤγαγεν ἀπὸ τῆς Καισαρείας ἐπὶ Ἀντιπατρίδος, ἔνθα δυσὶν ἡμέραις
καταστησάμενος[1] τὴν πόλιν τῇ τρίτῃ προῄει
444 πορθῶν καὶ καίων τὰς πέριξ πάσας. καταστρεψάμενος δὲ τὰ περὶ τὴν Θαμνᾶ τοπαρχίαν[2] ἐπὶ
Λύδδων καὶ Ἰαμνείας ἐχώρει καὶ προκεχειρω-
μέναις[3] ἑκατέραις ἐγκαταστήσας οἰκήτορας τῶν
προσκεχωρηκότων ἱκανοὺς εἰς Ἀμμαοῦντα ἀφ-
445 ικνεῖται. καταλαβόμενος δὲ τὰς ἐπὶ τὴν μητρόπολιν αὐτῶν εἰσβολὰς στρατόπεδόν τε τειχίζει
καὶ τὸ πέμπτον ἐν αὐτῇ τάγμα καταλιπὼν πρόεισι[4]
μετὰ τῆς ἄλλης δυνάμεως ἐπὶ τὴν Βεθλεπτηνφῶν
446 τοπαρχίαν. πυρὶ δὲ αὐτήν τε καὶ τὴν γειτνιῶσαν
ἀνελὼν καὶ τὰ πέριξ τῆς Ἰδουμαίας, φρούρια μὲν
447 τοῖς ἐπικαίροις τόποις ἐπετείχισε, καταλαβόμενος
δὲ δύο κώμας τὰς μεσαιτάτας τῆς Ἰδουμαίας,
Βήταβριν καὶ Καφάρτοβαν,[5] κτείνει μὲν ὑπὲρ
448 μυρίους, αἰχμαλωτίζεται δὲ ὑπὲρ χιλίους, καὶ
τὸ λοιπὸν πλῆθος ἐξελάσας ἐγκαθίστησιν τῆς
οἰκείας δυνάμεως οὐκ ὀλίγην, οἳ κατατρέχοντες

---

[1] L Lat. (composita): ἐγκαταστησάμενος the rest.
[2] τὰς π. τ. Θ. τοπαρχίας L Lat.
[3] προσκεχωρημέναις L Lat.   [4] L: πρόσεισι the rest.
[5] ed. pr.: Καταφάρτοβαν most mss.

[a] *Ras el-'Ain*, in the S. of the plain of Sharon, N.E. of
Joppa.   [b] "toparchy."
[c] S.E. of Antipatris. Here he turns S.W. towards the
coast to *Ludd* and *Yebnah*.

winter lasted, he employed himself in securing with garrisons the villages and smaller towns which had been reduced, posting decurions in the villages and centurions in the towns ; he also rebuilt many places that had been devastated. Then, at the first approach of spring, he marched the main body of his army from Caesarea to Antipatris.[a] After two days spent in restoring order in that town, on the third he advanced, laying waste and burning all the surrounding places. Having reduced the neighbourhood of the province [b] of Thamna,[c] he moved to Lydda and Jamnia ; both these districts being already subdued,[d] he quartered upon them an adequate number of residents from those who had surrendered, and passed to Ammaus.[e] Having occupied the approaches to the capital of this province, he fortified a camp and, leaving the fifth legion there, advanced with the rest of his forces to the province of Bethleptenpha.[f] After devastating with fire this and the neighbouring district and the outskirts of Idumaea, he built fortresses in suitable situations ; finally having taken two villages right in the heart of Idumaea, Betabris [g] and Caphartoba,[g] he put upwards of ten thousand of the inhabitants to death, made prisoners of over a thousand, expelled the remainder and stationed in the district a large division of his own troops, who overran and devastated

spring A.D. 68. He moves southward from Caesarea, subduing Judaea

and Idumaea.

---

 [d] § 130 (for Jamnia).
 [e] The toparchy (iii. 55) which took its name from Ammaus (or Emmaus), *Amwas*, N.W. of Jerusalem.
 [f] The correct form is probably Bethleptepha (or Bethletepha), Schürer, *G.J.V.* ii. 184 n. ; it is the modern *Beit Nettif*, S.W. of Jerusalem, and gave its name to one of the provinces of Judaea, *B*. iii. 54 n.
 [g] Unidentified.

449 ἐπόρθουν ἅπασαν τὴν ὀρεινήν. αὐτὸς δὲ μετὰ τῆς
λοιπῆς δυνάμεως ὑπέστρεψεν εἰς Ἀμμαοῦν, ὅθεν
διὰ τῆς Σαμαρείτιδος καὶ παρὰ τὴν Νέαν πόλιν[1]
καλουμένην, Μαβαρθὰ δ' ὑπὸ τῶν ἐπιχωρίων,
καταβὰς εἰς Κορέαν δευτέρᾳ Δαισίου μηνὸς
450 στρατοπεδεύεται. τῇ δ' ἑξῆς εἰς Ἱεριχοῦντα
ἀφικνεῖται, καθ' ἣν αὐτῷ συμμίσγει Τραϊανὸς εἷς
τῶν ἡγεμόνων τὴν ἐκ τῆς Περαίας ἄγων δύναμιν,
ἤδη τῶν ὑπὲρ τὸν Ἰορδάνην κεχειρωμένων.

451 (2) Τὸ μὲν οὖν πολὺ πλῆθος ἐκ τῆς Ἱεριχοῦς
φθάσαν τὴν ἔφοδον αὐτῶν εἰς τὴν ἄντικρυς Ἱεροσολύμων ὀρεινὴν διαπεφεύγει, καταλειφθὲν δ' οὐκ
452 ὀλίγον διαφθείρεται. τὴν δὲ πόλιν ἔρημον κατ-
ειλήφεσαν, ἥτις ἵδρυται μὲν ἐν πεδίῳ, ψιλὸν δὲ
ὑπέρκειται αὐτῇ καὶ ἄκαρπον ὄρος μήκιστον·
453 κατὰ γὰρ τὸ βόρειον κλίμα μέχρι τῆς Σκυθο-
πολιτῶν γῆς ἐκτείνεται, κατὰ δὲ τὸ μεσημβρινὸν
μέχρι τῆς Σοδομιτῶν χώρας καὶ τῶν περάτων τῆς
Ἀσφαλτίτιδος. ἔστιν δὲ ἀνώμαλόν τε πᾶν καὶ
454 ἀοίκητον διὰ τὴν ἀγονίαν. ἀντίκειται δὲ τούτῳ
τὸ περὶ[2] τὸν Ἰορδάνην ὄρος ἀρχόμενον ἀπὸ

---

[1] L : Νεάπολιν the rest.
[2] ὑπὲρ Destinon with Heg. (supra).

---

[a] Flavia Neapolis, mod. *Nablus*, the new town founded by
Vespasian c. A.D. 72 on the site of the older Mabartha
(Mamortha according to Pliny, *H.N.* v. 13. 69) in the immediate vicinity of Shechem. The most probable meaning
of Mabartha is " pass " or " passage " (*ma 'abartā*), the
name, like that of Shechem (" shoulder "), being taken from
the watershed on which both places stood, forming an easy

the whole of the hill country. He then returned
with the rest of his forces to Ammaus, and thence by
way of Samaria, passing Neapolis *a* or, as the natives
call it, Mabartha, he descended to Corea,*b* where he
encamped on the second of the month Daesius. On
the following day he reached Jericho, where he was
joined by Trajan,*c* one of his generals, with the force
which he had led from Peraea, all the country beyond
Jordan being now subjugated.

c. 20 June
A.D. 68.
Vespasian at
Jericho.

(2) The mass of the population, anticipating their
arrival, had fled from Jericho *d* to the hill country
over against Jerusalem, but a considerable number
remained behind and were put to death ; the city
itself the Romans found deserted. Jericho lies in
a plain, but above it hangs a bare and barren mountain range of immense length, extending northwards
as far as the territory of Scythopolis *e* and southwards
to the region of Sodom and the extremities of the
Lake Asphaltitis ; this hill district is all rugged
and owing to its sterility uninhabited. Opposite
to it and flanking the Jordan lies a second range,

Description
of neigh-
bourhood
of Jericho

pass between the Mediterranean and Jordan basins. Schürer,
G.J.V. i. 650, *Encycl. Bibl.*, and Hastings, *D.B.*

b From the pass of Shechem a Roman road followed the
course of a tributary of the Jordan in a S.E. direction down
to Corea or Coreae, *Tell el-Mazar*, on the N. frontier of
Judaea, *B.* i. 134, *A.* xiv. 49.

c Commander of the 10th legion and father of the future
emperor of that name, *B.* iii. 289 ff.

d Apparently the larger area of the toparchy (*B.* iii. 55) is
meant, as opposed to " the city itself " mentioned below.

e Bethshan, *Beisan*, the one city of Decapolis which lay W.
of the Jordan. The name Scythopolis may owe its origin to
the great Scythian invasion of Palestine in the 7th cent.
B.C., mentioned by Herodotus i. 105 ; Syncellus (quoted by
Schürer) writes Σκύθαι τὴν Παλαιστίνην κατέδραμον καὶ τὴν
Βασὰν κατέσχον τὴν ἐξ αὐτῶν κληθεῖσαν Σκυθόπολιν.

Ἰουλιάδος καὶ τῶν βορείων κλιμάτων, παρατεῖνον
δὲ εἰς μεσημβρίαν ἕως Σομόρων, ἥπερ ὁρίζει τὴν
Πέτραν τῆς Ἀραβίας. ἐν τούτῳ δ' ἐστὶ καὶ τὸ
Σιδηροῦν καλούμενον ὄρος μηκυνόμενον μέχρι τῆς
455 Μωαβίτιδος. ἡ μέση δὲ τῶν δύο ὀρέων χώρα τὸ
μέγα πεδίον καλεῖται, ἀπὸ κώμης Γινναβρὶν[1]
456 διῆκον μέχρι τῆς Ἀσφαλτίτιδος.[2] ἔστι δ' αὐτοῦ
μῆκος μὲν σταδίων χιλίων διακοσίων,[3] εὖρος δ'
εἴκοσι καὶ ἑκατόν, καὶ μέσον ὑπὸ τοῦ Ἰορδάνου
τέμνεται, λίμνας τε ἔχει τήν τε Ἀσφαλτῖτιν καὶ
τὴν Τιβεριέων φύσιν ἐναντίας· ἡ μὲν γὰρ ἁλ-
μυρώδης καὶ ἄγονος, ἡ Τιβεριέων δὲ γλυκεῖα καὶ
457 γόνιμος. ἐκπυροῦται δὲ ὥρᾳ θέρους τὸ πεδίον
καὶ δι' ὑπερβολὴν αὐχμοῦ περιέχει νοσώδη τὸν
458 ἀέρα· πᾶν γὰρ ἄνυδρον πλὴν τοῦ Ἰορδάνου, παρὸ
καὶ τοὺς μὲν ἐπὶ ταῖς ὄχθαις φοινικῶνας εὐθαλε-
στέρους καὶ πολυφορωτέρους εἶναι συμβέβηκεν,
ἧττον δὲ τοὺς πόρρω κεχωρισμένους.

459 (3) Παρὰ μέντοι τὴν Ἱεριχοῦν ἐστι πηγὴ δαψιλής
τε καὶ πρὸς ἀρδείας λιπαρωτάτη, παρὰ τὴν
παλαιὰν ἀναβλύζουσα πόλιν, ἣν Ἰησοῦς ὁ Ναυῆ

---

[1] Δενναβρὶ L; cf. iii. 447 Σενναβρίς, whence Σενναβρῖ Niese (ed. min.) here.
[2] P: + χώρας A: + λίμνης the rest.
[3] χιλ. διακοσ.] τριάκοντα καὶ διακοσίων L Lat. Heg., through misreading of ‚AC′ as ΛC′.

---

[a] Bethsaida Julias, et-Tell, at the head of the sea of Galilee, founded by Philip the Tetrarch, B. ii. 168.
[b] Literally " and the northern regions," perhaps=" or regions farther north."
[c] Perhaps Khirbat al Samra shown in map (facing p. 1) in Kennedy's Petra (1925).

134

which, beginning at Julias *a* in the north,*b* stretches parallel to the former chain southwards as far as Somora,*c* which borders on Petra in Arabia ; this range includes also the so-called Iron mountain *d* stretching into Moab. The region enclosed between these two mountain ranges is called the Great Plain.*e* This extends from the village of Ginnabris *f* to the Lake Asphaltitis, and is twelve hundred furlongs in length, and a hundred and twenty in breadth ; *g* it is intersected by the Jordan and contains two lakes, Asphaltitis and that of Tiberias, contrary in their nature, the former being salt and barren, the latter sweet and prolific. In summer the plain is burnt up, and the excessive drought renders the surrounding atmosphere pestilential ; for it is wholly without water, apart from the Jordan, which, moreover, explains why the palm-groves on the banks of that river are more luxuriant and productive than those further off.

(3) Hard by Jericho, however, is a copious spring *h* of excellent value for irrigation ; it gushes up near the old town, which was the first in the land of the

and of the Great Plain (Jordan valley).

Elisha's spring near Jericho.

d Unidentified ; " stretching " (μηκυνόμενον) probably means running out laterally from W. to E. (as in *B.* iii. 40).

e The *Ghōr* (=" Rift ") or Jordan valley. " The Great Plain " (similarly used in *A.* iv. 100) elsewhere is the name for the plain of Esdraelon.

f Called Sennabris (iii. 447), between Tiberias and Tarichaeae.

g *i.e.* (the " stade " being *c.* 606 feet) about 137 miles by 13. The actual length of the Jordan valley from the Sea of Galilee to the Dead Sea is 65 miles ; the breadth varies from 3 to 14 miles (G. A. Smith, *Hist. Geography of Holy Land*, 482). Josephus apparently includes the two lakes ; this would increase the length to *c.* 124 miles.

h Commonly identified with the Sultan's Spring, 1½ miles N. of the road from Jerusalem.

παῖς στρατηγὸς Ἑβραίων πρώτην εἷλε γῆς
460 Χαναναίων δορίκτητον. ταύτην τὴν πηγὴν λόγος
ἔχει κατ᾽ ἀρχὰς οὐ μόνον γῆς καὶ δένδρων καρποὺς
ἀπαμβλύνειν, ἀλλὰ καὶ γυναικῶν γονάς, καθόλου
τε πᾶσιν εἶναι νοσώδη τε καὶ φθαρτικήν, ἐξ-
ημερωθῆναι δὲ καὶ γενέσθαι τοὐναντίον ὑγιεινο-
τάτην τε καὶ γονιμωτάτην ὑπὸ Ἐλισσαίου τινὸς[1]
προφήτου· γνώριμος δ᾽ ἦν οὗτος Ἠλία καὶ
461 διάδοχος· ὃς ἐπιξενωθεὶς τοῖς κατὰ τὴν Ἱεριχοῦν,
περισσὸν δή τι φιλοφρονησαμένων αὐτὸν τῶν
ἀνθρώπων, αὐτούς τε ἀμείβεται καὶ τὴν χώραν
462 αἰωνίῳ χάριτι. προελθὼν γὰρ ἐπὶ τὴν πηγὴν
καὶ καταβαλὼν εἰς τὸ ῥεῦμα πλῆρες ἁλῶν ἀγγεῖον
κεραμοῦν,[2] ἔπειτα εἰς οὐρανὸν δεξιὰν ἀνατείνας
δικαίαν κἀπὶ γῆς[3] σπονδὰς μειλικτηρίους χεόμενος,
τὴν μὲν ᾐτεῖτο μαλάξαι τὸ ῥεῦμα καὶ γλυκυτέρας
463 φλέβας ἀνοῖξαι, τὸν δ᾽ ἐγκεράσασθαι τῷ ῥεύματι
γονιμωτέρους ἀέρας δοῦναί τε ἅμα καὶ καρπῶν
εὐθηνίαν τοῖς ἐπιχωρίοις καὶ τέκνων διαδοχήν, μηδ᾽
ἐπιλιπεῖν αὐτοῖς τὸ τούτων γεννητικὸν ὕδωρ,
464 ἕως μενοῦσι δίκαιοι. ταύταις ταῖς εὐχαῖς πολλὰ
προσχειρουργήσας[4] ἐξ ἐπιστήμης ἔτρεψε τὴν
πηγήν, καὶ τὸ πρὶν ὀρφανίας αὐτοῖς καὶ λιμοῦ
παραίτιον ὕδωρ ἔκτοτε εὐτεκνίας καὶ κόρου
465 χορηγὸν κατέστη. τοσαύτην γοῦν ἐν ταῖς ἀρδείαις
ἔχει δύναμιν ὡς, εἰ καὶ μόνον ἐφάψαιτο τῆς
χώρας, νοστιμώτερον εἶναι τῶν μέχρι κόρου
466 χρονιζόντων. παρὸ καὶ τῶν μέν, δαψιλεστέρως
χρωμένων, ἡ ὄνησίς ἐστιν ὀλίγη, τούτου δὲ τοῦ

---

[1] L Lat.: τοῦ the rest.   [2] Naber: κεράμου mss.
[3] καὶ ἐπὶ γῆς A[2]: καὶ πηγῆς or καὶ (τῇ) πηγῇ the rest.
[4] Destinon with Lat.: προ(περι- R)χειρουργήσας mss.

Canaanites to fall before the arms of Jesus the son of Naue,[a] general of the Hebrews. Tradition avers that this spring originally not only blighted the fruits of the earth and of trees but also caused women to miscarry, and that to everything alike it brought disease and destruction, until it was reclaimed and converted into a most salubrious and fertilizing source by a certain prophet Elisha, the disciple and successor of Elijah.[b] Having been the guest of the people of Jericho and been treated by them with extreme hospitality, he requited their kindness by conferring a boon for all time upon them and their country. For he went out to this spring and cast into the stream an earthenware vessel full of salt, and then raising his righteous right hand to heaven and pouring propitiatory libations upon the ground, he besought the earth to mollify the stream and to open sweeter channels, and heaven to temper its waters with more genial airs and to grant to the inhabitants alike an abundance of fruits, a succession of children, and an unfailing supply of water conducive to their production, so long as they remained a righteous people. By these prayers, supplemented by various ritual ceremonies,[c] he changed the nature of the spring, and the water which had before been to them a cause of childlessness and famine thenceforth became a source of fecundity and plenty. Such, in fact, are its powers of irrigation, that if it but skim the soil, it is more salubrious than waters which stand and saturate it. Hence, too, while the benefit derived from other streams is slight, though

[a] The Septuagint name for Joshua, son of Nun.
[b] *Cf.* 2 Kings. ii. 19-22.
[c] Literally "working many things besides with his hands from (professional) skill."

JOSEPHUS

467 ὀλίγου [χορηγία]¹ δαψιλής. ἄρδει γοῦν πλέονα
τῶν ἄλλων ἁπάντων, καὶ πεδίον μὲν ἔπεισιν
ἑβδομήκοντα σταδίων μῆκος εὖρος δ' εἴκοσιν,
ἐκτρέφει δ' ἐν αὐτῷ παραδείσους καλλίστους τε
468 καὶ πυκνοτάτους. τῶν δὲ φοινίκων ἐπαρδομένων
γένη πολλὰ ταῖς γεύσεσι καὶ ταῖς παρηγορίαις²
διάφορα· τούτων οἱ πιότεροι πατούμενοι καὶ μέλι
469 δαψιλὲς ἀνιᾶσιν οὐ πολλῷ τοῦ λοιποῦ χεῖρον. καὶ
μελιττοτρόφος δ' ἡ χώρα· φέρει δὲ καὶ ὀπο-
βάλσαμον, ὃ δὴ τιμιώτατον τῶν τῇδε καρπῶν,
κύπρον τε καὶ μυροβάλανον, ὡς οὐκ ἂν ἁμαρτεῖν
τινα εἰπόντα θεῖον εἶναι τὸ χωρίον, ἐν ᾧ δαψιλῆ τὰ
470 σπανιώτατα καὶ κάλλιστα γεννᾶται. τῶν μὲν
γὰρ ἄλλων αὐτῷ καρπῶν ἕνεκεν οὐκ ἂν ῥᾳδίως τι
παραβληθείη κλίμα τῆς οἰκουμένης· οὕτως τὸ
471 καταβληθὲν πολύχουν ἀναδίδωσιν. αἴτιόν μοι
δοκεῖ τὸ θερμὸν τῶν ἀέρων καὶ τὸ τῶν ὑδάτων
εὔτονον,³ τῶν μὲν προκαλουμένων⁴ τὰ φυόμενα
καὶ διαχεόντων, τῆς δ' ἰκμάδος ῥιζούσης ἕκαστον
ἰσχυρῶς καὶ χορηγούσης τὴν ἐν θέρει δύναμιν·
περικαὲς δέ ἐστιν οὕτως τὸ χωρίον, ὡς μηδένα
472 ῥᾳδίως προϊέναι. τὸ δὲ ὕδωρ πρὸ ἀνατολῆς

¹ PMA²: ἡ χορηγία L: om. the rest.
² προσηγορίαις Niese with Lat. nominibus.
³ Margin of PAM: εὔγονον the rest.
⁴ ed. pr. with Lat.: προσκαλουμένων mss.

·ᵃ The article τῶν (sc. ἄλλων ὑδάτων) must be dissociated from the following genitive absolute δαψιλεστέρως χρωμένων (cf. A. vii. 159).

ᵇ Jericho was " the city of palm-trees," Deut. xxxiv. 3, Judges i. 16.

ᶜ Legend said that the first roots of the balsam were imported into Palestine from Arabia by the Queen of Sheba, A. viii. 174; the method of collecting the juice is described
138

they use them more lavishly,[a] this little rill yields
an ample return. Indeed, this spring irrigates a
larger tract than all others, permeating a plain
seventy furlongs in length and twenty in breadth,
and fostering within that area the most charming
and luxuriant parks. Of the date-palms [b] watered
by it there are numerous varieties differing in flavour
and in medicinal properties ; the richer species of
this fruit when pressed under foot emit copious
honey, not much inferior to that of bees, which are
also abundant in this region. Here, too, grow the
juicy balsam,[c] the most precious of all the local products, the cypress and the myrobalanus [d] ; so that
it would be no misnomer to describe as " divine "
this spot in which the rarest and choicest plants are
produced in abundance.[e] For, with regard to its
other fruits, it would be difficult to find another
region in the habitable world comparable to this ;
so manifold are the returns from whatever is sown.
I attribute these results to the warmth of the air
and the bracing [f] effects of the water, the one calling
forth and diffusing the young plants, while the
moisture enables them all to take firm root and
supplies them with vitality in summer, when the
surrounding region is so parched up, that one can
scarcely venture out of doors. The water if drawn

The rich products of the region watered by it.

in *B.* i. 138, *A.* xiv. 54 ; Cleopatra appropriated from
Herod's realm " the palm grove of Jericho where the balsam
grows," *B.* i. 361, *A.* xv. 96 ; in the last passage Josephus
speaks of the balsam as peculiar to Jericho, but in *A.* ix. 7 he
mentions another habitat, Engedi on the Dead Sea.   Strabo
(xvi. 763) and other writers mention the balsam of Jericho.

    [d] " Perhaps the ben-nut." (Liddell and Scott).

    [e] *Cf.* the description of the fertile plain of Gennesareth,
iii. 516 ff.

    [f] Or, with the reading εὔγονον, " fertilizing."

ἀντλούμενον. ἔπειτα ἐξαιθριασθὲν γίνεται ψυχρό-
τατον καὶ τὴν ἐναντίαν πρὸς τὸ περιέχον φύσιν
λαμβάνει, χειμῶνος δὲ ἀνάπαλιν χλιαίνεται καὶ
473 τοῖς ἐμβαίνουσι γίνεται προσηνέστατον. ἔστι δὲ
καὶ τὸ περιέχον οὕτως εὔκρατον, ὡς λινοῦν
ἀμφιέννυσθαι τοὺς ἐπιχωρίους νιφομένης τῆς
474 ἄλλης Ἰουδαίας. ἀπέχει δ' ἀπὸ Ἱεροσολύμων
μὲν σταδίους ἑκατὸν πεντήκοντα, τοῦ δὲ Ἰορδάνου
ἑξήκοντα, καὶ τὸ μὲν μέχρι Ἱεροσολύμων αὐτῆς
ἔρημον καὶ πετρῶδες, τὸ δὲ μέχρι τοῦ Ἰορδάνου
καὶ τῆς Ἀσφαλτίτιδος χθαμαλώτερον μέν, ἔρημον
475 δὲ ὁμοίως καὶ ἄκαρπον. ἀλλὰ γὰρ τὰ μὲν περὶ
Ἱεριχοῦν εὐδαιμονεστάτην οὖσαν ἀποχρώντως
δεδήλωται.

476   (4) Ἄξιον δ' ἀφηγήσασθαι καὶ τὴν φύσιν τῆς
Ἀσφαλτίτιδος λίμνης, ἥτις ἐστὶ μέν, ὡς ἔφην,
πικρὰ καὶ ἄγονος, ὑπὸ δὲ κουφότητος καὶ τὰ
βαρύτατα τῶν εἰς αὐτὴν ῥιφέντων ἀναφέρει, κατα-
δῦναι δ' εἰς τὸν βυθὸν οὐδὲ ἐπιτηδεύσαντα ῥάδιον.
477 ἀφικόμενος γοῦν καθ' ἱστορίαν ἐπ' αὐτὴν Οὐεσπασιανὸς ἐκέλευσέ τινας τῶν νεῖν οὐκ ἐπιστα-
μένων, δεθέντας ὀπίσω τὰς χεῖρας, ῥιφῆναι κατὰ
τοῦ βυθοῦ, καὶ συνέβη πάντας ἐπινήξασθαι
478 καθάπερ ὑπὸ πνεύματος ἄνω βιαζομένους. ἔστι
δ' ἐπὶ τούτῳ καὶ ἡ τῆς χρόας μεταβολὴ θαυμάσιος·
τρὶς γὰρ ἑκάστης ἡμέρας τὴν ἐπιφάνειαν ἀλλάσ-
σεται καὶ πρὸς τὰς ἡλιακὰς ἀκτῖνας ἀνταυγεῖ ποι-
479 κίλως. τῆς μέντοι ἀσφάλτου κατὰ πολλὰ μέρη

before sunrise and then exposed to the air becomes intensely cold,[a] assuming a character the reverse of the surrounding atmosphere ; in winter, on the contrary, it is warm and quite pleasant to bathe in. Moreover, the climate is so mild that the inhabitants wear linen when snow is falling throughout the rest of Judaea. The distance from Jerusalem is a hundred and fifty furlongs and from the Jordan sixty.[b] The country from Jericho to Jerusalem is desert and rocky ; to the Jordan and the Lake Asphaltitis the ground is lower, though equally wild and barren. But of Jericho, that most favoured spot, enough has been said.

(4) The natural properties of the Lake Asphaltitis also merit remark. Its waters are, as I said,[c] bitter and unproductive, but owing to their buoyancy send up to the surface the very heaviest of objects cast into them, and it is difficult, even of set purpose, to sink to the bottom.[d] Thus, when Vespasian came to explore the lake, he ordered certain persons who were unable to swim to be flung into the deep water with their hands tied behind them ; with the result that all rose to the surface and floated, as if impelled upward by a current of air. Another remarkable feature is its change of colour : three times a day it alters its appearance and throws off a different reflection of the solar rays. Again, in many parts it

Description of the Lake Asphaltitis (Dead Sea).

Vespasian visits it.

---

[a] Cf. a similar statement on the water of the Sea of Galilee, iii. 508.

[b] i.e. 11½ and nearly 7 miles respectively. The actual distances appear to be about 16 and 5 miles.

[c] § 456.

[d] Cf. with this description Tac. Hist. v. 6 and Strabo, 763 f. (who confuses it with the Lake Sirbonis in Egypt ; context and details show that he refers to the Dead Sea).

βώλους μελαίνας ἀναδίδωσιν· αἱ δ' ἐπινήχονται
τό τε σχῆμα καὶ τὸ μέγεθος ταύροις ἀκεφάλοις
480 παραπλήσιαι. προσελαύνοντες δὲ οἱ τῆς λίμνης
ἐργάται καὶ δρασσόμενοι τοῦ συνεστῶτος ἕλκουσιν
εἰς τὰ σκάφη, πληρώσασι δὲ ἀποκόπτειν οὐ
ῥᾴδιον, ἀλλὰ δι' εὐτονίαν προσήρτηται τῷ μηρύ-
ματι τὸ σκάφος, ἕως ἂν ἐμμηνίῳ γυναικῶν αἵματι
καὶ οὔρῳ διαλύσωσιν αὐτήν, οἷς μόνοις εἴκει.
481 καὶ χρήσιμος δὲ οὐ μόνον εἰς ἁρμονίας νεῶν ἀλλὰ
καὶ πρὸς· ἄκεσιν σωμάτων· εἰς πολλὰ γοῦν τῶν
482 φαρμάκων παραμίσγεται. ταύτης τῆς λίμνης μῆκος μὲν ὀγδοήκοντα καὶ πεντακόσιοι στάδιοι,
καθὸ δὴ μέχρι Ζοάρων τῆς Ἀραβίας ἐκτείνεται,
483 εὖρος δὲ πεντήκοντα καὶ ἑκατόν. γειτνιᾷ δ' ἡ
Σοδομῖτις αὕτη, πάλαι μὲν εὐδαίμων γῆ καρπῶν
τε ἕνεκεν καὶ τῆς κατὰ πόλιν περιουσίας, νῦν δὲ
484 κεκαυμένη πᾶσα. φασὶ δ' ὡς δι' ἀσέβειαν οἰκητόρων κεραυνοῖς καταφλεγῆναι[1]· ἔστι γοῦν ἔτι
λείψανα τοῦ θείου πυρός, καὶ πέντε μὲν πόλεων
ἰδεῖν σκιάς, ἔτι δὲ κἂν τοῖς καρποῖς σποδιὰν
ἀναγεννωμένην, οἳ χροιὰν μὲν ἔχουσι τῶν ἐδωδίμων ὁμοίαν, δρεψαμένων δὲ χερσὶν εἰς καπνὸν

---

[1] κατεφλέγη L.

---

[a] So Tac. *loc. cit.* " fugit cruorem vestemque infectam
sanguine, quo feminae per menses exsolvuntur. Sic veteres
auctores." From Strabo 764 we learn that one of these
" ancient authors " was Poseidonius (2nd-1st cent. B.C.). *Cf.*

142

casts up black masses of bitumen, which float on the Its bitumen.
surface, in their shape and size resembling decapi-
tated bulls. The labourers on the lake row up to
these and catching hold of the lumps haul them into
their boats ; but when they have filled them it is no
easy task to detach their cargo, which owing to its
tenacious and glutinous character clings to the boat
until it is loosened by the monthly secretions of
women,[a] to which alone it yields. It is useful not
only for caulking ships, but also for the healing of the
body, forming an ingredient in many medicines. The
length of this lake is five hundred and eighty furlongs,[b] measured in a line reaching to Zoara[c] in
Arabia, and its breadth one hundred and fifty.[d]
Adjacent to it is the land of Sodom,[e] in days of old The blasted land of Sodom.
a country blest in its produce and in the wealth of
its various cities, but now all burnt up. It is said
that, owing to the impiety of its inhabitants, it was
consumed by thunderbolts ; and in fact vestiges of
the divine fire and faint traces of five cities are still
visible. Still, too, may one see ashes reproduced in
the fruits, which from their outward appearance
would be thought edible, but on being plucked with

also *B.* vii. 181, where the same secretions are named as
aids to the extraction of a certain root with medicinal
properties.

  [b] This figure (=about 66½ miles) is greatly exaggerated ;
the actual length is about 47 miles.

  [c] The Biblical Zoar, familiar as Lot's city of refuge, Gen.
xix. 22 ; perhaps (Smith and Bartholomew, *Atlas*) el-Keryeh,
a few miles S. of the Lake.

  [d] *i.e.* about 11½ miles ; the actual breadth at the broadest
part is about 10 miles.

  [e] Perhaps the modern *Jebel Usdum* at the S.W. corner of
the lake. Many older authorities located the cities of the
plain to the *north* of the Dead Sea.

485 διαλύονται[1] καὶ τέφραν. τὰ μὲν δὴ περὶ τὴν
Σοδομῖτιν μυθευόμενα τοιαύτην ἔχει πίστιν ἀπὸ
τῆς ὄψεως.

486 (ix. 1) Ὁ δὲ Οὐεσπασιανὸς πανταχόσε[2] περι-
τειχίζων[3] τοὺς ἐν τοῖς Ἱεροσολύμοις ἔν τε τῇ
Ἱεριχοῖ καὶ ἐν Ἀδίδοις ἐγείρει στρατόπεδα καὶ
φρουροὺς ἀμφοτέραις ἐγκαθίστησιν ἔκ τε τοῦ
487 Ῥωμαϊκοῦ καὶ συμμαχικοῦ τάγματος.[4] πέμπει
δὲ καὶ εἰς Γέρασα Λούκιον Ἄννιον παραδοὺς
488 μοῖραν ἱππέων καὶ συχνοὺς πεζούς. ὁ μὲν οὖν
ἐξ ἐφόδου τὴν πόλιν ἑλὼν ἀποκτείνει μὲν χιλίους
τῶν νέων, ὅσοι μὴ διαφυγεῖν ἔφθασαν, γενεὰς δὲ
ἠχμαλωτίσατο καὶ τὰς κτήσεις διαρπάσαι τοῖς
στρατιώταις ἐπέτρεψεν· ἔπειτα τὰς οἰκίας ἐμ-
489 πρήσας ἐπὶ τὰς πέριξ κώμας ἐχώρει. φυγαὶ δ'
ἦσαν τῶν δυνατῶν καὶ φθοραὶ τῶν ἀσθενεστέρων,
490 τὸ καταλειφθὲν δὲ πᾶν ἐνεπίμπρατο. καὶ δι-
ειληφότος τοῦ πολέμου τήν τε ὀρεινὴν ὅλην καὶ
τὴν πεδιάδα πάσας[5] οἱ ἐν τοῖς Ἱεροσολύμοις τὰς
ἐξόδους ἀφῄρηντο· τοὺς μὲν γὰρ[6] αὐτομολεῖν προ-
αιρουμένους οἱ ζηλωταὶ παρεφυλάσσοντο, τοὺς δὲ
οὔπω τὰ Ῥωμαίων φρονοῦντας εἶργεν ἡ στρατιὰ
πανταχόθεν τὴν πόλιν περιέχουσα.

---

[1] ἀναλύονται L.   [2] πανταχόθεν LC.
[3] ἐπιτειχίζων L.   [4] συντάγματος A.
     [5] Destinon : πᾶσαν mss.
     [6] μέντοι γε PA : μέν γε Destinon.

---

[a] Cf. Tac. Hist. v. 7 " et manere vestigia, terramque ipsam,
specie torridam, vim frugiferam perdidisse. Nam cuncta . . .
atra et inania velut in cinerem vanescunt "; and from a
writer of a thousand years later, Fulcher of Chartres, historian
of the first crusade, Hist. Hierosol. ii. 4 (Migne) "illic inter
arbores caeteras vidi quasdam poma ferentes, de quibus

144

the hand dissolve into smoke and ashes.[a] So far are the legends about the land of Sodom borne out by ocular evidence.

(ix. 1) Vespasian, with a view to investing Jerusalem on all sides, now established camps at Jericho and at Adida,[b] placing in each a garrison composed jointly of Romans and auxiliaries. He also sent Lucius Annius to Gerasa[c] with a squadron of cavalry and a considerable body of infantry. Annius, having carried the city by assault, put to the sword a thousand of the youth who had not already escaped, made prisoners of women and children, gave his soldiers licence to plunder the property, and then set fire to the houses and advanced against the surrounding villages. The able-bodied fled, the feeble perished, and everything left was consigned to the flames. The war having now embraced the whole region, both hill and plain, all egress from Jerusalem was cut off; for those who desired to desert were closely watched by the Zealots, while those who were not yet pro-Romans were confined by the army which hemmed in the city on every side.

Vespasian establishes camps at Jericho and Adida.

L. Annius takes Gerasa.

Jerusalem isolated.

cum collegissem, scire volens cujus naturae essent, inveni rupto cortice interius quasi pulverem atrum, et inde inanem prodire fumum." Dr. C. Geikie, *The Holy Land and the Bible*, ii. 117, writes that " the ' osher ' of the Arab is the true apple of Sodom. . . . Its fruit is like a large smooth apple or orange. . . . When ripe it is yellow and looks fair and attractive, and is soft to the touch, but if pressed, it bursts with a crack, and only the broken shell and a row of small seeds in a half-open pod, with a few dry filaments, remain in the hand."

[b] *Haditheh*, 3 miles E. of Lydda, and some 20 miles N.W. of Jerusalem.

[c] *Jerash*, in Gilead, on the N.E. frontier of Peraea, *B.* iii. 47.

491 (2) Οὐεσπασιανῷ δ᾽ εἰς Καισάρειαν ἐπιστρέ·
ψαντι καὶ παρασκευαζομένῳ μετὰ πάσης τῆς
δυνάμεως ἐπ᾽ αὐτῶν τῶν Ἱεροσολύμων ἐξ-
ελαύνειν ἀγγέλλεται Νέρων ἀνῃρημένος, τρία καὶ
δέκα βασιλεύσας ἔτη ⟨καὶ μῆνας ὀκτὼ⟩¹ καὶ
492 ἡμέρας ὀκτώ. περὶ οὗ λέγειν, ὃν τρόπον εἰς τὴν
ἀρχὴν ἐξύβρισεν πιστεύσας τὰ πράγματα τοῖς
493 πονηροτάτοις, Νυμφιδίῳ καὶ Τιγελλίνῳ, τοῖς γε²
ἀναξίοις τῶν ἐξελευθέρων, καὶ ὡς ὑπὸ τούτων
ἐπιβουλευθεὶς κατελείφθη μὲν ὑπὸ τῶν φυλάκων
ἁπάντων, διαδρὰς δὲ σὺν τέτρασι τῶν πιστῶν
ἀπελευθέρων ἐν τοῖς προαστείοις ἑαυτὸν ἀνεῖλεν,
καὶ ὡς οἱ καταλύσαντες αὐτὸν μετ᾽ οὐ³ πολὺν
494 χρόνον δίκας ἔδοσαν· τόν τε κατὰ τὴν Γαλατίαν
πόλεμον ὡς ἐτελεύτησε, καὶ πῶς Γάλβας ἀπο-
δειχθεὶς αὐτοκράτωρ εἰς Ῥώμην ἐπανῆλθεν ἐκ
τῆς Ἰσπανίας, καὶ ὡς ὑπὸ τῶν στρατιωτῶν
αἰτιαθεὶς ἐπὶ ταπεινοφροσύνῃ κατὰ μέσην ἐδολο-
φονήθη⁴ τὴν Ῥωμαίων ἀγοράν, ἀπεδείχθη τε
495 αὐτοκράτωρ Ὄθων· τήν τε τούτου στρατείαν⁵

¹ ins. Niese.   ² MRC: τε PAL: om. V.
³ μετ᾽ οὐ Cardwell: μετὰ MSS.
⁴ κατὰ μέσ. ἐδ. Niese (avoiding hiatus): ἐδ. κατὰ μέσην MSS.
⁵ Dindorf: στρατιὰν MSS.

ᵃ The actual length of his reign was 13 years 7 months 28
days (from 13th October 54 to 9th June 68). Dion Cassius
(lxiii. 29) reckons this in round numbers as 13 years 8 months.
With this figure the statement in Josephus may be brought
into conformity by altering ἡμέρας to μῆνας; more probably,
as suggested by Niese, καὶ μῆνας ὀκτὼ has dropped out
through homoioteleuton. With the insertion of those words,
Josephus makes the reign ten days too long; cf. similar
slight discrepancies in B. ii. 168, 180, 204.
ᵇ Nymphidius Sabinus, son of a freedwoman, was, along

146

(2) Vespasian had returned to Caesarea and was preparing to march in full strength upon Jerusalem itself, when the news reached him that Nero was slain, after a reign of thirteen years (eight months) and eight days.[a]   To tell how that emperor wantonly abused his authority by entrusting the administration to the vilest wretches, Nymphidius [b] and Tigellinus,[c] the most worthless of freedmen [d] ; how, when they conspired against him, he was abandoned by all his guards, and, escaping with four faithful freedmen,[e] put an end to himself [f] in the suburbs ; and how punishment ere long overtook those who had caused his overthrow—falls outside my purpose.   Nor do I propose to tell of the war in Gaul and its issue, of Galba's call to the imperial dignity and his return to Rome from Spain, of the charge of meanness [g] brought against him by the soldiers and how he was treacherously slain in the midst of the Roman forum [h] and Otho was made emperor ; of Otho's

with Tigellinus, prefect of the praetorian guards towards the end of Nero's reign. On Nero's death he attempted to seize the empire for himself, but was slain by the friends of Galba.

   [c] Sophonius Tigellinus. a man of obscure birth, appointed praetorian prefect A.D. 63, was the main instrument of the tyranny and profligacy which marked the end of Nero's reign ; he committed suicide on the accession of Otho. Juv. *Sat.* i. 155 " pone Tigellinum " etc., " dare to portray T. and you will be burnt alive."

   [d] Or, perhaps, " and to worthless freedmen."

   [e] Phaon, who offered him refuge at his villa 4 miles out of Rome, Epaphroditus, Sporus, and another. The dramatic story is told by Suetonius, *Nero* 47 f. and Dion Cass. lxiii. 27.

   [f] Epaphroditus assisting.

   [g] He alienated the praetorians by refusing the donative which Nymphidius had promised in his name.

   [h] Near the pool of Curtius.

ἐπὶ τοὺς Οὐιτελλίου στρατηγοὺς καὶ κατάλυσιν,
ἔπειτα τοὺς κατὰ Οὐιτέλλιον ταράχους καὶ τὴν
περὶ τὸ Καπετώλιον συμβολήν, ὅπως τε Ἀντώνιος
Πρῖμος καὶ Μουκιανός, διαφθείραντες Οὐιτέλλιον
καὶ τὰ Γερμανικὰ τάγματα, κατέστειλαν τὸν ἐμ-
496 φύλιον πόλεμον· πάντα ταῦτα διεξιέναι μὲν ἐπ᾽
ἀκριβὲς παρῃτησάμην, ἐπειδὴ δι᾽ ὄχλου πᾶσίν
ἐστιν καὶ πολλοῖς Ἑλλήνων τε καὶ Ῥωμαίων
ἀναγέγραπται, συναφείας δὲ ἕνεκεν τῶν πραγμάτων καὶ τοῦ μὴ διηρτῆσθαι τὴν ἱστορίαν
κεφαλαιωδῶς ἕκαστον ἐπισημαίνομαι.

497 Οὐεσπασιανὸς τοίνυν τὸ μὲν πρῶτον ἀνεβάλλετο
τὴν τῶν Ἱεροσολύμων στρατείαν, καραδοκῶν
498 πρὸς τίνα ῥέψει τὸ κρατεῖν μετὰ Νέρωνα· αὖθις
δὲ Γάλβαν ἀκούσας αὐτοκράτορα, πρὶν ἐπιστεῖλαί
τι περὶ τοῦ πολέμου κἀκεῖνον, οὐκ ἐπεχείρει,
πέμπει δὲ πρὸς αὐτὸν [καὶ]¹ τὸν υἱὸν Τίτον
ἀσπασόμενόν τε καὶ ληψόμενον τὰς περὶ Ἰουδαίων
ἐντολάς. διὰ δὲ τὰς αὐτὰς αἰτίας ἅμα Τίτῳ καὶ
499 Ἀγρίππας ὁ βασιλεὺς πρὸς Γάλβαν ἔπλει. καὶ
διὰ τῆς Ἀχαΐας,² χειμῶνος γὰρ ἦν ὥρα, μακραῖς
ναυσὶ περιπλεόντων³ φθάνει Γάλβας ἀναιρεθεὶς
μετὰ μῆνας ἑπτὰ καὶ ἴσας ἡμέρας· ἐξ οὗ καὶ τὴν
ἡγεμονίαν παρέλαβεν Ὄθων ἀντιποιούμενος τῶν
500 πραγμάτων. ὁ μὲν οὖν Ἀγρίππας εἰς τὴν Ῥώμην

---

¹ om. Havercamp with one ms. ² + αὐτῶν L.
³ παραπλεόντων Hudson with Lat. (praetervehuntur).

ᵃ These last incidents *are* narrated below, §§ 545-8, 585 ff.
ᵇ The meaning " *through* Achaea " is obscure. We might
expect, as has been suggested, " while [they were going by
land] through Achaea (for it was winter) [and the rest] were
sailing round " the Peloponnese; possibly there is a lacuna

148

campaign against the generals of Vitellius and his overthrow ; of the subsequent commotions under Vitellius and the fighting around the Capitol, and how Antonius Primus and Mucianus, by the destruction of Vitellius and his German legions, finally suppressed the civil war.[a]   All these matters I may be excused from narrating in detail, because they are commonly known and have been described by numerous Greek and Roman historians ; but to preserve the connexion of events and to avoid any break in the narrative, I have summarily touched upon each.

Vespasian, therefore, when the news first came, deferred his expedition against Jerusalem, anxiously waiting to see upon whom the empire would devolve after Nero's death ; nor when he subsequently heard that Galba was emperor would he undertake anything, until he had received further instructions from him concerning the war.   But he sent his son Titus to the new emperor to salute him and to receive his orders with reference to the Jews ; king Agrippa also embarked with Titus on the same errand to Galba.   However, before they reached their destination and while they were sailing round through Achaea [b] (for it was the winter season) in vessels of war, Galba was assassinated after a reign of seven months and as many days,[c] and was succeeded as emperor by Otho, the rival claimant to the sovereignty.   Agrippa decided, notwithstanding, to proceed to Rome, in

and defers his march to Jerusalem.

Titus sent to salute Galba,

in the text.   As the text stands, the parenthesis will account for the time taken over the voyage.   The canal through the isthmus of Corinth begun by Nero (iii. 540) was never completed.

   [c] From the death of Nero, 9th June 68, to that of Galba 15th January 69.   The calculation is correct.

149

ἀφικέσθαι διέγνω μηδὲν ὀρρωδήσας πρὸς τὴν
501 μεταβολήν· Τίτος δὲ κατὰ δαιμόνιον ὁρμὴν ἀπὸ
τῆς Ἑλλάδος εἰς τὴν Συρίαν ἀνέπλει καὶ κατὰ
τάχος εἰς Καισάρειαν ἀφικνεῖται πρὸς τὸν πατέρα.
502 καὶ οἱ μὲν μετέωροι περὶ τῶν ὅλων ὄντες ὡς ἂν
σαλευομένης τῆς Ῥωμαίων ἡγεμονίας ὑπερεώρων
τὴν ἐπὶ Ἰουδαίους στρατείαν,[1] καὶ διὰ τὸν περὶ
τῆς πατρίδος φόβον τὴν ἐπὶ τοὺς ἀλλοφύλους
ὁρμὴν ἄωρον ἐνόμιζον.
503 (3) Ἐπανίσταται δ' ἄλλος τοῖς Ἱεροσολύμοις
πόλεμος. υἱὸς ἦν Γιώρα Σίμων τις Γερασηνὸς τὸ
γένος, νεανίας πανουργίᾳ μὲν ἡττώμενος Ἰωάννου
504 τοῦ προκατέχοντος ἤδη τὴν πόλιν, ἀλκῇ δὲ
σώματος καὶ τόλμῃ διαφέρων, δι' ἣν καὶ ὑπὸ
Ἀνάνου τοῦ ἀρχιερέως φυγαδευθεὶς ἐξ ἧς εἶχε[2]
τοπαρχίας Ἀκραβετηνῆς πρὸς τοὺς κατειληφότας
505 τὴν Μασάδαν λῃστὰς παραγίνεται. τὸ μὲν οὖν
πρῶτον ἦν αὐτοῖς δι' ὑποψίας· εἰς τὸ κατωτέρω
γοῦν φρούριον ἐπέτρεψαν αὐτῷ παρελθεῖν ἅμα
ταῖς γυναιξίν, ἃς ἄγων ἧκεν, αὐτοὶ τὸ ὑψηλότερον
506 οἰκοῦντες· αὖθις δὲ διὰ συγγένειαν ἠθῶν καὶ ὅτι
πιστὸς ἐδόκει, συμπροενόμευε γοῦν αὐτοῖς ἐξιὼν
507 καὶ συνεπόρθει τὰ περὶ τὴν Μασάδαν. οὐ μὴν
ἐπὶ τὰ μείζω παρακαλῶν ἔπεισεν· οἱ μὲν γὰρ
ἐν ἔθει ὄντες τῷ φρουρίῳ, καθάπερ φωλεοῦ χω-
508 ρίζεσθαι μακρὰν ἐδεδοίκεσαν, ὁ δὲ τυραννιῶν
καὶ μεγάλων ἐφιέμενος ἐπειδὴ καὶ τὴν Ἀνάνου
τελευτὴν ἤκουσεν, εἰς τὴν ὀρεινὴν ἀφίσταται,

---

[1] LC: στρατηγίαν PAM: στρατίαν VR.
[2] ἦρχε Dindorf with one ms.

---

[a] Active in the opening attack on Cestius, *B.* ii. 521, he had afterwards become a marauder, ii. 652.

no way deterred by this change of affairs; but
Titus, under divine impulse, sailed back from Greece
to Syria and hastened to rejoin his father at Caesarea.
The two, being thus in suspense on these momentous
matters, when the Roman empire itself was reeling,
neglected the invasion of Judaea, regarding an
attack on a foreign country as unseasonable, while
in such anxiety concerning their own.

(3) But another war was now impending over
Jerusalem. There was a certain Simon,[a] son of
Gioras and a native of Gerasa,[b] a youth less cunning
than John, who was already in possession of the city,
but his superior in physical strength and audacity;
the latter quality had led to his expulsion by the
high priest Ananus from the province of Acrabetene,[c]
once under his command, whereupon he had joined
the brigands who had seized Masada.[d] At first they
regarded him with suspicion, and permitted him and
his following of women access only to the lower part
of the fortress, occupying the upper quarters themselves; but afterwards, as a man of congenial disposition and apparently to be trusted, he was allowed
to accompany them on their marauding expeditions
and took part in their raids upon the surrounding
district. His efforts to tempt them to greater enterprises were, however, unsuccessful; for they had
grown accustomed to the fortress and were afraid
to venture far, so to speak, from their lair. He, on
the contrary, was aspiring to despotic power and
cherishing high ambitions; accordingly on hearing
of the death of Ananus,[e] he withdrew to the hills,

rejoins Vespasian on hearing of accession of Otho.

Hostilities deferred.

Simon, son of Gioras, joins the brigands of Masada,

---

[b] *Jerash*, § 487.   [c] In the N. of Judaea.
[d] *Cf.* ii. 652 f., and for Masada, iv. 399.   [e] § 316.

151

καὶ προκηρύξας δούλοις μὲν ἐλευθερίαν, γέρας
δὲ ἐλευθέροις, τοὺς πανταχόθεν πονηροὺς συν-
ήθροιζεν.

509 (4) Ὡς δ᾽ ἦν αὐτῷ καρτερὸν ἤδη τὸ σύνταγμα,
τὰς ἀνὰ τὴν ὀρεινὴν κώμας κατέτρεχεν, ἀεὶ δὲ
προσγινομένων πλειόνων ἐθάρρει καταβαίνειν εἰς
510 τὰ χθαμαλώτερα. κἀπειδὴ πόλεσιν ἤδη φοβερὸς
ἦν, πολλοὶ πρὸς τὴν ἰσχὺν καὶ τὴν εὔροιαν τῶν
κατορθωμάτων ἐφθείροντο δυνατοί, καὶ οὐκέτι ἦν
δούλων μόνων οὐδὲ λῃστῶν στρατός, ἀλλὰ καὶ
δημοτικῶν οὐκ ὀλίγων ὡς πρὸς βασιλέα πειθαρχία.
511 κατέτρεχε δὲ τήν τε Ἀκραβετηνὴν τοπαρχίαν καὶ
τὰ μέχρι τῆς μεγάλης Ἰδουμαίας· κατὰ γὰρ
κώμην τινὰ καλουμένην Ναῒν[1] τεῖχος κατασκευάσας
512 ὥσπερ φρουρίῳ πρὸς ἀσφάλειαν ἐχρῆτο, κατὰ δὲ
τὴν φάραγγα προσαγορευομένην Φερεταὶ[2] πολλὰ
μὲν ἀνευρύνας σπήλαια, πολλὰ δ᾽ εὑρὼν ἕτοιμα
ταμιείοις ἐχρῆτο θησαυρῶν καὶ τῆς λείας ἐκ-
513 δοχείοις. ἀνετίθει δὲ καὶ τοὺς ἁρπαζομένους εἰς
αὐτὰ καρπούς, οἵ τε πολλοὶ τῶν λόχων δίαιταν
εἶχον ἐν ἐκείνοις· δῆλος δ᾽ ἦν τό τε σύνταγμα
προγυμνάζων καὶ τὰς παρασκευὰς κατὰ τῶν
Ἱεροσολύμων.

514 (5) Ὅθεν οἱ ζηλωταὶ δείσαντες αὐτοῦ τὴν ἐπιβολὴν[3] καὶ προλαβεῖν βουλόμενοι τὸν κατ᾽ αὐτῶν
τρεφόμενον ἐξίασι μετὰ τῶν ὅπλων οἱ πλείους·
ὑπαντιάζει δὲ Σίμων, καὶ παραταξάμενος συχνοὺς
μὲν αὐτῶν ἀναιρεῖ, συνελαύνει δὲ τοὺς λοιποὺς
515 εἰς τὴν πόλιν. οὔπω δὲ θαρρῶν τῇ δυνάμει τοῦ

___

[1] Ἀὶν PA : aiam Lat.
[2] φαρ. προσ. Φερεταί] Φαρὰ(ν) προσαγορευομένην φάραγγα
MVR(C).
[3] Destinon : ἐπιβουλὴν MSS.

where, by proclaiming liberty for slaves and rewards
for the free, he gathered around him the villains
from every quarter.

(4) Having now collected a strong force, he first
overran the villages in the hills, and then through
continual additions to his numbers was emboldened
to descend into the lowlands. And now when he
was becoming a terror to the towns, many men of
standing were seduced by his strength and career
of unbroken success into joining him; and his was
no longer an army of mere serfs or brigands, but
one including numerous citizen recruits, subservient
to his command as to a king. He now overran not
only the province of Acrabetene but the whole
district extending to greater Idumaea. For at a
village called Nain [a] he had thrown up a wall and
used the place as a fortress to secure his position;
while he turned to account numerous caves in the
valley known as Pheretae, [b] widening some and finding others adapted to his purpose, as store chambers
and repositories for plunder. Here, too, he laid up
his spoils of corn, and here most of his troops were
quartered. His object was evident: he was training
his force and making all these preparations for an
attack on Jerusalem.

and collects an army of marauders for an attack on the Zealots.

(5) The Zealots, in consequence, alarmed at his
designs and anxious to forestall one whose growing
strength was to their injury, went out with their
main body under arms; Simon met them and in
the ensuing fight killed many of them and drove
the remainder into the city. Misgivings about his

Simon repels attack of the Zealots

[a] Unidentified; apparently not far N. of the Idumaean
frontier, § 517 (not the Galilaean village so named).

[b] Perhaps *Khurbet Farah*, a gorge some 6 miles N.E. of
Jerusalem.

153

μὲν τοῖς τείχεσιν προσβάλλειν ἀπετράπη, χειρώ-
σασθαι δὲ πρότερον τὴν Ἰδουμαίαν ἐπεβάλετο·
καὶ δὴ δισμυρίους ἔχων ὁπλίτας ἤλαυνεν ἐπὶ τοὺς
516 ὅρους αὐτῆς. οἱ δὲ ἄρχοντες τῆς Ἰδουμαίας κατὰ
τάχος ἀθροίσαντες ἐκ τῆς χώρας τὸ μαχιμώτατον
περὶ πεντακισχιλίους καὶ δισμυρίους, τοὺς δὲ
πολλοὺς ἐάσαντες φρουρεῖν τὰ σφέτερα διὰ τὰς
τῶν ἐν Μασάδῃ σικαρίων καταδρομάς, ἐδέχοντο
517 τὸν Σίμωνα πρὸς τοῖς ὅροις. ἔνθα συμβαλὼν
αὐτοῖς καὶ δι᾽ ὅλης πολεμήσας ἡμέρας, οὔτε
νενικηκὼς οὔτε νενικημένος διεκρίθη, καὶ ὁ μὲν
εἰς τὴν Ναΐν,[1] οἱ δὲ Ἰδουμαῖοι διελύθησαν ἐπ᾽
518 οἴκου. καὶ μετ᾽ οὐ πολὺ Σίμων μείζονι δυνάμει
πάλιν εἰς τὴν χώραν αὐτῶν ὥρμητο, στρατοπεδευ-
σάμενος δὲ κατά τινα κώμην, Θεκουὲ καλεῖται,
πρὸς τοὺς ἐν Ἡρωδείῳ φρουρούς, ὅπερ ἦν πλησίον, Ἐλεάζαρόν τινα τῶν ἑταίρων ἔπεμψε
519 πείσοντα παραδοῦναι τὸ ἔρυμα. τοῦτον οἱ φύλακες ἑτοίμως[2] ἐδέξαντο, τὴν αἰτίαν ἀγνοοῦντες
δι᾽ ἣν ἥκοι, φθεγξάμενον δὲ περὶ παραδόσεως
ἐδίωκον σπασάμενοι τὰ ξίφη, μέχρι φυγῆς τόπον
οὐκ ἔχων ἔρριψεν ἀπὸ τοῦ τείχους ἑαυτὸν εἰς τὴν
520 ὑποκειμένην φάραγγα. καὶ ὁ μὲν αὐτίκα τελευτᾷ,
τοῖς δ᾽ Ἰδουμαίοις ἤδη κατορρωδοῦσι τὴν ἰσχὺν
τοῦ Σίμωνος ἔδοξε πρὸ τοῦ συμβαλεῖν κατα-
σκέψασθαι τὴν στρατιὰν τῶν πολεμίων.
521 (6) Εἰς τοῦτο δὲ ὑπηρέτην αὐτὸν ἑτοίμως ἐπεδίδου Ἰάκωβος, εἷς τῶν ἡγεμόνων, προδοσίαν
522 ἐνθυμούμενος. ὁρμήσας γοῦν ἀπὸ τῆς Ἀλούρου,

---

[1] aiam Lat.   [2] προθύμως P.

[a] Tekoa, 5 miles S. of Bethlehem.

forces, however, still deterred him from an assault
on the walls ; instead he resolved first to subdue
Idumaea, and now marched with an army of twenty   and invades
thousand men towards the frontiers of that country.   Idumaea.
The chieftains of Idumaea hastily mustered from
the country their most efficient troops, numbering
about twenty-five thousand, and leaving the mass of
the population to protect their property against
incursions of the *sicarii* of Masada, met Simon at the
frontier. There he fought them and, after a battle   A drawn
lasting all day, left the field neither victor nor   battle.
vanquished ; he then withdrew to Nain and the
Idumaeans disbanded to their homes. Not long
after, however, Simon with a yet larger force again
invaded their territory, and, encamping at a village
called Thekoue,[a] sent one of his comrades named
Eleazar to the garrison at Herodion,[b] which was not
far off, to persuade them to hand over that fortress.
The guards, ignorant of the object of his visit,
promptly admitted him, but at the first mention
of the word " surrender " drew their swords and
pursued him, until, finding escape impossible, he
flung himself from the ramparts into the valley
below and was killed on the spot. The Idumaeans,
now gravely alarmed at Simon's strength, decided
before risking an engagement to reconnoitre their
enemy's army.

(6) For this service James, one of their officers,   James the
promptly volunteered, meditating treachery. He   Idumaean
accordingly set out from Alurus,[c] the village where   country to
                                                      Simon.

[b] Some 3 miles N.E. of Tekoa ; the fortress built by Herod
the Great, i. 265, 419 ff., in which he was buried, i. 673.

[c] *Hulhul*, some 4 miles N. of Hebron, and 7 miles S.W. of
Simon's camp at Tekoa.

κατὰ γὰρ ταύτην συνήθροιστο τὴν κώμην τότε
τῶν Ἰδουμαίων τὸ στράτευμα, παραγίνεται πρὸς
523 Σίμωνα, καὶ πρώτην αὐτῷ παραδώσειν συντίθεται
τὴν αὑτοῦ πατρίδα,[1] λαβὼν ὅρκους ὡς ἀεὶ τίμιος
ὢν διατελέσει,[1] συνεργήσειν δὲ ὑπέσχετο καὶ περὶ
524 τῆς ὅλης Ἰδουμαίας. ἐφ᾽ οἷς ἑστιαθεὶς φιλοφρόνως ὑπὸ τοῦ Σίμωνος καὶ λαμπραῖς ἐπαρθεὶς
ὑποσχέσεσιν, ἐπειδήπερ εἰς τοὺς σφετέρους ὑπέστρεψε, τὸ μὲν πρῶτον πολλαπλασίονα τὴν στρα-
525 τιὰν ἐψεύδετο τοῦ Σίμωνος, ἔπειτα δεξιούμενος[2]
τούς τε ἡγεμόνας καὶ κατ᾽ ὀλίγους πᾶν τὸ πλῆθος
ἐνῆγεν ὥστε δέξασθαι τὸν Σίμωνα καὶ παραδοῦναι
526 δίχα μάχης αὐτῷ τὴν τῶν ὅλων ἀρχήν. ἅμα δὲ
ταῦτα διαπραττόμενος καὶ Σίμωνα δι᾽ ἀγγέλων
ἐκάλει σκεδάσειν ὑπισχνούμενος τοὺς Ἰδουμαίους·
527 ὃ δὴ παρέσχεν. ὡς γὰρ ἦν ἤδη πλησίον ἡ στρατιά,
πρῶτος ἀναπηδήσας ἐπὶ τὸν ἵππον μετὰ τῶν
528 συνδιεφθαρμένων ἔφευγε. πτόα δ᾽ ἐμπίπτει παντὶ
τῷ πλήθει, καὶ πρὶν εἰς χεῖρας ἐλθεῖν λυθέντες
ἐκ τῆς τάξεως ἀνεχώρουν ἕκαστοι πρὸς τὰ ἴδια.
529 (7) Σίμων δὲ παρὰ δόξαν εἰς τὴν Ἰδουμαίαν
εἰσήλασεν ἀναιμωτὶ καὶ προσβαλὼν ἀδοκήτως
πρώτην αἱρεῖ τὴν πολίχνην Χεβρών, ἐν ᾗ πλείστης
ἐκράτησε λείας, πάμπολυν δὲ διήρπασε καρπόν.
530 ὡς δέ φασιν οἱ ἐπιχώριοι τὴν Χεβρὼν οὐ μόνον
τῶν τῇδε πόλεων ἀλλὰ καὶ τῆς ἐν Αἰγύπτῳ Μέμ-
φεως ἀρχαιοτέραν· δισχίλια γοῦν αὐτῇ καὶ τρια-

---

[1] διατελεῖ L.
[2] perterritis Lat. (reading ? δεδισσόμενος, Destinon).

---

[a] Cf. Numbers xiii. 22 (23) " Hebron was built seven years
before Zoan (= Tanis, LXX and Josephus, A. i. 170) in Egypt."
Tanis " was in any case built before 2000 B.C." (G. B.

the Idumaean army was then concentrated, and repaired to Simon. With him he made a compact, first to deliver up his own native place, after receiving an assurance on oath that he should always hold some post of honour ; he further undertook to assist in the subjugation of the whole of Idumaea. Being thereupon hospitably entertained by Simon and elated with dazzling promises, he, on his return to his own people, began by immensely exaggerating the strength of that general's army ; and then, by giving receptions to the officers and to the whole rank and file, in small parties, he instigated them to receive Simon and to surrender to him, without a struggle, the whole direction of affairs. While these negotiations were proceeding, he sent a message to Simon, summoning him to come and promising to disperse the Idumaeans—a promise which he duly fulfilled. For, on the approach of the army, he was the first to spring to the saddle and fly, followed by his corrupted accomplices. Panic-stricken the whole multitude, before a blow was struck, broke from the ranks and made off to their several homes.

(7) Simon having thus, beyond expectation, marched into Idumaea without bloodshed, first of all by a surprise attack captured the little town of Hebron, where he gained abundant booty and laid hands on vast supplies of corn. According to the statements of its inhabitants, Hebron is a town of greater antiquity not only than any other in the country, but even than Memphis in Egypt,[a] being reckoned to be

Simon takes Hebron.

Antiquities of Hebron.

Gray, *Internat. Crit. Comm. in loc.*) ; the foundation of Memphis goes back to the beginnings of Egyptian history. The antiquity of Hebron is undetermined, " but it certainly seems of pre-Israelitish origin " (*ibid.*).

531 κόσια ἔτη συναριθμεῖται. μυθεύουσι δὲ αὐτὴν
καὶ οἰκητήριον Ἀβράμου τοῦ Ἰουδαίων προγόνου
γεγονέναι μετὰ τὴν ἐκ τῆς Μεσοποταμίας ἀπανά-
στασιν, τούς τε παῖδας αὐτοῦ λέγουσι καταβῆναι
532 εἰς Αἴγυπτον ἔνθεν· ὧν καὶ τὰ μνημεῖα μέχρι νῦν
ἐν τῇδε τῇ πολίχνῃ δείκνυται, πάνυ καλῆς μαρ-
533 μάρου καὶ φιλοτίμως εἰργασμένα. δείκνυται δ'
ἀπὸ σταδίων ἓξ τοῦ ἄστεος τερέβινθος μεγίστη,
καὶ φασὶ τὸ δένδρον ἀπὸ τῆς κτίσεως μέχρι νῦν
534 διαμένειν. ἔνθεν ὁ Σίμων διὰ πάσης ἐχώρει τῆς
Ἰδουμαίας, οὐ μόνον κώμας καὶ πόλεις πορθῶν,
λυμαινόμενος δὲ καὶ τὴν χώραν, ὡς μηδὲ τῶν
ἐπιτηδείων ἐξαρκούντων πρὸς τὸ πλῆθος·[1] δίχα
γὰρ τῶν ὁπλιτῶν τέσσαρες αὐτῷ συνείποντο
535 μυριάδες. προσῆν δὲ ταῖς χρείαις ὠμότης τε
αὐτοῦ καὶ πρὸς τὸ γένος ὀργή, δι' ἃ μᾶλλον
536 ἐξερημοῦσθαι συνέβαινε τὴν Ἰδουμαίαν. καθάπερ δὲ [ὑπὸ] τῶν ἀκρίδων κατόπιν ὕλην ἔστιν
ἰδεῖν ἐψιλωμένην πᾶσαν, οὕτω τὸ κατὰ νώτου τῆς
537 Σίμωνος στρατιᾶς ἐρημία κατελείπετο· καὶ τὰ
μὲν ἐμπιπρῶντες τὰ δὲ κατασκάπτοντες, πᾶν δὲ
τὸ πεφυκὸς ἀνὰ τὴν χώραν ἢ συμπατοῦντες
ἠφάνιζον ἢ νεμόμενοι καὶ τὴν ἐνεργὸν ὑπὸ τῆς
πορείας σκληροτέραν ἐποίουν τῆς ἀκάρπου, καθ-

---

[1] ὡς μηδὲ . . πλῆθος in the mss. stand after μυριάδες: transposed here by Bekker.

---

[a] Gen. xiii. 18.
[b] Jacob's residence in Hebron is mentioned in Gen. xxxv.
27, xxxvii. 14. The historian, however, is dependent on local
tradition, and ignores the Biblical narrative.
[c] The cave of Machpelah, the burial-place of Sarah

two thousand three hundred years old. They further relate that it was there that Abraham, the progenitor of the Jews, took up his abode after his migration from Mesopotamia,[a] and from here that his posterity went down into Egypt.[b] Their tombs are shown in this little town to this day, of really fine marble and of exquisite workmanship.[c] At a distance of six furlongs from the town there is also shown a huge terebinth-tree, which is said to have stood there ever since the creation.[d] From Hebron Simon pursued his march through the whole of Idumaea, not con-fining his ravages to villages and towns, but making havoc also of the country, since provisions proved insufficient for such a multitude ; for, exclusive of his troops, he had forty thousand followers. But, besides his needs, his cruelty and animosity against the nation contributed to complete the devastation of Idumaea. Just as a forest in the wake of locusts may be seen stripped quite bare, so in the rear of Simon's army nothing remained but a desert. Some places they burnt, others they razed to the ground ; all vegetation throughout the country vanished, either trodden under foot or consumed ; while the tramp of their march rendered cultivated land harder than the barren soil. In short, nothing

Simon devastates Idumaea.

(Gen. xxiii), Abraham (xxv. 9), Isaac (xxxv. 27 ff.), and Jacob (l. 13) is believed to be below the present mosque ; Jewish, Christian, and Moslem traditions are in agreement as to the site. The wall surrounding the mosque has been ascribed to the Herodian period (Conder, *Tent Work in Palestine*, 239).

[d] The " oak " of Abraham (so LXX; Heb. "oaks " or " terebinths ") is mentioned in Gen. xiii. 18, xiv. 13, xviii. 1. In the 5th cent. A.D. it was called Τερέβινθος, and was the scene of an annual feast and fair, Sozomen, *H.E.* ii. 4 (Robertson Smith).

ὅλου τε εἰπεῖν, οὐδὲ σημεῖόν τι κατελείπετο τοῖς
πορθουμένοις[1] τοῦ γεγονέναι.

538 (8) Ταῦτα πάλιν τοὺς ζηλωτὰς ἐπήγειρεν, καὶ
φανερῶς μὲν ἀντιπαρατάξασθαι κατέδεισαν, προ-
λοχίσαντες δ᾽ ἐν ταῖς παρόδοις ἁρπάζουσι τοῦ
Σίμωνος τὴν γυναῖκα καὶ τῆς περὶ αὐτὴν θεραπείας
539 συχνούς. ἔπειτα ὡς αὐτὸν αἰχμαλωτισάμενοι τὸν
Σίμωνα γεγηθότες εἰς τὴν πόλιν ὑπέστρεψαν καὶ
ὅσον οὐδέπω προσεδόκων καταθέμενον τὰ ὅπλα
540 περὶ τῆς γυναικὸς ἱκετεύσειν. τὸν δὲ οὐκ ἔλεος
εἰσῆλθεν ἀλλ᾽ ὀργὴ περὶ τῆς ἡρπασμένης, καὶ
πρὸς τὸ τεῖχος τῶν Ἱεροσολύμων ἐλθὼν καθάπερ
τὰ τρωθέντα τῶν θηρίων, ἐπειδὴ τοὺς τρώσαντας
οὐ κατέλαβεν, ἐφ᾽ οὓς εὗρε τὸν θυμὸν ἠφίει.
541 ὅσοι γοῦν λαχανείας ἔνεκεν ἢ φρυγανισμοῦ προ-
εληλύθεσαν ἔξω πυλῶν, ἀνόπλους καὶ γέροντας
συλλαμβάνων ᾐκίζετο καὶ διέφθειρεν, δι᾽ ὑπερβολὴν ἀγανακτήσεως μονονουχὶ καὶ νεκρῶν γευό-
542 μενος τῶν σωμάτων. πολλοὺς δὲ καὶ χειρο-
κοπήσας εἰσέπεμπε καταπλήξασθαι τοὺς ἐχθροὺς
ἅμα καὶ διαστῆσαι[2] τὸν δῆμον ἐπιχειρῶν πρὸς
543 τοὺς αἰτίους. ἐντέταλτο δ᾽ αὐτοῖς λέγειν ὅτι
Σίμων θεὸν ὄμνυσι τὸν πάντων ἔφορον, εἰ μὴ
θᾶττον ἀποδώσουσιν αὐτῷ τὴν γυναῖκα, ῥήξας τὸ
τεῖχος τοιαῦτα διαθήσειν πάντας τοὺς κατὰ τὴν
πόλιν, μηδεμιᾶς φεισάμενος ἡλικίας μηδ᾽ ἀπὸ
544 τῶν ἀναιτίων διακρίνας τοὺς αἰτίους. τούτοις οὐ
μόνον ὁ δῆμος ἀλλὰ καὶ οἱ ζηλωταὶ καταπλαγέντες ἀποπέμπουσιν αὐτῷ τὴν γυναῖκα· καὶ τότε
μὲν ἐκμειλιχθεὶς ὀλίγον ἀνεπαύσατο τοῦ συνεχοῦς
φόνου.

[1] + τούτοις PA.   [2] διαστασιάσαι L.

160

touched by their ravages left any sign of its having ever existed.

(8) These proceedings roused the Zealots anew ; and, though afraid to meet Simon in open battle, they laid ambushes in the passes and captured his wife and a large number of her attendants. Then, as if their prisoner had been Simon himself, they returned triumphant to the city, expecting that he would instantly lay down his arms and come to sue for his wife. It was, however, no tender feelings but indignation which her capture aroused in his breast, and advancing to the walls of Jerusalem like some wounded beast, when it has failed to catch its tormentors, he vented his wrath upon all whom he met. Any who had ventured outside the gates to gather herbs or fuel, unarmed and aged individuals, he seized, tortured and killed, in the extravagance of his rage almost gnawing their very corpses.[a] Many others he sent back into the city with their hands cut off, with the twofold object of intimidating his foes and of causing the people to rise against the responsible parties. These persons received injunctions to say that Simon had sworn by God, the overseer of all, that unless they restored his wife to him forthwith, he would break down the wall and inflict similar punishment on every soul in the city, sparing neither young nor old, and making no distinction between guilty and innocent. These threats so terrified not only the people but even the Zealots, that they sent him back his wife ; whereat, momentarily mollified, he paused for a while from his ceaseless slaughter.

The Zealots take Simon's wife prisoner

Simon by threats to Jerusalem recovers her.

---

[a] A similar " hyperbole " (the historian supplies the word !) occurs in vi. 373.

JOSEPHUS

545 (9) Οὐ μόνον δὲ κατὰ τὴν Ἰουδαίαν στάσις ἦν καὶ πόλεμος ἐμφύλιος, ἀλλὰ κἀπὶ τῆς Ἰταλίας.

546 ἀνήρητο μὲν γὰρ κατὰ μέσην τὴν Ῥωμαίων ἀγορὰν Γάλβας, ἀποδεδειγμένος δὲ αὐτοκράτωρ Ὄθων ἐπολέμει Οὐιτελλίῳ βασιλειῶντι· τοῦτον

547 γὰρ ᾕρητο τὰ κατὰ Γερμανίαν τάγματα. καὶ γενομένης συμβολῆς κατὰ Φρηγδίακον[1] τῆς Γαλατίας πρός τε Οὐάλεντα καὶ Καικίνναν[2] τοὺς Οὐιτελλίου στρατηγούς, τῇ πρώτῃ μὲν ἡμέρᾳ περιῆν Ὄθων, τῇ δὲ δευτέρᾳ τὸ Οὐιτελλίου

548 στρατιωτικόν· καὶ πολλοῦ φόνου γενομένου διεχρήσατο μὲν Ὄθων αὐτὸν ἐν Βριξέλλῳ[3] τὴν ἧτταν πυθόμενος, ἡμέρας δύο καὶ τρεῖς μῆνας

549 κρατήσας τῶν πραγμάτων, προσεχώρησε δὲ τοῖς Οὐιτελλίου στρατηγοῖς ἡ στρατιά, καὶ κατέβαινεν αὐτὸς εἰς τὴν Ῥώμην μετὰ τῆς δυνάμεως.

550 Ἐν δὲ τούτῳ καὶ Οὐεσπασιανὸς ἀναστὰς ἐκ τῆς Καισαρείας πέμπτῃ Δαισίου μηνὸς ὥρμησεν ἐπὶ τὰ μηδέπω κατεστραμμένα τῶν τῆς Ἰουδαίας

551 χωρίων. ἀναβὰς δ' εἰς τὴν ὀρεινὴν αἱρεῖ δύο τοπαρχίας, τήν τε Γοφνιτικὴν καὶ τὴν Ἀκραβετηνὴν καλουμένην, μεθ' ἃς Βήθηλά[4] τε καὶ Ἐφραὶμ πολίχνια, οἷς φρουροὺς ἐγκαταστήσας μέχρι Ἱεροσολύμων ἱππάζετο· φθορὰ δ' ἦν πολλῶν καταλαμβανομένων καὶ συχνοὺς ἠχμαλωτίζετο.

---

[1] Βηδριακὸν Hudson.   [2] ed. pr.: Κίννα(ν) mss.
[3] ed. pr.: Βριξέμῳ mss.
[4] VRC: Βαίθηλά M: Βήθηγά the rest.

---

[a] §§ 494, 499.
[b] A small town in Cisalpine Gaul, between Verona and

162

(9) Sedition and civil war were not, however, confined to Judaea, but were rampant also in Italy.
For Galba had been murdered in the midst of the
Roman forum,[a] and Otho, being proclaimed emperor,
was at war with Vitellius, now aspiring to imperial
sovereignty, having been elected by the legions in
Germany. In the battle fought at Bedriacum [b] in
Gaul against Valens and Caecinna,[c] the generals of
Vitellius, on the first day Otho had the advantage,
but on the second the troops of Vitellius ; and such
was the slaughter that Otho put an end to himself
at Brixellum,[d] where he learnt of his defeat, having
held the reins of government for three months and
two days.[e] His army went over to the generals of
Vitellius, who now descended in person upon Rome
with his entire force.

Meanwhile, Vespasian had moved from Caesarea
on the fifth of the month Daesius and advanced
against those districts of Judaea which had not yet
been reduced. Ascending into the hill country he
subdued two provinces, those which take their names
from Gophna [f] and Acrabetta [g] ; next he captured
the small towns of Bethela [h] and Ephraim [i] ; leaving
garrisons in these, he then rode with his cavalry up
to the walls of Jerusalem, killing many of those
encountered on the route, and taking numerous

Civil war in Italy.

Galba slain. 15 January A.D. 69.

Otho's death. 17 April A.D. 69.

Vitellius.

Vespasian again invades Judaea (c. 23) June A.D. 68,

Cremona ; the Vitellians in their turn were defeated soon
after in the same neighbourhood, §§ 634 ff. Tacitus, *Hist.* ii.
41-49, describes the battle and the death of Otho.

  [c] Fabius Valens and A. Caecina Alienus.
  [d] *Brescello*, about 12 miles N.E. of Parma.
  [e] From January 15 to April 17, 69.
  [f] Some 12 miles due N. of Jerusalem.
  [g] In the N.E. corner of Judaea.
  [h] Bethel (*Beitin*) a few miles S.E. of Gophna.
  [i] *et-Taiyibeh* N.E. of Bethel.

552 Κερεάλιος δ' αὐτῷ τῶν ἡγεμόνων, μοῖραν ἱππέων
καὶ πεζῶν ἀναλαβών, τὴν ἄνω καλουμένην Ἰδουμαίαν ἐπόρθει, καὶ Κάφεθρα¹ μὲν ψευδοπολίχνιον
ἐξ ἐφόδου λαβὼν ἐμπίπρησιν, ἑτέραν δὲ καλου-
553 μένην Καφαραβὶν² προσβαλὼν ἐπολιόρκει. πάνυ
δ' ἦν ἰσχυρὸν τὸ τεῖχος, καὶ τρίψεσθαι προσ-
δοκῶντι πλείω χρόνον αἰφνιδίως ἀνοίγουσιν οἱ
ἔνδον τὰς πύλας καὶ μεθ' ἱκετηριῶν προελθόντες
554 ἑαυτοὺς παρέδοσαν. Κερεάλιος δὲ τούτους παραστησάμενος ἐπὶ Χεβρὼν ἑτέρας πόλεως ἀρχαιο-
τάτης ἐχώρει· κεῖται δ', ὡς ἔφην, αὕτη κατὰ τὴν
ὀρεινὴν οὐ πόρρω Ἱεροσολύμων· βιασάμενος δὲ τὰς
εἰσόδους τὸ μὲν ἐγκαταλειφθὲν πλῆθος ἡβηδὸν ἀναιρεῖ,
555 τὸ δ' ἄστυ καταπίμπρησι. καὶ πάντων ἤδη κεχειρωμένων πλὴν Ἡρωδείου καὶ Μασάδας καὶ Μαχαιροῦντος, ταῦτα δ' ὑπὸ τῶν λῃστῶν κατείληπτο, σκοπὸς
ἤδη τὰ Ἱεροσόλυμα προύκειτο Ῥωμαίοις.
556 (10) Ὁ δὲ Σίμων ὡς ἐρρύσατο παρὰ τῶν
ζηλωτῶν τὴν γυναῖκα, πάλιν ἐπὶ τὰ λείψανα τῆς
Ἰδουμαίας ὑπέστρεψεν, καὶ περιελαύνων πανταχόθεν τὸ ἔθνος εἰς Ἱεροσόλυμα τοὺς πολλοὺς
557 φεύγειν συνηνάγκασεν. εἵπετο δὲ καὶ αὐτὸς ἐπὶ
τὴν πόλιν καὶ κυκλωσάμενος αὖθις τὸ τεῖχος
ὅντινα λάβοι τῶν προϊόντων κατὰ τὴν χώραν
558 ἐργατῶν διέφθειρεν. ἦν δὲ τῷ δήμῳ Σίμων μὲν
ἔξωθεν Ῥωμαίων φοβερώτερος, οἱ ζηλωταὶ δ'
ἔνδον ἑκατέρων χαλεπώτεροι, κἂν τούτοις ἐπινοίᾳ
κακῶν καὶ τόλμῃ τὸ σύνταγμα τῶν Γαλιλαίων

---

¹ Hudson : Καφαίορα L : further corruption in other mss.
² Χαφαραβεὶν· L : Χαραβὶν most mss.

ᵃ Sextus Cerealius Vetilianus, legate of the 5th legion,
who had defeated the Samaritans, iii. 310 ff.

prisoners. Furthermore, Cerealius,[a] one of his officers, with a detachment of horse and foot, laid waste what is known as upper Idumaea; here he carried at the first assault the petty town (as it falsely calls itself) of Caphethra[b] and burnt it to the ground, and then attacked and proceeded to besiege another town called Capharabis.[b] The wall of this place was exceptionally strong and he was anticipating a prolonged delay, when the inhabitants suddenly opened their gates and, approaching him with olive-branches as suppliants, surrendered. Cerealius, after their capitulation, advanced on Hebron, another city and one of great antiquity, situated, as I have said,[c] in the hill country not far[d] from Jerusalem; having forced the approaches he slew all whom he found there, young or old, and burnt down the town. Every fortress being now subdued except Herodion, Masada, and Machaerus, which were held by the brigands, Jerusalem was henceforth the one objective before the Romans.

and Cerealius Idumaea.

(10) Simon,[e] having now recovered his wife from the Zealots, returned once more to the relics of Idumaea and, harassing every quarter of the nation, drove multitudes to flee to Jerusalem. Thither he followed them himself, and again surrounding the wall killed any of the labouring class whom he caught going out into the country. The citizens thus found Simon without the walls a greater terror than the Romans, and the Zealots within more oppressive than either; while among the latter for mischievous ingenuity and audacity none surpassed the Galilaean contingent,

Jerusalem at the mercy of Simon without the walls

and the drunken horde of Zealots within.

---

[b] Unidentified. [c] *Cf.* § 530.
[d] Some 18 miles as the crow flies.
[e] Resuming the narrative from § 544.

559 διέφερεν[1]· τόν τε γὰρ Ἰωάννην παρήγαγον εἰς
ἰσχὺν οὗτοι, κἀκεῖνος αὐτοὺς ἐξ ἧς περιεποίησαν[2]
δυναστείας ἠμείβετο, πάντα ἐπιτρέπων δρᾶν ὧν
560 ἕκαστος ἐπεθύμει. πόθοι δ᾽ ἦσαν ἁρπαγῆς ἀ-
πλήρωτοι καὶ τῶν πλουσίων οἴκων ἔρευνα, φόνος
561 τε ἀνδρῶν καὶ γυναικῶν ὕβρεις ἐπαίζοντο, μεθ᾽
αἵματός τε τὰ συληθέντα κατέπινον καὶ μετ᾽
ἀδείας ἐνεθηλυπάθουν τῷ κόρῳ, κόμας συνθετι-
ζόμενοι καὶ γυναικείας ἐσθῆτας ἀναλαμβάνοντες,
καταντλούμενοι δὲ μύροις καὶ πρὸς εὐπρέπειαν
562 ὑπογράφοντες ὀφθαλμούς. οὐ μόνον δὲ κόσμον,
ἀλλὰ καὶ πάθη γυναικῶν ἐμιμοῦντο καὶ δι᾽ ὑπερβολὴν[3] ἀσελγείας ἀθεμίτους ἐπενόησαν ἔρωτας·
ἐνηλινδοῦντο δ᾽ ὡς πορνείῳ τῇ πόλει καὶ πᾶσαν
563 ἀκαθάρτοις ἐμίαναν ἔργοις. γυναικιζόμενοι δὲ
τὰς ὄψεις ἐφόνων ταῖς δεξιαῖς, θρυπτόμενοί τε
τοῖς βαδίσμασιν ἐπιόντες ἐξαπίνης ἐγίνοντο πολε-
μισταί, τά τε ξίφη προφέροντες ἀπὸ τῶν βε-
βαμμένων[4] χλανιδίων τὸν προστυχόντα διήλαυνον.
564 τοὺς ἀποδιδράσκοντας δὲ Ἰωάννην Σίμων φονικώ-
τερον ἐξεδέχετο, καὶ διαφυγών τις τὸν ἐντὸς
τείχους τύραννον ὑπὸ τοῦ πρὸ πυλῶν διεφθείρετο.
565 πᾶσα δὲ φυγῆς ὁδὸς τοῖς αὐτομολεῖν πρὸς Ῥωμαίους βουλομένοις ἀπεκέκοπτο.
566 (11) Διεστασίαζετο δὲ πρὸς τὸν Ἰωάννην ἡ
δύναμις, καὶ πᾶν ὅσον ἦν Ἰδουμαίων[5] ἐν αὐτῇ
χωρισθὲν ἐπεχείρει τῷ τυράννῳ φθόνῳ τε τῆς
567 ἰσχύος αὐτοῦ καὶ μίσει τῆς ὠμότητος. συμ-

---

[1] διέφθειρε(ν) mss.
[2] PAM : περιεποιήσαντο the rest : -ήσατο Lat.
[3] + ἀσωτίας P.
[4] L Exc. Lat. : περιβεβλημένων the rest.
[5] Ἰδουμαῖον ALR Exc.

for it was they who had promoted John to power, and he from the position of authority which they had won for him requited them by allowing every one to do whatever he desired. With an insatiable lust for loot, they ransacked the houses of the wealthy; the murder of men and the violation of women were their sport; they caroused on their spoils, with blood to wash them down,[a] and from mere satiety unscrupulously indulged in effeminate practices, plaiting their hair and attiring themselves in women's apparel, drenching themselves with perfumes and painting their eyelids to enhance their beauty. And not only did they imitate the dress, but also the passions[b] of women, devising in their excess of lasciviousness unlawful pleasures and wallowing as in a brothel in the city, which they polluted from end to end with their foul deeds. Yet, while they wore women's faces, their hands were murderous, and approaching with mincing steps they would suddenly become warriors and whipping out their swords from under their dyed mantles transfix whomsoever they met. Any who fled from John had a yet bloodier reception from Simon, and he who escaped the tyrant within the walls was slain by the other without the gates. Every avenue of escape was thus cut off from those desirous to desert to the Romans.

(11) But John's army now mutinied; and all the Idumaeans[c] within it broke away and made an attack on the tyrant, as much from envy of his power as from hatred of his cruelty. In the ensuing engage-

Sedition among the Zealots. John of Gischala is deserted by his Idumaean allies,

---

[a] Cf. vi. 372 ἐσύλων καὶ . . . τροφὴν ἁρπάζοντες αἵματι πεφυρμένην κατέπινον.   [b] or "experiences."

[c] It appears from this that some of the Idumaeans still remained in Jerusalem when the main body withdrew (§ 353).

βαλόντες δὲ ἀναιροῦσί τε πολλοὺς τῶν ζηλωτῶν
καὶ συνελαύνουσι τοὺς λοιποὺς εἰς τὴν βασιλικὴν
αὐλὴν κατασκευασθεῖσαν ὑπὸ Γραπτῆς· συγγενὴς
δ' ἦν αὕτη τοῦ τῶν Ἀδιαβηνῶν βασιλέως Ἰζᾶ·
568 συνεισπίπτουσι δ' οἱ Ἰδουμαῖοι, κἀκεῖθεν εἰς τὸ
ἱερὸν ἐξώσαντες[1] τοὺς ζηλωτὰς ἐφ' ἁρπαγὴν ἐτρά-
569 ποντο τῶν Ἰωάννου χρημάτων· κατὰ γὰρ τὴν
προειρημένην αὐλὴν αὐτός τε ᾤκει[2] καὶ τὰ λάφυρα
570 τῆς τυραννίδος κατέθετο. ἐν δὲ τούτῳ τὸ κατὰ
τὴν πόλιν ἐσκεδασμένον πλῆθος τῶν ζηλωτῶν εἰς
τὸ ἱερὸν πρὸς τοὺς διαπεφευγότας ἠθροίσθη, καὶ
κατάγειν αὐτοὺς παρεσκευάσατο Ἰωάννης ἐπί τε
571 τὸν δῆμον καὶ τοὺς Ἰδουμαίους. τοῖς δὲ οὐχ
οὕτω τὴν ἔφοδον αὐτῶν καταδεῖσαι παρέστη
μαχιμωτέροις οὖσιν ὡς τὴν ἀπόνοιαν, μὴ νύκτωρ
ἐκ τοῦ ἱεροῦ παρεισδύντες αὐτούς τε διαφθείρωσι
572 καὶ τὸ ἄστυ καταπιμπρῶσι. συνελθόντες οὖν
μετὰ τῶν ἀρχιερέων ἐβουλεύοντο, τίνα χρὴ τρόπον
573 φυλάξασθαι τὴν ἐπίθεσιν. θεὸς δ' ἄρα τὰς γνώμας
αὐτῶν εἰς κακὸν ἔτρεψε, καὶ χαλεπώτερον ἀπωλείας ἐπενόησαν τὸ πρὸς σωτηρίαν φάρμακον·
ἵνα γοῦν καταλύσωσιν Ἰωάννην, ἔκριναν δέχεσθαι
Σίμωνα καὶ μεθ' ἱκετηριῶν δεύτερον εἰσαγαγεῖν
574 ἑαυτοῖς τύραννον. ἐπεραίνετο δ' ἡ βουλή, καὶ
τὸν ἀρχιερέα Ματθίαν πέμψαντες ἐδέοντο Σίμωνος

---

[1] περιώσαντες C : περιεξώσαντες L.
[2] Destinon from Lat.: ὢν (ἦν C) ἐκεῖ MSS.

---

[a] Elsewhere (*B.* v. 147, vi. 356 ; *A.* xx. 17, etc.) called
Izates, which should perhaps be read here. The story of the
conversion to Judaism of Helena, Queen of Adiabene (in the
upper Tigris region), and of her son Izates is told in full in
A. xx. 17 ff. This royal family adorned Jerusalem with

ment they killed many of the Zealots and drove the
remainder into the palace built by Grapte, a relative
of Izas,[a] king of Adiabene. Rushing in along with
them the Idumaeans chased them thence into the
Temple, and then proceeded to plunder John's
treasures ; he having made this palace his residence
and the repository for the spoils of his tyranny.
Meanwhile, the rank and file of the Zealots who
were scattered about the city mustered to the
fugitives in the Temple, and John prepared to lead
them down against the people and the Idumaeans.
The latter, as the better soldiers, had less fear of
their attack than of their frenzy, lest they should
steal out of the temple by night and murder them
and burn down the town. They accordingly held a
meeting with the chief priests and deliberated how
they should guard against the assault. But God,
as events proved, perverted their judgement, and
they devised for their salvation a remedy more
disastrous than destruction : in other words, in order
to overthrow John, they decided to admit Simon *who invite*
and with suppliant appeals to introduce a second *Simon into*
tyrant over their heads. This resolution was carried *to oppose*
into effect, and the high priest Matthias [b] was *him.*
deputed to beg the Simon of whom they had such

buildings. We hear of her palace within the city (v. 253),
and of the pyramidal tombs 3 furlongs outside, in which she
and Izates were interred (*A.* xx. 95 ; *B.* v. 55, 119, 147) ; also
of the palace of another son, Monobazus (*B.* v. 252). Of
Grapte we hear no more. Queen Helena, like Paul and
Barnabas, brought relief to Jerusalem during the famine
under Claudius (*A.* xx. 51 ff.).

[b] Matthias, son of Boethus, belonging to one of the high-
priestly families (ἐκ τῶν ἀρχιερέων, *B.* v. 527 ; *cf.* iv. 148),
was afterwards, with his three sons, murdered by Simon
(v. 527 ff.).

εἰσελθεῖν ὃν πολλὰ¹ ἔδεισαν· συμπαρεκάλουν δ'
οἱ ἐκ τῶν Ἱεροσολύμων τοὺς ζηλωτὰς φεύγοντες
575 πόθῳ τῶν οἴκων καὶ τῶν κτημάτων. ὁ δ' αὐτοῖς
ὑπερηφάνως κατανεύσας τὸ δεσπόζειν εἰσέρχεται
μὲν ὡς ἀπαλλάξων τῶν ζηλωτῶν τὴν πόλιν,
σωτὴρ ὑπὸ τοῦ δήμου καὶ κηδεμὼν εὐφημούμενος,
576 παρελθὼν δὲ μετὰ τῆς δυνάμεως ἐσκόπει τὰ περὶ
τῆς ἑαυτοῦ δυναστείας καὶ τοὺς καλέσαντας οὐχ
ἧττον ἐχθροὺς ἐνόμιζεν ἢ καθ' ὧν ἐκέκλητο.
577 (12) Σίμων μὲν οὕτως ἐνιαυτῷ τρίτῳ τοῦ πολέμου Ξανθικῷ μηνὶ Ἱεροσολύμων ἐγκρατὴς γίνεται·
Ἰωάννης δὲ καὶ τὸ τῶν ζηλωτῶν πλῆθος εἰργό-
μενοι τῶν ἐξόδων τοῦ ἱεροῦ καὶ τὰ² τῆς πόλεως
ἀπολωλεκότες, παραχρῆμα γὰρ τὰ ἐκείνων οἱ
περὶ τὸν Σίμωνα διήρπασαν, ἐν ἀπόρῳ τὴν
578 σωτηρίαν εἶχον. προσέβαλλε δὲ τῷ ἱερῷ Σίμων
τοῦ δήμου βοηθοῦντος, κἀκεῖνοι καταστάντες ἐπὶ
τῶν στοῶν καὶ τῶν ἐπάλξεων ἠμύνοντο τὰς
579 προσβολάς. συχνοὶ δ' ἔπιπτον τῶν περὶ Σίμωνα
καὶ πολλοὶ τραυματίαι κατεφέροντο· ῥᾳδίως γὰρ
ἐξ ὑπερδεξίου τὰς βολὰς οἱ ζηλωταὶ καὶ οὐκ
580 ἀστόχους ἐποιοῦντο. πλεονεκτοῦντες δὲ τῷ τόπῳ
καὶ πύργους ἔτι προσκατεσκεύασαν τέσσαρας
μεγίστους, ὡς ἀφ' ὑψηλοτέρων ποιοῦντο τὰς
581 ἀφέσεις, τὸν μὲν κατὰ τὴν ἀνατολικὴν καὶ βόρειον
γωνίαν, τὸν δὲ τοῦ ξυστοῦ καθύπερθεν, τὸν δὲ
τρίτον κατὰ γωνίαν ἄλλην ἀντικρὺ τῆς κάτω
582 πόλεως· ὁ δὲ λοιπὸς ὑπὲρ τὴν κορυφὴν κατεσκεύαστο τῶν παστοφορίων, ἔνθα τῶν ἱερέων εἰς

---

¹ πολλάκις L Lat.   ² τάκ Bekker.

ᵃ On the W. side of the Temple ; the Xystus lay in or just
above the Tyropoeon valley (B. ii. 344 n.).

horror to enter the city ; the request was backed
by natives of Jerusalem who sought refuge from the
Zealots and yearned for their homes and possessions.
Haughtily consenting to be their master, he entered
as one who was to rid the city of the Zealots, acclaimed by the people as their saviour and protector ;
but, once admitted with his forces, his sole concern
was to secure his own authority, and he regarded
the men who had invited him as no less his enemies
than those whom he had been invited to oppose.

(12) Thus did Simon, in the third year of the war, Simon
in the month Xanthicus, become master of Jerusalem; master of
Jerusalem
while John and the Zealots, being debarred from all April–May
egress from the Temple, and having lost their posses- A.D. 69.
sions in the city—for these had been instantly
plundered by Simon's party—began to despair of
deliverance. Simon now attacked the Temple, with Simon
attacks the
the support of the citizens ; their adversaries posting Zealots
themselves on the porticoes and battlements and confined in
beating off their assaults. The casualties in Simon's the temple.
ranks were numerous, both in dead and wounded ;
for the Zealots from their higher ground could maintain an easy and well-directed fire. They, moreover,
improved this advantage of position by erecting
four huge towers in order to increase the elevation
from which their missiles were discharged : one at
the north-east corner, the second above the Xystus,[a]
the third at another corner opposite the lower town.[b]
The last was erected above the roof of the priests'
chambers,[c] at the point where it was the custom for

[b] At the S.W. angle of the Temple.
[c] Small chambers, for the use of the priests and storage of
utensils, ranged in stories round three sides of the inner
court.

ἐξ ἔθους ἱστάμενος ἑκάστην ἑβδομάδα εἰσιοῦσαν
προεσήμαινε σάλπιγγι δείλης καὶ τελεσθεῖσαν
αὖθις περὶ ἑσπέραν, ὅτε μὲν ἀνέργειαν τῷ λαῷ
583 καταγγέλλων, ὅτε δ᾽ ἔργων ἔχεσθαι. διέστησαν
δ᾽ ἐπὶ τῶν πύργων ὀξυβελεῖς τε καὶ λιθοβόλους
584 μηχανὰς τούς τε τοξότας καὶ σφενδονήτας. ἔνθα
δὴ τὰς μὲν προσβολὰς ὀκνηροτέρας ἐποιεῖτο ὁ
Σίμων, μαλακιζομένων αὐτῷ τῶν πλειόνων, ἀντ-
εῖχε δ᾽ ὅμως περιουσίᾳ δυνάμεως· τὰ δ᾽ ἀπὸ
τῶν ὀργάνων βέλη πορρωτέρω φερόμενα πολλοὺς
τῶν μαχομένων ἀνήρει.

585   (x. 1) Κατὰ δὲ τὸν αὐτὸν καιρὸν περιέσχε καὶ
586 τὴν Ῥώμην πάθη χαλεπά. παρῆν μὲν γὰρ ἀπὸ
Γερμανίας Οὐιτέλλιος ἅμα τῷ στρατιωτικῷ πολὺ
πλῆθος ἐπισυρόμενος ἕτερον, μὴ χωρούμενος δὲ
τοῖς ἀποδεδειγμένοις εἰς τοὺς στρατιώτας περιβόλοις ὅλην ἐποιήσατο τὴν Ῥώμην στρατόπεδον
587 καὶ πᾶσαν οἰκίαν ὁπλιτῶν ἐπλήρωσεν. οἱ δ᾽
ἀήθεσιν ὀφθαλμοῖς τὸν Ῥωμαίων πλοῦτον θεασά-
μενοι καὶ περιλαμφθέντες πάντοθεν ἀργύρῳ τε
καὶ χρυσῷ τὰς ἐπιθυμίας μόλις κατεῖχον, ὥστε
μὴ ἐφ᾽ ἁρπαγὰς τρέπεσθαί τε καὶ τοὺς ἐμποδὼν
γινομένους ἀναιρεῖν. καὶ τὰ μὲν κατὰ τὴν Ἰταλίαν
ἐν τούτοις ἦν.
588   (2) Οὐεσπασιανὸς δὲ ὡς τὰ πλησίον Ἱεροσολύμων καταστρεψάμενος ὑπέστρεψεν εἰς Καισά-

---

[a] *Cf.* Talmud Bab. *Sukkah* v. 5 (trans. Greenup, S.P.C.K.,
1925) " On the eve of the Sabbath they sounded (the trumpets)
six times in addition [to the 21 daily blasts]—3 to cause the
people to cease from work, and 3 to mark the separation
between the sacred and the secular day " ; the custom is also

one of the priests to stand and to give notice, by sound of trumpet, in the afternoon of the approach, and on the following evening of the close, of every seventh day, announcing to the people the respective hours for ceasing work and for resuming their labours.[a] Along these towers they posted catapults and *ballistae*, together with archers and slingers. Thenceforth Simon's attacks grew less strenuous, as most of his men lost heart; still by his superiority in numbers he was able to hold his ground, although the missiles from the engines with their longer range killed many of the combatants.

Custom of announcing the Sabbath by sound of trumpet.

(x. 1) About this very time [b] Rome also was beset by heavy calamities. Vitellius had arrived from Germany, dragging in the wake of his army a vast motley crowd besides; and not finding room enough in the quarters assigned to the troops, he converted the whole of Rome into a camp and filled every house with armed men. These, beholding with unaccustomed eyes the wealth of the Romans and surrounded on every side by the glitter of silver and gold, could scarce restrain their avarice or refrain from plundering right and left and slaughtering any who obstructed them.[c] Such was the condition of affairs in Italy.

Vitellius converts Rome into a camp.

(2) Vespasian,[d] after reducing the whole of the environs of Jerusalem, returned to Caesarea, where

Vespasian is exasperated at the news of the accession of Vitellius.

mentioned in T.B. *Shabbath* 35 b, Talm. Jer. *Shabbath*, xvii. 16 a.   [b] Resuming the narrative from § 549.

[c] The entry of Vitellius into Rome is described by Tacitus, *Hist.* ii. 89 (hardly prevented by his friends from marching in arms into Rome as into a captured city); Suetonius, *Vitell.* 11, represents him as entering in arms.

[d] Resuming the narrative from § 555.

ρειαν, ἀκούει τὰς κατὰ τὴν Ῥώμην ταραχὰς καὶ
589 Οὐιτέλλιον αὐτοκράτορα. τοῦτο αὐτόν, καίπερ
ἄρχεσθαι καθάπερ ἄρχειν καλῶς ἐπιστάμενον, εἰς
ἀγανάκτησιν προήγαγεν, καὶ τὸν μὲν ὡς ἐρήμου
καταμανέντα τῆς ἡγεμονίας ἠδόξει δεσπότην,
590 περιαλγήσας δὲ τῷ πάθει καρτερεῖν τὴν βάσανον
οὐχ οἷός τε ἦν καὶ τῆς πατρίδος πορθουμένης
591 ἑτέροις προσευσχολεῖν πολέμοις. ἀλλ᾽ ὅσον ὁ θυμὸς
ἤπειγεν ἐπὶ τὴν ἄμυναν, τοσοῦτον εἶργεν ἔννοια τοῦ
διαστήματος· πολλὰ γὰρ ⟨ἂν⟩[1] φθάσαι πανουργή-
σασαν[2] τὴν τύχην πρὶν αὐτὸν εἰς τὴν Ἰταλίαν
περαιωθῆναι, καὶ ταῦτα χειμῶνος ὥρα πλέοντα,
⟨καὶ⟩[3] σφαδάζουσαν ἤδη κατεῖχεν τὴν ὀργήν.
592 (3) Συνιόντες δὲ οἵ τε ἡγεμόνες καὶ στρατιῶται
καθ᾽ ἑταιρίαν φανερῶς ἤδη μεταβολὴν ἐβουλεύοντο καὶ διαγανακτοῦντες ἐβόων, ὡς οἱ μὲν
ἐπὶ τῆς Ῥώμης στρατιῶται τρυφῶντες καὶ μηδ᾽
ἀκούειν πολέμου φήμην ὑπομένοντες διαχειρο-
τονοῦσιν οἷς βούλονται τὴν ἡγεμονίαν καὶ πρὸς
ἐλπίδα λημμάτων ἀποδεικνύουσιν αὐτοκράτορας,
593 αὐτοὶ δὲ διὰ τοσούτων κεχωρηκότες πόνων καὶ
γηρῶντες ὑπὸ τοῖς κράνεσιν ἑτέροις χαρίζονται
τὴν ἐξουσίαν, καὶ ταῦτα τὸν ἀξιώτερον ἄρχειν
594 παρ᾽ αὐτοῖς ἔχοντες. ᾧ τίνα δικαιοτέραν ποτὲ
τῆς εἰς αὐτοὺς εὐνοίας ἀποδώσειν ἀμοιβήν, εἰ
τὴν νῦν καταπροοῖντο; τοσούτῳ δ᾽ εἶναι Οὐεσπασιανὸν ἡγεμονεύειν Οὐιτελλίου δικαιότερον, ὅσῳ
595 καὶ αὐτοὺς τῶν ἐκεῖνον ἀποδειξάντων· οὐ γὰρ
δὴ μικροτέρους τῶν ἀπὸ Γερμανίας διενηνοχέναι

---

[1] ins. Herwerden.
[2] nova facere (=καινουργήσασαν) Lat.: καλλιουργήσασαν L.
[3] ins. Destinon.

he heard of the disturbances in Rome and that
Vitellius was emperor. Though he knew full as well
how to obey as how to command, this news roused
his indignation : he scorned to own as master one
who laid mad hands upon the empire as though it
were forlorn, and such was his agony at this calamity [a]
that he could not endure the torture or, while his
own country was being devastated, devote attention
to other wars. But, much as anger impelled him
to avenge her, the thought of the distance no less
deterred him : for fortune might forestall him
by many a knavish trick before he could cross to
Italy, especially as he must sail in the winter season.
This reflection checked what was now becoming a
paroxysm of wrath.

(3) However, his officers and men, in friendly
gatherings, were already frankly discussing a revolution. " Those soldiers in Rome," they indignantly
exclaimed, " now living in luxury, who cannot bear
to hear even a rumour of war, are electing whom
they choose to the sovereignty and in hope of lucre
creating emperors ; whilst we, who have undergone
such numerous toils and are growing grey beneath
our helmets, are giving up this privilege to others,
when all the time we have among us one more
worthy of the government. What juster return
can we ever render him for his kindness to us, if we
fling away the present opportunity ? Vespasian's
claim to the empire is as far superior to that of
Vitellius, as are we to the electors of that emperor ;
for, surely, we have waged wars no less arduous than

His
indignant
soldiers
take
matters into
their own
hands

---

[a] The phrase, περιαλγήσας τῷ πάθει comes from Thuc.
iv. 14.

πολέμους οὐδὲ τῶν ἐκεῖθεν καταγαγόντων τὸν
596 τύραννον ἡττῆσθαι τοῖς ὅπλοις. ἀγῶνος ἐνδεήσειν
δὲ οὐδέν· οὐ γὰρ τὴν σύγκλητον ἢ τὸν Ῥωμαίων
δῆμον ἀνέξεσθαι τῆς Οὐιτελλίου λαγνείας ἀντὶ τῆς
Οὐεσπασιανοῦ σωφροσύνης, οὐδ' ἀντὶ μὲν ἡγεμόνος ἀγαθοῦ τύραννον ὠμότατον, ἄπαιδα[1] δὲ
ἀντὶ πατρὸς αἱρήσεσθαι προστάτην· μέγιστον γὰρ
δὴ πρὸς ἀσφάλειαν εἰρήνης εἶναι τὰς γνησίους
597 τῶν βασιλέων διαδοχάς.[2] εἴτε οὖν ἐμπειρίᾳ γήρως
προσήκει τὸ ἄρχειν, Οὐεσπασιανὸν αὐτοὺς ἔχειν,
εἴτε νεότητος ἀλκῇ, Τίτον· κραθήσεσθαι γὰρ τῆς
598 παρ' ἀμφοῖν ἡλικίας τὸ ὠφέλιμον. χορηγήσειν δ'
οὐ μόνον αὐτοὶ[3] τὴν ἰσχὺν τοῖς ἀποδειχθεῖσι τρία
τάγματα καὶ τὰς παρὰ τῶν βασιλέων συμμαχίας
ἔχοντες, συνεργήσειν δὲ[4] τά τε πρὸς ἕω πάντα καὶ
τῆς Εὐρώπης ὅσα τῶν ἀπὸ Οὐιτελλίου φόβων
κεχώρισται, καὶ τοὺς ἐπὶ τῆς Ἰταλίας δὲ συμμάχους, ἀδελφὸν Οὐεσπασιανοῦ καὶ παῖδα ἕτερον,
599 ὧν τῷ μὲν προσθήσεσθαι πολλοὺς τῶν ἐν ἀξιώματι
νέων, τὸν δὲ καὶ τὴν τῆς πόλεως φυλακὴν πεπιστεῦσθαι, μέρος οὐκ ὀλίγον εἰς ἐπιβολὴν[5] ἡγεμονίας.
600 καθόλου τε ἂν βραδύνωσιν αὐτοί, τάχα τὴν σύγκλητον ἀποδείξειν τὸν ὑπὸ τῶν συγγεγηρακότων[6]
στρατιωτῶν ἀτιμούμενον.

601 (4) Τοιαῦτα κατὰ συστροφὰς οἱ στρατιῶται

---

[1] ed. pr. : παῖδα mss.   [2] Bekker: ὑπεροχάς mss.
[3] αὐτοὺς most mss. (+ τότε VRC): αὐτοῖς L.
[4] συνεργήσειν δὲ M : συνετηρήσαμεν PAL : text doubtful.
[5] L: ἐπιβουλὴν the rest.
[6] Destinon: συντετηρηκότων "joint guardians (of the
empire)" mss.

---

[a] Or, with the ms. text, "is afforded by the sterling
excellences of princes."

176

the legions of Germany, nor are we inferior in arms
to the troops who have thence brought back this
tyrant. Besides, there will be no need for a contest ;
for neither senate nor Roman people would tolerate
the lewdness of Vitellius in place of the temperance
of Vespasian, nor prefer as president a most brutal
tyrant to a virtuous ruler, a childless prince to a
father, since the very best security for peace lies
in a legitimate succession to the throne.[a] If, then,
sovereignty calls for the experience of years, we
have Vespasian, if for the vigour of youth, there is
Titus ; the pair of them will combine the advantages
of their respective ages. Nor will the persons of our
choice be dependent solely on the strength which
we can supply, mustering as we can three legions [b]
and the auxiliaries furnished by the kings ; they will
have the further support of the whole eastern world
and of all in Europe too remote to be intimidated
by Vitellius, as also of our allies in Italy, a brother [c]
and another son [d] of Vespasian. Of these, one will
gain many recruits from the young men of rank,
while the other has actually been entrusted with
the charge of the city—a fact of no small importance
for any designs upon the empire. In short, if there
is any delay on our part, the senate will probably
elect the very man whom his own soldiers, who have
grown grey in his service, have disgracefully
neglected."

(4) Such was the conversation current in military

[b] V, X, and XV (*B.* iii. 65).
[c] Flavius Sabinus, who had served with Vespasian in
Britain, been for seven years governor of Moesia, and now
held the important post of *praefectus urbis* in Rome.
[d] Domitian.

διελάλουν· ἔπειτα συναθροισθέντες καὶ παρα-
κροτήσαντες ἀλλήλους ἀναγορεύουσι τὸν Οὐεσπασιανὸν αὐτοκράτορα καὶ σῴζειν τὴν κινδυνεύουσαν
602 ἡγεμονίαν παρεκάλουν. ·τῷ δὲ φροντὶς μὲν ἦν
πάλαι περὶ τῶν ὅλων, οὔτι γε μὴν αὐτὸς ἄρχειν
προῄρετο, τοῖς μὲν ἔργοις ἑαυτὸν ἄξιον ἡγού-
μενος, προκρίνων δὲ τῶν ἐν λαμπρότητι κινδύνων
603 τὴν ἐν ἰδιωτείαις ἀσφάλειαν. ἀρνουμένῳ δὲ μᾶλλον οἱ ἡγεμόνες ἐπέκειντο καὶ περιχυθέντες οἱ
στρατιῶται ξιφήρεις ἀναιρεῖν αὐτὸν ἠπείλουν, εἰ
604 μὴ βούλοιτο ζῆν ἀξίως. πολλὰ δὲ πρὸς αὐτοὺς
διατεινάμενος ἐξ ὧν διωθεῖτο τὴν ἀρχὴν τελευταῖον, ὡς οὐκ ἔπειθεν, εἴκει τοῖς ὀνομάσασι.

605 (5) Προτρεπομένων δ' αὐτὸν ἤδη Μουκιανοῦ τε
καὶ τῶν ἄλλων ἡγεμόνων ὡς αὐτοκράτορα καὶ
τῆς ἄλλης στρατιᾶς ἄγειν [βοώσης αὐτὴν]¹ ἐπὶ
πᾶν τὸ ἀντίπαλον, ὁ δὲ πρῶτον τῶν ἐπ' Ἀλεξανδρείας εἴχετο πραγμάτων, εἰδὼς πλεῖστον τῆς
ἡγεμονίας μέρος τὴν Αἴγυπτον οὖσαν διὰ τὴν τοῦ
606 σίτου χορηγίαν, ἧς κρατήσας εἰ παρέλκοι καὶ
βίᾳ καθαιρήσειν ἤλπιζεν Οὐιτέλλιον, οὐ γὰρ
ἀνέξεσθαι πείνης ἐπὶ Ῥώμης τὸ πλῆθος, τὰ δύο
τε ἐπὶ τῆς Ἀλεξανδρείας τάγματα προσποιή-
607 σασθαι βουλόμενος. ἐνεθυμεῖτο δὲ καὶ πρόβλημα
τὴν χώραν ἔχειν τῶν ἀπὸ τῆς τύχης ἀδήλων·
ἔστι γὰρ κατά τε γῆν δυσέμβολος καὶ τὰ πρὸς
608 θαλάσσης ἀλίμενος, κατὰ μὲν ἑσπέραν προβεβλη-

---

¹ ins. ed. pr. with some ms. support: om. PAM (probably
through homoioteleuton).

ᵃ Licinus Mucianus, legatus of Syria (§§ 32, 621), shortly
to be sent to Italy to secure the empire for Vespasian (632,

circles; and then banding together and encouraging one another, they proclaimed Vespasian emperor and urged him to save the endangered empire. and proclaim Vespasian emperor. Their general had long been concerned for the public weal, but had never purposed·his own promotion; for, though conscious that his career would justify such claim, he preferred the security of private life to the perils of illustrious station. But on his declining, the officers pressed him more insistently and the soldiers, flocking round with drawn swords, threatened him with death, if he refused to live with dignity. After forcibly representing to them his many reasons for rejecting imperial honours, finally, failing to convince them, he yielded to their call.

(5) He was now urged by Mucianus [a] and the other generals to act as emperor, and the rest of the army clamoured to be led against all opponents. Vespasian secures Egypt. His first object, however, was to secure a hold upon Alexandria. He realized the supreme importance of Egypt to the empire as its granary: [b] once master of it he hoped, by persistence,[c] to force Vitellius to surrender, as the populace of Rome would never submit to be starved. He also desired to annex the two legions [d] at Alexandria; while he further contemplated holding the country as a bulwark against the uncertain freaks of fortune. For Egypt [e] is at once difficult of access by land and on its sea-board destitute of harbours. It is protected on the west Description of Egypt.

654). His mixed character is tersely sketched by Tacitus (*Hist.* i. 10).

[b] Alexandria supplied corn sufficient to feed Rome for four months of the year (*B.* ii. 386).

[c] Or perhaps "if (the war) dragged on "; *cf. A.* xv. 148 εἰ παρέλκειν δέοι.

[d] III and XXII, ii. 387 note. [e] *Cf.* ii. 385 f.

179

μένη τὰ ἄνυδρα τῆς Λιβύης, κατὰ δὲ μεσημβρίαν
τὴν διορίζουσαν ἀπὸ Αἰθιόπων τὴν Συήνην καὶ
τοὺς ἀπλώτους τοῦ ποταμοῦ καταράκτας, ἀπὸ
δὲ τῆς ἀνατολῆς τὴν[1] ἐρυθρὰν θάλασσαν ἀναχεο-
609 μένην μέχρι Κοπτοῦ. βόρειον δὲ τεῖχος αὐτῆς[2] ἥ
τε μέχρι Συρίας γῆ καὶ τὸ καλούμενον Αἰγύπτιον
610 πέλαγος, πᾶν ἄπορον ὅρμων. τετείχισται μὲν
οὕτως ἡ Αἴγυπτος πάντοθεν· τὸ μεταξὺ δὲ Πηλουσίου καὶ Συήνης μῆκος αὐτῆς σταδίων δισχιλίων,
ὅ τε ἀπὸ τῆς Πλινθίνης ἀνάπλους εἰς τὸ Πηλούσιον
611 σταδίων τρισχιλίων ἑξακοσίων. ὁ δὲ Νεῖλος
ἀναπλεῖται μέχρι τῆς Ἐλεφάντων καλουμένης
πόλεως, ὑπὲρ ἣν εἴργουσι προσωτέρω χωρεῖν οὓς
612 προειρήκαμεν καταράκτας. δυσπρόσιτος δὲ λιμὴν
ναυσὶ καὶ κατ' εἰρήνην Ἀλεξανδρείας· στενός τε
γὰρ εἴσπλους καὶ πέτραις ὑφάλοις τὸν ἐπ' εὐθὺ
613 καμπτόμενος δρόμον. καὶ τὸ μὲν ἀριστερὸν αὐτοῦ
μέρος πέφρακται χειροκμήτοις σκέλεσιν, ἐν δεξιᾷ
δὲ ἡ προσαγορευομένη Φάρος νῆσος πρόκειται,
πύργον ἀνέχουσα μέγιστον ἐκπυρσεύοντα τοῖς
καταπλέουσιν ἐπὶ τριακοσίους σταδίους, ὡς ἐν
νυκτὶ πόρρωθεν ὁρμίζοιντο πρὸς τὴν δυσχέρειαν
614 τοῦ κατάπλου. περὶ ταύτην τὴν νῆσον κατα-

---

[1] τὴν Lat.: ἐπὶ τὴν MSS. [2] Niese: αὐτῇ MSS.

[a] *Assuan.*
[b] *Koft*, on the right bank of the Nile, N. of *Karnak*;
named perhaps as the place where the river most nearly
approaches the sea. The Red Sea, not including the Gulf of
Suez, actually penetrates considerably farther north.
[c] *Tell Farama*, alias *Tineh*, situate at or near what was
once the easternmost mouth of the Nile.

by the arid deserts of Libya, on the south by the
frontier separating it from Ethiopia—Syene [a] and
the unnavigable cataracts of the Nile—, on the east
by the Red Sea, which penetrates as far north as
Coptus [b] ; while its northern barriers are the land
towards Syria and the so-called Egyptian sea, totally
devoid of havens. Thus is Egypt walled off on every
side. Its length from Pelusium [c] to Syene is two
thousand furlongs [d] ; the passage from Plinthine [e] to
Pelusium is three thousand six hundred.[f] The Nile
is navigable up to the city called Elephantine,[g]
beyond which the cataracts already mentioned bar
further progress. The port [h] of Alexandria is difficult _The port of Alexandria_
for ships to approach even in peace-time, the en-
trance being narrow and diverted by submerged
rocks [i] which preclude direct passage. On the left
the channel is protected by artificial moles ; on the
right juts out the island called Pharos, supporting an _Pharos._
enormous tower, emitting a light visible three hundred
furlongs away to mariners making for port, to warn
them to anchor at night some distance off because
of the difficulty of the navigation. Round this island

[d] _i.e._ about 230 miles, a wholly inadequate figure ; the
actual distance was _c._ 650 miles.
[e] The Libyan frontier of Egypt, on the coast W. of
Alexandria ; exact site unidentified.
[f] _i.e._ about 414 miles ; this figure is nearly double the
actual distance of the sea voyage round the Delta basin
(_c._ 220 miles). Strabo 791 is nearer the mark in reckoning
the distance by sea from Pelusium to Pharos as 1450 stadia
(166 miles).
[g] The island below the First Cataract, opposite Assuan.
[h] _i.e._ the Great Harbour. Strabo, xvii. 791 ff., gives a
fuller account of the three harbours.
[i] _Cf._ Strabo 791 πρὸς δὲ τῇ στενότητι τοῦ μέταξυ πόρου καὶ
πέτραι εἰσὶν αἱ μὲν ὕφαλοι αἱ δὲ καὶ ἐξέχουσαι.

βέβληται χειροποίητα τείχη μέγιστα, προσαρασ-
σόμενον δὲ τούτοις τὸ πέλαγος καὶ τοῖς ἄντικρυς
ἔρκεσιν ἀμφηγνυμένον[1] ἐκτραχύνει τὸν πόρον καὶ
σφαλερὰν διὰ στενοῦ τὴν εἴσοδον ἀπεργάζεται.
615 ὁ μέντοι γε λιμὴν ἀσφαλέστατος ἔνδον καὶ τριάκοντα σταδίων τὸ μέγεθος, εἰς ὃν τά τε λείποντα
τῇ χώρᾳ πρὸς εὐδαιμονίαν κατάγεται καὶ τὰ
περισσεύοντα τῶν ἐπιχωρίων ἀγαθῶν[2] εἰς πᾶσαν
χωρίζεται[2] τὴν οἰκουμένην.
616 (6) Ἐφίετο μὲν οὖν εἰκότως τῶν ταύτῃ πραγμάτων Οὐεσπασιανὸς εἰς βεβαίωσιν τῆς ὅλης
ἡγεμονίας, ἐπιστέλλει δ᾽ εὐθὺς τῷ διέποντι τὴν
Αἴγυπτον καὶ τὴν Ἀλεξάνδρειαν Τιβερίῳ Ἀλεξάνδρῳ, δηλῶν τὸ τῆς στρατιᾶς πρόθυμον, καὶ
ὡς αὐτὸς ὑποδὺς ἀναγκαίως τὸ βάρος τῆς ἡγεμονίας συνεργὸν αὐτὸν καὶ βοηθὸν προσλαμβάνοι.
617 παραναγνοὺς δὲ τὴν ἐπιστολὴν Ἀλέξανδρος προθύμως τά τε τάγματα καὶ τὸ πλῆθος εἰς αὐτὸν
ὥρκωσεν. ἑκάτεροι δ᾽ ἀσμένως ὑπήκουσαν τὴν
ἀρετὴν τἀνδρὸς ἐκ τῆς ἐγγὺς στρατηγίας εἰδότες.
618 καὶ ὁ μὲν πεπιστευμένος ἤδη τὰ περὶ τὴν ἀρχὴν
προπαρεσκεύαζεν αὐτῷ καὶ τὰ πρὸς τὴν ἄφιξιν,
τάχιον δ᾽ ἐπινοίας διήγγελλον αἱ φῆμαι τὸν ἐπὶ
τῆς ἀνατολῆς αὐτοκράτορα, καὶ πᾶσα μὲν πόλις
ἑώρταζεν εὐαγγέλια [δὲ] καὶ θυσίας ὑπὲρ αὐτοῦ
619 ἐπετέλει. τὰ δὲ κατὰ Μυσίαν καὶ Παννονίαν

---

[1] Niese: ἀφικνύμενον, ἀφικν(ο)ύμενον mss.
[2] PA: μεριζόμενα L: μερίζεται the rest.

---

[a] The Great Harbour seems to have been only half this
length. The figure named (=c. 3½ miles) can barely be
reached by including the Eunostus Harbour ; the two were
originally separated by the causeway called the Hepta-
stadion, but this had perhaps now disappeared (Strabo 792).

immense walls have been reared by human hands; and the sea dashing against these and breaking around the piers opposite renders the passage rough and ingress through the strait perilous. The harbour inside is, however, perfectly safe and is thirty furlongs [a] in length. To this port are carried all the commodities which the country lacks for its welfare, and from it the surplus local products are distributed to every quarter of the world.[b]

(6) With good reason therefore was Vespasian eager to obtain control here, with a view to the stability of the empire at large. He accordingly at once wrote to Tiberius Alexander,[c] the governor of Egypt and Alexandria, informing him of the army's zeal and how, being forced to shoulder the burden of empire himself, he desired to enlist his co-operation and assistance. Having read this letter in public, Alexander promptly required the legions and the populace to take the oath of allegiance to Vespasian; a call to which they both gladly responded, knowing the sterling quality of the man from his generalship in their neighbourhood. Tiberius, now having the interests of the empire entrusted to his charge, made all preparations for Vespasian's arrival; and quicker than thought rumour spread the news of the new emperor in the east. Every city kept festival for the good news and offered sacrifices on his behalf; but the legions in Moesia and Pannonia,[d] recently

Tiberius Alexander secures Alexandria for Vespasian.

General acclamation at Vespasian's accession.

---

[b] Strabo 798 calls Alexandria μέγιστον ἐμπόριον τῆς οἰκουμένης and speaks of the precious wares of which she καὶ ὑποδοχεῖόν ἐστι καὶ χορηγεῖ τοῖς ἐκτός.

[c] *B.* ii. 220 note (summarizing his varied career).

[d] The provinces on the south bank of the Danube: Moesia covering the eastern portion (Serbia and Bulgaria), Pannonia the western (Austrian and neighbouring territory).

183

τάγματα, μικρῷ πρόσθεν κεκινημένα πρὸς τὴν
Οὐιτελλίου τόλμαν, μείζονι χαρᾷ Οὐεσπασιανῷ
620 τὴν ἡγεμονίαν ὤμνυον. ὁ δ' ἀναζεύξας ἀπὸ
Καισαρείας εἰς Βηρυτὸν παρῆν, ἔνθα πολλαὶ μὲν
ἀπὸ τῆς Συρίας αὐτῷ, πολλαὶ δὲ κἀπὸ τῶν ἄλλων
ἐπαρχιῶν πρεσβεῖαι συνήντων, στεφάνους παρ'
ἑκάστης πόλεως καὶ συγχαρτικὰ προσφέρουσαι
621 ψηφίσματα. παρῆν δὲ καὶ Μουκιανὸς ὁ τῆς
ἐπαρχίας ἡγεμών, τὸ πρόθυμον τῶν δήμων καὶ
τοὺς κατὰ πόλιν ὅρκους ἀπαγγέλλων.

622 (7) Προχωρούσης δὲ πανταχοῦ κατὰ νοῦν τῆς
τύχης καὶ τῶν πραγμάτων συννενευκότων ἐκ τοῦ
πλείστου μέρους, ἤδη παρίστατο τῷ Οὐεσπασιανῷ
νοεῖν, ὡς οὐ δίχα δαιμονίου προνοίας ἅψαιτο τῆς
ἀρχῆς, ἀλλὰ δικαία τις εἱμαρμένη περιαγάγοι τὸ
623 κρατεῖν τῶν ὅλων ἐπ' αὐτόν· ἀναμιμνήσκεται
γὰρ τά τε ἄλλα σημεῖα, πολλὰ δ' αὐτῷ γε-
γόνει πανταχοῦ προφαίνοντα τὴν ἡγεμονίαν, καὶ
τὰς τοῦ Ἰωσήπου φωνάς, ὃς αὐτὸν ἔτι ζῶντος
624 Νέρωνος αὐτοκράτορα προσειπεῖν ἐθάρσησεν. ἐξ-
επέπληκτο δὲ τὸν ἄνδρα δεσμώτην ἔτι ὄντα παρ'
αὑτῷ, καὶ προσκαλεσάμενος Μουκιανὸν ἅμα τοῖς
ἄλλοις ἡγεμόσι καὶ φίλοις πρῶτον μὲν αὐτοῦ τὸ
δραστήριον ἐκδιηγεῖτο καὶ ὅσα περὶ[1] τοῖς Ἰωτα-
625 πάτοις δι' αὐτὸν ἔκαμον, ἔπειτα τὰς μαντείας, ἃς
αὐτὸς μὲν ὑπώπτευσε τότε πλάσματα τοῦ δέους,
ἀποδειχθῆναι δὲ ὑπὸ τοῦ χρόνου καὶ τῶν πραγ-
626 μάτων θείας. "αἰσχρὸν οὖν," ἔφη, "τὸν προ-

---

[1] L: in Lat.: om. the rest.

[a] Tacitus, Hist. ii. 85 f. The legions in Moesia were

exasperated by the audacity of Vitellius, more gladly than any swore allegiance to Vespasian.[a] The latter, leaving Caesarea, proceeded to Berytus,[b] where numerous embassies, both from Syria and from the other provinces, waited upon him, bringing crowns and congratulatory decrees from the various cities. Thither too came Mucianus, the governor of the province, to report the popular enthusiasm and that every city had taken the oath.

(7) Now that fortune was everywhere furthering his wishes and that circumstances had for the most part conspired in his favour, Vespasian was led to think that divine providence had assisted him to grasp the empire and that some just destiny had placed the sovereignty of the world within his hands. Among many other omens,[c] which had everywhere foreshadowed his imperial honours, he recalled the words of Josephus, who had ventured, even in Nero's lifetime, to address him as emperor.[d] He was shocked to think that the man was still a prisoner in his hands, and summoning Mucianus with his other officers and friends, he first dwelt upon his doughty deeds and all the trouble that he had given them at Jotapata ; and then referred to his predictions, which at the time he himself had suspected of being fabrications prompted by fear, but which time and the event had proved to be divine. " It is disgraceful," he

Liberation of Josephus from bonds.

III Gallica (see § 633), VII Claudia, and VIII Augusta ; those in Pannonia, VII Galbiana and XIII Gemina.

[b] *Beirut.*

[c] Various *omina imperii* are mentioned by Tacitus (*Hist.* ii. 78), Suetonius (*Vesp.* 5), and Dion Cassius (lxvi. 1). The two last authorities include the prophecy of Josephus ; Weber, *Josephus and Vespasian* 45, believes that they drew upon some common source. *Cf. B.* iii. 404 n.   [d] iii. 401.

θεσπίσαντά μοι τὴν ἀρχὴν καὶ διάκονον τῆς τοῦ
θεοῦ φωνῆς ἔτι αἰχμαλώτου τάξιν ἢ δεσμώτου
τύχην ὑπομένειν," καὶ καλέσας τὸν Ἰώσηπον
627 λυθῆναι κελεύει. τοῖς μὲν οὖν ἡγεμόσιν ἐκ τῆς
εἰς τὸν ἀλλόφυλον ἀμοιβῆς λαμπρὰ καὶ περὶ
αὐτῶν ἐλπίζειν παρέστη, συνὼν δὲ τῷ πατρὶ
628 Τίτος " δίκαιον, ὦ πάτερ," ἔφη, " τοῦ Ἰωσήπου
καὶ τὸ ὄνειδος ἀφαιρεθῆναι σὺν τῷ σιδήρῳ·
γενήσεται γὰρ ὅμοιος τῷ μὴ δεθέντι τὴν ἀρχήν,
ἂν αὐτοῦ μὴ λύσωμεν ἀλλὰ κόψωμεν τὰ δεσμά."
τοῦτο γὰρ ἐπὶ τῶν μὴ δεόντως δεθέντων πράτ-
629 τεται. συνεδόκει ταῦτα, καὶ παρελθών τις πε-
λέκει διέκοψε τὴν ἄλυσιν. ὁ δὲ Ἰώσηπος εἰληφὼς
ὑπὲρ[1] τῶν προειρημένων γέρας τὴν ἐπιτιμίαν ἤδη
καὶ περὶ τῶν μελλόντων ἀξιόπιστος ἦν.
630 (xi. 1) Οὐεσπασιανὸς δὲ ταῖς πρεσβείαις χρη-
ματίσας καὶ καταστησάμενος ἑκάστοις τὰς ἀρχὰς
δικαίως καὶ διὰ τῶν ἀξίων, εἰς Ἀντιόχειαν
631 ἀφικνεῖται. καὶ βουλευόμενος ποῖ τρέπεσθαι,
προυργιαίτερα τῆς εἰς Ἀλεξάνδρειαν ὁρμῆς τὰ
κατὰ τὴν Ῥώμην ἔκρινε, τὴν μὲν βέβαιον οὖσαν
632 ὁρῶν, τὰ δ' ὑπὸ Οὐιτελλίου ταρασσόμενα. πέμπει δὴ Μουκιανὸν εἰς τὴν Ἰταλίαν παραδοὺς
ἱππέων τε καὶ πεζῶν συχνὴν δύναμιν. ὁ δὲ διὰ
τὴν τοῦ χειμῶνος ἀκμὴν δείσας τὸ πλεῖν[2] πεζῇ
τὴν στρατιὰν ἦγε διὰ Καππαδοκίας καὶ Φρυγίας.
633 (2) Ἐν δὲ τούτῳ καὶ Ἀντώνιος Πρῖμος ἀναλαβὼν τὸ τρίτον τάγμα τῶν κατὰ Μυσίαν, ἔτυχεν

---

[1] Niese: περὶ mss.   [2] Hudson from Lat.: πᾶν mss.

---

[a] Mucianus went ahead with some light-armed troops,
being followed by the 6th legion (Ferrata) and 13,000 veterans
(vexillarii), Tac. Hist. ii. 83.

said, " that one who foretold my elevation to power and was a minister of the voice of God should still rank as a captive and endure a prisoner's fate "; and calling for Josephus, he ordered him to be liberated. While the officers were only thinking that such requital of a foreigner augured brilliant honours for themselves, Titus, who was beside his father, said, "Justice demands, father, that Josephus should lose his disgrace along with his fetters. If instead of loosing, we sever his chains, he will be as though he had never been in bonds at all." For such is the practice in cases where a man has been unjustly put in irons. Vespasian approving, an attendant came forward and severed the chain with an axe. Thus Josephus won his enfranchisement as the reward of his divination, and his power of insight into the future was no longer discredited.

(xi. 1) Vespasian, having responded to the embassies and disposed of the various governorships with due regard to the claims of justice and the merits of the candidates, repaired to Antioch. Here deliberating in which direction to turn, he decided that affairs in Rome were more important than a march to Alexandria, seeing that the latter was secured, whereas at Rome Vitellius was creating general disorder. He accordingly dispatched Mucianus to Italy with a substantial force of cavalry and infantry ; [a] that officer, fearing the risk of a sea voyage in the depth of winter, led his army by land through Cappadocia and Phrygia.[b]

(2) Meanwhile Antonius Primus, along with the third legion from Moesia, where he was then in

Vespasian sends Mucianus with an army to Italy.

[b] Ordering the fleet from Pontus to concentrate at Byzantium, Tac. *ibid.*

187

δ' ἡγεμονεύων αὐτόθι, Οὐιτελλίῳ παραταξόμενος
634 ἠπείγετο. Οὐιτέλλιος δ' αὐτῷ συναντήσοντα μετὰ
πολλῆς δυνάμεως Καικίναν[1] Ἀλιηνὸν ἐκπέμπει,
μέγα θαρρῶν τἀνδρὶ διὰ τὴν ἐπ' Ὄθωνι νίκην.
ὁ δὲ ἀπὸ τῆς Ῥώμης ἐλαύνων διὰ τάχους περὶ
Κρέμωνα τῆς Γαλατίας τὸν Ἀντώνιον καταλαμ-
βάνει· μεθόριος δ' ἐστὶν ἡ πόλις αὕτη τῆς
635 Ἰταλίας. κατιδὼν δ' ἐνταῦθα τὸ πλῆθος τῶν
πολεμίων καὶ τὴν εὐταξίαν, συμβαλεῖν μὲν οὐκ
ἐθάρρει, σφαλερὰν δὲ τὴν ἀναχώρησιν λογιζό-
636 μενος προδοσίαν ἐβουλεύετο. συναγαγὼν δὲ τοὺς
ὑφ' αὑτὸν ἑκατοντάρχας καὶ χιλιάρχους ἐνῆγεν
μεταβῆναι πρὸς τὸν Ἀντώνιον, ταπεινῶν μὲν τὰ
Οὐιτελλίου πράγματα, τὴν Οὐεσπασιανοῦ δ' ἰσχὺν
637 ἐπαίρων, καὶ παρ' ᾧ μὲν εἶναι λέγων μόνον τῆς
ἀρχῆς ὄνομα, παρ' ᾧ δὲ τὴν δύναμιν, καὶ αὐτοὺς
δὲ ἄμεινον [εἶναι][2] προλαβόντας τὴν ἀνάγκην
ποιῆσαι χάριν καὶ μέλλοντας ἡττᾶσθαι τοῖς ὅπλοις
638 ταῖς γνώμαις τὸν κίνδυνον φθάσαι· Οὐεσπασιανὸν
μὲν γὰρ ἱκανὸν εἶναι καὶ χωρὶς αὐτῶν προσκτή-
σασθαι[3] καὶ τὰ λείποντα, Οὐιτέλλιον δ' οὐδὲ σὺν
αὐτοῖς τηρῆσαι τὰ ὄντα.

639 (3) Πολλὰ τοιαῦτα λέγων ἔπεισε καὶ πρὸς τὸν
640 Ἀντώνιον αὐτομολεῖ μετὰ τῆς δυνάμεως. τῆς δ'
αὐτῆς νυκτὸς ἐμπίπτει μετάνοια τοῖς στρατιώταις
καὶ δέος τοῦ προπέμψαντος, εἰ κρείσσων γένοιτο·

---

[1] C Lat. Heg. : Κικίλ(λ)ιον the rest.
[2] ins. L (Lat. ?): om. the rest.
[3] Dindorf: προκτήσασθαι L : προσθήσεσθαι the rest.

---

[a] M. Antonius Primus, in the sequel a rival of Mucianus,

188

command,[a] was also hastening to give battle to Vitellius ; and Vitellius had sent off Caecina Alienus with a strong force to oppose him, having great confidence in that general on account of his victory over Otho.[b] Caecina marching rapidly from Rome met Antonius near Cremona, a town in Gaul [c] on the frontiers of Italy ; but there, perceiving the numbers and discipline of the enemy, he would not venture on an engagement and, considering retreat hazardous, meditated treason.[d] Accordingly assembling the centurions and tribunes under his command, he urged them to go over to Antonius, disparaging the resources of Vitellius and extolling the strength of Vespasian.[e] " The one," he said, " has but the name, the other the power of sovereignty ; and it were better for you to forestall and make a virtue of necessity, and, as you are bound to be beaten in the field, to avert danger by policy. For Vespasian is capable, without your aid, of acquiring what he has yet to win ; while Vitellius, even with your support, cannot retain what he has already."

(3) Caecina's words, prolonged in the same strain, prevailed, and he and his army deserted to Antonius. But the same night the soldiers were overcome with remorse and fear of him who had sent them into the field, should he prove victorious ; and drawing their

Antonius Primus leads another army from Moesia against Vitellius.

Caecina, general of Vitellius, goes over to Antonius.

was now in command of the 7th legion (Galbiana ; Tac. *Hist.* ii. 86), in Pannonia, not in Moesia, as Josephus states ; but he was joined by the Moesian legions, the third (Gallica) taking the lead in revolt : "tertia legio exemplum ceteris Moesiae legionibus praebuit " (Tac. *H.* ii. 85).

[b] § 547.

[c] *i.e.* Gallia Cisalpina, Italy N. of the Po.

[d] Tacitus gives a fuller account, *Hist.* ii. 99, iii. 13 ff.

[e] " Vespasiani virtutem viresque partium extollit . . . atque omnia de Vitellio in deterius " (Tac. *Hist.* iii. 13).

189

σπασάμενοι δὲ τὰ ξίφη τὸν Καικίναν[1] ὥρμησαν
ἀνελεῖν, κἂν ἐπράχθη τὸ ἔργον αὐτοῖς, εἰ μὴ
προσπίπτοντες οἱ χιλίαρχοι καθικέτευσαν ἑκά-
641 στους.[2] οἱ δὲ τοῦ μὲν κτείνειν ἀπέσχοντο, δήσαντες
δὲ τὸν προδότην οἷοί τε ἦσαν ἀναπέμπειν[3] Οὐιτελλίῳ. ταῦτ᾿ ἀκούσας ὁ Πρῖμος αὐτίκα τοὺς
σφετέρους ἀνίστησι καὶ μετὰ τῶν ὅπλων ἦγεν
642 ἐπὶ τοὺς ἀποστάντας. οἱ δὲ παραταξάμενοι πρὸς
ὀλίγον μὲν ἀντέσχον, αὖθις δὲ τραπέντες ἔφευγον
εἰς τὴν Κρέμωνα. τοὺς δὲ ἱππεῖς ἀναλαβὼν
Πρῖμος ὑποτέμνεται τὰς εἰσόδους αὐτῶν, καὶ τὸ
μὲν πολὺ πλῆθος κυκλωσάμενος πρὸ τῆς πόλεως
διαφθείρει, τῷ δὲ λοιπῷ συνεισπεσὼν διαρπάσαι
643 τὸ ἄστυ τοῖς στρατιώταις ἐφῆκεν. ἔνθα δὴ
πολλοὶ μὲν τῶν ξένων ἔμποροι, πολλοὶ δὲ τῶν
ἐπιχωρίων ἀπώλοντο, πᾶσα δὲ [καὶ] ἡ Οὐιτελλίου
στρατιά, μυριάδες ἀνδρῶν τρεῖς καὶ διακόσιοι·
τῶν δ᾿ ἀπὸ τῆς Μυσίας Ἀντώνιος τετρακισχι-
644 λίους ἀποβάλλει καὶ πεντακοσίους. λύσας δὲ τὸν
Καικίναν πέμπει πρὸς Οὐεσπασιανὸν ἀγγελοῦντα
τὰ πεπραγμένα. καὶ ὃς ἐλθὼν ἀπεδέχθη τε ὑπ᾿
αὐτοῦ καὶ τὰ τῆς προδοσίας ὀνείδη ταῖς παρ᾿
ἐλπίδα τιμαῖς ἐπεκάλυψεν.

645   (4) Ἀνεθάρσει δὲ ἤδη καὶ κατὰ τὴν Ῥώμην
Σαβῖνος, ὡς πλησίον Ἀντώνιος ὢν ἀπηγγέλλετο,

---

[1] Lat. Heg. : Κικίλ(λ)ιον mss.
[2] L: αὐτοῖς or αὐτούς the rest.
[3] L: πέμπειν (πέμψειν) the rest.

swords they rushed off to kill Caecina and would have accomplished their purpose, had not the tribunes thrown themselves at the feet of their companies and implored them to desist.[a] The troops spared his life but bound the traitor and prepared to send him up to Vitellius. Primus, hearing of this, instantly called up his men and led them in arms against the rebels ; these forming in line of battle offered a brief resistance, but were then routed and fled for Cremona. Primus with his cavalry intercepted their entrance, surrounded and destroyed the greater part of them before the walls, and, forcing his way in with the remainder, permitted his soldiers to pillage the town. In the ensuing slaughter many foreign merchants [b] and many of the inhabitants perished, along with the whole army of Vitellius, numbering thirty thousand two hundred men ; of his troops from Moesia Antonius lost four thousand five hundred. Caecina, being liberated by him and sent to report these events to Vespasian, was on his arrival graciously received by the emperor, and covered the disgrace of his perfidy with unlooked for honours.

Antonius cuts the Vitellian army to pieces.

(4) In Rome, too, Sabinus [c] now regained courage on hearing of the approach of Antonius, and, muster-

Fights for the Capitol.

---

[a] Details not in Tacitus, who merely states that the soldiers bound Caecina and elected other leaders (*Hist.* iii. 14).

[b] " The occurrence of a fair (*tempus mercatus*) filled the colony, rich as it always was, with the appearance of still greater wealth " ; the sack of the town occupied four days (Tac. *Hist.* iii. 32 f.).

[c] § 598 note. The full story is told in Tacitus, *Hist.* iii. 64 ff. Sabinus attempted to negotiate conditions with Vitellius, who was prepared to abdicate ; but the Vitellianists prevented this, and a collision between them and the followers of Sabinus drove the latter to seek refuge in the temple of Jupiter on the Capitol.

καὶ συναθροίσας τὰ τῶν νυκτοφυλάκων στρατιωτῶν τάγματα νύκτωρ καταλαμβάνει τὸ Καπε-
646 τώλιον. μεθ' ἡμέραν δ' αὐτῷ πολλοὶ τῶν ἐπισήμων προσεγένοντο καὶ Δομετιανὸς ὁ τἀδελφοῦ
παῖς, μεγίστη μοῖρα τῶν εἰς τὸ κρατεῖν ἐλπίδων.
647 Οὐιτελλίῳ δὲ Πρίμου μὲν ἐλάττων φροντὶς ἦν,
τεθύμωτο[1] δ' ἐπὶ τοὺς συναποστάντας τῷ Σαβίνῳ,
καὶ διὰ τὴν ἔμφυτον ὠμότητα διψῶν αἵματος
εὐγενοῦς τοῦ στρατιωτικοῦ τὴν συγκατελθοῦσαν
648 αὐτῷ δύναμιν ἐπαφίησι τῷ Καπετωλίῳ. πολλὰ
μὲν οὖν ἔκ τε ταύτης καὶ τῶν ἀπὸ τοῦ ἱεροῦ
μαχομένων ἐτολμήθη, τέλος δὲ τῷ πλήθει περι-
όντες οἱ ἀπὸ τῆς Γερμανίας ἐκράτησαν τοῦ λόφου.
649 καὶ Δομετιανὸς μὲν[2] σὺν πολλοῖς τῶν ἐν τέλει
Ῥωμαίων δαιμονιώτερον διασώζεται, τὸ δὲ λοιπὸν
πλῆθος ἅπαν κατεκόπη, καὶ Σαβῖνος ἀναχθεὶς
ἐπὶ Οὐιτέλλιον ἀναιρεῖται, διαρπάσαντές τε οἱ
στρατιῶται τὰ ἀναθήματα τὸν ναὸν ἐνέπρησαν.
650 καὶ μετὰ μίαν ἡμέραν εἰσελαύνει μὲν Ἀντώνιος
μετὰ τῆς δυνάμεως, ὑπήντων δ' οἱ Οὐιτελλίου καὶ
τριχῇ κατὰ τὴν πόλιν συμβαλόντες ἀπώλοντο
651 πάντες. προέρχεται[3] δὲ μεθύων ἐκ τοῦ βασιλείου
Οὐιτέλλιος καὶ δαψιλέστερον ὥσπερ ἐν ἐσχάτοις
652 τῆς ἀσώτου τραπέζης κεκορεσμένος. συρεὶς δὲ

---

[1] τεθυμωμένος L Lat.   [2] Bekker with Lat.: δὲ MSS.
[3] rapitur Heg.: hence προέλκεται Destinon (cf. Tacitus,
Hist. iii. 84).

---

[a] "vigilum cohortes" (Tac. Hist. iii. 64). Seven corps of
night police had been instituted by Augustus " adversus
incendia," a sort of fire-brigade (Suet. Aug. 30, Dion Cass.
lv. 26).

ing the cohorts of the night-watch,[a] seized the Capitol 18 December
during the night. Early next day [b] he was joined A.D. 69
by many of the notables, including his nephew 19 December
Domitian, on whom mainly rested their hopes of
success. Vitellius, less concerned about Primus, was
infuriated at the rebels who had supported Sabinus,
and, from innate cruelty thirsting for noble blood,
let loose upon the Capitol that division of his army
which had accompanied him (from Germany).[c] Many
a gallant deed was done alike by them and by those
who fought them from the temple ; but at length
by superior numbers the German troops mastered
the hill. Domitian, with many eminent Romans,
miraculously escaped ; [d] but the rank and file were
all cut to pieces, Sabinus was brought a prisoner to
Vitellius and executed, and the soldiers after plundering the temple of its votive offerings set it on fire.
A day later Antonius marched in with his army ; he Antonius
was met by the troops of Vitellius, who gave battle Rome,
at three different quarters of the city [e] and perished 20 Dec.
to a man.[f] Then issued from the palace Vitellius The end of
drunk and, knowing the end was come, gorged with Vitellius.
a banquet more lavish and luxurious than ever ;

---

[b] " At dead of night " (*concubia nocte*), Sabinus, owing
to the careless watch of the Vitellianists and a rain storm, was
enabled to bring in his own children and Domitian and to
communicate with his followers (Tac. *H.* iii. 69).

[c] According to the fuller account of Tacitus (*H.* iii. 70 f.)
the soldiers acted without orders from Vitellius, now " neque
jubendi neque vetandi potens."

[d] Domitian disguised as an acolyte, *ib.* 74.

[e] The forces of Antonius advanced in three divisions :
along the Via Flaminia, along the Via Salaria to the Colline
Gate, and along the bank of the Tiber (Tac. *H.* iii. 82).

[f] " cecidere omnes contrariis vulneribus, versi in hostem "
Tac. *H.* iii. 84.

διὰ τοῦ πλήθους καὶ παντοδαπαῖς αἰκίαις ἐξ-
υβρισθεὶς ἐπὶ μέσης τῆς Ῥώμης ἀποσφάττεται,
μῆνας ὀκτὼ κρατήσας καὶ ἡμέρας πέντε, ὃν εἰ
συνέβη πλείω βιῶσαι χρόνον, ἐπιλιπεῖν ἂν αὐτοῦ
653 τῇ λαγνείᾳ τὴν ἡγεμονίαν οἶμαι. τῶν δ' ἄλλων
654 νεκρῶν ὑπὲρ πέντε μυριάδας[1] ἠριθμήθησαν. ταῦτα
μὲν τρίτῃ μηνὸς Ἀπελλαίου πέπρακτο, τῇ δ'
ὑστεραίᾳ Μουκιανὸς εἴσεισι μετὰ τῆς στρατιᾶς,
καὶ τοὺς σὺν Ἀντωνίῳ παύσας τοῦ κτείνειν, ἔτι
γὰρ ἐξερευνώμενοι τὰς οἰκίας πολλοὺς μὲν τῶν
Οὐιτελλίου στρατιωτῶν πολλοὺς δὲ τῶν δημοτικῶν
ὡς ἐκείνου ἀνῄρουν, φθάνοντες τῷ θυμῷ τὴν
ἀκριβῆ διάκρισιν, προαγαγὼν δὲ τὸν Δομετιανὸν
συνίστησι τῷ πλήθει μέχρι τῆς τοῦ πατρὸς
655 ἀφίξεως ἡγεμόνα. ὁ δὲ δῆμος ἀπηλλαγμένος ἤδη
τῶν φόβων αὐτοκράτορα Οὐεσπασιανὸν εὐφήμει,
καὶ ἅμα τήν τε τούτου βεβαίωσιν ἑώρταζε καὶ
τὴν Οὐιτελλίου κατάλυσιν.

656   (5) Εἰς δὲ τὴν Ἀλεξάνδρειαν ἀφιγμένῳ τῷ
Οὐεσπασιανῷ τὰ ἀπὸ τῆς Ῥώμης εὐαγγέλια ἧκε
καὶ πρέσβεις ἐκ πάσης τῆς ἰδίας οἰκουμένης
συνηδόμενοι· μεγίστη τε οὖσα μετὰ τὴν Ῥώμην
657 ἡ πόλις στενοτέρα[2] τοῦ πλήθους ἠλέγχετο. κε-
κυρωμένης δὲ ἤδη τῆς ἀρχῆς ἁπάσης καὶ σεσω-
σμένων παρ' ἐλπίδα Ῥωμαίοις τῶν πραγμάτων
Οὐεσπασιανὸς ἐπὶ τὰ λείψανα τῆς Ἰουδαίας τὸν
658 λογισμὸν ἐπέστρεφεν. αὐτὸς μέντοι [γε][3] εἰς τὴν

[1] μυριάδες PML.   [2] + τότε L.
[3] ins. L: om. the rest.

---

a He was haled from hiding in the palace, after attempting
escape, to the Gemonian stairs, where he was slain, the corpse
being then dragged to the Tiber (Tac. iii. 84 f., Suet.
Vitell. 17).

dragged through the mob and subjected to indignities of every kind, he was finally butchered in the heart of Rome.[a] He had reigned eight months and five days ; [b] and had fate prolonged his life, the very empire, I imagine, would not have sufficed for his lust. Of others slain, upwards of fifty thousand were counted. These events took place on the third of the month Apellaeus. On the following day Mucianus entered with his army and restrained the troops of Antonius from further slaughter ; for they were still searching the houses and massacring large numbers, not only of the soldiers of Vitellius, but of the populace, as his partisans, too precipitate in their rage for careful discrimination.[c] Mucianus then brought forward Domitian and recommended him to the multitude as their ruler pending his father's arrival. The people, freed at length from terrors, acclaimed Vespasian emperor, and celebrated with one common festival both his establishment in power and the overthrow of Vitellius.

(5) On reaching Alexandria Vespasian was greeted by the good news from Rome and by embassies of congratulation from every quarter of the world,[d] now his own ; and that city, though second only to Rome in magnitude, proved too confined for the throng. The whole empire being now secured and the Roman state saved beyond expectation, Vespasian turned his thoughts to what remained in Judaea. He was, however, anxious himself to take ship for Rome [e] as

---

[b] From 17 April to 21 (or 20) December.

[c] Cf. Tac. Hist. iv. 1, 11.

[d] Including one from King Vologesus, offering him 40,000 Parthian cavalry (Tac. Hist. iv. 51).

[e] He had received unfavourable reports of Domitian's conduct, ibid.

Ῥώμην ὥρμητο λήξαντος τοῦ χειμῶνος ἀνάγεσθαι
καὶ τάχος τὰ κατὰ τὴν Ἀλεξάνδρειαν διῴκει,
τὸν δὲ υἱὸν Τίτον μετὰ τῆς ἐκκρίτου δυνάμεως
659 ἀπέστειλεν ἐξαιρήσοντα τὰ Ἱεροσόλυμα. ὁ δὲ
προελθὼν πεζῇ μέχρι Νικοπόλεως, εἴκοσι δ' αὕτη
διέχει τῆς Ἀλεξανδρείας σταδίους, κἀκεῖθεν ἐπιβήσας τὴν στρατιὰν μακρῶν πλοίων ἀναπλεῖ διὰ
τοῦ Νείλου κατὰ¹ τὸν Μενδήσιον νομὸν μέχρι
660 πόλεως Θμούεως. ἐκεῖθεν δ' ἀποβὰς ὁδεύει καὶ
κατὰ πολίχνην [τινὰ]² Τάνιν αὐλίζεται. δεύτερος
αὐτῷ σταθμὸς Ἡρακλέους πόλις καὶ τρίτος
661 Πηλούσιον γίνεται. δυσὶ δ' ἡμέραις [ἐνταῦθα]³
τὴν στρατιὰν ἀναλαβὼν τῇ τρίτῃ διέξεισι τὰς
ἐμβολὰς τοῦ Πηλουσίου, καὶ προελθὼν σταθμὸν
ἕνα διὰ τῆς ἐρήμου πρὸς τῷ τοῦ Κασίου⁴ Διὸς
ἱερῷ στρατοπεδεύεται, τῇ δ' ὑστεραίᾳ κατὰ τὴν
Ὀστρακίνην· οὗτος ὁ σταθμὸς ἦν ἄνυδρος, ἐπ-
662 εισάκτοις δὲ ὕδασιν οἱ ἐπιχώριοι χρῶνται. μετὰ
ταῦτα πρὸς Ῥινοκορούροις ἀναπαύεται, κἀκεῖθεν

---

¹ L: μετὰ the rest. ² om. PA Lat.
³ om. L. ⁴ LC¹: Κασσίου the rest.

ᵃ Founded by Augustus in 24 B.C. on the scene of his final
defeat of M. Antonius and in commemoration of the surrender of Alexandria ; it lay on the coast some 2½ (Josephus)
or 3½ (Strabo) miles E. of that city (Strabo xvii. 795, Dion
Cass. li. 18).

ᵇ " Thirty " according to Strabo.

ᶜ Or " up and across " (διὰ τοῦ Νείλου, not ἀνὰ τὸν Νεῖλον);
he was crossing the Delta and part of the route would be by
canal.

ᵈ Or " over against."

soon as the winter was over and was now rapidly
settling affairs in Alexandria ; but he dispatched his sends Titus
against
Jerusalem.
son Titus with picked forces to crush Jerusalem.
Titus, accordingly, proceeding by land to Nicopolis [a]
(distant twenty [b] furlongs from Alexandria), there Itinerary of
march of
Titus from
Alexandria
to Caesarea.
embarked his army on ships of war and sailed up [c]
the Nile into [d] the Mendesian canton [e] to the city
of Thmuis.[f] Here he disembarked and, resuming
his march, passed a night at a small town called
Tanis.[g] His second day's march brought him to
Heracleopolis,[h] the third to Pelusium.[i] Having
halted here two days to refresh his army, on the
third he crossed the Pelusiac river-mouths, and,
advancing a day's march through the desert, encamped near the temple of the Casian Zeus,[j] and
on the next day at Ostracine [k] ; this station was
destitute of water, which is brought from elsewhere
for the use of the inhabitants. He next rested at
Rhinocorura,[l] whence he advanced to his fourth

[e] The " nome " of which Mendes (*Tell er-Rub̔*, S.W. of
Lake *Menzaleh*) was the capital.
[f] *Tmai* or (Smith and Bartholomew, *Atlas of Holy Land*,
Map 7) *Tell Ibu es-Salam* ; S.W. of Mendes.
[g] *San*, the Zoan of the Old Testament, some 20 miles E. of
Thmuis.
[h] Heracleopolis Parva ; site now covered by Lake
Menzaleh.
[i] *Tell Farama* alias *Tineh* (Biblical Sin, Ezek. xxx. 15),
§ 610.
[j] A temple of Zeus-Ammon near the summit of Mons
Casius (*Ras el-Kasrun*), a sandstone range adjoining Lake
Sirbonis and the Mediterranean : Pompey's tomb was on
the hill-side (Strabo xvii. 760).
[k] Unidentified.
[l] Or Rhinocolura, *el-'Arish*, on the confines of Egypt and
Palestine ; " the river of Egypt," *Wady el-'Arish*, marking
the boundary in Old Testament times.

εἰς Ῥάφειαν προελθὼν σταθμὸν τέταρτον, ἔστι δ᾽
ἡ πόλις αὕτη Συρίας ἀρχή, τὸ πέμπτον ἐν Γάζῃ
663 τίθεται στρατόπεδον, μεθ᾽ ἣν εἰς Ἀσκάλωνα
κἀκεῖθεν εἰς Ἰάμνειαν, ἔπειτα εἰς Ἰόππην κἀξ
Ἰόππης εἰς Καισάρειαν ἀφικνεῖται διεγνωκὼς αὐτόθι τὰς ἄλλας δυνάμεις ἀθροίζειν.

---

^a *Refaḥ*; Polybius likewise reckons it as the first city of

station, Raphia,[a] at which city Syria begins. His fifth camp he pitched at Gaza ; next he marched to Ascalon, and from there to Jamnia, then to Joppa, and from Joppa he finally reached Caesarea, the rendezvous fixed on for the concentration of his forces.

Syria, 'Ραφίας ἡ κεῖται μετὰ 'Ρινοκόλουρα πρώτη τῶν κατὰ Κοίλην Συρίαν πόλεων ὡς πρὸς τὴν Αἴγυπτον (v. 80).

ΒΙΒΛΙΟΝ Ε

1 (i. 1) Ὁ μὲν Τίτος ὃν προειρήκαμεν τρόπον
διοδεύσας τὴν ὑπὲρ Αἰγύπτου μέχρι Συρίας
ἐρημίαν εἰς Καισάρειαν παρῆν, ταύτῃ διεγνωκὼς
2 προσυντάξασθαι τὰς δυνάμεις. ἔτι δ᾽ αὐτοῦ κατὰ
τὴν Ἀλεξάνδρειαν συγκαθισταμένου τῷ πατρὶ
τὴν ἡγεμονίαν νέον[1] αὐτοῖς ἐγκεχειρισμένην ὑπὸ
τοῦ θεοῦ, συνέβη καὶ τὴν ἐν τοῖς Ἱεροσολύμοις
στάσιν ἀνακμάσασαν τριμερῆ γενέσθαι καὶ καθ᾽
αὐτοῦ θάτερον ἐπιστρέψαι μέρος, ὅπερ ἄν τις ὡς
3 ἐν κακοῖς ἀγαθὸν εἴποι καὶ δίκης ἔργον. ἡ μὲν
γὰρ κατὰ τοῦ δήμου τῶν ζηλωτῶν ἐπίθεσις,
ἥπερ κατῆρξεν ἁλώσεως τῇ πόλει, προδεδήλωται
μετὰ ἀκριβείας ὅθεν τε ἔφυ καὶ πρὸς ὅσον κακῶν
4 ἀνηυξήθη[2]· ταύτην δ᾽ οὐκ ἂν ἁμάρτοι τις εἰπὼν
στάσει στάσιν ἐγγενέσθαι, καὶ καθάπερ θηρίον λυσ-
σῆσαν ἐνδείᾳ τῶν ἔξωθεν ἐπὶ τὰς ἰδίας ἤδη σάρκας
5 ὁρμᾶν. (2) Ἐλεάζαρος γὰρ[3] ὁ τοῦ Σίμωνος, ὃς δὴ
καὶ τὰ πρῶτα τοῦ δήμου τοὺς ζηλωτὰς ἀπέστησεν
εἰς τὸ τέμενος, ὡς ἀγανακτῶν δῆθεν ἐπὶ τοῖς
ὁσημέραι τῷ Ἰωάννῃ τολμωμένοις, οὐ γὰρ ἀν-
επαύετο φονῶν οὗτος, τὸ δ᾽ ἀληθὲς αὐτοῦ μετα-

---

[1] V Lat. (nuper): νέαν the rest.
[2] ηὐξήθη PM.
[3] ὁρμᾶν· Ἐλεάζαρος γὰρ L: ὁρμᾷ, οὕτως Ἐλ. the rest.

BOOK V

(i. 1) Titus having thus, as described above, accom- plished the desert march across Egypt to Syria, arrived at Caesarea, the place where he had decided to marshal his forces before the campaign. But already, while he was still at Alexandria, assisting his father to establish the empire which God had recently committed to their hands, it so happened that the civil strife in Jerusalem had reached a fresh climax and become a triangular affair, one of the parties having turned its arms against itself; a discord which, as between criminals, might be called a blessing and a work of justice. Of the Zealots' attack upon the populace—the first step towards the city's ruin—a precise account has already been given, showing its origin and all the mischief in which it culminated.[a] This new development might be not inaccurately described as a faction bred within a faction, which like some raving beast for lack of other food at length preyed upon its own flesh.

(2) For Eleazar,[b] son of Simon, the man who had originally caused the Zealots to break with the citizens and withdraw into the sacred precincts, now —ostensibly from indignation at the enormities daily perpetrated by John, who continued unabated his murderous career, but, in reality, because he could

6 γενεστέρῳ τυράννῳ μὴ φέρων ὑποτετάχθαι, πόθῳ
τῶν ὅλων καὶ δυναστείας ἰδίας ἐπιθυμίᾳ διίσταται,
παραλαβὼν Ἰούδην τε τὸν Χελκία[1] καὶ Σίμωνα
τὸν Ἐσρῶνος τῶν δυνατῶν, πρὸς οἷς Ἐζεκίας
7 [ἦν] Χωβαρεῖ παῖς οὐκ ἄσημος. καθ' ἕκαστον
δὲ οὐκ ὀλίγοι τῶν ζηλωτῶν ἠκολούθησαν, καὶ
καταλαβόμενοι τὸν ἐνδότερον τοῦ νεὼ περίβολον
ὑπὲρ τὰς ἱερὰς πύλας ἐπὶ τῶν ἁγίων μετώπων[2]
8 τίθενται τὰ ὅπλα. πλήρεις μὲν οὖν ἐπιτηδείων
ὄντες ἐθάρρουν, καὶ γὰρ ἀφθονίᾳ τῶν ἱερῶν ἐγίνετο πραγμάτων τοῖς γε μηδὲν ἀσεβὲς ἡγουμένοις,
ὀλιγότητι δὲ[3] τῇ κατὰ σφᾶς ὀρρωδοῦντες ἐγ-
9 καθήμενοι[4] τὰ πολλὰ[5] κατὰ χώραν ἔμενον. ὁ δὲ
Ἰωάννης ὅσον ἀνδρῶν ὑπερεῖχε πλήθει, τοσοῦτον
ἐλείπετο τῷ τόπῳ, καὶ κατὰ κορυφὴν ἔχων τοὺς
πολεμίους οὔτ' ἀδεεῖς ἐποιεῖτο τὰς προσβολὰς
10 οὔτε δι' ὀργὴν ἠρέμει· κακούμενος δὲ πλέον
ἥπερ διατιθεὶς τοὺς περὶ τὸν Ἐλεάζαρον ὅμως
οὐκ ἀνίει, συνεχεῖς δ' ἐκδρομαὶ[6] καὶ βελῶν ἀφέσεις
ἐγίνοντο, καὶ φόνοις ἐμιαίνετο πανταχοῦ τὸ ἱερόν.
11 (3) Ὁ δὲ τοῦ Γιώρα Σίμων, ὃν ἐν ταῖς ἀμη-
χανίαις ἐπίκλητον αὐτῷ τύραννον ὁ δῆμος ἐλπίδι
βοηθείας προσεισήγαγε,[7] τήν τε ἄνω πόλιν ἔχων
καὶ τῆς κάτω πολὺ μέρος, ἐρρωμενέστερον ἤδη
τοῖς περὶ τὸν Ἰωάννην προσέβαλλεν ὡς ἂν καὶ
καθύπερθεν πολεμουμένοις· ἦν δ' ὑπὸ χεῖρα
προσιὼν αὐτοῖς,[8] ὥσπερ ἐκεῖνοι τοῖς ἄνωθεν.
12 καὶ τῷ Ἰωάννῃ διχόθεν πολεμουμένῳ συνέβαινε

---

[1] Hudson: Χέλικα (Chelicae Lat.) mss.
[2] μετώπων P Exc.   [3] δ' ἐν PA.
[4] P: ἐγκαθισάμενοι or ἐγκαθιστάμενοι the rest.
[5] ὅπλα L Exc.   [6] + κατ' ἀλλήλων C.

202

not brook submission to a tyrant junior to himself,
and craved absolute mastery and a despotism of his
own—seceded from the party, taking with him Judes
son of Chelcias, and Simon son of Esron, persons of
weight. along with a man of some distinction, Ezechias
son of Chobari. Each of these having a considerable
following of Zealots, the seceders took possession of
the inner court of the temple and planted their
weapons above the holy gates on the sacred façade.
Being amply supplied with necessaries they had no
fears on that ground, for there was an abundance of
consecrated articles for those who deemed nothing
impious ; but they were daunted by the paucity of
their numbers and as a rule sat still and held their
ground. On the other hand, John's numerical John holds
superiority was counterbalanced by the inferiority outer court
of his position : with his enemies over his head, he of temple.
could neither attack them with impunity, nor would
rage allow him to remain inactive. Though suffering
more injury than he inflicted on Eleazar and his men,
he nevertheless would not desist ; thus there were
continual sallies and showers of missiles, and the
temple on every side was defiled with carnage.

(3) Then there was Simon, son of Gioras, whom the Simon holds
people in their straits had summoned in hope of the city.
relief, only to impose upon themselves a further
tyrant.[a] He occupied the Upper and a large part of
the Lower City, and now attacked John's party more
vigorously, seeing that they were also assailed from
above ; but he was attacking them from beneath, as
were they their foes higher up.   John, thus between

[a] iv. 573.

---

[7] L : προσήγαγε most MSS.
[8] Hudson with Exc. : αὐτὸς MSS.

βλάπτεσθαί τε καὶ βλάπτειν [εὐκόλως],[1] καὶ
καθ᾽ ὅσον ἡττᾶτο τῶν ἀμφὶ τὸν Ἐλεάζαρον ὧν
ταπεινότερος, τοσοῦτον ἐπλεονέκτει τῷ ὑψηλῷ
13 τοῦ Σίμωνος. παρὸ καὶ χειρὶ μὲν τὰς κάτωθεν
προσβολὰς ἰσχυρῶς[2] εἶργε, τοὺς δ᾽ ἄνωθεν ἀπὸ
τοῦ ἱεροῦ κατακοντίζοντας ἀνέστελλε τοῖς ὀργάνοις·
14 ὀξυβελεῖς τε γὰρ αὐτῷ καὶ καταπέλται παρῆσαν οὐκ
ὀλίγοι καὶ λιθοβόλοι, δι᾽ ὧν οὐ μόνον ἠμύνετο
τοὺς πολεμοῦντας, ἀλλὰ καὶ πολλοὺς τῶν ἱερουρ-
15 γούντων ἀνήρει. καίπερ γὰρ πρὸς πᾶσαν ἀσέβειαν
ἐκλελυσσηκότες, ὅμως τοὺς θύειν ἐθέλοντας εἰσ-
ηφίεσαν, μεθ᾽ ὑποψιῶν μὲν καὶ φυλακῆς τοὺς
ἐπιχωρίους, διερευνώμενοι δὲ τοὺς ξένους·[3] οἳ
καίπερ περὶ τὰς εἰσόδους δυσωπήσαντες αὐτῶν
τὴν ὠμότητα παρανάλωμα τῆς στάσεως ἐγίνοντο.
16 τὰ γὰρ ἀπὸ τῶν ὀργάνων βέλη μέχρι τοῦ βωμοῦ
καὶ τοῦ νεὼ διὰ τὴν βίαν ὑπερφερόμενα τοῖς τε
17 ἱερεῦσι καὶ τοῖς ἱερουργοῦσιν ἐνέπιπτε, καὶ πολλοὶ
σπεύσαντες ἀπὸ γῆς περάτων περὶ[4] τὸν διώνυμον
καὶ πᾶσιν ἀνθρώποις χῶρον ἅγιον πρὸ τῶν
θυμάτων ἔπεσον αὐτοὶ καὶ τὸν Ἕλλησι πᾶσι καὶ
βαρβάροις σεβάσμιον βωμὸν κατέσπεισαν ἰδίῳ
18 φόνῳ, νεκροῖς δ᾽ ἐπιχωρίοις ἀλλόφυλοι καὶ ἱερεῦσι
βέβηλοι συνεφύροντο, καὶ παντοδαπῶν αἷμα
πτωμάτων ἐν τοῖς θείοις περιβόλοις ἐλιμνάζετο.
19 τί τηλικοῦτον, ὦ τλημονεστάτη πόλις, πέπονθας
ὑπὸ Ῥωμαίων, οἵ σου τὰ ἐμφύλια μύση πυρὶ

---

[1] om. Lat. [2] εὐμαρῶς LVRC.
[3] τοὺς ἐπιχωρίους διερευνώμενοι, τοὺς δὲ ξένους ἀδεέστερον LC
Exc. [4] ἐπὶ L Exc. Lat.

---

[a] "Stone-throwers"=*ballistae*. "Quick-firers"=a species
of catapult for discharging arrows, perhaps *scorpiones*
(Hudson); *cf*. iii. 80 note.

two fires, found losses befall him as easily as he inflicted them ; and the disadvantage from which he suffered in being lower than Eleazar was proportionate to his advantage over Simon in virtue of his higher position. Consequently, while he stoutly repelled attacks from below with hand missiles, he reserved his engines to check the hail of javelins from the temple above ; for he was amply supplied with " quick-firers," catapults and " stone-throwers," [a] with which he not only beat off his assailants but also killed many of the worshippers. For although these frenzied men had stopped short of no impiety, they nevertheless admitted those who wished to offer sacrifices, native Jews suspiciously and with precaution, strangers after a thorough search [b] ; yet these, though successful at the entrances in deprecating their cruelty, [c] often became casual victims of the sedition. For the missiles from the engines flew over with such force that they reached the altar and the sanctuary, lighting upon priests and sacrificers ; and many who had sped from the ends of the earth to gather round this farfamed spot, reverenced by all mankind, fell there themselves before [d] their sacrifices, and sprinkled with libations of their own blood that altar universally venerated by Greeks and barbarians. The dead bodies of natives and aliens, of priests and laity, were mingled in a mass, and the blood of all manner of corpses formed pools in the courts of God. What misery to equal that, most wretched city, hast thou suffered at the hands of the Romans, who entered to

Worshippers in temple killed while sacrificing.

[b] Or (with the other reading) " native Jews after a suspicious and cautious search, strangers with less apprehension."

[c] Or perhaps " successful in gaining entry by making them blush for their cruelty." [d] Or " before offering."

JOSEPHUS

καθαροῦντες[1] εἰσῆλθον; θεοῦ μὲν γὰρ οὔτε ἧς
ἔτι χῶρος οὔτε μένειν ἐδύνασο, τάφος οἰκείων
γενομένη σωμάτων καὶ πολέμου τὸν ναὸν ἐμφυλίου
ποιήσασα[2] πολυάνδριον· δύναιο δ' ἂν γενέσθαι
πάλιν ἀμείνων, εἴγε ποτὲ τὸν πορθήσαντα θεὸν
20 ἐξιλάσῃ. ἀλλὰ καθεκτέον γὰρ καὶ τὰ πάθη τῷ
νόμῳ τῆς γραφῆς,[3] ὡς οὐκ ὀλοφυρμῶν οἰκείων ὁ
καιρός, ἀλλ' ἀφηγήσεως πραγμάτων. δίειμι δὲ
τὰ ἑξῆς ἔργα τῆς στάσεως.

21 (4) Τριχῇ τῶν ἐπιβούλων τῆς πόλεως διῃρημένων οἱ μὲν περὶ τὸν Ἐλεάζαρον τὰς ἱερὰς
ἀπαρχὰς διαφυλάσσοντες κατὰ τοῦ Ἰωάννου τὴν
μέθην ἔφερον, οἱ δὲ σὺν τούτῳ διαρπάζοντες τοὺς
δημότας ἠγείροντο κατὰ τοῦ Σίμωνος· ἦν δὲ
κἀκείνῳ τροφὴ κατὰ τῶν ἀντιστασιαστῶν ἡ
22 πόλις. ὁπότε μὲν οὖν ἀμφοτέρωθεν ἐπιχειροῖτο,
τοὺς συνόντας ὁ Ἰωάννης ἀντέστρεφε, καὶ τοὺς
μὲν ἐκ τῆς πόλεως ἀνιόντας ἀπὸ τῶν στοῶν
βάλλων, τοὺς δ' ἀπὸ τοῦ ἱεροῦ κατακοντίζοντας
23 ἠμύνετο τοῖς ὀργάνοις· εἰ δ' ἐλευθερωθείη ποτὲ
τῶν καθύπερθεν ἐπικειμένων, διανέπαυε δ' αὐτοὺς
πολλάκις μέθη [τε] καὶ κάματος, ἀδεέστερον τοῖς
24 περὶ τὸν Σίμωνα μετὰ πλειόνων ἐπεξέθεεν. ἀεὶ
δ' ἐφ' ὅσον τρέψαιτο τῆς πόλεως ὑπεπίμπρα τὰς

---

[1] πυρὶ καθαροῦντες Lat. (πυρὶ καθαίροντες L Exc.), cf. iv.
323: περικαθαιροῦντες (περὶ καθ.) the rest.
[2] Hudson (constitueras Lat.): πλήσασα MSS.
[3] συγγραφῆς MVRC.

---

[a] Cf. Baruch iv. 18-21 : " For he that brought these
plagues upon you will deliver you from the hand of your
enemies. . . . Cry unto God and he shall deliver you."
Josephus would have countenanced the plea for penitence
206

purge with fire thy internal pollutions? For thou wert no longer God's place, nor couldest thou survive, after becoming a sepulchre for the bodies of thine own children and converting the sanctuary into a charnel-house of civil war. Yet might there be hopes for an amelioration of thy lot, if ever thou wouldst propitiate that God who devastated thee![a] However, the laws of history compel one to restrain even one's emotions, since this is not the place for personal lamentations but for a narrative of events.[b] I therefore proceed to relate the after history of the sedition.

(4) The conspirators against the city being now divided into three camps, Eleazar's party, having the keeping of the sacred first-fruits, directed their drunken fury against John; the latter with his associates plundered the townsfolk and wreaked their rage upon Simon; while Simon also to meet the rival factions looked to the city for supplies. Whenever John found himself attacked on both sides, he would face his men about in opposite directions, on the one hand hurling missiles from the porticoes upon those coming up from the town, on the other repelling with his engines those who were pouring their javelins upon him from the temple; but if ever he were relieved from pressure from above—and intoxication and fatigue often produced a cessation of this fire— he would sally out with more confidence and in greater strength against Simon. And, to whatever part of the city he turned his steps, his invariable

The civil war prepares the way for famine.

in the former portion of that book, but not the vindictive spirit which appears in the latter part (written after A.D. 70), and which ultimately led to the fierce outbreaks under Trajan and Hadrian.
[b] *Cf.* the proem to *B.J.* i. 11 f.

οἰκίας σίτου μεστὰς καὶ παντοδαπῶν ἐπιτηδείων·
τὸ δ' αὐτὸ πάλιν ὑποχωροῦντος ἐπιὼν ὁ Σίμων
ἔπραττεν, ὥσπερ ἐπίτηδες Ῥωμαίοις διαφθείροντες
ἃ παρεσκευάσατο πρὸς πολιορκίαν ἡ πόλις, καὶ
τὰ νεῦρα τῆς αὑτῶν ὑποκόπτοντες δυνάμεως.
25 συνέβη γοῦν τὰ [μὲν] περὶ τὸ ἱερὸν πάντα συμ-
φλεγῆναι καὶ μεταίχμιον ἐρημίας γενέσθαι παρατάξεως οἰκείας τὴν πόλιν, κατακαῆναι δὲ πλὴν
ὀλίγου πάντα τὸν σῖτον, ὃς ἂν αὐτοῖς οὐκ ἐπ'
26 ὀλίγα διήρκεσεν ἔτη πολιορκουμένοις. λιμῷ γοῦν
ἑάλωσαν, ὅπερ[1] ἥκιστα δυνατὸν ἦν, εἰ μὴ τοῦτον
αὑτοῖς προπαρεσκεύασαν.

27 (5) Πανταχόθεν δὲ τῆς πόλεως πολεμουμένης
ὑπὸ τῶν ἐπιβούλων καὶ συγκλύδων μέσος ὁ
28 δῆμος ὥσπερ μέγα σῶμα διεσπαράσσετο. γηραιοὶ
δὲ καὶ γυναῖκες ὑπ' ἀμηχανίας [τῶν εἴσω κακῶν][2]
ηὔχοντο Ῥωμαίους[3] καὶ τὸν ἔξωθεν πόλεμον ἐπ'
29 ἐλευθερίᾳ τῶν εἴσω κακῶν ἐκαραδόκουν. κατάπληξις δὲ δεινὴ καὶ δέος ἦν τοῖς γνησίοις, καὶ
οὔτε βουλῆς καιρὸς εἰς μεταβολὴν οὔτε συμβάσεως
30 ἐλπὶς οὔτε φυγῆς[4] τοῖς ἐθέλουσιν· ἐφρουρεῖτο γὰρ
πάντα, καὶ τὰ λοιπὰ στασιάζοντες οἱ ἀρχιλῃσταὶ
τοὺς εἰρηνικὰ Ῥωμαίοις φρονοῦντας ἢ πρὸς
αὐτομολίαν ὑπόπτους ὡς κοινοὺς πολεμίους ἀνῄρουν καὶ μόνον ὡμονόουν τὸ φονεύειν τοὺς σωτη-
31 ρίας ἀξίους. καὶ τῶν μὲν μαχομένων ἀδιάλειπτος
ἦν κραυγὴ μεθ' ἡμέραν τε καὶ νύκτωρ, δεινότεροι
32 δὲ οἱ τῶν πενθούντων ὀδυρμοὶ δέει.[5] καὶ θρήνων

[1] ὥσπερ PAL : qua Lat. : whence ᾧπερ Destinon.
[2] Perhaps accidentally repeated from below.
[3] Destinon : Ῥωμαίοις MSS.

practice was to set light to the buildings stocked with
corn and all kinds of provisions, and upon his retreat
Simon advanced and did the same ; as though they
were purposely serving the Romans by destroying
what the city had provided against a siege and severing the sinews of their own strength. At all events
the result was that all the environs of the temple
were reduced to ashes, the city was converted into a
desolate no man's land for their domestic warfare,
and almost all the corn, which might have sufficed
them for many years of siege, was burnt up. Through
famine certainly the city fell, a fate which would
have been practically impossible, had they not prepared the way for it themselves.

(5) The city being now on all sides beset by these
battling conspirators and their rabble, between them
the people, like some huge carcase, was torn in
pieces. Old men and women in their helplessness
prayed for the coming of the Romans and eagerly
looked for the external war to liberate them from
their internal miseries. Loyal citizens, for their
part, were in dire despondency and alarm, having no
opportunity for planning any change of policy, no
hope of coming to terms or of flight, if they had the
will ; for watch was kept everywhere, and the brigand
chiefs, divided on all else, put to death as their
common enemies any in favour of peace with the
Romans or suspected of an intention to desert, and
were unanimous only in slaughtering those deserving
of deliverance. The shouts of the combatants rang
incessantly by day and night, but yet more harrowing were the mourners' terrified lamentations. Their

Miseries of the populace.

---

⁴ LC Exc. Lat. : φυγὴ the rest.
⁵ PAM Lat. : ἀεὶ the rest.

μὲν αἰτίας ἐπαλλήλους αἱ συμφοραὶ προσέφερον,
τὰς δ' οἰμωγὰς ἐνέκλειεν ἡ κατάπληξις αὐτῶν,
φιμούμενοι δὲ τά γε πάθη τῷ φόβῳ μεμυκόσι
33 τοῖς στεναγμοῖς ἐβασανίζοντο. καὶ οὔτε πρὸς
τοὺς ζῶντας ἦν αἰδὼς ἔτι τοῖς προσήκουσιν οὔτε
πρόνοια τῶν ἀπολωλότων ταφῆς. αἴτιον δ' ἀμφοτέρων ἡ καθ' ἑαυτὸν ἀπόγνωσις ἑκάστου· παρεῖσαν
γὰρ εἰς πάντα τὰς προθυμίας οἱ μὴ στασιάζοντες
34 ὡς ἀπολούμενοι πάντως ὅσον οὐδέπω. πατοῦντες
δὴ τοὺς νεκροὺς ἐπ' ἀλλήλοις σεσωρευμένους οἱ
στασιασταὶ συνεπλέκοντο καὶ τὴν ἀπόνοιαν [ἀπὸ]¹
τῶν ἐν ποσὶ πτωμάτων σπῶντες ἦσαν ἀγριώτεροι.
35 προσεξευρίσκοντες δ' ἀεί τι καθ' αὑτῶν ὀλέθριον
καὶ πᾶν τὸ δοχθὲν ἀφειδῶς δρῶντες οὐδεμίαν οὔτ'
36 αἰκίας ὁδὸν οὔτε ὠμότητος παρέλειπον. ἀμέλει
Ἰωάννης τὴν ἱερὰν ὕλην εἰς πολεμιστηρίων κατασκευὴν ὀργάνων ἀπεχρήσατο· δόξαν γάρ ποτε τῷ
λαῷ καὶ τοῖς ἀρχιερεῦσιν ὑποστηρίξαντας τὸν
ναὸν εἴκοσι πήχεις προσυψῶσαι, κατάγει μὲν ἀπὸ
τοῦ Λιβάνου μεγίστοις ἀναλώμασι καὶ πόνοις
τὴν χρήσιμον ὕλην ὁ βασιλεὺς Ἀγρίππας, ξύλα
θέας ἄξια τήν τε εὐθύτητα καὶ τὸ μέγεθος·
37 μεσολαβήσαντος δὲ τοῦ πολέμου τὸ ἔργον Ἰωάννης
τεμὼν αὐτὰ πύργους κατεσκεύασεν, ἐξαρκοῦν
τὸ μῆκος εὑρὼν πρὸς τοὺς ἀπὸ τοῦ καθύπερθεν
38 ἱεροῦ μαχομένους, ἵστησί τε προσαγαγὼν κατόπιν
τοῦ περιβόλου τῆς πρὸς δύσιν ἐξέδρας ἄντικρυς,

¹ om. PA: so Destinon, reading ἀπόπνοιαν for ἀπόνοιαν,
" sniffing the exhalations from," etc.
210

calamities provided, indeed, perpetual cause for grief, but consternation locked their wailings within their breasts, and while fear suppressed all outward emotion they were tortured with stifled groans. No regard for the living was any longer paid by their relations, no thought was taken for the burial of the dead—negligences both due to personal despair ; for those who took no part in sedition lost interest in everything, momentarily expecting certain destruction. The rival parties, meanwhile, were at grips, trampling over the dead bodies that were piled upon each other, the frenzy inhaled from the corpses at their feet increasing their savagery ; and ever inventing some new instrument of mutual destruction and unsparingly putting every plan into practice, they left untried no method of outrage or brutality. Indeed John actually misappropriated the sacred timber for the construction of engines of war. For the people and the chief priests having decided in the past to underpin the sanctuary and to raise it twenty cubits higher, King Agrippa[a] had, at immense labour and expense, brought down from Mount Libanus the materials for that purpose, beams that for straightness and size were a sight to see. But the war having interrupted the work, John, finding them long enough to reach his assailants on the temple above, had them cut and made into towers, which he then brought up and placed in the rear of the inner court, opposite the western hall,[b] where

John constructs military towers from sacred timber.

---

[a] Agrippa II.

[b] Or " recess," opening from the portico surrounding the ναός, in the middle of the west wall of the inner court ; the translation " gate-room " (Hastings, *D.B.* s.v. " Temple ") is unsuitable, because there was no gate at this point (v. 200).

ἧπερ καὶ μόνη δυνατὸν ἦν, τῶν ἄλλων μερῶν
βαθμοῖς πόρρωθεν διειλημένων.

39 (6) Καὶ ὁ μὲν τοῖς κατασκευασθεῖσιν ἐξ ἀσεβείας ὀργάνοις κρατήσειν ἤλπισε τῶν ἐχθρῶν, ὁ δὲ
θεὸς ἄχρηστον αὐτῷ τὸν πόνον ἀπέδειξε πρὶν
ἐπιστῆσαί τινα τῶν πύργων Ῥωμαίους ἐπαγαγών.

40 ὁ γὰρ δὴ Τίτος ἐπειδὴ τὰ μὲν συνήγαγε τῆς
δυνάμεως πρὸς αὑτόν, τοῖς δ' ἐπὶ Ἱεροσολύμων
συναντᾶν ἐπιστείλας,[1] ἐξήλαυνε τῆς Καισαρείας.

41 ἦν δὲ τρία μὲν τὰ πρότερον αὐτοῦ τῷ πατρὶ
συνδῃώσαντα τὴν Ἰουδαίαν τάγματα καὶ τὸ πάλαι
σὺν Κεστίῳ πταῖσαν δωδέκατον, ὅπερ καὶ ἄλλως
ἐπίσημον δι' ἀνδρείαν ὑπάρχον τότε κατὰ μνήμην

42 ὧν ἔπαθεν εἰς ἄμυναν ᾔει προθυμότερον. τούτων
μὲν οὖν τὸ πέμπτον δι' Ἀμμαοῦς ἐκέλευσεν αὐτῷ
συναντᾶν καὶ διὰ Ἱεριχοῦντος τὸ δέκατον ἀνα-
βαίνειν, αὐτὸς δ' ἀνέζευξε μετὰ τῶν λοιπῶν,
πρὸς οἷς αἵ τε τῶν βασιλέων συμμαχίαι πολὺ[2]
πλείους καὶ συχνοὶ τῶν ἀπὸ τῆς Συρίας ἐπί-

43 κουροι συνῆλθον. ἀνεπληρώθη δὲ καὶ τῶν τεσσάρων ταγμάτων ὅσον Οὐεσπασιανὸς ἐπιλέξας
Μουκιανῷ συνέπεμψεν εἰς Ἰταλίαν ἐκ τῶν ἐπελ-

44 θόντων μετὰ Τίτου. δισχίλιοι μὲν γὰρ αὐτῷ τῶν
ἀπ' Ἀλεξανδρείας στρατευμάτων ἐπίλεκτοι, τρισ-
χίλιοι δὲ συνείποντο τῶν ἀπ' Εὐφράτου φυλάκων.

45 φίλων δὲ δοκιμώτατος εὔνοιάν τε καὶ σύνεσιν
Τιβέριος Ἀλέξανδρος, πρότερον μὲν αὐτοῖς τὴν

46 Αἴγυπτον διέπων, τότε δὲ τῶν στρατευμάτων

---

[1] L: ἐπέστειλεν (ἐπέστελλεν) the rest.
[2] P: πάλιν A: πάλαι L (? ἢ πάλαι Lat.): πᾶσαι the rest.

alone this was practicable, the other sides being cut off from approach by flights of steps.

(6) With the aid of the engines thus impiously constructed John hoped to master his foes, but God rendered his labour vain by bringing the Romans upon the scene before he had set a single man upon his towers. For Titus, having assembled part of his forces at headquarters and sent orders to the rest to join him at Jerusalem, was now on the march from Caesarea. He had the three legions [a] which under his father had previously ravaged Judaea, and the twelfth which under Cestius had once been defeated; [b] this legion, bearing a general reputation for valour, now, with the recollection of what it had suffered, advanced with the greater alacrity for revenge. Of these he directed the fifth to join him by the Emmaus route and the tenth to ascend by way of Jericho ; while he himself set out with the others, being further attended by the contingents from the allied kings, in greatly increased strength, and by a considerable body of Syrian auxiliaries. The gaps in the four legions caused by the drafts which Vespasian had sent with Mucianus to Italy [c] were filled by the new troops brought up by Titus. For two thousand picked men from the armies at Alexandria and three thousand guards from the Euphrates accompanied ·him. With these was the most tried of all his friends for loyalty and sagacity, Tiberius Alexander, [d] hitherto in charge of Egypt in the interests of Titus and his father, and now deemed worthy to take

Titus, with four legions, advances upon Jerusalem.

[a] V, X, and XV, B. iii. 65.
[b] ii. 500-555.   [c] iv. 632.
[d] For the diversified career of this distinguished Alexandrian Jew see ii. 220 note.

ἄρχειν[1] κριθεὶς ἄξιος ἐξ ὧν ἐδεξιώσατο πρῶτος
ἐγειρομένην ἄρτι τὴν ἡγεμονίαν καὶ μετὰ πίστεως
λαμπρᾶς ἐξ ἀδήλου[2] τῇ τύχῃ προσέθετο, σύμβου-
λός γε μὴν ταῖς τοῦ πολέμου χρείαις, ἡλικίᾳ τε
προύχων καὶ κατ' ἐμπειρίαν, εἵπετο.

47 (ii. 1) Προϊόντι δὲ εἰς τὴν πολεμίαν Τίτῳ
προῆγον μὲν οἱ βασιλικοὶ καὶ πᾶν τὸ συμμαχικόν,
ἐφ' οἷς ὁδοποιοὶ καὶ μετρηταὶ στρατοπέδων,
ἔπειτα τὰ τῶν ἡγεμόνων σκευοφόρα καὶ μετὰ τοὺς
τούτων ὁπλίτας αὐτὸς τούς τε ἄλλους ἐπιλέκτους
καὶ τοὺς λογχοφόρους ἔχων, κατόπιν δ' αὐτῷ
48 τοῦ τάγματος τὸ ἱππικόν· οὗτοι δὲ πρὸ τῶν
μηχανημάτων, κἀπ' ἐκείνοις μετ' ἐπιλέκτων χιλίαρχοι καὶ σπειρῶν ἔπαρχοι, μετὰ δὲ τούτους
περὶ τὸν αἰετὸν· αἱ σημαῖαι, καὶ ἔμπροσθεν οἱ
σαλπιγκταὶ τῶν σημαιῶν, ἐπὶ δὲ τούτοις ἡ φάλαγξ
49 τὸ στῖφος εἰς ἐξ πλατύνασα. τὸ δ' οἰκετικὸν
ἑκάστου τάγματος ὀπίσω καὶ πρὸ τούτων τὰ
σκευοφόρα, τελευταῖοι δὲ πάντων οἱ μίσθιοι καὶ
50 τούτων φύλακες οὐραγοί. προάγων δὲ τὴν δύναμιν
ἐν κόσμῳ, καθὰ Ῥωμαίοις σύνηθες, ἐμβάλλει διὰ
τῆς Σαμαρείτιδος εἰς Γόφνα κατειλημμένην τε
πρότερον ὑπὸ τοῦ πατρὸς καὶ τότε φρουρουμένην·
51 ἔνθα μίαν ἑσπέραν[3] αὐλισάμενος ὑπὸ τὴν ἕω
πρόεισι, καὶ διανύσας ἡμέρας σταθμὸν στρατοπεδεύεται κατὰ τὸν ὑπὸ Ἰουδαίων πατρίως
Ἀκανθῶν αὐλῶνα καλούμενον πρός τινι κώμῃ

---

[1] Hudson with Lat.: ἄρχων mss. (om. M).
[2] ἔτ' ἀδήλῳ Niese: ἐπ' ἀδήλῳ (cf. vii. 104) is possible.
[3] LC Lat.: ἡμέραν the rest.

command of these armies, because he had been the first to welcome the dynasty just arising and with splendid faith had attached himself to its fortunes while they were still uncertain. Pre-eminent moreover, through years and experience, as a counsellor in the exigencies of war, he now accompanied Titus.

(ii. 1) As Titus advanced [a] into enemy territory, his vanguard consisted of the contingents of the kings with the whole body of auxiliaries. Next to these were the pioneers and camp-measurers, then the officers' baggage-train ; behind the troops protecting these came the commander-in-chief, escorted by the lancers and other picked troops, and followed by the legionary cavalry. These were succeeded by the engines, and these by the tribunes and prefects of cohorts with a picked escort ; after them and surrounding the eagle [b] came the ensigns preceded by their trumpeters, and behind them the solid column, six abreast. The servants attached to each legion followed in a body, preceded by the baggage-train. Last of all came the mercenaries with a rearguard to keep watch on them. Leading his army forward in this orderly array, according to Roman usage, Titus advanced through Samaria to Gophna,[c] previously captured by his father and now garrisoned. After resting here one night he set forward at dawn, and at the end of a full day's march encamped in the valley which is called by the Jews in their native tongue "Valley of thorns," close to a village named

Order of the army on the march to Judaea.

---

[a] The following description should be compared with that of Vespasian's army on the march into Galilee, iii. 115-126.

[b] *Cf.* iii. 123.

[c] *Jufna*, some 13 miles N. of Jerusalem ; for Vespasian's capture of the " toparchy " of Gophna see iv. 551.

Γαβὰθ Σαοὺλ λεγομένῃ, σημαίνει δὲ τοῦτο λόφον
Σαούλου, διέχων ἀπὸ τῶν Ἱεροσολύμων ὅσον ἀπὸ
52 τριάκοντα σταδίων. ἀναλαβὼν δ' ἐντεῦθεν ὅσον
εἰς ἑξακοσίους τῶν ἐπιλέκτων ἱππέων ᾖει τήν τε
πόλιν περισκεψόμενος, ὅπως ὀχυρότητος ἔχοι,
καὶ τὰ φρονήματα τῶν Ἰουδαίων, εἰ πρὸς τὴν
ὄψιν αὐτοῦ πρὶν εἰς χεῖρας ἐλθεῖν ὑποδείσαντες
53 ἐνδοῖεν· πέπυστο[1] γάρ, ὅπερ ἦν ἀληθές, τοῖς
στασιώδεσι καὶ λῃστρικοῖς τὸν δῆμον ὑποπεπτη-
χότα ποθεῖν μὲν εἰρήνην, ἀσθενέστερον δὲ ὄντα
τῆς ἐπαναστάσεως ἠρεμεῖν.
54 (2) Ἕως μὲν οὖν ὄρθιον ἱππάζετο τὴν λεωφόρον
κατατείνουσαν πρὸς τὸ τεῖχος οὐδεὶς προυφαίνετο
55 τῶν πυλῶν, ἐπεὶ δ' ἐκ τῆς ὁδοῦ πρὸς τὸν Ψήφινον
πύργον ἀποκλίνας πλάγιον ἦγε τὸ τῶν ἱππέων
στῖφος, προπηδήσαντες ἐξαίφνης ἄπειροι κατὰ
τοὺς Γυναικείους καλουμένους πύργους διὰ τῆς
ἀντικρὺ τῶν Ἑλένης μνημείων πύλης διεκπαίουσι
56 τῆς ἵππου, καὶ τοὺς μὲν ἔτι κατὰ τὴν ὁδὸν θέοντας
ἀντιμέτωποι στάντες ἐκώλυσαν συνάψαι τοῖς
ἐκκλίνασι, τὸν δὲ Τίτον ἀποτέμνονται σὺν ὀλίγοις.
57 τῷ δὲ πρόσω μὲν ἦν χωρεῖν ἀδύνατον· ἐκτετά-
φρευτο γὰρ ἀπὸ τοῦ τείχους περὶ τὰς κηπείας
ἅπαντα, τοίχοις[2] τε ἐπικαρσίοις καὶ πολλοῖς ἔρκεσι
58 διειλημμένα· τὴν δὲ πρὸς τοὺς σφετέρους ἀναδρομὴν
πλήθει τῶν ἐν μέσῳ πολεμίων ἀμήχανον ἑώρα

---

[1] Hudson with Lat. and one MS.: πέπειστο the rest.
[2] PA: κήποις the rest.

---

[a] Gibeah of (i.e. birthplace of) Saul, 1 Sam. xi. 4, identified
with *Tell el-Ful*, about 4 miles N. of Jerusalem. The
" valley of thorns " may be a branch of the *Wady Suweinit*
(= " valley of the little acacias "); the main valley so

Gabath Saul,[a] which means " Saul's hill," at a distance of about thirty furlongs from Jerusalem. From here, with some six hundred picked horsemen, he rode forward to reconnoitre the city's strength and to test the mettle of the Jews, whether, on seeing him, they would be terrified into surrender before any actual conflict ; for he had learnt, as indeed was the fact, that the people were longing for peace, but were overawed by the insurgents and brigands and remained quiet merely from inability to resist.

Titus during reconnaissance of Jerusalem

(2) So long as he rode straight along the high road leading direct to the wall,[b] no one appeared outside the gates ; but when he diverged from the route and led his troop of horse in an oblique line towards the tower Psephinus,[c] the Jews suddenly dashed out in immense numbers at a spot called " the Women's towers," through the gate facing Helena's [d] monuments, broke through the cavalry, and placing themselves in front of those who were still galloping along the road, prevented them from joining their comrades who had left it, thus cutting off Titus with a handful of men.   For him to proceed was impossible, because the ground outside the ramparts was all cut up by trenches for gardening purposes and intersected by cross walls and numerous fences ; while to rejoin his own men was, he saw, impracticable owing to the intervening masses of the enemy and the retirement

is cut off and his life imperilled.

named, however, runs to the E. and N. of Gibeah of Saul (through another Gibeah or Geba, which cannot here be intended).

   [b] Probably towards the present Damascus gate.
   [c] At the N.W. angle of the third wall, v. 159.
   [d] Queen of Adiabene and a convert to Judaism, *A.* xx. 17 ff.   Her tomb is mentioned as a landmark in *B.* v. 119, 147, and her palace in v. 253.

217

καὶ τραπέντ᾽ ᾿ς τοὺς ἀνὰ τὴν λεωφόρον, ὧν οἱ
πολλοὶ μηδὲ γινώσκοντες τὸν τοῦ βασιλέως
κίνδυνον, ἀλλ᾽ οἰόμενοι συναναστραφῆναι κἀκεῖνον
59 ἀνέφευγον. ὁ δὲ κατιδὼν ὡς ἐν μόνῃ τῇ καθ᾽
αὑτὸν ἀλκῇ κεῖται τὸ σώζεσθαι τόν τε ἵππον
ἐπιστρέφει καὶ τοῖς περὶ αὐτὸν ἐμβοήσας ἕπεσθαι
μέσοις ἐμπηδᾷ τοῖς πολεμίοις, διεκπαῖσαι πρὸς
60 τοὺς σφετέρους βιαζόμενος. ἔνθα δὴ μάλιστα
παρέστη[1] νοεῖν, ὅτι καὶ πολέμων ῥοπαὶ καὶ
61 βασιλέων κίνδυνοι μέλονται θεῷ· τοσούτων γὰρ
ἐπὶ τὸν Τίτον ἀφιεμένων βελῶν μήτε κράνος
ἔχοντα μήτε θώρακα, προῆλθε γὰρ ὡς ἔφην οὐ
πολεμιστὴς ἀλλὰ κατάσκοπος, οὐδὲν ἥψατο τοῦ
σώματος, κενὰ δ᾽ ὥσπερ ἐπίτηδες ἀστοχούντων
62 παρερροιζεῖτο πάντα. ὃ[2] δὲ ξίφει τοὺς κατὰ
πλευρὸν ἀεὶ διαστέλλων καὶ πολλοὺς τῶν ἀντι-
προσώπων ἀνατρέπων ἤλαυνεν ὑπὲρ τοὺς ἐρειπο-
63 μένους τὸν ἵππον. τῶν δὲ κραυγή τε ἦν πρὸς
τὸ παράστημα τοῦ Καίσαρος καὶ παρακέλευσις
ὁρμᾶν ἐπ᾽ αὐτόν, φυγὴ δὲ καὶ χωρισμὸς[3] ἄθρους
64 καθ᾽ οὓς ἐπελαύνων γένοιτο. συνῆπτον δ᾽ οἱ τοῦ
κινδύνου μετέχοντες κατὰ νῶτα καὶ κατὰ πλευρὰν
νυσσόμενοι· μία γὰρ ἐλπὶς ἦν σωτηρίας ἑκάστῳ
τὸ συνεξανύτειν[4] τῷ Τίτῳ [καὶ] μὴ φθάσαντα
65 κυκλωθῆναι. δύο γοῦν τῶν ἀπωτέρω[5] τὸν μὲν
σὺν τῷ ἵππῳ περισχόντες κατηκόντισαν, θάτερον
δὲ καταπηδήσαντα διαφθείραντες τὸν ἵππον ἀπ-
ήγαγον, μετὰ δὲ τῶν λοιπῶν Τίτος ἐπὶ τὸ στρατό-
66 πεδον διασώζεται. τοῖς μὲν οὖν Ἰουδαίοις πλεο-
νεκτήσασι κατὰ τὴν πρώτην ἐπίθεσιν ἐπήγειρε

of his comrades on the highway, most of whom,
unaware of the prince's peril and believing that he
too had turned simultaneously, were in full retreat.
Perceiving that his safety depended solely on his
personal prowess, he turned his horse's head and
shouting to his companions to follow dashed into
the enemy's midst, struggling to cut his way through
to his own party. Then, more than ever, might the
reflection arise that the hazards of war and the perils
of princes are under God's care; for, of all that hail
of arrows discharged at Titus, who wore neither
helmet nor cuirass—for he had gone forward, as I
said, not to fight, but to reconnoitre—not one
touched his person, but, as if his assailants purposely
missed their mark, all whizzed harmless by. He,
meanwhile, with his sword constantly dispersing
those on his flank and prostrating multitudes who
withstood him to the face, rode his horse over his
fallen foes. At Caesar's intrepidity the Jews shouted
and cheered each other on against him, but wherever
he turned his horse there was flight and a general
stampede. His comrades in danger closed up to
him, riddled in rear and flank; for each man's
one hope of escape lay in pushing through with
Titus before he was cut off. Two, in fact, further
behind, thus fell: one with his horse was surrounded
and speared, the other who dismounted was killed
and his steed led off to the city; with the remainder
Titus safely reached the camp. The Jews thus
successful in their first onset were elated with in-

---

[1] After Lat. (*potuit*): παρέστι L: πάρεστί μοι PA: παρέστη
μοι the rest.
[2] P: τῷ the rest.　　[3] PAM: διαχωρισμὸς the rest.
[4] L: συνεξανοίγειν the rest.　　[5] ἀτονωτέρων L Lat.

τὰς διανοίας ἄσκεπτος ἐλπίς, καὶ πολὺ θάρσος
αὐτοῖς εἰς τὸ μέλλον [ἡ] πρόσκαιρος ῥοπὴ προυξένει.

67 (3) Καῖσαρ δ᾿ ὡς αὐτῷ συνέμιξε διὰ νυκτὸς
τὸ ἀπὸ τῆς Ἀμμαοῦς τάγμα, μεθ᾿ ἡμέραν ἐκεῖθεν
ἄρας ἐπὶ τὸν Σκοπὸν καλούμενον πρόεισιν,[1]
ἔνθεν ἥ τε πόλις ἤδη κατεφαίνετο καὶ τὸ τοῦ
ναοῦ μέγεθος ἐκλάμπον, καθὰ τῷ βορείῳ κλίματι
τῆς πόλεως χθαμαλὸς συνάπτων ὁ χῶρος ἐτύμως
68 Σκοπὸς ὠνόμασται. τῆς δὲ πόλεως σταδίους
ἑπτὰ διέχων ἐκέλευσε περιβαλέσθαι στρατόπεδον
τοῖς δύο τάγμασιν ἐμοῦ, τὸ δὲ πέμπτον τούτων
ὀπίσω τρισὶ σταδίοις· κόπῳ γὰρ τῆς διὰ νυκτὸς
πορείας τετριμμένους[2] ἐδόκει σκέπης ἀξίους εἶναι,
69 ὡς ἂν ἀδεέστερον τειχίσαιντο. καταρχομένων δ᾿
ἄρτι τῆς δομήσεως καὶ τὸ δέκατον τάγμα διὰ
Ἱεριχοῦντος ἤδη παρῆν, ἔνθα καθῆστό τις ὁπλιτικὴ
μοῖρα φρουροῦσα τὴν ἐμβολὴν ὑπὸ Οὐεσπασιανοῦ
70 προκατειλημμένην. προσετέτακτο δ᾿ αὐτοῖς ἐξ
ἀπέχοντας τῶν Ἱεροσολύμων σταδίους στρατοπεδεύσασθαι κατὰ τὸ Ἐλαιῶν καλούμενον ὄρος,
ὃ τῇ πόλει πρὸς ἀνατολὴν ἀντίκειται μέσῃ φάραγγι
βαθείᾳ διειργόμενον, ἣ Κεδρὼν ὠνόμασται.

71 (4) Τῶν δ᾿ ἀνὰ τὸ ἄστυ συρρηγνυμένων ἀδιαλείπτως τότε πρῶτον ἀνέπαυσεν τὴν ἐπ᾿ ἀλλήλοις
ἔριν ὁ ἔξωθεν πόλεμος ἐξαίφνης πολὺς ἐπελθών·

---

[1] πρόεισιν Bekker : πρόσεισιν mss.   [2] τετρυμένους Niese.

[a] The phrase θάρσος προυξένει comes from Soph. Trach. 726.
[b] Legion V, § 42.
[c] i.e. "Look-out man" (" look-out place "= Scopia) ; the
Semitic name was Saphein (cf. Mizpah, " look-out place ")
according to A. xi. 329. Here Cestius, with the 12th legion,

considerate hopes, and this transient turn of fortune
afforded them high confidence [a] as to the future.

(3) Caesar, being joined during the night by the
legion [b] from Emmaus, next day broke up his camp
and advanced to Scopus, as the place is called from
which was obtained the first view of the city and the
grand pile of the temple gleaming afar ; whence the
spot, a low prominence adjoining the northern
quarter of the city, is appropriately named Scopus.[c]
Here, at a distance of seven furlongs from the city,
Titus ordered one combined camp to be formed for
two of the legions,[d] and the fifth to be stationed
three furlongs in their rear ; considering that men
worn out with the fatigue of a night's march deserved
to be screened from molestation while throwing up
their entrenchments. Scarcely had they begun
operations when the tenth legion also arrived, having
come by way of Jericho,[e] where a party of soldiers
had been posted to guard the pass formerly taken by
Vespasian.[f] These troops had orders to encamp at a
distance of six furlongs from Jerusalem at the mount
called the Mount of Olives, which lies over against
the city on the east, being separated from it by a deep
intervening ravine called Kedron.

(4) And now for the first time the mutual dissension
of the factions within the town, hitherto incessantly
at strife, was checked by the war from without
suddenly bursting in full force upon them. The

He encamps at Mt. Scopus with three legions.

Legion X encamps on Mt. of Olives.

The factions join forces,

had encamped four years before, *B.* ii. 528, 542 ; here, too,
Alexander the Great on his approach to the city was met by
the high priest and people of Jerusalem, *A. loc. cit.*
  [d] XII and XV, §§ 41 f.
  [e] *Cf.* § 42.
  [f] Vespasian had established a camp with a permanent
garrison at Jericho, iv. 486 (*cf.* 450).

72 καὶ μετ' ἐκπλήξεως οἱ στασιασταὶ τοὺς Ῥωμαίους
ἀφορῶντες στρατοπεδευομένους τριχῇ κακῆς ὁμονοίας κατήρχοντο καὶ λόγον ἀλλήλοις ἐδίδοσαν,
73 τί μένοιεν ἢ τί παθόντες ἀνέχοιντο τρία ταῖς
ἀναπνοαῖς αὐτῶν ἐπιφρασσόμενα τείχη, καὶ τοῦ
πολεμίου[1] μετ' ἀδείας ἀντιπολίζοντος ἑαυτόν, οἱ
δ' ὥσπερ θεαταὶ καλῶν καὶ συμφόρων ἔργων
καθέζοιντο τειχήρεις, τὼ χεῖρε καὶ τὰς πανοπλίας
74 παρέντες· "καθ' αὑτῶν ἄρα γενναῖοι μόνον
ἡμεῖς," ἐξεβόησαν, "Ῥωμαῖοι δ' ἐκ τῆς ἡμετέρας
75 στάσεως κερδήσουσιν ἀναιμωτὶ τὴν πόλιν·" τούτοις ἀθροίζοντες ἀλλήλους παρεκρότουν, καὶ τὰς
πανοπλίας ἁρπάσαντες αἰφνιδίως ἐπεκθέουσι τῷ
δεκάτῳ τάγματι καὶ διὰ τῆς φάραγγος ἄξαντες
μετὰ κραυγῆς ἐξαισίου τειχιζομένοις προσπίπτουσι
76 τοῖς πολεμίοις. οἱ δὲ πρὸς τὸ ἔργον διῃρημένοι
καὶ διὰ τοῦτο τὰ πολλὰ τεθεικότες τῶν ὅπλων,
οὔτε γὰρ θαρρήσειν[2] τοὺς Ἰουδαίους πρὸς ἐκδρομὴν ὑπελάμβανον καὶ προθυμουμένων περι-
σπασθήσεσθαι τὰς ὁρμὰς τῇ στάσει, συνεταράχθη-
77 σαν ἀδοκήτως, καὶ τῶν ἔργων ἀφέμενοι τινὲς
μὲν ἀνεχώρουν εὐθέως, πολλοὶ δ' ἐπὶ τὰ ὅπλα
θέοντες πρὶν ἐπιστραφῆναι πρὸς τοὺς ἐχθροὺς
78 ἐφθάνοντο[3] παιόμενοι. προσεγίνοντο δὲ τοῖς Ἰουδαίοις ἀεὶ πλείους, ἐπὶ τῷ κρατεῖν τοὺς πρώτους
τεθαρρηκότες, καὶ τῶν ὄντων πολλαπλασίους
ἐδόκουν σφίσι τε καὶ τοῖς πολεμίοις δεξιᾷ χρώ-
79 μενοι τῇ τύχῃ. μάλιστα δὲ τοὺς ἐν ἔθει συντάξεως
ὄντας καὶ μετὰ κόσμου καὶ παραγγελμάτων

---

[1] M : πολέμου the rest.
[2] L Lat. : θαρσεῖν the rest.
[3] LC Lat. : ἐφονεύοντο the rest.

rival parties, beholding with dismay the Romans
forming three several encampments, started a sorry
alliance and began to ask each other what they were
waiting for, or what possessed them to let themselves
be choked by the erection of three fortifications ; the
enemy unmolested was building himself a rival city,
while they sat behind their ramparts, like spectators
of excellent and expedient operations, with hands
and weapons idle ! " Is then," they exclaimed,
" our valour to be displayed only against ourselves,
while the Romans, through our party strife, make a
bloodless conquest of the city ? " Stimulating each _{sally out}
other with such language and uniting forces, they _{and rout the tenth legion.}
seized their weapons, dashed out suddenly against
the tenth legion, and racing across the ravine with a
terrific shout, fell upon the enemy while engaged
upon his fortifications. The latter to facilitate their
work were in scattered groups and to this end had
laid aside most of their arms ; for they imagined
that the Jews would never venture upon a sally or
that, if moved to do so, their energies would be dis-
sipated by their dissensions. They were therefore
taken by surprise and thrown into disorder. Abandoning their work, some instantly retreated, while
many rushing for their arms were struck down before
they could round upon the foe. The Jews meanwhile were continually being reinforced by others
who were encouraged by the success of the first
party, and with fortune favouring them seemed both
to themselves and to the enemy far in excess of their
actual numbers. Moreover, men habituated to
discipline and proficient in fighting in ordered ranks
and by word of command, when suddenly confronted

πολεμεῖν εἰδότας ἀταξία φθάσασα θορυβεῖ. διὸ
καὶ τότε προληφθέντες οἱ Ῥωμαῖοι ταῖς ἐμβολαῖς
80 εἶκον. καὶ ὁπότε μὲν ἐπιστραφεῖεν οἱ καταλαμ-
βανόμενοι, τοῦ τε δρόμου τοὺς Ἰουδαίους ἐπεῖχον
καὶ διὰ τὴν ὁρμὴν ἧττον φυλαττομένους ἐτίτρωσκον,
ἀεὶ δὲ πληθυούσης τῆς ἐκδρομῆς μᾶλλον ταρατ-
τόμενοι τελευταῖον ἀπὸ τοῦ στρατοπέδου τρέ-
81 πονται. καὶ δοκεῖ τότε ἂν κινδυνεῦσαι τὸ τάγμα
πᾶν, εἰ μὴ Τίτος ἀγγελθὲν αὐτῷ τάχος ἐπεβοήθησε,
καὶ πολλὰ ὀνειδίσας εἰς ἀνανδρίαν ἐπιστρέφει μὲν
82 τοὺς φεύγοντας, αὐτὸς δὲ πλαγίοις τοῖς Ἰουδαίοις
προσπεσὼν μεθ᾽ ὧν ἧκεν ἐπιλέκτων συχνοὺς
μὲν ἀναιρεῖ, τιτρώσκει δὲ πλείους, τρέπεται δὲ
83 πάντας καὶ συνωθεῖ κατὰ τῆς φάραγγος. οἱ δ᾽ ἐν
τῷ κατάντει πολλὰ κακωθέντες, ὡς διεξέπεσον,
ἄντικρυς ἐπιστρέφονται καὶ μέσην ἔχοντες τὴν
84 χαράδραν τοῖς Ῥωμαίοις διεμάχοντο. μέχρι μὲν
δὴ μέσης ἡμέρας οὕτως ἐπολέμουν, ὀλίγον δ᾽
ἀπὸ μεσημβρίας ἐκκλίνοντος ἤδη, Τίτος τοὺς
μεθ᾽ αὑτοῦ προσβοηθήσαντας καὶ τοὺς ἀπὸ τῶν
σπειρῶν τοῖς ἐκτρέχουσιν ἀντιπαρατάξας τὸ λοιπὸν
τάγμα πρὸς τὸν τειχισμὸν ἀνέπεμπεν εἰς τὴν
ἀκρώρειαν.
85 (5) Ἰουδαίοις δὲ τοῦτ᾽ ἐδόκει φυγή, καὶ τοῦ
σκοποῦ κατασείσαντος θοἰμάτιον, ὃς αὐτοῖς ἐπὶ
τοῦ τείχους καθῆστο, προπηδῶσι πλῆθος ἀκραιφ-
νέστερον[1] μετὰ τοσαύτης ὁρμῆς, ὡς τὸν δρόμον
86 αὐτῶν τοῖς ἀγριωτάτοις εἰκάζειν θηρίοις. ἀμέλει
τῶν ἀντιπαραταχθέντων οὐδεὶς ἔμεινεν τὴν συμ-

---

[1] ἀκραιφνέστατον L (frequentissima Lat.).

with disorderly warfare, are peculiarly liable to be
thrown into confusion. Hence on this occasion too,
the Romans, being taken unawares, gave way to
repeated assaults. Whenever, indeed, any were
overtaken and turned upon the foe, they checked the
Jewish rush and wounded many who in the ardour of
pursuit were off their guard; but as more and more
Jews sallied out from the town, the disorder of the
Romans increased, until they were finally routed Titus coming to the
rescue
from the camp. Indeed, in all probability, the entire
legion would then have been in jeopardy, had not repels the
Jews.
Titus, hearing of their position, instantly come to
their aid. Roundly chiding their cowardice, he rallied
the fugitives and then falling upon the Jews in flank
with his band of picked followers, slew many, wounded
more, routed the whole body and drove them headlong down into the ravine. They suffered severely
on the declivity, but having reached the farther
bank turned to face the Romans and, with the brook
between them, renewed the combat. So the battle
raged till noon; and then shortly after midday
Titus, to check further sallies, deployed the reinforcements brought by himself, together with the
auxiliary cohorts, and dismissed the remainder of
the legion to the ridge to resume their fortification.

(5) The Jews, however, mistook this move for Fresh
Jewish
charge up
flight, and seeing the watchman, whom they had
posted on the ramparts, signalling by shaking his the slopes
of Olivet.
robe, another crowd, perfectly fresh, sprang forth
with such impetuosity that their rush was comparable
to that of the most savage of beasts. In fact not one
of the opposing line awaited their charge, but, as if

βολήν,¹ ἀλλ' ὥσπερ ἐξ ὀργάνου παιόμενοι διέρρηξαν
τὴν τάξιν καὶ πρὸς τὸ ὄρος τραπέντες ἀνέφευγον.
87 λείπεται δ' ἐν μέσῳ τῷ προσάντει Τίτος μετ'
ὀλίγων, καὶ πολλὰ τῶν φίλων παραινούντων, ὅσοι
δι' αἰδὼ τὴν πρὸς τὸν ἡγεμόνα τοῦ κινδύνου
88 καταφρονήσαντες ἔστησαν, εἶξαι θανατῶσιν Ἰουδαίοις καὶ μὴ προκινδυνεύειν τούτων, οὓς ἐχρῆν
πρὸ αὐτοῦ μένειν, λαμβάνειν δὲ ἔννοιαν τῆς καθ'
αὑτὸν τύχης καὶ μὴ στρατιώτου τάξιν ἀποπληροῦν
ὄντα καὶ τοῦ πολέμου καὶ τῆς οἰκουμένης δεσπότην,
μηδ' ὀξεῖαν οὕτως ὑφίστασθαι ῥοπὴν ἐν ᾧ σαλεύει
89 τὰ πάντα, τούτων οὐδ' ἀκούειν ἔδοξε, τοῖς δὲ καθ'
αὑτὸν ἀνατρέχουσιν ἀνθίσταται καὶ κατὰ στόμα
παίων βιαζομένους ἀνῄρει, κατά τε τοῦ πρανοῦς
90 ἀθρόοις ἐμπίπτων ἀνεώθει τὸ πλῆθος. οἱ δὲ πρός
τε τὸ παράστημα καὶ τὴν ἰσχὺν καταπλαγέντες
οὐδ' οὕτως μὲν ἀνέφευγον εἰς τὴν πόλιν, καθ'
ἑκάτερον² δ' ἐκκλίνοντες ἀπ' αὐτοῦ τοῖς ἀνωτέρω
φεύγουσι προσέκειντο. καὶ τούτοις δὲ κατὰ πλευ-
91 ρὰν προσβάλλων τὰς ὁρμὰς ὑπετέμνετο. κἀν
τούτῳ καὶ τοῖς ἄνω τειχίζουσι τὸ στρατόπεδον,
ὡς ἐθεάσαντο τοὺς κάτω φεύγοντας, πάλιν ἐμ-
92 πίπτει ταραχὴ καὶ δέος, καὶ διασκίδναται πᾶν τὸ
τάγμα, δοκούντων ἀνυπόστατον μὲν εἶναι τὴν τῶν
Ἰουδαίων ἐκδρομήν, τετράφθαι δ' αὐτὸν Τίτον·
οὐ γὰρ ἄν ποτε τοὺς ἄλλους φεύγειν ἐκείνου
93 μένοντος. καὶ καθάπερ πανικῷ δείματι κυκλω-
θέντες ἄλλος ἀλλαχῇ διεφέροντο, μέχρι τινὲς

---

¹ ἐμβολὴν LC.
² LVRC Lat.: ἕτερον PAM.

ᵃ i.e. apparently "(by a bolt) from an artillery engine"
226

struck from an engine,[a] they broke their ranks and
turned and fled up the mountain side, leaving Titus,
with a few followers, half way up the slope. The
friends who out of regard for the commander-in-chief
stood their ground indifferent to danger, all earnestly
entreated him to retire before these Jews who
courted death, and not to risk his life for men who
ought to have remained to protect him; he should
consider what he owed to fortune,[b] and not act the
part of a common soldier, lord as he was alike of the
war and of the world; he on whom all depended
ought not to face so imminent a risk. These ad-
visers Titus appeared not even to hear, but with-
standing the Jews who were rushing at him up the
hill, confronted, struck and slew them as they pressed
upon him, and then falling upon the masses thrust
them backward down the slope. Yet, terrified
though they were at his intrepidity and strength,
they did not even then retreat to the city, but inclining to either side to avoid him continued their
pursuit of those who were flying up the hill; whereupon he attacked them again in flank, and strove to
check the rush. Meanwhile the troops who were
fortifying the camp above, on seeing their comrades
below in flight, were themselves once more seized
with such consternation and alarm that the whole
legion scattered; for they imagined that the Jewish
charge was irresistible and that Titus himself had
been routed, because the rest would never, they
thought, have fled while he held his ground. Like
men beset by panic, they sped in all directions, until

Titus again
saves the
situation.

(ὄργανον ἀφετήριον, iii. 80). The ὄργανον in the obscure
simile in ii. 230 possibly bears the same meaning.
[b] Or " consider his peculiar fortune "; for Titus as the
favourite of Fortune cf. vi. 57.

κατιδόντες ἐν μέσῳ τοῦ πολέμου τὸν ἡγεμόνα
στρεφόμενον καὶ μέγα δείσαντες ἀμφ' αὐτῷ
94 διαβοῶσι τὸν κίνδυνον ὅλῳ τῷ τάγματι. τοὺς
δ' αἰδὼς ἐπέστρεφε, καὶ πλεῖόν τι φυγῆς κακίζοντες ἀλλήλους ἐπὶ τῷ καταλιπεῖν Καίσαρα
πάσῃ βίᾳ κατὰ τῶν Ἰουδαίων ἐχρῶντο καὶ
κλίναντες ἅπαξ ἀπὸ τοῦ κατάντους συνώθουν
95 αὐτοὺς εἰς τὸ κοῖλον. οἱ δ' ὑπὸ πόδα χωροῦντες
ἐμάχοντο, καὶ πλεονεκτοῦντες οἱ Ῥωμαῖοι τῷ
καθύπερθεν εἶναι συνελαύνουσι πάντας εἰς τὴν
96 φάραγγα. προσέκειτο δὲ τοῖς καθ' αὐτὸν ὁ Τίτος
καὶ τὸ μὲν τάγμα πάλιν ἐπὶ τὴν τειχοποιΐαν
ἔπεμψεν, αὐτὸς δὲ σὺν οἷς πρότερον ἀντιστὰς εἶργε
97 τοὺς πολεμίους· ὥστ', εἰ χρὴ μήτε θεραπείᾳ τι
προστιθέντα μήθ' ὑφελόντα φθόνῳ τἀληθὲς εἰπεῖν,
αὐτὸς Καῖσαρ δὶς μὲν ἐρρύσατο κινδυνεῦσαι ὅλον
τὸ τάγμα καὶ τοῦ περιβαλέσθαι τὸ στρατόπεδον
αὐτοῖς ἄδειαν παρέσχε.
98 (iii. 1) Λωφήσαντος δὲ πρὸς βραχὺ τοῦ θύραζε
πολέμου πάλιν τὸν ἔνδον ἡ στάσις ἐπήγειρεν.[1]
99 καὶ τῆς τῶν ἀζύμων ἐνστάσης ἡμέρας τεσσαρεσκαιδεκάτῃ Ξανθικοῦ μηνός, ἐν ᾗ δοκοῦσιν Ἰουδαῖοι
τὸν πρῶτον ἀπαλλαγῆναι καιρὸν Αἰγυπτίων, οἱ
μὲν περὶ τὸν Ἐλεάζαρον παρανοίγοντες τὰς
πύλας ἐδέχοντο ἐκ τοῦ δήμου τοὺς προσκυνεῖν
100 ἐθέλοντας εἴσω, Ἰωάννης δὲ προκάλυμμα τῆς
ἐπιβουλῆς ποιησάμενος τὴν ἑορτὴν τῶν σὺν αὐτῷ
κρυπτοῖς ὅπλοις ἐνσκευάσας[2] τοὺς ἀσημοτέρους,

---

[1] L Lat.: πάλιν ἔνδον ἡ στάσις ἐπηγείρετο the rest.
[2] L: συσκευάσας the rest.

^a § 82.

some, catching sight of their general in the thickest
of the fight and greatly alarmed on his account, with
shouts announced his danger to the whole legion.
Shame rallied them, and, upbraiding one another
with a worse guilt than flight in their desertion of
Caesar, they put forth their utmost energies against
the Jews and, having once made them give ground,
proceeded to thrust them off the slope into the valley.
The Jews retired step by step fighting, but the
Romans, having the advantage of position finally
drove them all into the ravine. Titus, still pressing
upon his immediate opponents, now sent the legion
back to resume their fortifications, while he, with
his former band,[a] withstood and held the enemy at
bay. Thus, if, without a syllable added in flattery
or withheld from envy, the truth must be told, Caesar
personally twice rescued the entire legion when in
jeopardy, and enabled them to intrench themselves
in their camp unmolested.

(iii. 1) During a temporary lull in the war without the walls, faction renewed its hostilities within.
When the day of unleavened bread came round on
the fourteenth of the month Xanthicus,[b] the reputed
anniversary of the Jews' first liberation from Egypt,[c]
Eleazar and his men partly opened the gates and
admitted citizens desiring to worship within the
building. But John, making the festival a cloak
for his treacherous designs, armed with concealed
weapons the less conspicuous of his followers, most

John, by a ruse at Passover (A.D. 70), gains entry to the inner temple.

[b] The Macedonian month corresponding to the Hebrew
Nisan (March-April).
[c] The words " reputed " and " first " (as though first of a
series of liberations from Egypt) rather suggest the hand of
a non-Jewish συνεργός ; but " first " may perhaps refer to
the later liberation from Babylon.

ὧν οἱ πλείους ἦσαν ἄναγνοι, διὰ σπουδῆς παρεισ-
πέμπει προκαταληψομένους τὸ ἱερόν. οἱ δ' ὡς
ἔνδον ἐγένοντο, τὰς ἐσθῆτας ἀπορρίψαντες ἐφά-
101 νησαν ἐξαπίνης ὁπλῖται. ταραχὴ δὲ μεγίστη
περὶ τὸν ναὸν αὐτίκα καὶ θόρυβος ἦν, τοῦ μὲν
ἔξω τῆς στάσεως λαοῦ κατὰ πάντων ἄκριτον
οἰομένων εἶναι τὴν ἐπίθεσιν, τῶν δὲ ζηλωτῶν
102 ἐπὶ σφίσι μόνοις. ἀλλ' οἱ μὲν ἀφέμενοι τὸ
φρουρεῖν ἔτι τὰς πύλας καὶ τῶν ἐπάλξεων κατα-
πηδήσαντες πρὶν εἰς χεῖρας ἐλθεῖν εἰς τοὺς ὑπονόμους τοῦ ἱεροῦ κατέφυγον· οἱ δ' ἀπὸ τοῦ δήμου
πρὸς τῷ βωμῷ καταπτήσσοντες καὶ περὶ τὸν
ναὸν συνειλούμενοι κατεπατοῦντο, ξύλοις τε ἀνέδην
103 παιόμενοι καὶ σιδήρῳ. πολλοὺς δὲ τῶν ἡσυχίων
κατ' ἔχθραν καὶ μῖσος ἴδιον ὡς ἀντιστασιαστὰς
ἀνῄρουν οἱ διάφοροι, καὶ πᾶς ὁ προσκρούσας τῳ
τῶν ἐπιβούλων πάλαι τηνικαῦτα ἐπιγνωσθεὶς ὡς
104 ζηλωτὴς πρὸς αἰκίαν ἀνήγετο. πολλὰ δὲ δεινὰ
τοὺς ἀναιτίους διαθέντες ἐκεχειρίαν τοῖς αἰτίοις
ἔδοσαν, καὶ προελθόντας ἐκ τῶν ὑπονόμων διίεσαν.
αὐτοὶ δὲ καὶ τὸ ἐνδοτέρω ἱερὸν κατασχόντες καὶ
τὰς ἐν αὐτῷ παρασκευὰς πάσας κατεθάρρουν ἤδη
105 τοῦ Σίμωνος. ἡ μὲν οὖν στάσις οὕτω τριμερὴς
οὖσα πρότερον εἰς δύο μοίρας περιίσταται.
106 (2) Ὁ δὲ Τίτος ἔγγιον ἀπὸ τοῦ Σκοποῦ τῇ
πόλει παραστρατοπεδεύσασθαι προαιρούμενος πρὸς
μὲν τοὺς ἐκτρέχοντας ἔστησεν ἐπιλέξας ἱππέων
τε καὶ πεζῶν ὅσους ἀρκέσειν ὑπελάμβανεν, τῇ
δ' ὅλῃ δυνάμει προσέταξεν ἐξομαλίζειν τὸ μέχρι
230

of whom were unpurified, and by his earnest endeavours got them stealthily passed into the temple to take prior possession of it. Once within, they cast off their garments and were suddenly revealed as armed men. The purlieus of the sanctuary were instantly a scene of the utmost disorder and confusion, the people who had no connexion with the party strife regarding this as an indiscriminate attack upon all, the Zealots as directed against themselves alone. The latter, however, neglecting any longer to guard the gates and not waiting to come to close quarters with the intruders, leapt down from the battlements and took refuge in the temple vaults ; while the visitors from the city, cowering beside the altar and huddled together around the sanctuary, were trampled under foot and mercilessly struck with clubs and swords. Many peaceable citizens from enmity and personal spite were slain by their adversaries as partisans of the opposite faction, and any who in the past had offended one of the conspirators, being now recognized as a Zealot, was led off to punishment. But while the innocent were thus brutally treated, the intruders granted a truce to the criminals and let them go when they emerged from the vaults. Being now in possession of the inner court of the temple and all the stores which it contained, they could bid defiance to Simon. The sedition, hitherto of a tripartite character, was thus again reduced to two factions. *John defeats Eleazar, and the two factions reunite.*

(2) Titus, now deciding to abandon Scopus and encamp nearer the city, posted a picked body of horse and foot of such strength as he deemed sufficient to check the enemy's sallies, and gave orders to his main army to level the intervening ground right up *Titus levels the ground from Scopus to Jerusalem.*

231

107 τοῦ τείχους διάστημα. καταβληθέντος δὲ παντὸς
ἔρκους καὶ περιφράγματος, ὅσα κήπων προαν-
εστήσαντο καὶ δένδρων[1] οἱ οἰκήτορες, ὕλης τε
ἡμέρου τῆς μεταξὺ πάσης ἐκκοπείσης ἀνεπλήσθη
108 μὲν τὰ κοῖλα καὶ χαραδρώδη τοῦ τόπου, τὰς δὲ
πετρώδεις ἐξοχὰς σιδήρῳ κατεργαζόμενοι χθαμαλὸν ἐποίουν πάντα τὸν τόπον ἀπὸ τοῦ Σκοποῦ
μέχρι τῶν Ἡρώδου μνημείων, ἃ προσέχει τῇ
τῶν ὄφεων ἐπικαλουμένῃ κολυμβήθρᾳ.

109 (3) Καὶ κατὰ ταύτας τὰς ἡμέρας ἐνέδραν οἱ
Ἰουδαῖοι κατὰ τῶν Ῥωμαίων συσκευάζονται
110 τοιάνδε. τῶν στασιαστῶν οἱ [μὲν] τολμηροὶ
προελθόντες ἔξω τῶν Γυναικείων καλουμένων
πύργων, ὡς ἐκβεβλημένοι δῆθεν ὑπὸ τῶν εἰρηνικὰ
φρονούντων καὶ δεδοικότες τὴν τῶν Ῥωμαίων
ἔφοδον ἀνειλοῦντο καὶ παρ' ἀλλήλους ὑπέπτησσον.
111 οἱ δὲ διαστάντες ἐπὶ τοῦ τείχους δῆμος εἶναι δοκῶν
εἰρήνην ἐβόων καὶ δεξιὰν ᾐτοῦντο καὶ τοὺς
Ῥωμαίους ἐκάλουν, ἀνοίξειν ὑπισχνούμενοι τὰς
πύλας· ἅμα δὲ ταῦτα κεκραγότες καὶ τοὺς σφετέρους ἔβαλλον λίθοις ὡς ἀπελαύνοντες τῶν
112 πυλῶν. κἀκεῖνοι βιάζεσθαι τὰς εἰσόδους ὑπεκρί-
νοντο καὶ τοὺς ἔνδον ἱκέτευεν, συνεχῶς τε πρὸς
τοὺς Ῥωμαίους ὁρμήσαντες[2] ἐπιστρεφόμενοι ταρατ-
113 τομένοις προσεῴκεισαν. παρὰ μὲν οὖν τοῖς στρατιώταις τὸ πανοῦργον αὐτῶν οὐκ ἐλείπετο πίστεως,
ἀλλ' ὡς τοὺς μὲν ἐν χερσὶν ἔχοντες ἑτοίμους πρὸς
τιμωρίαν, τοὺς δ' ἀνοίξειν τὴν πόλιν ἐλπίζοντες,

---

[1] δενδρώνων Destinon (probably rightly).
[2] AL Lat.: ὁρμήσαντας the rest.

---

a Unidentified ; cf. § 507. Niese thinks that the Herod
commemorated was the king of Chalcis, grandson of Herod

to the walls. Every fence and palisade with which
the inhabitants had enclosed their gardens and
plantations having accordingly been swept away, and
every fruit tree within the area felled, the cavities
and gullies on the route were filled up, the protuber-
ant rocks demolished with tools of iron, and the whole
intervening space from Scopus to Herod's monuments,[a] adjoining the spot called the Serpents' pool,[a]
was thus reduced to a dead level.

(3) During this period the Jews contrived the
following stratagem to trick the Romans. The more
daring of the insurgents, issuing forth from the so-
called Women's Towers,[b] as though they had been
ejected by the partisans of peace and were in terror
of being attacked by the Romans, kept close together
cowering in a bunch. Meanwhile their comrades,
lining the walls so as to be taken for the populace,
shouted " Peace," begged for protection, and invited
the Romans to enter, promising to open the gates ;
these cries they accompanied by showers of stones
aimed at their own men, as if to drive them from the
gates. The latter made a feint of forcing an entry
and petitioning those within, and constantly rushing
towards the Romans and again retreating showed
signs of extreme agitation. Their ruse did not fail
to impose on the rank and file : imagining that they
had one party at their mercy, to be punished at will,
and hoping that the other would throw open the
city, they were on the point of proceeding to action.

the Great ; the latter himself was buried at Herodion, 60
stades south of Jerusalem, B. i. 673. The Serpent's pool
has been uncertainly identified with the *Birket Mamilla*, to
the west of the city (G. A. Smith, *Jerusalem*, i. 114).
  [b] Unidentified : described in § 55 as opposite Queen
Helena's tomb, which is mentioned below, § 119.

114 ἐχώρουν ἐπὶ τὴν πρᾶξιν. Τίτῳ δὲ δι᾽ ὑποψίας
ἦν τὸ τῆς ἐπικλήσεως παράλογον· καὶ γὰρ πρὸ
μιᾶς ἡμέρας προκαλούμενος αὐτοὺς ἐπὶ συμβάσεις
διὰ τοῦ Ἰωσήπου μέτριον οὐδὲν εὕρισκε, καὶ τότε
τοὺς στρατιώτας κατὰ χώραν μένειν ἐκέλευσεν.
115 ἔφθασαν δέ τινες τῶν ἐπὶ τοῖς ἔργοις προτεταγμένων[1] ἁρπάσαντες τὰ ὅπλα πρὸς τὰς πύλας
116 ἐκδραμεῖν. τούτοις οἱ μὲν ἐκβεβλῆσθαι δοκοῦντες
τὸ πρῶτον ὑπεχώρουν, ἐπεὶ δὲ μεταξὺ τῶν τῆς
πύλης ἐγίνοντο πύργων, ἐκθέοντες ἐκυκλοῦντό
117 σφας καὶ προσέκειντο κατόπιν· οἱ δ᾽ ἀπὸ τοῦ
τείχους πλῆθος χερμάδων καὶ βελῶν παντοίων
ἄθρουν κατέχεαν, ὡς συχνοὺς μὲν ἀνελεῖν, τρῶσαι
118 δὲ πλείστους. ἦν γὰρ οὐ ῥᾴδιον τοῦ τείχους
διαφυγεῖν τῶν κατόπιν βιαζομένων, καὶ ἄλλως
αἰδὼς τῆς διαμαρτίας καὶ τῶν ἡγεμόνων δέος
119 παρεκελεύετο τῷ πταίσματι προσλιπαρεῖν. διὸ
δὴ μέχρι πλείστου διαδορατιζόμενοι καὶ πολλὰς
ὑπὸ τῶν Ἰουδαίων λαμβάνοντες πληγάς, ἀμέλει
δ᾽ οὐκ ἐλάττους ἀντιδιδόντες, τέλος ἀνωθοῦσι
τοὺς κυκλωσαμένους· ὑποχωροῦσι δ᾽ αὐτοῖς οἱ
Ἰουδαῖοι [καὶ] μέχρι τῶν Ἑλένης μνημείων
εἵποντο βάλλοντες.
120 (4) Ἔπειθ᾽ οἱ μὲν ἀπειροκάλως ἐξυβρίζοντες
εἰς τὴν τύχην ἔσκωπτόν τε τοὺς Ῥωμαίους
δελεασθέντας ἀπάτῃ καὶ τοὺς θυρεοὺς ἀνασείοντες
121 ἐσκίρτων καὶ μετὰ χαρᾶς ἀνεβόων. τοὺς δὲ
στρατιώτας ἀπειλῇ τε τῶν ταξιάρχων καὶ χαλε-
παίνων Καῖσαρ τούτοις ἐξεδέχετο, φάσκων ὡς
Ἰουδαῖοι μέν, οἷς ἀπόνοια μόνη στρατηγεῖ, πάντα
μετὰ προνοίας πράττουσι καὶ σκέψεως, ἐπιβουλάς

[1] ed. pr.: προστεταγμένων MSS.

Titus, on the contrary, viewed this surprising invitation with suspicion. For having only the day before, through Josephus, invited them to terms, he had met with no reasonable response; he therefore now ordered his men to remain where they were. However, some who were stationed in the forefront of the works had, without awaiting orders, seized their arms and rushed towards the gates. The pretended outcasts at first retired before them, but, as soon as the Romans came between the gateway towers, they darted out and surrounded and attacked them in rear; while those on the wall showered upon them a volley of stones and every species of missile, killing many and wounding most. For it was no easy matter to escape from the wall with the enemy pressing them behind; moreover, shame at their error and dread of their officers impelled them to persevere in their blunder. Consequently, it was only after a prolonged combat with spears and after receiving many wounds from the Jews—inflicting, to be sure, no fewer in return—that they eventually repelled their encircling enemy. Even when they retired, the Jews still followed and kept them under fire as far as the tomb of Helena.[a]

(4) Then, with vulgar abuse of their good fortune, they jeered at the Romans for being deluded by a ruse and brandishing their bucklers danced and shouted for joy. The soldiers, for their part, were met by threats from their officers and a furious Caesar. "These Jews," he protested, "with desperation for their only leader, do everything with forethought and circumspection: their stratagems

Titus reprimands his insubordinate troops.

---

[a] § 55 note.

JOSEPHUS

τε συντάσσοντες καὶ λόχους, ἕπεται δ' αὐτῶν
ταῖς ἐνέδραις καὶ τύχη διὰ τὸ πειθήνιον καὶ τὴν
122 πρὸς ἀλλήλους εὔνοιάν τε καὶ πίστιν· Ῥωμαῖοι δέ,
οἷς δι' εὐταξίαν καὶ τὸ πρὸς τοὺς ἡγεμόνας
εὐπειθὲς ἀεὶ δουλεύει καὶ τύχη, νῦν ὑπὸ τῶν
ἐναντίων πταίουσι καὶ διὰ χειρῶν ἀκρασίαν
ἁλίσκονται, τὸ πάντων αἴσχιστον, ἀστρατήγητοι
123 μαχόμενοι παρόντος Καίσαρος. ἦ μεγάλα μὲν
στενάξειν ἔφη τοὺς τῆς στρατείας νόμους, μεγάλα
δ' αὐτοῦ τὸν πατέρα τήνδε τὴν πληγὴν πυθόμενον,
124 εἴ γε ὁ μὲν ἐν πολέμοις γηράσας οὐδέποτ' ἔπταισεν
οὕτως, οἱ νόμοι δ' ἀεὶ καὶ τοὺς βραχύ τι τῆς
τάξεως παρακινήσαντας θανάτῳ κολάζουσιν, νῦν
125 δ' ὅλην στρατιὰν ἑωράκασι λιποτάκτην. γνώσεσθαί
γε μὴν αὐτίκα τοὺς ἀπαυθαδισαμένους ὅτι καὶ
τὸ νικᾶν παρὰ Ῥωμαίοις δίχα παραγγέλματος
126 ἀδοξεῖται. τοιαῦτα διατεινάμενος πρὸς τοὺς ἡγεμόνας δῆλος ἦν κατὰ πάντων χρήσεσθαι[1] τῷ
νόμῳ. καὶ οἱ μὲν παρεῖσαν τὰς ψυχὰς ὡς ὅσον
127 οὐδέπω τεθνηξόμενοι δικαίως, περιχυθέντα δὲ τὰ
τάγματα τῷ Τίτῳ περὶ τῶν συστρατιωτῶν ἱκέτευε
καὶ τὴν ὀλίγων προπέτειαν χαρίσασθαι τῇ πάντων
εὐπειθείᾳ κατηντιβόλουν· ἀναλήψεσθαι γὰρ τὸ
παρὸν πταῖσμα ταῖς εἰς τὸ μέλλον ἀρεταῖς.
128 (5) Πείθεται Καῖσαρ ἅμα ταῖς τε ἱκεσίαις
καὶ τῷ συμφέροντι· τὴν μὲν γὰρ καθ' ἑνὸς τιμωρίαν
ᾤετο χρῆναι μέχρις ἔργου προκόπτειν, τὴν δ'

---

[1] Destinon: χρήσασθαι or χρῆσθαι mss.

236

and ambuscades are carefully planned, and their
schemes are further favoured by fortune because of
their obedience and their mutual loyalty and confidence ; while Romans who, through orderly discipline and obedience to command, have ever found
even fortune their slave, are now brought to grief
by conduct the very opposite, are defeated through
their intemperate pugnacity, and—direst disgrace of
all—while fighting without a leader under the eyes of
Caesar !   Deeply indeed may the laws of the service
mourn,[a] deeply too my father when he hears of this
rebuff ; seeing that he, though grown grey in warfare,
never met with a like disaster, while those laws invariably punish with death the very slightest breach
of discipline, whereas now they have beheld a whole
corps quit the ranks !   However, these rash adven-
turers shall learn forthwith that, among Romans, even
a victory without orders given is held dishonourable.''
From such determined language to his officers it was
clear that Titus intended to put the law into force
against all.   The offenders, accordingly, gave themselves up for lost, expecting in a moment to meet their
merited death ; but the legions, flocking round Titus,
made intercession for their fellow-soldiers, imploring
him, in consideration of the obedience of them all,
to forgive the recklessness of a few, and assuring
him that these would retrieve their present error by
future meritorious deeds.

(5) To these entreaties, backed by considerations
of expediency, Caesar yielded ; for he held that,
while in the case of an individual punishment should
actually be carried into execution, where numbers

---

[a] Cf. the similar phrase used by the companions of
Josephus in the cave at Jotapata, iii. 356.

129 ἐπὶ πλήθους μέχρι λόγου. τοῖς μὲν οὖν στρατιώταις διηλλάττετο πολλὰ νουθετήσας αὖθις
εἶναι φρονιμωτέρους, αὐτὸς δ' ὅπως ἀμυνεῖται
130 τὴν Ἰουδαίων ἐπιβουλὴν ἐσκόπει. τέσσαρσι δ'
ἡμέραις ἐξισωθέντος τοῦ μέχρι τῶν τειχῶν
διαστήματος, βουλόμενος μετὰ ἀσφαλείας τάς
τε ἀποσκευὰς καὶ τὸ λοιπὸν πλῆθος παραγαγεῖν[1]
τὸ καρτερώτατον τῆς δυνάμεως ἀντιπαρεξέτεινεν
τῷ τείχει κατὰ τὸ βόρειον κλίμα καὶ πρὸς ἑσπέραν,
131 ἐφ' ἑπτὰ βαθύνας τὴν φάλαγγα, τῶν τε πεζῶν
προτεταγμένων καὶ κατόπιν τῶν ἱππέων, τρι-
στοίχων ἑκατέρων, ἕβδομοι κατὰ μέσον εἱστήκεσαν
132 οἱ τοξόται. τοσούτῳ δὲ στίφει πεφραγμένων
Ἰουδαίοις τῶν ἐκδρομῶν τά τε ὑποζύγια τῶν
τριῶν ταγμάτων καὶ ἡ πληθὺς ἀδεῶς παρώδευσεν.
133 αὐτὸς μὲν οὖν Τίτος ἀπέχων ὅσον εἰς σταδίους
δύο τοῦ τείχους κατὰ τὸ γωνιαῖον αὐτοῦ μέρος
ἀντικρὺ τοῦ καλουμένου Ψηφίνου πύργου στρατοπεδεύεται, πρὸς ὃν ὁ κύκλος τοῦ τείχους ἀπ'
134 ἄρκτον[2] καθήκων ἀνακάμπτει πρὸς δύσιν· ἡ δ'
ἑτέρα μοῖρα τῆς στρατιᾶς κατὰ τὸν Ἱππικὸν
προσαγορευθέντα πύργον τειχίζεται διεστῶσα τῆς
135 πόλεως ὁμοίως δύο σταδίους. τὸ μέντοι δέκατον
τάγμα κατὰ χώραν ἐπὶ τοῦ Ἐλαιῶν ὄρους ἔμενε.

136 (iv. 1) Τρισὶ δ' ὠχυρωμένη τείχεσιν ἡ πόλις
καθὰ[3] μὴ ταῖς ἀβάτοις φάραγξι κεκύκλωτο, ταύτῃ
γὰρ εἷς ἦν περίβολος, αὐτὴ μὲν ὑπὲρ δύο λόφων
ἀντιπρόσωπος ἔκτιστο μέσῃ φάραγγι διῃρημένων,
137 εἰς ἣν ἐπάλληλοι κατέληγον αἱ οἰκίαι. τῶν δὲ

---

[1] παράγειν PA.
[2] Destinon: ἄρκτον or ἄρκτου MSS.
[3] LVRC (cf. iii. 464, v. 223 etc.): καθ' ἣν the rest.

were concerned it should not go beyond reproof. He was therefore reconciled to the soldiers, after strictly admonishing them to be wiser in future ; while he privately reflected how best to avenge himself on the Jews for their stratagem. In four days all the intervening ground up to the walls was levelled ; and Titus, now anxious to secure a safe passage for the baggage and camp-followers, drew up the flower of his forces facing the northern and western portions of the wall, in lines seven deep : the infantry in front, the cavalry behind, each of these arms in three ranks, the archers forming a seventh line in the middle. The sallies of the Jews being held in check by this formidable array, the beasts of burden belonging to the three legions with their train of followers passed securely on. Titus himself encamped[a] about two furlongs from the ramparts, at the angle opposite the tower called Psephinus, where the circuit of the wall bends back from the north to the west. The other division of the army entrenched itself opposite the tower named Hippicus, likewise at a distance of two furlongs from the city. The tenth legion kept its position on the Mount of Olives.

Titus encamps in two divisions two furlongs from the walls.

(iv. 1) The city was fortified by three walls, except where it was enclosed by impassable ravines, a single rampart there sufficing. It was built, in portions facing each other, on two hills separated by a central valley,[b] in which the tiers of houses ended.

Description of Jerusalem.

---

[a] On the 14th of Xanthicus (1 May), as appears from § 567.
[b] The Tyropoeon, in the modern city a shallow glen known as *El-Wad.*

λόφων ὁ μὲν τὴν ἄνω πόλιν ἔχων ὑψηλότερός τε
πολλῷ καὶ τὸ μῆκος ἰθύτερος ἦν· διὰ γοῦν τὴν
ὀχυρότητα φρούριον μὲν ὑπὸ Δαυίδου τοῦ βασιλέως ἐκαλεῖτο, πατὴρ Σολομῶνος ἦν οὗτος τοῦ
πρώτου τὸν[1] ναὸν κτίσαντος, ἡ ἄνω δὲ ἀγορὰ
πρὸς ἡμῶν· ἅτερος δ᾽ ὁ καλούμενος Ἄκρα καὶ
138 τὴν κάτω πόλιν ὑφεστὼς ἀμφίκυρτος. τούτου
δ᾽ ἄντικρυς τρίτος ἦν λόφος, ταπεινότερός τε
φύσει τῆς Ἄκρας καὶ πλατείᾳ φάραγγι δι-
139 ειργόμενος ἄλλῃ πρότερον· αὖθίς γε μὴν καθ᾽ οὓς
οἱ Ἀσαμωναῖοι χρόνους ἐβασίλευον τήν τε φάραγγα ἔχωσαν, συνάψαι βουλόμενοι τῷ ἱερῷ τὴν
πόλιν, καὶ τῆς Ἄκρας κατεργασάμενοι τὸ ὕψος
ἐποίησαν χθαμαλώτερον, ὡς ὑπερφαίνοιτο καὶ
140 ταύτῃ[2] τὸ ἱερόν. ἡ δὲ τῶν τυροποιῶν προσαγορευομένη φάραγξ, ἣν ἔφαμεν τόν τε τῆς ἄνω
πόλεως καὶ τὸν κάτω λόφον διαστέλλειν, καθήκει
μέχρι Σιλωᾶς· οὕτω γὰρ τὴν πηγὴν γλυκεῖάν τε
141 καὶ πολλὴν οὖσαν ἐκαλοῦμεν. ἔξωθεν δ᾽ οἱ τῆς
πόλεως δύο λόφοι βαθείαις φάραγξιν περιείχοντο,
καὶ διὰ τοὺς ἑκατέρωθεν κρημνοὺς προσιτὸν
οὐδαμόθεν ἦν.

---

[1] πρώτου τὸν] τὸν πρῶτον P.   [2] ταύτης C.

---

[a] Cf. 2 Sam. v. 7.

[b] Most archaeologists now hold that Josephus here and in
his account of the capture of Jebus by David (A. vii. 65) is
in error as to the ancient topography, and that the " City of
David " or Sion lay, not on the western, but on the eastern
hill on the part called Ophel above the Virgin's spring
(G. A. Smith, *Jerusalem*, i. 134 f., 161 ff.). The historian's
error is perpetuated in modern nomenclature ; the so-called
" David's Tower " in the present citadel stands near the
Jaffa Gate on the basis of Herod's Tower of Phasael.

[c] Literally " gibbous," like the moon in its third quarter.

Of these hills that on which the upper city lay was The two
main hills. far higher and had a straighter ridge than the other ; consequently, owing to its strength it was called by King David—the father of Solomon the first builder of the temple—the Stronghold,[a] but we called it the upper agora.[b]   The second hill, which bore the name of Acra and supported the lower city, was a hog's back.[c] Opposite this was a third hill, by nature lower than Acra, and once divided from it by another broad ravine.   Afterwards, however, the Hasmonaeans, during the period of their reign, both filled up the ravine, with the object of uniting the city to the temple, and also reduced the elevation of Acra by levelling its summit, in order that it might not block the view of the temple.[d]   The Valley of the Cheesemakers,[e] as the ravine was called, which, as we said, divides the hill of the upper city from that of the lower, extends down to Siloam ; for so we called that fountain of sweet and abundant water. On the exterior the two hills on which the city stood were encompassed by deep ravines, and the precipitous cliffs on either side of it rendered the town nowhere accessible.

Cf. the name Ophel (= " hump ") given to a portion of this hill.

    [d] *Cf. B.* i. 50 and the more detailed description in *A.* xii. 215-217 ; in both those passages the levelling of Acra is ascribed to Simon.   But this is incompatible with 1 Macc. xiv. 37 which states that he fortified it.   Josephus is writing of what had disappeared two centuries before his day, and his description is probably in some points erroneous.   It has been suggested that the work was due to Hyrcanus I and that his erection of a Baris or castle at the N.W. corner of the temple led to the demolition of the Syrian Acra to the S. of it. (Smith, *Jerusalem,* i. 159 f., Schürer, *G.J.V.* (ed. 3), i. 247.)   [e] Tyropoeon.

142 (2) Τῶν δὲ τριῶν τειχῶν τὸ μὲν ἀρχαῖον διά τε
τὰς φάραγγας καὶ τὸν ὑπὲρ τούτων λόφον, ἐφ᾽ οὗ
143 κατεσκεύαστο, δυσάλωτον ἦν· πρὸς δὲ τῷ πλεο-
νεκτήματι τοῦ τόπου καὶ καρτερῶς ἐδεδόμητο,
Δαυίδου τε καὶ Σολομῶνος, ἔτι δὲ τῶν μεταξὺ
τούτων βασιλέων φιλοτιμηθέντων περὶ τὸ ἔργον.
144 ἀρχόμενον δὲ κατὰ βορρᾶν ἀπὸ τοῦ Ἱππικοῦ
καλουμένου πύργου καὶ διατεῖνον ἐπὶ τὸν ξυστόν,[1]
ἔπειτα τῇ βουλῇ συνάπτον ἐπὶ τὴν ἑσπέριον τοῦ
145 ἱεροῦ στοὰν ἀπηρτίζετο. κατὰ θάτερα δὲ πρὸς
δύσιν, ἀπὸ ταὐτοῦ μὲν ἀρχόμενον, διὰ δὲ τοῦ
Βηθσὼ[2] καλουμένου χώρου κατατεῖνον ἐπὶ τὴν
Ἐσσηνῶν πύλην, κἄπειτα πρὸς νότον ὑπὲρ τὴν
Σιλωὰν ἐπιστρέφον πηγήν, ἔνθεν τε πάλιν ἐκκλῖνον
πρὸς ἀνατολὴν ἐπὶ τὴν Σολομῶνος κολυμβήθραν
καὶ διῆκον μέχρι χώρου τινός, ὃν καλοῦσιν
Ὀφλᾶν,[3] τῇ πρὸς ἀνατολὴν στοᾷ τοῦ ἱεροῦ συν-
146 ῆπτε. τὸ δὲ δεύτερον τὴν μὲν ἀρχὴν ἀπὸ πύλης
εἶχεν, ἣν Γεννὰθ[4] ἐκάλουν τοῦ πρώτου τείχους
οὖσαν, κυκλούμενον δὲ τὸ προσάρκτιον κλίμα
147 μόνον ἀνήει μέχρι τῆς Ἀντωνίας. τῷ τρίτῳ δ᾽
ἀρχὴ ἦν ὁ Ἱππικὸς πύργος, ὅθεν μέχρι τοῦ
βορείου κλίματος κατατεῖνον ἐπὶ τὸν Ψήφινον
πύργον, ἔπειτα καθῆκον ἀντικρὺ τῶν Ἑλένης

---

[1] + λεγόμενον LVRC (Lat.): + καλούμενον M.
[2] Βησοῦ PA: Betiso Lat.
[3] Hudson with Lat. : Ὀφλᾶς (-ὰμ L) MSS.   [4] Γενὰθ PC.

---

[a] At the N.W. angle.
[b] Described below, § 163.   [c] Eastwards.
[d] The gymnasium, used for public speeches, and connected
with the temple by a bridge, B. ii. 344 note.
[e] A hall in or adjoining the S. part of the temple area, in
which the Sanhedrin usually met; Mishna, Middoth, v. 4 c

(2) Of the three walls, the most ancient, owing The first (or old) wall. to the surrounding ravines and the hill above them on which it was reared, was well-nigh impregnable. But, besides the advantage of its position, it was also strongly built, David and Solomon and their successors on the throne having taken pride in the work. Beginning on the north *a* at the tower called Hippicus,*b* it extended *c* to the Xystus,*d* and then joining the council-chamber *e* terminated at the western portico of the temple. Beginning at the same point in the other direction, westward, it descended past the place called Bethso *f* to the gate of the Essenes,*f* then turned southwards above the fountain of Siloam ; thence it again inclined to the east towards Solomon's pool,*f* and after passing a spot which they call Ophlas,*g* finally joined the eastern portico of the temple.

The second wall started from the gate in the first The second wall. wall which they called Gennath,*h* and, enclosing only the northern district of the town, went up as far as Antonia.

The third began at the tower Hippicus, whence it The third (or Agrippa's) wall stretched northwards to the tower Psephinus, and then descending opposite the monuments of Helena *i*

(Holtzmann), Schürer, *op. cit.* ii. 211. Its burning by the Romans is mentioned in vi. 354. The name by which it is called in the Mishna, *Lishkath hag-Gazith*, probably means, not, as usually translated, " Chamber of Hewn Stone," but " Chamber beside the Xystus " ; in the LXX Gazith= ξυστός (Schurer). *f* Unidentified.
    g The Biblical Ophel (= " hump "), Neh. iii. 26, etc. ; in Sir G. A. Smith's opinion probably a synonym for Sion, *Jerusalem*, i. 153.
    h Perhaps= Garden Gate. Its position, like the course of the second wall, is uncertain ; it has been " placed by some between the towers Hippicus and Phasael . . . by others at the latter tower," *ib.* i. 243.   *i* § 55.

μνημείων, Ἀδιαβηνὴ βασιλὶς ἦν αὕτη Ἰζάτου[1]
βασιλέως θυγάτηρ, καὶ διὰ σπηλαίων βασιλικῶν
μηκυνόμενον ἐκάμπτετο μὲν γωνιαίῳ πύργῳ κατὰ
τὸ τοῦ Γναφέως προσαγορευόμενον μνῆμα, τῷ
δ' ἀρχαίῳ περιβόλῳ συνάπτον εἰς τὴν Κεδρῶνα
148 καλουμένην φάραγγα κατέληγεν. τοῦτο τῇ προσ-
κτισθείσῃ πόλει περιέθηκεν Ἀγρίππας, ἥπερ ἦν
πᾶσα γυμνή· πλήθει γὰρ ὑπερχεομένη κατὰ
149 μικρὸν ἐξεῖρπε τῶν περιβόλων. καὶ τοῦ ἱεροῦ
τὰ προσάρκτια πρὸς τῷ λόφῳ συμπολίζοντες ἐπ'
οὐκ ὀλίγον προῆλθον[2] καὶ τέταρτον περιοικηθῆναι
λόφον, ὃς καλεῖται Βεζεθά, κείμενος μὲν ἀντικρὺ
τῆς Ἀντωνίας, ἀποτεμνόμενος δ' ὀρύγματι βαθεῖ·
150 διεταφρεύθη γὰρ ἐπίτηδες, ὡς μὴ τῷ λόφῳ συν-
άπτοντες οἱ θεμέλιοι τῆς Ἀντωνίας εὐπρόσιτοί τε
151 εἶεν καὶ ἧττον ὑψηλοί· διὸ δὴ καὶ πλεῖστον ὕψος
τοῖς πύργοις προσεδίδου τὸ βάθος τῆς τάφρου.
ἐκλήθη δ' ἐπιχωρίως βεζεθὰ τὸ νεόκτιστον μέρος,
ὃ μεθερμηνευόμενον Ἑλλάδι γλώσσῃ καινὴ λέγοιτ'
152 ἂν πόλις. δεομένων οὖν τῶν ταύτῃ σκέπης ὁ
πατὴρ τοῦ νῦν βασιλέως καὶ ὁμώνυμος Ἀγρίππας ἄρχεται μὲν οὗ προείπομεν τείχους, δείσας δὲ
Κλαύδιον Καίσαρα, μὴ τὸ μέγεθος τῆς κατασκευῆς ἐπὶ νεωτερισμῷ πραγμάτων ὑπονοήσῃ καὶ
στάσεως, παύεται θεμελίους μόνον βαλόμενος.
153 καὶ γὰρ οὐδ' ἂν ἦν ἁλώσιμος ἡ πόλις, εἰ προύκοπτε

---

[1] Ἰάζα τοῦ, Ἰζᾶ τοῦ or Ἀζα τοῦ MSS.; cf. iv. 567.
[2] + ὡς M.

---

[a] The course of the third wall after Psephinus is uncertain ; some identifying it with the present N. wall, others
making it embrace a wider area farther north. Recent
excavations (1926) favour the latter theory.

(queen of Adiabene and daughter of king Izates), and proceeding past the royal caverns it bent round a corner tower over against the so-called Fuller's tomb and joining the ancient rampart terminated at the valley called Kedron.[a] This wall was built by Agrippa to enclose the later additions to the city, which were quite unprotected; for the town, overflowing with inhabitants, had gradually crept beyond the ramparts. Indeed, the population, uniting to the hill [b] the district north of the temple, had encroached so far that even a fourth hill was surrounded with houses. This hill, which is called Bezetha, lay opposite Antonia, but was cut off from it by a deep fosse, dug on purpose to sever the foundations of Antonia from the hill and so to render them at once less easy of access and more elevated, the depth of the trench materially increasing the height of the towers. The recently built quarter was called in the vernacular Bezetha, which, might be translated into Greek as New Town.[c] Seeing then the residents of this district in need of defence, Agrippa, the father and namesake of the present king, began the above-mentioned wall; but, fearing that Claudius Caesar might suspect from the vast scale of the structure that he had designs of revolution and revolt, he desisted after merely laying the foundations. Indeed the city would have been impregnable, had the wall been continued as it

built to enclose Bezetha, the new quarter.

[b] On which the upper town lay.

[c] More correctly in ii. 530: " the district called Bezetha *and also* New Town (Caenopolis)." Bezetha probably= Beth-zaith= " house of olives " (Smith, *Jerusalem*, i. 244 note); it does not *mean* " New Town." Similar loose etymological statements occur in the *Antiquities*.

245

τὸ τεῖχος ὡς ἤρξατο· λίθοις μὲν γὰρ εἰκοσαπήχεσι
τὸ μῆκος καὶ τὸ εὖρος δεκαπήχεσι συνηρμόζετο,
μήθ' ὑπορυγῆναι σιδήρῳ ῥᾳδίως μήθ' ὑπ' ὀργάνοις
154 διασεισθῆναι δυνάμενον, δέκα δὲ πήχεις αὐτὸ[1]
τὸ τεῖχος ἐπλατύνετο, καὶ τὸ ὕψος πλεῖον μὲν ἄν,
ὡς εἰκός, ἔσχε μὴ διακωλυθείσης τῆς τοῦ καταρ-
155 ξαμένου φιλοτιμίας. αὖθις δὲ καίτοι μετὰ σπουδῆς
ἐγειρόμενον ὑπὸ Ἰουδαίων εἰς εἴκοσι πήχεις
ἀνέστη, καὶ διπήχεις μὲν τὰς ἐπάλξεις, τριπήχεις
δὲ τοὺς προμαχῶνας εἶχεν, ὡς τὸ πᾶν ὕψος εἰς
εἰκοσιπέντε πήχεις ἀνατετάσθαι.

156 (3) Τοῦ δὲ τείχους ὑπερεῖχον οἱ πύργοι πήχεις
εἴκοσι μὲν εἰς εὖρος, εἴκοσι δὲ εἰς ὕψος, τετράγωνοί
τε καὶ πλήρεις ὥσπερ αὐτὸ τὸ τεῖχος ὄντες· ἥ γε
μὴν ἁρμονία καὶ τὸ κάλλος τῶν λίθων οὐδὲν
157 ἀπέδει ναοῦ. μετὰ δὲ τὸ ναστὸν ὕψος τῶν πύργων,
ὅπερ ἦν εἰκοσάπηχυ, πολυτελεῖς ἦσαν οἶκοι, καὶ
καθύπερθεν ὑπερῷα, δεξαμεναί τε πρὸς τὰς τῶν
ὑετῶν ὑποδοχάς, ἕλικές τε καὶ πλατεῖαι καθ'
158 ἕκαστον ἄνοδοι. τοιούτους μὲν οὖν πύργους τὸ
τρίτον τεῖχος εἶχεν ἐνενήκοντα, τὰ μεταπύργια δὲ
τούτων ἀνὰ πήχεις διακοσίους· τὸ δ' αὖ μέσον
εἰς τέσσαρας καὶ δέκα πύργους, τὸ δ' ἀρχαῖον
159 εἰς ἑξήκοντα μεμέριστο. τῆς πόλεως δ' ὁ πᾶς
κύκλος σταδίων ἦν τριακοντατριῶν. θαυμασίου
δ' ὄντος ὅλου τοῦ τρίτου τείχους θαυμασιώτερος
ἀνεῖχε κατὰ γωνίαν βόρειός τε καὶ πρὸς δύσιν ὁ
Ψήφινος πύργος, καθ' ὃν ἐστρατοπεδεύσατο Τίτος.
160 ἐπὶ γὰρ ἑβδομήκοντα πήχεις ὑψηλὸς ὢν Ἀραβίαν
τε ἀνίσχοντος ἡλίου παρεῖχεν ἀφορᾶν καὶ μέχρι

[1] αὐτῷ M: αὐτῷ καὶ P: αὐτὸ καὶ A.

_____

[a] 33 stades = about 3⅘ miles. The circumference esti-

246

began; for it was constructed of stones twenty cubits long and ten broad, so closely joined that they could scarcely have been undermined with tools of iron or shaken by engines. The wall itself was ten cubits broad, and it would doubtless have attained a greater height than it did, had not the ambition of its founder been frustrated. Subsequently, although hurriedly erected by the Jews, it rose to a height of twenty cubits, besides having battlements of two cubits and bulwarks of three cubits high, bringing the total altitude up to twenty-five cubits.

(3) Above the wall, however, rose towers, twenty *The towers:* cubits broad and twenty high, square and solid as the wall itself, and in the joining and beauty of the stones in no wise inferior to a temple. Over this solid masonry, twenty cubits in altitude, were magnificent apartments, and above these, upper chambers and cisterns to receive the rain-water, each tower having broad spiral staircases. Of such towers the third wall had ninety, disposed at intervals of two hundred cubits; the line of the middle wall was broken by fourteen towers, that of the old wall by sixty. The whole circumference of the city was thirty-three furlongs.[a] But wonderful as was the third wall throughout, still more so was the tower Psephinus, which rose at its north-west angle and *Psephinus,* opposite to which Titus encamped. For, being seventy cubits high, it afforded from sunrise a prospect embracing both Arabia and the utmost limits

mated by " the land surveyor of Syria " (*ap.* Euseb. *Praep. Ev.* ix. 36) in the second century B.C. was 27 stades; for other exaggerated estimates of 40 and 50 stades see *Ap.* i. 197 note. The circumference here given for the larger city of the first century A.D. favours a more northerly position for the third wall than that of the existing north wall.

θαλάττης τὰ τῆς Ἑβραίων κληρουχίας ἔσχατα·
161 ὀκτάγωνος δ' ἦν. τούτου δ' ἄντικρυς ὁ Ἱππικὸς
καὶ παρ' αὐτὸν δύο κατεσκευάσθησαν μὲν ὑφ'
Ἡρώδου βασιλέως ἐν τῷ ἀρχαίῳ τείχει, μέγεθος
δὲ καὶ κάλλος ἦσαν καὶ ὀχυρότητα τῶν κατὰ τὴν
162 οἰκουμένην διάφοροι· πρὸς γὰρ τῷ φύσει μεγαλο-
ψύχῳ καὶ τῇ περὶ τὴν πόλιν φιλοτιμίᾳ τὴν
ὑπεροχὴν τῶν ἔργων ὁ βασιλεὺς πάθεσιν οἰκείοις
ἐχαρίζετο, καὶ τρισὶ τοῖς ἡδίστοις προσώποις,
ἀφ' ὧν ὠνόμασε τοὺς πύργους, ἀδελφῷ καὶ
φίλῳ καὶ γυναικί, τὴν μνήμην ἀνέθηκε, τὴν μὲν
ὡς προειρήκαμεν [καὶ]¹ κτείνας δι' ἔρωτα, τοὺς δ'
ἀποβαλὼν ἐν πολέμῳ γενναίως ἀγωνισαμένους.
163 ὁ μὲν οὖν Ἱππικὸς ἀπὸ τοῦ φίλου προσαγορευθεὶς
τετράγωνος μὲν ἦν, εὖρος δὲ καὶ μῆκος εἰκοσιπέντε πηχῶν ἕκαστον καὶ ὕψος τριάκοντα, οὐδαμοῦ
164 διάκενος. ὑπὲρ δὲ τὸ πλῆρες καὶ ταῖς πέτραις
συνηνωμένον εἰς ἐκδοχὴν ὄμβρων εἰκοσάπηχυς
165 λάκκος ἦν τὸ βάθος, ἐπάνω δὲ τούτου δίστεγος
οἶκος [ἦν]² εἴκοσι καὶ πέντε πηχῶν τὸ ὕψος εἰς
ποικίλα τέγη διῃρημένος, ὑπὲρ ὃν τύρσεις μὲν
διπήχεις προμαχῶνες δὲ περιβέβληντο τριπήχεις,
ὡς τὸ πᾶν ὕψος εἰς ὀγδοήκοντα πήχεις συναριθ-
166 μεῖσθαι. ὁ δὲ δεύτερος πύργος, ὃν ὠνόμασεν ἀπὸ
τἀδελφοῦ Φασάηλον, τὸ μὲν πλάτος καὶ τὸ μῆκος
ἴσον εἶχεν, τεσσαράκοντα πηχῶν ἕκαστον, ἐπὶ

---

¹ AL: om. the rest. ² om. L.

a Phasael, Hippicus (strangely ignored in the narrative of
Herod's reign), and Mariamme. b i. 443.
c Phasael, taken prisoner by the Parthians, committed
suicide, i. 271 ; of the other's end there is no record.
d Probably the N.W. tower of the present citadel (Smith,

248

of Hebrew territory as far as the sea; it was of octagonal form.

Over against this was the tower Hippicus, and close to it two others, all built by King Herod into the old wall, and for magnitude, beauty and strength without their equal in the world. For, apart from his innate magnanimity and his pride in the city, the king sought, in the super-excellence of these works, to gratify his private feelings; dedicating them to the memory of three persons to whom he was most fondly attached, and after whom he named these towers—brother, friend, and wife.[a] The last, as we have previously related, he had for love's sake actually slain [b]; the others he had lost in war, after valiant fight.[c]

Now Hippicus,[d] called after his friend, was quadrangular, its length and breadth being each twenty-five cubits, and to the height of thirty cubits it was solid throughout. But above this solid and compact mass of masonry was a reservoir, twenty cubits deep, to receive the rain-water, and over this a double-roofed chamber, twenty-five cubits high, with roofs of diverse colours; this again was crowned by turrets, two cubits, and battlements, three cubits high, so that the total altitude amounted to eighty cubits.

The second tower, which he named Phasael [e] after his brother, was of equal length and breadth, forty

and Herod's three towers:

Hippicus,

Phasael,

Jerusalem, i. 240). The three Herodian towers were preserved by Titus for the admiration of future ages, vii. 1 f.

[e] The N.E. tower of the present citadel, erroneously called "David's tower." The dimensions approximate to the round statement of Josephus (a cube of 40 cubits = c. 60 feet), being actually 65.6 ft. high × 55.78 broad × 70.21 long; *ib.* 191.

167 τεσσαράκοντα δ' αὐτοῦ τὸ ναστον ἦν ὕψος. ἐπάνω
δὲ αὐτοῦ περιήει στοὰ δεκάπηχυς τὸ ὕψος, θωρα-
168 κίοις τε καὶ προβόλοις σκεπομένη. μέσην δ'
ὑπερῳκοδόμητο τὴν στοὰν πύργος ἕτερος, εἴς
τε οἴκους πολυτελεῖς καὶ δὴ καὶ βαλανεῖον διῃρημένος, ὡς μηδὲν ἐνδέοι τῷ πύργῳ βασίλειον
δοκεῖν. τὰ δ' ἄκρα τοῖς προμαχῶσι καὶ ταῖς
169 τύρσεσιν †ἡ περιαυτοῦ†[1] κεκόσμητο. πηχῶν δ'
ἦν τὸ πᾶν ὕψος ὡς ἐνενήκοντα, καὶ τὸ μὲν σχῆμα
παρεῴκει τῷ κατὰ τὴν Φάρον ἐκπυρσεύοντι τοῖς
ἐπὶ 'Αλεξανδρείας πλέουσι, τῇ περιοχῇ δὲ πολὺ
μείζων ἦν· τηνικαῦτά γε μὴν τυραννεῖον ἀπεδείχθη
170 τοῦ Σίμωνος. ὁ δὲ τρίτος πύργος ἡ Μαριάμμη,
τοῦτο γὰρ ἡ βασιλὶς ἐκαλεῖτο, μέχρι μὲν εἴκοσι
πηχῶν ναστὸς ἦν, εἴκοσι δὲ πήχεις εἰς εὖρος
171 διέβαινε καὶ μῆκος ἴσον, πολυτελεστέραν δὲ καὶ
ποικιλωτέραν τῶν ἄλλων τὴν οἴκησιν εἶχεν ἐπάνω,
τοῦ βασιλέως οἰκεῖον ὑπολαβόντος τὸν ἀπὸ
γυναικὸς ὀνομασθέντα κεκοσμῆσθαι πλέον ἢ τοὺς
ἀπ' ἀνδρῶν, ὥσπερ ἐκείνους τοῦ τῆς γυναικὸς
ἰσχυροτέρους. τούτου τὸ πᾶν ὕψος πεντήκοντα
καὶ πέντε πηχῶν ἦν.

172 (4) Τηλικοῦτοι δ' ὄντες οἱ τρεῖς τὸ μέγεθος
173 πολὺ μείζονες ἐφαίνοντο διὰ τὸν τόπον· αὐτό τε
γὰρ τὸ ἀρχαῖον τεῖχος, ἐν ᾧ ἦσαν, ἐφ' ὑψηλῷ
λόφῳ δεδόμητο, καὶ τοῦ λόφου καθάπερ κορυφή
τις ὑψηλοτέρα προανεῖχεν εἰς τριάκοντα πήχεις,
ὑπὲρ ἦν οἱ πύργοι κείμενοι πολὺ δή τι τοῦ
174 μετεώρου προσελάμβανον. θαυμάσιον δὲ καὶ τῶν
λίθων ἦν τὸ μέγεθος· οὐ γὰρ ἐξ εἰκαίας χερμάδος
οὐδὲ φορητῶν ἀνθρώποις πετρῶν συνεστήκεσαν,

---

[1] PA: μᾶλλον ἤπερ ὁ πρὸ αὐτοῦ the rest: om. Lat.

cubits each ; forty cubits was also the height of its
solid base. Above and around this ran a cloister, ten
cubits high, protected by parapets and bulwarks.
Over this and rising from the centre of the cloister
was built another tower, apportioned into sumptuous
apartments, including a bath, in order that nothing
might be wanting to impart to this tower the appearance of a palace. Its summit was crowned with
battlements and turrets, and its total height was about
ninety cubits. In form it resembled the tower of
Pharos [a] that emits its beacon light to navigators
approaching Alexandria, but in circumference it was
much larger. It had now become the seat of Simon's
tyranny.

The third tower, Mariamme [b]—for such was the
queen's name—was solid to a height of but twenty
cubits, its breadth being also twenty cubits and its
length the same. But its upper residential quarters
were far more luxurious and ornate than those of
the other towers, the king considering it appropriate
that the one named after a woman should so far
surpass in decoration those called after men, as they
outdid the woman's tower in strength. The total
height of this last was fifty-five cubits.

(4) But while such were the proportions of these
three towers, they seemed far larger owing to their
site. For the old wall in which they stood was itself
built on a lofty hill, and above the hill rose as it were
a crest thirty cubits higher still ; on this the towers
stood and thus gained immensely in elevation.
Marvellous, too, were the dimensions of the stones ;
for these were not composed of ordinary blocks
or boulders such as men might carry, but were

*and
Mariamme.*

[a] iv. 613.   [b] Site unknown, apparently E. of Phasael.

175 λευκὴ δὲ μάρμαρος ἐτμήθη· καὶ τὸ μὲν μῆκος
ἑκάστης πηχῶν ἦν εἴκοσι, δέκα δὲ εὖρος καὶ
βάθος πέντε, συνήνωντο δ' ἐπ' ἀλλήλοις, ὡς
δοκεῖν ἕκαστον πύργον μίαν εἶναι πέτραν ἀνα-
πεφυκυῖαν, ἔπειτα δὲ περιεξέσθαι χερσὶ τεχνιτῶν
εἰς σχῆμα καὶ γωνίας· οὕτως οὐδαμόθεν ἡ συνά-
176 φεια τῆς ἁρμονίας διεφαίνετο. κειμένοις δὲ πρὸς
ἄρκτον αὐτοῖς ἔνδοθεν ἡ τοῦ βασιλέως αὐλὴ
177 προσέζευκτο παντὸς λόγου κρείσσων· οὔτε γὰρ
πολυτελείας οὔτε κατασκευῆς τινος ἔλειπεν ὑπερ-
βολήν, ἀλλὰ τετείχιστο μὲν ἅπασα τριάκοντα
πήχεις τὸ ὕψος κύκλῳ, κατ' ἴσον διάστημα κεκο-
σμημένοις δὲ[1] πύργοις διείληπτο ἀνδρῶσί τε
178 μεγίστοις καὶ εἰς ξενῶνας ἑκατοντακλίνους· ἐν
οἷς ἀδιήγητος μὲν ἡ ποικιλία τῶν λίθων ἦν, συνῆκτο
γὰρ πολὺς ὁ πανταχοῦ σπάνιος, θαυμασταὶ δ'
ὀροφαὶ μήκει τε δοκῶν καὶ λαμπρότητι προ-
179 κοσμημάτων, οἴκων δὲ πλῆθος καὶ διαφοραὶ
σχημάτων περὶ τούτους μυρίαι, πᾶσίν γε μὴν
ἀποσκευαὶ πλήρεις, καὶ τὰ πλείω τῶν ἐν ἑκάστοις
180 κειμένων ἐξ ἀργύρου τε καὶ χρυσοῦ. περίστοα
δὲ δι' ἀλλήλων ἐν κύκλῳ πολλά, καὶ στῦλοι πρὸς
ἑκάστῳ διάφοροι· τά γε μὴν τούτων ὕπαιθρα
181 πάντα[2] χλοερά, καὶ ποικίλαι μὲν ὗλαι μακροὶ δὲ δι'
αὐτῶν περίπατοι καὶ περὶ τούτους εὔριποι βαθεῖς
δεξαμεναί τε πανταχοῦ χαλκουργημάτων περί-
πλεοι, δι' ὧν τὸ ὕδωρ ἐξεχεῖτο, καὶ πολλοὶ περὶ τὰ
182 νάματα πύργοι πελειάδων ἡμέρων. ἀλλὰ γὰρ
οὔθ' ἑρμηνεῦσαι δυνατὸν ἀξίως τὰ βασίλεις., καὶ

---

[1] δὲ seems out of place and should probably stand before
(Niese) or after διάστημα : L places it after διείληπτο.
[2] PAM : πανταχοῦ the rest.

cut out of white marble. The length of each
block was twenty cubits, the breadth ten, and the
depth five, and so nicely were they joined to one
another that each tower seemed like one natural
rock, that had later been polished by the hands of
craftsmen into shape and angles ; so wholly imperceptible was the fitting of the joints.

Adjoining and on the inner side of these towers,   Herod's
which lay to the north of it, was the king's palace,   palace.
baffling all description : indeed, in extravagance
and equipment no building surpassed it. It was
completely enclosed within a wall thirty cubits high,
broken at equal distances by ornamental towers, and
contained immense banqueting-halls and bed-
chambers for a hundred guests. The interior fittings
are indescribable — the variety of the stones (for
species rare in every other country were here
collected in abundance), ceilings wonderful both for
the length of the beams and the splendour of their
surface decoration, the host of apartments with their
infinite varieties of design, all amply furnished, while
most of the objects in each of them were of silver or
gold. All around were many circular cloisters, leading one into another, the columns in each being
different, and their open courts all of greensward ;
there were groves of various trees intersected by
long walks, which were bordered by deep canals, and
ponds everywhere studded with bronze figures,
through which the water was discharged, and around
the streams were numerous cots for tame pigeons.
However, it is impossible adequately to delineate the
palace, and the memory of it is harrowing, recalling

φέρει βάσανον ἡ μνήμη, τὰς τοῦ ληστρικοῦ πυρὸς
183 δαπάνας ἀναφέρουσα· οὐ γὰρ ταῦτα Ῥωμαῖοι
κατέφλεξαν, ἀλλ' ὑπὸ τῶν ἔνδον ἐπιβούλων, ὡς
προειρήκαμεν, ἐν ἀρχῇ τῆς ἀποστάσεως[1] ἀπὸ
μὲν τῆς Ἀντωνίας ἤρξατο τὸ πῦρ, μετέβη δ' ἐπὶ
τὰ βασίλεια καὶ τῶν τριῶν πύργων τὰς στέγας
ἐπενεμήθη.
184   (v. 1) Τὸ δ' ἱερὸν ἵδρυτο μέν, ὥσπερ ἔφην, ἐπὶ
λόφου καρτεροῦ, κατ' ἀρχὰς δὲ μόλις ἐξήρκει τὸ
ἀνωτάτω χθαμαλὸν αὐτοῦ τῷ τε ναῷ καὶ τῷ
βωμῷ· τὰ γὰρ πέριξ ἀπόκρημνος ἦν καὶ κατάντης.
185 τοῦ δὲ βασιλέως Σολομῶνος, ὃς δὴ καὶ τὸν ναὸν
ἔκτισεν, τὸ κατ' ἀνατολὰς μέρος ἐκτειχίσαντος,
ἐπετέθη μία στοὰ τῷ χώματι· καὶ κατά γε τὰ
λοιπὰ μέρη γυμνὸς ὁ ναὸς ἦν. τοῖς δ' ἑξῆς αἰῶσιν
ἀεί τι τοῦ λαοῦ προσχωννύντος ἀνισούμενος ὁ
186 λόφος ηὐρύνετο. διακόψαντες δὲ καὶ τὸ προσάρκτιον τεῖχος τοσοῦτον προσελάμβανον ὅσον
ὕστερον ἐπεῖχεν ὁ τοῦ παντὸς ἱεροῦ περίβολος.
187 τειχίσαντες δ' ἐκ ῥίζης τριχῇ κυκλόθεν τὸν
λόφον καὶ μεῖζον ἐλπίδος ἐκπονήσαντες ἔργον, εἰς

[1] L: + καὶ (κατεφλέχθησαν καὶ C) the rest.

---

[a] B. ii. 430-440 ; the rebels first set fire to Antonia and then besieged the Roman garrison in Herod's palace and burnt their camp (September A.D. 66).

[b] For comparison with this account of Herod's temple we possess a second partial description in the tractate of the Mishna entitled *Middot*(h) (= " measures " sc. of the temple), written c. A.D. 150. The two accounts are in many particulars inconsistent. *Middoth* on some points usefully supplements Josephus ; but its author, whose information comes to him at second hand, writes without the strict regard for accuracy of a mere antiquarian. Like Ezekiel, he has before him a picture of the ideal temple of the future. Of

as it does the ravages of the brigands' fire. For it Its con-
flagration
by the
brigands. was not the Romans who burnt it to the ground, but this was done, as we have said already,[a] by conspirators within the walls at the opening of the revolt. The conflagration beginning at Antonia passed to the palace, and spread to the roofs of the three towers.

(v. 1) Though the temple,[b] as I said,[c] was Description
of the
temple.
Gradual
enlargement
of the
temple hill. seated on a strong hill, the level area on its summit originally barely sufficed for shrine and altar, the ground around it being precipitous and steep. But king Solomon, the actual founder of the temple, having walled up the eastern side, a single portico was reared on this made ground; on its other sides the sanctuary remained exposed. In course of ages, however, through the constant additions of the people to the embankment, the hill-top by this process of levelling up was widened. They further broke down the north wall and thus took in an area as large as the whole temple enclosure subsequently occupied.[d] Then, after having enclosed the hill from its base with a wall on three sides,[e] and accomplished a task greater than they could ever have

the two accounts, that of Josephus, who had seen the temple, is the more trustworthy; but the discrepancies between Josephus, *Middoth*, and archaeological discovery are so great that in the opinion of the most recent editor of the tractate " the true picture of the Herodian temple can no longer to-day be drawn." See O. Holtzmann, *Die Mischna, Middot* (Giessen, 1913), p. vi, and especially pp. 15–44, " Der Traktat Middot und Josephus."

[c] See §§ 138 f.

[d] According to *Middoth* ii. 1 the temple hill was 500 cubits square (a figure perhaps derived from Ezek. xlii. 16–20).

[e] Solomon having already walled up the E. side, as stated above, § 185.

ὃ μακροὶ μὲν ἐξαναλώθησαν αἰῶνες αὐτοῖς καὶ
οἱ ἱεροὶ δὲ θησαυροὶ πάντες, οὓς ἀνεπίμπλασαν οἱ
παρὰ τῆς οἰκουμένης δασμοὶ πεμπόμενοι τῷ θεῷ,
τούς τε ἄνω περιβόλους καὶ τὸ κάτω ἱερὸν ἀμφ-
188 εδείμαντο. τούτου τὸ ταπεινότατον ἀπὸ τρια-
κοσίων ἀνετείχισαν πηχῶν, κατὰ δέ τινας
τόπους καὶ[1] πλείονος. οὐ μέντοι πᾶν τὸ βάθος
ἐφαίνετο τῶν θεμελίων· ἐπὶ πολὺ γὰρ ἔχωσαν
τὰς φάραγγας, ἀνισοῦν βουλόμενοι τοὺς στενωποὺς
189 τοῦ ἄστεος. πέτραι δὲ τεσσαρακονταπήχεις τὸ
μέγεθος ἦσαν τοῦ δομήματος· ἥ τε γὰρ δαψίλεια
τῶν χρημάτων καὶ τοῦ λαοῦ φιλοτιμία λόγου
μείζονας ἐποιεῖτο τὰς ἐπιβολάς, καὶ τὸ μηδ'
ἐλπισθὲν ἕξειν πέρας ἐπιμονῇ καὶ χρόνοις ἦν ἀνύσιμον.

190 (2) Ἦν δὲ ἄξια τῶν τηλικούτων θεμελίων καὶ
τὰ ὑπὲρ αὐτῶν ἔργα· διπλαῖ μὲν γὰρ αἱ στοαὶ
πᾶσαι, κίονες δ' αὐταῖς εἰκοσιπέντε πηχῶν τὸ
ὕψος ἐφεστήκεσαν, μονόλιθοι λευκοτάτης μαρ-
191 μάρου, κεδρίνοις δὲ φατνώμασιν ὠρόφωντο. τούτων ἡ μὲν φυσικὴ πολυτέλεια καὶ τὸ εὔξεστον καὶ
τὸ ἁρμόνιον παρεῖχε θεωρίαν ἀξιόλογον, οὐδενὶ δ'
ἔξωθεν οὔτε ζωγραφίας οὔτε γλυφίδος ἔργῳ
192 προσηγλάιστο. καὶ πλατεῖαι μὲν ἦσαν ἐπὶ τριάκοντα πήχεις, ὁ δὲ πᾶς κύκλος αὐτῶν εἰς ἓξ
σταδίους συνεμετρεῖτο περιλαμβανομένης καὶ τῆς
Ἀντωνίας· τὸ δ' ὕπαιθρον ἅπαν πεποίκιλτο
193 παντοδαπῷ λίθῳ[2] κατεστρωμένον. διὰ τούτου
προϊόντων ἐπὶ τὸ δεύτερον ἱερὸν δρύφακτος

---

[1] L Lat. (etiam): ἐκ the rest.
[2] Destinon : παντοδαπῶν λίθων MSS.

hoped to achieve—a task upon which long ages
were spent by them as well as all their sacred
treasures, though replenished by the tributes offered
to God from every quarter of the world—they built
around the original block the upper courts and
the lower temple enclosure. The latter, where its
foundations were lowest, they built up from a depth
of three hundred cubits; at some spots this figure
was exceeded. The whole depth of the foundations
was, however, not apparent; for they filled up a
considerable part of the ravines, wishing to level the
narrow alleys of the town. Blocks of stone were Magnitude
used in the building measuring forty cubits; for of the stone
lavish funds and popular enthusiasm led to incred foundations
ible enterprises, and a task seemingly interminable
was through perseverance and in time actually
achieved.

(2) Nor was the superstructure unworthy of such The
foundations. The porticoes, all in double rows, were porticoes
supported by columns five and twenty cubits high— and the
each a single block of the purest white marble—and outer court
ceiled with panels of cedar. The natural magnificence of these columns, their excellent polish and fine
adjustment presented a striking spectacle, without
any adventitious embellishment of painting or
sculpture. The porticoes were thirty cubits broad,
and the complete circuit of them, embracing the
tower of Antonia, measured six furlongs. The open
court was from end to end variegated with paving
of all manner of stones.

Proceeding across this towards the second court The second
of the temple, one found it surrounded by a stone court
debarred to
foreigners.

περιβέβλητο λίθινος, τρίπηχυς μὲν ὕψος, πάνυ δὲ
194 χαριέντως διειργασμένος· ἐν αὐτῷ δ' εἱστήκεσαν
ἐξ ἴσου διαστήματος στῆλαι τὸν τῆς ἁγνείας
προσημαίνουσαι νόμον, αἱ μὲν Ἑλληνικοῖς αἱ δὲ
Ῥωμαϊκοῖς γράμμασιν, μηδένα ἀλλόφυλον ἐντὸς
τοῦ ἁγίου παριέναι· τὸ γὰρ δεύτερον ἱερὸν ἅγιον
195 ἐκαλεῖτο. καὶ τεσσαρεσκαίδεκα μὲν βαθμοῖς ἦν
ἀναβατὸν ἀπὸ τοῦ πρώτου, τετράγωνον δὲ ἄνω
196 καὶ τείχει περιπεφραγμένον ἰδίῳ. τούτου τὸ μὲν
ἔξωθεν ὕψος καίπερ τεσσαράκοντα πηχῶν ὑπάρχον
ὑπὸ τῶν βαθμῶν ἐκαλύπτετο, τὸ δ' ἔνδον εἴκοσι
καὶ πέντε πηχῶν ἦν· πρὸς γὰρ ὑψηλοτέρῳ δεδο-
μημένου τοῦ βάθρου[1] οὐκέτ' ἦν ἅπαν εἴσω κατα-
197 φανὲς καλυπτόμενον ὑπὸ τοῦ λόφου. μετὰ δὲ τοὺς
δεκατέσσαρας βαθμοὺς τὸ μέχρι τοῦ τείχους
198 διάστημα πηχῶν ἦν δέκα, πᾶν ἰσόπεδον. ἔνθεν
ἄλλοι πάλιν πεντέβαθμοι[2] κλίμακες ἀνῆγον ἐπὶ τὰς
πύλας, αἳ ἀπὸ μὲν ἄρκτου καὶ μεσημβρίας ὀκτώ,
καθ' ἑκάτερον τέσσαρες, δύο δ' ἦσαν ἐξ ἀνατολῆς
κατ' ἀνάγκην· διατετειχισμένου γὰρ κατὰ τοῦτο
τὸ κλίμα ταῖς γυναιξὶν ἰδίου πρὸς θρησκείαν

---

[1] τοῦ βάθρου Destinon : τοῦ βάθμου (or τοῖς βάθμοις) mss.
[2] ἑνδεκάβαθμοι PAML ; cf. § 206.

---

[a] Hebrew *soreg*, *Middoth* ii. 3 a.
[b] c. 4½ feet : according to *Middoth*, " ten handbreadths "
= c. 2⅓ feet.
[c] One of these slabs was discovered in 1871 by M. Clermont-Ganneau, and is now at Constantinople ; the inscription on it runs μηθένα ἀλλογενῆ εἰσπορεύεσθαι ἐντὸς τοῦ περὶ τὸ
ἱερὸν τρυφάκτου καὶ περιβόλου. ὃς δ' ἂν ληφθῇ ἑαυτῷ αἴτιος ἔσται
διὰ τὸ ἐξακολουθεῖν θάνατον. Josephus mentions it again in

balustrade,[a] three cubits[b] high and of exquisite workmanship; in this at regular intervals stood slabs giving warning, some in Greek, others in Latin characters, of the law of purification, to wit that no foreigner was permitted to enter the holy place,[c] for so the second enclosure of the temple was called. It was approached from the first by fourteen steps; the area above was quadrangular, and screened by a wall of its own. The exterior height of this, actually forty cubits, was disguised by the steps, the interior altitude was but five and twenty; for the floor being built on a higher level,[d] the whole was not visible from within, a portion being concealed by the hill. Beyond the fourteen steps there was a space of ten cubits between them and the wall, forming a level terrace.[e] From this again other flights of five steps led up to the gates. Of these there were eight on the north and south, four on either side, and two on the east [f]—necessarily; since in this quarter a special place of worship was walled off for the women,

---

A. xv. 417 ἑρκίον λιθίνου δρυφάκτου γραφῇ κωλῦον εἰσιέναι τὸν ἀλλοεθνῆ θανατικῆς ἀπειλουμένης τῆς ζημίας; *cf.* the allusion in Philo, *Leg. ad Gaium,* 31 (212 Cohn). St. Paul's arrest was due to a belief that he had brought Trophimus the Ephesian within the barrier, Acts xxi. 26 ff.

[d] Or (with the MSS.) "the staircase being built against rising ground."

[e] The steps, with the terrace above them, ran round three sides of the building; at the west end there were no steps (§ 38). *Middoth* ii. 3 b mentions the terrace (*Chel*), 10 cubits (broad), but speaks of 12 steps only, instead of the 14 + 5 of Josephus. In this and other discrepancies Josephus appears to be the more trustworthy authority.

[f] *i.e.* relatively to the ναός and the courts immediately surrounding it; the two gates were in the centre of the east and west walls respectively of the Women's Court, which formed the main access to the inner courts.

χώρου, ἔδει δευτέραν εἶναι πύλην· τέτμητο δ' αὕτη
199 τῆς πρώτης ἄντικρυς. κἀκ τῶν ἄλλων δὲ κλιμάτων
μία μεσημβρινὴ πύλη καὶ μία βόρειος, δι' ἧς[1] εἰς
τὴν γυναικωνῖτιν εἰσῆγον· κατὰ γὰρ τὰς ἄλλας
οὐκ ἐξῆν παρελθεῖν γυναιξίν, ἀλλ' οὐδὲ κατὰ τὴν
σφετέραν ὑπερβῆναι τὸ διατείχισμα. ἀνεῖτό γε
μὴν ταῖς τ' ἐπιχωρίοις καὶ ταῖς ἔξωθεν ὁμοφύλοις
200 ἐν ἴσῳ πρὸς θρησκείαν ὁ χῶρος. τὸ δὲ πρὸς δύσιν
μέρος οὐκ εἶχε πύλην, ἀλλὰ διηνεκὲς ἐδεδόμητο
ταύτῃ τὸ τεῖχος. αἱ στοαὶ δὲ μεταξὺ τῶν πυλῶν
ἀπὸ τοῦ τείχους ἔνδον ἐστραμμέναι πρὸ τῶν
γαζοφυλακίων σφόδρα μὲν καλοῖς καὶ μεγάλοις
ἀνείχοντο κίοσιν, ἦσαν δ' ἁπλαῖ, καὶ πλὴν τοῦ
μεγέθους τῶν κάτω κατ' οὐδὲν ἀπελείποντο.
201   (3) Τῶν δὲ πυλῶν αἱ μὲν ἐννέα χρυσῷ καὶ
ἀργύρῳ κεκαλυμμέναι πανταχόθεν ἦσαν, ὁμοίως
τε αἵ τε παραστάδες καὶ τὰ ὑπέρθυρα, μία δ' ἡ
ἔξωθεν τοῦ νεὼ Κορινθίου χαλκοῦ, πολὺ τῇ τιμῇ
τὰς καταργύρους καὶ περιχρύσους ὑπεράγουσα.
202 καὶ δύο μὲν ἑκάστου πυλῶνος θύραι, τριάκοντα
δὲ πηχῶν τὸ ὕψος ἑκάστης καὶ τὸ πλάτος ἦν
203 πεντεκαίδεκα. μετὰ μέντοι τὰς εἰσόδους ἐνδοτέρω
πλατυνόμενοι παρ' ἑκάτερον τριακονταπήχεις
ἐξέδρας εἶχον εὖρός τε καὶ μῆκος πυργοειδεῖς,

---

[1] δι' ἧς] quibus Lat.

---

[a] Or " facing inwards from."
[b] These lay round the walls of the whole inner court and
were used for the storage of temple property (Smith, *Jerusalem*, ii. 510 n., Hastings, *D.B.* iv. 714 a) ; they included
perhaps the strong-rooms for private wealth deposited here
for safety, *B.* vi. 282, *cf. A.* xix. 294 " the treasury." In the
N.T. (Mark xii. 41, etc.), on the other hand, " the treasury "

rendering a second gate requisite ; this approach The women's court.
opened opposite to the first. On the other sides
there was one gate on the south and one on the north
giving access to the women's court ; for women were
not permitted to enter by the others nor yet to pass
by way of their own gate beyond the partition wall.
This court was, however, thrown open for worship
to all Jewish women alike, whether natives of the
country or visitors from abroad. The west end of the
building had no gate, the wall there being unbroken.
The porticoes between the gates, on the inner side
of [a] the wall in front of the treasury chambers,[b] were
supported by exceedingly beautiful and lofty columns;
these porticoes were single, but, except in point of
size, in no way inferior to those in the lower court.

(3) Of the gates[c] nine were completely overlaid The gates
with gold and silver, as were also their door-posts
and lintels ; but one, that outside the sanctuary,
was of Corinthian bronze, and far exceeded in value
those plated with silver and set in gold.[d] Each
gateway had two doors, and each door was thirty
cubits in height and fifteen in breadth. Beyond and
within the entrances, however, the portals expanded,
embracing on either side turret-like chambers [e]
measuring thirty cubits in breadth and length, and

means the 13 trumpet-shaped receptacles for alms and
offerings which stood in the Women's Court.

[c] The 10 gates mentioned in § 198.

[d] " The Corinthian gate "=" the gate of Nicanor " of
Middoth (ii. 3 g, " All the gates were gilded except the gate
of Nicanor," mentioning its bronze), and probably " the
Beautiful gate " of Acts iii. 2, 10. From Josephus, though
his language is difficult, it seems clear that it was in the east
wall, not (as some have argued) in the west wall, of the
women's court. Corinthian bronze was famous.

[e] Or " gate-rooms."

ὑψηλὰς[1] δ' ὑπὲρ τεσσαράκοντα πήχεις· δύο δ'
ἀνεῖχον ἑκάστην κίονες, δώδεκα πηχῶν τὴν
204 περιοχὴν ἔχοντες. καὶ τῶν μὲν ἄλλων ἴσον ἦν
τὸ μέγεθος, ἡ δ' ὑπὲρ τὴν Κορινθίαν ἀπὸ τῆς
γυναικωνίτιδος ἐξ ἀνατολῆς ἀνοιγομένη τῆς τοῦ
205 ναοῦ πύλης ἀντικρὺ πολὺ μείζων· πεντήκοντα
γὰρ πηχῶν οὖσα τὴν ἀνάστασιν τεσσαρακονταπήχεις τὰς θύρας εἶχε καὶ τὸν κόσμον πολυ-
τελέστερον ἐπὶ δαψιλὲς πάχος ἀργύρου τε καὶ
χρυσοῦ. τοῦτον δὲ ταῖς ἐννέα πύλαις ἐπέχεεν ὁ
206 Τιβερίου πατὴρ Ἀλέξανδρος. βαθμοὶ δὲ δεκα-
πέντε πρὸς τὴν μείζονα πύλην ἀπὸ τοῦ τῶν
γυναικῶν διατειχίσματος ἀνῆγον· τῶν γὰρ κατὰ
τὰς ἄλλας πέντε βαθμῶν ἦσαν βραχύτεροι.

207 (4) Αὐτὸς δ' ὁ ναὸς κατὰ μέσον κείμενος, τὸ
ἅγιον ἱερόν, δώδεκα βαθμοῖς ἦν ἀναβατός, καὶ
τὸ μὲν κατὰ πρόσωπον ὕψος τε καὶ εὖρος ἴσον
ἀνὰ πήχεις ἑκατόν, κατόπιν δὲ τεσσαράκοντα
πήχεσι στενότερος· ἔμπροσθεν γὰρ ὥσπερ ὦμοι
208 παρ' ἑκάτερον εἰκοσαπήχεις διέβαινον. ἡ πρώτη
δ' αὐτοῦ πύλη, πηχῶν ἑβδομήκοντα τὸ ὕψος οὖσα
καὶ εὖρος εἴκοσι καὶ πέντε, θύρας οὐκ εἶχε· τοῦ
γὰρ οὐρανοῦ τὸ ἀχανὲς[2] καὶ ἀδιάκλειστον ἐνέφαινε·
κεχρύσωτο δὲ τὰ μέτωπα πάντα, καὶ δι' αὐτῆς
ὅ τε πρῶτος οἶκος ἔξωθεν πᾶς κατεφαίνετο μέ-
γιστος ὤν, καὶ τὰ περὶ τὴν εἴσω πύλην πάντα
209 λαμπόμενα χρυσῷ τοῖς ὁρῶσιν ὑπέπιπτεν. τοῦ
ναοῦ δὲ ὄντος εἴσω διστέγου μόνος ὁ πρῶτος

---

[1] Lat.: ὑψηλαὶ mss.   [2] Bekker: ἀφανὲς mss.

[a] i.e. west of.
[b] i.e. forming the eastern approach to the sanctuary, from
the west end of the Women's Court.

over forty cubits high, each supported by two columns, twelve cubits in circumference. The dimensions of the other gates were all alike, but the one beyond [a] the Corinthian gate, opening from the Women's Court on the east,[b] opposite the gate of the sanctuary, was far larger, having an altitude of fifty cubits, with doors of forty, and richer decoration, being overlaid with massive plates of silver and gold. The nine gates were thus plated by Alexander [c] the father of Tiberius. Fifteen steps led up from the women's compartment to the greater gate, these steps being shallower than the five at each of the other gates.[d]

(4) The sacred edifice itself, the holy temple, in the central position, was approached by a flight of twelve steps. The façade [e] was of equal height and breadth, each being a hundred cubits ; [f] but the building behind was narrower by forty cubits, for in front it had as it were shoulders extending twenty cubits on either side.[g] The first gate was seventy cubits high and twenty-five broad and had no doors, displaying unexcluded the void expanse of heaven; the entire face was covered with gold, and through it the first edifice was visible to a spectator without in all its grandeur and the surroundings of the inner gate all gleaming with gold fell beneath his eye. But, whereas the sanctuary within consisted of two

The temple buildings: the façade.

---

[c] Alabarch of Alexandria and brother of the philosopher Philo, *A.* xviii. 259 ; for his son, Tiberius Alexander, now a staff-officer in the Roman army, see *B.* ii. 220, v. 45.   [d] § 198.

[e] One must imagine a great propylaeon or porch.

[f] So *Middoth* iv. 6. In Nero's time King Agrippa had made preparations for raising the height to 120 cubits, but the work was prevented by the outbreak of war, *B.* v. 36 f., *cf. A.* xv. 391.

[g] *Middoth,* iv. 7 c: "The sanctuary was narrow behind and broad in front, like a lion."

οἶκος προύκειτο καὶ διηνεκὲς εἰς τὸ ὕψος, ἀνα-
τεινόμενος μὲν ἐπ᾽ ἐνενήκοντα πήχεις, μηκυνό-
μενος δὲ ἐπὶ πεντήκοντα καὶ διαβαίνων ἐπ᾽ εἴκοσιν.
210 ἡ δὲ διὰ τοῦ οἴκου πύλη κεχρύσωτο μέν, ὡς ἔφην,
πᾶσα καὶ ὅλος ὁ περὶ αὐτὴν τοῖχος, εἶχε δὲ καὶ
τὰς χρυσᾶς ὑπὲρ ἑαυτῆς ἀμπέλους, ἀφ᾽ ὧν βότρυες
211 ἀνδρομήκεις κατεκρέμαντο. [ὄντος δὲ ἤδη τοῦ
ναοῦ διστέγου, ταπεινοτέρα τῆς ἔξωθεν ὄψεως
ἡ ἔνδον ἦν]¹ καὶ θύρας εἶχε χρυσᾶς πεντήκοντα-
212 πέντε πήχεων τὸ ὕψος, εὖρος δ᾽ ἑκκαίδεκα. πρὸ
δὲ τούτων ἰσόμηκες καταπέτασμα πέπλος ἦν
Βαβυλώνιος ποικιλτὸς ἐξ ὑακίνθου καὶ βύσσου
κόκκου τε καὶ πορφύρας, θαυμαστῶς μὲν εἰρ-
γασμένος, οὐκ ἀθεώρητον δὲ τῆς ὕλης τὴν κρᾶσιν
213 ἔχων, ἀλλ᾽ ὥσπερ εἰκόνα τῶν ὅλων· ἐδόκει γὰρ
αἰνίττεσθαι τῇ κόκκῳ μὲν τὸ πῦρ, τῇ βύσσῳ δὲ
τὴν γῆν, τῇ δ᾽ ὑακίνθῳ τὸν ἀέρα, καὶ τῇ πορφύρᾳ
τὴν θάλασσαν, τῶν μὲν ἐκ τῆς χροίας ὁμοιουμένων,
τῆς δὲ βύσσου καὶ τῆς πορφύρας διὰ τὴν γένεσιν,
ἐπειδὴ τὴν μὲν ἀναδίδωσιν ἡ γῆ, τὴν δ᾽ ἡ θάλασσα.
214 κατεγέγραπτο δ᾽ ὁ πέπλος ἅπασαν τὴν οὐράνιον
θεωρίαν πλὴν τῶν ζῳδίων.
215 (5) Παριόντας δ᾽ εἴσω τὸ ἐπίπεδον τοῦ ναοῦ
μέρος ἐξεδέχετο. τούτου τοίνυν τὸ μὲν ὕψος
ἑξήκοντα πηχῶν καὶ τὸ μῆκος ἴσον, εἴκοσι² δὲ

---

¹ See note d.   ² εἰκοσιτεσσάρων L.

ᵃ δίστεγος must, from the context, here mean " with two
chambers *on the same floor*," *i.e.* the Holy Place and the Holy
of Holies ; not (as in § 211, note d below) " in two stories."
ᵇ § 208 fin.
ᶜ *Cf. A.* xv. 395. Tacitus, *Hist.* v. 5 alludes to the " vitis
aurea templo reperta " and to the inference drawn by some
that the Jews were worshippers of Father Liber (Bacchus)

separate chambers,[a] the first building alone stood
exposed to view, from top to bottom, towering to a
height of ninety cubits, its length being fifty and its
breadth twenty. The gate opening into the building
was, as I said,[b] completely overlaid with gold, as was
the whole wall around it. It had, moreover, above it
those golden vines,[c] from which depended grape-clusters as tall as a man ;[d] and it had golden doors The golden vine and the veil.
fifty-five cubits high and sixteen broad. Before
these hung a veil of equal length, of Babylonian
tapestry, with embroidery of blue and fine linen, of
scarlet also and purple, wrought with marvellous
skill. Nor was this mixture of materials without its
mystic meaning : it typified the universe. For the
scarlet seemed emblematical of fire, the fine linen of
the earth, the blue of the air, and the purple of the
sea ; the comparison in two cases being suggested
by their colour, and in that of the fine linen and
purple by their origin, as the one is produced by the
earth and the other by the sea. On this tapestry
was portrayed a panorama of the heavens, the signs
of the Zodiac excepted.

(5) Passing within one found oneself in the ground-floor of the sanctuary. This was sixty cubits in The sanctuary : interior.
height, the same in length, and twenty cubits in

---

[a] Here the mss. add : " But, as the sanctuary was now
in two stories, it appeared lower within than from without."
This irrelevant parenthesis interrupts the sentence, gives to
δίστεγος a meaning different from that in which it has just
been used, and is a premature reference to the *interior* of the
building, the description of which begins only at § 215 ; the
two stories are mentioned in § 221. I take the clause to be
a gloss on the opening words of § 209, perhaps a correction
of the author himself or of a συνεργός ; there are indications
that the text has been worked over.

216 πηχῶν τὸ πλάτος ἦν. τὸ δ' ἑξηκοντάπηχυ πάλιν
διῄρητο, καὶ τὸ μὲν πρῶτον μέρος ἀποτετμημένον
ἐπὶ τεσσαράκοντα πήχεις εἶχεν ἐν ἑαυτῷ τρία
τὰ θαυμασιώτατα καὶ περιβόητα πᾶσιν ἀνθρώποις
217 ἔργα, λυχνίαν τράπεζαν θυμιατήριον. ἐνέφαινον
δ' οἱ μὲν ἑπτὰ λύχνοι τοὺς πλανήτας· τοσοῦτοι
γὰρ ἀπ' αὐτῆς διῄρηντο τῆς λυχνίας· οἱ δ' ἐπὶ
τῆς τραπέζης ἄρτοι δώδεκα τόν τε ζῳδιακὸν
218 κύκλον καὶ τὸν ἐνιαυτόν. τὸ θυμιατήριον δὲ διὰ
τῶν τρισκαίδεκα θυμιαμάτων, οἷς ἐκ θαλάσσης
ἀνεπίμπλατο καὶ γῆς ἀοικήτου τε[1] καὶ οἰκουμένης,
219 ἐσήμαινεν ὅτι τοῦ θεοῦ πάντα καὶ τῷ θεῷ. τὸ
δ' ἐνδοτάτω μέρος εἴκοσι μὲν πηχῶν ἦν· διείργετο
δ' ὁμοίως καταπετάσματι πρὸς τὸ ἔξωθεν. ἔκειτο
δ' οὐδὲν ὅλως ἐν αὐτῷ, ἄβατον δὲ καὶ ἄχραντον
καὶ ἀθέατον ἦν πᾶσιν, ἁγίου δὲ ἅγιον ἐκαλεῖτο.
220 περὶ δὲ τὰ πλευρὰ τοῦ κάτω ναοῦ δι' ἀλλήλων
ἦσαν οἶκοι τρίστεγοι πολλοί, καὶ παρ' ἑκάτερον
221 εἰς αὐτοὺς ἀπὸ τῆς πύλης εἴσοδοι. τὸ δ' ὑπερῷον
μέρος τούτους μὲν οὐκέτ' εἶχεν τοὺς οἴκους,
παρόσον ἦν καὶ στενότερον, ὑψηλότερον[2] δ' ἐπὶ
τεσσαράκοντα πήχεις καὶ λιτότερον τοῦ κάτω·
συνάγεται γὰρ οὕτως πρὸς ἑξήκοντα τοῖς τοῦ
ἐπιπέδου πηχῶν ἑκατὸν τὸ πᾶν ὕψος.

---

[1] γῆς ἀοικήτου τε Niese : τῆς τε ἀοικήτου MSS. [2] ὑψηλὸν L.

---

[a] So the Talmud (as quoted in *Encycl. Bibl.* ii. 2167).
To the four ingredients prescribed in Exod. xxx. 34 (" stacte,
onycha, galbanum, frankincense ") there were added in
Rabbinic times nine more, viz. myrrh, cassia, spikenard,
saffron, costus, mace, cinnamon, salt and a herb which had
the property of causing the smoke to ascend vertically. An
incense of seven ingredients is mentioned in *Jubilees*, xvi. 24,
cf. Ecclus. xxiv. 15

breadth. But the sixty cubits of its length were again divided. The first portion, partitioned off at forty cubits, contained within it three most wonderful works of art, universally renowned : a lampstand, a table, and an altar of incense. The seven lamps (such being the number of the branches from the lampstand) represented the planets ; the loaves on the table, twelve in number, the circle of the Zodiac and the year ; while the altar of incense, by the thirteen [a] fragrant spices from sea and from land, both desert and inhabited, with which it was replenished, signified that all things are of God and for God.[b]

The Holy Place.

The innermost recess measured twenty cubits, and was screened in like manner from the outer portion by a veil. In this stood nothing whatever : unapproachable, inviolable, invisible to all, it was called the Holy of Holy.[c]

The Holy of Holies.

Around the sides of the lower part of the sanctuary were numerous chambers, in three stories, communicating with one another ; these were approached by entrances from either side of the gateway. The upper part of the building had no similar chambers, being proportionately narrower, but rose forty cubits higher in a severer style than the lower story. These forty cubits, added to the sixty of the ground-floor, amount to a total altitude of a hundred cubits.

Priests' chambers.

[b] To Philo the four Mosaic ingredients of the incense symbolize the four elements, *Quis rer. div. heres*, 197 (40). A similar " cosmical " interpretation of the tabernacle and of the priestly vestments (§ 231) is given by Josephus elsewhere (*A.* iii. 180 ff. ἕκαστα γὰρ τούτων εἰς ἀπομίμησιν καὶ διατύπωσιν τῶν ὅλων, *cf. B.* iv. 324 ἡ κοσμικὴ θρησκεία) and by Philo, *Vita Mosis* ii. 117 Cohn (iii. 12) ἀπεικόνισμα καὶ μίμημα τοῦ κόσμου.

[c] The Hebrew names for it were *debir* (" hindmost chamber ") or " Holy of Holies."

222 (6) Τὸ δ' ἔξωθεν αὐτοῦ πρόσωπον οὐδὲν οὔτ' εἰς ψυχῆς οὔτ' εἰς ὀμμάτων ἔκπληξιν ἀπέλειπεν· πλαξὶ γὰρ χρυσοῦ στιβαραῖς κεκαλυμμένος πάντοθεν, ὑπὸ τὰς πρώτας ἀνατολὰς πυρωδεστάτην ἀπέπαλλεν αὐγὴν καὶ τῶν βιαζομένων ἰδεῖν τὰς

223 ὄψεις ὥσπερ ἡλιακαῖς ἀκτῖσιν ἀπέστρεφεν. τοῖς γε μὴν ἀφικνουμένοις[1] ξένοις πόρρωθεν ὅμοιος ὄρει χιόνος πλήρει κατεφαίνετο· καὶ γὰρ καθὰ

224 μὴ κεχρύσωτο λευκότατος ἦν. κατὰ κορυφὴν δὲ χρυσέους ὀβελοὺς ἀνεῖχεν τεθηγμένους, ὡς μή τινι προσκαθεζομένῳ μολύνοιτο τῶν ὀρνέων. τῶν δ' ἐν αὐτῷ λίθων ἔνιοι μῆκος πέντε καὶ τεσσαράκοντα πηχῶν ἦσαν, ὕψος πέντε, εὖρος δ' ἕξ.

225 πρὸ αὐτοῦ δ' ὁ βωμὸς πεντεκαίδεκα μὲν ὕψος ἦν πήχεων, εὖρος δὲ καὶ μῆκος ἐκτείνων ἴσον ἀνὰ πεντήκοντα πήχεις τετράγωνος ἵδρυτο, κερατοειδεῖς προανέχων γωνίας, καὶ ἀπὸ μεσημβρίας ἐπ' αὐτὸν ἄνοδος ἠρέμα προσάντης ὑπτίαστο. κατεσκευάσθη δ' ἄνευ σιδήρου, καὶ οὐδέποτ'

226 ἔψαυεν αὐτοῦ σίδηρος. περιέστεφε δὲ τόν τε ναὸν καὶ τὸν βωμὸν εὔλιθόν τι καὶ χαρίεν γείσιον, ὅσον πηχυαῖον ὕψος, ὃ διεῖργεν ἐξωτέρω τὸν δῆμον

227 ἀπὸ τῶν ἱερέων. γονορροίοις μὲν δὴ καὶ λεπροῖς ἡ πόλις ὅλη, τὸ δ' ἱερὸν[2] γυναικῶν ἐμμήνοις

---

[1] εἰσαφικνουμένοις LVRC.

[2] τὸ δ' ἱερὸν Niese: τὸ διεῖργον or τὸ διεῖργον τὸ ἱερὸν most MSS.

---

[a] *Middoth* iv. 6 mentions a " raven-scarer " (scare-crow) one cubit high.

[b] These blocks, of almost incredible length, must have been exceptional ; *A.* xv. 392 gives the dimensions of the stones as about 25 cubits long, 8 high, and about 12 broad. *Cf.* the disciples' exclamation, " Master, behold what manner of stones ! " Mark xiii. 1.

(6) The exterior of the building wanted nothing Exterior of the temple. that could astound either mind or eye. For, being covered on all sides with massive plates of gold, the sun was no sooner up than it radiated so fiery a flash that persons straining to look at it were compelled to avert their eyes, as from the solar rays. To approaching strangers it appeared from a distance like a snow-clad mountain; for all that was not over-laid with gold was of purest white. From its summit protruded sharp golden spikes to prevent birds from settling upon and polluting the roof.[a] Some of the stones in the building were forty-five cubits in length, five in height and six in breadth.[b]

In front of it stood the altar, fifteen cubits high, The altar. and with a breadth and length extending alike to fifty cubits, in shape a square[c] with horn-like pro-jections at the corners, and approached from the south by a gently sloping acclivity.[d] No iron was used in its construction, nor did iron ever touch it.[e]

Surrounding both the sanctuary and the altar was a low stone parapet,[f] fair and graceful, about a cubit high, which separated the laity outside from the priests.

Persons afflicted with gonorrhoea or leprosy were Areas pro-hibited to excluded from the city altogether; the temple was particular closed to women during their menstruation, and even persons.

---

[c] *Middoth* iii. 1 a likewise describes the altar as a square with horns at the corners, but gives smaller dimensions, the base being a square of 32 cubits, the highest portion a square of 24 cubits, and the height 8 cubits; it mentions an older and still smaller altar.

[d] So *Middoth* iii. 3 b (adding dimensions).

[e] So *Middoth* iii. 4 a, b (no iron tool was used in cleaning it), adding the quaint explanation "for iron is created to shorten man's days and the altar is built to lengthen man's days." [f] Mentioned in *Midd.* ii. 7 b.

ἀπεκέκλειστο, παρελθεῖν δὲ ταύταις οὐδὲ καθαραῖς
ἐξῆν ὃν προείπαμεν ὅρον. ἀνδρῶν δ' οἱ μὴ
καθάπαν ἠγνευκότες εἴργοντο τῆς ἔνδον αὐλῆς,
καὶ τῶν ἱερέων πάλιν οἱ[1] καθαρεύοντες εἴργοντο.

228 (7) Τῶν δ' ἀπὸ γένους ἱερέων ὅσοι διὰ πήρωσιν
οὐκ ἐλειτούργουν παρῆσάν τε ἅμα τοῖς ὁλοκλήροις
ἐνδοτέρω τοῦ γεισίου καὶ τὰς ἀπὸ τοῦ γένους
ἐλάμβανον μερίδας, ταῖς γε μὴν ἐσθήσεσιν[2] ἰδιω-
τικαῖς ἐχρῶντο· τὴν γὰρ ἱερὰν ὁ λειτουργῶν

229 ἠμφιέννυτο μόνος. ἐπὶ δὲ τὸ θυσιαστήριον καὶ
τὸν ναὸν ἀνέβαινον οἱ τῶν ἱερέων ἄμωμοι, βύσσον
μὲν ἀμπεχόμενοι, μάλιστα δ' ἀπ' ἀκράτου νήφοντες
δέει τῆς θρησκείας, ὡς μή τι παραβαῖεν ἐν τῇ

230 λειτουργίᾳ. ὁ δὲ ἀρχιερεὺς ἀνῄει μὲν σὺν αὐτοῖς,
ἀλλ' οὐκ ἀεί, ταῖς δ' ἑβδομάσι καὶ νουμηνίαις
καὶ εἴ τις ἑορτὴ πάτριος ἢ πανήγυρις ἦν[3] πάνδημος

231 ἀγομένη δι' ἔτους. ἐλειτούργει δὲ τοὺς μηροὺς μὲν
ἄχρις αἰδοίου διαζώσματι καλύπτων, λινοῦν δὲ
ὑποδύτην ἔνδοθεν λαμβάνων καὶ ποδήρη καθύπερθεν ὑακίνθινον, ἔνδυμα στρογγύλον θυσανωτόν·
τῶν δὲ θυσάνων ἀπήρτηντο κώδωνες χρύσεοι καὶ
ῥοαὶ παράλληλοι, βροντῆς μὲν οἱ κώδωνες, ἀ-

232 στραπῆς δ' αἱ ῥοαὶ σημεῖον. ἡ δὲ τὸ ἔνδυμα τῷ
στέρνῳ προσηλοῦσα ταινία πέντε διηνθισμένη

---

[1] Destinon with Lat. : + μὴ mss.   [2] ἐσθῆσιν L.
[3] Destinon : ἢ PAL : om. the rest.

[a] § 199.
[b] Cf. with this paragraph Ap. ii. 103 f.
[c] A fuller description of the vestments both of the ordinary
priests and of the high priest, based on Exodus xxviii etc.,
is given in A. iii. 151-178.   Cf. Ecclus. xlv. 7-12.

when free from impurity they were not permitted
to pass the boundary which we have mentioned
above.[a]   Men not thoroughly clean were debarred
from admission to the inner court, from which even
priests were excluded when undergoing purification.[b]

(7) All who were of priestly lineage but were prevented from officiating by some physical defect, were
admitted within the parapet, along with those free
from any imperfection, and received the portions
which were their birthright, but wore ordinary
dress ; none but the officiating priest was clad in
the holy vestments.   The priests who were without
blemish went up to the altar and the sanctuary
clothed in fine linen, scrupulously abstaining from
strong drink through reverence for the ritual, lest
they should be guilty of any transgression in their
ministrations.

The high priest accompanied them, not on all
occasions, but on the seventh days and new moons,
and on any national festival or annual assemblage
of all the people.   When ministering, he wore[c]
breeches[d] which covered his thighs up to the loins,
an under vest of linen, and over that a blue robe[e]
reaching to the feet, full and tasselled ; and from the
tassels hung golden bells and pomegranates alternately, the bells symbolizing thunder and the pomegranates lightning.   The embroidered sash[f] which
attached this robe to the breast consisted of five

The
officiating
priests.

The high
priest's
vestments.

---

[d] " linen breeches " (*miknesei bad*), Ex. xxviii. 42, τὸν
μαναχάσην λεγόμενον *A*. iii. 152.
[e] " the robe of the ephod all of blue," Ex. xxviii. 31-35,
A. iii. 159-161 (μεεὶρ καλεῖται κατὰ τὴν ἡμετέραν γλῶσσαν=
Heb. *m'yil*).
[f] " A girdle the work of the embroiderer," Ex. xxviii. 39,
A. iii. 159.

ζώναις πεποίκιλτο, χρυσοῦ τε καὶ πορφύρας καὶ
κόκκου, πρὸς δὲ βύσσου καὶ ὑακίνθου, δι᾽ ὧν
ἔφαμεν καὶ τὰ τοῦ ναοῦ καταπετάσματα συνυφάνθαι.
233 τούτοις δὲ καὶ ἐπωμίδα κεκραμένην εἶχεν, ἐν ᾗ
πλείων χρυσὸς ἦν. σχῆμα μὲν οὖν ἐνδυτοῦ¹ θώ-
ρακος εἶχεν, δύο δ᾽ αὐτὴν ἐνεπόρπουν ἀσπιδίσκαι
χρυσαῖ, κατεκέκλειντο δ᾽ ἐν ταύταις κάλλιστοί
τε καὶ μέγιστοι σαρδόνυχες, τοὺς ἐπωνύμους τῶν
234 τοῦ ἔθνους φυλῶν ἐπιγεγραμμέναι. κατὰ δὲ
θάτερον ἄλλοι προσήρτηντο λίθοι δώδεκα, κατὰ
τρεῖς εἰς τέσσαρα μέρη διῃρημένοι, σάρδιον
τόπαζος σμάραγδος, ἄνθραξ ἴασπις σάπφειρος,
ἀχάτης ἀμέθυστος λιγύριον, ὄνυξ βήρυλλος χρυσό-
λιθος, ὧν ἐφ᾽ ἑκάστου πάλιν εἷς τῶν ἐπωνύμων
235 ἐγέγραπτο. τὴν δὲ κεφαλὴν βυσσίνη μὲν ἔσκεπεν
τιάρα, κατέστεπτο δ᾽ ὑακίνθῳ, περὶ ἣν χρυσοῦς
ἄλλος ἦν στέφανος ἔκτυπα φέρων τὰ ἱερὰ γράμ-
236 ματα· ταῦτα δ᾽ ἐστὶ φωνήεντα τέσσαρα. ταύτην

---

¹ ἐπενδύτου L.

ᵃ §§ 212 f. (excluding gold which is not mentioned in
connexion with the veil).

ᵇ Ex. xxviii. 6 ff., A. iii. 162 ff. Epomis, the Greek
rendering here and in the LXX of the Heb. ephod, means
the upper part of a woman's tunic attached by shoulder-
straps, a sort of " cape."   ᶜ i.e. at the shoulders.

ᵈ So A. iii. 165 ; the gem intended in Ex. xxviii. 9 is
uncertain, R.V. text " onyx," margin " beryl," LXX
σμάραγδος (? " emerald ").   ᵉ i.e. in front.

ᶠ Ex. xxviii. 17-20, A. iii. 168.

ᵍ A. iii. 168 " sardonyx."

ʰ In A. iii. 168 the stones in the two last rows are named
in another order, on which emphasis is laid : " The third row
begins with jacinth, then amethyst, and thirdly agate, being
the ninth in all ; in the fourth row chrysolite comes first,
next onyx, then beryl—it is the last."

bands of variegated colours, gold, purple, scarlet, fine linen and blue, with which, as we have said,[a] the veils in the sanctuary were also interwoven. Of the same mixture of materials, with gold preponderating, was the high-priest's ephod.[b] In form like an ordinary cuirass, it was fastened[c] by two golden brooches, set with very large and beautiful sardonyxes,[d] on which were engraved the names of those after whom the tribes of the nation were called. Attached to the other side[e] were twelve more stones,[f] in four rows of three each : sardius,[g] topaz, emerald ; carbuncle, jasper, sapphire ; agate, amethyst, jacinth ; onyx, beryl, chrysolite ;[h] on each of which, again, was engraved the name of one of the heads of the tribes. His head was covered by a tiara[i] of fine linen, wreathed with blue, encircling which was another crown, of gold, whereon were embossed the sacred letters, to wit, four vowels.[j] These robes were

---

[i] The " mitre of fine linen " or (R.V. margin) " turban of silk," Ex. xxviii. 37, 39 ; a fuller description of the head-dress is given in *A.* iii. 172-178, where it is compared to a cup-like flower.

[j] *i.e.* the tetragrammaton YHVH. That this was the inscription, and that the phrase in Ex. xxviii. 36 means " the sacred name Jahve," not " Holy (or ' Holiness ') to the LORD " is shown in two notes on Aaron's head-dress by Mr. J. E. Hogg and Prof. F. C. Burkitt in the *Journal of Theol. Studies*, vol. xxvi. 72, 180. The interpretation has the support of Philo, *De vita Mosis* ii. (iii.) 114 Cohn, τέτταρας ἔχον γλυφὰς ὀνόματος, Origen on Ps. ii. 2 and Bar Hebraeus ; *cf.* Jos. *A.* iii. 178 τελαμὼν . . . ἱεροῖς γράμμασι τοῦ θεοῦ τὴν προσηγορίαν ἐπιτετιμημένος, viii. 93 ἡ στεφάνη εἰς ἣν τὸν θεὸν Μωυσῆς ἔγραψε. Why Josephus speaks of " four *vowels* " is uncertain. The first and third letters are probably " by nature vowels " (=*i* and *u*), though by usage consonants (Gesenius, *Heb. Grammar*, ed. Cowley, pp. 26, 45). He is perhaps thinking of a *Greek* form ('Ιαυέ).

μὲν οὖν τὴν ἐσθῆτα οὐκ ἐφόρει χρόνιον, λιτοτέραν
δ' ἀνελάμβανεν, ὁπότε δ' εἰσίοι εἰς τὸ ἄδυτον·
εἰσῄει δ' ἅπαξ κατ' ἐνιαυτὸν μόνος ἐν ᾗ νηστεύειν
237 ἔθος ἡμέρᾳ πάντας τῷ θεῷ. καὶ τὰ μὲν περὶ τῆς
πόλεως καὶ τοῦ ναοῦ τῶν τε περὶ τούτου[1] ἐθῶν
καὶ νόμων αὖθις ἀκριβέστερον ἐροῦμεν· οὐ γὰρ
ὀλίγος περὶ αὐτῶν καταλείπεται λόγος.

238   (8) Ἡ δ' Ἀντωνία κατὰ γωνίαν μὲν δύο
στοῶν ἔκειτο τοῦ πρώτου ἱεροῦ, τῆς τε πρὸς
ἑσπέραν καὶ τῆς πρὸς ἄρκτον, δεδόμητο δ' ὑπὲρ
πέτρας πεντηκονταπήχους μὲν ὕψος, περικρήμνου
δὲ πάσης· ἔργον δ' ἦν Ἡρώδου τοῦ βασιλέως,
ἐν ᾧ μάλιστα τὸ φύσει μεγαλόνουν ἐπεδείξατο.
239 πρῶτον μὲν γὰρ ἐκ ῥίζης ἡ πέτρα πλαξὶ κεκάλυπτο
λείαις λίθοις, εἴς τε κάλλος καὶ ὡς ἀπολισθάνοι
240 πᾶς ὁ προσβαίνειν ἢ κατιέναι πειρώμενος. ἔπειτα
πρὸ τῆς τοῦ πύργου δομήσεως τριῶν πηχῶν
τεῖχος ἦν, ἐνδοτέρω δὲ τούτου τὸ πᾶν ἀνάστημα[2]
τῆς Ἀντωνίας ἐπὶ τεσσαράκοντα πήχεις ἠγείρετο.
241 τὸ δ' ἔνδον βασιλείων εἶχε χώραν καὶ διάθεσιν·
μεμέριστο γὰρ εἰς πᾶσαν οἴκων ἰδέαν τε καὶ
χρῆσιν περίστοά τε καὶ βαλανεῖα καὶ στρατοπέδων αὐλαῖς πλατείαις,[3] ὡς τῷ μὲν πάντ' ἔχειν
τὰ χρειώδη πόλις εἶναι δοκεῖν, τῇ πολυτελείᾳ

---

[1] περὶ τούτον L: ἐπὶ τούτοις the rest.
[2] L: διάστημα the rest.   [3] αὐλὰς πλατείας C.

---

[a] The Day of Atonement ; Lev. xvi.
[b] Doubtless in his projected work " On Customs and

274

not worn by the high priest in general, when he assumed plainer attire, but only when he penetrated to the innermost sanctuary ; this he entered alone once in the year, on the day on which it was the universal custom to keep fast to God.[a] Of the city and the temple and of the customs and laws relating to the latter we shall speak more minutely hereafter[b] ; for on these topics much yet remains to be told.

(8) The tower of Antonia lay at the angle where two porticoes, the western and the northern, of the first court of the temple met ; it was built upon a rock fifty cubits high and on all sides precipitous. It was the work of King Herod[c] and a crowning exhibition of the innate grandeur of his genius.[d] For, to begin with, the rock was covered from its base upwards with smooth flagstones, both for ornament and in order that anyone attempting to ascend or descend it might slip off. Next, in front of the actual edifice, there was a wall three cubits high ; and behind this the tower of Antonia rose majestic to an altitude of forty cubits. The interior resembled a palace in its spaciousness and appointments, being divided into apartments of every description and for every purpose, including cloisters, baths and broad courtyards for the accommodation of troops ; so that from its possession of all conveniences it seemed a town, from its magnificence a palace.[e] The general

The castle of Antonia.

Causes," often referred to in the *Antiquities*, but never apparently completed.

[c] Built on the site of an older castle (βᾶρις) erected by John Hyrcanus, *A.* xviii. 91, *cf.* xv. 403, *B.* i. 75, and named after Mark Antony, *B.* i. 401 ; it is the " castle " of Acts xxi. 34.

[d] The same phrase occurs in i. 408 (of Caesarea).

[e] *Cf.* i. 421 (of Herodion).

242 δὲ βασίλειον. πυργοειδὴς δὲ οὖσα τὸ πᾶν σχῆμα
κατὰ γωνίαν τέσσαρσιν ἑτέροις διείληπτο πύργοις,
ὧν οἱ μὲν ἄλλοι πεντήκοντα τὸ ὕψος, ὁ δ' ἐπὶ τῇ
μεσημβρινῇ καὶ κατὰ ἀνατολὴν γωνίᾳ κείμενος
ἑβδομήκοντα πηχῶν ἦν, ὡς καθορᾶν ὅλον ἀπ'
243 αὐτοῦ τὸ ἱερόν. καθὰ δὲ συνῆπτε ταῖς τοῦ ἱεροῦ
στοαῖς εἰς ἀμφοτέρας εἶχε καταβάσεις, δι' ὧν
244 κατῄεσαν οἱ φρουροί· καθῆστο γὰρ ἀεὶ¹ ἐπ' αὐτῆς
τάγμα Ῥωμαίων, καὶ διιστάμενοι περὶ τὰς στοὰς
μετὰ τῶν ὅπλων ἐν ταῖς ἑορταῖς τὸν δῆμον, ὡς
245 μή τι νεωτερισθείη, παρεφύλαττον· φρούριον γὰρ
ἐπέκειτο τῇ πόλει μὲν τὸ ἱερόν, τῷ ἱερῷ δ' ἡ
Ἀντωνία, κατὰ δὲ ταύτην οἱ τῶν τριῶν φύλακες
246 ἦσαν· καὶ τῆς ἄνω δὲ πόλεως ἴδιον φρούριον
ἦν τὰ Ἡρώδου βασίλεια. ἡ Βεζεθὰ² δὲ λόφος
διῄρητο μέν, ὡς ἔφην, ἀπὸ τῆς Ἀντωνίας, πάντων
δ' ὑψηλότατος ὢν μέρει τῆς καινῆς πόλεως
247 προσῴκιστο, καὶ μόνος τῷ ἱερῷ³ κατ' ἄρκτον
ἐπεσκότει. περὶ μὲν δὴ τῆς πόλεως καὶ τῶν τειχῶν
αὖθις εἰπεῖν ἀκριβέστερον ἕκαστα προτεθειμένοις
ἐπὶ τοῦ παρόντος ἀπόχρη.

248 (vi. 1) Τὸ μάχιμον δ' ἐν αὐτῇ καὶ στασιάζον
πλῆθος περὶ Σίμωνα μὲν ἦσαν μύριοι δίχα τῶν
Ἰδουμαίων, πεντήκοντα δ' ἡγεμόνες τῶν μυρίων,
249 ἐφ' οἷς οὗτος κύριος τῶν ὅλων. Ἰδουμαῖοι δ'
αὐτῷ συντελοῦντες εἰς πεντακισχιλίους ἄρχοντας
εἶχον δέκα· τούτων προύχειν ἐδόκουν ὅ τε τοῦ
250 Σωσᾶ Ἰάκωβος καὶ Σίμων υἱὸς Καθλᾶ.⁴ Ἰωάννης

¹ om. P.   ² Βεζαθὰ P: Βησσαθὴ L Lat. (cf. § 151).
³ τὸ ἱερὸν PA.   ⁴ Καθλέα L: Catiae Lat.; cf. iv. 235.

276

appearance of the whole was that of a tower with other towers at each of the four corners ; three of these turrets were fifty cubits high, while that at the south-east angle rose to seventy cubits, and so commanded a view of the whole area of the temple. At the point where it impinged upon the porticoes of the temple, there were stairs [a] leading down to both of them, by which the guards descended ; for a Roman cohort was permanently quartered there, and at the festivals took up positions in arms around the porticoes to watch the people and repress any insurrectionary movement. For if the temple lay as a fortress over the city, Antonia dominated the temple, and the occupants of that post were the guards of all three ; the upper town had its own fortress—Herod's palace.[b] The hill Bezetha was, as I said,[c] cut off from Antonia ; the highest of all the hills, it was encroached on by part of the new town and formed on the north the only obstruction to the view of the temple. As I propose hereafter [d] to give a fuller and more circumstantial description of the temple and the walls, these remarks shall for the present suffice.

The Roman garrison in Antonia.

(vi. 1) The strength of the combatants and insurgents within the city was as follows. Simon had an army, exclusive of the Idumaeans, of ten thousand men ; over these were fifty officers, Simon himself being commander - in - chief. His Idumaean contingent numbered five thousand and had ten chiefs, among whom James, son of Sosas, and Simon, son of

The strength and situation of the rival Jewish factions.

[a] From which St. Paul, when arrested, addressed the Jews, Acts xxi. 40.
[b] Described above, §§ 176 ff.
[c] § 149.
[d] See note b on § 237.

δὲ τὸ ἱερὸν κατειληφὼς ἑξακισχιλίους ὁπλίτας
εἶχεν ὑφ' ἡγεμόνας εἴκοσι. προσεγένοντο δ' αὐτῷ
τότε καὶ οἱ ζηλωταὶ παυσάμενοι τοῦ διαφέρεσθαι,
δισχίλιοι μὲν ὄντες καὶ τετρακόσιοι, χρώμενοι
δ' ἄρχοντι τῷ καὶ πρότερον Ἐλεαζάρῳ καὶ
251 Σίμωνι τῷ τοῦ Ἀρινοῦ.[1] πολεμούντων δὲ τούτων,
ὡς ἔφαμεν, ἆθλον ὁ δῆμος ἦν ἑκατέρων, καὶ τὸ
μὴ συναδικοῦν τοῦ λαοῦ μέρος ὑπ' ἀμφοῖν διηρπά-
252 ζετο. κατεῖχεν δ' ὁ μὲν Σίμων τήν τε ἄνω πόλιν
καὶ τὸ μέγα τεῖχος ἄχρι τοῦ Κεδρῶνος, τοῦ τε
ἀρχαίου τείχους ὅσον ἀπὸ τῆς Σιλωᾶς ἀνακάμπτον
εἰς ἀνατολὴν μέχρι τῆς Μονοβάζου κατέβαινεν
αὐλῆς· βασιλεὺς δ' οὗτος ἐστιν[2] τῶν ὑπὲρ Εὐφράτην
253 Ἀδιαβηνῶν· κατεῖχε δὲ καὶ τὴν πηγὴν καὶ τῆς
Ἄκρας, αὕτη δ' ἦν ἡ κάτω πόλις, τὰ μέχρι τῶν
Ἑλένης βασιλείων τῆς τοῦ Μονοβάζου μητρός,
254 ὁ δ' Ἰωάννης τό θ' ἱερὸν καὶ τὰ πέριξ ἐπ' οὐκ
ὀλίγον, τόν τε Ὀφλᾶν καὶ τὴν Κεδρῶνα καλουμένην φάραγγα. τὸ μεταξὺ δὲ τούτων ἐμπρήσαντες τῷ πρὸς ἀλλήλους πολέμῳ χώραν ἀνεῖσαν·
255 οὐδὲ γὰρ πρὸς τοῖς τείχεσιν ἐστρατοπεδευμένων
Ῥωμαίων ἔνδον ἡ στάσις ἠρέμει, βραχὺ δὲ πρὸς
τὴν πρώτην ὑπονήψαντες ἐκδρομὴν ἀνενόσουν καὶ

---

[1] Ἀρινοῦ L Lat. (cf. Ἀρὶ vi. 92, 148): Ἀρ(ε)ιάνου most mss.,
Ἰαείρου C.
[2] L Lat.: ἦν the rest.

---

[a] Cf. iv. 235, where four generals of the original Idumaean
army of 20,000, including James and Simon, are mentioned.
From the present passage it appears that not more than half
that force had withdrawn from Jerusalem ; iv. 353 implies
that the whole body had retired in disgust.
[b] § 27.   [c] The third (or Agrippa's) wall.
[d] Simon manned the walls at the two points where they

Cathlas, ranked highest.[a] John, at the time when
he seized the temple, had an army of six thousand
men, commanded by twenty officers ; but now the
Zealots also had joined him having abandoned their
quarrel, to the number of two thousand four hundred,
led by Eleazar, their former chief, and Simon, son of
Arinus. These two factions, being, as we said,[b] at
war with each other, the citizens were their common
prize, and those of the people who discountenanced
their iniquities became the prey of both. Simon
occupied the upper town, the great wall[c] as far as the
Kedron, and a portion of the old wall,[d] from the point
where it bent eastward at Siloam to its descent to
the court-house of Monobazus, king of Adiabene
beyond the Euphrates ; he held also the fountain[e]
and part of the Acra, that is to say, the lower town,
as far as the palace of Helena, the mother of Monobazus.[f] John held the temple with much of the environs, Ophla and the valley called Kedron. The
region between them they reduced to ashes and left
as the arena of their mutual conflicts. For not even
when the Romans were encamped beneath the walls,
did the civil strife slacken within ; the brief return to
comparative sanity when they made their first sally[g]

were exposed to Roman attack, on the N.W. against the main
army of Titus, on the S.E. against the tenth legion encamped
on the Mt. of Olives (§ 70).

[e] Siloam. The exhortation of Josephus a little later on
(§ 410) seems to imply that Siloam was *extra muros* and in
Roman hands ; but the apparent inconsistency (Smith,
Jerusalem, i. 224) may be explained by supposing that the
Romans held Gihon, the spring outside the walls, which fed
the pool of Siloam within, and were thus virtually, though
not actually, masters of Siloam as well.

[f] The positions of the palaces of Monobazus and Helena
are unidentified.   [g] §§ 71 ff.

κατὰ σφᾶς πάλιν διαστάντες ἐμάχοντο, τὰ κατ'
εὐχήν τε πάντα τοῖς πολιορκοῦσιν ἔπραττον.
256 οὔτε γοῦν αὐτοί τι χεῖρον ὑπὸ Ῥωμαίων ἔπαθον
ὧν ἀλλήλους ἔδρασαν, οὔτε μετὰ τούτους ἡ πόλις
ἐπειράθη καινοτέρου πάθους, ἀλλ' ἡ μὲν χαλεπώ-
τερόν τι πρὸ τοῦ πεσεῖν ἠτύχησεν, οἱ δ' ἑλόντες
257 αὐτὴν κατώρθωσάν τι μεῖζον. φημὶ γὰρ ὡς τὴν
μὲν πόλιν ἡ στάσις, Ῥωμαῖοι δ' εἷλον τὴν στάσιν,
ἥπερ ἦν πολὺ τῶν τειχῶν ὀχυρωτέρα· καὶ τὸ
μὲν σκυθρωπὸν τοῖς οἰκείοις, τὸ δίκαιον δ' ἄν
τις εὐλόγως Ῥωμαίοις προσγράφοι. νοείτω δ'
ὅπῃ τοῖς πράγμασιν ἕκαστος ἄγεται.
258   (2) Τῶν γε μὴν ἔνδον οὕτως διακειμένων ὁ
Τίτος μετ' ἐπιλέκτων ἱππέων περιιὼν ἔξωθεν ᾗ
259 προσβάλλοι τοῖς τείχεσι κατεσκέπτετο. ἀπορου-
μένῳ δὲ πάντοθεν, οὔτε γὰρ κατὰ τὰς φάραγγας
ἦν προσιτὸν καὶ κατὰ θάτερα τὸ πρῶτον τεῖχος
ἐφαίνετο τῶν ὀργάνων στερεώτερον, ἐδόκει κατὰ
τὸ Ἰωάννου τοῦ ἀρχιερέως μνημεῖον προσβαλεῖν·
260 ταύτῃ γὰρ τό τε πρῶτον ἦν ἔρυμα χθαμαλώτερον
καὶ τὸ δεύτερον οὐ συνῆπτεν, ἀμελησάντων καθὰ
μὴ λίαν ἡ καινὴ πόλις συνῴκιστο τειχίζειν, ἀλλ'
ἐπὶ τὸ τρίτον ἦν εὐπέτεια, δι' οὗ τήν τε ἄνω
πόλιν καὶ διὰ τῆς Ἀντωνίας τὸ ἱερὸν αἱρήσειν
261 ἐπενόει. ἐν δὲ τούτῳ περιόντος αὐτοῦ τοξεύεταί
τις τῶν φίλων, ὄνομα Νικάνωρ, κατὰ τὸν λαιὸν

---

[a] Analogous phrases recur repeatedly in the *Antiquities*,
e.g. i. 108 περὶ μὲν τούτων, ὡς ἂν ἑκάστοις ᾖ φίλον, οὕτω σκοπεί-
τωσαν, ii. 348, iii. 81, etc. They are probably derived
from Dionysius of Halicarnassus, who appends a similar
formula to an expression of his personal opinion (*e.g.* κρινέτω
δ' ἕκαστος ὡς βούλεται iii. 35. 6, ἐχέτω δ' ὅπῃ τις αὐτὸν πείθει
i. 48. 1).

was followed by a relapse, and the parties divided and fell to fighting once more, doing all that their besiegers could have desired. Certainly, they suffered nothing worse at the hands of the Romans than what they inflicted upon each other, nor after her experience of them did the city meet with any novel calamity; on the contrary, her more cruel disaster preceded her fall, and the relief which her captors brought her outweighed the loss. For I maintain that it was the sedition that subdued the city, and the Romans the sedition, a foe far more stubborn than her walls; and that all the tragedy of it may properly be ascribed to her own people, all the justice to the Romans. But let every one follow his own opinion whither the facts may lead him.[a]

(2) Such being the situation within the walls, Titus, with some picked cavalry, made a tour of inspection without, to select a spot against which to direct his attack. Baffled at all other points, the ravines rendering access impossible, while beyond them the first wall seemed too solid for his engines, he decided to make the assault opposite the tomb of John the high priest[b]; for here the first line of ramparts was on lower ground, and the second was disconnected with it, the builders having neglected to fortify the sparsely populated portions of the new town, while there was an easy approach to the third wall, through which his intention was to capture the upper town and so, by way of Antonia, the temple. In the meantime, while Titus was riding round the city, one of his friends, named Nicanor,[c] having approached too near

Titus selects point for attack and begins earthworks.

---

[b] John Hyrcanus (135–105 B.C.), *B.* i. 54, etc. His monument, often mentioned as a landmark (v. 304, 356, vi. 169), seems to have lain to the N.W. of the Jaffa gate.

[c] A tribune and an old friend of Josephus, iii. 346.

ὦμον, ἔγγιον μετὰ τοῦ Ἰωσήπου προσελθὼν καὶ
πειρώμενος εἰρηνικὰ τοῖς ἐπὶ τοῦ τείχους, οὐ
262 γὰρ ἄγνωστος ἦν, διαλέγεσθαι. διὰ τούτου τὰς
ὁρμὰς αὐτῶν ἐπιγνοὺς Καῖσαρ, εἰ μηδὲ τῶν ἐπὶ
σωτηρίᾳ προσιόντων ἀπέχοιντο, παροξύνεται πρὸς
τὴν πολιορκίαν, ἅμα τε οὖν¹ τοῖς τάγμασι δῃοῦν
τὰ πρὸ τῆς πόλεως ἠφίει καὶ συμφοροῦντας
263 ἐκέλευσε τὴν ὕλην ἐγείρειν χώματα. τριχῇ δὲ
διατάξας τὴν στρατιὰν πρὸς τὰ ἔργα μέσους
ἵστησι τῶν χωμάτων τούς τε ἀκοντιστὰς καὶ
τοξότας καὶ πρὸ τούτων τοὺς ὀξυβελεῖς καὶ
καταπέλτας καὶ τὰς λιθοβόλους μηχανάς, ὡς
τάς τ' ἐκδρομὰς εἴργοι τῶν πολεμίων ἐπὶ τὰ
ἔργα καὶ τοὺς ἀπὸ τοῦ τείχους κωλύειν πειρω-
264 μένους. κοπτομένων δὲ τῶν δένδρων τὰ προάστεια μὲν ἐν τάχει γεγύμνωτο, συμφορουμένων
δ' ἐπὶ τὰ χώματα τῶν ξύλων καὶ τῆς στρατιᾶς
ἁπάσης ἐπὶ τὸ ἔργον ὡρμημένης οὐδὲ τὰ παρὰ
265 τῶν Ἰουδαίων ἠρέμει. τὸν μὲν οὖν δῆμον ἐν
ἁρπαγαῖς ὄντα καὶ φόνοις συνέβαινε τότε θαρρεῖν·
ἀναπνεύσειν τε γὰρ περισπωμένων πρὸς τοὺς
ἔξωθεν ὑπελάμβανον καὶ λήψεσθαι παρὰ τῶν
αἰτίων αὐτοὶ δίκας, εἰ Ῥωμαῖοι περιγένοιντο.
266 (3) Ἰωάννης δέ, καίτοι χωρεῖν ἐπὶ τοὺς ἔξωθεν
πολεμίους τῶν περὶ αὐτὸν ὡρμημένων, δέει τοῦ
267 Σίμωνος ἔμενεν. οὐ μὴν ὁ Σίμων ἠρέμει, καὶ
γὰρ ἦν ἐγγίων τῇ πολιορκίᾳ, τὰ δ' ἀφετήρια
διίστησιν ἐπὶ τοῦ τείχους, ὅσα Κέστιόν τε ἀφῄρηντο
πρότερον καὶ τὴν ἐπὶ τῆς Ἀντωνίας φρουρὰν

¹ οὖν Holwerda: σὺν mss.: καὶ Destinon, Niese.

with Josephus, was wounded by an arrow in the left
shoulder while endeavouring to parley with those
on the wall, to whom he was not unknown, on the
subject of peace. Caesar apprised by this incident
of their animosity, since they would not refrain from
assaulting even those who approached them for their
welfare, was stimulated to undertake the siege. He
at once gave the legions permission to lay waste the
suburbs and issued orders to collect timber and erect
earthworks. Forming his army into three divisions
for these operations, he placed the javelin-men and
archers in the intervals between the embankments,
and in front of them the quick-firers,[a] catapults, and
stone-projectors,[b] to check any sallies of the enemy
against the works and any attempts from the ramparts to impede them. So the trees were felled and
the suburbs rapidly stripped; but while the timber
was being collected for the earthworks and the whole
army busily engaged in the work, the Jews on their
side were not inactive. The people who were
victims of rapine and massacre now began to take
heart, hoping to gain some respite while their
oppressors were occupied with the external foe and
to have their revenge on the culprits, should the
Romans prove victorious.

(3) But John, though his followers were impatient
for an encounter with the enemy outside, from fear
of Simon did not stir. Simon, however, being
nearer the besiegers, was not inactive, but posted
his artillery upon the ramparts, both the engines
which they had formerly taken from Cestius,[c] and
those captured when they overpowered the garrison

Jewish attacks on the builders.

---

[a] Or " scorpions."   [b] *ballistae.*
[c] In November of A.D. 66, ii. 554.

268 ἑλόντες ἔλαβον. ἀλλὰ τούτων μὲν τοῖς πολλοῖς
ἀχρεῖος ἡ κτῆσις ἦν δι' ἀπειρίαν· ὀλίγοι δ' ὑπὸ
τῶν αὐτομόλων διδαχθέντες ἐχρῶντο κακῶς τοῖς
ὀργάνοις, χερμάσι δὲ καὶ τόξοις τοὺς χωννύντας
ἔβαλλον ἀπὸ τοῦ τείχους καὶ κατὰ συντάξεις
269 ἐκτρέχοντες αὐτοῖς συνεπλέκοντο. τοῖς δ' ἐργα-
ζομένοις ἀπὸ μὲν τῶν βελῶν ἦν σκέπη γέρρα τῶν
χαρακωμάτων ὑπερτεταμένα, τὰ δ' ἀφετήρια πρὸς
τοὺς ἐκθέοντας· θαυμαστὰ δὲ πᾶσι μὲν κατεσκεύαστο τοῖς τάγμασι, διαφόρως δὲ τῷ δεκάτῳ
βιαιότεροί τε ὀξυβελεῖς καὶ μείζονα λιθοβόλα,
δι' ὧν οὐ μόνον τὰς ἐκδρομὰς ἀλλὰ καὶ τοὺς ἐπὶ
270 τοῦ τείχους ἀνέτρεπον. ταλαντιαῖοι μὲν γὰρ ἦσαν
αἱ βαλλόμεναι πέτραι, δύο δὲ καὶ πλείονας ἦσαν
σταδίους· ἡ πληγὴ δ' οὐ τοῖς προεντυχοῦσι μόνον,
ἐπὶ πολὺ δὲ καὶ τοῖς μετ' ἐκείνους ἦν ἀνυπόστατος.
271 οἵ γε μὴν Ἰουδαῖοι τὸ πρῶτον ἐφυλάττοντο τὴν
πέτραν· λευκὴ γὰρ ἦν, ὥστε μὴ τῷ ῥοίζῳ ση-
μαίνεσθαι μόνον, ἀλλὰ καὶ τῇ λαμπρότητι προορᾶ-
272 σθαι. σκοποὶ οὖν[1] αὐτοῖς ἐπὶ τῶν πύργων καθ-
εζόμενοι προεμήνυον, ὁπότε σχασθείη τὸ ὄργανον
καὶ ἡ πέτρα φέροιτο, τῇ πατρίῳ γλώσσῃ βοῶντες
"ὁ υἱὸς ἔρχεται." διίσταντο δὲ καθ' οὓς ᾔει[2]
καὶ προκατεκλίνοντο, καὶ συνέβαινε φυλαττομένων

---

[1] γοῦν Destinon (avoiding hiatus).
[2] ἵοι Niese.

---

[a] In August A.D. 66, ii. 430.
[b] Presumably from the ranks of the auxiliary (Syrian)
forces of the Roman army.
[c] The tenth legion had its camp on the Mt. of Olives, E.
of the city (§ 70); unless they had been moved, their attack
must have been meant to divert the Jews from their assault
on the earthworks being raised by the Romans on the W.

284

of Antonia [a] The possession of these, however, was for most of them useless owing to inexperience ; but some few, instructed by the deserters,[b] made a blundering use of them. They also assailed the builders with stones and arrows from the wall, and dashing out by companies engaged them in close combat. The workmen wére protected from the missiles by hurdles stretched over palisades, and from the enemy's sallies by the artillery. Wonderfully constructed as were the engines of all the legions, those of the tenth [c] were supreme. Their quick-firers [d] were more powerful and their stone-projectors [e] larger, enabling them to repel not only the sallying parties but also those on the ramparts. The rocks which they hurled weighed a talent [f] and had a range of two furlongs or more ; and their impact not only to those who first met it but even to those considerably in rear was irresistible. The Jews, however, at the first were on their guard against the stone, for, being white, its approach was intimated not only to the ear by the whiz, but also to the eye by its brilliance. Watchmen were accordingly posted by them on the towers, who gave warning whenever the engine was fired and the stone in transit, by shouting in their native tongue, " Sonny's [g] coming " ; whereupon those in the line of fire promptly made way and lay down, owing to which precautions the stone passed harmlessly through

The Roman artillery,

and Jewish precautions against it.

---

[a] Or " scorpions."   [e] *ballistae.*
[f] About three-quarters of a hundredweight (Attic standard); *cf.* iii. 167.
[g] Probably, as Reland suggests, *ha-eben* (" the stone ") was corrupted to *habben* (" the son "); compare similar jocose terms, such as " Black Maria," " Jack Johnson," used in the Great War.

273 ἄπρακτον διεκπίπτειν τὴν πέτραν. ἀντεπινοοῦσι
δὲ Ῥωμαῖοι μελαίνειν αὐτήν· τότε γὰρ οὐκέθ᾽
ὁμοίως προορωμένης εὐστόχουν καὶ πολλοὺς ἅμα
274 βολῇ μιᾷ διέφθειρον. ἀλλ᾽ οὐδὲ κακούμενοι μετ᾽
ἀδείας παρεῖχον Ῥωμαίοις ἐγείρειν τὰ χώματα,
πάσῃ δ᾽ ἐπινοίᾳ καὶ τόλμῃ χρώμενοι καὶ νύκτωρ
καὶ μεθ᾽ ἡμέραν εἶργον.
275 (4) Τῶν δ᾽ ἔργων συντετελεσμένων μολιβίδι μὲν
καὶ λίνῳ διαμετροῦσιν οἱ τέκτονες τὸ διάστημα
πρὸς τὸ τεῖχος, ἀπὸ τῶν χωμάτων ῥίψαντες· οὐ
γὰρ ἐνῆν ἄλλως ἄνωθεν βαλλομένοις· εὑρόντες δ᾽
ἐξικνεῖσθαι δυναμένας τὰς ἑλεπόλεις προσῆγον.
276 καὶ Τίτος ἐγγυτέρω τὰ ἀφετήρια διαστήσας, ὡς
μὴ τοὺς κριοὺς εἴργοιεν ἀπὸ τοῦ τείχους, ἐκέλευσε
277 τύπτειν. τριχόθεν δ᾽ ἐξαισίου κτύπου περιηχή-
σαντος αἰφνιδίως τὴν πόλιν κραυγή τε παρὰ τῶν
ἔνδον ἤρθη καὶ τοῖς στασιασταῖς ἴσον ἐμπίπτει
δέος. κοινὸν δ᾽ ἑκάτεροι τὸν κίνδυνον ἰδόντες
κοινὴν ἐπενόουν ἤδη ποιεῖσθαι καὶ τὴν ἄμυναν.
278 διαβοώντων δὲ πρὸς ἀλλήλους τῶν διαφόρων ὡς
πάντα πράττοιεν ὑπὲρ τῶν πολεμίων, δέον, εἰ
καὶ μὴ διηνεκῆ δίδωσιν αὐτοῖς ὁμόνοιαν ὁ θεός,
ἐν γοῦν τῷ παρόντι τὴν πρὸς ἀλλήλους φιλο-
νεικίαν ὑπερθεμένους κατὰ Ῥωμαίων συνελθεῖν,
κηρύσσει μὲν ἄδειαν ὁ Σίμων τοῖς ἀπὸ τοῦ ἱεροῦ
παρελθεῖν ἐπὶ τὸ τεῖχος, ἐπιτρέπει δὲ καίπερ
279 ἀπιστῶν ὁ Ἰωάννης. οἱ δὲ τοῦ μίσους καὶ τῶν
ἰδίων διαφορῶν λαβόντες ἀμνηστίαν ἓν σῶμα
γίνονται, καὶ τὸ μὲν τεῖχος περισχόντες ἀπ᾽ αὐτοῦ
πυρά τε παμπληθῆ κατὰ τῶν μηχανημάτων
ἵεσαν καὶ τοὺς ἐπιβρίθοντας τὰς ἑλεπόλεις ἀδια-

and fell in their rear. To frustrate this it occurred to the Romans to blacken it; when, as it was no longer equally discernible beforehand, they hit their mark and destroyed many with a single shot. Yet, though under this galling fire, the Jews did not suffer the Romans to raise their earthworks unmolested, but by every resource of ingenuity and daring strove, night and day, to thwart them.

(4) The works being completed, the engineers measured the distance to the wall with lead and line, which they cast from the embankments—the only practicable method for men under fire from above—and finding that the battering-rams could reach it, they brought them up. Titus then, after posting his artillery nearer the walls, to prevent the defenders from obstructing the rams, gave the order to strike. Suddenly, from three different quarters, a terrific din echoed round the city, a cry went up from the citizens within, and the rebels themselves were seized with a like alarm. Seeing themselves exposed to a common danger, both parties now bethought them of a common defence. The rival factions shouted across to each other that they were doing all they could to assist the enemy, when they ought, even if God denied them lasting concord, for the present at least to postpone their mutual strife and unite against the Romans; whereupon Simon proclaimed that all were at liberty to pass from the temple to the wall, and John, though mistrusting him, gave his permission. The parties, consigning their hatred and private quarrels to oblivion, thus became one body; and, lining the ramparts, they hurled from them showers of firebrands at the machines and kept those who were impelling the battering-engines

The battering-rams brought into action.

The rival factions join forces.

280 λείπτως ἔβαλλον, οἱ τολμηρότεροι δὲ κατὰ στίφη
προπηδῶντες τὰ γέρρα τῶν μηχανημάτων ἐσπάραττον καὶ τοῖς ἐπ' αὐτῶν προσπίπτοντες ἐπι-
στήμῃ μὲν ὀλίγα, τόλμῃ δὲ τὰ πλείω περιεγίνοντο.
281 προσεβοήθει δὲ τοῖς πονοῦσιν αὐτὸς ἀεὶ Τίτος,
καὶ παρ' ἑκάτερον τῶν ὀργάνων τούς τε ἱππέας
καὶ τοὺς τοξότας διαστήσας εἶργεν μὲν τοὺς τὸ
πῦρ ἐπιφέροντας, ἀνέστελλεν δὲ τοὺς ἀπὸ τῶν
πύργων βάλλοντας, ἐνεργοὺς δ' ἐποίει τὰς ἑλεπό-
282 λεις. οὐ μὴν ταῖς πληγαῖς ὑπήκουε τὸ τεῖχος,
εἰ μὴ καθόσον ὁ τοῦ πεντεκαιδεκάτου τάγματος
283 κριὸς γωνίαν διεκίνησε πύργου. τὸ δὲ τεῖχος
ἀκέραιον ἦν· οὐδὲ γὰρ εὐθέως συνεκινδύνευε τῷ
πύργῳ προύχοντι πολὺ καὶ μὴ δυναμένῳ συν-
απορρῆξαί τι ῥᾳδίως τοῦ περιβόλου.

284 (5) Παυσάμενοι δὲ τῶν ἐκδρομῶν πρὸς ὀλίγον
καὶ τοὺς Ῥωμαίους ἐπιτηρήσαντες ἐσκεδασμέ-
νους ἐπὶ τὰ ἔργα καὶ κατὰ τὰ στρατόπεδα,
καμάτῳ γὰρ ἀναχωρῆσαι καὶ δέει τοὺς Ἰουδαίους
ᾐξίουν, ἐκθέουσι κατὰ τὸν Ἱππικὸν πύργον διὰ
πύλης ἀφανοῦς πάντες, πῦρ τε τοῖς ἔργοις ἐπι-
φέροντες καὶ μέχρι τῶν ἐρυμάτων ἐπὶ τοὺς
285 Ῥωμαίους προελθεῖν ὡρμημένοι. πρὸς δὲ τὴν
κραυγὴν αὐτῶν οἵ τε πλησίον συνίσταντο ταχέως
καὶ οἱ πόρρωθεν συνέθεον. ἔφθανε δ' ἡ Ἰουδαίων
τόλμα τὴν Ῥωμαίων εὐταξίαν, καὶ τοὺς προεντυγ-
χάνοντας τρεψάμενοι προσέκειντο καὶ τοῖς συλ-
286 λεγομένοις. δεινὴ δὲ περὶ τὰς μηχανὰς συμπίπτει
μάχη, τῶν μὲν ὑποπιμπράναι, τῶν δὲ κωλύειν
βιαζομένων, κραυγή τε παρ' ἀμφοτέρων ἀσήμαντος
ἦν, καὶ πολλοὶ τῶν προαγωνιζομένων ἔπιπτον.
287 Ἰουδαῖοι δ' ὑπερεῖχον ἀπονοίᾳ, καὶ τῶν ἔργων

under incessant fire. The more venturesome, dashing out in bands, tore up the hurdles protecting the machines, and, falling upon the gunners, seldom through skill but generally through intrepidity, got the better of them. Titus, however, invariably came in person to the relief of those who were hard pressed and, posting his horsemen and archers on either side of the engines, kept the incendiaries at bay, beat back assailants from the towers, and brought the battering-rams into action. For all that, the wall did not succumb to the blows, save that the ram of the fifteenth legion dislodged the corner of a tower. But the wall itself was unimpaired; for it was not involved in immediate danger along with the tower, which projected far out and so could not easily bring down with it any of the main rampart.

(5) The Jews, having desisted from their sallies for a while and watched their opportunity when the Romans had dispersed about the works and their several encampments, in the belief that from exhaustion and terror their enemy had retired, suddenly all dashed out together through a concealed gate near the Hippicus tower, carrying firebrands to burn the works and determined to push their attack right up to the Roman entrenchments. At their shouts the legionaries near the spot instantly mustered and those further off came dashing up. But Jewish daring outstripped Roman discipline, and having routed those who first encountered them they pressed on against the assembling troops. A fierce conflict ensued around the engines, one side striving to set them alight, the other to prevent them; confused shouts arose from both and many of the foremost fighters fell. Jewish desperation, however, was

ἥπτετο τὸ πῦρ, καταφλεγῆναί τ᾽ ἂν ἐκινδύνευσε
πάντα μετὰ τῶν ὀργάνων, εἰ μὴ τῶν ἀπ᾽ Ἀλεξανδρείας ἐπιλέκτων ἀντέστησαν οἱ πολλοὶ παρὰ
τὴν σφετέραν ὑπόληψιν ἀνδρισάμενοι· καὶ γὰρ
τῶν ἐνδοξοτέρων διήνεγκαν κατὰ ταύτην τὴν
μάχην· μέχρι Καῖσαρ τοὺς τῶν ἱππέων δυνατω-
288 τάτους ἀναλαβὼν ἐμβάλλει τοῖς πολεμίοις. καὶ
δώδεκα μὲν αὐτὸς τῶν προμάχων ἀναιρεῖ, πρὸς
δὲ τὸ τούτων πάθος ἐγκλίναντος[1] τοῦ λοιποῦ
πλήθους ἑπόμενος συνελαύνει πάντας εἰς τὴν
289 πόλιν κἀκ τοῦ πυρὸς διασῴζει τὰ ἔργα. συνέβη
δ᾽ ἐν ταύτῃ τῇ μάχῃ καὶ ζωγρηθῆναί τινα τῶν
Ἰουδαίων, ὃν ὁ Τίτος ἀνασταυρῶσαι πρὸ τοῦ
τείχους ἐκέλευσεν, εἴ τι πρὸς τὴν ὄψιν ἐνδοῖεν
290 οἱ λοιποὶ καταπλαγέντες. μετὰ δὲ τὴν ἀναχώρησιν καὶ Ἰωάννης ὁ τῶν Ἰδουμαίων ἡγεμὼν
πρὸ τοῦ τείχους γνωρίμῳ τινὶ στρατιώτῃ δια-
λεγόμενος ὑπό τινος τῶν Ἀράβων κατὰ τοῦ
στέρνου τοξεύεται καὶ παραχρῆμα θνήσκει, μέγιστον τοῖς τε Ἰδουμαίοις πένθος καὶ λύπην τοῖς
στασιασταῖς ἀπολιπών· καὶ γὰρ κατά τε χεῖρα
καὶ συνέσει διάσημος ἦν.

291   (vii. 1) Τῇ δ᾽ ἐπιούσῃ νυκτὶ ταραχὴ καὶ τοῖς
292 Ῥωμαίοις ἐμπίπτει παράλογος. τοῦ γὰρ Τίτου
πύργους τρεῖς κατασκευάσαι κελεύσαντος πεν-
τηκονταπήχεις, ἵν᾽ ἑκάστου χώματος ἐπιστήσας
ἀπὸ τούτων τοὺς ἐπὶ τοῦ τείχους τρέποιτο,
συνέβη πεσεῖν αὐτομάτως ἕνα μέσης νυκτός.

---

[1] Bekker (after Zonaras ἐνέκλιναν): ἐκκλίνοντος (-αντος) mss.

---

[a] The first named of the four original Idumaean leaders,

proving superior, already the fire was gaining hold upon the works, and the whole would probably have perished in the flames, along with the engines, had not the picked troops from Alexandria in the main stood firm, displaying a gallantry which exceeded their own reputation (for indeed they surpassed on that occasion regiments of greater renown), until Caesar, bringing up the most stalwart of his cavalry, charged the enemy. A dozen of the foremost he slew with his own hand; terrified at their fate the remainder gave way; he followed, drove them all into the town, and rescued the works from the flames. One incident in this engagement was the capture of a Jewish prisoner, whom Titus ordered to crucifixion before the walls, in the hope that the spectacle might lead the rest to surrender in dismay. Moreover, after the retreat, John,[a] the chieftain of the Idumaeans, while talking before the wall to an acquaintance in the ranks, was pierced in the breast by an arrow from an Arab's bow and killed on the spot. This loss occasioned profound grief to the Idumaeans and sorrow to the Jewish insurgents; for he was distinguished alike for gallantry and sound judgement.

Death of Idumaean general.

(vii. 1) On the ensuing night the Romans themselves were thrown into unexpected[b] alarm. For Titus had given command for the construction of three towers, fifty cubits high, to be erected on the respective embankments, in order that from them he might repel the defenders of the ramparts; and one of these accidentally fell in the middle of the night.

A night panic in Roman camp.

iv. 235; he seems later to have been outshone by his brother James, v. 249 (where John is not mentioned).
   [b] Or " baseless."

293 μεγίστου δ' ἀρθέντος ψόφου δέος ἐμπίπτει τῷ
στρατῷ, καὶ τοὺς πολεμίους ἐπιχειρεῖν σφίσι
294 δόξαντες ἐπὶ τὰ ὅπλα πάντες ἔθεον. ταραχὴ δὲ
τῶν ταγμάτων καὶ θόρυβος ἦν, καὶ τὸ συμβὰν
οὐδενὸς εἰπεῖν ἔχοντος ἐπὶ πλεῖστον ἀπορούμενοι[1]
διεφέροντο, μηδενός τε φαινομένου πολεμίου δι'
295 ἀλλήλων ἐπτοοῦντο, καὶ τὸ σύνθημα μετὰ σπουδῆς
ἕκαστος τὸν πλησίον ἐπηρώτα καθάπερ Ἰουδαίων
ἐμβεβληκότων εἰς τὰ στρατόπεδα, πανικῷ τε
δείματι κυκλουμένοις παρεῴκεσαν, ἄχρι μαθὼν
τὸ συμβὰν Τίτος διαγγέλλειν ἐκέλευσε πᾶσι, καὶ
μόλις ἐπαύσαντο τῆς ταραχῆς.

296 (2) Ἰουδαίους γε μὴν πρὸς τὰ λοιπὰ καρτερῶς
ἀντέχοντας ἐκάκωσαν οἱ πύργοι· καὶ γὰρ τῶν
ὀργάνων τοῖς κουφοτέροις ἀπ' αὐτῶν ἐβάλλοντο
καὶ τοῖς ἀκοντισταῖς καὶ τοξόταις καὶ λιθοβόλοις.
297 οὔτε δὲ τούτων αὐτοὶ διὰ τὸ ὕψος ἐφικνοῦντο
καὶ τοὺς πύργους ἦν ἀμήχανον ἑλεῖν, μήτ' ἀνατραπῆναι ῥᾳδίως διὰ τὸ βρῖθος μήτ' ἐμπρησθῆναι
διὰ τὸν σίδηρον δυναμένους, ᾧ κατεκαλύπτοντο.
298 τρεπόμενοι δ' ἐξωτέρω βέλους οὐκέτ' ἐκώλυον
τῶν κριῶν τὰς ἐμβολάς, οἳ ἀδιαλείπτως παίοντες
299 ἤνυον κατ' ὀλίγον. ἤδη δὲ τῷ Νίκωνι τοῦ τείχους
ἐνδιδόντος, αὐτοὶ γὰρ τοῦτο Ἰουδαῖοι τὴν μεγίστην
ἐκάλεσαν Ῥωμαίων ἑλέπολιν ἀπὸ τοῦ πάντα
νικᾶν, ἀπέκαμνον μὲν πάλαι πρός τε τὰς μάχας
καὶ τὰς φυλακὰς πόρρωθεν τῆς πόλεως διανυκ-
300 τερεύοντες, ἄλλως δ' ὑπὸ ῥᾳστώνης καὶ τοῦ
βουλεύεσθαι πάντα κακῶς περιττὸν αὐτοῖς δόξαν
τὸ τεῖχος ἑτέρων μετ' αὐτὸ λειπομένων δύο,

---

[1] Holwerda with ms. authority : ἀποδυρόμενοι most mss.

The crash was tremendous, and the terrified troops, supposing that the enemy were upon them, all rushed to arms. Alarm and confusion pervaded the legions. None being able to say what had happened, they scattered far and wide in their perplexity, and sighting no enemy became scared of one another, and each hurriedly asked his neighbour the password, as though the Jews had invaded their camps. In fact they behaved like men beset by panic fright, until Titus, having learnt what had happened, gave orders to make it generally known; and thus, though with difficulty, was the alarm allayed.

(2) The Jews, stubbornly though they held out against everything else, suffered severely from these towers; for from them they became targets for the lighter artillery, the javelin-men, archers, and stone-throwers. Being so high up, these assailants were out of range, while there was no means of mastering the towers, their weight rendering it difficult to overturn them and their casing of iron impossible to set them on fire. If, on the other hand, they withdrew out of range of missiles, they could no longer check the impact of the rams, whose incessant battering was gradually taking effect. And now at length the wall began to succumb to Victor[a] (so the Jews themselves called the largest of the Roman engines from its victory over all obstacles); they had long been exhausted with fighting and watching, on night duty at a distance from the city; moreover, through indolence and their invariably misguided judgement, they decided that to defend this wall was superfluous, as two others remained behind it. Most

The Jews retire,

[a] Greek " Nicon."

301 μαλακισθέντες ἀνεχώρουν οἱ πολλοί. καὶ τῶν
Ῥωμαίων ἐπιβάντων καθὸ παρέρρηξεν ὁ Νίκων,[a]
καταλιπόντες τὰς φυλακὰς πάντες εἰς τὸ δεύτερον
τεῖχος ἀναφεύγουσιν. οἱ δ᾿ ὑπερβάντες τὰς πύλας
302 ἀνοίξαντες πᾶσαν εἰσδέχονται τὴν στρατιάν. καὶ
Ῥωμαῖοι μὲν οὕτω τοῦ πρώτου τείχους πεντεκαιδεκάτῃ κρατήσαντες ἡμέρᾳ, ἑβδόμη δὲ ἦν
Ἀρτεμισίου μηνός, αὐτοῦ τε πολὺ κατασκάπτουσι
καὶ τὰ προσάρκτια τῆς πόλεως, ἃ καὶ πρότερον
Κέστιος.

303   (3) Μεταστρατοπεδεύεται δὲ Τίτος εἴσω κατὰ
τὴν Ἀσσυρίων[d] παρεμβολὴν καλουμένην, ἐπισχὼν
πᾶν τὸ μεταξὺ μέχρι τοῦ Κεδρῶνος, ἀπὸ δὲ τοῦ
δευτέρου τείχους ὅσον ἐξωτέρω βέλους εἶναι·
304 προσβολὰς δ᾿ εὐθέως ἐποιεῖτο. ἐμμερισθέντες[1]
δ᾿ [οἱ] Ἰουδαῖοι καρτερῶς ἀπημύναντο τοῦ τείχους, οἱ μὲν περὶ τὸν Ἰωάννην ἀπό τε τῆς Ἀντωνίας καὶ τῆς προσαρκτίου στοᾶς τοῦ ἱεροῦ
καὶ πρὸ τῶν Ἀλεξάνδρου [τοῦ βασιλέως αὐτῶν][2]
μνημείων μαχόμενοι, τὸ δὲ τοῦ Σίμωνος τάγμα
τὴν παρὰ τὸ Ἰωάννου [τοῦ ἀρχιερέως][3] μνημεῖον
ἐμβολὴν διαλαβόντες ἐφράξαντο μέχρι πύλης,
καθ᾿ ἣν τὸ ὕδωρ ἐπὶ τὸν Ἱππικὸν πύργον εἰσῆκτο.

---

[1] PAM: καὶ μερισθέντες L: μερισθέντες the rest.
[2] om. Lat.: om. αὐτῶν L.
[3] om. L Lat.

---

[a] Greek "Nicon."
[b] From the Roman standpoint; previously called the third
wall from the Jewish and chronological point of view, § 147.
[c] ii. 530.
[d] The traditional site of the camp of Sennacherib's army,
unidentified; see 2 Kings xviii. 17, xix. 35. The calamity
which decimated his forces, though placed by Jewish tradition within or on the outskirts of the city (Ps. lxxvi. 2 f. " in

294

of them, accordingly, turned slack and retired ; and when the Romans mounted the breach which Victor [a] had made, all deserted their posts and fled back to the second wall. Those who had scaled the ramparts now opened the gates and admitted the whole army. The Romans having thus on the fifteenth day (of the siege), being the seventh of the month Artemisius, become masters of the first [b] wall, razed a large part of it along with the northern quarter of the city, previously destroyed by Cestius.[c]

(3) Titus now shifted his camp within the first wall to the so-called Camp of the Assyrians,[d] occupying all the ground between it and the Kedron, but keeping far enough back to be out of bowshot from the second wall, which he forthwith proceeded to attack. The Jews, dividing their forces, maintained a stubborn defence from the ramparts : John's division fighting from Antonia, from the north portico of the temple, and in front of the tomb of King Alexander [e] ; while Simon's troops occupied the approach [f] alongside the tomb of John the high priest [g] and manned the wall as far as the gate [h] through which water was conveyed to the Hippicus

and the Romans capture the first (Agrippa's) wall.

c. 25 May A.D. 70.

Titus encamps within the outer wall.

Salem "), probably befell elsewhere during his Egyptian campaign (2 Kings xix. 9), according to Herodotus ii. 141 at Pelusium.

[e] Alexander Jannaeus, 104–78 B.C., B. i. 85 ff. The site of his tomb is unidentified ; doubtless a conspicuous object, for, notwithstanding his unpopularity, the influence of his widow, Queen Alexandra, obtained for him a funeral more splendid than that of any of his predecessors, A. xiii. 406.

[f] Or " intercepted the assault," the brunt of which was here, § 259.

[g] John Hyrcanus, 135–105 B.C., father of Alexander ; for his tomb cf. § 259.

[h] Near the present Jaffa Gate.

305 προπηδῶντές τε πολλάκις ἐκ τῶν πυλῶν συστάδην
ἐπολέμουν καὶ συνδιωχθέντες ἐπὶ[1] τοῦ τείχους
κατὰ μὲν τὰς συμπλοκὰς ἡττῶντο, τῆς Ῥωμαίων
ἐπιστήμης ὄντες ἄπειροι, περιῆσαν δ' ἐν ταῖς
306 τειχομαχίαις. καὶ τοὺς μὲν μετ' ἰσχύος ἐμπειρία
παρεκρότει, Ἰουδαίους δὲ τόλμα δέει τρεφομένη
καὶ τὸ φύσει καρτερικὸν ἐν συμφοραῖς· προσῆν δ'
ἐλπὶς ἔτι σωτηρίας ᾗ[2] καὶ Ῥωμαίοις τοῦ ταχέως
307 κρατήσειν. οὐδετέρων δ' ἥπτετο κόπος, ἀλλὰ
προσβολαὶ καὶ τειχομαχίαι καὶ κατὰ λόχους
ἐκδρομαὶ συνεχεῖς δι' ὅλης ἡμέρας ἦσαν, οὐδ'
308 ἔστιν ἥτις ἰδέα μάχης ἀπελείπετο. νὺξ δ' ἀνέπαυε
μόλις ἕωθεν ἀρχομένους· ἦν δ' ἄυπνος ἀμφοτέροις
καὶ χαλεπωτέρα τῆς ἡμέρας, δέει τῶν μὲν ὅσον
οὔπω καταληφθήσεσθαι τὸ τεῖχος, τῶν δ' ἐπι-
θήσεσθαι Ἰουδαίους τοῖς στρατοπέδοις, ἔν τε τοῖς
ὅπλοις ἑκάτεροι διανυκτερεύοντες ὑπὸ τὰς πρώτας
309 αὐγὰς ἕτοιμοι πρὸς μάχην ἦσαν. καὶ παρὰ μὲν
Ἰουδαίοις ἔρις ἦν ὅστις προκινδυνεύσας χαρίσαιτο
τοῖς ἡγεμόσιν, μάλιστα δὲ τοῦ Σίμωνος αἰδὼς
ἦν καὶ δέος, οὕτως τε προσεῖχεν ἕκαστος αὐτῷ
τῶν ὑποτεταγμένων, ὡς καὶ πρὸς αὐτοχειρίαν
310 ἑτοιμότατος εἶναι κελεύσαντος· Ῥωμαίοις δ' ἐπ'
ἀνδρείαν ἦν προτροπὴ τοῦ τε κρατεῖν ἔθος καὶ ἥττης
ἀήθεια συνεχής τε στρατεία καὶ διηνεκεῖς μελέται
καὶ μέγεθος ἡγεμονίας, πρὸ δὲ πάντων Τίτος
311 ἀεὶ πᾶσιν πανταχοῦ παρατυγχάνων. τό τε γὰρ

[1] Hudson: ἀπὸ mss.
[2] After PA ᾗ: ἡ, ἦ or ἤ the rest.

[a] Cf. Thuc. iv. 55 τῆς πρὶν ἀηθείας τοῦ κακοπραγεῖν.
[b] In ἀεὶ πᾶσιν πανταχοῦ, an underlying Latin is traceable;
" quod semper, quod ubique, quod ab omnibus " (sc.
296

tower. Often they would dash out from the gates
and fight hand to hand, and though driven back on Desperate
to the walls and defeated in these close combats, fighting.
through lack of the Romans' military skill, they had
the advantage of them in the battles from the ramparts. Experience combined with strength was the
Romans' mainstay : daring, fostered by fear, along
with their innate fortitude under calamities, sustained
the Jews. Moreover, they still cherished hopes of
salvation, as did the Romans of speedy victory.
Neither army felt fatigue : assaults, battles at the
wall, sallies by companies continued incessantly
throughout the day, and no form of warfare was
omitted. Beginning at dawn, night scarcely brought
them respite : its hours were sleepless for both
and more terrible than day, one party dreading every
moment the capture of the wall, the other a Jewish
invasion of their camps. Both armies thus passed
the night under arms and at the first break of day
were ready for battle.

Among the Jews there was rivalry who should be Contrasted
foremost in the fray and so win favour with his motives
of the
officers ; Simon in particular was regarded with belligerents.
reverence and awe, and such was the esteem in which
he was held by all under his command, that each
was quite prepared to take his very own life had he
given the order. With the Romans, on the other
hand, the incentives to valour were their habit of
victory and inexperience of defeat,[a] their continuous
campaigns and perpetual training, the magnitude of
their empire, and above all Titus, ever and everywhere
present beside all.[b] For cowardice when Caesar was

creditur), the definition of the Catholic Faith attributed to
St. Vincent of Lerins (5th cent. A.D.), has older parallels.

μαλακισθῆναι παρόντος καὶ συναγωνιζομένου Καίσαρος δεινὸν ἐδόκει, καὶ τῷ καλῶς ἀγωνισαμένῳ
μάρτυς αὐτὸς ὁ καὶ τιμήσων παρῆν· κέρδος δ᾽
ἦν ἤδη καὶ τὸ γνωσθῆναι Καίσαρι γενναῖον ὄντα.
διὰ τοῦτο πολλοὶ τῆς κατὰ σφᾶς ἰσχύος ἀμείνους
312 τῇ προθυμίᾳ διεφάνησαν. παραταξαμένων γοῦν
κατὰ ταύτας τὰς ἡμέρας τῶν Ἰουδαίων πρὸ τοῦ
τείχους καρτερῷ στίφει καὶ διακοντιζομένων ἔτι
πόρρωθεν τῶν ταγμάτων ἑκατέρων, Λογγῖνός
τις τῶν ἱππέων ἐξαλλόμενος τῆς Ῥωμαϊκῆς
τάξεως ἐμπηδᾷ μέσῃ τῇ τῶν Ἰουδαίων φάλαγγι,
313 καὶ διασκεδασθέντων πρὸς τὴν ἐμβολὴν δύο τοὺς
γενναιοτάτους ἀναιρεῖ, τὸν μὲν κατὰ στόμα
πλήξας ὑπαντιάσαντα, τὸν δ᾽ ἀνασπάσας ἐκ τοῦ
προτέρου τὸ δόρυ κατὰ πλευρὰν διαπείρει τραπό-
μενον, ἐκ μέσων τε τῶν πολεμίων ἄτρωτος[1] εἰς
314 τοὺς σφετέρους ἔδραμεν. ὁ μὲν οὖν δι᾽ ἀρετὴν
ἐπίσημος ἦν, ζηλωταὶ δὲ τῆς ἀνδρείας[2] ἐγίνοντο
315 πολλοί. καὶ Ἰουδαῖοι μὲν ἀμελοῦντες τοῦ παθεῖν
τὸ διαθεῖναι μόνον ἐσκόπουν, ὅ τε θάνατος αὐτοῖς
ἐδόκει κουφότατος εἰ μετὰ τοῦ κτεῖναί τινα τῶν
316 πολεμίων προσπέσοι· Τίτος δὲ τῆς τῶν στρατιωτῶν ἀσφαλείας οὐχ ἧττον τοῦ κρατεῖν προυνόει,
καὶ τὴν μὲν ἀπερίσκεπτον ὁρμὴν ἀπόνοιαν λέγων,
μόνην δ᾽ ἀρετὴν τὴν μετὰ προνοίας καὶ τοῦ μηδὲν
τὸν δρῶντα παθεῖν, ἐν ἀκινδύνῳ τῷ κατὰ σφᾶς
ἐκέλευσεν ἀνδρίζεσθαι.
317 (4) Προσάγει δ᾽ αὐτὸς τοῦ βορείου τείχους τῷ
μέσῳ πύργῳ τὴν ἑλέπολιν, ἐν ᾧ τῶν Ἰουδαίων
τις ἀνὴρ γόης ὄνομα Κάστωρ ἐλόχα μεθ᾽ ὁμοίων
δέκα, τῶν λοιπῶν φυγόντων διὰ τοὺς τοξότας.

[1] Holwerda: πρῶτος MSS.　　　　[2] ἀνδραγαθίας L.

with them and sharing the contest seemed monstrous, while the man who fought bravely had as witness of his valour one who would also reward it ; nay, it was gain already to be known to Caesar as courageous. Hence many in their enthusiasm displayed greater valour than their strength warranted. Thus when, in the course of these days, the Jews were arrayed in stout force outside the walls and both armies were as yet engaged in distant combat with javelins, a certain trooper Longinus leapt out of the Roman lines and dashed into the midst of the Jewish phalanx. Breaking their ranks by his charge, he slew two of their bravest, piercing one in front as he advanced to meet him, and transfixing the other through the side, as he turned to flee, with the spear which he drew from his comrade's body ; he then escaped unscathed to his own lines from the midst of the enemy. His valour gained him distinction, and led many to emulate his gallantry. The Jews, for their part, regardless of suffering, thought only of the injury which they could inflict, and death seemed to them a trivial matter if it involved the fall of one of the enemy. Titus, on the other hand, cared as much for his soldiers' safety as for success ; and, pronouncing inconsiderate impetuosity to be mere desperation, and valour only deserving of the name when coupled with forethought and a regard for the actor's security, he ordered his troops to prove their manhood without running personal risks.

Feat of Longinus

(4) He now brought up the battering-ram against the central tower of the north wall, where a certain Jewish impostor, named Castor, lay in ambush with ten others of like character, the rest having been routed by the archers. Here for some time they

Ruse of Castor the Jew.

318 οὗτοι μέχρι μέν τινος ὑπεπτηχότες τοῖς θωρακίοις
ἠρέμουν, λυομένου¹ δὲ τοῦ πύργου διανίστανται,
καὶ προτείνας ὁ Κάστωρ τὰς χεῖρας ὡς ἱκετεύων
δῆθεν ἐκάλει τὸν Καίσαρα καὶ τῇ φωνῇ κατ-
319 οικτιζόμενος ἐλεῆσαι σφᾶς παρεκάλει. πιστεύσας
δ' ἐξ ἁπλότητος ὁ Τίτος καὶ μετανοεῖν ἤδη τοὺς
Ἰουδαίους ἐλπίσας, ἐπέχει μὲν τοῦ κριοῦ τὴν
ἐμβολὴν κωλύει τε τοξεύειν τοὺς ἱκέτας, λέγειν
320 δ' ἐκέλευεν ὅ τι βούλεται τῷ Κάστορι. τοῦ δ'
εἰπόντος ἐπὶ δεξιᾷ καταβῆναι θέλειν, ὁ Τίτος
συνήδεσθαι μὲν αὐτῷ τῆς εὐβουλίας ἔφη, συνήδεσθαι δέ, εἰ πάντες ταὐτὰ ἤδη φρονοῦσι, καὶ
321 τῇ πόλει διδόναι τε πίστιν ἑτοίμως. τῶν δέκα
δὲ οἱ πέντε μὲν αὐτῷ συνυπεκρίνοντο τὴν ἱκετηρίαν,
οἱ λοιποὶ δ' οὐκ ἄν ποτε δουλεύσειν Ῥωμαίοις
322 ἐβόων παρὸν ἐλευθέρους ἀποθανεῖν. καὶ μέχρι
πολλοῦ διαφερομένων ἐτρίβετο μὲν ἡ προσβολή,
πέμπων δ' ὁ Κάστωρ πρὸς τὸν Σίμωνα σχολῇ
βουλεύεσθαι περὶ τῶν ἐπειγόντων ἔλεγεν, ὡς
οὐκ ἐπ' ὀλίγον αὐτὸς διαπαίζοι² τὴν Ῥωμαίων
ἀρχήν. ἅμα δὲ ταῦτα πέμπων καταφανὴς ἦν
καὶ τοὺς ἀπειθοῦντας ἐπὶ τὴν δεξιὰν παρακαλῶν.
323 οἱ δ' ὥσπερ ἀγανακτοῦντες ὑπὲρ τὰ θωράκια
διήρουν τε τὰ ξίφη γυμνὰ καὶ τοὺς θώρακας
αὐτῶν πλήξαντες ὡς ἀπεσφαγμένοι κατέπεσον.
324 θάμβος δὲ τὸν Τίτον καὶ τοὺς περὶ αὐτὸν εἰσῄει
τοῦ τῶν ἀνδρῶν παραστήματος, καὶ μὴ δυνάμενοι
κάτωθεν ἀκριβῶς τὸ γεγενημένον ἰδεῖν ἐθαύμαζόν
τε τῆς εὐτολμίας αὐτοὺς καὶ τοῦ πάθους ἠλέουν.
325 τοξεύει δέ τις ἐν τούτῳ παρὰ τὴν ῥῖνα τὸν Κάστορα,
κἀκεῖνος εὐθέως ἀνασπάσας τὸ βέλος ἐπεδείκνυ

¹ σαλευομένου L.   ² διαπαίζει L Lat. (illudere).

300

remained motionless, crouching beneath the parapet, but when the tower began to rock they rose up, and Castor, stretching out his hands in suppliant pose, called upon Caesar and in piteous tones implored him to have mercy on them. Titus, in the simplicity of his heart, believed him, and, hoping that the Jews were at length repenting, stopped the battering of the ram, forbade the archers to shoot at the suppliants, and directed Castor to state what he wanted. The latter replying that he desired to come down under pledge of protection, Titus said that he congratulated him on his sound judgement, and would congratulate the city, if all were now of the same mind, and gladly offer them security. But while five of Castor's ten companions joined in this feigned supplication, the rest cried out that they would never be slaves of the Romans, so long as they might die free men. During this protracted dispute, the assault was suspended, and Castor sent word to Simon to take his time in deliberating on the necessary measures, as he could fool the Roman command for a long while yet. While dispatching this message he was to all appearance urging his recalcitrant comrades to accept the proffered pledge. They, on the other hand, in seeming indignation, brandished their naked swords above the breastworks and, striking their own breast-plates, fell down as though slain. Titus and his staff, amazed at the men's intrepidity, and unable from below to see exactly what had happened, admired their courage and commiserated their fate. Meanwhile, Castor was struck close to the nose with an arrow, which missile he instantly drew out and showed to Titus, complaining

τῷ Τίτῳ καὶ ὡς οὐ δίκαια πάσχων κατεμέμφετο.
πρὸς δὲ τὸν βαλόντα σχετλιάσας Καῖσαρ ἔπεμπε
παρεστῶτα τὸν Ἰώσηπον δοῦναι τῷ Κάστορι
326 δεξιάν. ἀλλ' ὁ μὲν οὔτ' αὐτὸς ἔφη προελεύσεσθαι,[1]
φρονεῖν γὰρ οὐδὲν ὑγιὲς τοὺς δεομένους, καὶ τοὺς
ὡρμημένους τῶν φίλων κατέσχεν· Αἰνείας δέ τις
327 τῶν αὐτομόλων αὐτὸς ἔφη προελεύσεσθαι.[1] καὶ
τοῦ Κάστορος καλοῦντος, ὅπως δέξαιτό τις καὶ
τὸ ἀργύριον ὃ φέροι μεθ' αὐτοῦ, σπουδαιότερον
ὁ Αἰνείας διαπετάσας τὸν κόλπον προσέδραμεν.
328 ἀράμενος δ' ὁ Κάστωρ πέτραν ἐπαφίησιν αὐτῷ,
καὶ τούτου μὲν διήμαρτε φυλαξαμένου, τιτρώσκει
329 δὲ στρατιώτην ἕτερον προσελθόντα. συννοήσας
δὲ Καῖσαρ τὴν ἀπάτην πρὸς βλάβης μὲν ἔγνω
τὸν ἐν πολέμοις ἔλεον, τὸ γὰρ ἀπηνέστερον ἧττον
ὑποπίπτειν τῷ πανούργῳ, τὰς δ' ἐμβολὰς τῆς
ἑλεπόλεως ὀργῇ τῆς χλεύης ἐποιεῖτο δυνατωτέρας.
330 ὑποδιδόντα δὲ τὸν πύργον ἐμπιπρᾶσιν οἱ περὶ τὸν
Κάστορα, καὶ διὰ τῆς φλογὸς εἰς τὴν ὑπ' αὐτῷ
κρυπτὴν ἁλλόμενοι πάλιν δόξαν ἀνδρείας Ῥωμαίοις
παρέσχον ὡς ῥίψαντες σφᾶς αὐτοὺς εἰς τὸ πῦρ.
331 (viii. 1) Αἱρεῖ δὲ Καῖσαρ ταύτῃ τὸ τεῖχος
ἡμέρᾳ πέμπτῃ μετὰ τὸ πρῶτον, καὶ τῶν Ἰουδαίων
φυγόντων ἀπ' αὐτοῦ παρέρχεται μετὰ χιλίων
ἔνδον ὁπλιτῶν καὶ τῶν περὶ αὐτὸν ἐπιλέκτων,
καθὸ καὶ τῆς καινῆς πόλεως ἐριοπώλιά τε ἦν καὶ
χαλκεῖα καὶ ἱματίων ἀγορά, πρός τε[2] τὸ τεῖχος
332 πλάγιοι κατέτεινον οἱ στενωποί. εἰ μὲν οὖν ἢ
τοῦ τείχους εὐθέως πλέον διέλυσεν ἢ πολέμου

---

[1] P: προσελεύσεσθαι the rest.
[2] Destinon: om. PA: δὲ the rest.

of being unfairly treated. Caesar sternly rebuked
the archer and commissioned Josephus, who was at
his side, to offer his hand to Castor. Josephus, however, not only declined to go himself, convinced that
these suppliants meant no good, but restrained those
of his friends who were anxious to step forward.
However, Aeneas, one of the deserters, volunteered
to go ; and Castor calling out for someone to take the
money which he was bringing with him, Aeneas ran
forward the more eagerly with robes extended to
receive it. Castor thereupon picked up a boulder
and hurled it at him ; it missed Aeneas who managed
to avoid it, but wounded another soldier who had
come up. Caesar, now that his eyes were opened· to
the trick, decided that in warfare compassion was
mischievous—severe measures affording less scope
for artifice—and, indignant at this mockery, put the
battering-ram more vigorously into action. When
the tower began to give way, Castor and his friends
set fire to it, and, leaping through the flames into
the vault beneath,[a] again impressed the Romans,
who imagined that they had plunged into the fire,
with a sense of their courage.

(viii. 1) At this spot,[b] on the fifth day after the
capture of the first wall, Caesar stormed the second ;
and, as the Jews had fled from it, he made his entry,
with a thousand legionaries and his own picked
troops, in that district of the new town where lay
the wool-shops, the braziers' smithies and the clothes-
market, and where the narrow alleys descended
obliquely to the ramparts. Now, had he either at
once broken down more of the wall or, by right of

The Romans
capture the
second wall,
c. 30 May,

---

[a] Cf. the similar escape of the Jewish general Niger, iii. 27.
[b] i.e. at " the central tower of the north wall," § 317.

νόμῳ παρελθὼν ἐπόρθει τὸ ληφθέν, οὐκ ἂν οἶμαί
333 τις ἐμίγη βλάβη τῷ κράτει. νῦν δὲ Ἰουδαίους
μὲν ἐλπίσας δυσωπήσειν ἐξὸν κακοῦν τῷ μὴ
θέλειν, πρὸς [δ']¹ ἀναχώρησιν εὐμαρῆ τὴν εἰσβολὴν
οὐκ ἐπλάτυνεν· οὐ γὰρ ἐπιβουλεύσειν οὓς εὐερ-
334 γετεῖν ὑπελάμβανεν. παρελθὼν γοῦν οὔτε κτείνειν
τινὰ τῶν καταλαμβανομένων ἐπέτρεψεν οὔθ' ὑποπιμπράναι τὰς οἰκίας, ἀλλ' ἅμα τοῖς μὲν στασιασταῖς, εἰ βούλοιντο μάχεσθαι δίχα τῆς τοῦ
δήμου βλάβης, ἄδειαν ἐξόδου, τῷ δήμῳ δὲ τὰς
κτήσεις ὑπισχνεῖτο δώσειν· περὶ πλείστου γὰρ
ἐποιεῖτο σῶσαι τὴν μὲν πόλιν αὑτῷ, τὸν δὲ ναὸν
335 τῇ πόλει. τὸν μὲν οὖν λαὸν ἕτοιμον εἶχεν εἰς
ἃ προύτρεπεν καὶ πάλαι, τοῖς μαχίμοις δ' ἐδόκει
τὸ φιλάνθρωπον ἀσθένεια, καὶ τὸν Τίτον ἀδυναμίᾳ
τοῦ τὴν ἄλλην πόλιν ἑλεῖν ταῦτα προτείνειν
336 ὑπελάμβανον. διαπειλοῦντες δὲ τοῖς δημόταις θάνατον, εἰ περὶ παραδόσεως μνησθείη τις αὐτῶν,
καὶ τοὺς παραφθεγγομένους εἰρήνην ἀποσφάττοντες, ἐπιτίθενται καὶ τοῖς εἰσελθοῦσι Ῥωμαίων,
οἳ μὲν κατὰ τοὺς στενωποὺς ὑπαντιάσαντες, οἳ
δ' ἀπὸ τῶν οἰκιῶν, ἄλλοι δ' ἔξω τοῦ τείχους κατὰ
337 τὰς ἄνω προπηδήσαντες πύλας. πρὸς οὓς ταραχ-
θέντες οἱ φρουροὶ τοῦ τείχους καθαλλόμενοι τῶν
338 πύργων ἀνεχώρουν εἰς τὰ στρατόπεδα. κραυγὴ
δ' ἦν τῶν μὲν εἴσω πάντοθεν πολεμίοις κεκυκλωμένων, τῶν δ' ἔξωθεν περὶ τοῖς ἀποληφθεῖσι²
δεδοικότων. πληθύνοντες δ' ἀεὶ Ἰουδαῖοι καὶ
πολλὰ πλεονεκτοῦντες κατ' ἐμπειρίαν τῶν στενω-
πῶν ἐτίτρωσκόν τε πολλοὺς καὶ προσπίπτοντες

¹ om. C. ² Destinon: ἀπολειφθεῖσι mss.

ᵃ Cf. his similar later offer, vi. 95.

war, followed up his entry by sacking what he had
captured, no loss, I imagine, would have attended
his triumph. But, in fact, because he hoped to
shame the Jews by his reluctance to injure when in a
position to do so, he omitted to widen the breach to
facilitate a retreat, never supposing that after such
treatment they would plot against their benefactor.
Accordingly, on entering, he would not allow his
troops to kill any persons caught or to fire the
houses; to the factions he offered a free exit from
the city to fight, if such was their desire, without
detriment to the people,[a] while to the people he
promised restoration of their property. For his
paramount object was to preserve the city for him-
self and the temple for the city. The people indeed but are soon
expelled.
had long been ready to act on his advice, but the
militants mistook his humanity for weakness and
regarded these overtures as due to his inability to
capture the rest of the town. Threatening, therefore, to kill any of the townsfolk who should mention
surrender, and butchering all who let fall a word
about peace, they attacked the Roman division that
had entered. Some confronted them in the streets,
some assailed them from the houses, while others,
rushing outside the wall by the upper gates, caused
such commotion among the sentries on the ramparts that they leapt down from the towers and
made off to their camp. There were cries from those
within, surrounded by a ring of enemies, from those
without, alarmed for their intercepted comrades.
The Jews, constantly growing in numbers and
greatly at an advantage through their knowledge of
the streets, wounded multitudes of the enemy and
with their charges thrust them before them. The

339 ἐξώθουν. οἱ δὲ κατ᾽ ἀνάγκην τὸ πλέον ἀντεῖχον,
οὐ γὰρ ἦν ἀθρόους διαφυγεῖν διὰ στενοῦ τοῦ
τείχους, δοκοῦσί τε ἂν κατακοπῆναι πάντες οἱ
340 παρελθόντες μὴ προσαμύναντος τοῦ Τίτου. διαστήσας γὰρ ἐπ᾽ ἄκροις τοῖς στενωποῖς τοὺς
τοξότας καὶ κατὰ τὸν μάλιστα πληθύοντα σταθεὶς
αὐτός, ἀνέστελλε τοῖς βέλεσι τοὺς πολεμίους,
καὶ σὺν αὐτῷ Δομέτιος Σαβῖνος, ἀνὴρ ἀγαθὸς
341 καὶ κατὰ ταύτην φανεὶς τὴν μάχην. παρέμεινε
δὲ συνεχῶς τοξεύων Καῖσαρ καὶ τοὺς Ἰουδαίους
κωλύων παρελθεῖν, μέχρι πάντες ἀνεχώρησαν οἱ
στρατιῶται.
342 (2) Ῥωμαῖοι μὲν οὕτως κρατήσαντες τοῦ δευτέρου τείχους ἐξεώσθησαν,[1] τῶν δ᾽ ἀνὰ τὸ ἄστυ
μαχίμων ἐπήρθη τὰ φρονήματα, καὶ μετέωροι
πρὸς τὴν εὐπραγίαν ἦσαν, οὔτ᾽ ἂν Ῥωμαίους εἰς
τὴν πόλιν τολμήσειν ἔτι παρελθεῖν οὔτ᾽ αὐτοὶ
343 παρελθόντων ἡττηθήσεσθαι δοκοῦντες. ἐπεσκότει
γὰρ αὐτῶν ταῖς γνώμαις διὰ τὰς παρανομίας ὁ
θεός, καὶ οὔτε τὴν Ῥωμαίων ἰσχὺν ὅσῳ πλείων
κατελείπετο τῆς ἐξελασθείσης ἔβλεπον οὔτε τὸν
344 ὑφέρποντα λιμὸν αὐτοῖς. ἔτι γὰρ παρῆν ἐσθίειν
ἐκ τῶν δημοσίων κακῶν καὶ τὸ τῆς πόλεως αἷμα
πίνειν· ἔνδεια δὲ τοὺς ἀγαθοὺς ἐπεῖχε πάλαι, καὶ
345 σπάνει τῶν ἐπιτηδείων διελύοντο πολλοί. τὴν
δὲ τοῦ λαοῦ φθορὰν ἑαυτῶν οἱ στασιασταὶ κου-
φισμὸν ὑπελάμβανον· μόνους γὰρ ἠξίουν σώζεσθαι
τοὺς μὴ ζητοῦντας[2] εἰρήνην καὶ κατὰ Ῥωμαίων

---

[1] Dindorf: ἐξεώθησαν or ἐξώσθησαν mss.
[2] ζηλοῦντας L.

Romans, on their side, mainly through sheer necessity continued to resist, as it was impossible for all to retire at once through the narrow breach ; and the entire invading force would probably have been annihilated, had not Titus come to their relief. Posting his archers at the ends of the streets and taking up a position himself where the throng was thickest, he with showers of arrows kept the enemy at bay, assisted by Domitius Sabinus,[a] a man who proved his gallantry in this as in other engagements, So Caesar stood his ground, incessantly shooting his arrows and stemming the advance of the Jews, until all his soldiers had retired.

(2) Thus, after gaining possession of the second wall, were the Romans ejected. Within the city the spirits of the war party, elated at their success, rose high ; since they imagined that the Romans would never again venture into the city, or that, if they did, they themselves would prove invincible. For God was blinding their minds because of their transgressions ; and they perceived neither how the forces still left to the Romans far outnumbered those which had been expelled, nor yet the stealthy approach of famine. For it was still possible to feed upon the public miseries and to drink of the city's life-blood ; but honest men had long since felt the pinch of want, and many were already failing for lack of necessaries. The factions, however, regarded the destruction of the people as a relief to themselves ; for they held that only those should be preserved who were enemies to peace and determined to devote their lives to resisting the Romans, and rejoiced at the wasting

had been the first to enter Jotapata, iii. 324. The personal prowess of Titus the hero is, as often, emphasized.

ζῆν προῃρημένους, τὸ δ' ἐναντίον πλῆθος ὥσπερ
346 βάρος[1] ἥδοντο δαπανώμενον. τοιοῦτοι μὲν δὴ
πρὸς τοὺς ἔνδον ἦσαν· Ῥωμαίους δὲ πάλιν τῆς
εἰσόδου πειρωμένους ἐκώλυον φραξάμενοι καὶ τὸ
καταρριφθὲν ἀντιτειχίσαντες τοῖς σώμασι τρισὶ
μὲν ἀντέσχον ἡμέραις καρτερῶς ἀμυνόμενοι, τῇ
τετάρτῃ δὲ προσβαλόντα γενναίως Τίτον οὐκ
ἤνεγκαν, ἀλλὰ βιασθέντες ᾗ καὶ πρότερον ἀνα-
347 φεύγουσιν. ὁ δὲ πάλιν τοῦ τείχους κρατήσας
τὸ προσάρκτιον μὲν εὐθέως κατέρριψε πᾶν, ἐπὶ
δὲ τοῦ κατὰ μεσημβρίαν φρουρὰς τοῖς πύργοις
ἐγκαταστήσας τῷ τρίτῳ προσβάλλειν ἐπενόει.

348 (ix. 1) Δόξαν δ' ἐπανεῖναι πρὸς ὀλίγον τὴν
πολιορκίαν καὶ διωρίαν βουλῆς τοῖς στασιασταῖς
παρασχεῖν, εἴ τι πρὸς τὴν καθαίρεσιν ἐνδοῖεν τοῦ
δευτέρου τείχους ἢ καὶ τὸν λιμὸν ὑποδείσαντες, οὐ
γὰρ εἰς πολὺ τὰς ἁρπαγὰς αὐτοῖς ἐξαρκέσειν, εἰς
349 δέον κατεχρῆτο τὴν ἄνεσιν· ἐνστάσης γὰρ τῆς
προθεσμίας, καθ' ἣν ἔδει διαδοῦναι τοῖς στρατιώταις τροφάς, ἐν ἀπόπτῳ τοῖς πολεμίοις ἐκέλευσε τοὺς ἡγεμόνας ἐκτάξαντας τὴν δύναμιν
350 ἀπαριθμεῖν ἑκάστῳ τἀργύριον. οἱ δ', ὥσπερ
ἔθος, ἀποκαλύψαντες τὰ ὅπλα θήκαις ἐσκεπα-
σμένα τέως, κατάφρακτοι προῄεσαν καὶ τοὺς
351 ἵππους ἄγοντες οἱ ἱππεῖς κεκοσμημένους. ἐπὶ
πλεῖστον δὲ τὰ πρὸ τῆς πόλεως ἀργύρῳ καὶ
χρυσῷ περιελάμπετο, καὶ τῆς ὄψεως ἐκείνης
οὐδὲν οὔτε τοῖς σφετέροις ἐπιτερπέστερον οὔτε τοῖς
352 πολεμίοις παρέστη φοβερώτερον. κατεπλήσθη

---

[1] After Lat. onus quoddam: βάρβαρον (-ων) PAML:
βαρβάρων βάρος C: ὑπὸ βαρβάρων βάρος VR; βάρος ἀργὸν
Destinon.

away of masses of their opponents who were only
an encumbrance. Such were their feelings towards
those within; while, having blocked and walled up
the breach with their own bodies, they were holding
up the Romans who were again attempting to break
through. For three days they maintained a stubborn
defence and held their ground; but on the fourth, The Romans
unable to withstand a gallant assault of Titus, they recapture
were compelled to fall back to their former refuge. wall.
Titus, once more master of the wall, immediately
razed the whole of the northern portion; and,
placing garrisons in the towers in the southern
quarter, laid his plans for an attack on the third
wall.[a]

(ix. 1) He now decided to suspend the siege for Suspension
a while and to afford the factions an interval for and parade
reflection, to see if the demolition of the second of Roman
wall or haply dread of famine might lead to any Jerusalem.
surrender, as the fruits of their rapine could not long
suffice them; and he turned the period of inaction
to good account. For the appointed day having
arrived for the distribution of the soldiers' pay,
he ordered his officers to parade the forces and
count out the money to each man in full view of the
enemy. So the troops, as was their custom, drew
forth their arms from the cases in which till now they
had been covered and advanced clad in mail, the
cavalry leading their horses which were richly caparisoned. The area in front of the city gleamed far
and wide with silver and gold, and nothing was more
gratifying to the Romans, or more awe-inspiring to
the enemy, than that spectacle. For the whole of

---

[a] *i.e.* the first or " old " wall from the Jewish standpoint,
§ 142.

γὰρ ἀφορώντων τό τε ἀρχαῖον τεῖχος ἅπαν καὶ
τοῦ ἱεροῦ τὸ βόρειον κλίμα, τάς τε οἰκίας
μεστὰς ἦν προκυπτόντων ὑπεριδεῖν,[1] καὶ τῆς
πόλεως .οὐδὲν ὃ μὴ κεκάλυπτο πλήθει διεφαίνετο.
353 κατάπληξις δὲ δεινὴ καὶ τοῖς τολμηροτάτοις
ἐνέπεσε τήν τε δύναμιν ἐπὶ ταὐτὸ πᾶσαν ὁρῶσι
καὶ τὸ κάλλος τῶν ὅπλων καὶ τὴν εὐταξίαν τῶν
354 ἀνδρῶν· δοκοῦσί τε ἄν μοι πρὸς ἐκείνην οἱ στασιασταὶ μεταβαλέσθαι τὴν ὄψιν, εἰ μὴ δι᾽ ὑπερβολὴν ὧν τὸν δῆμον ἔδρασαν κακῶν συγγνώμην
355 παρὰ Ῥωμαίοις ἀπήλπιζον. ἀποκειμένου δὲ τοῦ
μετὰ κολάσεως, εἰ παύσαιντο, πολὺ κρείττονα τὸν
ἐν πολέμῳ θάνατον ἡγοῦντο. καὶ τὸ χρεὼν δ᾽
ἐκράτει τούς τε ἀναιτίους τοῖς αἰτίοις συναπολέσθαι καὶ τῇ στάσει τὴν πόλιν.

356 (2) Τέσσαρσιν μὲν οὖν ἡμέραις οἱ Ῥωμαῖοι
καθ᾽ ἕκαστον τάγμα διετέλεσαν τὰς τροφὰς
κομιζόμενοι, τῇ πέμπτῃ δ᾽ ὡς οὐδὲν ἀπήντα
παρὰ τῶν Ἰουδαίων εἰρηνικόν, διχῇ διελὼν τὰ
τάγματα Τίτος ἤρχετο τῶν χωμάτων κατά τε τὴν
Ἀντωνίαν καὶ τὸ τοῦ Ἰωάννου μνημεῖον, ταύτῃ
μὲν τὴν ἄνω πόλιν αἱρήσειν ἐπινοῶν, τὸ δ᾽ ἱερὸν
357 κατὰ τὴν Ἀντωνίαν· τούτου γὰρ μὴ ληφθέντος
οὐδὲ τὸ ἄστυ κατέχειν ἀκίνδυνον ἦν· πρὸς ἑκατέρῳ
δὲ μέρει δύο χώματα ἠγείρετο καθ᾽ ἓν ἑκάστου
358 τάγματος. καὶ τοὺς μὲν παρὰ τὸ μνημεῖον ἐργαζομένους οἵ τε Ἰδουμαῖοι καὶ τὸ μετὰ τοῦ Σίμωνος
ὁπλιτικὸν εἶργον ἐπεκθέοντες, τοὺς δὲ πρὸ τῆς
Ἀντωνίας οἱ περὶ τὸν Ἰωάννην καὶ τὸ τῶν
359 ζηλωτῶν πλῆθος. ἐπλεονέκτουν δ᾽ οὐ κατὰ χεῖρα

---

[1] κατιδεῖν M : ἰδεῖν P.

310

the old wall and the north side of the temple were
thronged with spectators, the houses across the wall
were to be seen packed with craning heads, and
there was not a spot visible in the city which was not
covered by the crowd. Even the hardiest were
struck with dire dismay at the sight of this assemblage
of all the forces, the beauty of their armour and the
admirable order of the men ; and I cannot but think
that the rebels would have been converted by that
vision, had not the enormity of their crimes against
the people made them despair of obtaining pardon
from the Romans. But, death being the punishment in store for them if they desisted, they thought
it far better to die in battle. Fate, moreover, was
prevailing to involve both innocent and guilty, city
and sedition, in a common ruin.

(2) In four days the several Roman legions had all
received their pay. On the fifth, no overtures for
peace having come from the Jews, Titus formed the
legions into two divisions and began raising earthworks opposite Antonia and John's monument[a]
respectively ; his design being to carry the upper
town at the latter point, and the temple by way of
Antonia, for unless the temple were secured, to hold
even the town would be precarious. The erection
of two banks at each of these two quarters was
accordingly begun, one being assigned to each
legion. Those at work alongside the monument
were impeded by sallies of the Idumaeans and the
troops of Simon ; those before Antonia suffered
obstruction from John's followers and the Zealots.
Their adversaries, moreover, were successful, not
only with hand-missiles, owing to superiority of

The siege
renewed.
Earthworks
raised
opposite
Antonia
and John's
tomb.

* § 259.

μόνον ἀφ' ὑψηλοτέρων μαχόμενοι, καὶ τοῖς ὀργάν ιs
δ' ἤδη χρῆσθαι μεμαθηκότες· ἡ γὰρ καθ' ἡμέραν
τριβὴ κατὰ μικρὸν ἔθρεψε τὴν ἐμπειρίαν. εἶχον δ'
ὀξυβελεῖς μὲν τριακοσίους, τεσσαράκοντα δὲ τῶν
λιθοβόλων, δι' ὧν τὰ χώματα τοῖς Ῥωμαίοις
360 ἐποίουν δυσέργαστα.[1] Τίτος δὲ σώζεσθαί τε τὴν
πόλιν καὶ ἀπόλλυσθαι εἰδὼς ἑαυτῷ, ἅμα καὶ τῇ
πολιορκίᾳ προσέκειτο καὶ τοῦ παραινεῖν Ἰου-
361 δαίοις μετάνοιαν οὐκ ἠμέλει, τοῖς δ' ἔργοις
ἀνέμισγε συμβουλίαν, καὶ πολλάκις γινώσκων
ἀνυτικώτερον ὅπλων τὸν λόγον, αὐτός[2] τε σώζεσθαι
παρεκάλει παραδόντας τὴν πόλιν ἤδη[3] παρειλημμένην καὶ τὸν Ἰώσηπον καθίει τῇ πατρίῳ
γλώσσῃ διαλέγεσθαι, τάχ' ἂν[4] ἐνδοῦναι πρὸς
ὁμόφυλον δοκῶν αὐτούς.

362   (3) Οὗτος περιὼν τὸ τεῖχος καὶ πειρώμενος
ἔξω τε[5] βέλους εἶναι καὶ ἐν ἐπηκόῳ, πολλὰ κατ-
ηντιβόλει φείσασθαι μὲν αὐτῶν καὶ τοῦ δήμου,
φείσασθαι δὲ τῆς πατρίδος καὶ τοῦ ἱεροῦ μηδὲ
γενέσθαι πρὸς ταῦτα τῶν ἀλλοφύλων ἀπαθεστέ-
363 ρους. Ῥωμαίους μέν γε τοὺς μὴ μετέχοντας
ἐντρέπεσθαι τὰ τῶν πολεμίων ἅγια καὶ μέχρι νῦν
τὰς χεῖρας ἐπέχειν, τοὺς δ' ἐντραφέντας αὐτοῖς
κἂν περισωθῇ μόνους ἕξοντας ὡρμῆσθαι πρὸς
364 ἀπώλειαν αὐτῶν. ἦ μὴν τὰ καρτερώτερα μὲν
αὐτῶν ὁρᾶν τείχη πεπτωκότα, λειπόμενον δὲ τὸ

---

[1] δυσεργότερα LVRC (cf. § 496).
[2] Destinon : αὐτούς or αὐτοῖς mss.
[3] + ⟨παρ' ὀλίγον⟩ Destinon (cf. § 369).
[4] τάχ' ἂν Destinon : τάχα mss.
[5] ἔξω τε Niese (from Lat.) : ἔξω or ἐξωτέρω mss.

---

[a] §§ 267 f.   [b] Or " scorpions."

position, but also with their engines, which they had
now learnt to use,[a] daily practice having gradually
fostered their skill; and they possessed three
hundred quick-firers,[b] and forty stone-projectors,[c] by
means of which they seriously retarded the erection
of the Roman earthworks. Titus, conscious that the
preservation or destruction of the city vitally affected
himself, while pressing the siege did not omit to
urge the Jews to reconsider their policy. Blending
active operations with advice, and aware that speech
is often more effectual than arms, he not only personally exhorted them to seek salvation by the
surrender of the city, already practically[d] taken, but
also delegated Josephus to parley with them in their
native tongue, thinking that possibly they might
yield to the expostulation of a fellow-countryman.

(3) Josephus, accordingly, went round the wall,
and, endeavouring to keep out of range of missiles
and yet within ear-shot, repeatedly[e] implored them
to spare themselves and the people, to spare their
country and their temple, and not to display towards
them greater indifference than was shown by aliens.
The Romans, he urged, though without a share
in them, yet reverenced the holy places[f] of their
enemies, and had thus far restrained their hands
from them; whereas men who had been brought up
in them and, were they preserved, would alone enjoy
them, were bent on their destruction. Indeed, they
beheld their stoutest walls prostrate and but one

Josephus is commissioned to urge the Jews to surrender. "God is on the Roman side."

---

[c] *ballistae.*

[d] The preposition in παρειλημμένην possibly here has the
force of παρ' ὀλίγον, "almost."

[e] πολλά probably implies numerous speeches at different
spots rather than " at great length."

[f] Literally " things," including perhaps rites, etc.

τῶν ἑαλωκότων ἀσθενέστερον· γινώσκειν δὲ τὴν
Ῥωμαίων ἰσχὺν ἀνυπόστατον καὶ τὸ δουλεύειν
365 τούτοις οὐκ ἀπείραστον¹ αὐτοῖς. εἰ γὰρ δὴ καὶ
πολεμεῖν ὑπὲρ ἐλευθερίας καλόν, χρῆναι τὸ
πρῶτον· τὸ δ' ἅπαξ ὑποπεσόντας καὶ μακροῖς
εἴξαντας χρόνοις ἔπειτα ἀποσείεσθαι τὸν ζυγὸν
366 δυσθανατούντων, οὐ φιλελευθέρων εἶναι. δεῖν μέντοι καὶ δεσπότας ἀδοξεῖν ταπεινοτέρους, οὐχ οἷς
ὑποχείρια τὰ πάντα. τί γὰρ Ῥωμαίους διαπεφευγέναι, πλὴν εἰ μή τι διὰ θάλπος ἢ κρύος ἄχρηστον;
367 μεταβῆναι γὰρ πρὸς αὐτοὺς πάντοθεν τὴν τύχην,
καὶ κατὰ ἔθνος τὸν θεὸν ἐμπεριάγοντα τὴν ἀρχὴν
νῦν ἐπὶ τῆς Ἰταλίας εἶναι. νόμον γε μὴν ὡρίσθαι
καὶ παρὰ θηρσὶν ἰσχυρότατον καὶ παρ' ἀνθρώποις,
εἴκειν τοῖς δυνατωτέροις καὶ τὸ κρατεῖν παρ' οἷς
368 ἀκμὴ τῶν ὅπλων εἶναι. διὰ τοῦτο καὶ τοὺς
προγόνους αὐτῶν [πολὺ]² καὶ ταῖς ψυχαῖς καὶ τοῖς
σώμασιν ἔτι δὲ καὶ ταῖς ἄλλαις ἀφορμαῖς ἀμείνους
ὄντας, εἶξαι Ῥωμαίοις, οὐκ ἂν εἰ μὴ τὸν θεὸν
369 ᾔδεσαν σὺν αὐτοῖς τοῦθ' ὑπομείναντας. αὐτοὺς
δὲ τίνι καὶ πεποιθότας ἀντέχειν, ἑαλωκυίας μὲν
ἐκ πλείστου τῆς πόλεως μέρους, τῶν δ' ἔνδον, εἰ
καὶ τὰ τείχη παρέμενεν, ἁλώσεως χεῖρον δια-
370 κειμένων; οὐ γὰρ λανθάνειν Ῥωμαίους τὸν ἐν τῇ
πόλει λιμόν, ᾧ νῦν μὲν τὸν δῆμον, μετ' οὐ πολὺ
371 δὲ διαφθαρήσεσθαι καὶ τοὺς μαχίμους. εἰ γὰρ
δὴ καὶ παύσαιντο Ῥωμαῖοι τῆς πολιορκίας

¹ ἀπείρατον ML.
² L Lat.: om. the rest.

ᵃ Josephus, here and in the sequel, repeats what he has

remaining, weaker than those which had fallen; they knew that the might of the Romans was irresistible and that to serve them was no new experience for themselves. Be it granted that it was noble to fight for freedom, they should have done so at first; but, after having once succumbed and submitted for so long, to seek then to shake off the yoke was the part of men madly courting death, not of lovers of liberty.[a] To scorn meaner masters might, indeed, be legitimate, but not those to whom the universe was subject. For what was there that had escaped the Romans, save maybe some spot useless through heat or cold? Fortune, indeed, had from all quarters passed over to them, and God who went the round of the nations, bringing to each in turn the rod of empire, now rested over Italy. There was, in fact, an established law, as supreme among brutes as among men, " Yield to the stronger " and " The mastery is for those pre-eminent in arms." That was why their forefathers, men who in soul and body, aye and in resources to boot, were by far their superiors, had yielded to the Romans—a thing intolerable to them, had they not known that God was on the Roman side. As for them, on what did they rely in thus holding out, when the main part of the city was already captured, and when those within it, though their walls still stood, were in a plight even worse than capture? Assuredly, the Romans were not ignorant of the famine raging in the city, which was now consuming the populace, and would ere long consume the combatants as well. For, even were the Romans to desist from the siege

previously put into the mouth of Agrippa at the opening of the war, ii. 355 ff.

μηδ' ἐπιπίπτοιεν¹ τῇ πόλει ξιφήρεις, αὐτοῖς γε τὸν
ἄμαχον πόλεμον ἔνδον παρακαθῆσθαι καθ' ἑκάστην
ὥραν τρεφόμενον, εἰ μὴ καὶ πρὸς τὸν λιμὸν ἆραι
τὰ ὅπλα καὶ μάχεσθαι δύνανται, μόνοι .τε καὶ
372 παθῶν ἐπικρατεῖν. προσετίθει δὲ ὡς καλὸν πρὸ
ἀνηκέστου συμφορᾶς μεταβαλέσθαι καὶ πρὸς τὸ
σωτήριον ἕως ἔξεστι ῥέψαι· καὶ γὰρ οὐδὲ μνησι-
κακήσειν αὐτοῖς Ῥωμαίους τῶν γεγενημένων, εἰ
μὴ μέχρι τέλους ἀπαυθαδίσαιντο· φύσει τε γὰρ
ἐν τῷ κρατεῖν ἡμέρους εἶναι καὶ πρὸ τῶν θυμῶν
373 θήσεσθαι τὸ συμφέρον. τοῦτο δ' εἶναι μήτε τὴν
πόλιν ἀνδρῶν κενὴν μήτε τὴν χώραν ἔρημον ἔχειν.
διὸ καὶ νῦν Καίσαρα βούλεσθαι δεξιὰν αὐτοῖς
παρασχεῖν· οὐ γὰρ ἂν σῶσαί τινα βίᾳ λαβόντα τὴν
πόλιν, καὶ μάλιστα μηδ' ἐν ἐσχάταις συμφοραῖς
374 ὑπακουσάντων παρακαλοῦντι. τοῦ γε μὴν ταχέως
τὸ τρίτον τεῖχος ἁλώσεσθαι τὰ προεαλωκότα
πίστιν εἶναι· κἂν ἄρρηκτον δὲ ᾖ τὸ ἔρυμα, τὸν
λιμὸν ὑπὲρ Ῥωμαίων αὐτοῖς μαχεῖσθαι.²
375 (4) Ταῦτα τὸν Ἰώσηπον παραινοῦντα πολλοὶ
μὲν ἔσκωπτον ἀπὸ τοῦ τείχους, πολλοὶ δ' ἐβλασφήμουν, ἔνιοι δ' ἔβαλλον. ὁ δ' ὡς ταῖς φανεραῖς
οὐκ ἔπειθε συμβουλίαις, ἐπὶ τὰς ὁμοφύλους
376 μετέβαινεν ἱστορίας, " ἆ δειλοί,³ " βοῶν, " καὶ τῶν
ἰδίων ἀμνήμονες συμμάχων, ὅπλοις καὶ χερσὶ
πολεμεῖτε Ῥωμαίοις; τίνα γὰρ ἄλλον οὕτως
377 ἐνικήσαμεν; πότε δ' οὐ θεὸς ὁ κτίσας, ἂν ἀδι-

---

¹ ἐπεισπίπτοιεν LV.
² Niese from Lat.: μάχεσθαι mss.
³ PA: δείλαιοι the rest.

ᵃ Cf. Nicanor's words to Josephus himself at Jotapata,

316

and not fall upon the city with drawn swords, yet "It is
they had at their doors a war with which none could hopeless to fight the
contend, gaining strength every hour, unless indeed famine."
they could take arms and fight against famine itself
and, alone of all men, master even its pangs. They
would do well, he added, to repent ere irretrievable
disaster befell them and to incline to salutary counsels while they had the opportunity ; for the Romans
would bear them no malice for the past, unless they
persisted in their contumacy to the end : they were
naturally lenient in victory,[a] and would put above
vindictiveness considerations of expediency, which
did not consist in having on their hands either a
depopulated city or a devastated country. That was
why, even at this late hour, Caesar desired to grant
them terms ; whereas, if he took the city by storm,
he would not spare a man of them, especially after
the rejection of offers made to them when in extremities. That the third wall would be quickly
carried was vouched for by the fall of those already
captured ; and even were that defence impregnable,
the famine would fight for the Romans against them.

(4) Josephus, during this exhortation, was derided
by many from the ramparts, by many execrated, and
by some assailed with missiles. Failing to move
them by this direct advice, he passed to reminiscences
of their nation's history.

"Ah, miserable wretches," he cried, "unmindful The lessons of history.
of your own true allies, would you make war on
the Romans with arms and might of hand ? What
other foe have we conquered thus, and when did God Former
who created, fail to avenge, the Jews, if they were deliver-
ances:

iii. 347, and the Virgilian " parcere devictis " (*Aen.* vi. 853),
doubtless familiar to the author.

κῶνται, Ἰουδαίων ἔκδικος; οὐκ ἐπιστραφέντες
ὄψεσθε πόθεν ὁρμώμενοι μάχεσθε καὶ πηλίκον
ἐμιάνατε σύμμαχον; οὐκ ἀναμνήσεσθε πατέρων
ἔργα δαιμόνια, καὶ τὸν ἅγιον τόνδε χῶρον ἡλίκους
378 ἡμῖν πάλαι πολέμους¹ καθεῖλεν; ἐγὼ μὲν φρίττω
τὰ ἔργα τοῦ θεοῦ λέγων εἰς ἀναξίους ἀκοάς·
ἀκούετε δ' ὅμως, ἵνα γνῶτε μὴ μόνον Ῥωμαίοις
379 πολεμοῦντες ἀλλὰ καὶ τῷ θεῷ. βασιλεὺς ὁ τότε
Νεχαὼς Αἰγυπτίων, ὁ δ' αὐτὸς ἐκαλεῖτο καὶ
Φαραώ, μυρίᾳ χειρὶ καταβὰς ἥρπασε Σάρραν
380 βασιλίδα, τὴν μητέρα τοῦ γένους ἡμῶν. τί οὖν
ὁ ταύτης ἀνὴρ Ἀβραάμ, προπάτωρ δ' ἡμέτερος;
ἆρα τὸν ὑβριστὴν ἠμύνατο τοῖς ὅπλοις, καίτοι
ὀκτωκαίδεκα μὲν καὶ τριακοσίους ὑπάρχους ἔχων,
δύναμιν δ' ὑφ'² ἑκάστῳ τούτων ἄπειρον; ἢ αὐτοὺς
μὲν ἐρημίαν ἡγήσατο μὴ συμπαρόντος θεοῦ,
καθαρὰς δ' ἀνατείνας τὰς χεῖρας εἰς ὃν νῦν ἐμιάνατε
χῶρον ὑμεῖς, τὸν ἀνίκητον αὐτῷ βοηθὸν ἐστρατο-
381 λόγησεν; οὐ μετὰ μίαν ἑσπέραν ἄχραντος μὲν ἡ
βασίλισσα ἀνεπέμφθη πρὸς τὸν ἄνδρα, προσκυνῶν
δὲ τὸν ὑφ' ὑμῶν αἱμαχθέντα χῶρον ὁμοφύλῳ
φόνῳ καὶ τρέμων ἀπὸ τῶν ἐν νυκτὶ φαντασμάτων
ἔφευγεν ὁ Αἰγύπτιος, ἀργύρῳ δὲ καὶ χρυσῷ τοὺς
382 θεοφιλεῖς Ἑβραίους ἐδωρεῖτο; εἴπω τὴν εἰς

---

¹ πολεμίους Hudson (perhaps rightly).
² ἐφ' ALR.

ᵃ Or (with Hudson's text) " enemies."
ᵇ Again recalling Virgil, " horresco referens."
ᶜ Josephus here follows some strange version, doubtless
derived from Jewish legend (*Haggadah*), of the story in
Genesis xii. 10-20 (*cf.* the variant form of the story in xx. 1 ff.).
In the Biblical account Abraham goes down into Egypt;
here Pharaoh invades Palestine. Necho, moreover, was the

wronged ? Will you not turn your eyes and mark what place is that whence you issue to battle and reflect how mighty an Ally you have outraged ? Will you not recall your fathers' superhuman exploits and what mighty wars [a] this holy place has quelled for us in days of old ? For myself, I shudder at recounting [b] the works of God to unworthy ears ; yet listen, that you may learn that you are warring not against the Romans only, but also against God.

"Nechaos, also called Pharaoh,[c] the reigning king of Egypt, came down with a prodigious host and carried off Sarah, a princess [d] and the mother of our race. What action, then, did her husband Abraham, our forefather, take ? Did he avenge himself on the ravisher with the sword ? He had, to be sure, three hundred and eighteen officers under him,[e] each in command of a boundless army. Or did he not rather count these as nothing, if unaided by God, and uplifting pure hands towards this spot which you have now polluted enlist the invincible Ally on his side ? And was not the queen, after one night's absence, sent back immaculate to her lord, while the Egyptian, in awe of the spot which you have stained with the blood of your countrymen and trembling at his visions of the night, fled, bestowing silver and gold [f] upon those Hebrews beloved of God ?

(i.) Pharaoh Necho and Sarah.

name of a Pharaoh of far later date, the conqueror of Josiah, 2 Chron. xxxv. 20 ; no monarch of the name in patriarchal times is known.

[d] The name Sarah means " princess."

[e] The 318 " trained men, born in his house " whom he led out to the rescue of Lot, Gen. xiv. 14.

[f] Abimelech in similar circumstances bestowed gifts upon Abraham, Gen. xx. 14-16 ; no gifts from Pharaoh are recorded in xii. 20.

Αἴγυπτον μετοικίαν τῶν πατέρων; οὐ[1] τυραν-
νούμενοι καὶ βασιλεῦσιν ἀλλοφύλοις ὑποπεπτω-
κότες τετρακοσίοις ἔτεσι, παρὸν ὅπλοις ἀμύνεσθαι καὶ χερσί, σφᾶς αὐτοὺς ἐπέτρεψαν τῷ
383 θεῷ; τίς οὐκ οἶδεν τὴν παντὸς θηρίου καταπλησθεῖ-
σαν Αἴγυπτον καὶ πάσῃ φθαρεῖσαν νόσῳ, τὴν
ἄκαρπον γῆν, τὸν ἐπιλείποντα Νεῖλον, τὰς ἐπαλλήλους δέκα πληγάς, τοὺς διὰ ταῦτα μετὰ φρουρᾶς
προπεμπομένους πατέρας ἡμῶν ἀναιμάκτους ἀκιν-
384 δύνους, οὓς ὁ θεὸς αὑτῷ νεωκόρους ἦγεν; ἀλλὰ
τὴν ὑπὸ Σύρων ἁρπαγεῖσαν ἁγίαν ἡμῖν λάρνακα
οὐκ ἐστέναξε μὲν ἡ Παλαιστίνη καὶ Δαγὼν τὸ
ξόανον, ἐστέναξε δὲ πᾶν τὸ τῶν ἁρπασαμένων
385 ἔθνος, σηπόμενοι δὲ τὰ κρυπτὰ τοῦ σώματος καὶ
δι' αὐτῶν τὰ σπλάγχνα μετὰ τῶν σιτίων κατα-
φέροντες, χερσὶ ταῖς λησαμέναις ἀνεκόμισαν κυμ-
βάλων καὶ τυμπάνων ἤχῳ καὶ πᾶσι μειλικτηρίοις
386 ἱλασκόμενοι τὸ ἅγιον; θεὸς ἦν ὁ ταῦτα πατράσιν
ἡμετέροις στρατηγῶν, ὅτι τὰς χεῖρας καὶ τὰ ὅπλα
387 παρέντες αὐτῷ κρῖναι τὸ ἔργον ἐπέτρεψαν. βασιλεὺς Ἀσσυρίων Σενναχηρεὶμ ὅτε πᾶσαν τὴν
Ἀσίαν ἐπισυρόμενος τήνδε περιεστρατοπεδεύσατο
388 τὴν πόλιν, ἆρα χερσὶν ἀνθρωπίναις ἔπεσεν; οὐχ αἱ
μὲν ἀπὸ τῶν ὅπλων ἠρεμοῦσαι ἐν προσευχαῖς
ἦσαν, ἄγγελος δὲ τοῦ θεοῦ μιᾷ νυκτὶ τὴν ἄπειρον
στρατιὰν ἐλυμήνατο, καὶ μεθ' ἡμέραν ἀναστὰς ὁ
Ἀσσύριος ὀκτωκαίδεκα μυριάδας ἐπὶ πεντακισχιλίοις νεκρῶν εὗρε, μετὰ δὲ τῶν καταλειπομένων

---

[1] AM: οἱ the rest.

[a] The round number given in Gen. xv. 13 and followed
in Jos. *A.* ii. 204 and in St. Stephen's speech, Acts vii. 6 ;
Exodus xii. 40 more precisely " 430 years."

" Need I speak of the migration of our fathers to Egypt ? Oppressed and in subjection to foreign monarchs for four hundred years,[a] yet, though they might have defended themselves by resort to arms and violence, did they not commit themselves to God ? Who has not heard tell of Egypt overrun with all manner of beasts and wasted with every disease, of the barren land, the failing Nile, the ten successive plagues, and how in consequence our fathers were sent forth under escort,[b] without bloodshed, without risk, God conducting them as the future guardians of his shrine ? *(ii.) The plagues of Egyp and the Exodus.*

" Or again did not Philistia and the image Dagon rue the rape of our sacred ark by the Syrians ?[c] Did not the whole nation of those raiders rue the deed, ulcerated in their secret parts and excreting their entrails along with their food,[d] until with the hands which stole it they restored it, to the sound of cymbals and timbrels,[e] and with all manner of expiations propitiating the sanctuary ? God's leadership it was that brought our fathers this triumph, because, without resort to hand or weapon, they committed the issue to his decision. *(iii.) The recovery of the ark from the Philistines.*

" When Sennacherib, king of Assyria, with all Asia following in his train, encamped around this city,[f] was it by human hands he fell ? Were not those hands at rest from arms and raised in prayer, while God's angel, in one night, destroyed that countless host ? And when the Assyrian arose next morning, did he not find 185,000 corpses, and with the re- *(iv.) Overthrow of Sennacherib's host.*

[b] Cf. Wisdom xix. 2 μετὰ σπουδῆς προπέμψαντες αὐτούς, of the Egyptians speeding the Israelites on their way.

[c] 1 Sam. v.-vi.   [d] Rhetorical amplification of 1 Sam. v. 6.

[e] Another addition to the Biblical story.   [f] See § 303 n.

ἀνόπλους καὶ μὴ διώκοντας Ἑβραίους ἔφυγεν;
389 ἴστε καὶ τὴν ἐν Βαβυλῶνι δουλείαν, ἔνθα μετα-
νάστης ὁ λαὸς ὢν ἔτεσιν· ἑβδομήκοντα οὐ πρότερον
εἰς ἐλευθερίαν ἀνεχαίτισεν ἢ Κῦρον τοῦτο χαρίσασθαι τῷ θεῷ· προυπέμφθησαν γοῦν ὑπ' αὐτοῦ,
καὶ πάλιν ·τὸν αὐτῶν σύμμαχον ἐνεωκόρουν.
390 καθόλου δ' εἰπεῖν, οὐκ ἔστιν ὅ τι κατώρθωσαν οἱ
πατέρες ἡμῶν τοῖς ὅπλοις ἢ δίχα τούτων διήμαρ-
τον ἐπιτρέψαντες τῷ θεῷ· μένοντες μέν γε κατὰ
χώραν ἐνίκων ὡς ἐδόκει τῷ κριτῇ, μαχόμενοι δ'
391 ἔπταισαν ἀεί. τοῦτο μέν, ἡνίκα βασιλεὺς Βαβυλωνίων ἐπολιόρκει ταύτην τὴν πόλιν, συμβαλὼν
Σεδεκίας ὁ ἡμέτερος βασιλεὺς παρὰ τὰς Ἱερεμίου
προφητείας αὐτός θ' ἑάλω καὶ τὸ ἄστυ μετὰ τοῦ
ναοῦ κατασκαπτόμενον εἶδε· καίτοι πόσῳ με-
τριώτερος ὁ μὲν βασιλεὺς ἐκεῖνος τῶν ὑμετέρων
392 ἡγεμόνων ἦν, ὁ δ' ὑπ' αὐτῷ λαὸς ὑμῶν. βοῶντα
γοῦν τὸν Ἱερεμίαν, ὡς ἀπέχθοιντο μὲν τῷ θεῷ διὰ
τὰς εἰς αὐτὸν πλημμελείας, ἁλώσοιντο δ' εἰ μὴ
παραδοῖεν τὴν πόλιν, οὔθ' ὁ βασιλεὺς οὔθ' ὁ δῆμος
393 ἀνεῖλεν. ἀλλ' ὑμεῖς, ἵν' ἐάσω τἄνδον, οὐ γὰρ
⟨ἂν⟩[1] ἑρμηνεῦσαι δυναίμην τὰς παρανομίας ὑμῶν
ἀξίως, ἐμὲ τὸν παρακαλοῦντα πρὸς σωτηρίαν
ὑμᾶς βλασφημεῖτε καὶ βάλλετε, παροξυνόμενοι
πρὸς τὰς ὑπομνήσεις τῶν ἁμαρτημάτων καὶ μηδὲ
τοὺς λόγους φέροντες ὧν τἄργα δρᾶτε καθ'
394 ἡμέραν. τοῦτο δ', ἡνίκα Ἀντιόχου τοῦ κληθέντος

[1] ins. Destinon.

---

[a] 2 Kings xix. 35.
[b] Literally " manes "; the same metaphor occurs in
Agrippa's speech, ii. 370.
[c] 2 Kings xxv. 1-10. Zedekiah did not " see " the
destruction of town and temple, which in the Biblical account

322

mainder flee from the Hebrews who were neither armed nor pursuing ? [a]

" You know, moreover, of the bondage in Babylon, where our people passed seventy years in exile and never reared their heads [b] for liberty, until Cyrus granted it in gratitude to God ; yes, it was through him that they were sent forth and re-established the temple-worship of their Ally. In short, there is no instance of our forefathers having triumphed by arms or failed of success without them when they committed their cause to God : if they sat still they conquered, as it pleased their Judge, if they fought they were invariably defeated.

(v.) Cyrus and the restoration from exile.

" Thus, when the king of Babylon besieged this city, our king Zedekiah having, contrary to the prophetic warnings of Jeremiah, given him battle, was himself taken prisoner and saw the town and the temple levelled to the ground.[c] Yet, how much more moderate was that monarch than your leaders, and his subjects than you ! For, though Jeremiah loudly proclaimed that they were hateful to God for their transgressions against Him, and would be taken captive unless they surrendered the city, neither the king nor the people put him to death.[d] But you— to pass over those scenes within, for it would be beyond me adequately to portray your enormities— you, I say, assail with abuse and missiles me who exhort you to save yourselves, exasperated at being reminded of your sins and intolerant of any mention of those crimes which you actually perpetrate every day.

Former captures of the city : (i.) by the Babylonians,

" Or again, when our ancestors went forth in

(ii.) by Antiochus Epiphanes,

occurred ten years after he had been taken, a blinded prisoner, to Babylon.   [d] Cf. Jer. xxvii. 12 ff.

323

Ἐπιφανοῦς προσκαθεζομένου τῇ πόλει πολλὰ πρὸς τὸ θεῖον ἐξυβρικότος, οἱ πρόγονοι μετὰ τῶν ὅπλων προῆλθον, αὐτοὶ μὲν ἀπεσφάγησαν ἐν τῇ μάχῃ, διηρπάγη δὲ τὸ ἄστυ τοῖς πολεμίοις, ἠρημώθη δ' ἔτη τρία καὶ μῆνας ἓξ τὸ ἅγιον.

395 καὶ τί δεῖ τἆλλα λέγειν; ἀλλὰ Ῥωμαίους τίς ἐστρατολόγησε κατὰ τοῦ ἔθνους; οὐχ ἡ τῶν ἐπιχωρίων ἀσέβεια; πόθεν δ' ἠρξάμεθα δουλείας;

396 ἆρ' οὐχὶ ἐκ στάσεως τῶν προγόνων, ὅτε ἡ Ἀριστοβούλου καὶ Ὑρκανοῦ μανία καὶ πρὸς ἀλλήλους ἔρις Πομπήιον ἐπήγαγεν τῇ πόλει καὶ Ῥωμαίοις ὑπέταξεν ὁ θεὸς τοὺς οὐκ ἀξίους ἐλευθερίας;

397 τρισὶ γοῦν μησὶ πολιορκηθέντες ἑαυτοὺς παρέδοσαν, οὔθ' ἁμαρτόντες εἰς τὰ ἅγια καὶ τοὺς νόμους ἡλίκα ὑμεῖς καὶ πολὺ μείζοσιν ἀφορμαῖς

398 πρὸς τὸν πόλεμον χρώμενοι. τὸ δ' Ἀντιγόνου τέλος τοῦ Ἀριστοβούλου παιδὸς οὐκ ἴσμεν, οὗ βασιλεύοντος ὁ θεὸς ἁλώσει πάλιν τὸν λαὸν ἤλαυνε πλημμελοῦντα, καὶ Ἡρώδης μὲν ὁ Ἀντιπάτρου Σόσσιον, Σόσσιος δὲ Ῥωμαίων στρατιὰν ἤγαγεν, περισχεθέντες δ' ἐπὶ μῆνας ἓξ ἐπολιορκοῦντο, μέχρι δίκας τῶν ἁμαρτιῶν δόντες ἑάλωσαν καὶ διηρπάγη τοῖς πολεμίοις ἡ πόλις;

399 Οὕτως οὐδέποτε τῷ ἔθνει τὰ ὅπλα δέδοται, τῷ δὲ πολεμεῖσθαι καὶ τὸ ἁλώσεσθαι πάντως πρόσ-

400 εστι. δεῖ γάρ, οἶμαι, τοὺς χωρίον ἅγιον νεμομένους ἐπιτρέπειν πάντα τῷ θεῷ δικάζειν καὶ

---

a Cf. 1 Macc. i. 20 ff., Jos. A. xii. 246 ff., where, however, no contest is recorded ; according to the account in the *Antiquities* Jerusalem was twice captured by Antiochus, once without a battle (ἀμάχητί, 246), once by treachery (ἀπάτῃ, 248).

b c. December 168–June 164 B.C., the 1290 days of Dan.

arms against Antiochus,[a] surnamed Epiphanes, who
was blockading this city and had grossly outraged
the Deity, they were cut to pieces in the battle, the
town was plundered by the enemy and the sanctuary
for three years and six months [b] lay desolate.

"Why need I mention more? But, pray, who en- (iii.) by
listed the Romans against our country? Was it not Pompey,
the impiety of its inhabitants? Whence did our
servitude arise? Was it not from party strife among
our forefathers, when the madness of Aristobulus
and Hyrcanus and their mutual dissensions brought
Pompey against the city,[c] and God subjected to the 63 B.C.
Romans those who were unworthy of liberty? Yes,
after a three months' siege [d] they surrendered,
though innocent of such offences as yours against
the sanctuary and against the laws, and possessing
far ampler resources for war.

"Or know we not the fate of Antigonus, son of (iv.) by
Aristobulus, in whose reign God again smote the Herod and
people for their offences by the capture of this city; Sossius.
when Herod, son of Antipater, brought up Sossius,[e] 37 B.C.
and Sossius a Roman army, by whom they were for
six [f] months invested and besieged, until in retribution for their sins they were captured and the city
was sacked by the enemy?

"Thus invariably have arms been refused to our Arms have
nation, and warfare has been the sure signal for defeat. not been
For it is, I suppose, the duty of the occupants of holy the Jews.
ground to leave everything to the arbitrament of

---

xii. 11. 1 Macc., i. 54 with iv. 52, reckons the period as
3 years (to Dec. 165 B.C.).   [c] B. i. 131 ff.
   [d] B. i. 149, A. xiv. 66.   [e] B. i. 345, A. xiv. 468.
   [f] 5 months according to B. i. 351; under 2 months
according to A. xiv. 476, the two walls being captured in
40 and 15 days respectively.

καταφρονεῖν τότε χειρὸς ἀνθρωπίνης, ὅταν αὐτοὶ
401 πείθωσι τὸν ἄνω δικαστήν. ὑμῖν δὲ τί τῶν
εὐλογηθέντων ὑπὸ τοῦ νομοθέτου πέπρακται; τί
δὲ τῶν ὑπ' ἐκείνου κατηραμένων παραλέλειπται;
πόσῳ δ' ἐστὲ τῶν τάχιον ἁλόντων ἀσεβέστεροι;
402 οὐ τὰ κρυπτὰ μὲν τῶν ἁμαρτημάτων ἠδοξήκατε,
κλοπὰς λέγω καὶ ἐνέδρας καὶ μοιχείας, ἁρπαγαῖς
δ' ἐρίζετε καὶ φόνοις καὶ ξένας καινοτομεῖτε
κακίας ὁδούς, ἐκδοχεῖον δὲ πάντων τὸ ἱερὸν γέγονεν
καὶ χερσὶν ἐμφυλίοις ὁ θεῖος μεμίανται χῶρος,
ὃν καὶ Ῥωμαῖοι πόρρωθεν προσεκύνουν, πολλὰ
τῶν ἰδίων ἐθῶν εἰς τὸν ὑμέτερον παραλύοντες
403 νόμον.[1] εἶτ' ἐπὶ τούτοις τὸν ἀσεβηθέντα σύμμαχον
προσδοκᾶτε; πάνυ γοῦν ἐστὲ δίκαιοι ἱκέται καὶ
χερσὶ καθαραῖς τὸν βοηθὸν ὑμῶν παρακαλεῖτε.
404 τοιαύταις ὁ βασιλεὺς ἡμῶν ἱκέτευσεν ἐπὶ τὸν
Ἀσσύριον, ὅτε τὸν μέγαν ἐκεῖνον στρατὸν μιᾷ
νυκτὶ κατέστρωσεν ὁ θεός; ὅμοια δὲ τῷ Ἀσσυρίῳ
Ῥωμαῖοι δρῶσιν, ἵνα καὶ ἄμυναν ὑμεῖς ὁμοίαν
405 ἐλπίσητε; οὐχ ὁ μὲν χρήματα παρὰ τοῦ βασιλέως
ἡμῶν λαβὼν ἐφ' ᾧ μὴ πορθήσει τὴν πόλιν κατέβη
παρὰ τοὺς ὅρκους ἐμπρῆσαι τὸν ναόν, Ῥωμαῖοι
δὲ τὸν συνήθη δασμὸν αἰτοῦσιν, ὃν οἱ πατέρες

---

[1] εἰς . . . νόμον L (C similar, reading ἡμέτερον): παραλύοντες
καὶ νόμων the rest.

---

[a] Moses.
[b] For τάχιον = πρότερον cf. e.g. B. i. 284 (where the
parallel in A. has τὸ πρῶτον). The rendering " more
speedily defeated " would not be true, if the comparison
were between the duration of previous sieges of Jerusalem
alluded to and that of the present siege which had so far
lasted only some two months ; though it might apply to the
length of the war as a whole.

God and to scorn the aid of human hands, can they
but conciliate the Arbiter above. But as for you,
what have you done that is blessed by the lawgiver,[a]
what deed that he has cursed have you left undone?
How much more impious are you than those who
have been defeated in the past![b] Secret sins—I
mean thefts, treacheries, adulteries—are not beneath
your disdain,[c] while in rapine and murder you vie
with each other in opening up new and unheard of
paths of vice; aye and the temple has become the
receptacle[d] for all, and native hands have polluted
those divine precincts, which even Romans reverenced
from afar,[e] forgoing many customs of their own in
deference to your law. And after all this do you
expect Him, thus outraged, to be your ally? Righteous suppliants are ye, forsooth, and pure the hands
with which you appeal to your protector! With such,
I ween, our king besought aid against the Assyrian,[f]
when God in one night laid low that mighty host!
And so like are the deeds of the Romans to those of
the Assyrian, that you may look for a like vengeance
yourselves! Did not he accept money from our
king[g] on condition that he would not sack the city,
and then come down, in violation of his oaths, to
burn the sanctuary, whereas the Romans are but
demanding the customary tribute, which our fathers

Your
enormities
deprive you
of any hope
of deliver-
ance.

[c] Or perhaps interrogatively, " Have not secret sins . . .
been disdained by you . . .?," *i.e.* become too trivial to
satisfy you.

[d] Or " sink "; *cf.* Sallust, *Cat.* 37, " omnes . . . Romam
sicut in sentinam confluxerant."

[e] *i.e.* without passing the parapet marking the boundary
of the court of the Gentiles, §§ 193 f. *Cf.* ii. 341, where
Neapolitanus pays his devotions to the sanctuary " from the
permitted area."

[f] Sennacherib, § 387.   [g] 2 Kings xviii. 14 f.

406 ἡμῶν τοῖς ἐκείνων πατράσι παρέσχον; καὶ τούτου
τυχόντες οὔτε πορθοῦσι τὴν πόλιν οὔτε ψαύουσι
τῶν ἁγίων, διδόασι δ᾽ ὑμῖν τὰ ἄλλα, γενεάς τ᾽
ἐλευθέρας καὶ κτήσεις τὰς ἑαυτῶν νέμεσθαι καὶ
407 τοὺς ἱεροὺς νόμους σώζουσι. μανία δὴ τὸν θεὸν
προσδοκᾶν ἐπὶ δικαίοις οἷος ἐπ᾽ ἀδίκοις ἐφάνη.
καὶ παραχρῆμα δ᾽ ἀμύνειν οἶδεν ὅταν δέῃ· τοὺς
γοῦν Ἀσσυρίους κατὰ νύκτα τὴν πρώτην παρα-
408 στρατοπεδευσαμένους ἔκλασεν· ὥστ᾽ εἰ καὶ τὴν
ἡμετέραν γενεὰν ἐλευθερίας ἢ Ῥωμαίους κολάσεως
ἀξίους ἔκρινε, κἂν παραχρῆμα καθάπερ τοῖς
Ἀσσυρίοις ἐνέσκηψεν, ὅτε τοῦ ἔθνους ἥπτετο
Πομπήιος, ὅτε μετ᾽ αὐτὸν ἀνῄει Σόσσιος, ὅτε
Οὐεσπασιανὸς ἐπόρθει τὴν Γαλιλαίαν, τὰ τελευ-
409 ταῖα νῦν, ὅτε ἤγγιζε Τίτος τῇ πόλει. καίτοι
Μάγνος μὲν καὶ Σόσσιος πρὸς τῷ μηδὲν παθεῖν
καὶ ἀνὰ κράτος ἔλαβον τὴν πόλιν, Οὐεσπασιανὸς
δ᾽ ἐκ τοῦ πρὸς ἡμᾶς πολέμου καὶ βασιλείας ἤρξατο,
Τίτῳ μὲν γὰρ[1] καὶ πηγαὶ πλουσιώτεραι ῥέουσιν
410 αἱ ξηρανθεῖσαι πρότερον ὑμῖν· πρὸ γοῦν τῆς αὐτοῦ
παρουσίας τήν τε Σιλωὰν ἐπιλείπουσαν ἴστε καὶ
τὰς πρὸ τοῦ ἄστεος ἁπάσας, ὥστε πρὸς ἀμφορέας
ὠνεῖσθαι τὸ ὕδωρ· τὸ δὲ νῦν οὕτως πληθύουσι τοῖς
πολεμίοις ὑμῶν, ὡς μὴ μόνον αὐτοῖς καὶ κτήνεσιν,
411 ἀλλὰ καὶ κήποις διαρκεῖν. τό γε μὴν τέρας τοῦτο
πεπείραται[2] καὶ πρότερον ἐφ᾽ ἁλώσει τῆς πόλεως
γεγενημένον, ὅθ᾽ ὁ προειρημένος Βαβυλώνιος
ἐπεστράτευσεν, ὃς τήν τε πόλιν ἑλὼν ἐνέπρησε καὶ
τὸν ναόν, οὐδὲν οἶμαι τῶν τότε ἠσεβηκότων

---

[1] μὲν γὰρ] μέντοι or γε μὴν Niese.
[2] Niese: πεπείρασται or πεπείρασθε (-θαι) mss.

paid to theirs ?   Once they obtain this, they neither sack the city, nor touch the holy things, but grant you everything else, the freedom of your families, the enjoyment of your possessions and the protection of your sacred laws.   It is surely madness to expect God to show the same treatment to the just as to the unjust.   Moreover, He knows how, at need, to inflict instant vengeance, as when He broke the Assyrians on the very first night when they encamped hard by [a]; so that had he judged our generation worthy of freedom or the Romans of punishment, He would, as He did the Assyrians, have instantly visited them—when Pompey intermeddled with the nation, when after him Sossius came up, when Vespasian ravaged Galilee, and lastly now, when Titus was approaching the city.   And yet Magnus [b] and Sossius, far from sustaining any injury, took the city by storm ; Vespasian from his war against us mounted to a throne ; [c] while as for Titus, the very springs flow more copiously for him which had erstwhile dried up for you.   For before his coming, as you know, Siloam and all the springs outside the town were failing, insomuch that water was sold by the *amphora*[d] ; whereas now they flow so freely for your enemies as to suffice not only for themselves and their beasts but even for gardens.   This miracle, moreover, has been experienced ere now on the fall of the city, when the Babylonian whom I mentioned [e] marched against it and captured and burnt both the city and the sanctuary, although the Jews of that day were

---

[a] 2 Kings xix. 35, " that night," but see § 303 note.
[b] Pompey the Great.
[c] iv. 604.   [d] about 9 gallons.
[e] § 391. The " miracle " in his day is unrecorded in Scripture.

412 τηλικοῦτον ἡλίκα ὑμεῖς· ὥστ' ἐγὼ πεφευγέναι μὲν
ἐκ τῶν ἁγίων οἶμαι τὸ θεῖον, ἑστάναι δὲ παρ' οἷς
413 πολεμεῖτε νῦν. ἀλλ' ἀνὴρ μὲν ἀγαθὸς οἰκίαν
ἀσελγῆ φεύξεται καὶ τοὺς ἐν αὐτῇ στυγήσει, τὸν
δὲ θεὸν ἔτι πείθεσθε τοῖς οἰκείοις κακοῖς παραμένειν, ὃς τά τε κρυπτὰ πάντα ἐφορᾷ καὶ τῶν
414 σιγωμένων ἀκούει; τί δὲ σιγᾶται παρ' ὑμῖν ἢ τί
κρύπτεται; τί δ' οὐχὶ καὶ τοῖς ἐχθροῖς φανερὸν
γέγονε; πομπεύετε γὰρ παρανομοῦντες καὶ καθ'
ἡμέραν ἐρίζετε, τίς χείρων γένηται, τῆς ἀδικίας
415 ὥσπερ ἀρετῆς ἐπίδειξιν ποιούμενοι. καταλείπεται δ' ὅμως ἔτι σωτηρίας ὁδός, ἐὰν θέλητε, καὶ τὸ
θεῖον εὐδιάλλακτον ἐξομολογουμένοις καὶ μετα-
416 νοοῦσιν. ὦ σιδήρειοι, ῥίψατε τὰς πανοπλίας,
λάβετε ἤδη κατερειπομένης αἰδῶ πατρίδος, ἐπι-
στράφητε καὶ θεάσασθε τὸ κάλλος ἧς προδίδοτε,
417 οἷον ἄστυ, οἷον ἱερόν, ὅσων ἐθνῶν δῶρα. ἐπὶ
ταῦτά τις ὁδηγεῖ φλόγα; ταῦτά τις μηκέτ' εἶναι
θέλει; καὶ τί σώζεσθαι τούτων ἀξιώτερον, ἄτεγ-
418 κτοι¹ καὶ λίθων ἀπαθέστεροι. καὶ εἰ μὴ ταῦτα
γνησίοις ὄμμασιν βλέπετε, γενεὰς γοῦν ὑμετέρας
οἰκτείρατε, καὶ πρὸ ὀφθαλμῶν ἑκάστῳ γενέσθω
τέκνα καὶ γυνὴ καὶ γονεῖς, οὓς ἀναλώσει μετὰ
419 μικρὸν ἢ λιμὸς ἢ πόλεμος. οἶδ' ὅτι μοι συγκιν-
δυνεύει μήτηρ καὶ γυνὴ καὶ γένος οὐκ ἄσημον καὶ
πάλαι λαμπρὸς οἶκος, καὶ τάχα δοκῶ διὰ ταῦτα
συμβουλεύειν. ἀποκτείνατε αὐτούς, λάβετε μισθὸν

¹ ἄτεγκτοί γε L.

ᵃ After Aeschines (77. 25).
ᵇ His father, Matthias, though not mentioned here, was
still alive, his imprisonment being referred to below, § 533.

guilty, I imagine, of no such rank impiety as yours. My belief, therefore, is that the Deity has fled from the holy places and taken His stand on the side of those with whom you are now at war. God has fled to the Romans.

"Nay, an honourable man will fly from a wanton house and abhor its inmates, and can you persuade yourselves that God still remains with his household in their iniquity—God who sees every secret thing and hears what is buried in silence? And what is there veiled in silence or secrecy among you? Nay, what has not been exposed even to your foes? For you parade your enormities and daily contend who shall be the worst, making an exhibition of vice as though it were virtue.

"Yet a way of salvation is still left you, if you will: and the Deity is easily reconciled to such as confess and repent. Oh! iron-hearted men,[a] fling away your weapons, take compassion on your country even now tottering to its fall, turn round and behold the beauty of what you are betraying: what a city! what a temple! what countless nations' gifts! Against these would any man direct the flames? Is there any who wishes that these should be no more? What could be more worthy of preservation than these—ye relentless creatures, more insensible than stone! Yet if you look not on these with the eyes of genuine affection, at least have pity on your families, and let each set before his eyes his children, wife and parents, ere long to be the victims either of famine or of war. I know that I have a mother,[b] a wife, a not ignoble family, and an ancient and illustrious house involved in these perils; and maybe you think that it is on their account that my advice is offered. Slay them, take my blood as the price of your own Final appeal.

τῆς ἑαυτῶν σωτηρίας τὸ ἐμὸν αἷμα· κἀγὼ θνήσκειν
ἕτοιμος, εἰ μετ' ἐμὲ σωφρονεῖν μέλλετε."

420 (x. 1) Τοιαῦτα τοῦ Ἰωσήπου μετὰ δακρύων
ἐμβοῶντος οἱ στασιασταὶ μὲν οὔτ' ἐνέδοσαν οὔτ'
ἀσφαλῆ τὴν μεταβολὴν ἔκριναν, ὁ δὲ δῆμος
421 ἐκινήθη πρὸς αὐτομολίαν. καὶ οἱ μὲν τὰς κτήσεις
ἐλαχίστου πωλοῦντες, οἱ δὲ τὰ πολυτελέστερα
τῶν κειμηλίων, τοὺς μὲν χρυσοῦς, ὡς μὴ φωρα-
θεῖεν ὑπὸ τῶν λῃστῶν, κατέπινον, ἔπειτα πρὸς
τοὺς Ῥωμαίους διαδιδράσκοντες, ὁπότε κατ-
422 ενέγκαιεν εὐπόρουν πρὸς ἃ δέοιντο. διηφίει γὰρ
τοὺς πολλοὺς ὁ Τίτος εἰς τὴν χώραν ὅποι βούλοιτο
ἕκαστος, καὶ τοῦτ' αὐτὸ[1] μᾶλλον πρὸς αὐτομολίαν[2]
παρεκάλει, τῶν μὲν εἴσω κακῶν στερησομένους,
423 μὴ δουλεύσοντας δὲ Ῥωμαίοις. οἱ δὲ περὶ τὸν
Ἰωάννην καὶ τὸν Σίμωνα παρεφύλαττον[3] τὰς
τούτων ἐξόδους πλέον ἢ τὰς Ῥωμαίων εἰσόδους,
καὶ σκιάν τις ὑπονοίας παρασχὼν μόνον εὐθέως
ἀπεσφάττετο.

424 (2) Τοῖς γε μὴν εὐπόροις καὶ τὸ μένειν πρὸς
ἀπώλειαν ἴσον ἦν· προφάσει γὰρ αὐτομολίας
ἀνῃρεῖτό τις διὰ τὴν οὐσίαν. τῷ λιμῷ δ' ἡ
ἀπόνοια τῶν στασιαστῶν συνήκμαζε, καὶ καθ'
425 ἡμέραν ἀμφότερα προσεξεκαίετο τὰ δεινά. φα-
νερὸς μὲν γὰρ οὐδαμοῦ σῖτος ἦν, ἐπεισπηδῶντες
δὲ διηρεύνων τὰς οἰκίας, ἔπειθ' εὑρόντες μὲν ὡς
ἀρνησαμένους ᾐκίζοντο, μὴ εὑρόντες δ' ὡς ἐπι-
426 μελέστερον κρύψαντας ἐβασάνιζον. τεκμήριον δὲ
τοῦ τ' ἔχειν καὶ μὴ τὰ σώματα τῶν ἀθλίων, ὧν
οἱ μὲν ἔτι συνεστῶτες εὐπορεῖν τροφῆς ἐδόκουν,

---

[1] eos Lat.   [2] M: πρὸς (+ τὸ L) αὐτομολεῖν the rest.
[3] Niese (cf. §§ 493-6): περιεφύλαττον mss.

salvation! I too am prepared to die, if my death will lead to your learning wisdom."

(x. 1) Yet, though Josephus with tears thus loudly appealed to them, the insurgents neither yielded nor deemed it safe to alter their course. The people, however, were incited to desert; and selling for a trifling sum, some their whole property, others their most valuable treasures, they would swallow the gold coins [a] to prevent discovery by the brigands, and then, escaping to the Romans, on discharging their bowels, have ample supplies for their needs. For Titus dismissed the majority into the country, whithersoever they would; a fact which induced still more to desert, as they would be relieved from the misery within and yet not be enslaved by the Romans. The partisans of John and Simon, however, kept a sharper look-out for the egress of these refugees than for the ingress of Romans, and whoever afforded but a shadow of suspicion was instantly slaughtered.

Desertion of Jews to Titus.

(2) To the well-to-do, however, to remain in the city was equally fatal; for under pretext of desertion individuals were put to death for the sake of their property. The recklessness of the insurgents kept pace with the famine, and both horrors daily burst out in more furious flame. For, as corn was nowhere to be seen, they would rush in and search the houses, and then if they found any they belaboured the inmates as having denied the possession of it; if they found none they tortured them for more carefully concealing it. The personal appearance of the wretches was an index whether they had it or not: those still in good condition were presumed to be

The famine. House to house search.

[a] For the horrible nemesis which befell them see §§ 550 ff.

οἱ τηκόμενοι δὲ ἤδη παρῳδεύοντο, καὶ κτείνειν
ἄλογον ἐδόκει τοὺς ὑπ' ἐνδείας τεθνηξομένους
427 αὐτίκα. πολλοὶ δὲ λάθρα τὰς κτήσεις ἑνὸς
ἀντηλλάξαντο μέτρου, πυρῶν μὲν εἰ πλουσιώτεροι
τυγχάνοιεν ὄντες, οἱ δὲ πενέστεροι κριθῆς, ἔπειτα
κατακλείοντες αὑτοὺς εἰς τὰ μυχαίτατα τῶν
οἰκιῶν τινὲς μὲν ὑπ' ἄκρας ἐνδείας ἀνέργαστον
τὸν σῖτον ἤσθιον, οἱ δ' ἔπεσσον ὡς ἥ τε ἀνάγκη
428 καὶ τὸ δέος παρήνει. καὶ τράπεζα μὲν οὐδαμοῦ
παρετίθετο, τοῦ δὲ πυρὸς ὑφέλκοντες ἔτ' ὠμὰ
τὰ σιτία διήρπαζον.

429 (3) Ἐλεεινὴ δ' ἦν ἡ τροφὴ καὶ δακρύων ἄξιος
ἡ θέα, τῶν μὲν δυνατωτέρων πλεονεκτούντων,
τῶν δ' ἀσθενῶν ὀδυρομένων. πάντων μὲν δὴ
παθῶν ὑπερίσταται λιμός, οὐδὲν δ' οὕτως ἀπ-
όλλυσιν ὡς αἰδώ· τὸ γὰρ ἄλλως ἐντροπῆς ἄξιον ἐν
430 τούτῳ καταφρονεῖται. γυναῖκες γοῦν ἀνδρῶν καὶ
παῖδες πατέρων, καί, τὸ οἰκτρότατον, μητέρες
νηπίων ἐξήρπαζον ἐξ αὐτῶν τῶν στομάτων τὰς
τροφάς, καὶ τῶν φιλτάτων ἐν χερσὶ μαραινομένων
οὐκ ἦν φειδὼ τοὺς τοῦ ζῆν ἀφελέσθαι σταλαγμούς.
431 τοιαῦτα δ' ἐσθίοντες ὅμως οὐ διελάνθανον, πανταχοῦ δ' ἐφίσταντο [οἱ στασιασταὶ] καὶ τούτων
432 ταῖς ἁρπαγαῖς. ὁπότε γὰρ κατίδοιεν ἀποκεκλει-
σμένην οἰκίαν, σημεῖον ἦν τοῦτο τοὺς ἔνδον προσφέρεσθαι τροφήν· εὐθέως δ' ἐξαράξαντες τὰς
θύρας εἰσεπήδων, καὶ μόνον οὐκ ἐκ τῶν φαρύγγων
433 ἀναθλίβοντες τὰς ἀκόλους ἀνέφερον. ἐτύπτοντο
δὲ γέροντες ἀντεχόμενοι τῶν σιτίων, καὶ κόμης
ἐσπαράττοντο γυναῖκες συγκαλύπτουσαι τὰ ἐν
χερσίν. οὐδέ τις ἦν οἶκτος πολιᾶς ἢ νηπίων,
ἀλλὰ συνεπαίροντες τὰ παιδία τῶν ψωμῶν ἐκ-

well off for food, while those already emaciated were passed over, as it seemed senseless to kill persons so soon to die of starvation. Many clandestinely bartered their possessions for a single measure—of wheat, if they were rich, of barley, if they were poor ; then shutting themselves up in the most remote recesses of their houses, some in the extremity of hunger devoured the grain unground, others so baked it as necessity and fear dictated. Nowhere was any table laid ; they snatched the food half-cooked from the fire and tore it in pieces.

(3) Pitiful was the fare and lamentable the spectacle, the stronger taking more than their share, the weak whimpering. Famine, indeed, overpowers all the emotions, but of nothing is it so destructive as of shame : what at other times would claim respect is then treated with contempt. Thus, wives would snatch the food from husbands, children from fathers, and—most pitiable sight of all—mothers from the very mouths of their infants, and while their dearest ones were pining in their arms they scrupled not to rob them of the life-giving drops. Nor, though thus feeding, did they escape detection : everywhere the rebels hovered even over these wretches' prey. For, whenever they saw a house shut up, this was a signal that the inmates were taking food, and forthwith bursting open the doors they leapt in and forcing the morsels almost out of their very jaws brought them up again. Old men were beaten, clutching their victuals, and women were dragged by the hair, concealing what was in their hands. There was no compassion for hoary hairs or infancy : children were actually lifted up with the fragments to

Horrors of the famine and atrocities of the rebels.

434 κρεμάμενα κατέσειον εἰς ἔδαφος. τοῖς δὲ φθάσασι
τὴν εἰσδρομὴν αὐτῶν καὶ προκαταπιοῦσι τὸ
ἁρπαγησόμενον ὡς ἀδικηθέντες ἦσαν ὠμότεροι.
435 δεινὰς δὲ βασάνων ὁδοὺς ἐπενόουν πρὸς ἔρευναν
τροφῆς, ὀρόβοις μὲν ἐμφράττοντες τοῖς ἀθλίοις
τοὺς τῶν αἰδοίων πόρους, ῥάβδοις δ' ὀξείαις
ἀναπείροντες τὰς ἕδρας, τὰ φρικτὰ δὲ καὶ ἀκοαῖς
ἔπασχέ τις εἰς ἐξομολόγησιν ἑνὸς ἄρτου καὶ ἵνα
436 μηνύσῃ δράκα μίαν κεκρυμμένην ἀλφίτων. οἱ
βασανισταὶ δ' οὐκ ἐπείνων, καὶ γὰρ ἧττον ἂν
ὠμὸν ἦν τὸ μετ' ἀνάγκης, γυμνάζοντες δὲ τὴν
ἀπόνοιαν καὶ προπαρασκευάζοντες αὑτοῖς εἰς
437 τὰς ἑξῆς ἡμέρας ἐφόδια. τοῖς δ' ἐπὶ τὴν Ῥωμαίων φρουρὰν νύκτωρ ἐξερπύσασιν ἐπὶ λαχάνων
συλλογὴν ἀγρίων καὶ πόας ὑπαντῶντες, ὅτ' ἤδη
διαπεφευγέναι τοὺς πολεμίους ἐδόκουν, ἀφήρπαζον
438 τὰ κομισθέντα, καὶ πολλάκις ἱκετευόντων καὶ τὸ
φρικτὸν ἐπικαλουμένων ὄνομα τοῦ θεοῦ μεταδοῦναί
τι μέρος αὐτοῖς ὧν κινδυνεύσαντες ἤνεγκαν, οὐδ'
ὁτιοῦν μετέδοσαν· ἀγαπητὸν δ' ἦν τὸ μὴ καὶ
προσαπολέσθαι σεσυλημένον.
439 (4) Οἱ μὲν δὴ ταπεινότεροι τοιαῦτα πρὸς τῶν
δορυφόρων ἔπασχον, οἱ δ' ἐν ἀξιώματι καὶ πλούτῳ
πρὸς τοὺς τυράννους ἀνήγοντο. τούτων οἱ μὲν
ἐπιβουλὰς ψευδεῖς ἐπικαλούμενοι διεφθείροντο,
οἱ δὲ ὡς προδιδοῖεν Ῥωμαίοις τὴν πόλιν, τὸ δ'
ἑτοιμότατον ἦν μηνυτής τις[1] ὑπόβλητος ὡς
440 αὐτομολεῖν διεγνωκότων. ὁ δ' ὑπὸ Σίμωνος

[1] om. τις PAL Lat.

which they clung and dashed to the ground. To
those who had anticipated their raid and already
swallowed their expected spoil they were yet more
brutal, as defrauded of their due. Horrible were the
methods of torture which they devised in their search
for food, blocking with pulse the passages in their
poor victims' frames and driving sharp stakes up
their bodies; and one would shudder at the mere
recital of the pangs to which they were subjected to
make them confess to the possession of a single loaf
or to reveal the hiding-place of a handful of barley-
meal. Yet their tormentors were not famished:
their cruelty would have been less, had it had the
excuse of necessity; they were but practising their
recklessness and providing supplies for themselves
against the days to come. Again, if any under
cover of night had crept out to the Roman outposts
to gather wild herbs and grass, they would go to
meet them and, at the moment when these imagined
themselves clear of the enemy, snatch from them
what they had procured; and oft though their
victims implored them, invoking even the awful
name of God, to return them a portion of what
they had at their own peril obtained, not a morsel was
given them. They might congratulate themselves
if, when robbed, they were not killed as well.

(4) Such was the treatment to which the lower ^{Persecution}
classes were subjected by the satellites; the men ^{of wealthier}
of rank and wealth, on the other hand, were brought ^{Simon and}
up to the tyrants. Of them some were falsely ^{John.}
accused of conspiracy and executed, as were others
on the charge of betraying the city to the Romans;
but the readiest expedient was to suborn an informer
to state that they had decided to desert. One who

γυμνωθεὶς πρὸς Ἰωάννην ἀνεπέμπετο, καὶ τὸν
ὑπὸ Ἰωάννου σεσυλημένον ὁ Σίμων μετελάμβανεν·
ἀντιπρούπινον δ᾽ ἀλλήλοις τὸ αἷμα τῶν δημοτῶν
441 καὶ τὰ πτώματα τῶν ἀθλίων διεμερίζοντο. καὶ
τοῦ μὲν κρατεῖν στάσις ἦν ἐν ἀμφοτέροις, τῶν
δ᾽ ἀσεβημάτων ὁμόνοια· καὶ γὰρ ὁ μὴ μεταδοὺς
ἐκ τῶν ἀλλοτρίων κακῶν θατέρῳ μονοτρόπως
ἐδόκει πονηρός, καὶ ὁ μὴ μεταλαβὼν ὡς ἀγαθοῦ
τινος ἤλγει τὸν νοσφισμὸν τῆς ὠμότητος.

442 (5) Καθ᾽ ἕκαστον μὲν οὖν ἐπεξιέναι τὴν παρανομίαν αὐτῶν ἀδύνατον, συνελόντι[1] δ᾽ εἰπεῖν,
μήτε πόλιν ἄλλην τοιαῦτα πεπονθέναι μήτε γενεὰν
443 ἐξ αἰῶνος γεγονέναι κακίας γονιμωτέραν, οἵ γε
τελευταῖον καὶ τὸ γένος ἐφαύλιζον τῶν Ἑβραίων,
ὡς ἧττον ἀσεβεῖς δοκοῖεν πρὸς ἀλλοτρίους, ἐξ-
ωμολογήσαντο δ᾽ ὅπερ ἦσαν εἶναι δοῦλοι καὶ
444 σύγκλυδες καὶ νόθα τοῦ ἔθνους φθάρματα. τὴν
μέν γε πόλιν ἀνέτρεψαν αὐτοί, Ῥωμαίους δ᾽
ἄκοντας ἠνάγκασαν ἐπιγραφῆναι σκυθρωπῷ κατορθώματι καὶ μόνον οὐχ εἵλκυσαν ἐπὶ τὸν ναὸν
445 βραδῦνον τὸ πῦρ. ἀμέλει καιόμενον ἐκ τῆς ἄνω
πόλεως ἀφορῶντες οὔτ᾽ ἤλγησαν οὔτ᾽ ἐδάκρυσαν,
ἀλλὰ ταῦτα τὰ πάθη παρὰ Ῥωμαίοις εὑρέθη.
καὶ ταῦτα μὲν κατὰ χώραν ὕστερον μετ᾽ ἀπο-
δείξεως τῶν πραγμάτων ἐροῦμεν.

446 (xi. 1) Τίτῳ δὲ τὰ μὲν χώματα προύκοπτεν
καίτοι πολλὰ κακουμένων ἀπὸ τοῦ τείχους τῶν
στρατιωτῶν, πέμψας δ᾽ αὐτὸς μοῖραν τῶν ἱππέων
ἐκέλευσεν τοὺς κατὰ τὰς φάραγγας ἐπὶ συγκομιδῇ

---

[1] Niese: συνελόντα MSS.

had been fleeced by Simon was passed on to John, and he who had been plundered by John was taken over by Simon; they pledged each other in turn in the burghers' blood and shared the carcases of their unfortunate victims. As rivals for power they were divided, but in their crimes unanimous; for the one who gave his comrade no share in the proceeds of the miseries of others was ranked a scurvy villain, and he who received no share was aggrieved at his exclusion from the barbarity, as though defrauded of some good thing.

(5) To narrate their enormities in detail is impossible; but, to put it briefly, no other city ever endured such miseries, nor since the world began has there been a generation more prolific in crime. Indeed they ended by actually disparaging the Hebrew race, in order to appear less impious in so treating aliens,[a] and owned themselves, what indeed they were, slaves, the dregs of society and the bastard scum of the nation. It was they who overthrew the city, and compelled the reluctant Romans to register so melancholy a triumph, and all but attracted to the temple the tardy flames. Verily, when from the upper town they beheld it burning, they neither grieved nor shed a tear,[a] though in the Roman ranks these signs of emotion were detected. But this we shall describe hereafter in its place, with a full exposition of the facts.

Degradation of the Jewish race.

(xi. 1) Meanwhile the earthworks of Titus were progressing, notwithstanding the galling fire from the ramparts to which his men were exposed. The general, moreover, sent a detachment of horse with orders to lie in wait for any who issued from the town

Crucifixion of Jewish prisoners.

---

[a] *Cf.* vi. 364 καιομένην γοῦν ἀφορῶντες τὴν πόλιν ἱλαροῖς τοῖς προσώποις εὔθυμοι κτλ.

447 τροφῆς ἐξιόντας ἐνεδρεύειν. ἦσαν δέ τινες καὶ
τῶν μαχίμων, οὐκέτι διαρκούμενοι ταῖς ἁρπαγαῖς,
τὸ δὲ πλέον ἐκ τοῦ δήμου πένητες, οὓς αὐτομολεῖν
448 ἀπέτρεπε τὸ περὶ τῶν οἰκείων δέος· οὔτε γὰρ
λήσεσθαι τοὺς στασιαστὰς ἤλπιζον μετὰ γυναικῶν
καὶ παιδίων διαδιδράσκοντες καὶ καταλιπεῖν τοῖς
λῃσταῖς ταῦτα οὐχ ὑπέμενον ὑπὲρ αὐτῶν σφαγη-
449 σόμενα· τολμηροὺς δὲ πρὸς τὰς ἐξόδους ὁ λιμὸς
ἐποίει, καὶ κατελείπετο[1] λανθάνοντας εἰς[2] τοὺς
πολεμίους ἁλίσκεσθαι. λαμβανόμενοι δὲ κατ'
ἀνάγκην ἠμύνοντο,[3] καὶ μετὰ μάχην ἱκετεύειν
ἄωρον ἐδόκει. μαστιγούμενοι δὴ καὶ προβασανι-
ζόμενοι τοῦ θανάτου πᾶσαν αἰκίαν ἀνεσταυροῦντο
450 τοῦ τείχους ἀντικρύ. Τίτῳ μὲν οὖν οἰκτρὸν τὸ
πάθος κατεφαίνετο, πεντακοσίων ἑκάστης ἡμέρας
ἔστι δ' ὅτε καὶ πλειόνων ἁλισκομένων, οὔτε δὲ
τοὺς βίᾳ ληφθέντας ἀφεῖναι ἀσφαλὲς καὶ φυλάττειν
τοσούτους φρουρὰν τῶν φυλαξόντων ἑώρα· τό γε
μὴν πλέον οὐκ ἐκώλυεν τάχ' ἂν ἐνδοῦναι πρὸς
τὴν ὄψιν ἐλπίσας αὐτοὺς ⟨ὡς⟩,[4] εἰ μὴ παραδοῖεν,
451 ὅμοια πεισομένους. προσήλουν δ' οἱ στρατιῶται
δι' ὀργὴν καὶ μῖσος τοὺς ἁλόντας ἄλλον ἄλλῳ
σχήματι πρὸς χλεύην, καὶ διὰ τὸ πλῆθος χώρα
τ' ἐνέλειπε τοῖς σταυροῖς καὶ σταυροὶ τοῖς σώμασιν.
452   (2) Οἱ στασιασταὶ δὲ τοσοῦτον ἀπεδέησαν τοῦ
μεταβαλέσθαι πρὸς τὸ πάθος, ὥστε καὶ τοὐναντίον
453 αὐτοὶ σοφίσασθαι πρὸς τὸ λοιπὸν πλῆθος. σύ-

---

[1] + μὴ Bekker with one ms.
[2] εἰς (om. PA) is confirmed by the parallel in Plato, *Rep.*
468 A εἰς τοὺς πολεμίους ἁλόντα.
[3] + δέει τῆς κολάσεως L Lat.   [4] ins. Destinon after Lat.

into the ravines in quest of food. These included some of the combatants, no longer satisfied with their plunder, but the majority were citizens of the poorer class, who were deterred from deserting by fear for their families ; for they could neither hope to elude the rebels if they attempted to escape with their wives and children, nor endure to leave them to be butchered by the brigands on their behalf. Famine, however, emboldened them to undertake these excursions, and it but remained for them if they escaped unobserved from the town to be taken prisoners by the enemy. When caught, they were driven to resist,[a] and after a conflict it seemed too late to sue for mercy. They were accordingly scourged and subjected to torture of every description, before being killed, and then crucified opposite the walls. Titus indeed commiserated their fate, five hundred or sometimes more being captured daily ; on the other hand, he recognized the risk of dismissing prisoners of war, and that the custody of such numbers would amount to the imprisonment of their custodians ; but his main reason for not stopping the crucifixions was the hope that the spectacle might perhaps induce the Jews to surrender, for fear that continued resistance would involve them in a similar fate. The soldiers out of rage and hatred amused themselves by nailing their prisoners in different postures ; and so great was their number, that space could not be found for the crosses nor crosses for the bodies.

(2) The insurgents, however, far from relenting at these sufferings, deluded the remainder by inventing a contrary motive for them. Dragging the relatives

---

[a] Some authorities add " from fear of punishment."

ροντες γὰρ τοὺς τῶν αὐτομόλων οἰκείους ἐπὶ τὸ
τεῖχος καὶ τῶν δημοτῶν τοὺς ἐπὶ πίστιν ὡρμημένους, οἷα πάσχουσιν οἱ Ῥωμαίοις προσφεύγοντες
ἐπεδείκνυσαν καὶ τοὺς κεκρατημένους[1] ἱκέτας
454 ἔλεγον, οὐκ αἰχμαλώτους. τοῦτο πολλοὺς τῶν
αὐτομολεῖν ὡρμημένων μέχρι τἀληθὲς ἐγνώσθη
κατέσχεν· εἰσὶ δ᾽ οἳ καὶ παραχρῆμα διέδρασαν
ὡς ἐπὶ βέβαιον τιμωρίαν, ἀνάπαυσιν ἡγούμενοι
τὸν ἐκ τῶν πολεμίων θάνατον ἐν λιμοῦ συγκρίσει.
455 πολλοὺς δὲ καὶ χειροκοπῆσαι κελεύσας Τίτος
τῶν ἑαλωκότων, ὡς μὴ δοκοῖεν αὐτόμολοι καὶ
πιστεύοιντο διὰ τὴν συμφοράν, εἰσέπεμψε πρὸς
456 τὸν Σίμωνα καὶ τὸν Ἰωάννην, νῦν γε ἤδη παύσασθαι παραινῶν καὶ μὴ πρὸς ἀναίρεσιν τῆς
πόλεως αὐτὸν βιάζεσθαι, κερδῆσαι δ᾽ ἐκ τῆς ἐν
ὑστάτοις μεταμελείας τάς τε αὐτῶν ψυχὰς καὶ
τηλικαύτην πατρίδα καὶ ναὸν ἀκοινώνητον ἄλλοις.
457 περιιὼν δὲ τὰ χώματα τοὺς ἐργαζομένους ἅμα
κατήπειγεν, ὡς οὐκ εἰς μακρὰν ἀκολουθήσων
458 ἔργοις τῷ λόγῳ. πρὸς ταῦτα αὐτόν τ᾽ ἐβλασφήμουν
ἀπὸ τοῦ τείχους Καίσαρα καὶ τὸν πατέρα αὐτοῦ,
καὶ τοῦ μὲν θανάτου καταφρονεῖν ἐβόων, ᾑρῆσθαι
γὰρ αὐτὸν πρὸ δουλείας καλῶς, ἐργάσεσθαι δ᾽
ὅσα ἂν δύνωνται κακὰ Ῥωμαίους ἕως ἐμπνέωσι,
πατρίδος δ᾽ οὐ μέλειν τοῖς ὡς αὐτός φησιν ἀπολου-
μένοις, καὶ ναὸν[2] ἀμείνω τούτου τῷ θεῷ τὸν
459 κόσμον εἶναι. σωθήσεσθαί γε μὴν καὶ τοῦτον
ὑπὸ τοῦ κατοικοῦντος, ὃν καὶ αὐτοὶ σύμμαχον

[1] κρεμαμένους Destinon.
[2] ναὸν Bekker with Lat.: ναοῦ + ἀπολο(υ)μένου (om. Lat.
ed. pr.) MSS.

of the deserters to the wall, together with any citizens who were anxious to accept the offer of terms, they showed them what was the fate of those who sought refuge with the Romans, asserting that the arrested victims were not captives, but suppliants. This, until the truth became known, kept back many who were eager to desert; some, however, instantly fled, as to certain punishment, regarding death at the enemy's hands as rest in comparison with starvation. But Titus now gave orders to cut off the hands of several of the prisoners, that they might not be mistaken for deserters and that their calamity might add credit to their statements, and then sent them in to Simon and John, exhorting them now at least to pause, and not compel him to destroy the city, but by repentance at the eleventh hour to gain their own lives, their magnificent city, and a temple unshared by others. At the same time he went round the embankments, urging on the workmen, as if intending shortly to follow up his threats by action. To this message the Jews retorted by heaping abuse from the ramparts upon Caesar himself, and his father, crying out that they scorned death, which they honourably preferred to slavery; that they would do Romans every injury in their power while they had breath in their bodies; that men so soon, as he himself said, to perish, were unconcerned for their native place, and that the world was a better temple for God than this one.[a] But, they added, it would yet be saved by Him who dwelt therein, and

Admonitions of Titus

and retorts of the Jewish leaders.

---

[a] *Cf.* Baruch iii. 24, " O Israel, how great is the house of God ! and how large is the place of his possession ! " etc. Writing after the tragedy of A.D. 70 the author of that work says in effect " The house of God is not the ruined Temple but the broad universe."

ἔχοντες πᾶσαν χλευάσειν ἀπειλὴν ὑστεροῦσαν
ἔργων· τὸ γὰρ τέλος εἶναι τοῦ θεοῦ. τοιαῦτα
ταῖς λοιδορίαις ἀναμίσγοντες ἐκεκράγεσαν.

460 (3) Ἐν δὲ τούτῳ καὶ ὁ Ἐπιφανὴς Ἀντίοχος
παρῆν ἄλλους τε ὁπλίτας συχνοὺς ἔχων καὶ περὶ
αὑτὸν στῖφος Μακεδόνων καλούμενον, ἥλικας
πάντας, ὑψηλούς, ὀλίγον ὑπὲρ ἀντίπαιδας, τὸν
Μακεδονικὸν τρόπον ὡπλισμένους τε καὶ πεπαιδευμένους, ὅθεν καὶ τὴν ἐπίκλησιν εἶχον, ὑστε-
461 ροῦντες οἱ πολλοὶ τοῦ γένους. εὐδαιμονῆσαι γὰρ
δὴ μάλιστα τῶν ὑπὸ Ῥωμαίοις βασιλέων τὸν
Κομμαγηνὸν συνέβη πρὶν γεύσασθαι μεταβολῆς·
ἀπέφηνε δὲ κἀκεῖνος ἐπὶ γήρως ὡς οὐδένα χρὴ
462 λέγειν πρὸ θανάτου μακάριον. ἀλλ' ὅ γε παῖς
ἀκμάζοντος αὐτοῦ τηνικαῦτα παρὼν θαυμάζειν
ἔφασκε, τί δήποτε Ῥωμαῖοι κατοκνοῖεν προσιέναι
τῷ τείχει· πολεμιστὴς δέ τις αὐτὸς ἦν καὶ φύσει
παράβολος κατά τε [τὴν] ἀλκὴν τοσοῦτος, ὡς
463 ὀλίγων¹ τὰ τῆς τόλμης διαμαρτάνειν. μειδιά-
σαντος δὲ τοῦ Τίτου καὶ " κοινὸς ὁ πόνος "
εἰπόντος, ὡς εἶχεν ὥρμησεν ὁ Ἀντίοχος μετὰ
464 τῶν Μακεδόνων πρὸς τὸ τεῖχος. αὐτὸς μὲν οὖν
διά τε ἰσχὺν καὶ κατ' ἐμπειρίαν ἐφυλάττετο τὰ
τῶν Ἰουδαίων βέλη τοξεύων εἰς αὐτούς, τὰ
μειράκια δ' αὐτῷ συνετρίβη πάντα πλὴν ὀλίγων·
διὰ γὰρ αἰδῶ τῆς ὑποσχέσεως προσεφιλονείκει

---

¹ Bekker: ὀλίγῳ mss.

ᵃ Son of Antiochus IV, King of Commagene; he appears
again in *B.* vii. 232, with his brother Ephialtes, fighting in
defence of his father's kingdom.
ᵇ Antiochus IV. He had previously sent supports to
Cestius, *B.* ii. 500, and to Vespasian in Galilee, iii. 68.
ᶜ A petty kingdom on the upper Euphrates, between

344

while they had Him for their ally they would deride all menaces unsupported by action; for the issue rested with God. Such, with invectives interspersed, were their exclamations.

(3) Meanwhile there appeared on the scene Antiochus Epiphanes,[a] bringing with him, besides numerous other forces, a bodyguard calling themselves "Macedonians," all of the same age, tall, just emerged from adolescence, and armed and trained in the Macedonian fashion, from which circumstance indeed they took their title, most of them lacking any claim to belong to that race. For of all the monarchs owning allegiance to Rome the king[b] of Commagene[c] enjoyed the highest prosperity, before he experienced reverse; but he too proved in old age how no man should be pronounced happy before his death.[d] However, the father's fortunes were at their zenith at the time when his son arrived and expressed his surprise that a Roman army should hesitate to attack the ramparts; something of a warrior himself, he was of an adventurous nature and withal so robust that his daring was seldom unsuccessful. Titus replying with a smile, "The field is open," Antiochus, without further ado, dashed with his Macedonians at the wall. His own strength and skill enabled him to avoid the missiles of the Jews, while raining arrows upon them, but his young comrades with few exceptions were all overpowered. For, out of respect for their engagement, they

Cilicia and Armenia, with Samosata for capital. Annexed by Rome under Tiberius, the kingdom was revived by Gaius, but was finally annexed to Syria by Vespasian, when Antiochus was accused of an intention to revolt from Rome, B. vii. 219 ff.

[d] Allusion to Solon's saying, Herodotus i. 32.

465 μαχόμενα· καὶ τέλος ἀνεχώρουν τραυματίαι πολλοί,
συννοοῦντες ὅτι καὶ τοῖς ἀληθῶς Μακεδόσιν, εἰ
μέλλοιεν κρατεῖν, δεῖ τῆς Ἀλεξάνδρου τύχης.

466 (4) Τοῖς δὲ Ῥωμαίοις ἀρξαμένοις δωδεκάτῃ
μηνὸς Ἀρτεμισίου συνετελέσθη τὰ χώματα μόλις
ἐνάτῃ καὶ εἰκάδι, ταῖς δεχεπτὰ συνεχῶς πονου-
467 μένων ἡμέραις· μέγιστα γὰρ ἐχώσθη τὰ τέσσαρα,
καὶ θάτερον μὲν τὸ ἐπὶ τὴν Ἀντωνίαν ὑπὸ τοῦ
πέμπτου τάγματος ἐβλήθη κατὰ μέσον τῆς
Στρουθίου¹ καλουμένης κολυμβήθρας, τὸ δ' ἕτερον
ὑπὸ τοῦ δωδεκάτου διεστῶτος ὅσον εἰς πήχεις
468 εἴκοσι. τῷ δεκάτῳ δὲ τάγματι διέχοντι πολὺ
τούτων κατὰ τὸ βόρειον κλίμα τὸ ἔργον ἦν καὶ
κολυμβήθραν Ἀμύγδαλον προσαγορευομένην· τούτου δὲ τὸ πεντεκαιδέκατον ἀπὸ τριάκοντα πηχῶν
469 ἔχου κατὰ τὸ τοῦ ἀρχιερέως μνημεῖον. προσ-
αγομένων δ' ἤδη τῶν ὀργάνων² ὁ μὲν Ἰωάννης
ἔνδοθεν ὑπορύξας τὸ κατὰ τὴν Ἀντωνίαν μέχρι
τῶν χωμάτων καὶ διαλαβὼν σταυροῖς τοὺς ὑπονόμους ἀνακρήμνησιν τὰ ἔργα, πίσσῃ δὲ καὶ
ἀσφάλτῳ διακεχρισμένην [τὴν] ὕλην εἰσκομίσας
470 ἐνίησι πῦρ. καὶ τῶν σταυρῶν ὑποκαέντων ἥ τε
διῶρυξ ἐνέδωκεν ἀθρόα, καὶ μετὰ μεγίστου ψόφου
471 κατεσείσθη τὰ χώματα εἰς αὐτήν. τὸ μὲν οὖν
πρῶτον μετὰ τοῦ κονιορτοῦ καπνὸς ἠγείρετο βαθὺς
πνιγομένου τῷ πταίσματι³ τοῦ πυρός, τῆς δὲ
θλιβούσης ὕλης διαβιβρωσκομένης ἤδη φανερὰ
472 φλὸξ ἐρρήγνυτο. καὶ τοῖς Ῥωμαίοις ἔκπληξις

¹ C: τοῦ Στρουθίου L: τοῦ θείου the rest.
² τῶν ὀργάνων] αὐτῶν PA. ³ πτώματι LC.

___

ᵃ Identified by M. Clermont-Ganneau with the so-called

emulously maintained the fight, until at length, mainly wounded, they retired, reflecting that even genuine Macedonians, if they are to conquer, must have Alexander's fortune.

(4) Though the Romans had begun their earth-works on the twelfth of the month Artemisius, they were scarcely completed on the twenty-ninth, after seventeen days of continuous toil. For the four embankments were immense. Of the first two, that at Antonia was thrown up by the fifth legion over against the middle of the pool called Struthion,[a] the other by the twelfth legion about twenty cubits away. The tenth legion, at a considerable distance from these, was employed in the northern region and over against the pool termed Amygdalon[b]; while, thirty cubits from them, the fifteenth were at work opposite the high priest's monument.[c] But while the engines were now being brought up, John from within had undermined the ground from Antonia right up to the earthworks, supporting the tunnels with props, and thus leaving the Roman works suspended; having then introduced timber be-smeared with pitch and bitumen he set the whole mass alight. The props being consumed, the mine collapsed in a heap, and with a tremendous crash the earthworks fell in. At first dense volumes of smoke arose with clouds of dust, the fire being smothered by the debris, but as the materials which crushed it were eaten away, a vivid flame now burst forth. The Romans were in consternation at this sudden cata-

Completion of Roman earthworks.

c. 30 May
c. 16 June
A.D. 70.

John under-mines and burns up one portion of them,

Twin Pools, adjoining the N.W. corner of Antonia (G. A. Smith, *Jerusalem*, i. 116).
  [b] Probably to be identified with the " Pool of the Patri-arch's Bath," near the Jaffa Gate. *ib.* 115.   [c] § 259.

μὲν πρὸς τὸ αἰφνίδιον, ἀθυμία δὲ πρὸς τὴν ἐπίνοιαν ἐμπίπτει, καὶ κρατήσειν οἰομένοις ἤδη τὸ
συμβὰν καὶ πρὸς τὸ μέλλον ἔψυξε τὴν ἐλπίδα·
τὸ δὲ ἀμύνειν ἀχρεῖον ἐδόκει πρὸς τὸ πῦρ, καὶ εἰ
σβεσθείη τῶν χωμάτων καταποθέντων.

473 (5) Μετὰ δ' ἡμέρας δύο καὶ τοῖς ἄλλοις ἐπιτίθενται χώμασιν οἱ περὶ τὸν Σίμωνα· καὶ γὰρ δὴ
προσαγαγόντες ταύτῃ τὰς ἑλεπόλεις οἱ Ῥωμαῖοι
474 διέσειον [ἤδη] τὸ τεῖχος. Γεφθαῖος[1] δέ τις ἀπὸ
Γάρις πόλεως τῆς Γαλιλαίας, καὶ Μαγάσσαρος
τῶν βασιλικῶν Μαριάμμης θεράπων, μεθ' ὧν
Ἀδιαβηνός τις υἱὸς Ναβαταίου, τοὔνομα κληθεὶς
ἀπὸ τῆς τύχης Κεαγίρας,[2] ὅπερ σημαίνει χωλός,
ἁρπάσαντες λαμπάδας προεπήδησαν ἐπὶ τὰς μη-
475 χανάς. τούτων τῶν ἀνδρῶν οὔτε τολμηρότεροι
κατὰ τόνδε τὸν πόλεμον ἐκ τῆς πόλεως ἐφάνησαν
476 οὔτε φοβερώτεροι· καθάπερ γὰρ εἰς φίλους ἐκτρέχοντες οὐ πολεμίων στῖφος,[3] οὔτ' ἐμέλλησαν
οὔτ' ἀπέστησαν,[4] ἀλλὰ διὰ μέσων ἐνθορόντες τῶν
477 ἐχθρῶν ὑφῆψαν τὰς μηχανάς. βαλλόμενοι δὲ καὶ
τοῖς ξίφεσιν ἀνωθούμενοι πάντοθεν οὐ πρότερον
ἐκ τοῦ κινδύνου μετεκινήθησαν ἢ δράξασθαι τῶν
478 ὀργάνων τὸ πῦρ. αἰρομένης δ' ἤδη τῆς φλογὸς
Ῥωμαῖοι μὲν ἀπὸ τῶν στρατοπέδων συνθέοντες
ἐβοήθουν, Ἰουδαῖοι δ' ἐκ τοῦ τείχους ἐκώλυον
καὶ τοῖς σβεννύειν πειρωμένοις συνεπλέκοντο κατὰ
479 μηδὲν τῶν ἰδίων φειδόμενοι σωμάτων. καὶ οἱ

---

[1] From vi. 148 (cf. 92): Τεφθαῖος mss.
[2] With Lat, : καὶ Ἀγίρας or καὶ Ἀγήρας etc. mss.: Χαγείρας
Hudson.
[3] + οὔτ(ε) ἔδεισαν some mss.   [4] om. οὔτ' ἀπέστησαν L.

strophe and dispirited by the enemy's ingenuity ;
moreover, coming at the moment when they imagined
victory within their grasp, the casualty damped their
hopes of ultimate success. It seemed useless to
fight the flames, when even if they were extinguished
their earthworks were overwhelmed.

(5) Two days later Simon's party launched a *and Simon attacks*
further attack on the other earthworks, for the *the other.*
Romans had there brought up the rams and were
already battering the wall. A certain Gephthaeus,
of Garis, a town in Galilee, and Magassarus, a soldier
of the king and henchman of Mariamme,[a] along with
the son of a certain Nabataeus from Adiabene, called
from his misfortune by the name of Ceagiras, signify-
ing " lame," [b] snatched up torches and rushed forth
against the engines. No bolder men than these
three sallied from the town throughout this war or
inspired greater terror ; for, as though racing for
friendly ranks and not into a mass of enemies, they
neither slackened nor turned aside, but, plunging
through the midst of the foe, set light to the machines.
Assailed by shots and sword-thrusts from every
quarter, nothing could move them from the field of
danger until the fire had caught hold of the engines.
The flames now towering aloft, the Romans came
rushing from their encampments to the rescue ;
while the Jews obstructed them from the ramparts
and, utterly regardless of their own lives, struggled
hand to hand with those who were endeavouring to
extinguish the conflagration. On the one side were

---

[a] Or " one of the royal henchmen of Mariamme." Mariamme was daughter of Agrippa I and sister of Agrippa II
" the king," *B.* ii. 220 ; the man must have been a deserter.

[b] Aramaic *ḥaggera'*, "lame man."

μὲν εἷλκον ἐκ τοῦ πυρὸς τὰς ἑλεπόλεις τῶν ὑπὲρ
αὐτὰς γέρρων φλεγομένων, οἱ δ' Ἰουδαῖοι καὶ
διὰ τῆς φλογὸς ἀντελαμβάνοντο καὶ τοῦ σιδήρου
ζέοντος δρασσόμενοι τοὺς κριοὺς οὐ μεθίεσαν·
διέβαινε δ' ἀπὸ τούτων ἐπὶ τὰ χώματα τὸ πῦρ
480 καὶ τοὺς ἀμύνοντας προελάμβανεν. ἐν τούτῳ δ'
οἱ μὲν Ῥωμαῖοι κυκλούμενοι τῇ φλογὶ καὶ τὴν
σωτηρίαν τῶν ἔργων ἀπογνόντες ἀνεχώρουν ἐπὶ
481 τὰ στρατόπεδα, Ἰουδαῖοι δὲ προσέκειντο πλείους
ἀεὶ γινόμενοι τῶν ἔνδοθεν προσβοηθούντων καὶ
τῷ κρατεῖν τεθαρρηκότες ἀταμιεύτοις ἐχρῶντο
ταῖς ὁρμαῖς,[1] προελθόντες[2] δὲ μέχρι τῶν ἐρυμάτων
482 ἤδη συνεπλέκοντο τοῖς φρουροῖς. τάξις ἐστὶν
ἐκ διαδοχῆς ἱσταμένη πρὸ τοῦ στρατοπέδου,[3] καὶ
δεινὸς ἐπ' αὐτῇ Ῥωμαίων νόμος τὸν ὑποχωρή-
483 σαντα καθ' ἣν δήποτ' οὖν αἰτίαν θνήσκειν. οὗτοι
τοῦ μετὰ κολάσεως τὸν μετ' ἀρετῆς θάνατον
προκρίναντες ἵστανται, καὶ πρὸς τὴν τούτων
ἀνάγκην πολλοὶ τῶν τραπέντων ἐπεστράφησαν
484 αἰδούμενοι. διαθέντες δὲ καὶ τοὺς ὀξυβελεῖς ἐπὶ
τοῦ τείχους εἶργον τὸ προσγινόμενον πλῆθος ἐκ
τῆς πόλεως, οὐδὲν εἰς ἀσφάλειαν ἢ φυλακὴν τῶν
σωμάτων προνοουμένους· συνεπλέκοντο γὰρ [οἱ]
Ἰουδαῖοι τοῖς προστυχοῦσι καὶ ταῖς αἰχμαῖς[4]
ἀφυλάκτως ἐμπίπτοντες αὐτοῖς τοῖς σώμασι τοὺς
485 ἐχθροὺς ἔπαιον. οὔτε δ' ἔργοις αὐτοὶ πλέον ἢ
τῷ θαρρεῖν περιῆσαν καὶ Ῥωμαῖοι τῇ τόλμῃ
πλέον εἶκον ἢ τῷ κακοῦσθαι.
486 (6) Παρῆν δ' ἤδη Τίτος ἀπὸ τῆς Ἀντωνίας,
ὅπου[5] κεχώριστο κατασκεπτόμενος τόπον ἄλλοις

---

[1] Cf. iv. 44, vi. 171: ὀργαῖς PA.
[2] Niese with Lat.: προσελθόντες mss.

the Romans striving to drag the battering-engines out of the fire, their wicker shelters all ablaze; on the other, the Jews holding on to them through the flames, clutching the red-hot iron and refusing to relinquish the rams. From these the fire spread to the earth-works, outstripping the defenders. Thereupon the Romans, enveloped in flames and despairing of the preservation of the works, beat a retreat to their camps; while the Jews, hotly pursuing, their numbers continually augmented by fresh reinforcements from the city, and flushed with success, pressed on with uncontrolled impetuosity right up to the entrenchments, and finally grappled with the sentries. There is a line of troops, relieved from time to time, who are stationed in front of every camp and come under a severe Roman law that he who quits his post under any pretext whatsoever dies. These men, preferring an heroic death to capital punishment, stood firm; and seeing the straits of their comrades many of the fugitives for very shame returned. Posting the "quick-firers" [a] along the camp-wall, they kept at bay the masses who, without a thought for safety or personal defence, were surging up from the town; for the Jews grappled with any whom they met, and all unguardedly flinging themselves bodily upon the spear-points, struck at their antagonists. But their superiority lay less in deeds than in daring, and the Romans yielded rather to intrepidity than to injuries received.

(6) But now Titus appeared from Antonia, whither he had gone to inspect a site for fresh earthworks.

The Jews invade the Roman camp.

Titus repels them.

[a] Or "scorpions."

---

[3] + μετὰ τῶν ὅπλων LC Lat. Suid.
[4] L: ἀκμαῖς the rest.   [5] quo (= ὅποι) Lat.

χώμασι, καὶ πολλὰ τοὺς στρατιώτας φαυλίσας, ε
κρατοῦντες τῶν πολεμίων τειχῶν κινδυνεύουσ
τοῖς ἰδίοις καὶ πολιορκουμένων ὑπομένουσιν αὐτο
τύχην, ὥσπερ ἐκ δεσμωτηρίου καθ᾽ αὑτῶν Ἰουδαίους ἀνέντες, περιῄει μετὰ τῶν ἐπιλέκτων κατὰ
487 πλευρὰ τοὺς πολεμίους αὐτός· οἱ δὲ κατὰ στόμα
παιόμενοι καὶ πρὸς τοῦτον ἐπιστραφέντες ἐκαρτέ-
ρουν. μιγείσης δὲ τῆς παρατάξεως ὁ μὲν κονιορτὸς τῶν ὀμμάτων, ἡ κραυγὴ δὲ τῶν ἀκοῶν ἐπεκράτει, καὶ οὐδετέρῳ παρῆν ἔτι τεκμήρασθαι τὸ
488 ἐχθρὸν ἢ τὸ φίλιον. Ἰουδαίων δὲ οὐ τοσοῦτον
ἔτι κατ᾽ ἀλκὴν ὅσον ἀπογνώσει σωτηρίας παρα-
μενόντων καὶ Ῥωμαίους ἐτόνωσεν αἰδὼς δόξης
τε καὶ τῶν ὅπλων καὶ προκινδυνεύοντος Καίσαρος
489 ὥστε μοι δοκοῦσι τὰ τελευταῖα δι᾽ ὑπερβολὴν
θυμῶν κἂν [ὅλον] ἁρπάσαι[1] τὸ τῶν Ἰουδαίων
πλῆθος, εἰ μὴ τὴν ῥοπὴν τῆς παρατάξεως φθά-
490 σαντες ἀνεχώρησαν εἰς τὴν πόλιν. διεφθαρμένων
δὲ τῶν χωμάτων Ῥωμαῖοι μὲν ἦσαν ἐν ἀθυμίαις
τὸν μακρὸν κάματον ἐπὶ μιᾶς ὥρας ἀπολέσαντες
καὶ πολλοὶ μὲν ταῖς συνήθεσι μηχαναῖς ἀπήλπιζον
ἁλώσεσθαι τὴν πόλιν.

491 (xii. 1) Τίτος δὲ μετὰ τῶν ἡγεμόνων ἐβουλεύετο,
καὶ τοῖς μὲν θερμοτέροις πᾶσαν ἐδόκει προσφέρειν
τὴν δύναμιν ἀποπειρᾶσθαί τε τοῦ τείχους βίᾳ
492 μέχρι μὲν γὰρ νῦν κατὰ σπάσμα Ἰουδαίοις [τῆς
στρατιᾶς] συμπεπλέχθαι, προσιόντων δ᾽ ἀθρόων
οὐδὲ τὴν ἔφοδον οἴσειν· καταχωσθήσεσθαι γὰρ
493 ὑπὸ τῶν βελῶν. τῶν δ᾽ ἀσφαλεστέρων οἱ μὲν
καὶ τὰ χώματα ποιεῖν πάλιν, οἱ δὲ καὶ δίχα τούτων
προσκαθέζεσθαι μόνον παραφυλάττοντας τάς τε

---

[1] ἀναρπάσαι conj. Niese, cf. ii. 550 (some mss.).

Severely reprimanding his troops for having, while
mastering the enemy's fortifications, thus jeopardized
their own, and put themselves in the position of the
besieged, by letting loose the Jews upon them from
their prison house, he then with his picked force,
himself at their head, got round and took the enemy
in flank; but though attacked in front as well,
they turned and resolutely withstood him. In the
medley of the fight, blinded by the dust and deafened
by the din, neither side could any longer distinguish
friend from foe. The Jews still held out, though
now less through prowess than from despair of
salvation, while the Romans were braced by a regard
for glory, for the honour of their arms, and for Caesar
foremost in danger; insomuch that I imagine that,
in the excess of their fury, they would have ended
by wiping out the entire Jewish host, had not their
enemy, anticipating the turn of the battle, retreated
into the city. The Romans, however, with their
earthworks demolished, were in deep dejection,
having lost in one hour the fruit of their long labour,
and many despaired of ever carrying the town by
the ordinary appliances.

(xii. 1) Titus now held a consultation with his
officers. The more sanguine were of opinion that
he should bring up his entire force and essay to carry
the wall by storm; for hitherto separate sections
only had been engaged with the Jews, whereas
under a mass attack the Jews would be powerless to
resist their onset, as they would be overwhelmed by
the hail of missiles. Of the more cautious, some
were for reconstructing the earthworks; others
advised that they should dispense with these and
resort to a blockade, merely guarding against the

Titus holds a council of war.

ἐξόδους αὐτῶν καὶ τὰς εἰσκομιδὰς τῶν ἐπιτηδείων
παρήνουν καὶ τῷ λιμῷ καταλείπειν τὴν πόλιν,
μηδὲ συμπλέκεσθαι κατὰ χεῖρα τοῖς πολεμίοις·
494 ἄμαχον γὰρ εἶναι τὴν ἀπόγνωσιν οἷς εὐχὴ μὲν τὸ[1]
σιδήρῳ πεσεῖν, ἀπόκειται δὲ καὶ δίχα τούτου
495 πάθος χαλεπώτερον. αὐτῷ δὲ τὸ μὲν ἀργεῖν
καθόλου μετὰ τοσαύτης δυνάμεως οὐκ ἐδόκει
πρέπειν καὶ τὸ μάχεσθαι περιττὸν πρὸς ἀλλήλων
496 φθαρησομένοις, βάλλεσθαι δὲ χώματα δύσεργοι
ἀπέφαινεν ὕλης ἀπορίᾳ καὶ τὸ παραφυλάττειν τὰς
ἐξόδους δυσεργότερον· κυκλώσασθαί τε γὰρ τῇ
στρατιᾷ τὴν πόλιν διὰ μέγεθος καὶ δυσχωρίαι
οὐκ εὐμαρὲς εἶναι καὶ σφαλερὸν ἄλλως πρὸς τὰς
497 ἐπιθέσεις. τῶν δὲ φανερῶν φυλαττομένων ἀφανεῖς
ἐπινοηθήσεσθαι[2] Ἰουδαίοις ὁδοὺς κατά τε ἀνάγκην
καὶ δι' ἐμπειρίαν· εἰ δέ τι λάθρα παρεισκομι-
σθήσοιτο, τριβὴν ἔσεσθαι πλείω τῇ πολιορκίᾳ.
498 δεδιέναι τε μὴ τὴν δόξαν τοῦ κατορθώματος αὐτῷ
τὸ μῆκος ἐλαττώσῃ τοῦ χρόνου· τούτῳ μὲν γὰρ
εἶναι πᾶν ἀνύσιμον, πρὸς δὲ τῆς εὐκλείας τὸ τάχος·
499 δεῖν γε μήν, εἰ καὶ τῷ τάχει μετ' ἀσφαλείας
βούλοιντο[3] χρήσασθαι, περιτειχίζειν ὅλην τὴν πόλιν
μόνως γὰρ οὕτως ἂν πάσας ἀποφράξαι τὰς ἐξόδους,
καὶ Ἰουδαίους ἢ πρὸς ἅπαντα ἀπογνόντας τὴν
σωτηρίαν παραδώσειν τὴν πόλιν ἢ λιμώττοντας
500 χειρωθήσεσθαι ῥᾳδίως· οὐδὲ γὰρ ἠρεμήσειν αὐτὸς[4]
ἄλλως, ἀλλὰ καὶ τῶν χωμάτων ἐπιμελήσεσθαι
πάλιν χρώμενος τοῖς κωλύουσιν ἀτονωτέροις.
501 εἰ δέ τῳ μέγα δοκεῖ καὶ δυσήνυτον τὸ ἔργον,

---

[1] L: τῷ the rest.
[2] After Lat. (excogitaturos): ἐπινοεῖσθαι mss.
[3] L: βούλοιτο the rest.
[4] Destinon: αὐτὸν L: αὐτοὺς the rest.

egress of the besieged and the introduction of supplies, and that, leaving the city to the famine, they should avoid direct conflict with the foe; for there was no contending with desperate men whose prayer was to fall by the sword, and for whom, if that was denied them, a harder fate was in store. To Titus, however, to remain totally inactive with so large a force appeared undignified, while to contend with men who would soon destroy each other seemed superfluous. At the same time he pointed out the extreme difficulty of throwing up earthworks, owing to lack of materials, and the even greater difficulty of guarding against sallies; for to encompass the city with troops would, owing to its extent and the obstacles presented by the ground, be no easy matter, and would, moreover, expose them to the risk of enemy attacks. They might guard the obvious outlets, but the Jews from necessity and their knowledge of the locality would contrive secret routes; and, should supplies be furtively smuggled in, the siege would be still further protracted. He feared, moreover, that the glory of success would be diminished by the delay; for though time could accomplish everything, yet rapidity was essential to renown. If, however, they wished to combine speed and security, they must throw a wall round the whole city: only thus could every exit be blocked, and the Jews would then either in utter despair of salvation surrender the city, or, wasted by famine, fall an easy prey; for he himself would not remain altogether inactive, but would once more turn his attention to the earthworks when he had an enfeebled foe to obstruct him. And if anyone considered this a great and arduous

Decision to build a wall round Jerusalem.

χρῆναι σκοπεῖν, ὡς οὔτε Ῥωμαίοις τι μικρὸν
ἐνεργεῖν πρέπει, καὶ δίχα πόνου κατορθοῦν τι τῶν
μεγάλων οὐδενὶ ῥᾴδιον.

502 (2) Τούτοις πείσας τοὺς ἡγεμόνας διανέμειν
ἐκέλευσε τὰς δυνάμεις ἐπὶ τὸ ἔργον. ὁρμὴ δέ τις
ἐμπίπτει δαιμόνιος τοῖς στρατιώταις, καὶ μερι-
σαμένων τὸν περίβολον οὐ μόνον τῶν ταγμάτων
ἦν ἔρις, ἀλλὰ καὶ τῶν ἐν αὐτοῖς τάξεων πρὸς
503 ἀλλήλας, καὶ στρατιώτης μὲν δεκαδάρχην, δεκαδ-
άρχης δ' ἑκατοντάρχην, οὗτος δ' ἐσπούδαζεν
ἀρέσασθαι χιλίαρχον, τῶν δὲ χιλιάρχων ἐπὶ τοὺς
ἡγεμόνας ἔτεινεν ἡ φιλοτιμία καὶ τῶν ἡγεμόνων
τὴν ἅμιλλαν ἐβράβευε Καῖσαρ· περιὼν γὰρ
αὐτὸς ἑκάστης ἡμέρας πολλάκις ἐπεσκόπει τὸ
504 ἔργον. ἀρξάμενος δ' ἀπὸ τῆς Ἀσσυρίων παρεμ-
βολῆς, καθ' ἣν αὐτὸς ἐστρατοπεδεύσατο, ἐπὶ τὴν
κατωτέρω Καινόπολιν ἦγε τὸ τεῖχος, ἔνθεν διὰ τοῦ
505 Κεδρῶνος ἐπὶ τὸ Ἐλαιῶν ὄρος· εἶτ' ἀνακάμπτων
κατὰ μεσημβρίαν περιλαμβάνει τὸ ὄρος ἄχρι τῆς
Περιστερεῶνος καλουμένης πέτρας τόν τε ἑξῆς
λόφον, ὃς ἐπίκειται τῇ κατὰ τὴν Σιλωὰμ φάραγγι,
κἀκεῖθεν ἐκκλίνας πρὸς δύσιν εἰς τὴν τῆς πηγῆς
506 κατήει φάραγγα. μεθ' ἣν ἀναβαίνων κατὰ τὸ
Ἀνάνου τοῦ ἀρχιερέως μνημεῖον καὶ διαλαβὼν

---

[a] Probably a reminiscence of Soph. *El.* 945 ὅρα πόνου τοι
χωρὶς οὐδὲν εὐτυχεῖ, of which a similar paraphrase is put into
the mouth of Titus elsewhere, iii. 495. Titus was familiar
with Greek literature (" Latine Graeceque, vel in orando vel
in fingendis poematibus, promptus," Suet. *Tit.* 3), and the
356

operation, let him reflect that it ill became Romans to undertake a trivial task and that without toil nothing great could lightly be achieved by any man.[a]

(2) Having by these arguments convinced his officers, Titus ordered them to distribute the task among the forces. The troops thereupon were seized with a sort of preternatural enthusiasm, and, the circuit of the wall being respectively apportioned, not only the legions, but their component companies vied with one another : the soldier studied to please his decurion, the decurion the centurion, and he the tribune, while the emulation of the tribunes extended to the staff-officers, and in the rivalry between the officers Caesar himself was umpire ; for he went round himself frequently every day and inspected the work. Beginning at the camp of the Assyrians [b] —the site of his own encampment—he directed the wall towards the lower region of the New Town and thence across the Kedron to the Mount of Olives ; then, bending round to the south, he enclosed the mount as far as the rock called Peristereon [c] together with the adjoining hill, which overhangs the Siloam ravine ; thence, inclining westwards, the line [d] descended into the Valley of the Fountain,[e] beyond which it ascended over against the tomb of Ananus the high priest [f] and, taking in [g] the mountain where

Line of the Roman wall.

Sophoclean phrase possibly in these two instances comes from the Emperor himself.

  [b] § 303.   [c] = " Dovecote " ; unidentified.

  [d] Literally " he descended " and so on.

  [e] Siloam is apparently meant.

  [f] Probably the elder Ananus, son of Sethi, the father of five high priests, *A.* xviii. 26, xx.197 f., including the younger and more famous Ananus who was slain by the Zealots, iv. 315 f.

  [g] Or, perhaps, " cutting across."

τὸ ὄρος, ἔνθα Πομπήιος ἐστρατοπεδεύσατο, πρὸς
507 κλίμα βόρειον ἐπέστρεφε, καὶ προελθὼν μέχρι
κώμης τινός, Ἐρεβίνθων οἶκος καλεῖται, καὶ
μετ' ἐκείνην τὸ Ἡρώδου μνημεῖον περισχὼν κατὰ
ἀνατολὴν τῷ ἰδίῳ στρατοπέδῳ συνῆπτεν, ὅθεν
508 ἤρξατο. τὸ μὲν οὖν τεῖχος ἑνὸς δέοντος τεσσαράκοντα σταδίων ἦν, ἔξωθεν δ' αὐτῷ προσ-
ῳκοδομήθη τρισκαίδεκα φρούρια, καὶ τούτων οἱ
509 κύκλοι δέκα συνηριθμοῦντο σταδίων. τρισὶ δ' ᾠκο-
δομήθη τὸ πᾶν ἡμέραις, ὡς τὸ μὲν ἔργον μηνῶν
[εἶναι] ἄξιον, τὸ τάχος δ' ἡττᾶσθαι πίστεως.
510 περικλείσας δὲ τῷ τείχει τὴν πόλιν καὶ δύναμιν
τοῖς φρουρίοις ἐγκαταστήσας, τὴν μὲν πρώτην
φυλακὴν τῆς νυκτὸς περιιὼν αὐτὸς ἐπεσκέπτετο,
τὴν δευτέραν δ' ἐπέτρεψεν Ἀλεξάνδρῳ, τὴν τρίτην
511 δ' ἔλαχον οἱ τῶν ταγμάτων ἡγεμόνες. διεκληροῦντο
δ' οἱ φύλακες τοὺς ὕπνους, καὶ δι' ὅλης νυκτὸς
περιῄεσαν κατὰ [τὰ] διαστήματα τῶν φρουρίων.
512 (3) Ἰουδαίοις δὲ μετὰ τῶν ἐξόδων ἀπεκόπη
πᾶσα σωτηρίας ἐλπίς, καὶ βαθύνας αὐτὸν ὁ λιμὸς
κατ' οἴκους καὶ γενεὰς τὸν δῆμον ἐπεβόσκετο.
513 καὶ τὰ μὲν τέγη πεπλήρωτο γυναικῶν καὶ βρεφῶν
λελυμένων, οἱ στενωποὶ δὲ γερόντων νεκρῶν,
παῖδες δὲ καὶ νεανίαι διοιδοῦντες ὥσπερ εἴδωλα
κατὰ τὰς ἀγορὰς ἀνειλοῦντο καὶ κατέπιπτον ὅπῃ
514 τινὰ τὸ πάθος καταλαμβάνοι. θάπτειν δὲ τοὺς
προσήκοντας οὔτ' ἴσχυον οἱ κάμνοντες καὶ τὸ
διευτονοῦν ὤκνει διά τε πλῆθος τῶν νεκρῶν καὶ
τὸ κατὰ σφᾶς ἄδηλον· πολλοὶ γοῦν τοῖς ὑπ' αὐτῶν

---

a According to *A.* xiv. 60 Pompey encamped "to the
north of the temple" (*cf. A.* xiv. 466, *B.* i. 343, "before the
temple"); the present passage appears to locate his camp
rather to the west of the temple.
358

Pompey encamped,[a] turned northwards, and proceeded to a village called " House of pulse," [b] after passing which it encompassed Herod's monument,[c] and so joined the east side of the general's own camp from which it had started. The wall was thirty-nine furlongs in length and had attached to its outer side thirteen forts, whose united circumferences amounted to ten furlongs. The whole was built in three days, such rapidity, over a work that might well have occupied months, being well-nigh incredible. Having enclosed the city within this wall and posted garrisons in the forts, Titus went round himself during the first watch of the night and inspected everything ; the second watch he entrusted to Alexander [d] ; for the third the commanders of the legions drew lots. The sentries, too, had their allotted hours of rest and all night long patrolled the intervals between the forts.

(3) For the Jews, along with all egress, every hope of escape was now cut off ; and the famine, enlarging its maw,[e] devoured the people by households and families. The roofs were thronged with women and babes completely exhausted, the alleys with the corpses of the aged ; children and youths, with swollen figures, roamed like phantoms through the market-places and collapsed wherever their doom overtook them. As for burying their relatives, the sick had not the strength, while those with vigour still left were deterred both by the multitude of the dead and by the uncertainty of their own fate.

Increased Jewish mortality.

Neglect of burial.

[b] Unidentified ; *cf.* the name Bethlehem (" house of bread ").   [c] § 108.
[d] Tiberius Alexander, § 45.
[e] Literally " deepening itself " ; perhaps " deepening (*i.e.* tightening) its grip." Famine is pictured as a bird of prey.

JOSEPHUS

θαπτομένοις ἐπαπέθνησκον, πολλοὶ δ' ἐπὶ τὰς
515 θήκας πρὶν ἐπιστῆναι τὸ χρεὼν προῆλθον. οὔτε
δὲ θρῆνος ἐν ταῖς συμφοραῖς οὔτ' ὀλοφυρμὸς ἦν,
ἀλλ' ὁ λιμὸς ἤλεγχε τὰ πάθη, ξηροῖς δὲ τοῖς
ὄμμασι καὶ σεσηρόσι τοῖς στόμασιν οἱ δυσθανα-
τοῦντες ἐφεώρων τοὺς φθάσαντας ἀναπαύσασθαι,
βαθεῖα δὲ περιεῖχεν τὴν πόλιν σιγὴ καὶ νὺξ θανάτου
γέμουσα καὶ τούτων οἱ λῃσταὶ χαλεπώτεροι.
516 τυμβωρυχοῦντες γοῦν τὰς οἰκίας ἐσύλων τοὺς
νεκροὺς καὶ τὰ καλύμματα τῶν σωμάτων περι-
σπῶντες μετὰ γέλωτος ἐξήεσαν, τάς τε αἰχμὰς[1] τῶν
ξιφῶν ἐδοκίμαζον ἐν τοῖς πτώμασιν, καί τινας
τῶν ἐρριμμένων ἔτι ζῶντας διήλαυνον ἐπὶ πείρᾳ
517 τοῦ σιδήρου· τοὺς δ' ἱκετεύοντας χρῆσαι σφίσι
δεξιὰν καὶ ξίφος τῷ λιμῷ κατέλειπον ὑπερηφανοῦν-
τες, καὶ τῶν ἐκπνεόντων ἕκαστος ἀτενίσας εἰς
τὸν ναὸν ἀφεώρα τοὺς στασιαστὰς ζῶντας ἀπο-
518 λιπών. οἱ δὲ τὸ μὲν πρῶτον ἐκ τοῦ δημοσίου
θησαυροῦ τοὺς νεκροὺς θάπτειν ἐκέλευον, τὴν ὀσμὴν
οὐ φέροντες, ἔπειθ' ὡς οὐ διήρκουν ἀπὸ τῶν
τειχῶν ἔρριπτον εἰς τὰς φάραγγας.
519 (4) Περιιὼν δὲ ταύτας ὁ Τίτος ὡς ἐθεάσατο
πεπλησμένας τῶν νεκρῶν καὶ βαθὺν ἰχῶρα μυδών-
των[2] ὑπορρέοντα τῶν σωμάτων, ἐστέναξέ τε καὶ
τὰς χεῖρας ἀνατείνας κατεμαρτύρατο τὸν θεόν,
520 ὡς οὐκ εἴη τὸ ἔργον αὐτοῦ. τὰ μὲν δὴ κατὰ τὴν
πόλιν εἶχεν οὕτως, Ῥωμαῖοι δὲ μηδενὸς ἔτι τῶν
στασιαστῶν ἐκτρέχοντος, ἤδη γὰρ καὶ τούτων
ἀθυμία καὶ λιμὸς ἐφήπτετο, πρὸς[3] εὐθυμίαις
ἦσαν σίτου τε ἀφθονίαν καὶ τῶν ἄλλων ἐπιτη-

---

[1] ἀκμὰς L Eus.   [2] + τὸν mss. (om. Bekker).
[3] After L: ἐπ' the rest.

360

For many fell dead while burying others, and many went forth to their tombs ere fate was upon them.[a] And amidst these calamities there was neither lamentation nor wailing : famine stifled the emotions, and with dry eyes and grinning mouths these slowly dying victims looked on those who had gone to their rest before them. The city, wrapped in profound silence and night laden with death, was in the grip of a yet fiercer foe—the brigands. For breaking into habitations that were now mere charnel-houses, they rifled the dead and stripping the coverings from the bodies departed with shouts of laughter ; they tried the points of their swords on the corpses and ran them through some of the prostrate but still living wretches, to test the temper of the blade, but any who implored them to lend them their hand and sword they disdainfully left to the mercy of the famine. And each victim expired with his eyes fixed on the temple and averted from the rebels whom he left alive. The latter at the outset ordered the bodies to be buried at the public expense, finding the stench intolerable ; afterwards, when incapable of continuing this, they flung them from the ramparts into the ravines.

(4) When Titus, going his rounds, beheld these valleys choked with dead and the thick matter oozing from under the clammy carcases, he groaned and, raising his hands to heaven, called God to witness that this was not his doing. Such was the situation within the city. Meanwhile the Romans, relieved from further sallies of the rebels (for now even these felt the grip of despondency and famine) were in the highest spirits, with abundant supplies of corn

---

[a] *i.e.* hastened their own end by attending the funeral of others.

δείων ἐκ τῆς Συρίας καὶ τῶν πλησίον ἐπαρχιῶν
521 ἔχοντες· ἱστάμενοι δὲ πολλοὶ τοῦ τείχους πλησίον
καὶ πολὺ πλῆθος τῶν ἐδωδίμων ἐπιδεικνύμενοι
τῷ κατὰ σφᾶς κόρῳ τὸν λιμὸν τῶν πολεμίων
522 ἐξέκαιον. πρὸς δὲ τὸ πάθος τῶν στασιαστῶν
μηδὲν ἐνδιδόντων, Τίτος οἰκτείρων τὰ λείψανα
τοῦ δήμου καὶ σπουδάζων τὸ γοῦν περιὸν ἐξ-
αρπάσαι, πάλιν ἤρχετο χωμάτων χαλεπῶς αὐτῷ
523 τῆς ὕλης ποριζομένης· ἡ μὲν γὰρ περὶ τὴν πόλιν
πᾶσα τοῖς προτέροις ἔργοις ἐκέκοπτο, συνεφόρουν
δ' ἄλλην ἀπ' ἐνενήκοντα σταδίων οἱ στρατιῶται.
καὶ πρὸς μόνης ὕψουν τῆς Ἀντωνίας κατὰ μέρη
τέσσαρα πολὺ μείζονα τῶν προτέρων χώματα.
524 περιὼν δ' ὁ Καῖσαρ τὰ τάγματα καὶ κατεπείγων
τὸ ἔργον ἐπεδείκνυ τοῖς λῃσταῖς, ὡς ἐν χερσὶν
525 εἴησαν αὐτοῦ. μόνοις δ' ἐκείνοις ἄρα κακῶν
ἀπολώλει μεταμέλεια, καὶ τὰς ψυχὰς χωρίσαντες
ἀπὸ τῶν σωμάτων ἀμφοτέροις ὡς ἀλλοτρίοις
526 ἐχρῶντο. οὔτε γὰρ πάθος αὐτῶν ἡμέρου τὴν
ψυχὴν οὔτ' ἀλγηδὼν ἥπτετο τοῦ σώματος, οἵ γε
καὶ νεκρὸν τὸν δῆμον ὥσπερ κύνες ἐσπάραττον
καὶ τὰ δεσμωτήρια τῶν ἀρρώστων ἐνεπίμπλασαν.
527 (xiii. 1) Σίμων γοῦν οὐδὲ Ματθίαν, δι' ὃν
κατέσχε τὴν πόλιν, ἀβασάνιστον ἀνεῖλε· Βοηθοῦ
παῖς ἦν οὗτος ἐκ τῶν ἀρχιερέων, ἐν τοῖς μάλιστα
528 τῷ δήμῳ πιστὸς καὶ τίμιος· ὃς ὑπὸ τοῖς ζηλωταῖς
κακουμένου τοῦ πλήθους, οἷς ἤδη καὶ Ἰωάννης
προσῆν, πείθει τὸν δῆμον εἰσαφεῖναι τὸν Σίμωνα

ᵃ *i.e.* becoming like brute beasts, they treated soul and
body as of no concern to them, they did not care what
happened to anyone's soul or body. I owe this suggestion

and other necessaries from Syria and the adjoining provinces; and many of them would approach the ramparts and, displaying masses of victuals, inflame by their superabundance the pangs of the enemy's hunger. The rebels still remaining unmoved by these sufferings, Titus, commiserating the remnants of the people and anxious at least to rescue the survivors, recommenced the erection of earth-works, though timber was now procured with difficulty; for, all the trees round the city having been felled for the previous works, the troops had to collect fresh material from a distance of ninety furlongs. The new mounds were raised only opposite Antonia, in four sections, and were much larger than the former embankments. Caesar, meanwhile, making the round of the legions and expediting operations, plainly showed the brigands that they were now in his hands. In them alone, however, all remorse for evils was extinct; and divorcing soul from body they treated both as aliens.[a] For neither could suffering tame their souls nor anguish affect their bodies, seeing that they continued, like dogs, to maul the very carcase of the people and to pack the prisons with the feeble.

New earthworks begun.

(xiii. 1) Simon indeed did not suffer even Matthias, to whom he owed his possession of the city, to go untortured to his death. This Matthias was the son of Boethus, claimed high-priestly ancestry, and had won the special confidence and esteem of the people. At the time when the multitude were being maltreated by the Zealots, to whom John had now attached himself, he had persuaded the citizens to

Simon murders Matthias, his former patron, and others.

to Dr T. E. Page; but the meaning of this artificial passage is doubtful.

βοηθόν, οὐδὲν οὔτε προσυνθέμενος οὔτε προσ-
529 δοκήσας φαῦλον ἐξ αὐτοῦ. παρελθὼν δ᾽ ἐκεῖνος
ὡς ἐκράτησε τῆς πόλεως, ἐχθρὸν ἐν ἴσῳ τοῖς
ἄλλοις ἡγεῖτο καὶ τὸν ὑπὲρ αὐτοῦ σύμβουλον
530 ὡς ἂν ἐξ ἁπλότητος γεγενημένον. ἀχθέντα δὲ
τηνικαῦτα καὶ κατηγορούμενον τὰ τῶν Ῥωμαίων
φρονεῖν κατακρίνει μὲν θανάτῳ, μηδ᾽ ἀπολογίας
ἀξιώσας, σὺν τρισὶν υἱοῖς· ὁ γὰρ τέταρτος ἔφθη
διαδρὰς πρὸς Τίτον· ἱκετεύοντα δ᾽ ἀναιρεθῆναι
πρὸ τῶν τέκνων καὶ ταύτην αἰτούμενον τὴν χάριν
ἀνθ᾽ ὧν ἀνοίξειεν αὐτῷ τὴν πόλιν, τελευταῖον
531 ἀνελεῖν ἐκέλευσεν. ὁ μὲν οὖν ἐν ὄψει φονευθεῖσιν[1]
ἐπεσφάγη τοῖς παισὶν ἀντικρὺς Ῥωμαίων προαχ-
θείς· οὕτω γὰρ ὁ Σίμων Ἀνάνῳ τῷ Βαγαδάτου[2]
προσέταξεν, ὃς ἦν ὠμότατος αὐτῷ τῶν δορυφόρων,
ἐπειρωνευόμενος, εἴ τι βοηθήσουσιν αὐτῷ πρὸς
οὓς ἐξελθεῖν εἵλετο, θάπτειν τ᾽ ἀπεῖπε τὰ σώματα.
532 μετὰ τούτους ἱερεύς τις Ἀνανίας υἱὸς Μασβάλου[3]
τῶν ἐπισήμων καὶ ὁ γραμματεὺς τῆς βουλῆς
Ἀριστεύς, γένος ἐξ Ἀμμαοῦς, καὶ σὺν τούτοις
πεντεκαίδεκα τῶν ἀπὸ τοῦ δήμου λαμπρῶν
533 ἀναιροῦνται. τὸν δὲ τοῦ Ἰωσήπου πατέρα συγ-
κλείσαντες ἐφύλαττον, κηρύττουσι δὲ μηδένι τῶν
κατὰ τὴν πόλιν μήτε συνομιλεῖν μήτ᾽ ἐπὶ ταὐτὸ
συναθροίζεσθαι δέει προδοσίας, καὶ τοὺς συν-
ολοφυρομένους πρὸ ἐξετάσεως ἀνῄρουν.

---

[1] φονευθεῖσιν Hudson from Lat.: φονευθεὶς MSS.
[2] PAM: Μαγαδάτου should perhaps be read, cf. vi. 229.
[3] Μασαμβάλου L Lat.

[a] iv. 574.

admit Simon as an ally,[a] without making any previous stipulation with him or anticipating foul play on his part. But when Simon had once entered and become master of the town, he considered the very man who had advocated his cause an enemy, equally with the rest, as having done so from pure simplicity. And now he had him brought up, accused him of siding with the Romans, and, without even granting him an opportunity of defence, condemned him to death, along with three of his sons; the fourth having already fled to Titus. Moreover, when Matthias entreated that he might be slain before his children, begging this favour in return for his having opened the gates to him, Simon ordered that he should be slain last. He was, accordingly, butchered over the bodies of his sons, who had been slaughtered before his eyes, after having been led out in view of the Romans; for such were the instructions given by Simon to Ananus,[b] son of Bagadates, the most truculent of his satellites, with the ironical remark, " Let him see whether his friends to whom he intended to desert will assist him." He moreover refused burial to the bodies. After these a priest named Ananias, son of Masbalus, a person of distinction, and Aristeus, the secretary of the council,[c] a native of Emmaus, and along with them fifteen eminent men from among the people were executed. They further detained the father of Josephus in prison, issued a proclamation forbidding any throughout the city to confabulate or congregate in one spot —for fear of treason—and put to death without inquiry persons taking part in joint lamentation.

[b] A native of Emmaus who afterwards deserted to the Romans, vi. 229.   [c] The Sanhedrin.

534 (2) Ταῦτα ὁρῶν Ἰούδης τις υἱὸς Ἰούδου, τῶν
ὑπάρχων τοῦ Σίμωνος εἷς ὢν καὶ πεπιστευμένος
ὑπ' αὐτοῦ πύργον φυλάττειν, τάχα μέν τι καὶ
οἴκτῳ τῶν ὠμῶς ἀπολλυμένων, τὸ δὲ πλέον αὐτοῦ
προνοίᾳ, συγκαλέσας τοὺς πιστοτάτους τῶν ὑπ'
535 αὐτὸν δέκα, "μέχρι τίνος ἀνθέξομεν," ἔφη,
"τοῖς κακοῖς; ἢ τίνα σωτηρίας ἔχομεν ἐλπίδα
536 πιστοὶ πονηρῷ μένοντες; οὐχ ὁ μὲν λιμὸς ἤδη
καθ' ἡμῶν, Ῥωμαῖοι δὲ παρὰ μικρὸν ἔνδον,
Σίμων δὲ καὶ πρὸς εὐεργέτας ἄπιστος, καὶ
δέος μὲν ἤδη παρ' αὐτοῦ κολάσεως, ἡ δὲ παρὰ
Ῥωμαίοις δεξιὰ βέβαιος; φέρε, παραδόντες τὸ
537 τεῖχος σώσωμεν ἑαυτοὺς καὶ τὴν πόλιν. πείσεται
δ' οὐδὲν δεινὸν Σίμων, ἐὰν ἀπεγνωκὼς ἑαυτὸν
538 τάχιον δῷ δίκην." τούτοις τῶν δέκα πεισθέντων
ὑπὸ τὴν ἕω τοὺς λοιποὺς τῶν ὑποτεταγμένων
ἄλλον ἀλλαχόσε διέπεμπεν, ὡς μὴ φωραθείη τι
τῶν βεβουλευμένων, αὐτὸς δὲ περὶ τρίτην ὥραν
539 ἀπὸ τοῦ πύργου τοὺς Ῥωμαίους ἐκάλει. τῶν δ'
οἱ μὲν ὑπερηφάνουν, οἱ δὲ ἠπίστουν, οἱ πολλοὶ δ'
ὤκνουν ὡς μετὰ μικρὸν ἀκινδύνως ληψόμενοι τὴν
540 πόλιν. ἐν ὅσῳ δὲ Τίτος μεθ' ὁπλιτῶν παρῄει
πρὸς τὸ τεῖχος, ἔφθη γνοὺς ὁ Σίμων, καὶ μετὰ
τάχους τόν τε πύργον προκαταλαμβάνει καὶ τοὺς
ἄνδρας συλλαβὼν ἐν ὄψει τῶν Ῥωμαίων ἀναιρεῖ
καὶ πρὸ τοῦ τείχους λωβησάμενος ἔρριψε τὰ
σώματα.

541 (3) Κἀν τούτῳ περιὼν Ἰώσηπος, οὐ γὰρ ἀνίει
παρακαλῶν, βάλλεται τὴν κεφαλὴν λίθῳ καὶ
παραχρῆμα πίπτει καρωθείς. ἐκδρομὴ δὲ ἐπὶ τὸ

(2) A spectator of these scenes, Judes, son of Judes, Plot to surrender the city discovered by Simon. one of Simon's lieutenants and entrusted by him with the custody of a tower, partly perhaps out of compassion for the victims thus cruelly slain, but mainly thinking of his own safety, called together ten of the men under him on whom he could most rely and said : " How long are we to tolerate these crimes ? Or what prospect have we of escaping by keeping faith with this villain ? Is not the famine already upon us, the Roman army all but in the town, and Simon treacherous even to his benefactors ? Have we not reason to fear that he will soon punish us, while a Roman pledge can be trusted ? Come, let us surrender the ramparts and save ourselves and the city ! Simon will suffer no great hardship if, despairing of his life, he is brought sooner to justice." The ten assenting to these proposals, early next morning he dispatched the rest of the men under his command in various directions, to prevent any discovery of the plot, and about the third hour called to the Romans from the tower. Of the latter some disdained him, others were incredulous, while the majority shrank from interfering, certain of taking the city ere long without running any risks. However, while Titus was preparing to advance to the wall with a body of troops, Simon, receiving timely intelligence, forestalled him by promptly occupying the tower, arrested and slew the men in full view of the Romans, and after mutilating their bodies flung them over the ramparts.

(3) Meanwhile, Josephus while going his rounds— Josephus is hit and reported killed. for he was unremitting in his exhortations—was struck on the head with a stone and instantly dropped insensible. The Jews made a rush for the body, and

πτῶμα[1] τῶν Ἰουδαίων γίνεται, κἂν ἔφθη συρεὶς
εἰς τὴν πόλιν, εἰ μὴ ταχέως Καῖσαρ ἔπεμψε τοὺς
542 ὑπερασπίζοντας. μαχομένων δὲ τούτων ὁ Ἰώσηπος μὲν αἴρεται βραχύ τι τῶν πραττομένων
ἐπαΐων, οἱ στασιασταὶ δ᾽ ὡς ἀνελόντες ὃν ἐπ-
543 εθύμουν μάλιστα μετὰ χαρᾶς ἀνεβόων. διαγ-
γέλλεταί τε εἰς τὴν πόλιν, καὶ τὸ καταλειπόμενον
πλῆθος ἐπέσχεν ἀθυμία, πεπεισμένους οἴχεσθαι
544 τῷ ὄντι δι᾽ ὃν αὐτομολεῖν ἐθάρρουν. ἀκούσασα
δ᾽ ἡ τοῦ Ἰωσήπου μήτηρ ἐν τῷ δεσμωτηρίῳ
τεθνάναι τὸν υἱόν, πρὸς μὲν τοὺς φύλακας ἀπὸ Ἰωταπάτων τοῦτ᾽ ἔφη πεπεῖσθαι· καὶ γὰρ οὐδὲ
545 ζῶντος ἀπολαύειν· ἰδίᾳ δ᾽ ὀλοφυρομένη πρὸς τὰς
θεραπαινίδας τοῦτον εἰληφέναι τῆς εὐτεκνίας ἔλεγε
καρπὸν τὸ μηδὲ θάψαι τὸν υἱόν, ὑφ᾽ οὗ ταφή-
546 σεσθαι προσεδόκησεν. ἀλλὰ γὰρ οὔτε ταύτην
ἐπὶ πλέον ὠδύνα τὸ ψεῦδος οὔτε τοὺς λῃστὰς
ἔθαλπε· ταχέως γὰρ ἐκ τῆς πληγῆς ἀνήνεγκεν ὁ
Ἰώσηπος, καὶ προελθὼν τοὺς μὲν οὐκ εἰς μακρὰν
ἐβόα δίκας αὐτῷ δώσειν τοῦ τραύματος, τὸν δὲ
547 δῆμον ἐπὶ πίστιν πάλιν προυκαλεῖτο. θάρσος δὲ
τῷ λαῷ καὶ τοῖς στασιασταῖς ἔκπληξις ἐμπίπτει
πρὸς τὴν ὄψιν αὐτοῦ.
548 (4) Τῶν δ᾽ αὐτομόλων οἱ μὲν ὑπ᾽ ἀνάγκης ἀπὸ
τοῦ τείχους ἐπήδων ταχέως, οἱ δὲ προϊόντες ὡς
ἐπὶ μάχῃ μετὰ χερμάδων ἔπειτα πρὸς τοὺς
Ῥωμαίους ἔφευγον. συνείπετο δὲ τούτοις τύχη
τῶν εἴσω χαλεπωτέρα, καὶ τοῦ παρὰ σφίσι λιμοῦ
συντομώτερον[2] εὕρισκον πρὸς ὄλεθρον τὸν παρὰ

---

[1] τὸ πτῶμα] τῷ πτώματι MVRC.
[2] L Lat. (velociorem): συντονώτερον the rest.

he would have been dragged into the city, had not
Caesar promptly sent out a rescue party. During
the ensuing conflict Josephus was borne away, little
conscious of what was passing; while the rebels,
supposing that they had killed the man for whose
blood they thirsted most, shouted with delight. The
rumour spreading to the town, the residue of the
populace were deeply dejected, believing that he
who gave them courage to desert had really perished.
The mother of Josephus, hearing in prison that her
son was dead, remarked to her warders, " Ever since
Jotapata[a] I was sure of it; indeed I had no joy of
him in his lifetime "; but in private lamentation to
her handmaidens she said, " This, then, is the fruit
that I reap of my blessed child-bearing that I am to
be denied the burial of the son by whom I hoped to
have been buried." Happily, however, neither the
distress which this false report occasioned her nor
the solace which it brought to the brigands was of
long duration; for Josephus, quickly recovering from
the blow, came forward and, shouting to his foes
that he would ere long be avenged on them for his
wound, renewed his exhortations to the citizens to
accept his assurances. The sight of him animated
the people and filled the rebels with dismay.

(4) As for the deserters, some, having no alter-
native, hastily leapt from the ramparts; others,
starting out with stones, as for a skirmish, then fled
to the Romans. Hither, however, a harsher fate
pursued them than that of their comrades within;
and they found satiety in the Roman camp more
rapidly[b] fatal than the famine which they had left

Horrible fate of Jewish refugees ripped open by Syrians and Arabs.

---

[a] Or perhaps " when the news came from Jotapata ";
cf. iii. 432 ff.   [b] Or (with the other reading) " drastically."

549 Ῥωμαίοις κόρον. παρεγίνοντο μὲν γὰρ ἀπὸ τῆς
ἐνδείας πεφυσημένοι καὶ ὥσπερ ὑδρωπιῶντες,
ἔπειτα ἀθρόως κενοῖς ὑπερεμπιπλάμενοι τοῖς
σώμασιν ἐρρήγνυντο, πλὴν τῶν δι' ἐμπειρίαν
ταμιευσαμένων τὰς ὀρέξεις καὶ κατ' ὀλίγον προσ-
θέντων τροφὴν ἀπειθισμένῳ τῷ σώματι φέρειν.

550 καὶ τοὺς οὕτω δὲ σωζομένους ἑτέρα πληγὴ μετ-
ελάμβανε· τῶν γὰρ παρὰ τοῖς Σύροις τις αὐτομόλων φωρᾶται τῶν τῆς γαστρὸς λυμάτων χρυσοῦς
ἐκλέγων· καταπιόντες[1] δ', ὡς ἔφαμεν, αὐτοὺς
προήεσαν, ἐπειδὴ διηρεύνων[2] πάντας οἱ στασιασταί,
καὶ πολὺ πλῆθος ἦν ἐν τῇ πόλει χρυσοῦ· δώδεκα
γοῦν Ἀττικῶν ὠνοῦντο πρότερον ἰσχύοντας[3] πέντε

551 καὶ εἴκοσιν. ἀλλά τοι τῆς ἐπινοίας ἐλεγχθείσης
δι' ἑνός, ἀναπίμπλαται μὲν φήμης[4] τὰ στρατόπεδα,
ὡς μεστοὶ χρυσίου παρεῖεν οἱ αὐτόμολοι, τὸ δὲ τῶν
Ἀράβων πλῆθος καὶ οἱ Σύροι τοὺς ἱκέτας ἀνα-

552 τέμνοντες ἠρεύνων τὰς γαστέρας. καὶ τούτου
τοῦ πάθους οὐδὲν ἔμοιγε δοκεῖ συμβῆναι Ἰουδαίοις χαλεπώτερον· μιᾷ γοῦν ἀνεσχίσθησαν νυκτὶ
πρὸς δισχιλίους.

553 (5) Καὶ γνοὺς τὴν παρανομίαν Τίτος ὀλίγου
μὲν ἐδέησε τὸ ἱππικὸν περιστήσας κατακοντίσαι
τοὺς αἰτίους, εἰ μὴ πολὺ πλῆθος ἐνείχετο καὶ
τῶν ἀνῃρημένων πολλαπλασίους ἦσαν οἱ κολα-

554 σθησόμενοι. συγκαλέσας δὲ τούς τε τῶν συμμάχων
ἡγεμόνας καὶ τοὺς τῶν ταγμάτων, συνδιεβάλλοντο
γὰρ καὶ τῶν στρατιωτῶν τινες, πρὸς ἑκατέρους

---

[1] Herwerden : καταπίνοντες mss.
[2] Destinon (avoiding hiatus): ἀνηρεύνων mss.
[3] PAL: ἰσχύοντα the rest.
[4] Holwerda : φήμη εἰς mss.

at home. For they arrived swollen from hunger, like persons afflicted with dropsy, and then, overcharging at a gulp their empty stomachs, burst asunder; though some had learnt by experience to restrain their appetites and little by little administered nourishment to bodies unused to the load. But even those who thus escaped were overtaken later by another catastrophe. For one of the refugees in the Syrian ranks was discovered picking gold coins from his excrements; these pieces, as we have said,[a] they had swallowed before their departure, because they were all searched by the rebels and gold was so abundant in the town that they could purchase for twelve Attic drachmas coin formerly worth five-and-twenty.[b] This artifice being, however, detected in one instance, a rumour ran through the camps that the deserters had come full of gold, whereupon the Arab rabble with the Syrians proceeded to cut open the suppliants and search their intestines. No more cruel calamity, in my opinion, befell the Jews than this: actually in one night no less than two thousand were ripped up.

(5) On learning of this outrage Titus very nearly ordered his horse to surround the culprits and shoot them down, being only checked by the multitude of persons implicated, those who would have to be punished far outnumbering their victims. Summoning, however, the commanders both of the auxiliaries and of the legions (for some of his own soldiers also were involved in the charge) and addressing both

Titus severely reprimands his troops.

---

[a] § 421.
[b] *Cf.* vi. 317 (in consequence of the plunder of Jerusalem) "throughout Syria the standard of gold was depreciated to half its former value."

371

555 ἀγανακτεῖν[1] ἔλεγεν, εἰ τῶν μὲν σὺν αὐτῷ στρατευομένων τινὲς τοιαῦτα δρῶσιν κέρδους ἕνεκεν
ἀδήλου, μηδὲ τὰ ὅπλα σφῶν αὐτῶν αἰδούμενοι
556 πεποιημένα ἀργύρου τε καὶ χρυσοῦ, τοῖς δ'
Ἄραψι καὶ τοῖς Σύροις, εἰ πρῶτον μὲν ἐν ἀλλοτρίῳ
πολέμῳ τοῖς πάθεσιν αὐτεξουσίως χρῶνται, ἔπειτα
τῇ περὶ φόνους ὠμότητι καὶ τῷ πρὸς Ἰουδαίους
μίσει Ῥωμαίους ἐπιγράφουσι· καὶ γὰρ νῦν ἐνίους
αὐτῶν[2] τῶν στρατιωτῶν συναπολαύειν τῆς κακο-
557 δοξίας. τούτοις μὲν οὖν διηπείλησε θάνατον, εἴ
τις εὑρεθείη πάλιν τὸ αὐτὸ τολμῶν, τοῖς δ' ἀπὸ
τῶν ταγμάτων ἐπέστελλεν ἐρευνήσαντας τοὺς
558 ὑπόπτους ἀνάγειν ἐπ' αὐτόν. καταφρονεῖ[3] δ',
ὡς ἔοικε, φιλοχρηματία πάσης κολάσεως, καὶ
δεινὸς ἐμπέφυκεν ἀνθρώποις τοῦ κερδαίνειν ἔρως,
οὐδέν τε οὕτως πάθος ⟨ὡς⟩[4] πλεονεξία παρα-
559 βάλλεται. ἢ ταῦτα μὲν ἄλλως καὶ μέτρον ἔχει
καὶ φόβοις ὑποτάσσεται, θεὸς δ' ἦν ὁ τοῦ λαοῦ
παντὸς κατακρίνας καὶ πᾶσαν αὐτοῖς σωτηρίας
560 ὁδὸν εἰς ἀπώλειαν ἀποστρέφων. ὃ γοῦν μετ'
ἀπειλῆς ἀπεῖπεν ὁ Καῖσαρ λάθρα κατὰ τῶν
αὐτομόλων ἐτολμᾶτο, καὶ τοὺς διαδιδράσκοντας
πρὶν πᾶσιν ὀφθῆναι προαπαντῶντες ἀπέσφαττον
οἱ βάρβαροι, περισκοπούμενοι δέ, μή τις ἐπίδοι
Ῥωμαίων, ἀνέσχιζον κἀκ τῶν σπλάγχνων τὸ
561 μιαρὸν κέρδος εἷλκον. ὀλίγοις δ' ἐνευρίσκετο, καὶ
τοὺς πολλοὺς παρανήλισκεν ἐλπὶς μόνη. τοῦτο μὲν
δὴ τὸ πάθος πολλοὺς τῶν αὐτομόλων ἐπανήγαγεν.
562 (6) Ἰωάννης δ' ὡς ἐπέλειπον αἱ ἁρπαγαὶ παρὰ

---

[1] ἀγανακτεῖν Bekker: ἀγανακτῶν mss.   [2] αὐτῷ VRC.
[3] Destinon with Lat.: κατεφρόνει mss.
[4] ins. Hudson: Niese omits πλεονεξία.

372

groups, he said that he was indignant that soldiers in his service should be guilty of such acts for the sake of uncertain lucre, and did not blush for their own arms, made of silver and gold. To the Arabs and Syrians he expressed his wrath, first at the idea that in a foreign war they should give unrestrained licence to their passions, and next that they should induce Romans to lend their name to their own murderous brutality and hatred of the Jews, seeing that some of the very legionaries now shared their infamy. These foreigners he threatened with death, should any be found daring to repeat the crime; the legionaries he directed to search for suspected offenders and to bring them up to him. But avarice, it seems, defies all punishment and a dire love of gain is ingrained in human nature, no other passion being so headstrong as greed; though, in truth, in other circumstances these passions observe some bounds and submit to deterrents, but here God and no other had condemned His whole people and was turning every avenue of salvation to their destruction. Thus what Caesar had prohibited with threats men still ventured furtively to practise upon the deserters: advancing to meet the fugitives before the troops had caught sight of them, these barbarians would massacre them, and then, looking round to see that no Roman eye was upon them, rip them up and extract the filthy lucre from their bowels. In few only was it found: the bare hope of finding it caused the wanton destruction of most. This calamity in fact drove many of the deserters back.

(6) John when the plunder from the people failed

τοῦ δήμου, πρὸς ἱεροσυλίαν ἐτρέπετο, καὶ πολλὰ
μὲν τῶν ἀναθημάτων κατεχώνευεν ἐκ τοῦ ναοῦ,
πολλὰ δὲ τῶν πρὸς τὰς λειτουργίας ἀναγκαίων
σκεύη, κρατῆρας [τε] καὶ πίνακας καὶ τραπέζας·
ἀπέσχετο δ' οὐδὲ τῶν ὑπὸ τοῦ Σεβαστοῦ καὶ
563 τῆς γυναικὸς αὐτοῦ πεμφθέντων ἀκρατοφόρων. οἱ
μέν γε Ῥωμαίων βασιλεῖς ἐτίμησάν τε καὶ προσ-
εκόσμησαν τὸ ἱερὸν ἀεί, τότε δ' ὁ Ἰουδαῖος
564 καὶ τὰ τῶν ἀλλοφύλων κατέσπα. πρὸς δὲ τοὺς
συνόντας ἔλεγεν, ὡς δεῖ μετ' ἀδείας καταχρήσασθαι
τοῖς θείοις ὑπὲρ τοῦ θείου καὶ τοὺς τῷ ναῷ στρα-
565 τευομένους ἐξ αὐτοῦ τρέφεσθαι. διὰ τοῦτο καὶ
τὸν ἱερὸν οἶνον καὶ τὸ ἔλαιον, ὃ τοῖς ὁλοκαυτώμασιν
οἱ ἱερεῖς ἐφύλαττον [ἐπιχεῖν],[1] ἐκκενώσας, ἦν
δ' ἐν τῷ ἔνδον ἱερῷ, διένεμε τῷ πλήθει, κἀκεῖνοι
δίχα φρίκης[2] ἠλείφοντο καὶ ἔπινον [ἐξ αὐτῶν].[3]
566 οὐκ ἂν ὑποστειλαίμην εἰπεῖν ἅ μοι κελεύει τὸ
πάθος· οἶμαι Ῥωμαίων βραδυνόντων ἐπὶ τοὺς
ἀλιτηρίους ἢ καταποθῆναι ἂν ὑπὸ χάσματος ἢ
κατακλυσθῆναι τὴν πόλιν ἢ τοὺς τῆς Σοδομηνῆς
μεταλαβεῖν κεραυνούς· πολὺ γὰρ τῶν ταῦτα
παθόντων ἤνεγκε γενεὰν ἀθεωτέραν· τῇ γοῦν
τούτων ἀπονοίᾳ πᾶς ὁ λαὸς συναπώλετο.
567 (7) Καὶ τί δεῖ κατὰ μέρος ἐκδιηγεῖσθαι τὰς
συμφοράς; ἀλλὰ πρὸς Τίτον ἐν ταύταις ταῖς
ἡμέραις Μανναῖος ὁ Λαζάρου φυγὼν διὰ μιᾶς
ἔλεγεν ἐκκεκομίσθαι πύλης, ἣν αὐτὸς ἐπεπίστευ-

---

[1] LVRC: ἐπεισχεῖν, ἐπεῖχεν or ἐπέχεεν the rest: om. Lat.
[2] PA Lat. Exc.: + πλέον τοῦ ἵν the rest.
[3] om. Lat.

---

[a] Cf. 1 Cor. ix. 13.
[b] According to the Mishna, *Middoth* ii. 6, the wine and

him, had recourse to sacrilege, melting down many John's sacrilegious plundering of the temple. of the temple-offerings and many of the vessels required for public worship, bowls and salvers and tables ; nor did he abstain from the vessels for pure wine sent by Augustus and his consort. For the Roman sovereigns ever honoured and added embellishment to the temple, whereas this Jew now pulled down even the donations of foreigners, remarking to his companions that they should not scruple to employ divine things on the Divinity's behalf, and that those who fought for the temple should be supported by it.^{a} He accordingly drew every drop of the sacred wine and of the oil, which the priests kept for pouring upon the burnt-offerings and which stood in the inner temple,^{b} and distributed these to his horde, who without horror anointed themselves and drank therefrom.^{c} Nor can I here refrain from uttering what my emotion bids me say. I believe that, had the Romans delayed to punish these reprobates, either the earth would have opened and swallowed up the city,^{d} or it would have been swept away by a flood,^{e} or have tasted anew the thunderbolts of the land of Sodom. For it produced a generation far more godless than the victims of those visitations, seeing that these men's frenzy involved the whole people in their ruin.

(7) But why need I severally recount the calamities ? Why, indeed, when Mannaeus, son of Lazarus, who sought refuge in those days with Titus, reported that there were carried out through a single gate, oil were stored in a chamber at the S.W. corner of the Women's Court.

Numbers of the dead in Jerusalem.

^{c} Some mss. add " more than a hin."
^{d} Like Korah and his company, Numb. xvi. 32.
^{e} Like the generation of Noah.

το, μυριάδας ἔνδεκα νεκρῶν ἐπὶ πεντακισχιλίοις
ὀκτακοσίοις ὀγδοήκοντα, ἀφ' ἧς αὐτοῖς ἡμέρας
παρεστρατοπεδεύσατο τεσσαρεσκαιδεκάτῃ Ξανθικοῦ
568 μηνὸς ἄχρι Πανέμου νουμηνίας. τοῦτο δ' ἦν
πλῆθος ἀπόρων· καὶ οὐδὲ αὐτὸς ἐφεστώς, ἀλλὰ
δημοσίᾳ μισθὸν διδοὺς ἐξ ἀνάγκης ἠρίθμει. τοὺς
δὲ λοιποὺς οἱ προσήκοντες ἔθαπτον· ταφὴ δ'
569 ἦν τὸ προκομίσαντας ἐκ τοῦ ἄστεος ῥῖψαι. μετὰ
δὲ τοῦτον διαδράντες πολλοὶ τῶν ἐπισήμων τὰς
πάσας τῶν ἀπόρων νεκρῶν ἀπήγγελλον μυριάδας
ἑξήκοντα διὰ τῶν πυλῶν ἐκριφῆναι, τῶν δ' ἄλλων
570 ἀνεξερεύνητον εἶναι τὸν ἀριθμόν. μηκέτι δ' εὐ-
τονούντων τοὺς πτωχοὺς ἐκφέρειν, [ἔλεγον]¹ συσ-
σωρεύοντας εἰς τοὺς μεγίστους οἴκους τὰ πτώματα
571 ἀποκλείειν. καὶ τοῦ μὲν σίτου τὸ μέτρον πραθῆναι
ταλάντου, μετὰ ταῦτα δ' ὡς οὐδὲ ποηλογεῖν ἔθ'
οἷόν τ' ἦν περιτειχισθείσης τῆς πόλεως, προελθεῖν
τινας εἰς τοσοῦτον ἀνάγκης, ὥστε τὰς ἀμάρας
ἐρευνῶντας καὶ παλαιὸν ὄνθον βοῶν προσφέρεσθαι
τὰ ἐκ τούτων σκύβαλα, καὶ τὸ μηδ' ὄψει φορητὸν
572 πάλαι τότε γενέσθαι τροφήν. ταῦτα Ῥωμαῖοι
μὲν ἀκούοντες ἠλέησαν, οἱ στασιασταὶ δὲ καὶ
βλέποντες οὐ μετενόουν, ἀλλ' ἠνείχοντο μέχρις
αὐτῶν προελθεῖν· πεπήρωντο γὰρ ὑπὸ τοῦ χρεών,
ὃ τῇ τε πόλει καὶ αὐτοῖς ἤδη παρῆν.

¹ om. P Lat.

ᵃ § 133.
ᵇ *i.e.* between 1 May and 20 July, A.D. 70 (Niese).
ᶜ Or " chambers."
ᵈ These two rare words are Homeric (ἀμαρά *Il.* xxi. 259 ; ὄνθος xxiii. 775-7).

which had been entrusted to him, 115,880 corpses, between the fourteenth of the month Xanthicus, on which the general encamped before their walls,[a] and the new moon of Panemus[b]? All these were of the poorer class; nor had he undertaken this charge himself, but being responsible for the payment of public funds he was bound to keep count. The remainder were buried by their relatives, burial consisting merely in bringing them forth and casting them out of the town. This refugee was followed by many eminent citizens, who reported that the corpses of the lower classes thrown out through the gates amounted in all to 600,000; of the rest it was impossible to discover the number. They added that, when strength failed them to carry out the poor, they piled the bodies in the largest mansions[c] and shut them up; also that a measure of corn had been sold for a talent, and that later when it was no longer possible to gather herbs, the city being all walled in, some were reduced to such straits that they searched the sewers[d] and for old cow dung[d] and ate the offal therefrom, and what once would have disgusted them to look at had now become food. The tale of these horrors aroused the compassion of the Romans; yet the rebels who witnessed them relented not, but endured to go even to these extremes.[e] For they were blinded by Fate, which, alike for the city and for themselves, was now imminent.

---

[e] Or, taking αὐτῶν, as masculine, = αὐτῶν with Hudson and others, "patiebantur ea usque ad ipsos progredi." For αὐτῶν neuter, as translated above, cf. e.g. A. xv. 182 μέχρι τοῦδε προελθεῖν.

ΒΙΒΛΙΟΝ ς

1 (i. 1) Τὰ μὲν οὖν τῶν Ἱεροσολύμων πάθη
προύκοπτεν καθ᾿ ἡμέραν ἐπὶ τὸ χεῖρον, τῶν τε
στασιαστῶν μᾶλλον παροξυνομένων [ἐν][1] ταῖς συμφοραῖς καὶ τοῦ λιμοῦ μετὰ τὸν δῆμον ἤδη κἀκείνους
2 νεμομένου. τό γε μὴν πλῆθος τῶν σεσωρευμένων
ἀνὰ τὴν πόλιν πτωμάτων ὄψει τε φρικῶδες ἦν καὶ
λοιμώδη προσέβαλλεν ὀσμήν, πρός τε τὰς ἐκδρομὰς
ἐμπόδιον τοῖς μαχομένοις· ὥσπερ γὰρ διὰ παρατάξεως φόνῳ μυρίῳ γεγυμνασμένους[2] χωροῦντας
3 ἔδει τὰ σώματα πατεῖν. οἱ δ᾿ ἐπιβαίνοντες οὔτ᾿
ἔφριττον οὔτ᾿ ἠλέουν οὔτε κληδόνα κακὴν σφῶν
αὐτῶν ὑπελάμβανον τὴν εἰς τοὺς κατοιχομένους
4 ὕβριν, πεφυρμένοι δ᾿ ὁμοφύλῳ φόνῳ τὰς δεξιὰς
ἐπὶ τὸν πρὸς τοὺς ἀλλοφύλους πόλεμον ἐξέθεον,
ὀνειδίζοντες ἔμοιγε δοκεῖν τὸ θεῖον εἰς βραδυτῆτα
τῆς ἐπ᾿ αὐτῶν[3] κολάσεως· οὐ γὰρ ἐλπίδι νίκης ὁ
πόλεμος, ἤδη δὲ ἀπογνώσει σωτηρίας ἐθρασύνετο.
5 Ῥωμαῖοι δὲ καίτοι πολλὰ περὶ τὴν τῆς ὕλης
συγκομιδὴν ταλαιπωρούμενοι τὰ χώματα διήγειραν
μιᾷ καὶ εἴκοσιν ἡμέραις, κείραντες, ὡς προείρηται,
τὴν περὶ τὸ ἄστυ χώραν ἐπ᾿ ἐνενήκοντα σταδίους
6 ἐν κύκλῳ πᾶσαν. ἦν δ᾿ ἐλεεινὴ καὶ τῆς γῆς ἡ θέα·

---

[1] om. L Lat. Exc.
[2] PALC: γεγυμνασμένης MVR (Lat.).
[3] PA: αὐτοὺς L Exc.: αὐτοῖς the rest.

378

BOOK VI

(i. 1) THE sufferings of Jerusalem thus daily grew New Roman earthworks completed. worse, the fury of the rebels being intensified by the calamities in which they were involved, and the famine now extending its ravages from the people to themselves. The piles of corpses throughout the city, presenting a horrible spectacle and emitting a pestilential stench, were, moreover, an impediment to the combatants in their sallies; for, like men inured to countless carnage on the battlefield, they were compelled on the march to trample over the bodies.[a] Yet, they set foot on them without a shudder, without pity, without a thought of any evil omen to themselves from this outrage to the departed. With hands imbrued with the blood of their countrymen they rushed forth to war with the foreigner, upbraiding the Deity (so I cannot but think) for His tardiness in punishing them; for it was no hope of victory but despair of escape which now nerved them to the battle. The Romans, meanwhile, though sorely harassed in the collection of timber, had completed their earthworks in one and twenty days, having, as already stated,[b] cleared the whole district around the town to a distance of ninety furlongs. Pitiful too was the aspect of the country,

[a] Or (with the other reading) " like men advancing over a battlefield strewn (literally ' exercised ') with countless carnage they were compelled to trample," etc.   [b] v. 523.

τὰ γὰρ πάλαι δένδρεσι καὶ παραδείσοις κεκοσμη-
μένα τότε πανταχόθεν ἠρήμωτο καὶ περικέκοπτο
7 τὴν ὕλην, οὐδείς τε τὴν πάλαι Ἰουδαίαν καὶ τὰ
περικαλλῆ προάστεια τῆς πόλεως ἑωρακὼς ἀλλό-
φυλος, ἔπειτα τὴν τότε βλέπων ἐρημίαν οὐκ
ὠλοφύρατο καὶ κατεστέναξεν τὴν μεταβολὴν παρ'
8 ὅσον γένοιτο· πάντα γὰρ ἐλυμήνατο τὰ σημεῖα τοῦ
κάλλους ὁ πόλεμος, καὶ οὐκ ἄν τις ἐξαπίνης ἐπι-
στὰς τῶν προεγνωκότων ἐγνώρισε τὸν τόπον, ἀλλὰ
παρὼν ἐζήτει τὴν πόλιν.
9   (2) Ῥωμαίοις δὲ καὶ Ἰουδαίοις τὸ τέλος τῶν
10 χωμάτων ἴσην ἐνεποίει δέους ἀρχήν· οἱ μὲν γάρ,
εἰ μὴ καὶ ταῦτα καύσειαν, ἁλώσεσθαι τὴν πόλιν
προσεδόκων, Ῥωμαῖοι δ' οὐκέθ'[1] αἱρήσειν κἀκείνων
11 διαφθαρέντων. ὕλης τε γὰρ ἦν ἀπορία, καὶ τῶν
μὲν πόνων ἤδη τὸ σῶμα,[2] τῶν δ' ἐπαλλήλων πται-
12 σμάτων αἱ ψυχαὶ τοῖς στρατιώταις ἐλείποντο. τάς
γε μὴν κατὰ τὴν πόλιν συμφορὰς Ῥωμαίοις πλέον
εἶναι συνέβαινε πρὸς ἀθυμίας ἢ τοῖς ἐν αὐτῇ·
παρὰ γὰρ τὰ τηλικαῦτα πάθη τοῖς μαχομένοις
13 οὐδὲν ἐχρῶντο μαλακωτέροις, ἀλλ' ἐθραύοντο
πάντοτε τὰς ἐλπίδας, τῶν μὲν χωμάτων ταῖς
ἐπιβουλαῖς, τῶν δ' ὀργάνων στερρότητι τοῦ τείχους,
τῆς δὲ κατὰ χεῖρα μάχης ταῖς τῶν συμπλεκομένων
τόλμαις πλεονεκτούμενοι, τὸ δὲ μέγιστον, στάσεώς
τε καὶ λιμοῦ καὶ πολέμου καὶ τοσούτων κακῶν
εὑρίσκοντες ἐπάνω τὸ παράστημα τῆς ψυχῆς
14 Ἰουδαίους ἔχοντας. ὑπελάμβανόν τε[3] τῶν ἀνδρῶν
ἀμάχους μὲν τὰς ὁρμάς, ἀνάλωτον δὲ τὴν ἐπὶ
συμφοραῖς εὐθυμίαν εἶναι· τί γὰρ ἂν μὴ ὑποστῆναι

---

[1] οὐκέθ' Herwerden : οὐκ ἂν ἔθ' mss.
[2] τὰ σώματα M Lat.
[3] om. Lat. Syr.

sites formerly beautified with trees and parks now Judaea and
reduced to an utter desert and stripped bare of Jerusalem unrecogniz-
timber ; and no stranger who had seen the old able.
Judaea and the entrancingly beautiful suburbs of
her capital, and now beheld her present desolation,
could have refrained from tears or suppressed a sigh
at the greatness of the change. For the war had
ruined all the marks of beauty, and no one who
knew it of old, coming suddenly upon it, would have
recognized the place, but, though beside it, he would
have looked for the city.

(2) The completion of the earthworks proved, to Dejection of
the Romans no less than to the Jews, a source of the Romans.
apprehension. For, while the latter thought that,
should they fail to burn these also, the city would
be taken, the Romans feared that they would never
take it, should these embankments too be destroyed.
For there was a dearth of materials, and the soldiers'
bodies were now sinking beneath their toils, and their
minds under a succession of reverses. Indeed, the
calamities of the city caused more despondency to
the Romans than to the citizens, for they found
their opponents in no wise chastened by their severe
misfortunes, while their own hopes were continually
dashed, their earthworks mastered by the enemy's
stratagems, their engines by the solidity of the walls,
their close combat by the daring of their antagonists.
But worst of all was the discovery that the Jews
possessed a fortitude of soul that could surmount
faction, famine, war and such a host of calamities.
They fancied the impetuosity of these men to
be irresistible and their cheerfulness in distress
invincible ; for what would they not endure if

δεξιᾷ τύχῃ χρωμένους τοὺς ὑπὸ κακῶν πρὸς ἀλκὴν
τρεπομένους; οἱ μὲν οὖν ἐρρωμενεστέρας διὰ ταῦτα
τῶν χωμάτων ἐποιοῦντο τὰς φυλακάς.

15 (3) Οἱ δὲ περὶ τὸν Ἰωάννην κατὰ τὴν Ἀντωνίαν
ἅμα καὶ πρὸς τὸ μέλλον, εἰ καταρριφθείη τὸ τεῖχος,
ἠσφαλίζοντο καὶ πρὶν ἐπιστῆναι τοὺς κριοὺς ἐπ-
16 έθεντο τοῖς ἔργοις. οὐ μὴν ἐκράτησάν γε τῆς
ἐπιχειρήσεως, ἀλλὰ προελθόντες[1] μετὰ λαμπάδων
πρὶν ἐγγίσαι τοῖς χώμασι ψυχρότεροι τῆς ἐλπίδος
17 ὑπέστρεψαν. πρῶτον μὲν γὰρ οὐδ' ὁμονοεῖν ἡ
σκέψις αὐτῶν ἐῴκει κατὰ μέρος ἐκπηδώντων κἀκ
διαλειμμάτων καὶ μεμελλημένως μετὰ δέους,
καθόλου τ' εἰπεῖν οὐκ Ἰουδαϊκῶς· τὰ γὰρ ἴδια τοῦ
ἔθνους ὑστέρητο ἅμα ἡ τόλμα καὶ ὁρμὴ καὶ
δρόμος ὁμοῦ πάντων καὶ τὸ μηδὲ πταίοντας
18 ἀναστρέφειν. ἀτονώτεροι δ' ἑαυτῶν προελθόντες
καὶ τοὺς Ῥωμαίους εὗρον ἐρρωμενέστερον τοῦ
19 συνήθους παρατεταγμένους· τοῖς μέν γε σώμασι
καὶ ταῖς πανοπλίαις οὕτως ἐφράξαντο τὰ χώματα
πάντοθεν, ὡς τῷ πυρὶ μηδαμόθεν καταλιπεῖν
παράδυσιν, τὴν δὲ ψυχὴν ἐτόνωσαν ἕκαστος μὴ
20 μετακινηθῆναι τῆς τάξεως πρὸ θανάτου. πρὸς
γὰρ τῷ πάσας αὐτῶν ὑποκόπτεσθαι τὰς ἐλπίδας,
εἰ κἀκεῖνα καταφλεγείη τὰ ἔργα, δεινὴ τοὺς
στρατιώτας εἶχεν αἰδώς, εἰ πάντα κρατήσειαν
πανουργίᾳ μὲν ἀρετῆς, ἀπόνοια δ' ὅπλων, πλῆθος
21 δ' ἐμπειρίας, Ἰουδαῖοι δὲ Ῥωμαίων. ἅμα δέ τι
καὶ[2] τἀφετήρια συνήργει τῶν προπηδώντων ἐφικνού-
μενα, καὶ πεσών τις τῷ μεθ' αὐτὸν ἐμπόδιον ἦν,
ὅ τε κίνδυνος τοῦ πρόσω χωρεῖν ἐποίει μαλακω-

---

[1] ed. pr. Heʒ.: προσελθόντες MSS.
[2] τι καὶ C: ἔτι καὶ MVR: καὶ L: om. PA.

favoured by fortune, who were impelled to valour
by disasters ? For these reasons, then, the Romans
strengthened yet more their guard upon the
earthworks.

(3) John and his party within Antonia, on the
other hand, while taking precautions for the future,
in the event of the demolition of the wall, also
made an attack on the works before the rams were
brought up. In this enterprise, however, they did
not succeed, but, having advanced with torches, returned with ardent hopes grown cold,[a] ere they had
approached the earthworks. For, to begin with,
there seemed to be no unanimity in their design :
they dashed out in small parties, at intervals, hesitat-
ingly and in alarm, in short not like Jews : the
characteristics of the nation—daring, impetuosity,
the simultaneous charge, the refusal to retreat even
when worsted[b]—were all lacking. But while their own
advance was abnormally spiritless, they found the
Romans drawn up in stouter array than usual, with
their bodies and armour so completely screening the
earthworks as to leave no loophole for firebrands from
any quarter whatever, and each man's heart braced
to die rather than quit his post. For not only would
all their hopes be cut off, should these works also be
burnt up, but the soldiers felt it a dire disgrace
that craft should invariably triumph over valour,
desperation over arms, numbers over experience,
and Jews over Romans. The artillery, moreover,
rendered assistance, reaching the sallying parties
with their missiles ; each enemy who fell obstructed
the man in his rear, and the risk of advancing damped

---

[a] Literally "colder than their hope."
[b] Or perhaps "the retreat without so much as a hitch."

22 τέρους. τῶν δ' ἐνδοτέρω βέλους ὑποδραμόντων
οἱ μὲν πρὶν εἰς χεῖρας ἐλθεῖν τὴν εὐταξίαν καὶ τὸ
πύκνωμα τῶν πολεμίων καταπλαγέντες, οἱ δὲ
νυττόμενοι τοῖς ξυστοῖς ἐπαλινδρόμουν· καὶ τέλος
ἀλλήλους κακίζοντες εἰς δειλίαν ἀνεχώρουν ἄπρα-
κτοι. νουμηνίᾳ Πανέμου μηνὸς ἡ ἐπιχείρησις ἦν.
23 ἀναχωρησάντων δὲ τῶν Ἰουδαίων προσῆγον οἱ
Ῥωμαῖοι τὰς ἑλεπόλεις, βαλλόμενοι πέτραις τε
ἀπὸ τῆς Ἀντωνίας καὶ πυρὶ καὶ σιδήρῳ καὶ παντὶ
τῷ χορηγουμένῳ Ἰουδαίοις ὑπὸ τῆς ἀνάγκης
24 βέλει· καίπερ γὰρ πολὺ τῷ τείχει πεποιθότες καὶ
τῶν ὀργάνων καταφρονοῦντες ὅμως ἐκώλυον τοὺς
25 Ῥωμαίους προσάγειν. οἱ δὲ τὴν σπουδὴν τῶν
Ἰουδαίων τοῦ μὴ πληγῆναι τὴν Ἀντωνίαν ὑπολαμβάνοντες γίνεσθαι δι' ἀσθένειαν τοῦ τείχους
καὶ σαθροὺς ἐλπίσαντες εἶναι τοὺς θεμελίους ἀντ-
26 εφιλονείκουν. οὐ μὴν ὑπήκουε τὸ τυπτόμενον, ἀλλ'
οἱ μὲν συνεχῶς βαλλόμενοι καὶ πρὸς μηδένα τῶν
καθύπερθεν κινδύνων ἐνδιδόντες ἐνεργοὺς παρεῖχον
27 τὰς ἑλεπόλεις· ὡς δ' ἦσαν ἐλάττους καὶ περι-
εθραύοντο ταῖς πέτραις, ἕτεροι τοὺς θυρεοὺς ὀρο-
φώσαντες ὑπὲρ τῶν σωμάτων χερσὶ καὶ μοχλοῖς
ὑπώρυττον τοὺς θεμελίους, καὶ τέσσαράς γε λίθους
28 προσκαρτερήσαντες ἐξέσεισαν. ἀνέπαυσε δὲ νὺξ
ἑκατέρους, κἂν ταύτῃ τὸ τεῖχος ὑπὸ τῶν κριῶν
σεσαλευμένον, καὶ¹ καθ' ὃ τοῖς προτέροις ἐπι-
βουλεύων χώμασιν ὁ Ἰωάννης ὑπώρυξεν ἐνδούσης
τῆς διώρυχος, ἐξαπίνης κατερείπεται.

¹ om. Lat.

ᵃ i.e. long range projectiles ; cf. iii. 212 τῶν δὲ πόρρω βαλ-
λομένων ἐνδοτέρω γινόμενοι προσέκειτο κτλ.
ᵇ pila.   ᶜ Iron arrow-heads : cf. iii. 240.

their ardour. Of those who did penetrate past the reach of these projectiles,[a] some sped back, before coming to close quarters, dismayed by the admirable order and serried ranks of their antagonists, others only when pricked by the points of the javelins.[b] Finally, reviling each other for cowardice, they all retired, their object unattained. This attack took place on the new moon of the month Panemus.

c. 20 July A.D. 70.

On the retreat of the Jews, the Romans brought up the siege-engines, being assailed from Antonia with rocks, fire, iron [c] and every species of missile with which necessity supplied the Jews, who, notwithstanding their confident reliance on their ramparts and their contempt of the engines, yet strove to prevent the Romans from bringing them up. The latter, surmising that the anxiety of the Jews to save Antonia from assault arose from some weakness in the wall and hoping that the foundations were rotten, redoubled their efforts. Nevertheless it resisted the battering ; but the Romans, under an incessant fire and undeterred by the perils to which they were exposed from above, brought the siege-engines effectively into action. As, however, they were at a disadvantage and crushed by the boulders, another party, locking their bucklers over their bodies, with hands and crowbars started undermining the foundations and by perseverance succeeded in dislodging four stones. Night suspended the labours of both combatants, but in the course of it the wall, whose shaking by the rams was followed by the collapse of the mine, at the point where John in his designs on the former earthworks had dug beneath it,[d] suddenly fell to the ground.

The Roman batter Antonia.

Collapse of part of the wall

[d] v. 469.

385

29 (4) Τούτου συμβάντος παραδόξως ἑκατέροις
30 διετέθη τὰ φρονήματα· Ἰουδαίους μὲν γάρ, οὓς
ἀθυμεῖν εἰκὸς ἦν, τῷ μὴ παρ' ἐλπίδα γενέσθαι τὸ
πτῶμα καὶ προησφαλίσθαι πρὸς αὐτὸ θαρρεῖν ὡς
31 μενούσης συνέβαινε τῆς Ἀντωνίας· Ῥωμαίων δέ
γε τὴν παρ' ἐλπίδα χαρὰν ἐπὶ τῷ καταρριφθέντι
ταχέως ἔσβεσεν ὄψις ἑτέρου τείχους, ὅπερ ἔνδοθεν
32 οἱ περὶ τὸν Ἰωάννην ἀντῳκοδομήκεσαν. εὐμαρε-
στέρα γε μὴν τῆς πρότερον ἡ προσβολὴ κατεφαί-
νετο· τό τε γὰρ ἀναβῆναι διὰ τῶν καταρριφθέντων
ῥᾶον ἐδόκει, καὶ τὸ τεῖχος ἀσθενέστερόν τε πολλῷ
τῆς Ἀντωνίας καὶ ταχέως τῷ πρόσκαιρον εἶναι
λύσειν[1] ὑπελάμβανον. οὐ μὴν ἐτόλμα τις ἀναβῆναι·
πρόυπτος γὰρ τοῖς ἀρξαμένοις ἦν ἀπώλεια.

33 (5) Νομίζων δ' ὁ Τίτος ἐγείρεσθαι μάλιστα τὰς
τῶν πολεμούντων προθυμίας ἐλπίδι καὶ λόγῳ, τάς
τε προτροπὰς καὶ τὰς ὑποσχέσεις πολλάκις μὲν
λήθην ἐνεργάζεσθαι τῶν κινδύνων, ἔστι δ' ὅτε καὶ
θανάτου καταφρόνησιν, συναγαγὼν ἐπὶ ταὐτὸ τοὺς
34 ἀλκίμους ἐπειρᾶτο τῶν ἀνδρῶν, "ὦ συστρατιῶ-
ται," λέγων, "τὸ μὲν παρακελεύειν ἐπὶ τὰ μὴ
φέροντα κίνδυνον αὐτόθεν τοῖς παρακελευομένοις
ἀκλεές, ἀμέλει δὲ καὶ τῷ παρακελεύοντι φέρει
35 κατάγνωσιν ἀνανδρίας. δεῖ δ', οἶμαι, προτροπῆς
εἰς μόνα τὰ σφαλερὰ τῶν πραγμάτων, ὡς ἐκεῖνά
36 γε καθ' αὑτοὺς πράττειν ἄξιον.[2] ὥστ' ἔγωγε τὸ
μὲν ὑπάρχειν χαλεπὴν τὴν ἐπὶ τὸ τεῖχος ἄνοδον
αὐτὸς ὑμῖν προτίθημι· τὸ δ' ὅτι μάλιστα προσήκει
μάχεσθαι τοῖς δυσκόλοις τοὺς ἀρετῆς ἐφιεμένους
καὶ ὅτι καλὸν ἐν εὐκλείᾳ τελευτὴ καὶ ὡς οὐκ
ἄκαρπον ἔσται τοῖς καταρξαμένοις τὸ γενναῖον,

[1] Bekker: λύσιν L : λύειν the rest.   [2] + ὃν Destinon.

(4) The effect of this incident on the spirits of both belligerents was surprising. For the Jews, who might reasonably have been disheartened by it, were, in consequence of their being prepared for this catastrophe and having taken precautions to meet it, quite confident, as Antonia still remained; whereas the unlooked-for joy of the Romans at the downfall was extinguished by the appearance of a second wall which John and his party had built within. True, the assault of this one looked easier than that of the first, as the ascent would be facilitated by the debris; they also imagined the wall itself to be far weaker than that of Antonia and that, being a temporary structure, it would be rapidly destroyed. Still, none ventured to mount; for manifest destruction awaited the first assailants.

(5) Titus, believing that the ardour of troops in warfare is best roused by hope and encouraging words, and that exhortations and promises often induce forgetfulness of danger and sometimes even contempt of death, called his stalwarts together and put to the proof the mettle of his men. "Fellow-soldiers," he said, "to deliver an oration inciting to enterprises involving no risk is to cast a direct slur on the persons addressed, while it assuredly convicts him who delivers it of unmanliness. Exhortation, in my opinion, is needed only for hazardous affairs, since in other circumstances men may be expected to act of their own accord. That the scaling of this wall is arduous I, therefore, myself grant you at the outset; but that to contend with difficulties best becomes those who aspire to heroism, that it is glorious to die with renown, and that the gallantry of those who lead the way will not go unrewarded—

37 διέξειμι. πρῶτον μὲν οὖν ὑμῶν γενέσθω προτροπὴ
τό τινας ἴσως ἀποτρέπον, ἡ Ἰουδαίων μακροθυμία
38 καὶ τὸ καρτερικὸν ἐν οἷς κακοπαθοῦσιν· αἰσχρὸν
γὰρ Ῥωμαίους τε ὄντας καὶ στρατιώτας ἐμούς,
καὶ διδακτὸν μὲν ἐν εἰρήνῃ τὸ πολεμεῖν, ἔθιμον δ᾽
ἐν πολέμῳ τὸ κρατεῖν ἔχοντας, ἡττᾶσθαι κατὰ
χεῖρα Ἰουδαίων ἢ κατὰ ψυχήν, καὶ ταῦτα πρὸς τῷ
τέλει τῆς νίκης καὶ συνεργουμένους ὑπὸ τοῦ θεοῦ.
39 τὰ [μὲν][1] γὰρ ἡμέτερα πταίσματα τῆς Ἰουδαίων
ἐστὶν ἀπονοίας, τὰ δ᾽ ἐκείνων πάθη ταῖς τε ὑμετέ-
ραις ἀρεταῖς καὶ ταῖς τοῦ θεοῦ συνεργίαις αὔξεται·
40 στάσις γὰρ καὶ λιμὸς καὶ πολιορκία καὶ δίχα
μηχανημάτων πίπτοντα τείχη τί ἂν ἀλλ᾽ ἢ θεοῦ
41 μὲν εἴη μῆνις ἐκείνοις, βοήθεια δ᾽ ἡμετέρα; τὸ
τοίνυν μὴ μόνον ἐλαττοῦσθαι χειρόνων, ἀλλὰ καὶ
τὴν θείαν συμμαχίαν προδιδόναι πρὸς ἡμῶν οὐκ
42 ἂν εἴη. πῶς δ᾽ οὐκ αἰσχρὸν Ἰουδαίοις[2] μέν, οἷς
οὐ[3] πολλὴν αἰσχύνην φέρει τὸ λείπεσθαι μαθοῦσι
δουλεύειν, ὑπὲρ τοῦ μηκέτι τοῦτο πάσχειν θανάτου
καταφρονεῖν καὶ πολλάκις εἰς μέσους ἡμᾶς ἐκτρέ-
χειν, οὐκ ἐλπίδι τοῦ κρατήσειν, ἀλλὰ διὰ ψιλὴν
43 ἐπίδειξιν ἀνδρείας· ὑμᾶς δὲ τοὺς γῆς ὀλίγου δεῖν
ἁπάσης καὶ θαλάσσης κρατοῦντας, οἷς καὶ τὸ μὴ
νικᾶν ὄνειδος, μηδ᾽ ἅπαξ εἰς τοὺς πολεμίους παρα-
44 βάλλεσθαι, περιμένειν δὲ τὸν λιμὸν κατ᾽ αὐτῶν καὶ
τὴν τύχην ἀργοὺς καθεζομένους μετὰ τοιούτων
ὅπλων, καὶ ταῦτα δι᾽ ὀλίγου τοῦ παραβόλου τὸ
45 πᾶν κατορθῶσαι δυναμένους· ἀναβάντες γοῦν ἐπὶ
τὴν Ἀντωνίαν ἔχομεν τὴν πόλιν· καὶ γὰρ ἂν
γίνηταί τις ἔτι πρὸς τοὺς ἔνδον, ὅπερ οὐκ οἶμαι,

---

[1] ins. L: omit the rest.   [2] L: Ἰουδαίοις the rest.
[3] οὐ L: om. PA: insert before φέρει the rest.

on those points I would now dwell. In the first place, then, let that be an incentive to you which to some might perhaps be a deterrent, I mean the long-suffering of the Jews and their fortitude in adversity. For shameful were it that Romans, soldiers of mine, men who in peace are trained for war, and in war are accustomed to conquer, should be outdone, either in strength or courage, by Jews, and that when final victory is in sight and we are enjoying the co-opera-tion of God. For our reverses are but the outcome of the Jews' desperation, while their sufferings are increased by your valiant exploits and the constant co-operation of the Deity. For faction, famine, siege, the fall of ramparts without impact of engines—what can these things mean but that God is wroth with them and extending His aid to us ? Surely, then, to allow ourselves not merely to be surpassed by inferiors but to betray a divine Ally would be beneath our dignity. It would indeed be disgraceful that Jews, to whom defeat brings no serious discredit since they have learnt to be slaves, should, in order to end their servitude, scorn death and constantly charge into our midst, not from any hope of victory, but for the sheer display of bravery ; and yet that you, masters of well nigh every land and sea, to whom not to conquer is disgrace, should never once venture into the enemy's ranks, but should wait for famine and fortune to bring them down, sitting idle with weapons such as these, and that though at a little hazard you have it in your power to achieve everything. Yes, Antonia once mounted, and the city is ours ; for, even if—and I do not expect it—any further battle awaits us with those within,

JOSEPHUS

μάχη, τό γε κατὰ κορυφὴν εἶναι καὶ ταῖς ἀναπνοαῖς
ἐπικαθῆσθαι τῶν πολεμίων ταχέως τὴν ὁλοσχερῆ
46 νίκην ἐγγυᾶται. καὶ ἔγωγε τὸ μὲν ὑμνεῖν ἄρτι τὴν
ἐν πολέμῳ τελευτὴν καὶ τὴν ἐπὶ τοῖς ἀρειμανίοις
πεσοῦσιν ἀθανασίαν παραλιπὼν ἐπαρασαίμην ἂν
τοῖς ἄλλως ἔχουσι τὸν κατ' εἰρήνην ἐκ νόσου
θάνατον, οἷς μετὰ τοῦ σώματος καὶ ἡ ψυχὴ τάφῳ
47 κατακρίνεται. τίς γὰρ οὐκ οἶδε τῶν ἀγαθῶν
ἀνδρῶν ὅτι τὰς μὲν ἐν παρατάξει ψυχὰς σιδήρῳ
τῶν σαρκῶν ἀπολυθείσας τὸ καθαρώτατον στοι-
χεῖον αἰθὴρ ξενοδοχῶν ἄστροις ἐγκαθιδρύει, δαί-
μονες δ' ἀγαθοὶ καὶ ἥρωες εὐμενεῖς ἰδίοις ἐγγόνοις
48 ἐμφανίζονται, τὰς δ' ἐν νοσοῦσι τοῖς σώμασι συν-
τακείσας, κἂν τὰ μάλιστα κηλίδων ἢ μιασμάτων
ὦσι καθαραί, νὺξ ὑπόγειος ἀφανίζει καὶ λήθη
βαθεῖα δέχεται, λαμβανούσας ἅμα τοῦ τε βίου καὶ
49 τῶν σωμάτων, ἔτι δὲ τῆς μνήμης περιγραφήν; εἰ
δὲ κέκλωσται μὲν ἀνθρώποις ἀναγκαία τελευτή,
κουφότερον δ' εἰς αὐτὴν νόσου πάσης σίδηρος
ὑπηρέτης, πῶς οὐκ ἀγεννὲς μὴ διδόναι ταῖς χρεί-
50 αις ὃ τῷ χρεὼν ἀποδώσομεν; καὶ ταῦτα μὲν ὡς
οὐ δυναμένων σωθῆναι τῶν ἐπιχειρησόντων διεξ-
ῆλθον· ἔνεστι δὲ σώζεσθαι τοῖς ἀνδριζομένοις κἀκ
51 τῶν σφαλερωτάτων. πρῶτον μὲν γὰρ τὸ καταρριφθὲν εὐεπίβατον, ἔπειτα πᾶν τὸ οἰκοδομηθὲν
εὐδιάλυτον, ὑμεῖς τε πλείους θαρσήσαντες ἐπὶ τὴν
πρᾶξιν ἀλλήλοις προτροπὴ καὶ βοήθεια γίνεσθε,
καὶ τοῖς πολεμίοις τὸ ὑμέτερον παράστημα ταχέως
52 κλάσει τὰ φρονήματα. καὶ τάχ' ἂν ὑμῖν ἀν-
αίμακτον τὸ κατόρθωμα γένοιτο μόνον καταρξα-
390

your position over their heads commanding the very air your enemies breathe would ensure a complete and speedy victory.

"I refrain on this occasion from an encomium on the warrior's death and the immortality reserved for those who fall in the frenzy of battle, but for any who think otherwise the worst I could wish is that they may die in peace of disease, soul and body alike condemned to the tomb. For what brave man knows not that souls released from the flesh by the sword on the battlefield are hospitably welcomed by that purest of elements, the ether, and placed among the stars, and that as good genii and benignant heroes they manifest their presence to their posterity; while souls which pine away in bodies wasted by disease, however pure they may be from stain or pollution, are obliterated in subterranean night and pass into profound oblivion, their life, their bodies, aye and their memory, brought simultaneously to a close? But if men are doomed to an inevitable end and the sword is a gentler minister thereof than any disease, surely it were ignoble to deny to the public service what we must surrender to fate.

"Thus far I have spoken on the assumption that any who may attempt this feat must necessarily perish. Yet the valiant may come safe through even the most hazardous of enterprises. For in the first place, the ruined wall will be easy to mount; again, all that has been built up will be easy to overthrow; do you but summon courage for the task, with growing numbers stimulating and supporting one another, and your determination will soon break the enemy's spirit. Peradventure you may find the exploit bloodless, if you but begin; for, though they will in all

μένοις· ἀναβαίνοντας μὲν γὰρ κωλύειν πειράσονται
κατὰ τὸ εἰκός, λαθόντας δὲ καὶ βιασαμένους ἅπαξ
53 οὐκ ἂν ὑποσταῖεν ἔτι, κἂν ὀλίγοι φθάσητε. τὸν δὲ
καταρξάμενον αἰσχυνοίμην ἂν εἰ μὴ ποιήσαιμι
ζηλωτὸν ἐν ταῖς ἐπικαρπίαις, καὶ ὁ μὲν ζῶν ἄρξει
τῶν νῦν ὁμοίων, μακαριστὰ δ' ἀκολουθήσει καὶ
τοῖς πεσοῦσι τὰ ἀριστεῖα.''

54 (6) Τοιαῦτα τοῦ Τίτου διεξιόντος τὸ μὲν ἄλλο
πλῆθος ἔδεισε τοῦ κινδύνου τὸ μέγεθος, τῶν δ' ἐν
ταῖς σπείραις[1] στρατευομένων Σαβῖνος τοὔνομα,
γένος ἀπὸ Συρίας, ἀνὴρ καὶ κατὰ χεῖρα καὶ κατὰ
55 ψυχὴν ἄριστος ἐφάνη. καίτοι προϊδὼν ἄν τις
αὐτὸν ἀπό γε τῆς σωματικῆς ἕξεως οὐδ' εἰκαῖον
εἶναι στρατιώτην ἔδοξε· μέλας μὲν γὰρ ἦν τὴν
χροίαν, ἰσχνός, τὴν σάρκα πεπιλημένος, ἀλλ'
ἐνῴκει τις ἡρωικὴ ψυχὴ λεπτῷ σώματι καὶ πολὺ
56 τῆς ἰδίας ἀλκῆς στενοτέρῳ.[2] πρῶτος γοῦν ἀναστὰς
''ἐπιδίδωμί σοι, Καῖσαρ,'' ἔφη, '' προθύμως
57 ἐμαυτόν· πρῶτος ἀναβαίνω τὸ τεῖχος. καὶ εὔχομαι
μέν μου τῇ τε ἰσχύι καὶ τῇ γνώμῃ τὴν σὴν ἀκολου-
θῆσαι τύχην, εἰ δὲ νεμεσηθείην τῆς ἐπιβολῆς, ἴσθι
με μὴ[3] πταίσαντα παρ' ἐλπίδας, ἀλλ' ὑπὲρ σοῦ
58 κρίσει τὸν θάνατον ᾑρημένον.'' ταῦτ' εἰπὼν· καὶ
τῇ μὲν ἀριστερᾷ χειρὶ τὸν θυρεὸν ὑπὲρ τῆς κεφαλῆς
προανατείνας,[4] τῇ δεξιᾷ δὲ τὸ ξίφος σπασάμενος
ἐχώρει πρὸς τὸ τεῖχος περὶ ὥραν μάλιστα τῆς
59 ἡμέρας ἕκτην. εἵποντο δ' αὐτῷ καὶ τῶν ἄλλων
ἕνδεκα μόνοι ζηλωταὶ τῆς ἀνδρείας γενόμενοι·

---

[1] + τις L Lat. (Zon. ut vid.).
[2] Lat. : γενναιοτέρῳ (-τέρᾳ) mss.
[3] με μὴ LC: μὴ με the rest.
[4] LVRC: ἀνατείνας the rest.

probability endeavour to thwart your ascent, yet if unperceived you once force a way through, their resistance may well break down, though but a handful of you elude them. As for him who leads the assault, I should blush were I not to make him an enviable man in the award of honours ; and while the survivor shall command those who are now his equals, the blessed meed of valour shall follow the fallen to the grave."

(6) Thus harangued by Titus, the troops in general were deterred by the gravity of the danger ; but among those serving in the cohorts [a] was one named Sabinus, a native of Syria, who showed himself both in might of hand and in spirit the bravest of men. Yet anyone seeing him before that day and judging from his outward appearance would not have taken him even for a common soldier. His skin was black, his flesh shrunk and emaciated ; but within that slender frame, far too strait for its native prowess, there dwelt an heroic soul. He was the first to rise. " Caesar," he said, " to you I gladly offer myself ; I am the first to scale the wall. And I pray that my strength and resolution may be attended by your good fortune.[b] Yet, should some nemesis balk me of my intent, know that my failure will not surprise me, but that for your sake I have deliberately preferred to die." Having spoken thus, with his left hand he extended his buckler over his head and with his right drew his sword and advanced towards the wall, almost exactly at the sixth hour of the day He was followed by eleven others, who alone were found to emulate his gallantry ; but the hero, im-

---

[a] Auxiliary troops.
[b] For Titus as the favourite of Fortune cf. v. 88.

προῆγε δὲ πολὺ πάντων ὁ ἀνὴρ ὁρμῇ τινι δαιμονίῳ
60 χρώμενος. οἱ φρουροὶ δ' ἀπὸ τοῦ τείχους κατ-
ηκόντιζόν τε αὐτοὺς καὶ βέλεσι πάντοθεν ἀπείροις
ἔβαλλον καὶ πέτρας ἐξαισίους κατεκύλιον, αἳ ἐκ
61 τῶν μὲν ἕνδεκα παρέσυραν ἐνίους, ὁ δὲ Σαβῖνος
ἀπαντῶν τοῖς ἀφιεμένοις καὶ καταχωννύμενος ὑπὸ
τῶν βελῶν οὐ · πρότερον ἐπέσχε τὴν ὁρμὴν ἢ
γενέσθαι τε ἐπ' ἄκρῳ καὶ τρέψασθαι τοὺς πολε-
62 μίους· καταπλαγέντες γὰρ αὐτοῦ τήν τε δύναμιν
οἱ Ἰουδαῖοι καὶ τὸ παράστημα τῆς ψυχῆς, ἅμα δὲ
καὶ πλείους ἀναβεβηκέναι δόξαντες ἐτράπησαν.
63 ἔνθα δὴ καταμέμψαιτ' ἄν τις ὡς φθονερὰν ἐπὶ ταῖς
ἀρεταῖς τὴν τύχην καὶ κωλύουσαν ἀεὶ τὰ παράδοξα
64 τῶν κατορθωμάτων. ὁ γοῦν ἀνὴρ οὗτος, ὅτ'
ἐκράτησε τῆς ἐπιβολῆς, ἐσφάλη καὶ πταίσας πρός
τινι πέτρᾳ πρηνὴς ἐπ' αὐτὴν μετὰ μεγίστου ψόφου
κατέπεσεν· ἐπιστραφέντες δ' οἱ Ἰουδαῖοι καὶ κατιδόντες μόνον τε αὐτὸν καὶ πεπτωκότα, πάντοθεν
65 ἔβαλλον. ὁ δ' ἐς γόνυ διαναστὰς καὶ προκαλυψά-
μενος τὸν θυρεὸν τὸ μὲν πρῶτον ἠμύνετο καὶ πολ-
66 λοὺς τῶν πλησιασάντων ἔτρωσεν· αὖθις δ' ὑπὸ πλήθους τραυμάτων παρῆκε τὴν δεξιὰν καὶ τέλος πρὶν
ἀποδοῦναι τὴν ψυχὴν κατεχώσθη τοῖς βέλεσιν, ἀνὴρ
ἄξιος μὲν ἀμείνονι χρῆσθαι δι' ἀνδρείαν καὶ τύχῃ,
67 πεσὼν δὲ τῆς ἐπιβολῆς ἀναλόγως. τῶν δὲ ἄλλων
τρεῖς μὲν τοὺς ἤδη πρὸς τοῖς ἄκροις ὄντας συν-
τρίψαντες ἀπέκτειναν τοῖς λίθοις, οἱ δ' ὀκτὼ τραυματίαι κατασυρέντες ἀνεκομίσθησαν εἰς τὸ στρατόπεδον. ταῦτα μὲν οὖν τρίτῃ μηνὸς Πανέμου ἐπράχθη.
68 (7) Μετὰ δ' ἡμέρας δύο τῶν προκοιτούντων
τινὲς ἐπὶ τοῖς χώμασι φυλάκων εἴκοσι συνελθόντες
προσποιοῦνται¹ μὲν τὸν τοῦ πέμπτου τάγματος
394

pelled by some preternatural stimulus, far outstripped
them all. From the ramparts the guards hurled
their javelins at the party, assailed them from all
quarters with showers of arrows, and rolled down
enormous boulders which swept away some of the
eleven ; but Sabinus, facing the missiles and buried
beneath the darts, yet never slackened his pace until
he had gained the summit and routed the enemy.
For the Jews, dumbfounded at his strength and intrepidity and, moreover, imagining that more had
ascended, turned and fled. And here one cannot
but censure Fortune as envious of feats of valour and
ever thwarting marvellous achievements. For at the
moment when this hero had attained his object, he
slipped and stumbling over a rock fell headlong upon
it with a tremendous crash. The Jews, turning and
seeing him alone and prostrate, assailed him from
all sides. Rising upon his knee and screening himself with his buckler, he for a while kept them at
bay and wounded many of those who approached
him ; but soon under his numerous wounds his arm
was paralysed, and he was at length, before giving
up his life, buried under the missiles : a man whose
gallantry deserved a better fortune, but whose fall
was in keeping with his enterprise. Of his comrades
three after gaining the summit were crushed to death
by the stones ; the remaining eight were drawn down
wounded and conveyed to the camp. These events
took place on the third of the month of Panemus.

His untimely end.

c. 22 July.

(7) Two days later, twenty of the guards on
outpost duty at the earthworks came together and
enlisting the services of the standard-bearer of the

---

¹ PA Syr.: προσκαλοῦνται the rest.

σημαιαφόρον καὶ δύο τινὰς τῶν ἐν ταῖς ἴλαις
ἱππέων καὶ σαλπικτὴν ἕνα, κατὰ δ' ὥραν τῆς
νυκτὸς ἐνάτην προσβαίνουσι[1] μὲν ἡσυχῇ διὰ τῶν
ἐρειπίων ἐπὶ τὴν Ἀντωνίαν, ἀποσφάξαντες δὲ τοὺς
πρώτους τῶν φρουρῶν κοιμωμένους κρατοῦσι τοῦ
τείχους καὶ τῷ σαλπικτῇ σημαίνειν ἐκέλευσαν.

69 πρὸς ὃ τῶν μὲν ἄλλων φυλάκων ἐξανάστασίς τε[2]
αἰφνίδιος ἦν καὶ φυγὴ πρίν τινα τὸ πλῆθος ἐπιδεῖν
τῶν ἐπιβεβηκότων· ὅ τε γὰρ φόβος καὶ ἡ σάλπιγξ
φαντασίαν αὐτοῖς τοῦ πλήθους ἀναβεβηκέναι πολε-

70 μίων παρεῖχε. Καῖσαρ δὲ τοῦ σημείου κατακούσας
ἐξοπλίζει τήν τε δύναμιν διὰ τάχους[3] καὶ μετὰ τῶν
ἡγεμόνων πρῶτος ἀναβαίνει τοὺς ἐπιλέκτους ἔχων.

71 καταπεφευγότων δ' Ἰουδαίων εἰς τὸ ἱερὸν καὶ
αὐτοὶ διὰ τῆς διώρυγος εἰσέπιπτον, ἣν ὁ Ἰωάννης

72 ἐπὶ τὰ χώματα τῶν Ῥωμαίων ὑπώρυξε. καὶ
διαστάντες[4] ἐπ'[5] ἀμφοτέρων οἱ στασιασταὶ τῶν
ταγμάτων, τοῦ τε Ἰωάννου καὶ τοῦ Σίμωνος,
εἶργον αὐτοὺς οὐδεμίαν οὔτε ἰσχύος οὔτε προθυμίας

73 ἐλλείποντες ὑπερβολήν· πέρας γὰρ ἁλώσεως ὑπελάμβανον τὸ Ῥωμαίους παρελθεῖν εἰς τὸ ἅγιον, ὃ δὴ

74 κἀκεῖνοι τοῦ κρατεῖν ἀρχήν. συρρήγνυται δὲ περὶ
τὰς εἰσόδους μάχη καρτερά, τῶν μὲν καταλαβέσθαι
καὶ τὸ ἱερὸν εἰσβιαζομένων, τῶν δ' Ἰουδαίων

75 ἐξωθούντων αὐτοὺς ἐπὶ τὴν Ἀντωνίαν. καὶ τὰ
βέλη μὲν ἦν ἀμφοτέροις ἄχρηστα καὶ τὰ δόρατα,
σπασάμενοι δὲ τὰ ξίφη συνεπλέκοντο, καὶ περὶ τὴν
συμβολὴν ἄκριτον ἦν ὁποτέρωθεν ἕκαστοι μάχοιντο,
πεφυρμένων μὲν τῶν ἀνδρῶν καὶ περὶ τὴν στενο-

---

[1] προβαίνουσι Lat. (procedunt).   [2] τε L: om. the rest.
[3] κατὰ τάχος L.   [4] διαναστάντες L.
[5] ὑπ' L: ἀπ' ed. pr. (perhaps rightly).

396

fifth legion, two troopers from the squadrons [a] and a Another scaling party successful, c. 24 July.
trumpeter, at the ninth hour of the night advanced
noiselessly over the ruins towards Antonia. The
first sentinels whom they encountered they cut down
in their sleep and, taking possession of the wall,
ordered the trumpeter to sound. Thereupon, the
other guards suddenly started to their feet and fled,
before any had noted what number had ascended;
for their panic and the trumpet-call led them to
imagine that the enemy had mounted in force.
Caesar, hearing the signal, promptly called the forces Fierce night battle for the Temple.
to arms, and with the generals and his body of picked
men was the first to mount. The Jews had fled to
the temple, into which the Romans also were pene-
trating through the mine excavated by John to
reach their earthworks.[b] The rebels of both factions,
those of John and of Simon, drawn up in separate
divisions sought to stem their advance, with a prodigious exhibition of strength and spirit; for they
held that the entry of the Romans into the sanctuary
meant final capture, while the latter regarded it as
the prelude to victory. So the armies clashed in
desperate struggle round the entrances, the Romans
pressing on to take possession also of the temple,
the Jews thrusting them back upon Antonia. Missiles
and spears were useless to both belligerents. Drawing their swords, they closed with each other, and
in the mêlée it was impossible to tell on which side
either party was fighting, the men being all jumbled

[a] *alae*, auxiliary cavalry.   [b] § 28.

χωρίαν διηλλαγμένων, τῆς δὲ βοῆς ἀσημάντου
76 προσπιπτούσης διὰ τὸ μέγεθος. φόνος τε ἦν
ἑκατέρωθεν πολύς, καὶ τῶν πεσόντων τά τε
σώματα καὶ τὰς πανοπλίας πατοῦντες ἔθραυον οἱ
77 μαχόμενοι. ἀεὶ δ' ἐφ' ὁπότερον βρίσειεν ῥέων ὁ
πόλεμος, παρακέλευσις μὲν ἦν τῶν πλεονεκτούντων,
οἰμωγαὶ δὲ τῶν τρεπομένων. οὔτε δ' αἱ φυγαὶ
τόπον εἶχον οὔθ' αἱ διώξεις, ἀλλ' ἀγχώμαλοι
ῥοπαὶ καὶ μετακλίσεις μεμιγμένης ἐγίνοντο τῆς
78 παρατάξεως. τοῖς δ' ἔμπροσθεν γινομένοις ἢ τοῦ
θνήσκειν ἢ τοῦ κτείνειν[1] ἀνάγκη παρῆν οὐκ οὔσης
ἀναφυγῆς· οἱ γὰρ κατὰ νώτου πρόσω βιαζόμενοι
τοὺς σφετέρους παρ' ἀμφοῖν οὐδὲ τῇ μάχῃ μετ-
79 αίχμιον κατέλειπον. πλεονεκτούντων δὲ τῶν Ἰουδαίων τοῖς θυμοῖς τὴν Ῥωμαίων ἐμπειρίαν καὶ
κλινομένης καθάπαν ἤδη τῆς παρατάξεως, ἀπὸ
γὰρ ἐνάτης ὥρας τῆς νυκτὸς εἰς ἑβδόμην τῆς
80 ἡμέρας ἐπολέμουν, οἱ μὲν ἀθρόοι καὶ τὸν τῆς ἁλώσεως
κίνδυνον ἔχοντες ἀνδρείας ἐφόδιον, Ῥωμαῖοι δὲ
μέρει τῆς δυνάμεως, οὔπω γὰρ ἐπαναβεβήκει τὰ
τάγματα, κἀκείνοις ἐπανεῖχον οἱ μαχόμενοι τότε,
κρατεῖν τῆς Ἀντωνίας ἀποχρῆν ἐπὶ τοῦ παρόντος
ἐδόκει.
81   (8) Ἰουλιανὸς δέ τις ἑκατοντάρχης τῶν ἀπὸ τῆς
Βιθυνίας, οὐκ ἄσημος ὢν ἀνήρ, ὧν[2] ἐγὼ κατ'
ἐκεῖνον ἱστόρησα τὸν πόλεμον ὅπλων τ' ἐμπειρίᾳ
καὶ ἀλκῇ σώματος καὶ ψυχῆς παραστήματι
82 πάντων ἄριστος, ὁρῶν τοὺς Ῥωμαίους ἐνδιδόντας
ἤδη καὶ κακῶς ἀμυνομένους, παρειστήκει δὲ Τίτῳ
κατὰ τὴν Ἀντωνίαν, προπηδᾷ καὶ νικῶντας ἤδη
τοὺς Ἰουδαίους τρέπεται μόνος μέχρι τῆς τοῦ

---

[1] ἢ τοῦ κτείνειν ἢ τοῦ θνήσκειν L Lat.

together and intermingled in the confined area, and
their shouts, owing to the terrific din, falling con-
fusedly on the ear. There was great slaughter on
either side, and the bodies and armour of the fallen
were trampled down and crushed by the combatants.
And always, in whichever direction rolled the veering
tide of war, were heard the cheers of the victors,
the wailings of the routed. Room for flight or
pursuit there was none ; dubious turns of the scale
and shifting of position were the sole incidents in
the confused contest. Those in front had either to
kill or to be killed, there being no retreat ; for those
in rear in either army pressed their comrades forward,
leaving no intervening space between the combatants.
At length, Jewish fury prevailing over Roman skill, Romans
the whole line began to waver. For they had been fall back or Antonia.
fighting from the ninth hour of the night until the
seventh of the day ; the Jews in full strength, with
the peril of capture as an incentive to gallantry,
the Romans with but a portion of their forces, the
legions upon whom the present combatants were
dependent having not yet come up. It was therefore
considered sufficient for the present to hold Antonia.

(8) But one Julianus, a centurion in the Bithynian Fate of
contingent, a man of some mark, and distinguished another hero
above all whose acquaintance I made during that Julianus.
war in the science of arms, strength of body and
intrepidity of soul, seeing the Romans beginning to
give way and offering but a sorry resistance, sprang
forward—he had been standing beside Titus on
Antonia—and single-handed drove back the Jews,
already victorious, to the corner of the inner temple.

---

² C : δν the rest, the Lat. and Syr. versions apparently
reading ἄριστον below.

399

ἐνδοτέρω ἱεροῦ γωνίας. ἔφευγε δὲ τὸ πλῆθος
ἄθρουν, οὔτε τὴν ἰσχὺν οὔτε τὴν τόλμαν ἀνθρωπίνην
83 ὑπολαμβάνοντες. ὁ δὲ διὰ μέσων τῶν σκεδαννυ-
μένων ἄλλοτε ἄλλῃ διᾴττων ἐφόνευε τοὺς καταλαμβανομένους, καὶ τῆς ὄψεως ἐκείνης οὐδὲν οὔτε τῷ
Καίσαρι θαυμασιώτερον οὔτε τοῖς ἄλλοις παρέστη
84 φρικωδέστερον. ἐδιώκετο δ' ἄρα καὶ αὐτὸς ὑπὸ
τῆς εἱμαρμένης, ἣν ἀμήχανον διαφυγεῖν θνητὸν
85 ὄντα. τὰ γὰρ ὑποδήματα πεπαρμένα πυκνοῖς καὶ
ὀξέσιν ἥλοις ἔχων, ὥσπερ τῶν ἄλλων στρατιωτῶν ἕκαστος, καὶ κατὰ λιθοστρώτου τρέχων ὑπ-
ολισθάνει, πεσὼν δ' ὕπτιος μετὰ μεγίστου τῆς παν-
86 οπλίας ἤχου τοὺς φεύγοντας ἐπιστρέφει. καὶ τῶν
μὲν ἀπὸ τῆς Ἀντωνίας Ῥωμαίων ἤρθη βοὴ περὶ
τἀνδρὶ δεισάντων, οἱ δὲ Ἰουδαῖοι περιστάντες
αὐτὸν ἀθρόοι τοῖς τε ξυστοῖς καὶ ταῖς ῥομφαίαις
87 πάντοθεν ἔπαιον. ὁ δὲ πολὺν μὲν τῷ θυρεῷ σίδηρον
ἐξεδέχετο, πολλάκις δὲ ἀναστῆναι πειράσας ὑπὸ
τοῦ πλήθους τῶν τυπτόντων ἀνετράπη, καὶ κεί-
88 μενος δ' ὅμως ἔνυττε τῷ ξίφει πολλούς· οὐδὲ γὰρ
ἀνῃρέθη ταχέως, τῷ τε κράνει καὶ τῷ θώρακι
πεφραγμένος πάντα τὰ καίρια πρὸς σφαγὴν καὶ
τὸν αὐχένα συνέλκων· μέχρι κοπτομένων αὐτῷ
τῶν ἄλλων μελῶν καὶ μηδενὸς προσαμῦναι τολ-
89 μῶντος ἐνέδωκε. δεινὸν δὲ πάθος εἰσῄει Καίσαρα
ἀνδρὸς οὕτως ἐναρέτου καὶ ἐν ὄψει τοσούτων
φονευομένου· καὶ αὐτὸν μὲν ὁ τόπος διέκλειε
βοηθεῖν θέλοντα, τοὺς δυναμένους δὲ κατάπληξις.
90 Ἰουλιανὸς μὲν οὖν πολλὰ δυσθανατήσας καὶ τῶν
κτεινόντων ὀλίγους ἀπλῆγας καταλιπὼν μόλις
ἀποσφάττεται, μέγιστον οὐ παρὰ Ῥωμαίοις καὶ
Καίσαρι μόνον ἀλλὰ καὶ παρὰ τοῖς πολεμίοις κλέος

The multitude fled in crowds before him, regarding such strength and courage as superhuman ; while he, dashing this way and that through the midst of their scattering ranks, slew all whom he overtook, and no spectacle that met the eye of Caesar was more wonderful than that, nor more terrifying to his foes. Yet, after all, he too was to be dogged by Destiny, whom no mortal man may escape. For, wearing, like any other soldier, shoes thickly studded with sharp nails,[a] while running across the pavement he slipped and fell on his back, with a loud clash of armour, which made the fugitives turn. A cry of concern for the hero went up from the Romans in Antonia, while the Jews crowding round him struck at him from all sides with spears and swords. Many a weapon he parried with his buckler, many a time he tried to rise but was thrown back by the number of his assailants, and, prostrate though he was, many a one did he stab with his sword ; for, being protected in every vital part by helmet and cuirass and drawing in his neck, he was not quickly dispatched. At length, when all his other limbs were hacked and no comrade ventured to his aid, he succumbed. Caesar was deeply moved at the fall of so valiant a soldier, butchered too under the eyes of so many ; and though anxious personally to assist him, he was debarred by his situation, while those who might have done so were withheld by terror. Thus Julianus, after a hard struggle with death and letting few of those who slew him go unscathed, was with difficulty slaughtered, leaving behind him the highest reputation, not only with the Romans and Caesar,

---

[a] " studded with nails " : the Greek phrase is Homeric, *Il.* i. 246, xi. 633.

91 καταλιπών· Ἰουδαῖοι δὲ καὶ τὸν νεκρὸν ἁρπασά-
μενοι πάλιν τοὺς Ῥωμαίους τρέπονται καὶ κατα-
92 κλείουσιν εἰς τὴν Ἀντωνίαν. ἠγωνίσαντο δὲ ἐξ
αὐτῶν ἐπισήμως κατὰ ταύτην τὴν μάχην Ἀλεξᾶς
μέν τις καὶ Γυφθαῖος τοῦ Ἰωάννου τάγματος, ἐκ
δὲ τῶν περὶ Σίμωνα Μαλαχίας τε καὶ ὁ τοῦ
Μέρτωνος Ἰούδας, καὶ Σωσᾶ υἱὸς Ἰάκωβος τῶν
Ἰδουμαίων ἡγεμών, τῶν δὲ ζηλωτῶν ἀδελφοὶ δύο,
παῖδες Ἀρί, Σίμων τε καὶ Ἰούδης.
93 (ii. 1) Τίτος δὲ τοῖς μὲν σὺν αὐτῷ στρατιώταις
κατασκάπτειν προσέταξε τοὺς θεμελίους τῆς
Ἀντωνίας καὶ τῇ δυνάμει πάσῃ ῥᾳδίαν τὴν ἄνοδον
94 εὐτρεπίζειν, αὐτὸς δὲ τὸν Ἰώσηπον παραστησά-
μενος· ἐπέπυστο γὰρ ἐπ᾽ ἐκείνης τῆς ἡμέρας,
Πανέμου δ᾽ ἦν ἑπτακαιδεκάτη, τὸν ἐνδελεχισμὸν
καλούμενον ἀνδρῶν[1] ἀπορίᾳ διαλελοιπέναι τῷ θεῷ
95 καὶ τὸν δῆμον ἐπὶ τούτῳ δεινῶς ἀθυμεῖν· λέγειν τῷ
Ἰωάννῃ πάλιν ἐκέλευσεν ἃ καὶ πρότερον, ὡς εἰ καί
τις αὐτὸν ἔρως κακὸς ἔχοι τοῦ μάχεσθαι, προ-
ελθόντι μεθ᾽ ὅσων βούλεται πολεμεῖν ἐξείη[2] δίχα
τοῦ συναπολέσθαι τήν τε πόλιν καὶ τὸν ναὸν αὐτῷ,
μηκέτι μέντοι μιαίνειν τὸ ἅγιον μηδὲ εἰς τὸν θεὸν
πλημμελεῖν, παρεῖναι δ᾽ αὐτῷ τὰς ἐπιλελοιπυίας
θυσίας ἐκτελεῖν δι᾽ ὧν ἂν ἐπιλέξηται Ἰουδαίων.
96 καὶ ὁ Ἰώσηπος, ὡς ἂν εἴη μὴ τῷ Ἰωάννῃ μόνον
ἀλλὰ καὶ τοῖς πολλοῖς ἐν ἐπηκόῳ στάς,[3] τά τε τοῦ
97 Καίσαρος διήγγελλεν ἑβραΐζων, καὶ πολλὰ προσ-

---

[1] Read probably ἀρνῶν.
[2] ἐξῆν PAML : ἐξεῖναι Destinon.
[3] om. P ; for text cf. iii. 471.

---

[a] iv. 235.
[b] Perhaps = Jairus, as read by cod. C.
[c] The daily, morning and evening sacrifice, Heb. *Tamid* :

but even with his enemies. The Jews, after snatching up the body, again routed the Romans and shut
them up in Antonia. On their side those who distinguished themselves in this engagement were, in
John's army, a certain Alexas and Gyphthaeus; in
Simon's division Malachias, Judas, son of Merton,
with James, son of Sosas,[a] commander of the
Idumaeans ; and of the Zealots two brothers, Simon
and Judes, sons of Ari.[b]

(ii. 1) Titus now ordered the troops that were Antonia razed to the ground.
with him to raze the foundations of Antonia and to
prepare an easy ascent for the whole army. Then, August A.D. 70.
having learnt that on that day—it was the seven-
teenth of Panemus—the so-called continual sacrifice [c] Cessation of the daily sacrifices.
had for lack of men [d] ceased to be offered to God
and that the people were in consequence terribly
despondent, he put Josephus forward with instructions to repeat to John [e] the same message as before,
namely " that if he was obsessed by a criminal
passion for battle, he was at liberty to come out
with as many as he chose and fight, without involving
the city and the sanctuary in his own ruin ; but that
he should no longer pollute the Holy Place nor sin
against God ; and that he had his permission to
perform the interrupted sacrifices with the help of
such Jews as he might select."

Josephus, standing so that his words might reach Josephus addresses John and the Jews.
the ears not only of John but also of the multitude,
delivered Caesar's message in Hebrew,[f] with earnest

---

[c] cf. Numb. xxviii. 6. The cessation of the daily offering was
one of the five calamities associated by Jewish tradition with
the 17th of the month Tammuz (Panemus in the Syrian
calendar), Talm. Bab. *Taanith*, iv. 6.

[d] Or (with corrected text) "lambs." [e] J. of Gischala.

[f] *i.e.* Aramaic ; *cf.* Acts xxi. 40, xxii. 2.

ηντιβόλει φείσασθαι τῆς πατρίδος καὶ διασκεδάσαι
τοῦ ναοῦ γευόμενον ἤδη τὸ πῦρ, τούς τ᾽ ἐναγι-
98 σμοὺς ἀποδοῦναι τῷ θεῷ. πρὸς ταῦτα τοῦ δήμου
μὲν ἦν κατήφεια καὶ σιγή, πολλὰ δ᾽ ὁ τύραννος
λοιδορηθείς τε τῷ Ἰωσήπῳ καὶ καταρασάμενος τὸ
τελευταῖον προσέθηκεν, ὡς οὐκ ἄν ποτε δείσειεν
99 ἅλωσιν· θεοῦ γὰρ ὑπάρχειν τὴν πόλιν. καὶ ὁ
Ἰώσηπος πρὸς ταῦτ᾽ ἀνέκραγεν " πάνυ γοῦν
καθαρὰν τῷ θεῷ τετήρηκας αὐτήν, ἀμίαντον δὲ
μένει τὸ ἅγιον, εἰς ὅν τ᾽ ἐλπίζεις σύμμαχον οὐδὲν
ἠσέβησας, τὰς δ᾽ ἐθίμους θυσίας ἀπολαμβάνει.
100 κἂν μὲν σοῦ τις ἀφέλῃ τὴν καθ᾽ ἡμέραν τροφήν,
ἀσεβέστατε, τοῦτον ἡγήσαι[1] πολέμιον, αὐτὸν δ᾽ ὃν
τῆς αἰωνίου θρησκείας ἐστέρησας θεὸν ἐλπίζεις
101 σύμμαχον ἔχειν ἐν τῷ πολέμῳ; καὶ Ῥωμαίοις
τὰς ἁμαρτίας ἀνατίθης, οἳ μέχρι νῦν κήδονται
τῶν ἡμετέρων νόμων καὶ τὰς ὑπὸ σοῦ διακοπείσας
102 θυσίας ἀποδίδοσθαι τῷ θεῷ βιάζονται; τίς οὐκ ἂν
στενάξειε καὶ κατολοφύραιτο τῆς παραδόξου μεταβολῆς τὴν πόλιν, εἴ γε ἀλλόφυλοι μὲν καὶ πολέμιοι
τὴν σὴν ἀσέβειαν ἐπανορθοῦνται, σὺ δ᾽ ὁ Ἰουδαῖος,
ὁ τοῖς νόμοις ἐντραφείς, κἀκείνων πρὸς αὐτοὺς
103 γίνῃ χαλεπώτερος; ἀλλά τοι, Ἰωάννη, καὶ μετανοῆσαι μὲν ἐκ κακῶν οὐκ αἰσχρὸν ἐν ἐσχάτοις καὶ
καλὸν ὑπόδειγμα βουλομένῳ σώζειν τὴν πατρίδα
104 σοι πρόκειται βασιλεὺς Ἰουδαίων Ἰεχονίας, ὃς
ποτε στρατεύσαντι τῷ Βαβυλωνίῳ δι᾽ αὐτὸν ἑκὼν
ἐξέστη πρὶν ἁλῶναι τῆς πόλεως καὶ μετὰ γενεᾶς
αἰχμαλωσίαν ὑπέμεινεν ἐθελούσιον ὑπὲρ τοῦ μὴ
παραδοῦναι ταῦτα πολεμίοις τὰ ἅγια καὶ τὸν οἶκον

---

[1] ἡγήσει C Lat.: ἡγήσῃ VR.

appeals to them " to spare their country, to disperse the flames that were already licking the sanctuary and to restore to God the expiatory sacrifices." [a] His words were received by the people in dejection and silence ; but the tyrant,[b] after many invectives and imprecations upon Josephus, ended by saying that he " could never fear capture, since the city was God's."

At this Josephus cried aloud : " Pure indeed have you kept it for God ! The Holy Place too remains undefiled ! Your looked-for Ally has suffered no impiety from you and still receives His customary sacrifices ! Most impious wretch, should anyone deprive you of your daily food, you would consider him an enemy ; and do you hope to have God, whom you have bereft of His everlasting worship, for your Ally in this war ? And do you impute your sins to the Romans, who, to this day, are concerned for our laws and are trying to force you to restore to God those sacrifices which *you* have interrupted ? Who would not bewail and lament for the city at this amazing inversion, when aliens and enemies rectify your impiety, while you, a Jew, nurtured in her laws, treat them more harshly even than your foes ?

" Yet, be sure, John, it is no disgrace to repent of misdeeds, even at the last ; and, if you desire to save your country, you have a noble example set before you in Jeconiah, king of the Jews. He, when of old his conduct had brought the Babylonian's army upon him, of his own free will left the city before it was taken, and with his family endured voluntary captivity, rather than deliver up these holy places

---

[a] *Cf.* i. 32 note.   [b] John.

105 τοῦ θεοῦ περιιδεῖν φλεγόμενον. διὰ τοῦτο λόγος
τε αὐτὸν πρὸς ἁπάντων Ἰουδαίων ἱερὸς ὑμνεῖ¹ καὶ
μνήμη ῥέουσα δι' αἰῶνος ἀεὶ νέα τοῖς ἐπιγινομένοις
106 παραδίδωσιν ἀθάνατον. καλόν, ὦ Ἰωάννη, ὑπόδειγμα, κἂν προσῇ κίνδυνος· ἐγὼ δέ σοι καὶ τὴν
107 ἀπὸ Ῥωμαίων συγγνώμην ἐγγυῶμαι. μέμνησο δ'
ὡς ὁμόφυλος ὢν παραινῶ καὶ Ἰουδαῖος ὢν ἐπ-
αγγέλλομαι, καὶ χρὴ σκοπεῖν τίς ὁ συμβουλεύων καὶ
πόθεν. μὴ γὰρ ἔγωγέ ποτε γενοίμην ζῶν οὕτως
αἰχμάλωτος, ἵνα παύσωμαι² τοῦ γένους ἢ τῶν
108 πατρίων ἐπιλάθωμαι. πάλιν ἀγανακτεῖς καὶ κέκρα-
γάς μοι λοιδορούμενος, ἀξίω γε καὶ χαλεπωτέρων,
ὃς ἀντικρὺς εἱμαρμένης τι παραινῶ καὶ τοὺς ὑπὸ
109 τοῦ θεοῦ βιάζομαι κατακρίτους σώζειν. τίς οὐκ
οἶδεν τὰς τῶν παλαιῶν προφητῶν ἀναγραφὰς καὶ
τὸν ἐπιρρέποντα τῇ τλήμονι πόλει χρησμὸν ἤδη
ἐνεστῶτα; τότε γὰρ ἅλωσιν αὐτῆς προεῖπον,
110 ὅταν ὁμοφύλου τις ἄρξῃ φόνου. τῶν ὑμετέρων
δὲ πτωμάτων οὐχ ἡ πόλις καὶ τὸ ἱερὸν δὲ πᾶν
πεπλήρωται; θεὸς ἄρα, θεὸς αὐτὸς ἐπάγει μετὰ
Ῥωμαίων καθάρσιον³ αὐτῷ πῦρ καὶ τὴν τοσούτων
μιασμάτων γέμουσαν πόλιν ἀναρπάζει."
111 (2) Ταῦτα λέγων ὁ Ἰώσηπος μετ' ὀδυρμοῦ καὶ

¹ ἀνυμνεῖ L.
² om. Lat.; possibly corrupt.
³ C, cf. Lat. lustrationis: κάθαρσιν the rest.

ᵃ Amplification of the narrative in 2 Kings xxiv. 12, " And
Jehoiachin the king of Judah went out to the king of Babylon,
he and his mother and his servants and his princes and his
officers : and the king of Babylon took him," etc. ; cf. Jos.
Ant. x. 100.

ᵇ Reference uncertain, but cf. Orac. Sibyll. iv. 115 ff.
ἥξει καὶ Σολύμοισι κάκη πολέμοιο θύελλα | Ἰταλόθεν, νηὸν δὲ θεοῦ

to the enemy and see the house of God in flames.[a] Therefore is he celebrated in sacred story by all Jews, and memory, in a stream that runs down the ages ever fresh, passes him on to posterity immortal. A noble example, John, even were it dangerous to follow ; but I can warrant you even pardon from the Romans. Remember, too, that I who exhort you am your countryman, that I who make this promise am a Jew ; and it is right that you should consider who is your counsellor and whence he comes. For never may I live to become so abject a captive as to abjure my race or to forget the traditions of my forefathers !

" Once again are you indignant and shout your abuse at me ; and indeed I deserve even harsher treatment for offering advice in fate's despite and for struggling to save those whom God has condemned. Who knows not the records of the ancient prophets and that oracle which threatens this poor city and is even now coming true ? For they foretold that it would then be taken whensoever one should begin to slaughter his own countrymen.[b] And is not the city, aye and the whole temple, filled with your corpses ? God it is then, God Himself. who with the Romans is bringing the fire to purge His temple and exterminating a city so laden with pollutions."

(2) At these words, spoken with lamentation and

μέγαν ἐξαλαπάξει. | ἡνίκα δ' ἀφροσύνῃσι πεποιθότες εὐσεβίην τε | ῥίψουσιν στυγερούς τε τελοῦσι φόνους περὶ νηόν, | καὶ τότ' ἀπ' Ἰταλίης . . . (an allusion follows to Nero's flight and the Roman civil war). . . . | ἐκ Συρίης δ' ἥξει Ῥώμης πρόμος, ὃς πυρὶ νηὸν | συμφλέξας Σολύμων κτλ. The fourth book of Sibylline Oracles dates from c. A.D. 80, and is therefore almost contemporary with the *Jewish War* of Josephus.

112 δακρύων λυγμῷ τὴν φωνὴν ἐνεκόπη. καὶ Ῥωμαῖοι
μὲν ᾤκτειράν τε τοῦ πάθους καὶ τῆς προαιρέσεως
αὐτὸν ἐθαύμασαν, οἱ δὲ περὶ τὸν Ἰωάννην παρ-
ωξύνοντο μᾶλλον ἐπὶ τοὺς Ῥωμαίους ἐπιθυμοῦντες
113 ἐγκρατεῖς γενέσθαι κἀκείνου. τῶν γε μὴν εὐγενῶν
πολλοὺς ἐκίνησεν ὁ λόγος, καὶ τινὲς μὲν ὀρρωδοῦντες τὰς φυλακὰς τῶν στασιαστῶν κατὰ χώραν
ἔμενον, ἀπώλειαν μέντοι σφῶν τε αὐτῶν καὶ τῆς
πόλεως κατεγνώκεσαν, εἰσὶ δ' οἳ καιροφυλακή-
σαντες ἄδειαν ἀναχωρήσεως πρὸς τοὺς Ῥωμαίους
114 κατέφυγον. ὧν ἦσαν ἀρχιερεῖς μὲν Ἰώσηπός τε
καὶ Ἰησοῦς, υἱοὶ δ' ἀρχιερέων τρεῖς μὲν Ἰσμαήλου
τοῦ καρατομηθέντος ἐν Κυρήνῃ, καὶ τέσσαρες
Ματθίου καὶ εἷς ἑτέρου Ματθίου, διαδρὰς μετὰ τὴν
τοῦ πατρὸς ἀπώλειαν, ὃν ὁ τοῦ Γιώρα Σίμων
ἀπέκτεινεν σὺν τρισὶν υἱοῖς, ὡς προείρηται.
πολλοὶ δὲ καὶ τῶν [ἄλλων]¹ εὐγενῶν τοῖς ἀρχιερεῦσι
115 συμμετεβάλοντο. Καῖσαρ δ' αὐτοὺς τά τε ἄλλα
φιλοφρόνως ἐδέξατο καὶ γινώσκων ἀλλοφύλοις
ἤθεσιν ἀηδῆ τὴν διατριβὴν ἕξειν ἀπέπεμψεν αὐτοὺς
εἰς Γόφναν, τέως ἐκεῖ παραινῶν μένειν· ἀποδώσειν
γὰρ ἑκάστῳ τὰς κτήσεις κατὰ σχολὴν ἀπὸ τοῦ
116 πολέμου γενόμενος. οἱ μὲν οὖν εἰς τὸ δοθὲν
πολίχνιον μετὰ πάσης ἀσφαλείας ἀνεχώρουν ἄσμενοι·
μὴ φαινομένων δ' αὐτῶν διεφήμισαν οἱ στασιασταὶ
πάλιν ὡς ἀποσφαγεῖεν ὑπὸ Ῥωμαίων οἱ αὐτόμολοι,
δηλονότι τοὺς λοιποὺς ἀποτρέποντες τῷ φόβῳ

¹ om. C Lat.

ᵃ Possibly Ishmael, son of Phabi, whose tenure of the
high-priesthood and detention in Rome by Nero as a hostage
are mentioned elsewhere, *A.* xviii. 34, xx. 179, 194 f.

408

tears, Josephus's voice broke down with sobs. Even Effect of the Romans pitied him in his emotion and admired the speech : desertion his resolution ; but John and his followers were only of many the more exasperated against the Romans, being Jewish nobles eager to get Josephus also into their power. Many, however, of the upper class were moved by the speech. Some of these, indeed, intimidated by the rebels' guards, remained where they were, though convinced that they themselves and the city were both doomed to destruction ; but there were others who, watching their opportunity for escaping in safety, made off to the Romans. Among these were the chief priests Joseph and Jesus, and certain sons of chief priests : namely three sons of Ishmael ^a who was beheaded in Cyrene, four of Matthias, and one son of another Matthias ^b ; the last had escaped after the death of his father, who was slain with three of his sons by Simon, son of Gioras, as related above.^c Many others also of the aristocracy went over with the chief priests. Caesar both received them with all other courtesy, and, recognizing that they would find life distasteful amidst foreign customs, dispatched them to Gophna,^d advising them to remain there for the present, and promising to restore every man's property, so soon as he had leisure after the war. They accordingly retired, gladly and in perfect security, to the small town assigned ; but when nothing more was seen of them, the rebels again ^e circulated a report that the deserters had been slaughtered by the Romans, with the evident intention of deterring

^b Matthias, son of Boethus.
^c v. 527-531.
^d *Jufna,* some 12 miles due N. of Jerusalem.
^e *Cf.* v. 453 f.

JOSEPHUS

117 διαδιδράσκειν. ἤνυστο δ' ὡς καὶ πρότερον αὐτοῖς
τὸ πανούργημα[1] πρὸς καιρόν· ἐπεσχέθησαν γὰρ
ὑπὸ τοῦ δέους αὐτομολεῖν.

118 (3) Αὖθις δ' ὡς ἀνακαλέσας τοὺς ἄνδρας ἀπὸ
τῆς Γόφνα Τίτος ἐκέλευσε μετὰ τοῦ Ἰωσήπου
περιελθόντας τὸ τεῖχος ὀφθῆναι τῷ δήμῳ, πλεῖστοι
119 πρὸς τοὺς Ῥωμαίους ἔφευγον. γινόμενοι[2] δ'
ἀθρόοι καὶ πρὸ τῶν Ῥωμαίων ἱστάμενοι μετ'
οἰμωγῆς καὶ δακρύων ἱκέτευον τοὺς στασιαστὰς
τὸ μὲν πρῶτον ὅλῃ τοὺς Ῥωμαίους δέξασθαι τῇ
120 πόλει καὶ τὴν πατρίδα σῶσαι [πάλιν],[3] εἰ δὲ μή,
τοῦ γε ἱεροῦ πάντως ὑπεξελθεῖν καὶ ῥύσασθαι τὸν
ναὸν αὐτοῖς· οὐ γὰρ ἂν τολμῆσαι Ῥωμαίους μὴ
μετὰ μεγίστης ἀνάγκης καταφλέξαι τὰ ἅγια.
121 τούτοις μᾶλλον ἀντεφιλονείκουν, καὶ πολλὰ βλάσ-
φημα τοῖς αὐτομόλοις ἀντικεκραγότες ἐπὶ τῶν
ἱερῶν πυλῶν τούς τε ὀξυβελεῖς καὶ καταπέλτας
καὶ λιθοβόλους μηχανὰς διέστησαν, ὡς τὸ κύκλῳ
μὲν ἱερὸν ἀπὸ πλήθους νεκρῶν προσεοικέναι
122 πολυανδρίῳ, τὸν δὲ ναὸν αὐτὸν φρουρίῳ. τοῖς δ'
ἁγίοις καὶ ἀβάτοις μετὰ τῶν ὅπλων εἰσεπήδων
θερμὰς ἔτι τὰς χεῖρας ἐξ ὁμοφύλων ἔχοντες
φόνων, καὶ προύκοψαν εἰς τοσοῦτον παρανομίας,
ὥσθ' ἣν ἂν εἰκὸς ἀγανάκτησιν γενέσθαι Ἰουδαίων,
εἰ Ῥωμαῖοι ταῦτ' ἐξυβρίζοιεν[4] εἰς αὐτούς, ταύτην
εἶναι παρὰ Ῥωμαίων τότε πρὸς Ἰουδαίους ἀσε-
123 βοῦντας εἰς τὰ ἴδια. τῶν μέν γε στρατιωτῶν οὐκ
ἔστιν ὅστις οὐ μετὰ φρίκης εἰς τὸν ναὸν ἀφεώρα

---

[1] LC (cf. vi. 230, 321) : πανοῦργον the rest.
[2] γενόμενοι P.
[3] om. Lat., probably rightly : πόλιν was perhaps written
as a gloss on πατρίδα and then corrected to πάλιν.
[4] ἐξύβριζον P.

410

the rest from attempting to escape. The ruse, as before,[a] was successful for a while, terror checking desertions.

(3) Subsequently, however, Titus recalled these men from Gophna and ordered them to go round the ramparts with Josephus and let the people see them ; whereupon great numbers fled to the Romans. Grouped together and standing before the Roman lines, the refugees, with lamentation and tears, implored the rebels, as their best course, to admit the Romans freely to the city and to save the fatherland ; or, failing that, at all events to withdraw from the temple and to preserve the sacred edifice for them, since the Romans would never venture, except under the direst necessity, to set fire to the holy places. These appeals only excited fiercer opposition, and retorting by heaping abuse upon the deserters, they ranged their quick-firers,[b] catapults, and *ballistae* above the holy gates, so that the surrounding temple-court from the multitude of dead resembled a common burial-ground and the temple itself a fortress. Into those hallowed and inviolable precincts they rushed in arms, their hands yet hot with the blood of their countrymen ; and to such lengths of crime did they proceed, that the indignation which the Jews might naturally have displayed had the Romans inflicted such wanton outrages upon them, was now manifested by the Romans against the Jews, for profaning their own sacred places. Of the soldiers, indeed, there was not one who did not regard the temple with awe and reverence and pray that the

who appeal to their countrymen to surrender.

---

[a] *Cf.* v. 453 f.   [b] Or " scorpions."

411

JOSEPHUS

καὶ προσεκύνει τούς τε λῃστὰς ηὔχετο πρὶν ἀνηκέστου πάθους μετανοῆσαι.

124 (4) Τίτος δὲ ὑπερπαθήσας πάλιν ἐξωνείδιζε τοὺς
περὶ τὸν Ἰωάννην, λέγων " ἆρ' οὐχ ὑμεῖς, ὦ
μιαρώτατοι, τὸν δρύφακτον τοῦτον προυβάλεσθε
125 τῶν ἁγίων; οὐχ ὑμεῖς δὲ τὰς ἐν αὐτῷ στήλας
διεστήσατε, γράμμασιν Ἑλληνικοῖς καὶ ἡμετέροις
κεχαραγμένας,[1] μηδένα τὸ γείσιον ὑπερβαίνειν[2]
126 παραγγέλλειν[3]; οὐχ ἡμεῖς δὲ τοὺς ὑπερβάντας ὑμῖν
ἀναιρεῖν ἐπετρέψαμεν, κἂν Ῥωμαῖός τις ᾖ; τί οὖν
νῦν, ἀλιτήριοι, καὶ νεκροὺς ἐν αὐτῷ καταπατεῖτε;
τί δὲ τὸν ναὸν αἵματι ξένῳ καὶ ἐγχωρίῳ φύρετε;
127 μαρτύρομαι θεοὺς ἐγὼ πατρίους καὶ εἴ τις ἐφεώρα
ποτὲ τόνδε τὸν χῶρον, νῦν μὲν γὰρ οὐκ οἴομαι,
μαρτύρομαι δὲ καὶ στρατιὰν [τὴν][4] ἐμὴν καὶ τοὺς
παρ' ἐμοὶ Ἰουδαίους καὶ ὑμᾶς αὐτούς, ὡς οὐκ ἐγὼ
128 ταῦθ' ὑμᾶς ἀναγκάζω μιαίνειν. κἂν ἀλλάξητε τῆς
παρατάξεως τὸν τόπον, οὔτε προσελεύσεταί τις
Ῥωμαίων τοῖς ἁγίοις οὔτ' ἐνυβρίσει, τηρήσω δὲ
τὸν ναὸν ὑμῖν καὶ μὴ θέλουσι."

129 (5) Ταῦτα τοῦ Ἰωσήπου διαγγέλλοντος ἐκ τοῦ
Καίσαρος, οἱ λῃσταὶ καὶ ὁ τύραννος οὐκ ἀπ'
εὐνοίας ἀλλὰ κατὰ δειλίαν γίνεσθαι τὰς παρα-
130 κλήσεις δοκοῦντες ὑπερηφάνουν. Τίτος δὲ ὡς οὔτε
οἶκτον ἑαυτῶν τοὺς ἄνδρας οὔτε φειδὼ[5] τοῦ ναοῦ
ποιουμένους ἑώρα, πάλιν πρὸς πόλεμον ἄκων
131 ἐχώρει. πᾶσαν μὲν οὖν τὴν δύναμιν ἐπάγειν αὐτοῖς
οὐχ οἷόν τε ἦν μὴ χωρουμένην τῷ τόπῳ, τριάκοντα
δ' ἐπιλέξας ἀφ' ἑκάστης ἑκατονταρχίας τοὺς

---

[1] + ἃ MV[2] (ἃς MV[1]RC).
[2] + ἀλλογενῆ Destinon (cf. v. 194).
[3] παραγγέλλει MVRC.

412

brigands might relent ere it met with irretrievable calamity.

(4) Titus, yet more deeply distressed, again upbraided John and his friends. " Was it not you," he said, " most abominable wretches, who placed this balustrade ^a before your sanctuary ? Was it not you that ranged along it those slabs, engraved in Greek characters and in our own, proclaiming that none may pass the barrier ? And did we not permit you to put to death any who passed it, even were he a Roman ? Why then, you miscreants, do you now actually trample corpses underfoot within it ? Why do you defile your temple with the blood of foreigner and native ? I call the gods of my fathers to witness and any deity that once watched over this place— for now I believe that there is none—I call my army, the Jews within my lines, and you yourselves to witness that it is not I who force you to pollute these precincts. Exchange the arena of conflict for another and not a Roman shall approach or insult your holy places ; nay, I will preserve the temple for you, even against your will."

Unavailing appeal of Titus.

(5) This message from Caesar being transmitted through Josephus, the brigands and their tyrant,^b attributing his exhortations rather to cowardice than goodwill, treated them with contempt. Titus, thereupon, seeing that these men had neither compassion for themselves nor regard for the temple, once more reluctantly resumed hostilities. It was impossible to bring up his whole force against them owing to the confined nature of the ground ; he therefore selected thirty of the best men from each century,

Roman night attack watched by Titus from Antonia.

<hr>

^a v. 193 f.   ^b John of Gischala.

<hr>

⁴ L: om. the rest.   ⁵ φειδώ τινα LVRC.

ἀρίστους καὶ τοῖς χιλιάρχοις ἀνὰ χιλίους παραδούς,
τούτων δ' ἐπιτάξας ἡγεμόνα Κερεάλιον, ἐπιθέσθαι
προσέταξε ταῖς φυλακαῖς περὶ ὥραν τῆς νυκτὸς
132 ἐνάτην. ὄντα δὲ καὶ αὐτὸν ἐν τοῖς ὅπλοις καὶ
συγκαταβαίνειν παρεσκευασμένον οἵ τε φίλοι διὰ
τὸ μέγεθος τοῦ κινδύνου κατέσχον καὶ τὰ παρὰ
133 τῶν ἡγεμόνων λεγόμενα· πλεῖον γαρ αὐτὸν ἀνύσειν
ἔφασαν ἐπὶ τῆς Ἀντωνίας καθεζόμενον καὶ τὴν
μάχην ἀγωνοθετοῦντα τοῖς στρατιώταις ἢ εἰ καταβὰς προκινδυνεύοι· πάντας γὰρ ὁρῶντος Καίσαρος
134 ἀγαθοὺς πολεμιστὰς ἔσεσθαι. τούτοις πεισθεὶς
Καῖσαρ καὶ δι' ἓν τοῦτο τοῖς στρατιώταις ὑπομένειν εἰπών, ἵνα κρίνῃ τὰς ἀρετὰς αὐτῶν καὶ μήτε
τῶν ἀγαθῶν τις ἀγέραστος μήτε τῶν ἐναντίων
ἀτιμώρητος διαλάθῃ, γένηται δ' αὐτόπτης καὶ
μάρτυς ἁπάντων ὁ καὶ τοῦ κολάζειν καὶ τοῦ
135 τιμᾶν κύριος, τοὺς μὲν ἐπὶ τὴν πρᾶξιν ἔπεμπε καθ'
ἣν ὥραν προείρηται, προελθὼν δ' αὐτὸς εἰς τὸ
εὐκάτοπτον ἀπὸ τῆς Ἀντωνίας ἐκαραδόκει τὸ
μέλλον.

136 (6) Οὐ μὴν οἵ γε πεμφθέντες τοὺς φύλακας εὗρον
κοιμωμένους, ὡς ἤλπισαν, ἀλλ' ἀναπηδήσασι μετὰ
κραυγῆς εὐθέως συνεπλέκοντο· πρὸς δὲ τὴν βοὴν
τῶν ἐκκοιτούντων ἔνδοθεν οἱ λοιποὶ κατὰ στῖφος
137 ἐξέθεον. τῶν μὲν δὴ πρώτων τὰς ὁρμὰς ἐξ-
εδέχοντο Ῥωμαῖοι· περιέπιπτον δ' οἱ μετ' ἐκείνους
τῷ σφετέρῳ τάγματι, καὶ πολλοὶ τοῖς οἰκείοις ὡς
138 πολεμίοις ἐχρῶντο. τὴν μὲν γὰρ διὰ βοῆς ἐπί-
γνωσιν ἡ κραυγὴ συγχυθεῖσα παρ' ἀμφοῖν, τὴν δὲ δι'

---

[a] Sextus Cerealis Vettulenus, commander of Legion V,
iii. 310, etc.
414

entrusted every thousand to a tribune, and appointing Cerealius[a] commander-in-chief gave orders to attack the guards about the ninth hour of the night. He was himself in arms and prepared to descend with them, but was restrained[b] by his friends on account of the gravity of the risk and the observations of the officers, who remarked that he would achieve more by sitting still in Antonia as director of the contest of his troops than by going down and exposing himself in the forefront; for under the eyes of Caesar all would play the man. To this persuasion Caesar yielded, telling his men that his sole reason for remaining behind was that he might judge of their gallantry, so that none of the brave might go unnoticed and unrewarded nor any of an opposite character escape the penalty, but that he, who had power both to punish and to reward, might be a spectator and witness of all. At the hour mentioned he dispatched them upon their enterprise, while he himself advanced to a spot from which he could see all below, and from Antonia anxiously awaited the issue.

(6) The force thus dispatched did not, however, find the guards asleep, as they had hoped, but, the latter springing up with a shout, they were instantly involved in a close struggle; and at the cry of the sentries their comrades dashed out in a dense body from within. The Romans met the charge of the front ranks; while those behind fell foul of their own party, and many treated their friends as foes. For recognition by the voice was rendered impossible for any by the confused din on either

[b] *Cf.* 2 Sam. xviii. 2 ff. (David restrained from going forth to war against Absalom).

ὀμμάτων ἡ νὺξ ἕκαστον ἀφείλετο, καὶ τυφλώττειν
ἄλλως οὓς μὲν οἱ θυμοὶ παρεσκεύαζον οὓς δ' ο
φόβοι· διὰ τοῦτο τὸν προστυχόντα πλήττειν ἦ
139 ἄκριτον. Ῥωμαίους μὲν οὖν συνησπικότας κα
κατὰ συντάξεις προπηδῶντας ἧττον ἔβλαπτεν ἡ
ἄγνοια· καὶ γὰρ ἦν παρ' ἑκάστῳ μνήμη τοῦ
140 συνθήματος· Ἰουδαῖοι δ' ἀεὶ σκεδαννύμενοι καὶ
τάς τε προσβολὰς καὶ τὰς ὑποχωρήσεις ἀνέδην ποιούμενοι πολλάκις φαντασίαν παρεῖχον ἀλλήλοις
πολεμίων· τὸν ὑποστρέφοντα γὰρ ἕκαστος οἰκεῖον
διὰ σκότους ὡς ἐπιόντα Ῥωμαῖον ἐξεδέχετο.
141 πλείους γοῦν ὑπὸ τῶν ἰδίων ἢ τῶν πολεμίων
ἐτρώθησαν, ἕως ἡμέρας γενομένης ὄψει τὸ λοιπὸν
ἡ μάχη διεκρίνετο, καὶ κατὰ φάλαγγα διαστάντες
τοῖς τε βέλεσιν εὐτάκτοις ἐχρῶντο καὶ ταῖς ἀμύναις.
142 οὐδέτεροι δὲ οὔτ' εἶκον οὔτ' ἐκοπίων, ἀλλ' οἱ μὲν
ὡς ἐφορῶντος Καίσαρος[1] κατ' ἄνδρα καὶ κατὰ
συντάξεις ἤριζον ἀλλήλοις, καὶ προκοπῆς ἕκαστος
ἐκείνην αὑτῷ τὴν ἡμέραν ἄρξειν ὑπελάμβανεν, εἰ
143 γενναίως ἀγωνίσαιτο· Ἰουδαίοις δ' ἐβράβευε τὰς
τόλμας ὅ τε περὶ σφῶν αὐτῶν καὶ τοῦ ἱεροῦ φόβος
καὶ ὁ τύραννος ἐφεστὼς καὶ τοὺς μὲν παρακαλῶν,
144 τοὺς δὲ μαστιγῶν καὶ διεγείρων ἀπειλαῖς. συνέβαινε δὲ τὸ μὲν πλεῖστον σταδιαίαν[2] εἶναι τὴν μάχην,
ἐν ὀλίγῳ δὲ καὶ ταχέως ἀντιστρέφεσθαι τὰς ῥοπάς·
οὐδέτεροι γὰρ οὔτε φυγῆς οὔτε διώξεως μῆκος
145 εἶχον. ἀεὶ δὲ πρὸς τὸ συμβαῖνον οἰκεῖος[3] ἀπὸ τῆς
Ἀντωνίας ὁ θόρυβος ἦν, θαρρεῖν δὲ καὶ κρατοῦσι

---

[1] P Lat. (imperatoris): Τίτου the rest.   [2] σταδιαίαν MSS.
[3] C: om. L: οἰκείοις (τοῖς οἰκείοις M) the rest.

---

[a] Or " was separated (or ' decided ') by the eye."

side, as was ocular recognition by the darkness of
the night; moreover, some were so blinded by
passion and others by fear as to strike indiscriminately all who fell in their way. The Romans, who
interlocked their shields and charged by companies,
suffered less from such ignorance; each man, too,
recollected the watchword. But the Jews, constantly
scattering and alike attacking and retreating at
random, were frequently taken by each other for
enemies: each man in the darkness receiving a
returning comrade as if he were an advancing Roman.
Indeed more were wounded by their own friends
than by the foe, until, with the dawn of day, the
battle thenceforward was discernible to the eye [a] and,
parting into their respective lines, they could employ
their missiles and maintain their defence in good
order. Nor did either side give way or relax their
efforts. The Romans, as under the eye of Caesar,
vied man with man and company with company,
each believing that that day would lead to his
promotion, if he but fought with gallantry. The
Jews had as arbiter of their own daring deeds their
fear for themselves and for the temple and the
looming presence of the tyrant,[b] encouraging some,
rousing others by the lash and by menaces into
action. The contest was perforce for the most
part stationary,[c] the manœuvres to and fro being
limited to a narrow space and quickly over; for
neither side had room for flight or pursuit. And at
every incident of the fight an appropriate roar went
up from Antonia: were their comrades gaining they

[b] John of Gischala.
[c] The MSS. read " was perforce confined at most within
a furlong."

τοῖς σφετέροις ἐπεβόων καὶ μένειν τρεπομένοις.
146 ἦν δ' ὥσπερ τι πολέμου θέατρον· οὐδὲν γὰρ οὔτε
Τίτον οὔτε τοὺς περὶ αὐτὸν ἐλάνθανε τῶν κατὰ τὴν
147 μάχην. τὸ δὲ πέρας, ἀρξάμενοι τῆς νυκτὸς ἐνάτης
ὥρας περὶ[1] πέμπτην τῆς ἡμέρας διελύθησαν, ἀφ'
οὗπερ ἤρξαντο τόπου τῆς συμβολῆς μηδέτεροι
βεβαίως κλίναντες τοὺς ἑτέρους, ἀλλὰ τὴν νίκην
148 μέσην ἐν ἀγχωμάλῳ[2] καταλιπόντες. καὶ Ῥωμαίων
μὲν ἐπισήμως ἠγωνίσαντο πολλοί, Ἰουδαίων δ' ἐκ
μὲν τῶν περὶ Σίμωνα Ἰούδης ὁ τοῦ Μαρεώτου καὶ
Σίμων ὁ τοῦ Ὁσαΐα, τῶν δὲ Ἰδουμαίων Ἰάκωβος
καὶ Σίμων, Ἀκατελᾶ[3] μὲν οὗτος παῖς, Σωσᾶ δὲ
ὁ Ἰάκωβος, τῶν δὲ μετὰ Ἰωάννου Γεφθαῖος καὶ
Ἀλεξᾶς, τῶν δὲ ζηλωτῶν Σίμων υἱὸς Ἀρί.
149 (7) Ἐν τούτῳ δ' ἡ λοιπὴ τῶν Ῥωμαίων δύναμις
ἡμέραις ἑπτὰ καταστρεψαμένη τοὺς τῆς Ἀντωνίας
θεμελίους μέχρι τοῦ ἱεροῦ πλατεῖαν ἄνοδον[4] εὐ-
150 τρεπίσαντο. πλησιάσαντα δὲ τῷ πρώτῳ περιβόλῳ
τὰ τάγματα κατήρχετο χωμάτων, τὸ μὲν ἀντικρὺς
τῆς τοῦ εἴσω ἱεροῦ γωνίας, ἥτις ἦν κατ' ἄρκτον
καὶ δύσιν, τὸ δὲ κατὰ τὴν βόρειον ἐξέδραν, ἣ
151 μεταξὺ τῶν δύο πυλῶν ἦν· τῶν δὲ λοιπῶν δύο
θάτερον μὲν κατὰ τὴν ἑσπέριον στοὰν τοῦ ἔξωθεν
ἱεροῦ, τὸ δ' ἕτερον [ἔξω][5] κατὰ τὴν βόρειον. προύκοπτεν μέντοι μετὰ πολλοῦ καμάτου καὶ ταλαιπωρίας αὐτοῖς τὰ ἔργα [καὶ][6] τὴν ὕλην ἀφ' ἑκατὸν
152 σταδίων συγκομίζουσιν, ἐκακοῦντο δ' ἔσθ' ὅπη καὶ
κατ' ἐπιβουλάς, αὐτοὶ διὰ περιουσίαν τοῦ κρατεῖν

---

[1] Niese: ὑπὲρ MSS.   [2] P: + τῇ παρατάξει the rest.
[3] PA: Νακατελα MVR: Καθθαια L: Καθλᾶ C ; cf. v. 249.
[4] ὁδὸν PM Lat. Heg. ; for text cf. vi. 93.
[5] om. Lat.   [6] om. C Lat.

shouted to them to be of good cheer, were they falling back, to stand fast. It was like a battle on the stage, for nothing throughout the engagement escaped the eyes of Titus or of those around him. At length, after an action which opened at the ninth hour of the night, they broke off about the fifth hour of the day, neither side having seriously repelled their adversaries from the very spot on which the conflict began, and victory remaining undecided in this drawn battle. Of the Romans many distinguished themselves; the Jewish heroes were, of the party of Simon, Judes son of Mareotes, and Simon son of Hosaias; of the Idumaeans, James and Simon, the latter the son of Acatelas,[a] the former of Sosas; of John's contingent, Gephthaeus and Alexas; of the Zealots, Simon son of Ari.

A drawn contest.

(7) Meanwhile the rest of the Roman army, having in seven days overthrown the foundations of Antonia, had prepared a broad ascent to the temple. The legions now approaching the first wall began to raise embankments: one facing the north-west angle of the inner temple, a second over against the northern hall which stood between the two gates, and two more, one opposite the western portico of the outer court of the temple, the other outside [b] opposite the northern portico. The works, however, did not advance without causing the troops great fatigue and hardship, the timber being conveyed from a distance of a hundred furlongs; [c] they also suffered occasionally from stratagems, being themselves owing to their overwhelming superiority less on their

A road engineered to the temple and new embankments begun.

---

[a] The name elsewhere appears as Caathas or Cathlas, iv. 271, v. 249.

[b] Perhaps " further out."   [c] *Cf.* § 5.

ὄντες ἀδεέστεροι καὶ δι' ἀπόγνωσιν ἤδη σωτηρίας
153 χρώμενοι τολμηροτέροις τοῖς Ἰουδαίοις. τῶν γὰρ
ἱππέων τινὲς ὁπότε προέλθοιεν ἐπὶ ξυλείαν ἢ
χόρτου συλλογήν, τὸν τῆς συγκομιδῆς[1] χρόνον
ἀνίεσαν βόσκεσθαι τοὺς ἵππους ἀποχαλινοῦντες,
οὓς οἱ Ἰουδαῖοι κατὰ στῖφος ἐκπηδῶντες ἥρπαζον.
154 καὶ τούτου συνεχῶς γινομένου νομίσας Καῖσαρ,
ὅπερ ἦν, ἀμελείᾳ τῶν σφετέρων πλέον ἢ τῇ Ἰουδαίων ἀνδρείᾳ γίνεσθαι τὰς ἁρπαγάς, ἔγνω σκυ-
θρωπότερον τοὺς λοιποὺς πρὸς φυλακὴν τῶν
155 ἵππων[2] ἐπιστρέψαι. καὶ κελεύσας ἀπαχθῆναι τὴν
ἐπὶ θανάτῳ τῶν ἀπολεσάντων στρατιωτῶν ἕνα,
φόβῳ τοῖς ἄλλοις ἐτήρησε τοὺς ἵππους· οὐκέτι γὰρ
εἴων νέμεσθαι, καθάπερ δὲ συμπεφυκότες αὐτοῖς
156 ἐπὶ τὰς χρείας ἐξῇεσαν. οἱ μὲν οὖν προσεπολέμουν
τῷ ἱερῷ καὶ τὰ χώματα διήγειρον.[3]
157 (8) Μετὰ δὲ μίαν ἡμέραν αὐτῶν τῆς ἀνόδου
πολλοὶ τῶν στασιαστῶν, οἷς ἁρπαγαί τε ἐπέλειπον
ἤδη καὶ ὁ λιμὸς ἤπειγε, συνελθόντες ταῖς κατὰ τὸ
Ἐλαιῶν ὄρος Ῥωμαίων φυλακαῖς ἐπιτίθενται περὶ
ὥραν ἑνδεκάτην τῆς ἡμέρας, οἰόμενοι πρῶτον μὲν
ἀδοκήτων, ἔπειτα πρὸς θεραπείαις[4] ἤδη τοῦ
158 σώματος ὄντων ῥᾳδίως διεκπαίσειν.[5] προαισθό-
μενοι δὲ τὴν ἔφοδον αὐτῶν οἱ Ῥωμαῖοι καὶ
ταχέως ἐκ τῶν πλησίον φρουρίων συνδραμόντες
εἶργον ὑπερπηδᾶν καὶ διακόπτειν τὸ περιτείχισμα
159 βιαζομένους. γενομένης δὲ καρτερᾶς τῆς συμβολῆς ἄλλα τε πολλὰ παρ' ἑκατέρων γενναίως

---

[1] PA : κομιδῆς the rest.
[2] A Lat. : ἱππέων the rest.
[3] L : διήγειραν the rest. [4] Niese : θεραπείας mss.
[5] Destinon : διεκπεσεῖν C : διεκπαίειν the rest.

guard, while they found the Jews through their present despair of escape more daring than before. Thus, some of the cavalry, whenever they went out to collect wood or fodder, used to take the bridles off their horses and turn them loose to graze while they were foraging; and these the Jews, sallying out in companies, carried off. This happening repeatedly, Caesar, correctly believing that these raids were due rather to the negligence of his own men than to the courage of the Jews, determined by an act of unusual severity to make the rest more attentive to the care of their horses. He accordingly ordered off one of the troopers who had lost his horse to capital punishment, and by that fearful example preserved the steeds of the others; for they no longer let them graze, but went forth on their errands clinging to them as though man and beast were by nature inseparable. The assault on the temple and the erection of the earthworks thus occupied the energies of the Romans.

Jewish horse-stealers.

(8) The day after the ascent of the legions many of the rebels, who with plunder now failing them were hard pressed by famine, joined forces and attacked the Roman sentries on the Mount of Olives [a] at about the eleventh hour of the day; expecting firstly to find them off their guard, and secondly to catch them while taking refreshment, and thus easily to break through. The Romans, however, fore-warned of their approach, promptly rushed from the neighbouring forts to the spot and checked their forcible efforts to scale or to cut their way through the camp wall. A sharp contest ensued, in which many gallant feats were performed on either side;

Jewish attack on Roman camp on Mount Olivet.

[a] Where the tenth legion were encamped, v. 69 f.

ἐπράχθη, Ῥωμαίων μὲν μετὰ τῆς ἰσχύος ἐμπειρίᾳ
τοῦ πολεμεῖν χρωμένων, Ἰουδαίων δ' ἀφειδέσι ταῖς
160 ὁρμαῖς καὶ τοῖς θυμοῖς ἀκατασχέτοις· ἐστρατήγει
δὲ τῶν μὲν αἰδώς, τῶν δ' ἀνάγκη· τό τε γὰρ
ἐξαφεῖναι Ἰουδαίους ὥσπερ ἄρκυσιν ἐνειλημένους[1]
Ῥωμαίοις αἴσχιστον ἐδόκει, κἀκεῖνοι μίαν ἐλπίδα
σωτηρίας εἶχον, εἰ βιασάμενοι ῥήξειαν τὸ τεῖχος·
161 καὶ τῶν ἀπὸ σπείρας τις ἱππέων, Πεδάνιος τοὔνομα,
τρεπομένων ἤδη τῶν Ἰουδαίων καὶ κατὰ τῆς
φάραγγος συνωθουμένων, ῥόθιον ἐκ πλαγίου παρελαύνων τὸν ἵππον ἁρπάζει τινὰ φεύγοντα τῶν
πολεμίων, νεανίαν στιβαρόν τε ἄλλως τὸ σῶμα
καὶ καθωπλισμένον, δραξάμενος ἐκ τοῦ σφυροῦ·
162 τοσοῦτον μὲν ἑαυτὸν ἐκ τρέχοντος ἐπέκλινε τοῦ
ἵππου, τοσοῦτον δ' ἐπεδείξατο τῆς[2] δεξιᾶς τὸν
τόνον καὶ τοῦ λοιποῦ σώματος ἔτι δ' ἐμπειρίαν[3]
163 ἱππικῆς. ὁ μὲν οὖν ὥσπερ τι κειμήλιον ἁρπασά-
μενος ἧκε φέρων Καίσαρι τὸν αἰχμάλωτον· Τίτος
δὲ τὸν μὲν λαβόντα τῆς δυνάμεως θαυμάσας, τὸν
δὲ ληφθέντα τῆς περὶ τὸ τεῖχος ἐπιχειρήσεως
κολάσαι κελεύσας, αὐτὸς ἐν ταῖς περὶ τὸ ἱερὸν
διαμάχαις ἦν καὶ τὰ χώματα κατήπειγεν.
164 (9) Ἐν ᾧ Ἰουδαῖοι κακούμενοι ταῖς συμβολαῖς,
ἀεὶ κατ' ὀλίγον κορυφουμένου τοῦ πολέμου καὶ τῷ
ναῷ προσέρποντος, καθάπερ σηπομένου σώματος
ἀπέκοπτον τὰ προειλημμένα μέλη φθάνοντες τὴν
165 εἰς τὸ πρόσω νομήν. τῆς γὰρ βορείου καὶ κατὰ
δύσιν στοᾶς τὸ συνεχὲς πρὸς τὴν Ἀντωνίαν
ἐμπρήσαντες ἔπειτα ἀπέρρηξαν ὅσον πήχεις εἴκοσι,
ταῖς ἰδίαις χερσὶν ἀρξάμενοι καίειν τὰ ἅγια.

---

[1] ἐνειλημένους Destinon : ἐνειλημμένους mss.
[2] + τε AVRC.
[3] Syr. Suidas : ἐμπειρίας mss.

422

the Romans displaying military skill combined with
strength, the Jews reckless impetuosity and unbridled
rage. Shame commanded the one party, necessity
the other; for to let loose the Jews, now caught
as it were in a net, seemed to the Romans most disgraceful, while their enemy's one hope of safety lay
in forcing their way through the wall. Among other Equestrian
incidents, a trooper from one of the cohorts, named feat of
Pedanius—when the Jews were at last repulsed Pedanius.
and being driven down into the ravine—urging
his horse at top speed along their flank, snatched up
one of the flying foe, a youth of sturdy frame and
in full armour, grasping him by the ankle; so far
did he stoop from his horse, when at the gallop,
and such muscular strength of arm and body, along
with consummate horsemanship, did he display.
Carrying off his captive like some precious treasure,
he came with his prize to Caesar. Titus expressed
his admiration of the captor's strength, ordered his
captive to punishment for his assault on the wall,
and then devoted his attention to the struggle for
the temple and the acceleration of the earthworks.

(9) Meanwhile the Jews, sorely suffering from Burning of
their encounters, as the war slowly, yet steadily, the temple
rose to a climax and crept towards the sanctuary, porticoes
cut away, as from a mortifying body, the limbs and con-
already affected, to arrest further ravages of the the Romans.
disease. In other words, they set fire to that portion
of the north-west portico which was connected with
Antonia, and afterwards hacked away some twenty
cubits, their own hands thus beginning the conflagration of the holy places. Two days later, on the 24 Panemus
c. 12 August

166 μετὰ δ' ἡμέρας δύο, τετράδι καὶ εἰκάδι τοῦ προ-
εἰρημένου μηνός, τὴν πλησίον στοὰν ὑποπιμπρᾶσι
Ῥωμαῖοι, καὶ μέχρι πεντεκαίδεκα πηχῶν προ-
κόψαντος τοῦ πυρὸς ἀποκόπτουσιν ὁμοίως Ἰουδαῖοι
τὴν ὀροφήν, μήτε καθάπαν[1] ἐξιστάμενοι τῶν ἔργων
καὶ τὸ πρὸς τὴν Ἀντωνίαν συναφὲς αὐτῶν δι-
167 αιροῦντες· διὸ καὶ παρὸν κωλύειν ὑποπιμπράντας,
οἱ δὲ πρὸς τὴν ἐμβολὴν τοῦ πυρὸς ἠρεμήσαντες
168 τὴν νομὴν ἐμέτρησαν τῷ σφίσι χρησίμῳ.[2] περὶ
μὲν δὴ τὸ ἱερὸν οὐ διέλειπον αἱ συμβολαί, συνεχὴς
δ' ἦν κατὰ μέρος ἐκθεόντων ἐπ' ἀλλήλους ὁ
πόλεμος.

169 (10) Τῶν Ἰουδαίων δέ τις κατὰ ταύτας τὰς
ἡμέρας ἀνὴρ τό τε σῶμα βραχὺς καὶ τὴν ὄψιν
εὐκαταφρόνητος, γένους θ' ἕνεκα καὶ τῶν ἄλλων
ἄσημος, Ἰωνάθης ἐκαλεῖτο, προελθὼν κατὰ τὸ
τοῦ ἀρχιερέως Ἰωάννου μνημεῖον ἄλλα τε πολλὰ
πρὸς τοὺς Ῥωμαίους ὑπερηφάνως ἐφθέγγετο καὶ
τὸν ἄριστον αὐτῶν εἰς μονομαχίαν προυκαλεῖτο.
170 τῶν δὲ ταύτῃ παρατεταγμένων οἱ πολλοὶ μὲν
ὑπερηφάνουν, ἦσαν δ' οἳ κατὰ τὸ εἰκὸς ἐδεδοίκεσαν,
ἥπτετό γε μὴν τινῶν καὶ λογισμὸς οὐκ ἀσύνετος
171 θανατῶντι μὴ συμπλέκεσθαι· τοὺς γὰρ ἀπεγνω-
κότας τὴν σωτηρίαν ἅμα[3] καὶ τὰς ὁρμὰς ἀταμιεύ-
τους ἔχειν καὶ τὸ θεῖον εὐδυσώπητον, τό τε παρα-
βάλλεσθαι πρὸς οὓς καὶ τὸ νικᾶν οὐ μέγα καὶ μετ'
αἰσχύνης τὸ λειφθῆναι σφαλερόν, οὐκ ἀνδρείας

---

[1] καθάπαξ PAM.

[2] τῷ σφίσι χρησ. Niese : αὐτῷ σφίσι χρησίμως mss.

[3] ἅμα Destinon : ἀλλὰ PAL, perhaps rightly = " yet " : τά
τε ἄλλα (ταῦτ' ἄλλα) the rest.

---

[a] i.e., to cut the connexion with Antonia.

twenty-fourth of the month above mentioned, the Romans set light to the adjoining portico ; and when the flames had spread to a distance of fifty cubits, it was again the Jews who cut away the roof, and with no reverence whatever for these works of art severed the connexion thereby formed with Antonia. For that reason,[a] though they might have prevented the building from being set alight, instead when the fire attacked it they remained motionless and merely measured the extent of its ravages by their own convenience. Thus conflicts around the temple raged incessantly, and fights between small parties sallying out upon each other were continuous.

(10) In the course of these days a Jew, named Jonathan, a man of mean stature and despicable appearance, undistinguished by birth or otherwise, coming forward opposite the tomb of the high-priest John,[b] and addressing the Romans in much opprobrious language, challenged the best of them to single combat. Of those in the adverse ranks at this point, the majority regarded him with contempt, some probably with apprehension, while others were influenced by the not unreasonable reflection that it was wise to avoid a conflict with one who courted death ; being aware that men who despaired of their lives had not only ungovernable passions but also the ready compassion of the Deity,[c] and that to risk life in an encounter with persons whom to defeat were no great exploit, while to be beaten would involve ignominy as well as danger, would be an

Single combat of Jew and Roman.

---

[b] John Hyrcanus ; the neighbourhood of his monument was the point selected by Titus for his first attack, v. 259.

[c] Literally "had the Deity easily put out of countenance," *i.e.* "easily moved by entreaty."

172 ἀλλὰ θρασύτητος εἶναι. μηδενὸς δ' ἐπὶ πολὺ
προϊόντος καὶ τοῦ Ἰουδαίου πολλὰ κατακερτο-
μοῦντος αὐτοὺς εἰς δειλίαν, ἀλαζὼν γάρ τις ἦν
αὐτῷ σφόδρα καὶ τῶν Ῥωμαίων ὑπερήφανος,
Πούδης τις ὄνομα τῶν ἐξ ἴλης ἱππέων βδελυξά-
μενος αὐτοῦ τά τε ῥήματα καὶ τὸ αὔθαδες, εἰκὸς
δὲ καὶ πρὸς τὴν βραχύτητα τοῦ σώματος αὐτὸν
173 ἀσκέπτως ἐπαρθῆναι, προπηδᾷ, καὶ τὰ μὲν ἄλλα
περιῆν συμβαλών, προεδόθη δ' ὑπὸ τῆς τύχης·
πεσόντα γὰρ αὐτὸν ὁ Ἰωνάθης ἀποσφάττει προσ-
174 δραμών. ἔπειτα ἐπιβὰς τῷ νεκρῷ τό τε ξίφος
ᾑμαγμένον ἀνέσειε καὶ τῇ λαιᾷ τὸν θυρεόν, ἐπηλά-
λαξέ τε τῇ στρατιᾷ πολλὰ καὶ πρὸς τὸν πεσόντα
κομπάζων καὶ τοὺς ὁρῶντας Ῥωμαίους ἐπισκώ-
175 πτων, ἕως αὐτὸν ἀνασκιρτῶντα καὶ ματαΐζοντα
Πρῖσκός τις ἑκατοντάρχης τοξεύσας διήλασε βέλει·
πρὸς ὃ τῶν τε Ἰουδαίων καὶ τῶν Ῥωμαίων κραυγὴ
176 συνεξήρθη διάφορος. ὁ δὲ δινηθεὶς ἐκ τῶν ἀλγη-
δόνων ἐπὶ τὸ σῶμα τοῦ πολεμίου κατέπεσεν,
ὠκυτάτην ἀποφήνας ἐν πολέμῳ τὴν ἐπὶ τοῖς
ἀλόγως εὐτυχοῦσι[1] νέμεσιν.

177 (iii. 1) Οἱ δ' ἀνὰ τὸ ἱερὸν στασιασταὶ φανερῶς
τε οὐκ ἀνίεσαν τοὺς ἐπὶ τῶν χωμάτων στρατιώτας
ἀμυνόμενοι καθ' ἑκάστην ἡμέραν, καὶ τοῦ προειρημένου μηνὸς ἑβδόμῃ καὶ εἰκάδι δόλον ἐνσκευά-
178 ζονται τοιόνδε. τῆς ἑσπερίου στοᾶς τὸ μεταξὺ
τῶν δοκῶν καὶ τῆς ὑπ' αὐταῖς[2] ὀροφῆς ὕλης
ἀναπιμπλᾶσιν αὔης, πρὸς δὲ ἀσφάλτου τε καὶ
πίσσης· ἔπειθ' ὡς καταπονούμενοι δῆθεν ὑπεχώ-
179 ρουν. πρὸς ὃ τῶν μὲν ἀσκέπτων πολλοὶ ταῖς
ὁρμαῖς φερόμενοι προσέκειντο τοῖς ὑποχωροῦσιν

[1] τῷ (τὸ A) ἀλόγως εὐτυχοῦντι PA.

act, not of bravery, but of recklessness. For long
no antagonist came forward and the Jew continued
to rail at them as cowards—for the fellow was
supremely conceited and contemptuous of the
Romans—until a trooper from one of the squadrons,[a]
named Pudens, disgusted at his language and
arrogance, perhaps also thoughtlessly presuming on
his puny stature, leapt forward, and was otherwise
gaining on his adversary in the encounter, , when he
was betrayed by fortune : for he fell, whereupon
Jonathan sprang upon him and dispatched him.
Then, trampling on the corpse, brandishing his
bloody sword and with his left hand waving his
buckler, he shouted lustily to the army, glorying
over his prostrate foe and jeering at his Roman
spectators ; until, in the midst of his dancing and
buffoonery, Priscus, a centurion, bent his bow and
transfixed him with an arrow, calling forth from
Jews and Romans simultaneous cries of a contrary
nature. The victim, writhing in agony, fell upon
the body of his foe, illustrating how swift in war is
the nemesis that overtakes irrational success.

(iii. 1) The rebels in the temple, while never
relaxing their undisguised daily efforts to repel the
troops on the earthworks, on the twenty-seventh
of the above-named month contrived, moreover, the
following ruse. They filled the space between the
rafters of the western portico and the ceiling beneath
them with dry tinder, along with bitumen and pitch,
and then, as though utterly exhausted, retired.
Thereupon many of the inconsiderate legionaries,
carried away by impetuosity, started in pursuit of

A Jewish ruse causes great Roman loss on a burning portico.
27 Panemus c. 15 August.

---

[a] Of the auxiliary cavalry (*alae*).

ἐπί τε τὴν στοὰν ἀνεπήδων προσθέμενοι κλίμακας,
οἱ δὲ συνετώτεροι τὴν ἄλογον τροπὴν τῶν Ἰου-
180 δαίων ὑπονοήσαντες ἔμενον. κατεπλήσθη μέντοι
τῶν ἀναπηδησάντων ἡ στοά, κἂν τούτῳ Ἰουδαῖοι[1]
πᾶσαν ὑποπιμπρᾶσιν αὐτήν. αἰρομένης δ' αἰφνιδίως πάντοθεν τῆς φλογὸς τούς τε ἔξω τοῦ
κινδύνου Ῥωμαίους ἔκπληξις ἐπέσχε δεινὴ καὶ
181 τοὺς περισχεθέντας ἀμηχανία. κυκλούμενοι δ'
ὑπὸ τῆς φλογὸς οἱ μὲν εἰς τὴν πόλιν ὀπίσω κατεκρήμνιζον ἑαυτούς, οἱ δ' εἰς τοὺς πολεμίους, πολλοὶ
δ' ἐλπίδι σωτηρίας εἰς τοὺς σφετέρους καταπη-
δῶντες ἐκλῶντο τὰ μέλη, πλείστων δ' ἔφθανε τὰς
ὁρμὰς τὸ πῦρ καί τινες τὴν φλόγα σιδήρῳ.
182 περιεῖχε δ' εὐθέως καὶ τοὺς ἄλλως φθειρομένους
τὸ πῦρ ἐπὶ πλεῖστον ἐκφερόμενον. Καίσαρα δὲ
καίπερ χαλεπαίνοντα τοῖς ἀπολλυμένοις, ἐπειδὴ
δίχα παραγγέλματος ἀναβεβήκεσαν, ὅμως οἶκτος
183 εἰσῄει τῶν ἀνδρῶν· καὶ μηδενὸς προσαμύνειν
δυναμένου, τοῦτο γοῦν παραμύθιον ἦν τοῖς φθειρο-
μένοις τὸ βλέπειν ὑπὲρ οὗ τις ἠφίει τὴν ψυχὴν
ὀδυνώμενον· βοῶν τε γὰρ αὐτοῖς καὶ προπηδῶν
καὶ τοῖς περὶ αὐτὸν ἐκ τῶν ἐνόντων ἐπαμύνειν
184 παρακαλῶν δῆλος ἦν. τὰς δὲ φωνὰς ἕκαστος καὶ
τὴν διάθεσιν ὥσπερ τι λαμπρὸν ἀποφέρων ἐντάφιον
185 εὔθυμος ἀπέθνησκεν. ἔνιοί γε μὴν ἐπὶ τὸν τοῖχον
τῆς στοᾶς ὄντα πλατὺν ἀναχωρήσαντες ἐκ μὲν τοῦ
πυρὸς διεσώθησαν, ὑπὸ δὲ τῶν Ἰουδαίων περισχεθέντες ἐπὶ πολὺ μὲν ἀντέσχον διατιτρωσκό-

---

[1] PL: οἱ Ἰουδαῖοι the rest.

the fugitives and, applying ladders, sprang up them on to the portico; the more prudent, however, suspecting the unaccountable withdrawal of the Jews, remained where they were. The portico, nevertheless, was packed with those who had mounted, at the moment when the Jews from below set the whole building alight. The flames suddenly shooting up on every side, those of the Romans who were out of danger were seized with dire consternation, while those involved in it were utterly helpless. Surrounded by the flames, some precipitated themselves into the city behind them, some into the enemy's midst; many in hope of saving themselves leapt down among their friends and fractured their limbs; but most in their rush to escape were caught by the fire, while some with the sword anticipated the flames. The fire, moreover, spreading far and wide, instantly enveloped even those already doomed to some other form of death. Caesar, though angry with his perishing soldiers for mounting the portico without orders, was yet filled with compassion for them; and, impossible though it was for any to relieve them, it was at least a consolation to the doomed men to behold the grief of him in whose service they were giving up their lives. For he was plainly visible, shouting to them and rushing forward and exhorting those around him to do their utmost to rescue them. And every man, carrying with him, like some splendid obsequies, those cries, that emotion of Caesar, thus cheerfully expired. Some, indeed, got back to the wall of the portico, which was broad, and escaped the conflagration, but were there surrounded by the Jews and, after maintaining

186 μένοι, τέλος δὲ πάντες· ἔπεσον, (2) καὶ τελευταῖός
τις αὐτῶν νεανίας, ὀνόματι Λόγγος,[1] ὅλον ἐπι-
κοσμήσας τὸ πάθος καὶ κατ' ἄνδρα μνήμης ἀξίων
ὄντων πάντων τῶν ἀπολωλότων ἄριστος φανείς.
187 ὃν οἱ μὲν Ἰουδαῖοι τῆς τε ἀλκῆς ἀγάμενοι καὶ
ἄλλως ἀνελεῖν ἀσθενοῦντες καταβῆναι πρὸς αὐτοὺς
ἐπὶ δεξιᾷ παρεκάλουν, ὁ δὲ ἀδελφὸς Κορνήλιος ἐκ
θατέρου μὴ καταισχῦναι τὸ σφέτερον κλέος καὶ
τὴν Ῥωμαίων στρατιάν. τούτῳ πεισθεὶς καὶ
διαράμενος φανερὸν ἑκατέροις τοῖς τάγμασι τὸ
188 ξίφος αὐτὸν ἀναιρεῖ. τῶν δὲ τῷ πυρὶ περι-
σχεθέντων Ἀρτώριός[2] τις πανουργίᾳ διασώζεται·
προσκαλεσάμενος γάρ τινα τῶν συστρατιωτῶν[3]
Λούκιον, ᾧ συνεσκήνει, μεγάλῃ τῇ φωνῇ "κληρο-
νόμον," ἔφη, "καταλείπω σε τῶν ἐμαυτοῦ κτη-
189 μάτων, εἰ προσελθών με δέξαιο." τοῦ δὲ ἑτοίμως προσδραμόντος ὁ μὲν ἐπ' αὐτὸν κατενεχθεὶς
ἔζησεν, ὁ δὲ δεξάμενος ὑπὸ τοῦ βάρους τῷ λιθο-
190 στρώτῳ προσαραχθεὶς παραχρῆμα θνήσκει. τοῦτο
τὸ πάθος πρὸς καιρὸν μὲν Ῥωμαίοις ἐνεποίησεν
ἀθυμίαν, πρὸς δὲ τὸ μέλλον ὅμως ἀπαρακλήτους[4]
κατασκευάσαν[5] φυλακτικωτέρους τε[6] πρὸς τὰς
Ἰουδαίων ἀπάτας ὠφέλησεν, ἐν αἷς τὰ πολλὰ δι'
ἄγνοιαν τῶν τόπων καὶ τὸ ἦθος τῶν ἀνδρῶν
191 ἐβλάπτοντο. κατεκάη δ' ἡ στοὰ μέχρι τοῦ Ἰωάννου
πύργου, ὃν ἐκεῖνος ἐν τῷ πρὸς Σίμωνα πολέμῳ
κατεσκεύασεν ὑπὲρ τὰς ἐξαγούσας ὑπὲρ τὸν ξυστὸν
πύλας· τὸ δὲ λοιπὸν ἐπὶ διεφθαρμένοις ἤδη

---

[1] Longinus Heg. Syr.   [2] Σερτώριος C.
[3] ML Lat.: στρατιωτῶν the rest.   [4] PAL: om. the rest.
[5] Destinon: κατεσκεύασεν (προκατεσκεύασεν L) the rest.
[6] PA: καὶ the rest.

a prolonged resistance, riddled with wounds, all at length fell.

(2) The last survivor of them, a youth named Longus, shed lustre on the whole tragedy, and, memorable as was every single man that perished, proved himself the bravest of all. The Jews, as well from admiration of his prowess as from their inability to kill him, besought him to come down to them, pledging him his life ; his brother Cornelius, on the other hand, implored him not to disgrace his own reputation or the Roman arms. Influenced by his words, he brandished his sword in view of both armies and slew himself. Among those enveloped in the flames one, Artorius, saved his life by an artifice. Calling at the top of his voice to Lucius, a fellow-soldier with whom he shared a tent, " I leave you," he said, " heir to my property if you come and catch me." Lucius promptly running up, Artorius plunged down on top of him and was saved ; while he who received him was dashed by his weight against the pavement and killed on the spot.

This disaster, while it created for the time despondency in the Roman ranks, nevertheless had a beneficial effect for the future in rendering them less responsive to such invitations and more cautious against Jewish stratagems, their injuries from which were mainly due to their ignorance of the ground and the character of the men. The flames consumed the portico as far as the tower[a] which John, during his feud with Simon, had erected over the gates leading out above the Xystus ; the remainder, after the destruction of the troops that had mounted it, was hacked away

[a] The second of four towers erected by John of Gischala, iv. 580 f.

431

192 Ἰουδαῖοι[1] τοῖς ἀναβᾶσιν ἀπέκοψαν. τῇ δ᾽ ὑστεραίᾳ
καὶ Ῥωμαῖοι τὴν βόρειον στοὰν ἐνέπρησαν μέχρι
τῆς ἀνατολικῆς ὅλην, ὧν ἡ συνάπτουσα γωνία τῆς
Κεδρῶνος καλουμένης φάραγγος ὑπερδεδόμητο,
παρ᾽ ὃ καὶ φοβερὸν ἦν τὸ βάθος. καὶ τὰ μὲν περὶ
τὸ ἱερὸν ἐν τούτοις ἦν.

193 (3) Τῶν δ᾽ ὑπὸ τοῦ λιμοῦ φθειρομένων κατὰ
τὴν πόλιν ἄπειρον μὲν ἔπιπτε τὸ πλῆθος, ἀδιήγητα
194 δὲ συνέβαινε τὰ πάθη. καθ᾽ ἑκάστην γὰρ οἰκίαν,
εἴ που τροφῆς παραφανείη σκιά, πόλεμος ἦν, καὶ
διὰ χειρῶν ἐχώρουν οἱ φίλτατοι πρὸς ἀλλήλους
ἐξαρπάζοντες τὰ ταλαίπωρα τῆς ψυχῆς ἐφόδια.
195 πίστις δ᾽ ἀπορίας οὐδὲ τοῖς θνήσκουσιν ἦν, ἀλλὰ
καὶ τοὺς ἐκπνέοντας οἱ λῃσταὶ διηρεύνων, μή τις
ὑπὸ κόλπον ἔχων τροφὴν σκήπτοιτο τὸν θάνατον
196 αὐτῷ. οἱ δ᾽ ὑπ᾽ ἐνδείας κεχηνότες ὥσπερ
λυσσῶντες κύνες ἐσφάλλοντο, καὶ παρεφέροντο
ταῖς τε θύραις ἐνσειόμενοι μεθυόντων τρόπον καὶ
ὑπ᾽ ἀμηχανίας εἰς τοὺς αὐτοὺς οἴκους εἰσπηδῶντες
197 δὶς ἢ τρὶς ὥρα μιᾷ. πάντα δ᾽ ὑπ᾽ ὀδόντας ἦγεν ἡ
ἀνάγκη, καὶ τὰ μηδὲ τοῖς ῥυπαρωτάτοις τῶν ἀλόγων ζῴων πρόσφορα συλλέγοντες ἐσθίειν ὑπέφερον·
ζωστήρων γοῦν καὶ ὑποδημάτων τὸ τελευταῖον οὐκ
ἀπέσχοντο καὶ τὰ δέρματα τῶν θυρεῶν ἀποδέροντες
198 ἐμασῶντο. τροφὴ δ᾽ ἦν καὶ χόρτου τισὶ παλαιοῦ
σπαράγματα[2]· τὰς γὰρ ἶνας ἔνιοι συλλέγοντες
ἐλάχιστον σταθμὸν ἐπώλουν Ἀττικῶν τεσσάρων.
199 καὶ τί δεῖ τὴν ἐπ᾽ ἀψύχοις ἀναίδειαν τοῦ λιμοῦ
λέγειν; εἶμι γὰρ αὐτοῦ δηλώσων ἔργον οἷον μήτε

---

[1] Hudson with Heg. Lat.: Ἰουδαίοις MSS.
[2] LC Eus. Lat.: σπάραγμα the rest.

---

[a] Cf. the Psalmist's simile, " They snarl like a dog and

by the Jews. The next day the Romans also burnt c. 16 August. the whole northern portico right up to that on the east, where the angle connecting the two was built over the ravine called Kedron, the depth at that point being consequently terrific. Such was the condition of affairs in the vicinity of the temple.

(3) Meanwhile, the victims perishing of famine *Further* throughout the city were dropping in countless *horrors of* numbers and enduring sufferings indescribable. In *the famine.* every house, the appearance anywhere of but a shadow of food was a signal for war, and the dearest of relatives fell to blows, snatching from each other the pitiful supports of life. The very dying were not credited as in want ; nay, even those expiring were searched by the brigands, lest any should be concealing food beneath a fold of his garment and feigning death. Gaping with hunger, like mad dogs,[a] these ruffians went staggering and reeling along, battering upon the doors in the manner of drunken men, and in their perplexity bursting into the same house twice or thrice within a single hour. Necessity drove the victims to gnaw anything, and objects which even the filthiest of brute beasts would reject they condescended to collect and eat : thus in the end they abstained not from belts and shoes and stripped off and chewed the very leather of their bucklers. Others devoured tufts of withered grass : indeed some collectors of stalks sold a trifling quantity for four Attic drachmas.[b] But why tell of the shameless resort to inanimate articles of food induced by the famine, seeing that I am here about to

go round about the city : they wander up and down for meat," Ps. lix. 14 f.   [b] The coin is unexpressed in the Greek, as elsewhere (ii. 592). The Attic drachma was the ordinary day's wage for a labourer.

παρ' Ἕλλησιν μήτε παρὰ βαρβάροις ἱστόρηται,
200 φρικτὸν μὲν εἰπεῖν, ἄπιστον δ' ἀκοῦσαι. καὶ ἔγωγε
μὴ δόξαιμι τερατεύεσθαι τοῖς αὖθις ἀνθρώποις,
κἂν παρέλειπον τὴν συμφορὰν ἡδέως, εἰ μὴ τῶν
κατ' ἐμαυτὸν εἶχον ἀπείρους μάρτυρας. ἄλλως τε
καὶ ψυχρὰν ἂν καταθείμην τῇ πατρίδι χάριν
καθυφέμενος τὸν λόγον ὧν πέπονθεν τὰ ἔργα.

201 (4) Γυνή τις τῶν ὑπὲρ τὸν Ἰορδάνην κατοικούντων, Μαρία τοὔνομα, πατρὸς Ἐλεαζάρου,
κώμης Βηθεζουβᾶ,[1] σημαίνει δὲ τοῦτο οἶκος
ὑσσώπου, διὰ γένος καὶ πλοῦτον ἐπίσημος, μετὰ
τοῦ λοιποῦ πλήθους εἰς τὰ Ἱεροσόλυμα κατα-
202 φυγοῦσα συνεπολιορκεῖτο. ταύτης τὴν μὲν ἄλλην
κτῆσιν οἱ τύραννοι διήρπασαν, ὅσην ἐκ τῆς
Περαίας ἀνασκευασαμένη μετήνεγκεν εἰς τὴν πόλιν,
τὰ δὲ λείψανα τῶν κειμηλίων καὶ εἴ τι τροφῆς
ἐπινοηθείη καθ' ἡμέραν εἰσπηδῶντες ἥρπαζον οἱ
203 δορυφόροι. δεινὴ δὲ τὸ γύναιον ἀγανάκτησις
εἰσῄει, καὶ πολλάκις λοιδοροῦσα καὶ καταρωμένη
204 τοὺς ἅρπαγας ἐφ' αὑτὴν ἠρέθιζεν. ὡς δ' οὔτε
παροξυνόμενός τις οὔτ' ἐλεῶν αὐτὴν ἀνῄρει, καὶ
τὸ μὲν εὑρεῖν τι σιτίον ἄλλοις ἐκοπία, πανταχόθεν
δ' ἄπορον ἦν ἤδη καὶ τὸ εὑρεῖν, ὁ λιμὸς δὲ διὰ
σπλάγχνων καὶ μυελῶν ἐχώρει καὶ τοῦ λιμοῦ
μᾶλλον ἐξέκαιον οἱ θυμοί, σύμβουλον λαβοῦσα τὴν
205 ὀργὴν μετὰ τῆς ἀνάγκης ἐπὶ τὴν φύσιν ἐχώρει, καὶ

---

[1] L : Βεθεζώρ M, Βαθεζώρ Eus., Βαθεχώρ the rest.

[a] Josephus strangely ignores the parallel incident at the
siege of Samaria, recorded in 2 Kings vi. 28 f. *Cf.* Deut.
xxviii. 57 and Baruch ii. 2 f. (" great plagues, such as never
happened under the whole heaven, as it came to pass in
Jerusalem . . . that we should eat . . . every man the flesh
of his own daughter ").

describe an act unparalleled [a] in the history whether
of Greeks or barbarians, and as horrible to relate
as it is incredible to hear ? For my part, for fear
that posterity might suspect me [b] of monstrous
fabrication, I would gladly have omitted this tragedy,
had I not innumerable witnesses among my con-
temporaries. Moreover, it would be a poor com-
pliment that I should pay my country in suppressing
the narrative of the woes which she actually endured.

(4) Among the residents of the region beyond
Jordan was a woman named Mary, daughter of
Eleazar, of the village of Bethezuba (the name means
" House of Hyssop " [c]), eminent by reason of her
family and fortune, who had fled with the rest of the
people to Jerusalem and there become involved in
the siege. The bulk of her property, which she had
packed up and brought with her from Peraea [d] to the
city, had been plundered by the tyrants; while the
relics of her treasures, with whatever food she had
contrived to procure, were being carried off by their
satellites in their daily raids. With deep indignation
in her heart, the poor woman constantly abused and
cursed these extortioners and so incensed them
against her. But when no one either out of exasperation or pity put her to death, weary of finding for
others food, which indeed it was now impossible
from any quarter to procure, while famine coursed
through her intestines and marrow and the fire of
rage was more consuming even than the famine,
impelled by the promptings alike of fury and
necessity, she proceeded to an act of outrage upon

Mary, the
mother who
devoured
her child.

[b] Or " I hope that I shall not be suspected by posterity
 . . . and indeed I would gladly," etc.
[c] Heb. Beth Ezob : site unidentified.
[d] Transjordania, B. iii. 44 ff.

435

τὸ τέκνον, ἦν δ' αὐτῇ παῖς ὑπομάστιος, ἁρπα-
σαμένη " βρέφος," εἶπεν, "ἄθλιον, ἐν πολέμῳ καὶ
206 λιμῷ καὶ στάσει τίνι σε τηρήσω; τὰ μὲν παρὰ
Ῥωμαίοις δουλεία, κἂν ζήσωμεν ἐπ' αὐτούς,[1]
φθάνει δὲ καὶ δουλείαν ὁ λιμός, οἱ στασιασταὶ δ'
207 ἀμφοτέρων χαλεπώτεροι. ἴθι, γενοῦ μοι τροφὴ
καὶ τοῖς στασιασταῖς ἐρινὺς καὶ τῷ βίῳ μῦθος ὁ
208 μόνος ἐλλείπων ταῖς Ἰουδαίων συμφοραῖς." καὶ
ταῦθ' ἅμα λέγουσα κτείνει τὸν υἱόν, ἔπειτ' ὀπτή-
σασα τὸ μὲν ἥμισυ κατεσθίει, τὸ δὲ λοιπὸν κατα-
209 καλύψασα ἐφύλαττεν. εὐθέως δ' οἱ στασιασταὶ
παρῆσαν, καὶ τῆς ἀθεμίτου κνίσης σπάσαντες ἠπείλουν, εἰ μὴ δείξειεν τὸ παρασκευασθέν, ἀποσφάξειν
αὐτὴν εὐθέως. ἡ δὲ καὶ μοῖραν αὐτοῖς εἰποῦσα
καλὴν τετηρηκέναι τὰ λείψανα τοῦ τέκνου δι-
210 εκάλυψεν. τοὺς δ' εὐθέως φρίκη καὶ παρέκστασις[2]
ᾕρει καὶ παρὰ τὴν ὄψιν ἐπεπήγεσαν. ἡ δ' "ἐμόν,"
ἔφη, "τοῦτο τὸ τέκνον γνήσιον καὶ τὸ ἔργον ἐμόν.
211 φάγετε, καὶ γὰρ ἐγὼ βέβρωκα. μὴ γένησθε μήτε
μαλακώτεροι γυναικὸς μήτε συμπαθέστεροι μητρός.
εἰ δ' ὑμεῖς εὐσεβεῖς καὶ τὴν ἐμὴν ἀποστρέφεσθε
θυσίαν, ἐγὼ μὲν ὑμῖν βέβρωκα, καὶ τὸ λοιπὸν δ'
212 ἐμοὶ μεινάτω." μετὰ ταῦθ' οἱ μὲν τρέμοντες
ἐξῄεσαν, πρὸς ἓν τοῦτο δειλοὶ καὶ μόλις ταύτης τῆς
τροφῆς τῇ μητρὶ παραχωρήσαντες, ἀνεπλήσθη δ'
εὐθέως ὅλη τοῦ μύσους ἡ πόλις, καὶ πρὸ ὀμμάτων
ἕκαστος τὸ πάθος λαμβάνων ὥσπερ[3] αὐτῷ τολ-
213 μηθὲν ἔφριττε. σπουδὴ δὲ τῶν λιμωττόντων ἐπὶ
τὸν θάνατον ἦν, καὶ μακαρισμὸς τῶν φθασάντων
πρὶν ἀκοῦσαι καὶ θεάσασθαι κακὰ τηλικαῦτα.

---

[1] Text doubtful: ἐπ' αὐτοῖς Hudson: ὑπ' αὐτούς A².
[2] A: παρέκστασις P: φρενῶν ἔκστασις the rest.

436

nature. Seizing her child, an infant at the breast,
"Poor babe," she cried, "amidst war, famine, and
sedition, to what end should I preserve thee ? With
the Romans slavery awaits us, should we live till they
come ; but famine is forestalling slavery, and more
cruel than both are the rebels. Come, be thou food
for me, to the rebels an avenging fury, and to the
world a tale such as alone is wanting to the calamities
of the Jews." With these words she slew her son,
and then, having roasted the body and devoured
half of it, she covered up and stored the remainder.
At once the rebels were upon her and, scenting the
unholy odour, threatened her with instant death
unless she produced what she had prepared. Replying that she had reserved a goodly portion for
them also, she disclosed the remnants of her child.
Seized with instant horror and stupefaction, they
stood paralysed by the sight. She, however, said,
"This is my own child, and this my handiwork. Eat,
for I too have eaten. Show not yourselves weaker
than a woman, or more compassionate than a mother.
But if you have pious scruples and shrink from my
sacrifice, then let what I have eaten be your portion
and the remainder also be left for me." At that
they departed trembling, in this one instance
cowards, though scarcely yielding even this food to
the mother. The whole city instantly rang with
the abomination, and each, picturing the horror of
it, shuddered as though it had been perpetrated by
himself. The starving folk longed for death, and
felicitated those who had gone to their rest ere they
had heard or beheld such evils.

---

[a] L : ὡς παρ' the rest.

214 (5) Ταχέως δὲ καὶ Ῥωμαίοις διηγγέλθη τὸ
πάθος. τῶν δ' οἱ μὲν ἠπίστουν, οἱ δὲ ᾤκτειρον,
τοὺς δὲ πολλοὺς εἰς μῖσος τοῦ ἔθνους σφοδρότερον
215 συνέβη προελθεῖν. Καῖσαρ δ' ἀπελογεῖτο καὶ περὶ
τούτου τῷ θεῷ, φάσκων παρὰ μὲν αὐτοῦ Ἰουδαίοις
εἰρήνην καὶ αὐτονομίαν προτείνεσθαι καὶ πάντων
216 ἀμνηστίαν τῶν τετολμημένων, τοὺς δ' ἀντὶ μὲν
ὁμονοίας στάσιν, ἀντὶ δ' εἰρήνης πόλεμον, πρὸ
κόρου δὲ[1] καὶ εὐθηνίας λιμὸν αἱρουμένους, ἰδίαις δὲ
χερσὶν ἀρξαμένους καίειν τὸ συντηρούμενον ὑφ'
ἡμῶν ἱερὸν αὐτοῖς, εἶναι καὶ τοιαύτης τροφῆς
217 ἀξίους. καλύψειν μέντοι τὸ τῆς τεκνοφαγίας μύσος
αὐτῷ τῷ τῆς πατρίδος πτώματι καὶ οὐ καταλείψειν
ἐπὶ τῆς οἰκουμένης ἡλίῳ καθορᾶν πόλιν, ἐν ᾗ
218 μητέρες οὕτω τρέφονται. προσήκειν μέντοι πρὸ
μητέρων πατράσιν τὴν τοιαύτην τροφήν, οἳ καὶ
μετὰ τηλικαῦτα πάθη μένουσιν ἐν τοῖς ὅπλοις.
219 ταῦθ' ἅμα διεξιὼν ἐνενόει καὶ τὴν ἀπόγνωσιν τῶν
ἀνδρῶν· οὐ γὰρ ἂν ἔτι σωφρονῆσαι τοὺς πάντα
προπεπονθότας ἐφ' οἷς εἰκὸς ἦν μεταβαλέσθαι μὴ
παθοῦσιν.[2]

220 (iv. 1) Ἤδη δὲ τῶν δύο ταγμάτων συντετε-
λεκότων τὰ χώματα Λώου μηνὸς ὀγδόῃ προσάγειν
ἐκέλευσε τοὺς κριοὺς κατὰ τὴν ἑσπέριον ἐξέδραν
221 τοῦ ἔξωθεν[3] ἱεροῦ. πρὸ δὲ τούτων ἐξ ἡμέρας[4]
ἀδιαλείπτως ἡ στερροτάτη πασῶν ἑλέπολις τύπ-
τουσα τὸν τοῖχον οὐδὲν ἤνυσεν, ἀλλὰ καὶ ταύτης
καὶ τῶν ἄλλων τὸ μέγεθος καὶ ἡ ἁρμονία τῶν
222 λίθων ἦν ἀμείνων. τῆς δὲ βορείου πύλης ὑπώρυττον

---

[1] δέ τοι L. [2] πάθωσιν Naber.
[3] Lat.: ἔωθεν PA[1]: ἔσωθεν the rest; cf. §§ 151, 244.
[4] PL: ἡμέραις the rest.

(5) The horrible news soon spread to the Romans. Protestation of Titus. Of them some were incredulous, others were moved to pity, but the effect on the majority was to intensify their hatred of the nation. Caesar declared himself innocent in this matter also in the sight of God, protesting that *he* had offered the Jews peace, independence, and an amnesty for all past offences, while *they*, preferring sedition to concord, peace to war, famine to plenty and prosperity, and having been the first to set fire with their own hands to that temple which he and his army were preserving for them, were indeed deserving even of such food as this. He, however, would bury this abomination of infant-cannibalism beneath the ruins of their country, and would not leave upon the face of the earth, for the sun to behold, a city in which mothers were thus fed. Yet, he added, such food was less meet for mothers than for fathers, who even after such horrors still remained in arms. While expressing these sentiments, he had, moreover, in mind the desperation of these men, being convinced that they were past being brought to reason who had already endured all the miseries, to be spared the experience of which they might have been expected to relent.

(iv. 1) Two of the legions having now completed their earthworks,[a] on the eighth of the month Lous, Titus ordered the rams to be brought up opposite the western hall of the outer court of the temple. Rams and ladders proving unavailing c. 27 August Before their arrival, the most redoubtable of all the siege-engines had for six days incessantly battered the wall without effect, the massiveness and nice adjustment of the stones being proof against it as against the rest. Another party endeavoured to

[a] *Cf.* §§ 150 f.

ἕτεροι τοὺς θεμελίους καὶ πολλὰ ταλαιπωρήσαντες
τοὺς ἔμπροσθεν λίθους ἐξεκύλισαν. ἀνείχετο[1] δ᾽
ὑπὸ τῶν ἐνδοτέρω καὶ διέμεινεν ἡ πύλη, μέχρι τὰς
δι᾽[2] ὀργάνων καὶ τῶν μοχλῶν ἐπιχειρήσεις ἀπο-
223 γνόντες κλίμακας ταῖς στοαῖς προσέφερον. οἱ δὲ
Ἰουδαῖοι κωλῦσαι μὲν οὐκ ἔφθασαν, ἀναβᾶσι δὲ
συμπεσόντες ἐμάχοντο, καὶ τοὺς μὲν ἀνωθοῦντες
εἰς τοὐπίσω κατεκρήμνιζον, τοὺς δ᾽ ὑπαντιάζοντας[3]
224 ἀνήρουν· πολλοὺς δὲ τῶν κλιμάκων ἀποβαίνοντας,
πρὶν φράξασθαι τοῖς θυρεοῖς, παίοντες ταῖς ῥομφαίαις ἔφθανον, ἐνίας δὲ γεμούσας ὁπλιτῶν κλί-
225 μακας παρακλίνοντες ἄνωθεν κατέσειον· ἦν δ᾽ οὐκ
ὀλίγος καὶ αὐτῶν φόνος. οἱ δὲ ἀνενεγκόντες τὰς
σημαίας περὶ αὐτῶν ἐπολέμουν, δεινὴν ἡγούμενοι
226 καὶ πρὸς αἰσχύνης τούτων τὴν ἁρπαγήν. τέλος
δὲ καὶ τῶν σημαιῶν οἱ Ἰουδαῖοι κρατοῦσιν καὶ
τοὺς ἀναβάντας διαφθείρουσιν· οἱ δὲ λοιποὶ πρὸς
τὸ τῶν ἀπολωλότων πάθος ὀρρωδοῦντες ἀνεχώρουν.
227 τῶν μὲν οὖν Ῥωμαίων ἄπρακτος οὐδεὶς ἀπέθανεν,
τῶν δὲ στασιαστῶν οἱ κατὰ τὰς προτέρας μάχας
ἠγωνίσαντο γενναίως καὶ τότε, καὶ Ἐλεάζαρος
228 ἀδελφιδοῦς τοῦ τυράννου Σίμωνος. ὁ δὲ Τίτος ὡς
ἑώρα τὴν ἐπὶ τοῖς ἀλλοτρίοις ἱεροῖς φειδὼ πρὸς
βλάβης τοῖς στρατιώταις γινομένην καὶ φόνου, τὰς
πύλας προσέταξεν ὑφάπτειν.
229   (2) Ἐν δὲ τούτῳ πρὸς αὐτὸν αὐτομολοῦσιν
Ἄνανός τε ὁ ἀπ᾽ Ἀμμαοῦς,[4] τῶν Σίμωνος δορυ-

---

[1] ἀνείχοντο PA.   [2] PM: διὰ τῶν the rest.
  [3] ὑπαντιάζοντες L.
  [4] C: ἀφαμμαούς PA: ἀφ᾽ Ἀμμαοῦς other mss.

undermine the foundations of the northern gate, and by great exertions succeeded in extricating the stones in front ; but the gate, supported by the inner stones, stood firm. Finally, despairing of all attempts with engines and crowbars, the Romans applied ladders to the porticoes. The Jews made no haste to prevent this, but as soon as they mounted vigorously attacked them. Some they thrust back and hurled down headlong, others who encountered them they slew[a] ; many as they stepped off the ladders they cut down with their swords, before they could shield themselves with their bucklers; some ladders, again, laden with armed men, they tilted sideways from above and dashed to the ground ; not, however, without suffering considerable slaughter themselves. The Romans who had brought up the standards fought fiercely around these, deeming their loss a dire disaster and disgrace ; yet, eventually, these ensigns also were taken by the Jews, who destroyed all who had mounted. The remainder, intimidated by the fate of the fallen, then retired. Of the Romans, not one had not achieved something ere he fell ; of the rebels, those who had gained distinction in previous engagements fought gallantly also in this, as did also Eleazar, nephew of the tyrant Simon. Titus, now that he saw that his endeavour to spare a foreign temple led only to the injury and slaughter of his troops, issued orders to set the gates on fire. *Titus orders the temple gates to be fired.*

(2) Meanwhile two deserters had joined him, Ananus of Emmaus, the most bloodthirsty of Simon's *Two prominent deserters.*

---

[a] Or, with the other reading, " they encountered and slew."

φόρων ὁ φονικώτατος, καὶ Ἀρχέλαος υἱὸς Μαγαδ-
δάτου, συγγνώμην ἐλπίσαντες ἐπειδὴ κρατούντων
230 Ἰουδαίων ὑπεχώρουν.[1] Τίτος δὲ καὶ τοῦτο[2] πανούργημα προυβάλλετο[3] τῶν ἀνδρῶν, καὶ τὴν ἄλλην
περὶ τοὺς ἰδίους[4] ὠμότητα πεπυσμένος ὥρμητο
κτείνειν ἑκατέρους, ὑπ᾽ ἀνάγκης ἦχθαι λέγων
αὐτούς, οὐκ ἐκ προαιρέσεως παρεῖναι, καὶ σωτηρίας
οὐκ ἀξίους εἶναι τοὺς φλεγομένης ἤδη δι᾽ αὐτοὺς
231 τῆς πατρίδος ἐξαλλομένους. ἐκράτει δ᾽ ὅμως τοῦ
θυμοῦ ἡ πίστις, καὶ ἀφίησι τοὺς ἄνδρας, οὐ μὴν ἐν
232 ἴσῃ μοίρᾳ κατέτασσε τοῖς ἄλλοις. ἤδη δὲ ταῖς
πύλαις οἱ στρατιῶται προσῆγον τὸ πῦρ, καὶ
περιτηκόμενος ὁ ἄργυρος διεδίδου ταχέως εἰς τὴν
ξυλείαν τὴν φλόγα, ἔνθεν ἀθρόως ἐκφερομένη τῶν
233 στοῶν ἐπελαμβάνετο. τοῖς δ᾽ Ἰουδαίοις ὁρῶσι τὸ
πῦρ ἐν κύκλῳ μετὰ τῶν σωμάτων παρείθησαν αἱ
ψυχαί, καὶ διὰ τὴν κατάπληξιν ἀμύνειν μὲν ἢ
σβεννύειν ὥρμησεν οὐδείς, αὖοι δ᾽ ἐστῶτες ἀφεώ-
234 ρων. οὐ μὴν πρὸς τὸ δαπανώμενον ἀθυμοῦντες
εἰς γοῦν τὸ λοιπὸν ἐσωφρόνουν, ἀλλ᾽ ὡς ἤδη καὶ
τοῦ ναοῦ καιομένου τοὺς θυμοὺς ἐπὶ Ῥωμαίους
235 ἔθηγον. ἐκείνην μὲν οὖν τὴν ἡμέραν καὶ τὴν
ἐπιοῦσαν νύκτα τὸ πῦρ ἐπεκράτει· κατὰ μέρος
γάρ, οὐχ ὁμοῦ πάντοθεν ἴσχυσαν ὑφάψαι τὰς
στοάς.
236 (3) Τῇ δ᾽ ἐπιούσῃ Τίτος μέρει τῆς δυνάμεως

---

[1] PAM: ἀνέχωρουν L: ἀπέχωρουν the rest.
[2] + τὸ L.   [3] προβάλλεται PA: προυβάλετο L.
[4] Ἰουδαίους LC Lat.

---

[a] Employed by him as executioner of the chief priest
Matthias, Simon's former patron, v. 531. Ananus is there
called son of Bagadatus, a name probably identical with

442

lieutenants,[a] and Archelaus, son of Magaddatus, hoping for pardon because they were leaving the Jews at a moment of success. Titus, however, censured their action as a further knavish trick; and, having heard of their cruelty in general to their countrymen, he was strongly minded to put them both to death, observing that they had been driven by necessity, not led by inclination, to come over, and that men who leapt from their native city only when enveloped in the flames, for which they were themselves responsible, did not deserve to live. Nevertheless, his good faith overcame his animosity, and he let them go, though he did not put them on an equal footing with the rest.

The troops were by now setting fire to the gates, and the silver melting all around quickly admitted the flames to the woodwork, whence they spread in dense volumes and caught hold of the porticoes. The Jews, seeing the fire encircling them, were deprived of all energy of body and mind; in utter consternation none attempted to ward off or extinguish the flames; paralysed[b] they stood and looked on. Yet, though dismayed by the ravage being wrought, they learnt no lesson with regard to what was left, but, as if the very sanctuary were now ablaze, only whetted their fury against the Romans. So throughout that day and the ensuing night the fire prevailed; for they could only set light to portions of the porticoes, and not to the whole range at once.

Burning of gates and porticoes.

(3) On the following day Titus, after giving orders *c. 28 August.*

---

[a] Magaddatus, here assigned to the father of the other deserter, Archelaus.

[b] Literally " dry " (*cf.* i. 381. " dry with fright ").

σβεννύειν τε καὶ τὰ[1] παρὰ τὰς πύλας ὁδοποιεῖν εἰς
εὐμαρεστέραν τῶν ταγμάτων ἄνοδον κελεύσας
237 αὐτὸς συνῆγε τοὺς ἡγεμόνας. καὶ συνελθόντων ἐξ
τῶν κορυφαιοτάτων, Τιβερίου τε Ἀλεξάνδρου τοῦ
πάντων τῶν στρατευμάτων ἐπάρχοντος, καὶ Σέξτου
Κερεαλίου τοῦ τὸ πέμπτον ἄγοντος τάγμα, καὶ
Λαρκίου Λεπίδου τὸ δέκατον, καὶ Τίτου Φρυγίου
238 τὸ πεντεκαιδέκατον, πρὸς οἷς Φρόντων ἦν Ἀτέριος[2]
στρατοπεδάρχης τῶν ἀπὸ Ἀλεξανδρείας δύο ταγμάτων, καὶ Μᾶρκος Ἀντώνιος Ἰουλιανὸς ὁ τῆς
Ἰουδαίας ἐπίτροπος, καὶ μετὰ τούτους ἐπιτρόπων
καὶ χιλιάρχων ἀθροισθέντων, βουλὴν περὶ τοῦ
239 ναοῦ προυτίθει. τοῖς μὲν οὖν ἐδόκει χρῆσθαι τῷ
τοῦ πολέμου νόμῳ· μὴ γὰρ ἂν ποτε Ἰουδαίους
παύσασθαι νεωτερίζοντας τοῦ ναοῦ μένοντος, ἐφ᾽
240 ὃν οἱ πανταχόθεν συλλέγονται. τινὲς δὲ παρῄνουν,
εἰ μὲν καταλίποιεν αὐτὸν Ἰουδαῖοι καὶ μηδεὶς ἐπ᾽
αὐτοῦ τὰ ὅπλα θείη, σώζειν, εἰ δὲ πολεμοῖεν[3] ἐπιβάντες, καταφλέγειν· φρούριον γάρ, οὐκέτι ναὸν
εἶναι, καὶ τὸ λοιπὸν ἔσεσθαι τῶν ἀναγκασάντων
241 [τὴν][4] ἀσέβειαν, οὐκ αὐτῶν. ὁ δὲ Τίτος οὐδ᾽ ἂν
ἐπιβάντες ἐπ᾽ αὐτοῦ πολεμῶσιν[5] Ἰουδαῖοι φήσας[6]
ἀντὶ τῶν ἀνδρῶν ἀμυνεῖσθαι[7] τὰ ἄψυχα οὐδὲ
καταφλέξειν ποτὲ τηλικοῦτον ἔργον· Ῥωμαίων
γὰρ ἔσεσθαι τὴν βλάβην, ὥσπερ καὶ κόσμον τῆς
242 ἡγεμονίας αὐτοῦ μένοντος· θαρροῦντες δ᾽ ἤδη
προσετίθεντο τῇ γνώμῃ Φρόντων τε καὶ Ἀλέξ-

---

[1] τὰ L : om. the rest.
[2] Renier (quoted by Niese): Ἐτέριος PA, Ἐτέρνιος, etc., the rest.
[3] πολεμῶεν MSS.
[4] ins. L : om. the rest.
[5] L Zon.: πολεμῶεν the rest.
[6] Text doubtful: ἔφη has weak ms. support: Niese suspects a lacuna.
[7] Niese: ἀμύνεσθαι MSS.

to a division of his army to extinguish the fire and make a road to the gates to facilitate the ascent of the legions, called together his generals. Six of his chief staff-officers were assembled, namely, Tiberius Alexander, the prefect of all the forces,[a] Sextus Cerealius, Larcius Lepidus, and Titus Phrygius, the respective commanders of the fifth, tenth, and fifteenth legions ; Fronto Haterius, prefect of the two legions [b] from Alexandria, and Marcus Antonius Julianus, procurator of Judaea ; and the procurators and tribunes being next collected, Titus brought forward for debate the subject of the temple. Some were of opinion that the law of war should be enforced, since the Jews would never cease from rebellion while the temple remained as the focus for concourse from every quarter. Others advised that if the Jews abandoned it and placed no weapons whatever upon it, it should be saved, but that if they mounted it for purposes of warfare, it should be burnt ; as it would then be no longer a temple, but a fortress, and thenceforward the impiety would be chargeable, not to the Romans but to those who forced them to take such measures. Titus, however, declared that, even were the Jews to mount it and fight therefrom, he would not wreak vengeance on inanimate objects instead of men, nor under any circumstances burn down so magnificent a work ; for the loss would affect the Romans, inasmuch as it would be an ornament to the empire if it stood.[c] Fortified by this pronouncement, Fronto, Alexander, and Cerealius

---

[a] *Praefectus castrorum*, a sort of quartermaster general, with control over all the camps ; *cf.* v. 45 f.

[b] v. 44.

[c] For a conflicting account of the verdict of Titus at this council see Introduction to vol. ii. pp. xxiv f.

243 ἀνδρὸς καὶ Κερεάλιος. τότε μὲν οὖν διαλύει τὸ
συνέδριον καὶ τὰς ἄλλας δυνάμεις διαναπαῦσαι
κελεύσας τοῖς ἡγεμόσιν, ὅπως ἐρρωμενεστέροις[1]
ἐν τῇ παρατάξει χρήσαιτο, τοῖς ἀπὸ τῶν σπειρῶν
ἐπιλέκτοις ὁδοποιεῖν διὰ τῶν ἐρειπίων προσέταξε
καὶ τὸ πῦρ σβεννύειν.

244 (4) Κατ᾽ ἐκείνην μὲν δὴ τὴν ἡμέραν [τῶν][2]
Ἰουδαίων κάματός τε καὶ κατάπληξις ἐκράτησε
τὰς ὁρμάς· τῇ δ᾽ ἐπιούσῃ συλλεξάμενοί τε τὴν
ἰσχὺν καὶ ἀναθαρσήσαντες ἐπεκθέουσι διὰ τῆς
ἀνατολικῆς πύλης τοῖς φύλαξι τοῦ ἔξωθεν ἱεροῦ
245 περὶ δευτέραν ὥραν. οἱ δὲ καρτερῶς μὲν ἐδέξαντο
αὐτῶν τὴν ἐμβολὴν καὶ φραξάμενοι τοῖς θυρεοῖς
κατὰ μέτωπον ὥσπερ τεῖχος ἐπύκνωσαν τὴν
φάλαγγα, δῆλοι δ᾽ ἦσαν οὐκ ἐπὶ πολὺ συμμενοῦντες[3]
πλήθει τε τῶν ἐκτρεχόντων καὶ θυμοῖς ἡττώμενοι.
246 φθάσας δὲ τῆς παρατάξεως τὴν ῥοπὴν Καῖσαρ,
καθεώρα γὰρ ἀπὸ τῆς Ἀντωνίας, ἐπήμυνε μετὰ
247 τῶν ἐπιλέκτων ἱππέων. Ἰουδαῖοι δὲ τὴν ἔφοδον οὐχ ὑπέμειναν, ἀλλὰ τῶν πρώτων πεσόντων
248 ἐτράπησαν οἱ πολλοί· καὶ ὑποχωροῦσι μὲν τοῖς
Ῥωμαίοις ἐπιστρεφόμενοι προσέκειντο, μεταβαλ-
λομένων δ᾽ ἀνέφευγον πάλιν, ἕως περὶ πέμπτην τῆς
ἡμέρας ὥραν οἱ μὲν βιασθέντες εἰς τὸ ἔνδον
249 συνεκλείσθησαν ἱερόν, (5) Τίτος δ᾽ ἀνεχώρησεν
εἰς τὴν Ἀντωνίαν διεγνωκὼς τῆς ἐπιούσης ἡμέρας
ὑπὸ τὴν ἔω μετὰ πάσης ἐμβαλεῖν τῆς δυνάμεως
250 καὶ τὸν ναὸν περικατασχεῖν. τοῦ δ᾽ ἄρα κατ-
εψήφιστο μὲν τὸ πῦρ ὁ θεὸς πάλαι, παρῆν δ᾽ ἡ
εἱμαρμένη χρόνων περιόδοις ἡμέρα δεκάτη Λώου

---

[1] Destinon from Lat.: ἐρρωμένοις L: ἐρρωμενέστερον the
rest.

ow came over to his view. He then dissolved the
ouncil, and, directing the officers to allow the other
roops an interval of repose, that he might find them *and gives*
einvigorated in action, he gave orders to the picked *orders to*
nen from the cohorts to open a road through the *extinguish*
ruins and extinguish the fire. *the fire.*

(4) Throughout that day fatigue and consternation
crushed the energies of the Jews ; but, on the follow- *c. 29 August.*
ing day, with recruited strength and renewed
courage, they sallied out through the eastern gate
upon the guards of the outer court of the temple,
at about the second hour. The Romans stubbornly
met their charge and, forming a screen in front with
their shields like a wall, closed up their ranks ; it
was evident, however, that they could not long hold
together, being no match for the number and fury
of their assailants. Caesar, who was watching the
scene from Antonia, anticipating the breaking of the
line, now brought up his picked cavalry to their
assistance. The Jews could not withstand their
onset : the fall of the foremost led to a general
retreat. Yet whenever the Romans retired they
returned to the attack, only to fall back once
more when their opponents wheeled round ; until,
about the fifth hour of the day, the Jews were
overpowered and shut up in the inner court of the
temple.

(5) Titus then withdrew to Antonia, determined *Conflagra-*
on the following day, at dawn, to attack with his *tion of the*
temple in
whole force, and invest the temple. That building, *despite of*
however, God, indeed long since, had sentenced *Titus.*
to the flames ; but now in the revolution of the years
had arrived the fated day, the tenth of the month *c. 30 (Niese*
29) August.

---

² om. AL.   ³ Bekker with Lat.: συμμένοντες MSS.

μηνός, καθ' ἣν καὶ πρότερον ὑπὸ τοῦ τῶν Βαβυ-
251 λωνίων βασιλέως ἐνεπρήσθη. λαμβάνουσι δ' α
φλόγες ἐκ τῶν οἰκείων τὴν ἀρχὴν καὶ τὴν αἰτίαν
ὑποχωρήσαντος γὰρ τοῦ Τίτου πρὸς ὀλίγον λω-
φήσαντες οἱ στασιασταὶ πάλιν τοῖς Ῥωμαίοις ἐπιτίθενται, καὶ τῶν τοῦ ναοῦ φρουρῶν γίνεται συμ
βολὴ πρὸς τοὺς σβεννύντας τὸ πῦρ [τοῦ ἔνδοθει
ἱεροῦ],[1] οἳ τρεψάμενοι τοὺς Ἰουδαίους μέχρι τοῦ
252 ναοῦ παρηκολούθουν. ἔνθα δὴ τῶν στρατιωτῶ
τις, οὔτε παράγγελμα περιμείνας οὔτ' ἐπὶ τηλικούτῳ δείσας ἐγχειρήματι, δαιμονίῳ[3] ὁρμῇ τιν
χρώμενος ἁρπάζει μὲν ἐκ τῆς φλεγομένης ὕλης,
ἀνακουφισθεὶς δ' ὑπὸ συστρατιώτου[5] τὸ πῦρ ἐνίησ
θυρίδι χρυσῇ, καθ' ἣν εἰς τοὺς περὶ τὸν ναὸν οἴκους
253 εἰσιτὸν ἦν ἐκ τοῦ βορείου κλίματος. αἰρομένης δε
τῆς φλογὸς Ἰουδαίων μὲν ἐγείρεται κραυγὴ τοῦ
πάθους ἀξία, καὶ πρὸς τὴν ἄμυναν συνέθεον, οὔτε
τοῦ ζῆν ἔτι φειδὼ λαμβάνοντες οὔτε ταμιευόμενο
τὴν ἰσχύν, δι' ὃν[6] φυλακτικοὶ πρότερον ἦσαι
οἰχομένου.

254 (6) Δραμὼν δέ τις ἀγγέλλει Τίτῳ· κἀκεῖνος
ἔτυχεν δὲ κατὰ σκηνὴν ἀναπαυόμενος ἐκ τῆς
μάχης, ὡς εἶχεν ἀναπηδήσας ἔθει πρὸς τὸν ναὸι
255 εἴρξων τὸ πῦρ. κατόπιν δ' οἵ τε ἡγεμόνες εἴποντο
πάντες, καὶ πτοηθέντα τούτοις ἠκολούθει τὸ

---

[1] om. Syr.   [2] + ἔνδοθεν A Syr.   [3] + δ' Destinon
[4] φλογός PA (Syr. ?): text uncertain.
[5] Bekker with Lat. : στρατιώτου mss.
[6] δι' ὃν Destinon, cf. iii. 196, v. 543, vi. 322: δι' οὗ or δι' ὃ
καὶ mss.

---

[a] This is in accordance with Jer. lii. 12 f., where the
burning of the temple by Nebuzaradan, captain of Nebuchadrezzar's guard, is stated to have occurred on the 10th day

Lous, the day on which of old it had been burnt by
the king of Babylon.[a] The flames, however, owed
their origin and cause to God's own people.[b] For,
on the withdrawal of Titus, the insurgents, after a
brief respite, again attacked the Romans, and an
engagement ensued between the guards of the
sanctuary and the troops who were endeavouring
to extinguish the fire in the inner court ; the latter
routing the Jews and pursuing them right up to
the sanctuary. At this moment, one of the soldiers,
awaiting no orders and with no horror of so dread
a deed, but moved by some supernatural impulse,
snatched a brand from the burning timber and,
hoisted up by one of his comrades, flung the fiery
missile through a low golden door,[c] which gave access
on the north side to the chambers surrounding the
sanctuary. As the flame shot up, a cry, as poignant
as the tragedy, arose from the Jews, who flocked
to the rescue, lost to all thought of self-preservation,
all husbanding of strength, now that the object of
all their past vigilance was vanishing.

(6) Titus was resting in his tent after the engagement, when a messenger rushed in with the tidings.
Starting up just as he was, he ran to the temple to
arrest the conflagration ; behind him followed his
whole staff of generals, while in their train came the
excited legionaries, and there was all the hubbub and

of the 5th month (Heb. Ab = Lous in the Syrian calendar).
In 2 Kings xxv. 8, on the other hand, the day is given as
the 7th Ab ; while, in Jewish tradition, the anniversary of
the double burning has always been kept on the 9th Ab. A
fictitious symmetry between corresponding events in the two
sieges has probably been at work.

[b] Or " to their own people."

[c] Or " through a golden window."

τάγματα· βοὴ δ' ἦν καὶ θόρυβος ἅτε τηλικαύτης
256 δυνάμεως ἀτάκτως κεκινημένης. ὁ μὲν οὖν Καῖσαρ
τῇ τε φωνῇ[1] καὶ τῇ δεξιᾷ διεσήμαινε τοῖς μαχομένοις τὸ πῦρ σβεννύειν, οὔτε δὲ βοῶντος ἤκουον
μείζονι κραυγῇ τὰς ἀκοὰς προκατειλημμένοι καὶ
τοῖς νεύμασι τῆς χειρὸς οὐ προσεῖχον, οἱ μὲν τῷ
257 πολεμεῖν, οἱ δ' ὀργῇ περισπώμενοι. τῶν δὲ ταγμάτων εἰσθεόντων οὔτε παραίνεσις οὔτ' ἀπειλὴ
κατεῖχεν τὰς ὁρμάς, ἀλλ' ὁ θυμὸς ἁπάντων ἐστρα-
τήγει· καὶ περὶ τὰς εἰσόδους συνωθούμενοι πολλοὶ
μὲν ὑπ' ἀλλήλων κατεπατοῦντο, πολλοὶ δὲ θερμοῖς
ἔτι καὶ τυφομένοις τοῖς ἐρειπίοις τῶν στοῶν ἐμ-
258 πίπτοντες ἡττωμένων συμφοραῖς ἐχρῶντο. πλησίον
δὲ τοῦ ναοῦ γινόμενοι τῶν μὲν τοῦ Καίσαρος
παραγγελμάτων προσεποιοῦντο μηδὲ κατακούειν,
τοῖς πρὸ αὐτῶν δὲ τὸ πῦρ ἐνιέναι παρεκελεύοντο.
259 τῶν δὲ στασιαστῶν ἀμηχανία μὲν ἦν ἤδη τοῦ
βοηθεῖν, φόνος δὲ πανταχοῦ καὶ τροπή. τὸ δὲ
πλέον ἀπὸ τοῦ δήμου λαὸς ἀσθενὴς καὶ ἄνοπλος
ὅπου καταληφθείη τις ἀπεσφάττετο, καὶ περὶ μὲν
τὸν βωμὸν πλῆθος ἐσωρεύετο νεκρῶν, κατὰ δὲ τῶν
τοῦ ναοῦ βάθρων αἷμά τ' ἔρρει πολὺ καὶ τὰ τῶν
ἄνω φονευομένων σώματα κατωλίσθανε.
260 (7) Καῖσαρ δ' ὡς οὔτε τὰς ὁρμὰς ἐνθουσιώντων
τῶν στρατιωτῶν κατασχεῖν οἷός τε ἦν καὶ τὸ πῦρ
ἐπεκράτει, παρελθὼν μετὰ τῶν ἡγεμόνων ἔνδον
ἐθεάσατο τοῦ ναοῦ τὸ ἅγιον καὶ τὰ ἐν αὐτῷ, πολὺ
μὲν τῆς παρὰ τοῖς ἀλλοφύλοις φήμης ἀμείνω, τοῦ
δὲ κόμπου καὶ τῆς παρὰ τοῖς οἰκείοις δόξης οὐκ
261 ἐλάττω. τῆς φλογὸς δ' οὐδέπω δικνουμένης

---

[1] L (Lat. voce): βοῇ the rest.

confusion attending the disorderly movement of so large a force. Caesar, both by voice and hand, signalled to the combatants to extinguish the fire ; but they neither heard his shouts, drowned in the louder din which filled their ears, nor heeded his beckoning hand, distracted as they were by the fight or their fury. The impetuosity of the legionaries, when they joined the fray, neither exhortation nor threat could restrain ; passion was for all the only leader. Crushed together about the entrances, many were trampled down by their companions ; many, stumbling on the still hot and smouldering ruins of the porticoes, suffered the fate of the vanquished. As they drew nearer to the sanctuary they pretended not even to hear Caesar's orders and shouted to those in front of them to throw in the firebrands. The insurgents, for their part, were now powerless to help ; and on all sides was carnage and flight. Most of the slain were civilians, weak and unarmed people, each butchered where he was caught. Around the altar a pile of corpses was accumulating ; down the steps of the sanctuary flowed a stream of blood, and the bodies of the victims killed above went sliding to the bottom.

(7) Caesar, finding himself unable to restrain the impetuosity of his frenzied soldiers and the fire gaining the mastery, passed with his generals within the building and beheld the holy place of the sanctuary and all that it contained—things far exceeding the reports current among foreigners and not inferior to their proud reputation among ourselves.[a] As the flames had nowhere yet penetrated to the interior,

His unavailing efforts to save it.

---

[a] *Cf.* the account of Pompey's similar visit to the Holy Place, i. 152.

οὐδαμόθεν εἴσω, τοὺς δὲ περὶ τὸν ναὸν οἴκους
νεμομένης, νομίσας, ὅπερ ἦν, ἔτι σώζεσθαι τὸ
262 ἔργον δύνασθαι προπηδᾷ, καὶ αὐτός τε παρακαλεῖν
τοὺς στρατιώτας ἐπειρᾶτο τὸ πῦρ σβεννύειν καὶ
Λιβεράλιον ἑκατοντάρχην τῶν περὶ αὐτὸν λογχο-
φόρων ξύλοις παίοντα τοὺς ἀπειθοῦντας ἐκέλευσεν
263 εἴργειν. τῶν δὲ καὶ τὴν πρὸς τὸν Καίσαρα αἰδῶ
καὶ τὸν ἀπὸ τοῦ κωλύοντος φόβον ἐνίκων οἱ θυμοὶ
καὶ τὸ πρὸς Ἰουδαίους μῖσος καὶ πολεμική τις
264 ὁρμὴ λαβροτέρα· τοὺς δὲ πολλοὺς ἐνῆγεν ἁρπαγῆς
ἐλπίς, δόξαν [τε]¹ ἔχοντας ὡς τὰ ἔνδον ἅπαντα
χρημάτων μεστὰ εἴη καὶ τὰ πέριξ ὁρῶντας χρυσοῦ
265 πεποιημένα. φθάνει δέ τις καὶ τῶν εἴσω παρεληλυ-
θότων, ἐκπηδήσαντος τοῦ Καίσαρος πρὸς ἐποχὴν
τῶν στρατιωτῶν, πῦρ εἰς τοὺς στροφέας ἐμβαλὼν
266 τῆς πύλης [ἐν σκότῳ]²· τότε γὰρ ἐξαπίνης ἔνδοθεν
ἐκφανείσης φλογὸς οἵ τε ἡγεμόνες μετὰ τοῦ
Καίσαρος ἀνεχώρουν, καὶ τοὺς ἔξωθεν οὐδεὶς
ὑφάπτειν ἐκώλυεν. ὁ μὲν οὖν ναὸς οὕτως ἄκοντος
Καίσαρος ἐμπίπραται.

267 (8) Πολλὰ δ᾽ ἄν τις ἐπολοφυράμενος ἔργῳ
πάντων ὧν ὄψει καὶ ἀκοῇ παρειλήφαμεν θαυμα-
σιωτάτῳ κατασκευῆς τε ἕνεκα καὶ μεγέθους, ἔτι
τε τῆς καθ᾽ ἕκαστον πολυτελείας καὶ τῆς περὶ τὰ
ἅγια δόξης, μεγίστην λάβοι παραμυθίαν τὴν εἱμαρ-
μένην, ἄφυκτον οὖσαν ὥσπερ ἐμψύχοις οὕτω καὶ
268 ἔργοις καὶ τόποις. θαυμάσαι³ δ᾽ ἄν τις ἐν αὐτῇ
τῆς περιόδου τὴν ἀκρίβειαν· καὶ μῆνα γοῦν, ὡς
ἔφην, καὶ ἡμέραν ἐτήρησεν τὴν αὐτήν, ἐν ᾗ

---

¹ om. P Lat.
² om. Lat. Zon.: ἐν κόντῳ (" with a pole ") M margin.
³ θαυμάσειε L Zon.

but were consuming the chambers surrounding the
temple, Titus, correctly assuming that the structure
might still be saved, rushed out and by personal
appeals endeavoured to induce the soldiers to quench
the fire ; while he directed Liberalius, a centurion
of his bodyguard of lancers, to restrain, by resort to
clubs, any who disobeyed orders. But their respect
for Caesar and their fear of the officer who was
endeavouring to check them were overpowered by
their rage, their hatred of the Jews, and a lust for
battle more unruly still. Most of them were further
stimulated by the hope of plunder, believing that the
interior was full of money and actually seeing that
all the surroundings were made of gold. However,
the end was precipitated by one of those who
had entered the building, and who, when Caesar
rushed out to restrain the troops, thrust a firebrand,
in the darkness,[a] into the hinges of the gate. At
once a flame shot up from the interior, Caesar
and his generals withdrew, and there was none
left to prevent those outside from kindling a blaze.
Thus, against Caesar's wishes, was the temple set
on fire.

(8) Deeply as one must mourn for the most marvellous edifice which we have ever seen or heard of,
whether we consider its structure, its magnitude, the
richness of its every detail, or the reputation of its
Holy Places, yet may we draw very great consolation
from the thought that there is no escape from Fate,
for works of art and places any more than for living
beings. And one may well marvel at the exactness
of the cycle of Destiny ; for, as I said, she waited
until the very month and the very day on which in

The
anniversary
of a previous
conflagra-
tion.

---

[a] Text uncertain.

πρότερον ὑπὸ Βαβυλωνίων ὁ ναὸς ἐνεπρήσθη.
269 καὶ ἀπὸ μὲν τῆς πρώτης αὐτοῦ κτίσεως, ἣν
κατεβάλετο Σολομὼν ὁ βασιλεύς, μέχρι τῆς νῦν
ἀναιρέσεως, ἣ γέγονεν ἔτει δευτέρῳ τῆς Οὐεσπασιανοῦ ἡγεμονίας, ἔτη συνάγεται χίλια ἑκατὸν
τριάκοντα, πρὸς δὲ μῆνες ἑπτὰ καὶ πεντεκαίδεκα
270 ἡμέραι· ἀπὸ δὲ τῆς ὕστερον, ἣν ἔτει δευτέρῳ
Κύρου βασιλεύοντος ἐποιήσατο Ἀγγαῖος, ἔτη
μέχρι τῆς ὑπὸ Οὐεσπασιανοῦ ἁλώσεως τριακοντα-
εννέα πρὸς ἑξακοσίοις καὶ ἡμέραι τεσσαρακοντα-
πέντε.

271 (v. 1) Καιομένου δὲ τοῦ ναοῦ τῶν μὲν προσ-
πιπτόντων ἦν ἁρπαγή, φόνος δὲ τῶν καταλαμβανομένων μυρίος καὶ οὔτε ἡλικίας ἦν ἔλεος οὔτ᾽
ἐντροπὴ σεμνότητος, ἀλλὰ καὶ παιδία καὶ γέροντες
καὶ βέβηλοι καὶ ἱερεῖς ὁμοίως ἀνῃροῦντο, καὶ πᾶν
γένος ἐπεξῄει περισχὼν ὁ πόλεμος, ὁμοῦ τούς τε
272 ἱκετεύοντας καὶ τοὺς ἀμυνομένους. συνήχει δ᾽ ἡ
φλὸξ ἐπὶ πλεῖστον ἐκφερομένη τοῖς τῶν πιπτόντων
στεναγμοῖς, καὶ διὰ μὲν τὸ ὕψος τοῦ λόφου καὶ τὸ
τοῦ φλεγομένου μέγεθος ἔργου πᾶσαν ἄν τις
ἔδοξε καίεσθαι τὴν πόλιν, τῆς δὲ βοῆς ἐκείνης
οὐδὲν ἐπινοηθῆναι δύναιτ᾽ ἂν ἢ μεῖζον ἢ φοβερώ-
273 τερον. τῶν τε γὰρ Ῥωμαϊκῶν ταγμάτων ἀλαλαγ-
μὸς ἦν συμφερομένων, καὶ τῶν στασιαστῶν πυρὶ
καὶ σιδήρῳ κεκυκλωμένων κραυγή, τοῦ τε ἀπο-
ληφθέντος ἄνω λαοῦ τροπή τε μετ᾽ ἐκπλήξεως εἰς
τοὺς πολεμίους καὶ πρὸς τὸ πάθος οἰμωγαί.
274 συνεβόα δὲ τοῖς ἐπὶ τοῦ λόφου τὸ κατὰ τὴν πόλιν
πλῆθος· ἤδη δὲ πολλοὶ τῷ λιμῷ μαραινόμενοι καὶ
μεμυκότες ὡς εἶδον τὸ τοῦ ναοῦ πῦρ, εἰς ὀδυρμοὺς

bygone times the temple had been burnt by the Babylonians.[a] From its first foundation by King Solomon up to its present destruction, which took place in the second year of Vespasian's reign, the total period amounts to one thousand one hundred and thirty years seven months and fifteen days; from its rebuilding by Haggai in the second year of the reign of Cyrus until its fall under Vespasian to six hundred and thirty-nine years and forty-five days.[b]

(v. 1) While the temple blazed, the victors plundered everything that fell in their way and slaughtered wholesale all who were caught. No pity was shown for age, no reverence for rank; children and greybeards, laity and priests, alike were massacred; every class was pursued and encompassed in the grasp of war, whether suppliants for mercy or offering resistance. The roar of the flames streaming far and wide mingled with the groans of the falling victims; and, owing to the height of the hill and the mass of the burning pile, one would have thought that the whole city was ablaze. And then the din—nothing more deafening or appalling could be conceived than that. There were the war-cries of the Roman legions sweeping onward in mass, the howls of the rebels encircled by fire and sword, the rush of the people who, cut off above, fled panic-stricken only to fall into the arms of the foe, and their shrieks as they met their fate. With the cries on the hill were blended those of the multitude in the city below; and now many who were emaciated and tongue-tied from starvation, when they beheld the

Sounds and scenes attending the fire.

---

[a] § 250 note. [b] Chronological system uncertain.

πάλιν καὶ κραυγὴν εὐτόνησαν· συνήχει δ' ἥ τε
Περαία καὶ τὰ πέριξ ὄρη βαρυτέραν ποιοῦντα τὴν
275 βοήν. ἦν δὲ τοῦ θορύβου τὰ πάθη φοβερώτερα·
τὸν μέν γε τοῦ ἱεροῦ λόφον ἐκ ῥιζῶν ἄν τις ἔδοξε
βράττεσθαι πάντοθεν τοῦ πυρὸς καταγέμοντα,
δαψιλέστερον δὲ τὸ αἷμα τοῦ πυρὸς εἶναι καὶ τῶν
276 φονευόντων πλείους τοὺς φονευομένους· οὐδαμοῦ
γὰρ ἡ γῆ διεφαίνετο τῶν νεκρῶν, ἀλλὰ [καὶ]¹
σωροῖς ἐπεμβαίνοντες² οἱ στρατιῶται σωμάτων
277 ἐπὶ τοὺς διαφεύγοντας ἔθεον. τὸ μὲν οὖν ληστρικὸν
πλῆθος ὠσάμενοι τοὺς Ῥωμαίους μόλις εἰς τὸ
ἔξω διεκπίπτουσιν ἱερὸν κἀκεῖθεν εἰς τὴν πόλιν,
τοῦ δημοτικοῦ δὲ τὸ λειφθὲν ἐπὶ τὴν ἔξω στοὰν
278 κατέφυγε. τῶν δ' ἱερέων τινὲς τὸ μὲν πρῶτον
ἀπὸ τοῦ ναοῦ τούς τε ὀβελοὺς καὶ τὰς ἕδρας αὐτῶν
μολίβου πεποιημένας ἀνασπῶντες εἰς τοὺς Ῥω-
279 μαίους ἠφίεσαν, αὖθις δ' ὡς οὔτ' ἤνυόν τι καὶ τὸ
πῦρ ἐπ' αὐτοὺς ἀνερρήγνυτο, ἐπὶ τὸν τοῖχον
ἀναχωρήσαντες, ὄντα ὀκτάπηχυν τὸ εὖρος, ἔμενον.
280 δύο γε μὴν τῶν ἐπισήμων, παρὸν σωθῆναι πρὸς
Ῥωμαίους μεταστάσιν ἢ διακαρτερεῖν πρὸς τὴν
μετὰ τῶν ἄλλων τύχην, ἑαυτοὺς ἔρριψαν εἰς τὸ
πῦρ καὶ τῷ ναῷ συγκατεφλέγησαν, Μηΐρός τε υἱὸς
Βελγᾶ καὶ Ἰώσηπος Δαλαίου.
281 (2) Ῥωμαῖοι δὲ μάταιον τὴν ἐπὶ τοῖς πέριξ
φειδὼ κρίναντες τοῦ ναοῦ φλεγομένου πάντα συν-
επίμπρασαν, τά τε λείψανα τῶν στοῶν καὶ τὰς

¹ om. LC Zon.　　　² ἐπιβαίνοντες PA.

ᵃ Cf. the similar catalogue of horrible sounds, including
456

sanctuary on fire, gathered strength once more for lamentations and wailing. Peraea and the surrounding mountains contributed their echoes, deepening the din.[a] But yet more awful than the uproar were the sufferings. You would indeed have thought that the temple-hill was boiling over from its base, being everywhere one mass of flame, but yet that the stream of blood was more copious than the flames and the slain more numerous than the slayers. For the ground was nowhere visible through the corpses; but the soldiers had to clamber over heaps of bodies in pursuit of the fugitives. The brigand crowd succeeded in pushing through the Romans and with difficulty forcing their way into the outer court of the temple, and thence to the city; while what was left of the populace took refuge on the outer portico.[b] Of the priests some, at the first, tore up the spikes from the sanctuary, with their leaden sockets, and hurled them at the Romans, but afterwards, finding their efforts unavailing and the flames breaking out against them, they retired to the wall, which was eight cubits broad, and there remained. Two persons of distinction, however, having the choice of saving their lives by going over to the Romans or of holding out and sharing the fortune of the rest, plunged into the fire and were consumed with the temple, namely Meirus, son of Belgas, and Josephus, son of Dalaeus.

(2) The Romans, thinking it useless, now that the temple was on fire, to spare the surrounding buildings, set them all alight, both the remnants of the porticoes and the gates, excepting two, one on the

Burning of the treasury and other buildings.

the mountain echoes, in the account of the siege of Jotapata, iii. 247-250. [b] Their fate is described below, §§ 283 f.

πύλας πλὴν δύο, τῆς μὲν ἐκ τῶν ἀνατολικῶν, τῆς
δὲ μεσημβρινῆς· καὶ ταύτας¹ ὕστερον κατέσκαψαν.
282 ἔκαιον δὲ καὶ τὰ γαζοφυλάκια, ἐν οἷς ἄπειρον μὲν
χρημάτων πλῆθος ἄπειροι δ' ἐσθῆτες καὶ ἄλλα
κειμήλια, συνελόντι δ' εἰπεῖν, πᾶς ὁ 'Ιουδαίων
σεσώρευτο πλοῦτος, ἀνεσκευασμένων ἐκεῖ τοὺς
283 οἴκους τῶν εὐπόρων. ἧκον δὲ καὶ ἐπὶ τὴν λοιπὴν
στοὰν τοῦ ἔξωθεν ἱεροῦ· καταπεφεύγει² δ' ἐπ'
αὐτὴν ἀπὸ τοῦ δήμου γύναια καὶ παιδία καὶ
284 σύμμικτος ὄχλος εἰς ἑξακισχιλίους. πρὶν δὲ Καίσαρα κρῖναί τι περὶ αὐτῶν ἢ κελεῦσαι τοὺς ἡγεμόνας, φερόμενοι τοῖς θυμοῖς οἱ στρατιῶται τὴν
στοὰν ὑφάπτουσι, καὶ συνέβη τοὺς μὲν ῥιπτοῦντας
αὐτοὺς ἐκ τῆς φλογὸς διαφθαρῆναι, τοὺς δ' ἐν
285 αὐτῇ· περιεσώθη δ' ἐκ τοσούτων οὐδείς. τούτοις
αἴτιος τῆς ἀπωλείας ψευδοπροφήτης τις κατέστη
κατ' ἐκείνην κηρύξας τὴν ἡμέραν τοῖς ἐπὶ τῆς
πόλεως, ὡς ὁ θεὸς ἐπὶ τὸ ἱερὸν ἀναβῆναι κελεύει
286 δεξομένους τὰ σημεῖα τῆς σωτηρίας. πολλοὶ δ'
ἦσαν ἐγκάθετοι παρὰ τῶν τυράννων τότε πρὸς τὸν
δῆμον προφῆται, προσμένειν τὴν ἀπὸ τοῦ θεοῦ
βοήθειαν καταγγέλλοντες, ὡς ἧττον αὐτομολοῖεν
καὶ τοὺς ἐπάνω δέους καὶ φυλακῆς γενομένους
287 ἐλπὶς παρακροτοίη. πείθεται δὲ ταχέως³ ἄνθρωπος
ἐν συμφοραῖς, ὅταν δ' ἤδη⁴ καὶ τῶν κατεχόντων
δεινῶν ἀπαλλαγὴν ὁ ἐξαπατῶν ὑπογράφῃ, τόθ'
ὁ πάσχων ὅλος γίνεται τῆς ἐλπίδος.
288 (3) Τὸν γοῦν ἄθλιον δῆμον οἱ μὲν ἀπατεῶνες καὶ
καταψευδόμενοι τοῦ θεοῦ τηνικαῦτα παρέπειθον,

¹ + δ' Destinon.
² Bekker with one ms. and Lat. (confugerant): καταφεύγει
the rest.   ³ δ' εὐθέως L.   ⁴ δὲ ἤδη L: δὲ δὴ most mss.

east and the other on the south; these also they subsequently razed to the ground. They further burnt the treasury-chambers,[a] in which lay vast sums of money, vast piles of raiment, and other valuables; for this, in short, was the general repository of Jewish wealth, to which the rich had consigned the contents of their dismantled houses. They then proceeded Destruction to the one remaining portico of the outer court, on of six which the poor women and children of the populace refugees and a mixed multitude had taken refuge, numbering six thousand. And before Caesar had come to any decision or given any orders to the officers concerning these people, the soldiers, carried away by rage, set fire to the portico from below; with the result that some were killed plunging out of the flames, others perished amidst them, and out of all that multitude not a soul escaped. They owed their destruction to deluded by a false prophet, who had on that day proclaimed to a false the people in the city that God commanded them to prophet. go up to the temple court, to receive there the tokens of their deliverance. Numerous prophets, indeed, were at this period suborned by the tyrants to delude the people, by bidding them await help from God, in order that desertions might be checked and that those who were above fear and precaution might be encouraged by hope. In adversity man is quickly persuaded; but when the deceiver actually pictures release from prevailing horrors, then the sufferer wholly abandons himself to expectation.

(3) Thus it was that the wretched people were Portents deluded at that time by charlatans and pretended of the end.

---

[a] v. 200; it was here that Herod Agrippa suspended the golden chain given him by Caligula on his release from imprisonment, A. xix. 294.

τοῖς δ' ἐναργέσι καὶ προσημαίνουσι τὴν μέλλουσαν
ἐρημίαν τέρασιν οὔτε προσεῖχον οὔτ' ἐπίστευον,
ἀλλ' ὡς ἐμβεβροντημένοι καὶ μήτ' ὄμματα μήτε
ψυχὴν ἔχοντες τῶν τοῦ θεοῦ κηρυγμάτων παρ-
289 ήκουσαν, τοῦτο μὲν ὅτε ὑπὲρ τὴν πόλιν ἄστρον ἔστη
ῥομφαίᾳ παραπλήσιον καὶ παρατείνας ἐπ' ἐνιαυτὸν
290 κομήτης, τοῦτο δ' ἡνίκα πρὸ τῆς ἀποστάσεως καὶ
τοῦ πρὸς τὸν πόλεμον κινήματος ἀθροιζομένου τοῦ
λαοῦ πρὸς τὴν τῶν ἀζύμων ἑορτήν, ὀγδόῃ δ' ἦν
Ξανθικοῦ μηνός, κατὰ νυκτὸς ἐνάτην ὥραν τοσοῦτο
φῶς περιέλαμψε τὸν βωμὸν καὶ τὸν ναόν, ὡς
δοκεῖν ἡμέραν εἶναι λαμπράν, καὶ τοῦτο παρέτεινεν
291 ἐφ' ἡμίσειαν ὥραν· ὃ τοῖς μὲν ἀπείροις ἀγαθὸν
ἐδόκει, τοῖς δ' ἱερογραμματεῦσι πρὸς τῶν ἀποβεβη-
292 κότων εὐθέως ἐκρίθη. καὶ κατὰ τὴν αὐτὴν ἑορτὴν
βοῦς μὲν ἀχθεῖσα ὑπό του πρὸς τὴν θυσίαν ἔτεκεν
293 ἄρνα ἐν τῷ ἱερῷ μέσῳ, ἡ δ' ἀνατολικὴ πύλη τοῦ
ἐνδοτέρω ναοῦ χαλκῆ μὲν οὖσα καὶ στιβαρωτάτη,
κλειομένη δὲ περὶ δείλην μόλις ὑπ' ἀνθρώπων
εἴκοσι, καὶ μοχλοῖς μὲν ἐπερειδομένη σιδηροδέτοις,
κατάπηγας δ' ἔχουσα βαθυτάτους εἰς τὸν οὐδὸν
ὄντα διηνεκοῦς λίθου καθιεμένους, ὤφθη κατὰ
294 νυκτὸς ὥραν ἕκτην αὐτομάτως ἠνοιγμένη·[1] δραμόντες δ' οἱ τοῦ ἱεροῦ φύλακες ἤγγειλαν τῷ
στρατηγῷ, κἀκεῖνος ἀναβὰς μόλις αὐτὴν ἴσχυσεν
295 κλεῖσαι. πάλιν τοῦτο τοῖς μὲν ἰδιώταις κάλλιστον

---

[1] PA Eus.: ἠνεῳγμένη the rest.

[a] Tac. *Hist.* v. 13, "evenerant prodigia, quae neque hostiis
neque votis piare fas habet gens superstitioni obnoxia,
religionibus adversa." "Tacitus means that the Jews were
much under the influence of their religion (which he calls
superstitio), but, unlike the Romans, did not feel that pro-
digies involved any obligations (*religiones*) to avert them."

messengers of the deity ; while they neither heeded
nor believed in the manifest portents that foretold
the coming desolation, but, as if thunderstruck and
bereft of eyes and mind, disregarded the plain
warnings of God.[a] So it was when a star, resembling The star
a sword, stood over the city, and a comet which and comet.
continued for a year. So again when, before the The
revolt and the commotion that led to war, at the midnight
time when the people were assembling for the feast light round the altar.
of unleavened bread, on the eighth of the month
Xanthicus,[b] at the ninth hour of the night, so brilliant
a light shone round the altar and the sanctuary that
it seemed to be broad daylight ; and this continued
for half an hour. By the inexperienced this was
regarded as a good omen, but by the sacred scribes
it was at once interpreted in accordance with after
events. At that same feast a cow that had been A monstrous
brought by some one for sacrifice gave birth to a birth in the temple.
lamb in the midst of the court of the temple ; more-
over, the eastern gate of the inner court—it was of Spontane-
brass and very massive, and, when closed towards ous opening of the
evening, could scarcely be moved by twenty men ; brazen gate.
fastened with iron-bound bars, it had bolts which
were sunk to a great depth into a threshold consisting of a solid block of stone—this gate was observed
at the sixth hour of the night to have opened of its
own accord.[c] The watchmen of the temple ran
and reported the matter to the captain,[d] and he
came up and with difficulty succeeded in shutting it.
This again to the uninitiated seemed the best of

[b] March-April ; " 25 April of the Julian year if Josephus
follows his usual system, but here he seems to have used a
more ancient Jewish reckoning " (Niese).
[c] Tac. ibid. " apertae repente delubri fores."
[d] " The captain of the temple," Acts iv. 1, v. 24.

ἐδόκει τέρας· ἀνοῖξαι γὰρ τὸν θεὸν αὐτοῖς τὴν τῶν
ἀγαθῶν πύλην· οἱ λόγιοι δὲ λυομένην αὐτομάτως
τοῦ ναοῦ τὴν ἀσφάλειαν ἐνενόουν, καὶ πολεμίοις
296 δῶρον ἀνοίγεσθαι τὴν πύλην, δηλωτικόν τ' ἐρημίας
ἀπέφαινον ἐν αὑτοῖς τὸ σημεῖον. μετὰ δὲ τὴν
ἑορτὴν οὐ πολλαῖς ἡμέραις ὕστερον, μιᾷ καὶ εἰκάδι
297 Ἀρτεμισίου μηνός, φάσμα τι δαιμόνιον ὤφθη
μεῖζον πίστεως· τερατεία δὲ ἂν ἔδοξεν οἶμαι τὸ
ῥηθησόμενον, εἰ μὴ καὶ παρὰ τοῖς θεασαμένοις
298 ἱστόρητο καὶ τὰ ἐπακολουθήσαντα πάθη τῶν
σημείων ἦν ἄξια· πρὸ γὰρ ἡλίου δύσεως ὤφθη
μετέωρα περὶ πᾶσαν τὴν χώραν ἅρματα καὶ
299 φάλαγγες ἔνοπλοι διάττουσαι τῶν νεφῶν καὶ κυ-
κλούμεναι τὰς πόλεις. κατὰ δὲ τὴν ἑορτήν, ἣ
πεντηκοστὴ καλεῖται, νύκτωρ οἱ ἱερεῖς παρελθόντες εἰς τὸ ἔνδον ἱερόν, ὥσπερ αὐτοῖς ἔθος[1]
πρὸς τὰς λειτουργίας, πρῶτον μὲν κινήσεως ἔφασαν
300 ἀντιλαβέσθαι καὶ κτύπου, μετὰ δὲ ταῦτα φωνῆς
ἀθρόας "μεταβαίνομεν[2] ἐντεῦθεν." τὸ δὲ τούτων
φοβερώτερον, Ἰησοῦς γάρ τις υἱὸς Ἀνανίου[3] τῶν
ἰδιωτῶν ἄγροικος, πρὸ τεσσάρων ἐτῶν τοῦ πολέμου
τὰ μάλιστα τῆς πόλεως εἰρηνευομένης[4] καὶ εὐθη-
νούσης, ἐλθὼν εἰς τὴν ἑορτήν, ἐν ᾗ σκηνοποιεῖσθαι
301 πάντας ἔθος τῷ θεῷ, κατὰ τὸ ἱερὸν ἐξαπίνης
ἀναβοᾶν ἤρξατο "φωνὴ ἀπ' ἀνατολῆς, φωνὴ ἀπὸ

---

[1] P (cf. § 300): + ἦν the rest.
[2] μεταβαίνωμεν Lat. Zon. Eus. *Dem. Ev.*
[3] PA Heg. Eus.: Ἀνάνου the rest.   [4] εἰρηνευούσης PL.

[a] c. May (" 8 June," Niese as above).
[b] Tac. *ibid.* " visae per caelum concurrere acies, rutilantia
arma et subito nubium igne conlucere templum " (partly
based on Virgil, *Aen.* viii. 528 f.).
[c] Tac. *ibid.* " apertae repente delubri fores et audita major

462

omens, as they supposed that God had opened to
them the gate of blessings ; but the learned understood that the security of the temple was dissolving
of its own accord and that the opening of the gate
meant a present to the enemy, interpreting the
portent in their own minds as indicative of coming
desolation. Again, not many days after the festival, Celestial
on the twenty-first of the month Artemisium,[a] there armies.
appeared a miraculous phenomenon, passing belief.
Indeed, what I am about to relate would, I imagine,
have been deemed a fable, were it not for the narra-
tives of eyewitnesses and for the subsequent calamities
which deserved to be so signalized. For before
sunset throughout all parts of the country chariots
were seen in the air and armed battalions hurtling
through the clouds and encompassing the cities.[b]
Moreover, at the feast which is called Pentecost, The voice
the priests on entering the inner court of the temple temple.
by night, as their custom was in the discharge of
their ministrations, reported that they were conscious, first of a commotion and a din, and after that
of a voice as of a host, " We are departing hence." [c]

But a further portent was even more alarming. The
Four years before the war, when the city was enjoy- cries of
ing profound peace and prosperity, there came to Jesus for
the feast at which it is the custom of all Jews to before
erect tabernacles to God,[d] one Jesus, son of Ananias, the war.
a rude peasant, who, standing in the temple, suddenly
began to cry out, " A voice from the east, a voice

humana vox, excedere deos ; simul ingens motus exceden-
tium." This supports the reading, μεταβαίνομεν, in the text,
rather than the variant, " let us depart hence."
   [d] The Feast of Tabernacles, *Sukkoth*, autumn of A.D. 62,
as appears from § 308. Hostilities opened four years later
with the defeat of Cestius in the autumn of A.D. 66.

δύσεως, φωνὴ ἀπὸ τῶν τεσσάρων ἀνέμων, φωνὴ
ἐπὶ Ἱεροσόλυμα καὶ τὸν ναόν, φωνὴ ἐπὶ νυμφίους
καὶ νύμφας, φωνὴ ἐπὶ τὸν λαὸν πάντα.'' τοῦτο
μεθ' ἡμέραν καὶ νύκτωρ κατὰ πάντας τοὺς στενω-
302 ποὺς περιῄει κεκραγώς. τῶν δὲ ἐπισήμων τινὲς
δημοτῶν ἀγανακτήσαντες πρὸς τὸ κακόφημον
συλλαμβάνουσι τὸν ἄνθρωπον καὶ πολλαῖς αἰκί-
ζονται πληγαῖς. ὁ δ' οὔθ' ὑπὲρ αὑτοῦ φθεγξά-
μενος οὔτ' ἰδίᾳ πρὸς τοὺς παίοντας, ἃς καὶ πρότερον
303 φωνὰς βοῶν διετέλει. νομίσαντες δ' οἱ ἄρχοντες,
ὅπερ ἦν, δαιμονιώτερον τὸ κίνημα τἀνδρὸς ἀν-
άγουσιν αὐτὸν ἐπὶ τὸν παρὰ Ῥωμαίοις ἔπαρχον.
304 ἔνθα μάστιξι μέχρι ὀστέων ξαινόμενος οὔθ' ἱκέτευσεν οὔτ' ἐδάκρυσεν, ἀλλ' ὡς ἐνῆν μάλιστα τὴν
φωνὴν ὀλοφυρτικῶς παρεγκλίνων πρὸς ἑκάστην
305 ἀπεκρίνατο πληγὴν "αἰαῖ Ἱεροσολύμοις.'' τοῦ
δ' Ἀλβίνου διερωτῶντος, οὗτος γὰρ ἔπαρχος ἦν,
τίς τ' εἴη καὶ πόθεν, καὶ διὰ τί ταῦτα φθέγγοιτο,
πρὸς ταῦτα μὲν οὐδ' ὁτιοῦν ἀπεκρίνατο, τὸν δ' ἐπὶ
τῇ πόλει θρῆνον εἴρων οὐ διέλειπεν, μέχρι κατα-
306 γνοὺς μανίαν ὁ Ἀλβῖνος ἀπέλυσεν αὐτόν. ὁ δὲ τὸν
μέχρι τοῦ πολέμου χρόνον οὔτε προσῄει τινὶ τῶν
πολιτῶν οὔτε ὤφθη λαλῶν, ἀλλὰ καθ' ἡμέραν
ὥσπερ εὐχὴν μεμελετηκὼς "αἰαῖ Ἱεροσολύμοις''
307 ἐθρήνει. οὔτε δέ τινι τῶν τυπτόντων αὐτὸν ὁσημέραι κατηρᾶτο οὔτε τοὺς τροφῆς μεταδιδόντας
εὐλόγει, μία δὲ πρὸς πάντας ἦν ἡ σκυθρωπὴ κληδὼν
308 ἀπόκρισις. μάλιστα δ' ἐν ταῖς ἑορταῖς ἐκεκράγει·
καὶ τοῦτ' ἐφ' ἑπτὰ ἔτη καὶ μῆνας πέντε εἴρων οὔτ'
ἤμβλυνεν τὴν φωνὴν οὔτ' ἔκαμεν, μέχρις οὗ κατὰ

---

from the west, a voice from the four winds ; a voice against Jerusalem and the sanctuary, a voice against the bridegroom and the bride,[a] a voice against all the people." Day and night he went about all the alleys with this cry on his lips. Some of the leading citizens, incensed at these ill-omened words, arrested the fellow and severely chastised him. But he, without a word on his own behalf or for the private ear of those who smote him, only continued his cries as before. Thereupon, the magistrates, supposing, as was indeed the case, that the man was under some supernatural impulse, brought him before the Roman governor ; there, although flayed to the bone with scourges, he neither sued for mercy nor shed a tear, but, merely introducing the most mournful of variations into his ejaculation, responded to each stroke with " Woe to Jerusalem ! " When Albinus,[b] the governor, asked him who and whence he was and why he uttered these cries, he answered him never a word, but unceasingly reiterated his dirge over the city, until Albinus pronounced him a maniac and let him go. During the whole period up to the outbreak of war he neither approached nor was seen talking to any of the citizens, but daily, like a prayer that he had conned, repeated his lament, " Woe to Jerusalem ! " He neither cursed any of those who beat him from day to day, nor blessed those who offered him food : to all men that melancholy presage was his one reply. His cries were loudest at the festivals. So for seven years and five months he continued his wail, his voice never flagging nor his strength exhausted, until in the siege, having seen to cease from . . . the streets of Jerusalem . . . the voice of the bridegroom and the voice of the bride " (vii. 34, etc.).

[b] Procurator A.D. 62–64, B. ii. 272-6.

τὴν πολιορκίαν ἔργα τῆς κληδόνος ἰδὼν ἀνεπαύσατο.
περιιὼν γὰρ ἀπὸ[1] τοῦ τείχους "αἰαὶ πάλιν τῇ
309 πόλει καὶ τῷ λαῷ καὶ τῷ ναῷ" διαπρύσιον ἐβόα,
ὡς δὲ τελευταῖον προσέθηκεν "αἰαὶ δὲ κἀμοί,"
λίθος ἐκ τοῦ πετροβόλου σχασθεὶς καὶ πλήξας
αὐτὸν παραχρῆμα κτείνει, φθεγγομένην δ' ἔτι τὰς
κληδόνας ἐκείνας τὴν ψυχὴν ἀφῆκε.

310 (4) Ταῦτά τις ἐννοῶν εὑρήσει τὸν μὲν θεὸν
ἀνθρώπων κηδόμενον καὶ παντοίως προσημαίνοντα
τῷ σφετέρῳ γένει τὰ σωτήρια, τοὺς δ' ὑπ' ἀνοίας
311 καὶ κακῶν αὐθαιρέτων ἀπολλυμένους, ὅπου γε
Ἰουδαῖοι καὶ τὸ ἱερὸν μετὰ τὴν καθαίρεσιν τῆς
Ἀντωνίας τετράγωνον ἐποίησαν, ἀναγεγραμμένον
ἐν τοῖς λογίοις ἔχοντες ἁλώσεσθαι τὴν πόλιν καὶ
τὸν ναόν, ἐπειδὰν τὸ ἱερὸν γένηται τετράγωνον.
312 τὸ δ' ἐπᾶραν αὐτοὺς μάλιστα πρὸς τὸν πόλεμον ἦν
χρησμὸς ἀμφίβολος ὁμοίως ἐν τοῖς ἱεροῖς εὑρη-
μένος γράμμασιν, ὡς κατὰ τὸν καιρὸν ἐκεῖνον ἀπὸ
313 τῆς χώρας αὐτῶν τις ἄρξει τῆς οἰκουμένης. τοῦθ'
οἱ μὲν ὡς οἰκεῖον ἐξέλαβον καὶ πολλοὶ τῶν σοφῶν
ἐπλανήθησαν περὶ τὴν κρίσιν, ἐδήλου δ' ἄρα τὴν
Οὐεσπασιανοῦ τὸ λόγιον ἡγεμονίαν ἀποδειχθέντος
314 ἐπὶ Ἰουδαίας αὐτοκράτορος. ἀλλὰ γὰρ οὐ δυνατὸν

---

[1] PA: ἐπὶ the rest.

---

[a] Authority unknown.
[b] So Tacitus, *Hist.* v. 13 " pluribus persuasio inerat anti-
quis sacerdotum litteris contineri, eo ipso tempore fore ut
valesceret Oriens profectique Judaea rerum poterentur.
quae ambages Vespasianum ac Titum praedixerat, sed vulgus
more humanae cupidinis sibi tantam fatorum magnitudinem
interpretati ne adversis quidem ad vera mutabantur." *Cf.*
the similar statement in Suetonius, *Vesp.* 4 " percrebruerat

his presage verified, he found his rest. For, while going his round and shouting in piercing tones from the wall, " Woe once more to the city and to the people and to the temple," as he added a last word, " and woe to me also," a stone hurled from the *ballista* struck and killed him on the spot. So with those ominous words still upon his lips he passed away.

(4) Reflecting on these things one will find that God has a care for men, and by all kinds of pre-monitory signs shows His people the way of salvation, while they owe their destruction to folly and calamities of their own choosing. Thus the Jews, after the demolition of Antonia, reduced the temple to a square, although they had it recorded in their oracles that the city and the sanctuary would be taken when the temple should become four-square.[a] But what more than all else incited them to the war was an ambiguous oracle, likewise found in their sacred scriptures, to the effect that at that time one from their country would become ruler of the world. This they understood to mean someone of their own race, and many of their wise men went astray in their interpretation of it. The oracle, however, in reality signified the sovereignty of Vespasian, who was proclaimed Emperor on Jewish soil.[b] For all

Two oracles.

Oriente toto vetus et constans opinio, esse in fatis ut eo tempore Judaea profecti rerum potirentur. Id de imperatore Romano, quantum postea eventu paruit, praedictum Judaei ad se trahentes rebellarunt." For discussions on this (Messi-anic) prophecy and the relations between Josephus and Tacitus see E. Norden in *Neue Jahrbücher für das klassische Altertum*, 1913, xxxi. 637 ff., and P. Corrsen in *Zeitschrift für die N.T. Wissenschaft*, 1914, 114 ff. Tacitus is not likely to have read Josephus: both are apparently dependent on a common source.

ἀνθρώποις τὸ χρεὼν διαφυγεῖν οὐδὲ προορωμένοις.
315 οἱ δὲ καὶ τῶν σημείων ἃ μὲν ἔκριναν πρὸς ἡδονὴν ἃ
δ' ἐξουθένησαν, μέχρις οὗ τῇ τε ἁλώσει τῆς πατρίδος καὶ τῷ σφῶν αὐτῶν ὀλέθρῳ διηλέγχθησαν
τὴν ἄνοιαν.
316 (vi. 1) Ῥωμαῖοι δὲ τῶν μὲν στασιαστῶν καταπεφευγότων εἰς τὴν πόλιν, καιομένου δὲ αὐτοῦ τε
τοῦ ναοῦ καὶ τῶν πέριξ ἁπάντων, κομίσαντες τὰς
σημαίας εἰς τὸ ἱερὸν καὶ θέμενοι τῆς ἀνατολικῆς
πύλης ἄντικρυς ἔθυσάν τε αὐταῖς αὐτόθι καὶ τὸν
Τίτον μετὰ μεγίστων εὐφημιῶν ἀπέφηναν αὐτο-
317 κράτορα. ταῖς δὲ ἁρπαγαῖς οὕτως ἐνεπλήσθησαν
οἱ στρατιῶται πάντες, ὥστε κατὰ τὴν Συρίαν πρὸς
ἥμισυ τῆς πάλαι τιμῆς τὸν σταθμὸν τοῦ χρυσίου
318 πιπράσκεσθαι. τῶν δ' ἀνὰ τὸν τοῖχον τοῦ ναοῦ
ἱερέων διακαρτερούντων παῖς διψήσας ἱκέτευε τοὺς
φύλακας τῶν Ῥωμαίων δοῦναι δεξιὰν αὐτῷ καὶ τὸ
319 δίψος ἐξωμολογεῖτο. τῶν δὲ τῆς ἡλικίας καὶ τῆς
ἀνάγκης οἶκτον λαβόντων καὶ δόντων δεξιὰς
καταβὰς αὐτός τε πίνει καὶ ὃ φέρων ἧκεν ἀγγεῖον
πλήσας ὕδατος ᾤχετο φεύγων ἄνω πρὸς τοὺς
320 σφετέρους. τῶν δὲ φυλάκων καταλαβεῖν μὲν
οὐδεὶς ἴσχυσε, πρὸς δὲ τὴν ἀπιστίαν ἐβλασφήμουν.
κἀκεῖνος οὐδὲν ἔφη παραβεβηκέναι τῶν συνθηκῶν·
λαβεῖν γὰρ δεξιὰν οὐ τοῦ μένειν παρ' αὐτοῖς ἀλλὰ
τοῦ καταβῆναι μόνον καὶ λαβεῖν ὕδωρ, ἅπερ
321 ἀμφότερα πεποιηκὼς πιστὸς ἔδοξεν εἶναι. τὸ μὲν
δὴ πανούργημα διὰ τὴν ἡλικίαν μάλιστα τοῦ
παιδὸς ἀπεθαύμαζον οἱ πλανηθέντες· πέμπτῃ δ'

ᵃ Havercamp quotes Tertullian's *Apology*, xvi. "sed et
Victorias adoratis. . . . Religio Romanorum tota castrensis
signa veneratur, signa jurat, signa omnibus diis praeponit."

that, it is impossible for men to escape their fate, even though they foresee it. Some of these portents, then, the Jews interpreted to please themselves, others they treated with contempt, until the ruin of their country and their own destruction convicted them of their folly.

(vi. 1) The Romans, now that the rebels had fled to the city, and the sanctuary itself and all around it were in flames, carried their standards into the temple court and, setting them up opposite the eastern gate, there sacrificed to them,[a] and with rousing acclamations hailed Titus as imperator. So glutted with plunder were the troops, one and all, that throughout Syria the standard of gold was depreciated to half its former value. Among the priests still holding out on the wall of the sanctuary [b] a lad, who was parched with thirst, confessed his condition to the Roman guards and besought them to pledge him security. Taking pity on his youth and distress, they promised him protection ; whereupon he came down and drank, and then, after filling with water a vessel which he had brought with him, raced back to his comrades above. The guards all failing to catch him and cursing his perfidy, he replied that he had broken no covenant ; for the accepted pledge did not bind him to remain with them, but merely permitted him to descend and procure water ; both these actions he had done, and therefore considered that he had been true to his word. Such cunning, especially in so young a boy, astonished the Romans whom he had outwitted ; however, on the fifth day, the priests, now famishing,

The Romans sacrifice to the standards and hail Titus imperator.

Surrender and execution of the priests.

For the practice here mentioned Josephus seems to be the sole authority.   [b] § 279.

JOSEPHUS

ἡμέρᾳ λιμώττοντες οἱ ἱερεῖς καταβαίνουσι καὶ
πρὸς Τίτον ἀναχθέντες ὑπὸ τῶν φυλάκων ἱκέτευον
322 τυχεῖν σωτηρίας. ὁ δὲ τὸν μὲν τῆς συγγνώμης
καιρὸν αὐτοῖς παρῳχηκέναι φήσας, οἴχεσθαι δὲ
δι' ὃν εὐλόγως ἂν αὐτοὺς ἔσῳζε, πρέπειν δὲ τοῖς
ἱερεῦσι τῷ ναῷ συναπολέσθαι, κελεύει κολάσαι
τοὺς ἄνδρας.
323   (2) Οἱ δὲ περὶ τοὺς τυράννους ὡς τῷ τε πολέμῳ
πάντοθεν ἐκρατοῦντο καὶ περιτετειχισμένοις διαφυγεῖν οὐδαμόθεν ἦν, προκαλοῦνται¹ τὸν Τίτον εἰς
324 λόγους. ὁ δὲ καὶ διὰ τὸ φιλάνθρωπον φύσει τὸ
γοῦν ἄστυ περισῶσαι προαιρούμενος καὶ τῶν
φίλων ἐναγόντων, ἤδη γὰρ μετριάζειν τοὺς λῃστὰς
ὑπελάμβανον,² ἵσταται κατὰ τὸ πρὸς δύσιν μέρος
325 τοῦ ἔξωθεν ἱεροῦ· ταύτῃ γὰρ ὑπὲρ τὸν ξυστὸν
ἦσαν πύλαι, καὶ γέφυρα συνάπτουσα τῷ ἱερῷ τὴν
ἄνω πόλιν· αὕτη τότε μέση τῶν τυράννων ἦν καὶ
326 τοῦ Καίσαρος. τὸ δὲ πλῆθος ἑκατέροις βύζην
ἐφεστήκει, Ἰουδαῖοι μὲν περὶ Σίμωνα καὶ Ἰωάννην
μετέωροι συγγνώμης ἐλπίδι, Ῥωμαῖοι δὲ Καίσαρι
327 καραδοκοῦντες αὐτῶν τὴν ἀξίωσιν. παραγγείλας
δὲ τοῖς στρατιώταις Τίτος θυμοῦ τε καὶ βελῶν
μένειν ἐγκρατεῖς, καὶ τὸν ἑρμηνέα παραστησάμενος,
ὅπερ ἦν τεκμήριον τοῦ κρατεῖν, πρῶτος ἤρξατο
328 λέγειν· "ἆρά γε ἤδη κεκόρεσθε τῶν τῆς πατρίδος
κακῶν,³ ἄνδρες, οἱ μήτε τῆς ἡμετέρας δυνάμεως
μήτε τῆς ἑαυτῶν ἀσθενείας ἔννοιαν λαβόντες, ὁρμῇ
δὲ ἀσκέπτῳ καὶ μανίᾳ τόν τε δῆμον καὶ τὴν πόλιν
καὶ τὸν ναὸν ἀπολωλεκότες, ἀπολούμενοι δὲ καὶ

¹ Naber with Lat.: προσκαλοῦνται mss.
² Hudson with Lat.: ὑπελάμβανεν mss.
³ + ὦ P Lat.

470

came down and, being conducted by the guards to Titus, implored him to spare their lives. But he told them that the time for pardon had for them gone by, that the one thing for whose sake he might with propriety have spared them was gone, and that it behoved priests to perish with their temple, and so ordered them to execution.

(2) The tyrants and their followers, beaten on all sides in the war and surrounded by a wall [a] preventing any possibility of escape, now invited Titus to a parley. Anxious, with his innate humanity, at all events to save the town, and instigated by his friends, who supposed that the brigands had at length been brought to reason, Titus took up a position on the west of the outer court of the temple ; there being at this point gates opening above the Xystus and a bridge [b] which connected the upper city with the temple and now parted the tyrants from Caesar. The multitude stood in crowds on either side : the Jews around Simon and John, excited by hopes of pardon, the Romans beside Caesar eagerly waiting to hear their claim. Titus, after charging his troops to keep a check on their rage and their missiles, and stationing an interpreter beside him, proceeded, in token of his conquest, to address them first.

Simon and John ask for parley with Titus.

" Well, sirs, are you at length sated with your country's woes :—you who, without bestowing a thought on our strength or your own weakness, have through inconsiderate fury and madness lost your people, your city, and your temple, and are yourselves justly doomed to perish ;—you who from the

Titus addresses the tyrants

---

[a] v. 502 ff.
[b] For Xystus and bridge *cf.* ii. 344. This speech of Titus at the close is delivered almost on the same spot as that of Agrippa before the outbreak of war.

329 αὐτοὶ δικαίως, οἳ πρῶτον μὲν ἀφ' οὗ Πομπήιος
εἷλεν ὑμᾶς κατὰ κράτος οὐκ ἐπαύσασθε νεωτεροποιίας, ἔπειτα καὶ φανερὸν ἐξηνέγκατε πρὸς
330 Ῥωμαίους πόλεμον; ἆρά γε πλήθει πεποιθότες;
καὶ μὴν ἐλάχιστον ὑμῖν μέρος ἀντήρκεσεν τοῦ
Ῥωμαίων στρατιωτικοῦ. πίστει τοιγαροῦν συμμάχων; καὶ τί τῶν ἔξω τῆς ἡμετέρας ἡγεμονίας
ἐθνῶν ἔμελλεν αἱρήσεσθαι Ἰουδαίους πρὸ Ῥωμαίων;
331 ἀλλ' ἀλκῇ σωμάτων; καὶ μὴν ἴστε Γερμανοὺς
δουλεύοντας ἡμῖν. ὀχυρότητι δὲ τειχῶν; καὶ τί
μεῖζον ὠκεανοῦ τεῖχος[1] κώλυμα, ὃν περιβεβλη-
μένοι Βρεττανοὶ τὰ Ῥωμαίων ὅπλα προσκυνοῦσιν;
332 καρτερίᾳ ψυχῆς καὶ πανουργίᾳ στρατηγῶν; ἀλλὰ
333 μὴν ᾔδειτε καὶ Καρχηδονίους ἁλόντας. τοιγαροῦν
ὑμᾶς ἐπήγειρε κατὰ Ῥωμαίων ἡ Ῥωμαίων φιλαν-
θρωπία, οἳ πρῶτον μὲν ὑμῖν τήν τε χώραν ἔδομεν
νέμεσθαι καὶ βασιλεῖς ὁμοφύλους ἐπεστήσαμεν,
334 ἔπειτα τοὺς πατρίους νόμους ἐτηρήσαμεν, καὶ ζῆν
οὐ μόνον καθ' ἑαυτοὺς ἀλλὰ καὶ πρὸς[2] τοὺς ἄλλους
335 ἐπετρέψαμεν ὡς ἐβούλεσθε· τὸ δὲ μέγιστον, δασμο-
λογεῖν τε ὑμῖν ἐπὶ τῷ θεῷ καὶ ἀναθήματα συλ-
λέγειν ἐπετρέψαμεν, καὶ τοὺς ταῦτα φέροντας οὔτ'
ἐνουθετήσαμεν οὔτε ἐκωλύσαμεν, ἵν' ἡμῖν γένησθε
πλουσιώτεροι[3] καὶ παρασκευάσησθε τοῖς ἡμετέροις
336 χρήμασιν καθ' ἡμῶν. ἔπειτα τηλικούτων ἀγαθῶν
ἀπολαύοντες ἐπὶ τοὺς παρασχόντας ἠνέγκατε τὸν
κόρον καὶ δίκην τῶν ἀτιθασεύτων ἑρπετῶν τοῖς
337 σαίνουσι τὸν ἰὸν ἐναφήκατε. ἔστω γοῦν, κατ-
εφρονήσατε τῆς Νέρωνος ῥᾳθυμίας, καὶ καθάπερ
ῥήγματα ἢ σπάσματα τὸν ἄλλον χρόνον κακοήθως

---

[1] PM: + atque Lat.: τείχους the rest.
[2] L ("cum" Lat.): om. the rest.

first, ever since Pompey reduced you by force never ceased from revolution, and have now ended by declaring open war upon the Romans? Did you rely on numbers? Nay, a mere fraction of the Roman soldiery has proved your match. On the fidelity of allies? Pray, what nation beyond the limits of our empire would prefer Jews to Romans? On physical strength, perhaps? Yet you are aware that the Germans are our slaves. On the solidity of your walls? But what wall could be a greater obstacle than the ocean, encompassed by which the Britons yet do homage to the Roman arms? On the determination of spirit and the astuteness of your generals? Yet you knew that even Carthaginians were defeated.

"No, assuredly you were incited against the Romans by Roman humanity. To begin with, we allowed you to occupy this land and set over you kings of your own blood; then we maintained the laws of your forefathers and permitted you, not only among yourselves but also in your dealings with others, to live as you willed; above all, we permitted you to exact tribute for God and to collect offerings, without either admonishing or hindering those who brought them—only that you might grow richer at our expense and make preparations with our money to attack us! And then, enjoying such privileges, you turned your superabundance against the donors, and like untameable reptiles spat your venom upon those who caressed you.

"You held, be it granted, Nero's indolence in contempt, and, like fractures or ruptures, remained for a time malignantly quiescent, only to show your true

---

³ + πολέμιοι L Lat.

ἠρεμοῦντες ἐν τῇ μείζονι νόσῳ διεφάνητε καὶ πρὸς
ἐλπίδας ἀναιδεῖς[1] ἀμέτρους ἐξετείνατε τὰς ἐπι-
338 θυμίας. ἧκεν ὁ πατὴρ οὑμὸς εἰς τὴν χώραν, οὐ
τιμωρησόμενος ὑμᾶς τῶν κατὰ Κέστιον, ἀλλὰ
339 νουθετήσων· δέον γοῦν, εἴπερ ἐπ᾽ ἀναστάσει τοῦ
ἔθνους παρῆν, ἐπὶ τὴν ῥίζαν ὑμῶν δραμεῖν καὶ
ταύτην ἐκπορθεῖν τὴν πόλιν εὐθέως, ὁ δὲ Γαλιλαίαν
ἐδῄου καὶ τὰ πέριξ, ἐπιδιδοὺς ὑμῖν χρόνον εἰς μετα-
340 μέλειαν. ἀλλ᾽ ὑμῖν ἀσθένεια τὸ φιλάνθρωπον
ἐδόκει κἀκ τῆς ἡμετέρας πραότητος τὴν τόλμαν
341 ἐπεθρέψατε. Νέρωνος οἰχομένου τοῦθ᾽ ὅπερ ἐχρῆν
τοὺς πονηροτάτους ἐποιήσατε, ταῖς ἐμφυλίοις ἡμῶν
ταραχαῖς ἐπεθαρρήσατε, καὶ χωρισθέντων εἰς τὴν
Αἴγυπτον ἐμοῦ τε καὶ τοῦ πατρὸς εἰς παρασκευὰς
τοῦ πολέμου κατεχρήσασθε τοῖς καιροῖς, καὶ οὐκ
ᾐδέσθητε ταράσσειν αὐτοκράτορας γεγενημένους
οὓς καὶ στρατηγοὺς φιλανθρώπους ἐπειράσατε.
342 προσφυγούσης γοῦν ἡμῖν τῆς ἡγεμονίας, καὶ τῶν
μὲν κατὰ ταύτην ἠρεμούντων πάντων, πρεσβευο-
μένων δὲ καὶ συνηδομένων τῶν ἔξωθεν ἐθνῶν,
343 πάλιν οἱ Ἰουδαῖοι πολέμιοι, καὶ πρεσβεῖαι μὲν
ὑμῶν πρὸς τοὺς ὑπὲρ Εὐφράτην ἐπὶ νεωτερισμῷ,
περίβολοι δὲ τειχῶν ἀνοικοδομούμενοι καινοί,
στάσεις δὲ καὶ τυράννων φιλονεικίαι καὶ πόλεμος
ἐμφύλιος, μόνα τοῖς οὕτω πονηροῖς πρέποντα.
344 ἧκον ἐπὶ τὴν πόλιν ἐγὼ παρὰ τοῦ πατρὸς ἄκοντος
λαβὼν σκυθρωπὰ παραγγέλματα. τὸν δῆμον ἀκού-
345 σας εἰρηνικὰ φρονεῖν ἥσθην. ὑμᾶς παύσασθαι πρὸ
πολέμου παρεκάλουν, μέχρι πολλοῦ πολεμούντων

---

[1] ἀναιδείας P : + καὶ MLC.

character on the outbreak of a more serious malady,[a] when you let your ambitions soar unbounded to shameless expectations. My father came into the country, not to punish you for events under Cestius,[b] but to admonish you. Had he come to extirpate the nation, his duty surely was to hasten to the root of your strength and to sack this city forthwith; whereas he proceeded to ravage Galilee and the surrounding district, thus affording you time for repentance. But by you his humanity was taken for weakness, and upon our clemency you nursed your audacity. On Nero's decease, you acted like the basest scoundrels. Emboldened by our intestine troubles, when I and my father had departed for Egypt, you abused your opportunities by preparing for hostilities, and were not ashamed to harass those, now made emperors, whose humanity as generals you had experienced. Thus, when the empire found refuge in us, when throughout its length was universal tranquillity, and foreign nations were sending embassies of congratulation, once again the Jews were in arms. There were embassies from you to your friends beyond the Euphrates fostering revolt; fortifications being built up anew; seditions, contentions of tyrants, and civil war—the only things befitting men so base. I came to this city, the bearer of gloomy injunctions from my reluctant father. The news that the townsfolk were disposed to peace rejoiced my heart. As for you, before hostilities began I urged you to pause; for a long while after you had begun them I spared

---

[a] Roman internal disorders and turbulence in east and west after Nero's death, *cf.* the proem, *B.* i. 4 f.
[b] ii. 499 ff.

ἐφειδόμην, δεξιὰς αὐτομόλοις ἔδωκα, καταφυγοῦσι
πίστεις ἐτήρησα, πολλοὺς αἰχμαλώτους ἠλέησα,
τοὺς ἐπείγοντας βασανίσαι[1] ἐκώλυσα,[2] τείχεσιν
ὑμετέροις μηχανὰς ἄκων προσήγαγον, ἀεὶ φονῶντας
τοὺς στρατιώτας ἐφ᾽ ὑμῖν κατέσχον, καθ᾽ ἑκάστην
νίκην ὡς ἡττώμενος ὑμᾶς εἰς εἰρήνην προυκαλε-
346 σάμην. τοῦ ἱεροῦ πλησίον γενόμενος πάλιν ἑκὼν
ἐξελαθόμην τῶν τοῦ πολέμου νόμων, φείσασθαι δὲ
παρεκάλουν τῶν ἰδίων ὑμᾶς ἁγίων καὶ σῶσαι τὸν
ναὸν ἑαυτοῖς, διδοὺς ἄδειάν τε ἐξόδου καὶ πίστιν
σωτηρίας, εἰ δ᾽ ἐβούλεσθε, καὶ μάχης καιρὸν ἐν
ἄλλῳ τόπῳ· πάντων ὑπερείδετε καὶ τὸν ναὸν ἰδίαις
347 χερσὶν ἐνεπρήσατε. ἔπειτα, μιαρώτατοι, προκα-
λεῖσθέ[3] με πρὸς λόγους νῦν; ἵνα τί σώσητε τοιοῦτον
οἷον ἀπόλωλεν; ποίας[4] ὑμᾶς αὐτοὺς ἀξιοῦτε μετὰ
348 τὸν ναὸν σωτηρίας; ἀλλὰ καὶ νῦν μετὰ τῶν ὅπλων
ἑστήκατε καὶ οὐδ᾽ ἐν ἐσχάτοις ὑποκρίνεσθε γοῦν
349 ἱκέτας, ὦ ταλαίπωροι, τίνι πεποιθότες; οὐ νεκρὸς
μὲν ὑμῶν ὁ δῆμος, οἴχεται δ᾽ ὁ ναός, ὑπ᾽ ἐμοὶ δ᾽ ἡ
πόλις, ἐν χερσὶ δὲ ταῖς ἐμαῖς ἔχετε τὰς ψυχάς;
εἶθ᾽ ὑπολαμβάνετε δόξαν ἀνδρείας τὸ δυσθανατᾶν;
350 οὐ μὴν ἐγὼ φιλονεικήσω πρὸς τὴν ἀπόνοιαν ὑμῶν,
ῥίψασι δὲ τὰ ὅπλα καὶ παραδοῦσι τὰ σώματα χα-
ρίζομαι τὸ ζῆν, ὥσπερ ἐν οἰκίᾳ πρᾷος δεσπότης τὰ
μὲν ἀνήκεστα κολάσας, τὰ δὲ λοιπὰ σώζων ἐμαυτῷ.''
351   (3) Πρὸς ταῦτα ἀποκρίνονται δεξιὰν μὲν μὴ
δύνασθαι παρ᾽ αὐτοῦ λαβεῖν, ὀμωμοκέναι γὰρ
μήποτε τοῦτο ποιήσειν, ἔξοδον δ᾽ ᾐτοῦντο διὰ τοῦ

---

[1] Destinon (whom I follow with hesitation): βασανίσας
mss.   [2] L: ἐκόλασα the rest.
[3] ed. pr. with Lat.: προσκαλεῖσθε mss.
[4] Bekker: οἴας mss.

476

you : I gave pledges of protection to deserters, I kept faith with them when they fled to me ; many were the prisoners whom I compassionated, forbidding their oppressors to torture them ; with reluctance I brought up my engines against your walls ; my soldiers, thirsting for your blood, I invariably restrained ; after every victory, as if defeated myself, I invited you to peace. On approaching the temple, again in deliberate forgetfulness of the laws of war, I besought you to spare your own shrines and to preserve the temple for yourselves, offering you unmolested egress and assurance of safety, or, if you so wished, an opportunity for battle on some other arena.[a] All offers you scorned and with your own hands set fire to the temple.[b]

"And after all this, most abominable wretches, do you now invite me to a parley ? What have you to save comparable to what is lost ? What protection do you think you deserve after losing your temple ? Nay, even now you stand in arms and, at the last extremity, do not so much as pretend to be suppliants. Miserable men, on what do you rely ? Is not your folk dead, your temple gone, your city at my mercy, are not your very lives in my hands ? And do you yet deem it glorious bravery to die in the last ditch ? I, however, will not emulate your frenzy. Throw down your arms, surrender your persons, and I grant you your lives, like a lenient master of a household punishing the incorrigible and preserving the rest for myself."

(3) To this they replied that they could not accept a pledge from him, having sworn never to do so ; but they asked permission to pass through his line

His offers being rejected,

---

[a] v. 360 ff., vi. 128.   [b] vi. 165.

477

περιτειχίσματος μετὰ γυναικῶν καὶ τέκνων· ἀπ-
ελεύσεσθαι γὰρ εἰς τὴν ἔρημον καὶ καταλείψειν
352 αὐτῷ τὴν πόλιν. πρὸς ταῦτα ἀγανακτήσας Τίτος,
εἰ τύχην ἑαλωκότων ἔχοντες αἱρέσεις αὐτῷ προ-
τείνουσι νενικηκότων, κηρῦξαι μὲν ἐκέλευσεν εἰς
αὐτοὺς μήτε αὐτομολεῖν ἔτι μήτε δεξιὰν ἐλπίζειν,
353 φείσεσθαι γὰρ οὐδενός, ἀλλὰ πάσῃ δυνάμει μάχεσθαι καὶ σῴζειν ἑαυτοὺς ὅπως ἂν δύνωνται· πάντα
γὰρ αὐτὸς ἤδη πράξειν πολέμου νόμῳ· τοῖς δὲ
στρατιώταις ἐμπιπράναι καὶ διαρπάζειν ἐπέτρεψεν
354 τὴν πόλιν. οἱ δ᾽ ἐκείνην μὲν ἐπέσχον τὴν ἡμέραν,
τῇ δ᾽ ὑστεραίᾳ τό τε ἀρχεῖον καὶ τὴν ἄκραν καὶ
τὸ βουλευτήριον καὶ τὸν Ὀφλᾶν καλούμενον
355 ὑφῆψαν· καὶ προύκοψε τὸ πῦρ μέχρι τῶν Ἑλένης
βασιλείων, ἃ δὴ κατὰ μέσην τὴν ἄκραν ἦν, ἐκαίοντο
δ᾽ οἱ στενωποὶ καὶ αἱ οἰκίαι νεκρῶν ὑπὸ τοῦ λιμοῦ
διεφθαρμένων πλήρεις.
356 (4) Κατὰ ταύτην τὴν ἡμέραν οἵ τε Ἰζάτου
βασιλέως υἱοὶ καὶ ἀδελφοί, πρὸς οἷς πολλοὶ τῶν
ἐπισήμων δημοτῶν [ἐκεῖ][1] συνελθόντες, ἱκέτευσαν
Καίσαρα δοῦναι δεξιὰν αὐτοῖς. ὁ δὲ καίτοι πρὸς
πάντας τοὺς ὑπολοίπους διωργισμένος οὐκ ἤλλαξε
357 τὸ ἦθος, δέχεται δὲ τοὺς ἄνδρας. καὶ τότε μὲν ἐν
φρουρᾷ πάντας εἶχε, τοὺς δὲ τοῦ βασιλέως παῖδας
καὶ συγγενεῖς δήσας ὕστερον εἰς Ῥώμην ἀνήγαγεν
πίστιν ὁμήρων παρέξοντας.
358 (vii. 1) Οἱ στασιασταὶ δ᾽ ἐπὶ τὴν βασιλικὴν
ὁρμήσαντες αὐλήν, εἰς ἣν δι᾽ ὀχυρότητα πολλοὶ τὰς

---

[1] om. Lat.: ἐκείνοις Destinon (followed by συνεξελθόντες).

[a] The site of the building intended is uncertain. The
"archives" themselves (τὰ ἀρχεῖα, money-lenders' bonds, etc.)

f circumvallation with their wives and children, un-
ertaking to retire to the desert and to leave the
ity to him. Thereupon Titus, indignant that men
n the position of captives should proffer proposals to
im as victors, ordered proclamation to be made to
hem neither to desert nor to hope for terms any
onger, for he would spare none ; but to fight with
ll their might and save themselves as best they
ould, because all his actions henceforth would be
overned by the laws of war. He then gave his
roops permission to burn and sack the city. For
hat day they refrained ; but on the next they set
re to the Archives,[a] the Acra, the council-chamber,[b]
nd the region called Ophlas, the flames spreading
s far as the palace of Queen Helena,[c] which was in
he centre of the Acra. The streets also were burnt
nd the houses, packed with the bodies of the victims
f the famine.

Titus permits the destruction of the city. September A.D. 70.

(4) On the same day the sons and brothers of king
zates,[d] who were joined by many of the eminent
ownsfolk, entreated Caesar to grant them a pledge
f protection. Though infuriated at all the survivors,
Titus, with the unalterable humanity of his character,
eceived them. For the present he kept them all in
ustody ; the king's sons and kinsmen he subsequently brought up in chains to Rome as hostages
or the allegiance of their country.

Fate of the kinsmen of King Izates.

(vii. 1) The rebels now rushed to the royal
palace,[e] in which, owing to its solidity, many had
had been burnt by the insurgents four years before at the
pening of hostilities, ii. 427.

The rebels loot the palace and take two Roman prisoners.

[b] The usual meeting-place of the Sanhedrin, v. 144 note.
[c] v. 253.
[d] King of Adiabene and a convert to Judaism, iv. 567 note.
[e] Herod's palace on the Upper City (*cf.* § 376).

κτήσεις ἀπέθεντο, τούς τε Ῥωμαίους ἀπ᾽ αὐτῆ
τρέπονται καὶ τὸ συνηθροισμένον αὐτόθι τοῦ δήμοι
πᾶν φονεύσαντες, ὄντας εἰς ὀκτακισχιλίους κα
359 τετρακοσίους, τὰ χρήματα διήρπασαν. ἐζώγρησα
δὲ καὶ Ῥωμαίων δύο, τὸν μὲν ἱππέα τὸν δὲ πεζόν
καὶ τὸν μὲν πεζὸν ἀποσφάξαντες εὐθέως ἔσυρα
περὶ τὴν πόλιν, ὥσπερ ἑνὶ σώματι πάντας Ῥω
360 μαίους ἀμυνόμενοι, ὁ δ᾽ ἱππεὺς ὠφέλιμόν τι αὐτοῖ
πρὸς σωτηρίαν ὑποθήσεσθαι λέγων ἀνάγεται πρὸ
Σίμωνα· παρ᾽ ᾧ μηδὲν εἰπεῖν ἔχων Ἀρδάλᾳ τιν
361 τῶν ἡγεμόνων παραδίδοται κολασθησόμενος. ὁ δ
αὐτὸν[1] ὀπίσω τὼ χεῖρε δήσας καὶ ταινίᾳ τοὺ
ὀφθαλμοὺς ἀντικρὺ τῶν Ῥωμαίων προήγαγεν ὡ
καρατομήσων· φθάνει δ᾽ ἐκεῖνος εἰς τοὺς Ῥω
μαίους διαφυγὼν ἐν ὅσῳ τὸ ξίφος ἐσπάσατο [2]
362 Ἰουδαῖος. τοῦτον διαφυγόντα ἐκ τῶν πολεμίω
ἀνελεῖν μὲν οὐχ ὑπέμεινεν Τίτος, ἀνάξιον δ
Ῥωμαίων εἶναι στρατιώτην κρίνας, ὅτι ζῶ
ἐλήφθη, τά τε ὅπλα ἀφείλετο καὶ τοῦ τάγματος
ἐξέβαλεν, ἅπερ ἦν αἰσχυνομένῳ θανάτου χα
λεπώτερα.

363 (2) Τῇ δ᾽ ἑξῆς Ῥωμαῖοι τρεψάμενοι τοὺς λῃστὰς
ἐκ τῆς κάτω πόλεως τὰ μέχρι τοῦ Σιλωᾶ [πάντα]
ἐνέπρησαν, καὶ τοῦ μὲν ἄστεος ἥδοντο δαπανω
μένου, τῶν δ᾽ ἁρπαγῶν διημάρτανον, ἐπειδὴ πάνθ᾽
οἱ στασιασταὶ προκενοῦντες ἀνεχώρουν εἰς τὴ
364 ἄνω πόλιν. ἦν γὰρ αὐτοῖς μετάνοια μὲν οὐδεμιά
τῶν κακῶν, ἀλαζονεία δ᾽ ὡς ἐπ᾽ ἀγαθοῖς· καιο
μένην γοῦν ἀφορῶντες τὴν πόλιν ἱλαροῖς τοῖς
προσώποις εὔθυμοι προσδέχεσθαι τὴν τελευτὴν
ἔλεγον, πεφονευμένου μὲν τοῦ δήμου, κεκαυμένου

---

[1] Niese with Lat.: αὐτοῦ MSS.   [2] om. PAM.

deposited their property ; and, having beaten off
the Romans, they slew the whole mass of people
who had congregated there, to the number of eight
thousand four hundred, and looted the money.
They also made prisoners of two Romans, one a
trooper, the other a foot-soldier. The latter they
slaughtered on the spot and dragged round the city,
as though in the person of one they were wreaking
vengeance on all the Romans. The trooper, who
declared that he had a suggestion to make conducive
to their safety, was brought up to Simon, but having
nothing to tell him was handed over to Ardalas, one
of the officers, for execution. Ardalas, having bound
his hands behind his back and bandaged his eyes,
led him forth in view of the Romans to be beheaded ;
but the prisoner, at the moment when the Jew drew
his sword, managed to escape to the Romans. After
such an escape from the enemy, Titus could not
bring himself to put him to death ; but judging him
unfit to be a Roman soldier after being taken alive,
he deprived him of his arms and dismissed him from
the legion—a penalty to one with any sense of shame
severer than death.

(2) On the following day the Romans, having The Romans
burn the
lower town.
routed the brigands from the lower town, set the
whole on fire as far as Siloam ; the consuming of the
town rejoiced their hearts, but they were disappointed
of plunder, the rebels having cleared out everything
before they retired to the upper city. For the latter
showed no remorse for their evils, but rather bragged
of them as blessings. Indeed, when they beheld
the city burning, they declared with beaming faces
that they cheerfully awaited the end, seeing that,
with the people slaughtered, the temple in ashes,

481

δὲ τοῦ ναοῦ, φλεγομένου δὲ τοῦ ἄστεος μηδὲν
365 καταλείποντες[1] τοῖς πολεμίοις. οὐ μὴν ὅ γε
Ἰώσηπος ἐν ἐσχάτοις ἱκετεύων αὐτοὺς ὑπὲρ τῶν
λειψάνων τῆς πόλεως ἔκαμνεν, ἀλλὰ πολλὰ μὲν
πρὸς τὴν ὠμότητα καὶ τὴν ἀσέβειαν εἰπών, πολλὰ
δὲ συμβουλεύσας πρὸς σωτηρίαν οὐδὲν τοῦ χλευα-
366 σθῆναι πλέον ἀπηνέγκατο. ἐπεὶ δ' οὔτε παραδοῦναι διὰ τὸν ὅρκον ἑαυτοὺς ὑπέμενον οὔτε
πολεμεῖν ἐξ ἴσου Ῥωμαίοις ἔθ' οἷοί τε ἦσαν,
ὥσπερ εἱρκτῇ περιειλημμένοι, τό τε τοῦ φονεύειν
ἔθος ἐκίνει τὰς δεξιάς, σκιδνάμενοι κατὰ τὰ
ἔμπροσθεν τῆς πόλεως τοῖς ἐρειπίοις ὑπελόχων
367 τοὺς αὐτομολεῖν ὡρμημένους. ἡλίσκοντο δὲ πολλοί,
καὶ πάντας ἀποσφάττοντες, ὑπὸ γὰρ ἐνδείας οὐδὲ
φεύγειν ἴσχυον, ἐρρίπτουν αὐτῶν κυσὶ τοὺς νεκρούς.
368 ἐδόκει δὲ πᾶς τρόπος ἀπωλείας τοῦ λιμοῦ κου-
φότερος, ὥστε καὶ Ῥωμαίοις ἀπηλπικότες ἤδη
τὸν ἔλεον ὅμως προσέφευγον καὶ φονεύουσι[2] τοῖς
369 στασιασταῖς ἑκόντες ἐνέπιπτον. τόπος τ' ἐπὶ
τῆς πόλεως οὐδεὶς γυμνὸς ἦν, ἀλλὰ πᾶς λιμοῦ
νεκρὸν εἶχεν ἢ στάσεως [καὶ πεπλήρωτο νεκρῶν ἢ
διὰ στάσιν ἢ διὰ λιμὸν ἀπολωλότων].[3]
370 (3) Ἔθαλπε δὲ τούς τε τυράννους καὶ τὸ σὺν
αὐτοῖς ληστρικὸν ἐλπὶς ἐσχάτη περὶ τῶν ὑπονόμων,
εἰς οὓς καταφεύγοντες οὐ προσεδόκων ἐρευνηθή-
σεσθαι, μετὰ δὲ τὴν παντελῆ τῆς πόλεως ἅλωσιν
ἀναζευξάντων Ῥωμαίων προελθόντες ἀποδράσε-
371 σθαι ἐπεχείρουν. τὸ δ' ἦν ἄρα ὄνειρος αὐτοῖς·
οὔτε γὰρ τὸν θεὸν οὔτε Ῥωμαίους λήσειν ἔμελλον.

[1] PA : καταλιπόντες the rest.
[2] φονῶσι Herwerden.
[3] The bracketed tautological clause, omitted in the

and the town in flames, they were leaving nothing to their foes. Josephus, however, even at the last, never flagged in his entreaties to them on behalf of the relics of the town; yet for all his denunciation of their cruelty and impiety, for all the counsel offered to secure their salvation, the only return which he obtained was ridicule. Since they could not think of surrender, owing to their oath, and were now incapable of fighting the Romans on equal terms, being caged as in a prison-house, while their hands through habit yet itched for slaughter, they dispersed about the outskirts of the city and lay in wait among the ruins for any who were eager to desert. Many, indeed, were caught, and, the famine having deprived them even of strength for flight, they were all massacred and their bodies flung to the dogs. But death in any form seemed lighter than famine; so that, though now despairing of mercy from the Romans, they fled to them nevertheless and, though the rebels were murderous, voluntarily fell into their hands. Not a spot in the city was left bare: every corner had its corpse, the victim of famine or sedition.

The rebels waylay deserters.

(3) A last and cherished hope of the tyrants and their brigand comrades lay in the underground passages, as a place of refuge where they expected that no search would be made for them, intending after the complete capture of the city and the departure of the Romans to come forth and make their escape. But this proved to be but a dream: for they were not destined to elude either God or the Romans. For the time, however,

The mines their last hope of escape.

___

translation, and, according to Hudson, deleted in one MS., must be rejected as a "doublet."

372 τηνικαῦτά γε μὴν τοῖς ὑπογείοις πεποιθότες αὐτοὶ
πλείονα τῶν Ῥωμαίων ἐνεπίμπρασαν, καὶ τοὺς ἐκ
τῶν καιομένων καταφεύγοντας εἰς τὰς διώρυχας
ἔκτεινόν τε ἀνέδην καὶ ἐσύλων, καὶ εἴ τινος εὕροιεν
τροφὴν ἁρπάζοντες αἵματι πεφυρμένην κατέπινον.

373 ἦν δὲ καὶ πρὸς ἀλλήλους ἐν ταῖς ἁρπαγαῖς ἤδη
πόλεμος αὐτοῖς, δοκοῦσί τε ἄν μοι μὴ φθασθέντες[1]
ὑπὸ τῆς ἁλώσεως δι᾽ ὑπερβολὴν ὠμότητος γεύσασθαι καὶ τῶν νεκρῶν.

374 (viii. 1) Καῖσαρ δ᾽, ὡς ἀμήχανον ἦν ἐξελεῖν
δίχα χωμάτων τὴν ἄνω πόλιν περίκρημνον οὖσαν,
διανέμει τοῖς ἔργοις τὴν δύναμιν Λώου μηνὸς

375 εἰκάδι. χαλεπὴ δ᾽ ἦν τῆς ὕλης ἡ κομιδὴ πάντων,
ὡς ἔφην, τῶν περὶ τὴν πόλιν ἐφ᾽ ἑκατὸν σταδίους

376 ἐψιλωμένων εἰς τὰ πρότερον χώματα. τῶν μὲν
οὖν τεσσάρων ταγμάτων ἠγείρετο τὰ ἔργα κατὰ
τὸ πρὸς δύσιν κλίμα τῆς πόλεως ἀντικρὺ τῆς

377 βασιλικῆς αὐλῆς, τὸ δὲ συμμαχικὸν πλῆθος καὶ ὁ
λοιπὸς ὄχλος κατὰ τὸν ξυστὸν ἔχου[2] καὶ τὴν
γέφυραν καὶ τὸν Σίμωνος πύργον, ὃν ᾠκοδόμησε
πρὸς Ἰωάννην πολεμῶν ἑαυτῷ φρούριον.

378 (2) Κατὰ ταύτας τὰς ἡμέρας οἱ τῶν Ἰδουμαίων
ἡγεμόνες κρύφα συνελθόντες ἐβουλεύσαντο περὶ
παραδόσεως σφῶν αὐτῶν, καὶ πέμψαντες ἄνδρας
πέντε πρὸς Τίτον ἱκέτευον δοῦναι δεξιὰν αὐτοῖς.

379 ὁ δὲ καὶ τοὺς τυράννους ἐνδώσειν ἐλπίσας ἀπο-

---

[1] So one (Berlin) ms. with Syr. Lat.: φθαρθέντες or φθαρέντες
the rest.
[2] Destinon: ἐξοῦ or ἐξ οὗ mss.: om. C Lat.

---

[a] Cf. iv. 541 (the same hyperbole).   [b] Cf. § 151.
[c] Of Herod the Great.

trusting to these subterranean retreats, they were more active incendiaries than the Romans ; all who fled from the flames into these trenches they mercilessly slew and plundered ; and if ever they found a victim with food, they snatched it from him and devoured it, all defiled with blood. At last they fought with one another over their spoils ; and I verily believe that, had not capture forestalled them, they would in their excess of savagery have tasted the very corpses.[a]

(viii. 1) Caesar, finding it impracticable to reduce the upper city without earthworks, owing to the precipitous nature of the site, on the twentieth of the month Lous apportioned the task among his forces. The conveyance of timber was, however, arduous, all the environs of the city to a distance of a hundred furlongs having, as I said,[b] been stripped bare for the former embankments. The works now raised by the four legions were on the west side of the city, opposite the royal palace[c] ; while the auxiliaries and the other units threw up embankments[d] adjoining the Xystus, the bridge and the tower which Simon, when at war with John, had built as a fortress for himself.[e]

(2) During these days the chiefs of the Idumaeans[f] met in secret to deliberate about surrendering themselves, and dispatching five delegates to Titus besought his protection. Titus, hoping that the tyrants also would be induced to yield through the

The Romans prepare to attack the upper town c. 8th September.

Overtures of the Idumaeans to Titus frustrated by Simon.

[d] To the east of the Upper City.
[e] *Cf.* § 191 for the tower erected by John when at war with Simon ; if, as appears, the same tower is intended, the names have here been incorrectly transposed.
[f] Some of whom had remained in Jerusalem when the main body withdrew, iv. 566.

σπασθέντων [τῶν][1] Ἰδουμαίων, οἳ πολὺ τοῦ πολέμου
μέρος ἦσαν, βραδέως μέν, ἀλλ' οὖν κατανεύει τε
τὴν σωτηρίαν αὐτοῖς καὶ τοὺς ἄνδρας ἀνέπεμψε.
380 παρασκευαζομένων δ' ἀποχωρεῖν αἰσθάνεται Σίμων,
καὶ πέντε μὲν τοὺς ἀπελθόντας πρὸς Τίτον εὐθέως
ἀναιρεῖ, τοὺς δ' ἡγεμόνας, ὧν ἐπισημότατος ἦν
381 ὁ τοῦ Σωσᾶ Ἰάκωβος, συλλαβὼν εἵργνυσι· τὸ δὲ
πλῆθος τῶν Ἰδουμαίων ἀμηχανοῦν διὰ τὴν ἀφ-
αίρεσιν τῶν ἡγεμόνων οὐκ ἀφύλακτον εἶχε καὶ
382 τὸ τεῖχος φρουραῖς ἐπιμελεστέραις διελάμβανεν. οὐ
μὴν ἀντέχειν οἱ φρουροὶ πρὸς τὰς αὐτομολίας
ἴσχυον, ἀλλὰ καίτοι πλείστων φονευομένων πολὺ
383 πλείους οἱ διαφεύγοντες ἦσαν. ἐδέχοντο δὲ Ῥωμαῖοι πάντας, τοῦ τε Τίτου διὰ πρᾳότητα τῶν
προτέρων ἀμελήσαντος παραγγελμάτων, καὶ αὐτοὶ
κόρῳ τοῦ κτείνειν ἀπεχόμενοι καὶ κέρδους ἐλπίδι·
384 τοὺς γὰρ δημοτικοὺς καταλιπόντες μόνους τὸν
ἄλλον ὄχλον ἐπώλουν σὺν· γυναιξὶ καὶ τέκνοις,
ἐλαχίστης τιμῆς ἕκαστον πλήθει τε τῶν πιπρασκο-
385 μένων καὶ ὀλιγότητι τῶν ὠνουμένων. καίπερ δὲ
προκηρύξας μηδένα μόνον αὐτομολεῖν, ὅπως καὶ
τὰς γενεὰς ἐξαγάγοιεν, ὅμως καὶ τούτους ἐδέχετο·
ἐπέστησε μέντοι τοὺς διακρινοῦντας ἀπ' αὐτῶν, εἴ
386 τις εἴη κολάσεως ἄξιος. καὶ τῶν μὲν ἀπεμπολη-
θέντων ἄπειρον ἦν τὸ πλῆθος, οἱ δημοτικοὶ δὲ
διεσώθησαν ὑπὲρ τετρακισμυρίους, οὓς διαφῆκεν
Καῖσαρ ᾗ φίλον ἦν ἑκάστῳ.
387 (3) Ἐν δὲ ταῖς αὐταῖς ἡμέραις καὶ τῶν ἱερέων
τις Θεβουθεῖ παῖς, Ἰησοῦς ὄνομα, λαβὼν περὶ
σωτηρίας ὅρκους παρὰ Καίσαρος ἐφ' ᾧ παραδώσει

---

[1] ins. L Zon.: om. the rest.

defection of the Idumaeans, who formed an important factor in the war, after some hesitation consented to spare them and sent the men back. But as they were preparing to depart Simon detected the plot. The five emissaries to Titus he at once put to death; the chiefs, of whom the most distinguished was James, son of Sosas,[a] he arrested and imprisoned; while the rank and file of the Idumaeans, rendered helpless by the loss of their leaders, were narrowly watched by him and the walls manned with more vigilant guards. The sentries, however, were powerless to check desertion; for, although multitudes were slain, a far larger number escaped. The Romans received them all, Titus out of clemency disregarding his former orders,[b] and his men from satiety and in hope of gain abstaining from slaughter. For the citizens alone were allowed to remain: the rest with the women and children were sold, for a trifling sum per head, owing to the glut of the market and the dearth of purchasers. Moreover, notwithstanding his previous proclamation that none should desert alone, to the end that they should bring out their families with them, Titus yet received even such persons; appointing, however, officers to discriminate from among them any who might deserve punishment. The number of those sold was prodigious; of the citizens there were spared upwards of forty thousand, whom Caesar allowed to retire whither each one's fancy led him.

Numerous deserters to the Romans.

(3) During those same days, one of the priests named Jesus, son of Thebuthi, after obtaining a sworn pledge of protection from Caesar, on condition

Temple treasures delivered up by their custodians.

---

[a] One of the leaders of the original expedition and often mentioned, iv. 235, etc.   [b] § 352.

487

388 τινὰ τῶν ἱερῶν κειμηλίων, ἔξεισι καὶ παραδίδωσιν
ἀπὸ τοῦ τοίχου τοῦ ναοῦ λυχνίας δύο τῶν κατὰ τὸν
ναὸν κειμένων[1] παραπλησίας, τραπέζας τε καὶ
κρατῆρας καὶ φιάλας, πάνθ᾽ ὁλόχρυσα καὶ στι-
389 βαρώτατα, παραδίδωσι δὲ καὶ τὰ καταπετάσματα
καὶ τὰ ἐνδύματα τῶν ἀρχιερέων σὺν τοῖς λίθοις
καὶ πολλὰ τῶν πρὸς τὰς ἱερουργίας σκευῶν ἄλλα.
390 συλληφθεὶς δὲ καὶ ὁ γαζοφύλαξ τοῦ ἱεροῦ Φινέας
ὄνομα τούς τε χιτῶνας καὶ τὰς ζώνας ὑπέδειξε[2]
τῶν ἱερέων, πορφύραν τε πολλὴν καὶ κόκκον, ἃ
πρὸς τὰς χρείας ἀπέκειτο τοῦ καταπετάσματος,
σὺν οἷς κιννάμωμόν τε πολὺ καὶ κασσίαν καὶ
πλῆθος ἑτέρων ἀρωμάτων, ἃ συμμίσγοντες ἐθυμίων
391 ὁσημέραι τῷ θεῷ. παρεδόθη δὲ ὑπ᾽ αὐτοῦ πολλὰ
καὶ τῶν ἄλλων κειμηλίων κόσμος θ᾽ ἱερὸς οὐκ
ὀλίγος, ἅπερ αὐτῷ βίᾳ ληφθέντι τὴν τῶν αὐτομόλων συγγνώμην ἔδωκε.
392   (4) Συντετελεσμένων δ᾽ ἤδη καὶ τῶν χωμάτων
ἐν ὀκτωκαίδεκα ἡμέραις ἑβδόμῃ Γορπιαίου μηνὸς
Ῥωμαῖοι μὲν προσῆγον τὰς μηχανάς, τῶν δὲ
στασιαστῶν οἱ μὲν ἀπεγνωκότες ἤδη τὴν πόλιν
ἀνεχώρουν τοῦ τείχους εἰς τὴν ἄκραν, οἱ δ᾽ ἐγκατ-
393 εδύοντο τοῖς ὑπονόμοις· πολλοὶ δὲ διαστάντες
ἠμύνοντο τοὺς προσάγοντας τὰς ἑλεπόλεις. ἐκρά-
τουν δὲ καὶ τούτων Ῥωμαῖοι πλήθει τε καὶ βίᾳ
καὶ τὸ μέγιστον, εὐθυμοῦντες ἀθύμων ἤδη καὶ
394 παρειμένων. ὡς δὲ παρερράγη[3] μέρος τι τοῦ
τείχους, καί τινες τῶν πύργων τυπτόμενοι τοῖς

---

[1] ταῖς κατα ς. ν. κειμέναις C : Niese suspects a lacuna after
κειμένων.
[2] PA : ἐπέδειξε the rest.
[3] Herwerden : περιερράγη mss.

488

of his delivering up some of the sacred treasures, came out and handed over from the wall of the sanctuary two lampstands similar to those deposited in the sanctuary, along with tables, bowls, and platters, all of solid gold and very massive [a]; he further delivered up the veils, the high-priests' vestments, including the precious stones, and many other articles used in public worship. Furthermore, the treasurer of the temple, by name Phineas, being taken prisoner, disclosed the tunics and girdles worn by the priests, an abundance of purple and scarlet kept for necessary repairs to the veil of the temple, along with a mass of cinnamon and cassia and a multitude of other spices, which they mixed and burnt daily as incense to God. Many other treasures also were delivered up by him, with numerous sacred ornaments ; those services procuring for him, although a prisoner of war, the pardon accorded to the refugees.

(4) The earthworks having now been completed after eighteen days' labour, on the seventh of the month Gorpiaeus the Romans brought up the engines. Of the rebels, some already despairing of the city retired from the ramparts to the Acra, others slunk down into the mines ; many, however, posting themselves along the wall, attempted to repel those who were bringing up the siege-engines. But these too the Romans overpowered by numbers and force, but, above all, by the high spirits in which they faced men already dispirited and unnerved. And when a portion of the wall broke down and some of the

The Romans attack the upper town. c. 25th September.

---

[a] The table of shew-bread with incense-cups and two silver trumpets are depicted on the Arch of Titus in Rome as borne in the triumphal procession.

κριοῖς ἐνέδοσαν, φυγὴ μὲν ἦν εὐθέως τῶν ἀμυνο-
μένων, δέος δὲ καὶ τοῖς τυράννοις ἐμπίπτει σφο-
395 δρότερον τῆς ἀνάγκης· πρὶν γὰρ ὑπερβῆναι τοὺς
πολεμίους ἐνάρκων τε καὶ μετέωροι πρὸς φυγὴν
ἦσαν, ἦν δ' ἰδεῖν τοὺς πάλαι σοβαροὺς καὶ τοῖς
ἀσεβήμασιν ἀλαζόνας τότε ταπεινοὺς καὶ τρέ-
μοντας, ὡς ἐλεεινὴν εἶναι καίπερ ἐν πονηροτάτοις
396 τὴν μεταβολήν. ὥρμησαν μὲν οὖν ἐπὶ τὸ περιτείχισμα δραμόντες ὤσασθαί τε τοὺς φρουροὺς καὶ
397 διακόψαντες ἐξελθεῖν· ὡς δὲ τοὺς μὲν πάλαι
πιστοὺς ἑώρων οὐδαμοῦ, διέφυγον γὰρ ὅπῃ τινὶ
συνεβούλευεν ἡ ἀνάγκη, προσθέοντες δὲ οἱ μὲν
ὅλον ἀνατετράφθαι τὸ πρὸς δύσιν τεῖχος ἤγγελλον,
οἱ δ' ἐμβεβληκέναι τοὺς Ῥωμαίους ἤδη[1] τε πλησίον
398 εἶναι ζητοῦντας αὐτούς, ἕτεροι δὲ καὶ ἀφορᾶν ἀπὸ[2]
τῶν πύργων πολεμίους ἔλεγον πλάζοντος τὰς
ὄψεις τοῦ δέους, ἐπὶ στόμα πεσόντες ἀνῴμωζον
τὴν ἑαυτῶν φρενοβλάβειαν καὶ καθάπερ ὑποκεκομ-
399 μένοι τὰ νεῦρα τῆς φυγῆς ἠπόρουν. ἔνθα δὴ
μάλιστ' ἄν τις καταμάθοι τήν τε τοῦ θεοῦ δύναμιν
ἐπὶ τοῖς ἀνοσίοις καὶ τὴν Ῥωμαίων τύχην· οἱ μέν
γε τύραννοι τῆς ἀσφαλείας ἐγύμνωσαν αὑτοὺς κἀκ
τῶν πύργων κατέβησαν ἑκόντες, ἐφ' ὧν βίᾳ μὲν
400 οὐδέποθ' ἁλῶναι, μόνῳ δ' ἐδύναντο λιμῷ. Ῥωμαῖοι δὲ τοσαῦτα περὶ τοῖς ἀσθενεστέροις τείχεσι
καμόντες παρέλαβον τύχῃ τὰ μὴ δυνατὰ τοῖς
ὀργάνοις· παντὸς γὰρ ἰσχυρότεροι μηχανήματος
ἦσαν οἱ τρεῖς πύργοι, περὶ ὧν ἀνωτέρω δεδηλώκαμεν.

---

[1] Destinon after Lat.: οἱ δ' ἤδη MSS.
[2] Herwerden with Heg.: ἐπὶ MSS.

---

[a] § 323. [b] Hippicus, Phasael, and Mariamme, v. 161 ff.

towers succumbed to the battering of the rams, the defenders at once took flight, and even the tyrants were seized with a needlessly serious alarm. For before the enemy had surmounted the breach they were paralysed and on the verge of flight; and those men, erstwhile so haughty and proud of their impious crimes, might then be seen abject and trembling—a transformation which, even in such villains, was pitiable. They were indeed eager to make a dash for the wall enclosing them,[a] repel the guards, cut their way through and escape; but when they could nowhere see their old faithful henchmen—for these had fled whithersoever the crisis suggested—and when men came running up with tidings, some that the whole western wall was overthrown, others that the Romans had broken through and were even now at hand in search of them, while yet others, whose eyes were bewildered by fright, declared that they could actually see the enemy from the towers, they fell upon their faces, bemoaning their own infatuation, and as though their sinews had been cut from under them were impotent to fly. Here may we signally discern at once the power of God over unholy men and the fortune of the Romans. For the tyrants stripped themselves of their security and descended of their own accord from those towers, whereon they could never have been overcome by force, and famine alone could have subdued them; while the Romans, after all the toil expended over weaker walls, mastered by the gift of fortune those that were impregnable to their artillery. For the three towers, which we have described above,[b] would have defied every engine of war.

The rebels fly

491

401 (5) Καταλιπόντες δὴ τούτους, μᾶλλον δ' ὑπὸ
τοῦ θεοῦ καταβληθέντες ἀπ' αὐτῶν, παραχρῆμα
μὲν εἰς τὴν ὑπὸ τῇ Σιλωᾷ φάραγγα καταφεύγουσιν,
αὖθις δ' ὀλίγον ἀνακύψαντες ἐκ τοῦ δέους ὥρμησαν
402 ἐπὶ τὸ τῇδε περιτείχισμα. χρησάμενοι δὲ ταῖς
τόλμαις ἀγενεστέραις τῆς ἀνάγκης, κατεάγησαν
γὰρ ἤδη τὴν ἰσχὺν ἅμα τῷ δέει καὶ ταῖς συμφοραῖς, ὑπὸ τῶν φρουρῶν ἀνωθοῦνται καὶ σκεδασθέντες ὑπ' ἀλλήλων[1] κατέδυσαν εἰς τοὺς ὑπονόμους.
403 Ῥωμαῖοι δὲ τῶν τειχῶν κρατήσαντες τάς τε
σημαίας ἔστησαν ἐπὶ τῶν πύργων καὶ μετὰ κρότου
καὶ χαρᾶς ἐπαιάνιζον ἐπὶ τῇ νίκῃ, πολὺ τῆς
ἀρχῆς κουφότερον τοῦ πολέμου τὸ τέλος εὑρηκότες·
ἀναιμωτὶ γοῦν τοῦ τελευταίου τείχους ἐπιβάντες
ἠπίστουν, καὶ μηδένα βλέποντες ἀντίπαλον ἀληθῶς[2]
404 ἠπόρηντο. εἰσχυθέντες δὲ τοῖς στενωποῖς ξιφήρεις
τούς τε καταλαμβανομένους ἐφόνευον ἀνέδην καὶ
τῶν συμφευγόντων τὰς οἰκίας αὐτάνδρους ὑπ-
405 επίμπρασαν. πολλὰς δὲ κεραΐζοντες ὁπότ' ἔνδον
παρέλθοιεν ἐφ' ἁρπαγήν, γενεὰς ὅλας νεκρῶν κατ-
ελάμβανον καὶ τὰ δωμάτια πλήρη τῶν τοῦ
λιμοῦ πτωμάτων, ἔπειτα πρὸς τὴν ὄψιν πεφρικότες
406 κεναῖς χερσὶν ἐξῄεσαν. οὐ μὴν οἰκτείροντες τοὺς
οὕτως ἀπολωλότας ταὐτὸ καὶ πρὸς τοὺς ζῶντας
ἔπασχον, ἀλλὰ τὸν ἐντυγχάνοντα διελαύνοντες
ἀπέφραξαν μὲν τοὺς στενωποὺς νεκροῖς, αἵματι δ'
ὅλην τὴν πόλιν κατέκλυσαν, ὡς πολλὰ [καὶ][3] τῶν
407 φλεγομένων σβεσθῆναι τῷ φόνῳ. καὶ οἱ μὲν
κτείνοντες ἐπαύσαντο πρὸς ἑσπέραν, ἐν δὲ τῇ

[1] ἀπ' ἀλλήλων should perhaps be read with one ms.: " per
diversa " Lat.

(5) Having then abandoned these, or rather and take refuge in the mines. been driven down from them by God, they found immediate refuge in the ravine below Siloam ; but afterwards, having recovered a little from their panic, they rushed upon the adjoining section of the barrier. Their courage, however, proving unequal to the occasion (for their strength was now broken alike by terror and misfortune), they were repulsed by the guards and dispersing hither and thither slunk down into the mines.

The Romans, now masters of the walls, planted Roman victory complete. their standards on the towers, and with clapping of hands and jubilation raised a paean in honour of their victory. They had found the end of the war a much lighter task than the beginning ; indeed, they could hardly believe that they had surmounted the last wall without bloodshed, and, seeing none to oppose them, were truly perplexed. Pouring into the alleys, sword in hand, they massacred indiscriminately all whom they met, and burnt the houses with all who had taken refuge within. Often in the course of their raids, on entering the houses for loot, they would find whole families dead and the rooms filled with the victims of the famine, and then, shuddering at the sight, retire empty-handed. Yet, while they pitied those who had thus perished, they had no similar feelings for the living, but, running everyone through who fell in their way, they choked the alleys with corpses and deluged the whole city with blood, insomuch that many of the fires were extinguished by the gory stream. Towards evening they ceased slaughtering, but when night fell the

---

[2] AM (Lat. " pro certo "): ἀήθως, "unusually," the rest.
[3] ins. A: om. the rest.

νυκτὶ τὸ πῦρ ἐπεκράτει, φλεγομένοις δ' ἐπανέτειλεν
Ἱεροσολύμοις ἡμέρα Γορπιαίου μηνὸς ὀγδόη,
408 πόλει τοσαύταις χρησαμένη συμφοραῖς κατὰ τὴν
πολιορκίαν, ὅσοις ἀπὸ [τῆς]¹ κτίσεως ἀγαθοῖς
κεχρημένη πάντως ἂν ἐπίφθονος ἔδοξεν, οὐ μὴν
ἀξίᾳ κατ' ἄλλο τι τῶν τηλικούτων ἀτυχημάτων ἢ
τῷ² γενεὰν τοιαύτην ἐνεγκεῖν, ὑφ' ἧς ἀνετράπη.
409 (ix. 1) Παρελθὼν δὲ Τίτος εἴσω τά τε ἄλλα
τῆς ὀχυρότητος τὴν πόλιν καὶ τῶν πύργων ἀπεθαύ-
410 μασεν, οὓς οἱ τύραννοι κατὰ φρενοβλάβειαν ἀπ-
έλιπον. κατιδὼν γοῦν τό τε ναστὸν αὐτῶν ὕψος
καὶ τὸ μέγεθος ἑκάστης πέτρας τήν τε ἀκρίβειαν
τῆς ἁρμονίας, καὶ ὅσοι μὲν εὖρος ἡλίκοι δὲ ἦσαν
411 τὴν ἀνάστασιν, "σὺν θεῷ γ' ἐπολεμήσαμεν," ἔφη,
"καὶ θεὸς ἦν ὁ τῶνδε τῶν ἐρυμάτων Ἰουδαίους
καθελών, ἐπεὶ χεῖρες ἀνθρώπων ἢ μηχαναὶ τί πρὸς
412 τούτους τοὺς πύργους δύνανται;" τότε μὲν οὖν
πολλὰ τοιαῦτα διελέχθη πρὸς τοὺς φίλους, τοὺς δὲ
τῶν τυράννων δεσμώτας, ὅσοι κατελήφθησαν ἐν
413 τοῖς φρουρίοις, ἀνῆκεν. αὖθις δὲ τὴν ἄλλην ἀφανί-
ζων πόλιν καὶ τὰ τείχη κατασκάπτων τούτους τοὺς
πύργους κατέλιπε μνημεῖον εἶναι τῆς αὑτοῦ τύχης,
ᾗ συστρατιώτιδι χρησάμενος ἐκράτησε τῶν ἁλῶναι
μὴ δυναμένων.
414 (2) Ἐπεὶ δ' οἱ στρατιῶται μὲν ἔκαμνον ἤδη
φονεύοντες, πολὺ δ' ἔτι³ πλῆθος τῶν περιόντων
ἀνεφαίνετο, κελεύει Καῖσαρ μόνους μὲν τοὺς
ἐνόπλους καὶ χεῖρας ἀντίσχοντας κτείνειν, τὸ δὲ
415 λοιπὸν πλῆθος ζωγρεῖν. οἱ δὲ μετὰ τῶν παρηγ-
γελμένων τό τε γηραιὸν καὶ τοὺς ἀσθενεῖς ἀνῄρουν·

¹ om. A.   ² Niese: τὸ mss.
³ δ' ἔτι L Lat.: δέ τι the rest.

fire gained the mastery, and the dawn of the eighth All Jerusalem in flames. day of the month Gorpiaeus broke upon Jerusalem in flames—a city which had suffered such calamities c. 26th September. during the siege, that, had she from her foundation enjoyed an equal share of blessings, she would have been thought unquestionably enviable; a city undeserving, moreover, of these great misfortunes on any other ground, save that she produced a generation such as that which caused her overthrow.

(ix. 1) Titus, on entering the town, was amazed Entry of Titus. at its strength, but chiefly at the towers, which the tyrants, in their infatuation, had abandoned. Indeed, when he beheld their solid lofty mass, the magnitude of each block and the accuracy of the joinings, and marked how great was their breadth, how vast their height, " God indeed," he exclaimed, " has been with us in the war. God it was who brought down the Jews from these strongholds; for what power have human hands or engines against these towers ? " He made many similar observations to his friends at that time, when he also liberated all prisoners of the tyrants who were found in the forts. And when, at a later period, he demolished the rest of the city and razed the walls, he left these towers [a] as a memorial of his attendant fortune, to whose co-operation he owed his conquest of defences which defied assault.

(2) Since the soldiers were now growing weary of Fate of the captives. slaughter, though numerous survivors still came to light, Caesar issued orders to kill only those who were found in arms and offered resistance, and to make prisoners of the rest. The troops, in addition to those specified in their instructions, slew the old

---

[a] Phasael, under the erroneous name of " David's tower," still stands.

τὸ δ᾽ ἀκμάζον καὶ χρήσιμον εἰς τὸ ἱερὸν συνελά-
σαντες ἐγκατέκλεισαν τῷ τῶν γυναικῶν περιτειχί-
416 σματι. καὶ φρουρὸν μὲν ἐπέστησε Καῖσαρ ἕνα τῶν
ἀπελευθέρων, Φρόντωνα δὲ τῶν φίλων ἐπικρινοῦντα
417 τὴν ἀξίαν ἑκάστῳ τύχην. ὁ δὲ τοὺς μὲν στασιώδεις
καὶ λῃστρικοὺς πάντας ὑπ᾽ ἀλλήλων ἐνδεικνυ-
μένους ἀπέκτεινε, τῶν δὲ νέων τοὺς ὑψηλοτάτους
418 καὶ καλοὺς ἐπιλέξας ἐτήρει τῷ θριάμβῳ. τοῦ δὲ
λοιποῦ πλήθους τοὺς ὑπὲρ ἑπτακαίδεκα ἔτη δήσας
ἔπεμψεν εἰς τὰ κατ᾽ Αἴγυπτον ἔργα, πλείστους δ᾽
εἰς τὰς ἐπαρχίας διεδωρήσατο Τίτος φθαρησο-
μένους ἐν τοῖς θεάτροις σιδήρῳ καὶ θηρίοις· οἱ δ᾽
419 ἐντὸς ἑπτακαίδεκα ἐτῶν ἐπράθησαν. ἐφθάρησαν
δὲ αὐτῶν, ἐν αἷς διέκρινεν ὁ Φρόντων ἡμέραις, ὑπ᾽
ἐνδείας χίλιοι πρὸς τοῖς μυρίοις, οἱ μὲν ὑπὸ μίσους
τῶν φυλάκων μὴ μεταλαμβάνοντες τροφῆς, οἱ δ᾽
οὐ προσιέμενοι διδομένην· πρὸς δὲ τὸ πλῆθος ἦν
ἔνδεια καὶ σίτου.

420 (3) Τῶν μὲν οὖν αἰχμαλώτων πάντων, ὅσα καθ᾽
ὅλον ἐλήφθη τὸν πόλεμον, ἀριθμὸς ἐννέα μυριάδες
καὶ ἑπτακισχίλιοι συνήχθη, τῶν δὲ ἀπολομένων
κατὰ πᾶσαν τὴν πολιορκίαν μυριάδες ἑκατὸν καὶ
421 δέκα. τούτων τὸ πλέον ὁμόφυλον μὲν ἀλλ᾽ οὐκ
ἐπιχώριον· ἀπὸ γὰρ τῆς χώρας ὅλης ἐπὶ τὴν τῶν
ἀζύμων ἑορτὴν συνεληλυθότες ἐξαπίνης τῷ πολέμῳ
περιεσχέθησαν, ὥστε τὸ μὲν πρῶτον αὐτοῖς τὴν
στενοχωρίαν γενέσθαι λοιμώδη φθοράν, αὖθις δὲ
422 καὶ λιμὸν ὠκύτερον. ὅτι δ᾽ ἐχώρει τοσούτους ἡ
πόλις, δῆλον ἐκ τῶν ἐπὶ Κεστίου συναριθμηθέντων,

ᵃ Perhaps " mines " (Whiston). *Cf.* the sending of

and feeble; while those in the prime of life and serviceable they drove together into the temple and shut them up in the court of the women. Caesar appointed one of his freedmen as their guard, and his friend Fronto to adjudicate upon the lot appropriate to each. Fronto put to death all the seditious and brigands, information being given by them against each other; he selected the tallest and most handsome of the youth and reserved them for the triumph; of the rest, those over seventeen years of age he sent in chains to the works [a] in Egypt, while multitudes were presented by Titus to the various provinces, to be destroyed in the theatres by the sword or by wild beasts; those under seventeen were sold. During the days spent by Fronto over this scrutiny, eleven thousand of the prisoners perished from starvation, partly owing to their jailers' hatred, who denied them food, partly through their own refusal of it when offered; moreover, for so vast a multitude even corn failed.

(3) The total number of prisoners taken throughout the entire war amounted to ninety-seven thousand, and of those who perished during the siege, from first to last, to one million one hundred thousand. Of these the greater number were of Jewish blood, but not natives of the place; for, having assembled from every part of the country for the feast of unleavened bread, they found themselves suddenly enveloped in the war, with the result that this over crowding produced first pestilence, and later the added and more rapid scourge of famine. That the city could contain so many is clear from the count

Statistics of prisoners and dead.

Vespasian's prisoners to work on Nero's Corinthian canal, iii. 540.

ὃς τὴν ἀκμὴν τῆς πόλεως διαδηλῶσαι Νέρωνι
βουλόμενος καταφρονοῦντι τοῦ ἔθνους παρεκάλεσεν
τοὺς ἀρχιερεῖς, εἴ πως δυνατὸν εἴη τὴν πληθὺν
423 ἐξαριθμήσασθαι· οἱ δ' ἐνστάσης ἑορτῆς, πάσχα
καλεῖται, καθ' ἣν θύουσιν μὲν ἀπὸ ἐνάτης ὥρας
μέχρις ἑνδεκάτης, ὥσπερ δὲ φατρία[1] περὶ ἑκάστην
γίνεται θυσίαν οὐκ ἐλάσσων ἀνδρῶν δέκα, μόνον
γὰρ οὐκ ἔξεστιν δαίνυσθαι, πολλοὶ δὲ καὶ συν-
424 είκοσιν ἀθροίζονται, τῶν μὲν θυμάτων εἰκοσιπέντε
μυριάδας ἠρίθμησαν, πρὸς δὲ πεντακισχίλια ἑξα-
425 κόσια,[2] γίνονται δ' ἀνδρῶν, ἵν' ἑκάστου δέκα δαιτυ-
μόνας θῶμεν, μυριάδες ἑβδομήκοντα καὶ διακόσιαι
426 καθαρῶν ἁπάντων καὶ ἁγίων· οὔτε γὰρ λεπροῖς
οὔτε γονορροϊκοῖς οὔτε γυναιξὶν ἐπεμμήνοις οὔτε
τοῖς ἄλλως μεμιασμένοις ἐξὸν ἦν τῆσδε τῆς θυσίας
427 μεταλαμβάνειν, ἀλλ' οὐδὲ τοῖς ἀλλοφύλοις, ὅσοι
κατὰ θρησκείαν παρῆσαν, (4) πολὺ δὲ τούτων
428 πλῆθος ἔξωθεν συλλέγεται. τότε γε μὴν ὥσπερ
εἰς εἱρκτὴν ὑπὸ τῆς εἱμαρμένης πᾶν συνεκλείσθη
τὸ ἔθνος, καὶ ναστὴν ὁ πόλεμος τὴν πόλιν ἀνδρῶν
429 ἐκυκλώσατο. πᾶσαν γοῦν ἀνθρωπίνην καὶ δαι-
μονίαν φθορὰν ὑπερβάλλει τὸ πλῆθος τῶν ἀπολω-
λότων· ἐπεὶ γοῦν τῶν φανερῶν οὓς μὲν ἀνεῖλον οὓς
δ' ἠχμαλωτίσαντο Ῥωμαῖοι, τοὺς δ'[3] ἐν τοῖς
ὑπονόμοις ἀνηρεύνων καὶ τοὔδαφος ἀναρρηγνύντες
430 ὅσοις μὲν ἐνετύγχανον ἔκτεινον, εὑρέθησαν δὲ
κἀκεῖ νεκροὶ πλείους δισχιλίων, οἱ μὲν ὑπὸ σφῶν
αὐτῶν οἱ δ' ὑπ' ἀλλήλων, τὸ πλέον δ' ὑπὸ τοῦ

---

[1] So the mss.: φρατρία Hudson.
[2] πεντακισχίλια ἑξακόσια] ἑξακισχίλια καὶ πεντακόσια L Lat.
[3] τοὺς δ'] τοὺς ML Zon.: οὓς δ(ὲ) the rest.

taken under Cestius. For he, being anxious to convince Nero, who held the nation in contempt, of the city's strength, instructed the chief priests, if by any means possible, to take a census of the population. Accordingly, on the occasion of the feast called Passover, at which they sacrifice from the ninth to the eleventh hour, and a little fraternity, as it were, gathers round each sacrifice, of not fewer than ten persons (feasting alone not being permitted), while the companies often include as many as twenty, the victims were counted and amounted to two hundred and fifty-five thousand six hundred; allowing an average of ten diners to each victim, we obtain a total of two million seven hundred thousand,[a] all pure and holy. For those afflicted with leprosy or gonorrhoea, or menstruous women, or persons otherwise defiled were not permitted to partake of this sacrifice, nor yet any foreigners present for worship, (4) and a large number of these assemble from abroad. But now the whole nation had been shut up by fate as in a prison, and the city when war encompassed it was packed with inhabitants. The victims thus outnumbered those of any previous visitation, human or divine. For when all who showed themselves had been either slain or made prisoners by the Romans, the victors instituted a search for those in the mines, and, tearing up the ground, slew all whom they met; here too were found upwards of two thousand dead, of whom some had been destroyed by their own, and some by one another's hands, but the greater number by

Marginal notes: Census of population taken under Cestius.

Search for those concealed underground.

---

[a] Text or arithmetic is at fault; the total should be 2,556,000.

431 λιμοῦ διεφθαρμένοι. δεινὴ δ' ὑπήντα τοῖς ἐπεισ-
πίπτουσιν ὀδμὴ τῶν σωμάτων, ὡς πολλοὺς μὲν
ἀναχωρεῖν εὐθέως, τοὺς δ' ὑπὸ πλεονεξίας εἰσ-
432 δύεσθαι νεκροὺς σεσωρευμένους ἐμπατοῦντας· πολλὰ
γὰρ τῶν κειμηλίων ἐν ταῖς διώρυξιν εὑρίσκετο, καὶ
πᾶσαν θεμιτὴν ὁδὸν ἐποίει τὸ κέρδος· ἀνήγοντο
δὲ καὶ δεσμῶται πολλοὶ τῶν τυράννων, οὐδὲ γὰρ
433 ἐν ἐσχάτοις ἐπαύσαντο τῆς ὠμότητος. ἀπετίσατό
γε μὴν ὁ θεὸς ἀμφοτέρους ἀξίως, καὶ Ἰωάννης μὲν
λιμώττων μετὰ τῶν ἀδελφῶν ἐν τοῖς ὑπονόμοις
ἦν πολλάκις ὑπερηφάνησε παρὰ Ῥωμαίων δεξιὰν
λαβεῖν ἱκέτευσε, Σίμων δὲ πολλὰ διαμαχήσας πρὸς
τὴν ἀνάγκην, ὡς διὰ τῶν ἑξῆς δηλώσομεν, αὐτὸν
434 παραδίδωσιν. ἐφυλάχθη δ' ὁ μὲν τῷ θριάμβῳ σφά-
γιον, ὁ δ' Ἰωάννης δεσμοῖς αἰωνίοις. Ῥωμαῖοι δὲ
τάς τ' ἐσχατιὰς τοῦ ἄστεος ἐνέπρησαν καὶ τὰ τείχη
κατέσκαψαν.

435 (x. 1) Ἑάλω μὲν οὕτως Ἱεροσόλυμα ἔτει
δευτέρῳ τῆς Οὐεσπασιανοῦ ἡγεμονίας Γορπιαίου
μηνὸς ὀγδόῃ, ἁλοῦσα δὲ καὶ πρότερον πεντάκις
436 τοῦτο δεύτερον ἠρημώθη. Ἀσωχαῖος μὲν γὰρ ὁ
τῶν Αἰγυπτίων βασιλεὺς καὶ μετ' αὐτὸν Ἀντίοχος,
ἔπειτα Πομπήιος καὶ ἐπὶ τούτοις σὺν Ἡρώδῃ
437 Σόσσιος ἑλόντες ἐτήρησαν τὴν πόλιν. πρὸ δὲ
τούτων ὁ τῶν Βαβυλωνίων βασιλεὺς κρατήσας
ἠρήμωσεν αὐτὴν μετὰ · ἔτη τῆς κτίσεως χίλια
438 τετρακόσια ἑξηκονταοκτὼ μῆνας ἕξ. ὁ δὲ πρῶτος
κτίσας ἦν Χαναναίων δυνάστης ὁ τῇ πατρίῳ

ᵃ vii. 25-36.   ᵇ c. 26th September, A.D. 70.
ᶜ i.e., the Biblical Shishak, who plundered Jerusalem in
the reign of Rehoboam, c. 969 B.C., 1 Kings xiv. 25 ff. In

famine. So horrible was the stench from the bodies
which met the intruders, that many instantly withdrew, but others penetrated further through avarice,
trampling over heaps of corpses ; for many precious
objects were found in these passages, and lucre
legalized every expedient. Many also of the tyrants'
prisoners were brought up ; for even at the last
they did not abandon their cruelty. God, however, _{Fate of the}
visited both with fit retribution : for John, perishing _{leaders.}
of hunger with his brethren in the mines, implored
from the Romans that protection which he had so
often spurned, and Simon, after a long struggle with
necessity, to be related hereafter,[a] surrendered ;
the latter was reserved for execution at the triumph,
while John was sentenced to perpetual imprisonment. The Romans now set fire to the outlying
quarters of the town and razed the walls to the
ground.

(x. 1) Thus was Jerusalem taken in the second _{Previous}
year of the reign of Vespasian on the eighth of the _{captures of} _{Jerusalem.}
month Gorpiaeus.[b] Captured on five previous occa- _{Concise} _{chrono-}
sions, it was now for the second time devastated. _{logical} _{record of}
Asochaeus,[c] king of Egypt, and after him Antiochus,[d] _{its history.}
then Pompey,[e] and subsequently Sossius in league
with Herod[f] took the city but preserved it. But
before their days the king of Babylon[g] had subdued
it and laid it waste, fourteen hundred and sixty-eight
years and six months after its foundation.[h] Its
original founder was a Canaanite chief, called in the

the *Jewish Antiquities* the name appears as Ἴσωκος (Ἴσακος)
or Σούσακος.
[a] Antiochus Epiphanes, *c.* 170 B.C.
[e] In 63 B.C., *B.* i. 141 ff.   [f] 37 B.C., i. 345 ff.
[g] Nebuchadrezzar, in 587 B.C., 2 Kings xxv.
[h] Chronological system uncertain.

JOSEPHUS

γλώσσῃ κληθεὶς βασιλεὺς δίκαιος· ἦν γὰρ δὴ τοιοῦτος. διὰ τοῦτο ἱεράσατό τε τῷ θεῷ πρῶτος καὶ τὸ ἱερὸν πρῶτος δειμάμενος Ἱεροσόλυμα τὴν πόλιν προσηγόρευσεν Σόλυμα καλουμένην πρότερον.

439 τὸν μὲν δὴ τῶν Χαναναίων λαὸν ἐκβαλὼν ὁ τῶν Ἰουδαίων βασιλεὺς Δαυίδης[1] κατοικίζει τὸν ἴδιον, καὶ μετὰ τοῦτον ἔτεσι τετρακοσίοις ἑβδομήκοντα καὶ ἑπτὰ μησὶν ἐξ ὑπὸ Βαβυλωνίων κατασκάπτεται.

440 ἀπὸ δὲ Δαυίδου τοῦ βασιλέως, ὃς πρῶτος αὐτῆς ἐβασίλευσεν Ἰουδαῖος, μέχρι τῆς ὑπὸ Τίτου γενομένης κατασκαφῆς ἔτη χίλια καὶ ἑκατὸν ἑβδο-

441 μηκονταεννέα· ἀπὸ δὲ τῆς πρώτης κτίσεως ἔτη μέχρι τῆς ἐσχάτης ἁλώσεως δισχίλια ἑκατὸν ἑβδο-

442 μήκοντα καὶ ἑπτά. ἀλλὰ γὰρ οὔθ' ἡ ἀρχαιότης οὔθ' ὁ πλοῦτος ὁ βαθὺς οὔτε τὸ διαπεφοιτηκὸς ὅλης τῆς οἰκουμένης ἔθνος οὔθ' ἡ μεγάλη δόξα τῆς θρησκείας ἤρκεσέ τι πρὸς ἀπώλειαν αὐτῇ. τοιοῦτο μὲν δὴ τὸ τέλος τῆς Ἱεροσολύμων πολιορκίας.

[1] C: δᾱδ (= Δαυὶδ) the rest, and so in § 440.

---

[a] Melchi-zedek. The name is similarly interpreted, "king of righteousness," in the Ep. to the Hebrews, vii. 2; in

native tongue ' Righteous King ' [a]; for such indeed he was. In virtue thereof he was the first to officiate as priest of God and, being the first to build the temple, gave the city, previously called Solyma, the name of Jerusalem.[b] The Canaanite population was expelled by David, the king of the Jews, who established his own people there ; and four hundred and seventy-seven years and six months after his time it was razed to the ground by the Babylonians. The period from king David, its first Jewish sovereign, to its destruction by Titus was one thousand one hundred and seventy-nine years ; and from its first foundation until its final overthrow, two thousand one hundred and seventy-seven. Howbeit, neither its antiquity, nor its ample wealth, nor its people spread over the whole habitable world, nor yet the great glory of its religious rites, could aught avail to avert its ruin. Thus ended the siege of Jerusalem.

reality it apparently meant " my king is Zedek," Z. being the name of a Phoenician deity, *cf.* Adoni-zedek " my lord is Z.," Jos. x. 1. Melchizedek is " king of Salem " (Gen. xiv. 18), probably an archaic name for Jerusalem.

[b] Greek " Hierosolyma " ; for the names Solyma, Hierosolyma and the popular Greek etymology, uncritically taken over by Josephus, see G. A. Smith, *Jerusalem*, i. 261 f.

1 (i. 1) Ἐπεὶ δ' οὔτε φονεύειν οὔτε διαρπάζειν
εἶχεν ἡ στρατιὰ πάντων τοῖς θυμοῖς ἐπιλειπόντων,
οὐ γὰρ δή γε φειδοῖ τινος ἔμελλον ἀφέξεσθαι δρᾶν
ἔχοντες, κελεύει Καῖσαρ ἤδη τήν τε πόλιν ἅπασαν
καὶ τὸν νεὼν κατασκάπτειν, πύργους μὲν ὅσοι
τῶν ἄλλων ὑπερανειστήκεσαν καταλιπόντας, Φασάηλον Ἱππικὸν Μαριάμμην, τεῖχος δ' ὅσον ἦν
2 ἐξ ἑσπέρας τὴν πόλιν περιέχον, τοῦτο μέν, ὅπως
εἴη τοῖς ὑπολειφθησομένοις φρουροῖς στρατόπεδον,
τοὺς πύργους δέ, ἵνα τοῖς ἔπειτα σημαίνωσιν οἵας
πόλεως καὶ τίνα τρόπον ὀχυρᾶς ὅμως¹ ἐκράτησεν
3 ἡ Ῥωμαίων ἀνδραγαθία. τὸν δ' ἄλλον ἅπαντα
τῆς πόλεως περίβολον οὕτως ἐξωμάλισαν οἱ
κατασκάπτοντες, ὡς μηδεπώποτ' οἰκηθῆναι πίστιν
4 ἂν ἔτι παρασχεῖν τοῖς προσελθοῦσι. τοῦτο μὲν
οὖν τὸ τέλος ἐκ τῆς τῶν νεωτερισάντων ἀνοίας
Ἱεροσολύμοις ἐγένετο, λαμπρᾷ τε πόλει καὶ παρὰ
πᾶσιν ἀνθρώποις διαβοηθείσῃ.
5 (2) Καῖσαρ δὲ φυλακὴν μὲν αὐτόθι καταλιπεῖν
ἔγνω τῶν ταγμάτων τὸ δέκατον καί τινας ἴλας
ἱππέων καὶ λόχους πεζῶν, πάντα δ' ἤδη τὰ τοῦ
πολέμου διῳκηκὼς ἐπαινέσαι τε σύμπασαν ἐπόθει
τὴν στρατιὰν ἐπὶ τοῖς κατορθώμασιν καὶ τὰ

¹ Niese and others: οὕτως mss. (om. L).

504

BOOK VII

(i. 1) The army now having no victims either for slaughter or plunder, through lack of all objects on which to vent their rage—for they would assuredly never have desisted through a desire to spare anything so long as there was work to be done—Caesar ordered the whole city and the temple to be razed to the ground, leaving only the loftiest of the towers, Phasael, Hippicus, and Mariamme, and the portion of the wall enclosing the city on the west: the latter as an encampment for the garrison that was to remain, and the towers to indicate to posterity the nature of the city and of the strong defences which had yet yielded to Roman prowess. All the rest of the wall encompassing the city was so completely levelled to the ground as to leave future visitors to the spot no ground for believing that it had ever been inhabited. Such was the end to which the frenzy of revolutionaries brought Jerusalem, that splendid city of worldwide renown.

(2) As the local garrison Caesar decided to leave the tenth legion, along with some squadrons of cavalry and companies of infantry; and having now settled everything relating to the war, he was anxious to commend the army in general for their achievements and to confer the appropriate rewards on those

Jerusalem razed to the ground.

Titus commends his troops,

505

προσήκοντα γέρα τοῖς ἀριστεύσασιν ἀποδουναι.
6 ποιηθέντος οὖν αὐτῷ μεγάλου κατὰ μέσην τὴν
πρότερον παρεμβολὴν βήματος, καταστὰς ἐπὶ
τοῦτο μετὰ τῶν ἡγεμόνων[1] εἰς ἐπήκοον ἁπάσῃ
τῇ στρατιᾷ, χάριν μὲν ἔφη[2] πολλὴν ἔχειν αὐτοῖς
τῆς πρὸς αὐτὸν εὐνοίας, ᾗ χρώμενοι διατελοῦσιν·
7 ἐπήνει δὲ τῆς ἐν παντὶ ⟨τῷ⟩[3] πολέμῳ πειθαρχίας,
ἣν ἐν πολλοῖς καὶ μεγάλοις κινδύνοις ἅμα τῇ
κατὰ σφᾶς ἀνδρείᾳ παρέσχον, τῇ μὲν πατρίδι
καὶ δι' αὐτῶν τὸ κράτος αὔξοντες, φανερὸν δὲ
πᾶσιν ἀνθρώποις καθιστάντες, ὅτι μήτε πλῆθος
πολεμίων μήτε χωρίων ὀχυρότητες ἢ μεγέθη
πόλεων ἢ τῶν ἀντιτεταγμένων ἀλόγιστοι τόλμαι
καὶ θηριώδεις ἀγριότητες δύναιντ' ἄν ποτε τὴν
Ῥωμαίων ἀρετὴν διαφυγεῖν, κἂν εἰς πολλά τινες
8 τὴν τύχην εὕρωνται συναγωνιζομένην. καλὸν μὲν
οὖν ἔφη καὶ τῷ πολέμῳ τέλος αὐτοὺς ἐπιθεῖναι
πολλῷ χρόνῳ[4] γενομένῳ· μηδὲ γὰρ εὔξασθαί τι
9 τούτων ἄμεινον, ὅτ' εἰς αὐτὸν καθίσταντο· τούτου
δὲ κάλλιον αὐτοῖς καὶ λαμπρότερον ὑπάρχειν,
ὅτι τοὺς ἡγησομένους καὶ τῆς Ῥωμαίων ἀρχῆς
ἐπιτροπεύσοντας αὐτῶν χειροτονησάντων εἴς τε
τὴν πατρίδα προπεμψάντων ἄσμενοι πάντες προσ-
ίενται καὶ τοῖς ὑπ' αὐτῶν ἐγνωσμένοις ἐμμένουσι
10 χάριν ἔχοντες τοῖς ἑλομένοις. θαυμάζειν μὲν οὖν
ἔφη πάντας καὶ ἀγαπᾶν, εἰδὼς ὅτι τοῦ δυνατοῦ
11 τὴν προθυμίαν οὐδεὶς ἔσχε βραδυτέραν· τοῖς μέν-

---

[1] ἡγεμονικωτάτων L Lat.
[2] χάριν μὲν ἔφη Niese (avoiding hiatus): ἔλεγεν χάριν μὲν
ἔφη L: ἔλεγε χάριν μὲν the rest.
[3] ins. Herwerden.   [4] πολλῷ χρόνῳ] πολυχρονίῳ Bekker.

who had specially distinguished themselves. A
spacious tribunal having accordingly been constructed for him in the centre of his former camp,
he here took his stand with his principal officers, so
as to be heard by the whole army. He expressed
his deep gratitude to them for the loyalty which they
had continuously shown him. He commended them
for that ready obedience which, along with personal
courage in many grave dangers, they had displayed
throughout the war, thus by their own actions
enhancing the might of their country and demon-
strating to all mankind that neither the numbers of
the enemy, the strength of fortresses, the magnitude
of cities, nor the reckless daring [a] and bestial savagery
of antagonists could ever baffle the valour of Romans,
however often some of their foes might have found an
ally in fortune. Glorious, indeed, it was (he said) to
have brought to a close a war of such long duration;
for they could never have prayed for any happier
issue when they entered upon it.[b] But a yet more
glorious and splendid tribute to them than this was
the fact that those[c] whom they had themselves elected
to be the governors and administrators of the Roman
empire, and had sent off to the capital, were being
hailed with universal satisfaction, their rulings
adhered to, and their electors regarded with gratitude. Therefore (he continued) he admired and held
them all in affection, knowing that there was not one
whose alacrity had fallen short of his ability; but

[a] ἀλόγιστοι τόλμαι after Thuc. iii. 82. 3 (τόλμα ἀλόγιστος).
[b] εἰς αὐτὸν καθίσταντο: another Thucydidean phrase (iv. 23
ἐς πόλεμον καθίσταντο).
[c] The plural of Vespasian and his party or the Flavian
dynasty: the soldiers' choice included Titus, B. iv. 597.

τοι διαπρεπέστερον ἀγωνισαμένοις ὑπὸ ῥώμης
πλείονος καὶ τὸν μὲν αὐτῶν βίον ἀριστείαις κεκο-
σμηκόσι, τὴν δ' αὐτοῦ στρατείαν ἐπιφανεστέραν
διὰ τῶν κατορθωμάτων πεποιηκόσιν ἔφη τὰ γέρα
καὶ τὰς τιμὰς εὐθὺς ἀποδώσειν, καὶ μηδένα τῶν
πλέον πονεῖν ἑτέρου θελησάντων τῆς δικαίας
12 ἀμοιβῆς ἁμαρτήσεσθαι. πλείστην γὰρ αὐτῷ τούτου γενήσεσθαι τὴν ἐπιμέλειαν, ἐπεὶ καὶ μᾶλλον
ἐθέλειν τὰς ἀρετὰς τιμᾶν τῶν συστρατευομένων
ἢ κολάζειν τοὺς ἁμαρτάνοντας.
13 (3) Εὐθέως οὖν ἐκέλευσεν ἀναγινώσκειν τοῖς
ἐπὶ τοῦτο τεταγμένοις ὅσοι τι λαμπρὸν ἦσαν ἐν
14 τῷ πολέμῳ κατωρθωκότες. καὶ κατ' ὄνομα καλῶν
ἐπῄνει τε παριόντας ὡς ἂν ὑπερευφραινόμενός
τις ἐπ' οἰκείοις κατορθώμασι καὶ στεφάνους
ἐπετίθει χρυσοῦς, περιαυχένιά τε χρυσᾶ καὶ
δόρατα μικρὰ[1] χρυσᾶ καὶ σημαίας ἐδίδου πεποιη-
15 μένας ἐξ ἀργύρου, καὶ τὴν ἑκάστου τάξιν ἤλλαττεν
εἰς τὸ κρεῖττον, οὐ μὴν ἀλλὰ κἀκ τῶν λαφύρων
ἄργυρον καὶ χρυσὸν ἐσθῆτάς τε καὶ τῆς ἄλλης
16 αὐτοῖς λείας δαψιλῶς ἀπένειμε. πάντων δὲ τε-
τιμημένων ὅπως [ἂν][2] αὐτὸς ἕκαστον ἠξίωσε, τῇ
συμπάσῃ στρατιᾷ ποιησάμενος εὐχὰς ἐπὶ πολλῇ
κατέβαινεν εὐφημίᾳ τρέπεταί τε πρὸς θυσίας
ἐπινικίους, καὶ πολλοῦ βοῶν πλήθους τοῖς βωμοῖς
παρεστηκότος καταθύσας ἅπαντας τῇ στρατιᾷ
17 διαδίδωσιν εἰς εὐωχίαν. αὐτὸς δὲ τοῖς ἐν τέλει
τρεῖς ἡμέρας συνεορτάσας τὴν μὲν ἄλλην στρατιὰν
διαφίησιν ᾗ καλῶς εἶχεν ἑκάστους ἀπιέναι, τῷ
δεκάτῳ δὲ τάγματι τὴν τῶν Ἱεροσολύμων ἐπ-

---

[1] A : μακρὰ the rest.   [2] om. Dindorf and Niese.

upon those who had more eminently distinguished themselves in the fight by superior energy, and had not only shed a lustre on their own lives by deeds of gallantry but rendered his campaign more famous by their achievements, he would forthwith confer their rewards and honours, and not a man who had chosen to exert himself more than his fellows should miss his due recompense. For to this he would devote his special attention, since he was more concerned to reward the valorous deeds, than to punish the delinquencies, of his fellow-soldiers.

(3) He accordingly forthwith gave orders to the appointed officers to read out the names of all who had performed any brilliant feat during the war. Calling up each by name he applauded them as they came forward, no less exultant over their exploits than if they were his own. He then placed crowns of gold upon their heads, presented them with golden neck-chains, little golden spears and standards made of silver, and promoted each man to a higher rank; he further assigned to them out of the spoils silver and gold and raiments and other booty in abundance. When all had been rewarded as he judged each to have deserved, after invoking blessings upon the whole army he descended amidst many acclamations and proceeded to offer sacrifices of thanksgiving for his victory. A vast number of oxen being brought up beside the altars, he sacrificed them all and distributed them to the troops for a banquet. Having himself for three days joined in festivities with his staff officers, he dismissed the rest of the troops to their several appropriate destinations; the tenth legion,[a] however, he entrusted with the custody of

and awards honours.

Destination of the legions.

---

[a] *Fretensis,* Mommsen, *Provinces* ii. 63 note.

ἔτρεψε φυλακὴν οὐκέτ᾽ αὐτοὺς ἐπὶ τὸν Εὐφράτην
18 ἀποστείλας, ἔνθα πρότερον ἦσαν. μεμνημένος δὲ
τοῦ δωδεκάτου τάγματος, ὅτι Κεστίου στρα-
τηγοῦντος ἐνέδωκαν τοῖς Ἰουδαίοις, τῆς μὲν
Συρίας αὐτὸ παντάπασιν ἐξήλασεν, ἦν γὰρ τὸ
παλαιὸν ἐν Ῥαφαναίαις,[1] εἰς δὲ τὴν Μελιτηνὴν·
καλουμένην ἀπέστειλε· παρὰ τὸν Εὐφράτην ἐν
μεθορίοις τῆς Ἀρμενίας ἐστὶ καὶ Καππαδοκίας.
19 δύο δ᾽ ἠξίωσεν αὐτῷ μέχρι τῆς εἰς Αἴγυπτον
ἀφίξεως, τὸ πέμπτον καὶ τὸ πεντεκαιδέκατον,
20 παραμένειν. καὶ καταβὰς ἅμα τῷ στρατῷ πρὸς
τὴν ἐπὶ τῇ θαλάττῃ Καισάρειαν εἰς ταύτην τό τε
πλῆθος τῶν λαφύρων ἀπέθετο καὶ τοὺς αἰχμαλώτους προσέταξεν ἐν αὐτῇ φυλάττεσθαι· τὸν γὰρ
εἰς τὴν Ἰταλίαν πλοῦν ὁ χειμὼν ἐκώλυε.
21 (ii. 1) Καθ᾽ ὃ δὲ καιροῦ Τίτος Καῖσαρ τοῖς
Ἱεροσολύμοις πολιορκῶν προσήδρευεν, ἐν τούτῳ
νεὼς φορτίδος Οὐεσπασιανὸς ἐπιβὰς ἀπὸ τῆς
22 Ἀλεξανδρείας εἰς Ῥόδον διέβαινεν.[3] ἐντεῦθεν δὲ
πλέων ἐπὶ τριήρων καὶ πάσας τὰς ἐν τῷ παράπλῳ
πόλεις ἐπελθών, εὐκταίως αὐτὸν δεχομένας, ἀπὸ
τῆς Ἰωνίας εἰς τὴν Ἑλλάδα περαιοῦται, κἀκεῖθεν
ἀπὸ Κερκύρας ἐπ᾽ ἄκραν Ἰαπυγίαν, ὅθεν ἤδη
23 κατὰ γῆν ἐποιεῖτο τὴν πορείαν. Τίτος δ᾽ ἀπὸ
τῆς ἐπὶ θαλάττῃ Καισαρείας ἀναζεύξας εἰς τὴν
Φιλίππου καλουμένην Καισάρειαν ἧκε συχνόν τ᾽
ἐν αὐτῇ χρόνον ἐπέμεινεν παντοίας θεωρίας
24 ἐπιτελῶν· καὶ πολλοὶ τῶν αἰχμαλώτων ἐνταῦθα
διεφθάρησαν, οἱ μὲν θηρίοις παραβληθέντες, οἱ
δὲ κατὰ πληθὺν ἀλλήλοις ἀναγκαζόμενοι χρήσασθαι

---

[1] Ῥαφαναῖς A.   [2] After C (Μελιτινην): Μελίτην the rest.
[3] διέβαλεν L.

Jerusalem,[a] not sending them back to their former
station on the Euphrates. Recollecting too that the
twelfth [b] legion had under the command of Cestius
succumbed to the Jews,[c] he banished them from
Syria altogether—for they had previously been
quartered at Raphanaeae [d]—and sent them to the
district called Melitene, beside the Euphrates, on the
confines of Armenia and Cappadocia. Two legions,
the fifth [e] and the fifteenth,[f] he thought fit to retain
with himself until his arrival in Egypt. Then
descending with his army to Caesarea-on-sea, he
there deposited the bulk of his spoils and directed
that his prisoners should be kept in custody ; for the
winter season prevented his sailing for Italy. *Titus leaves for Caesarea-on-sea.*

(ii. 1) Now at the time when Titus Caesar was
assiduously besieging Jerusalem, Vespasian, embarking on a merchant-vessel, crossed from Alexandria to Rhodes. From there he sailed on triremes ;
and touching at all towns on his route, and being
everywhere received with ovations, he passed over
from Ionia into Greece, and thence from Corcyra to
the Iapygian promontory, whence he pursued his
journey by land. *Vespasian's journey to Italy.*

Titus, removing his troops from Caesarea-on-sea,
now passed to Caesarea Philippi so called, where he
remained for a considerable time, exhibiting all
kinds of spectacles. Here many of the prisoners
perished, some being thrown to wild beasts, others
compelled in opposing masses to engage one another *Titus exhibits shows at Caesarea Philippi.*

---

[a] § 5.   [b] *Fulminata.*   [c] *B.* ii. 500 ff.
[d] Or Raphanaea (§ 97) or Raphaneia ; in upper Syria,
W. of Emessa (*Homs*).
[e] *Macedonica.*   [f] *Apollinaris.*

25 πολεμίοις. ἐνταῦθα καὶ τὴν Σίμωνος τοῦ Γιώρα
σύλληψιν ἐπύθετο τοῦτον γενομένην τὸν τρόπον.

26 (2) Σίμων οὗτος Ἱεροσολύμων πολιορκουμένων
ἐπὶ τῆς ἄνω πόλεως ὤν, ἐπεὶ τῶν τειχῶν ἐντὸς
ἡ Ῥωμαίων στρατιὰ γενομένη πᾶσαν ἐπόρθει
τὴν πόλιν, τότε τῶν φίλων τοὺς πιστοτάτους
παραλαβὼν καὶ σὺν αὐτοῖς λιθοτόμους τε καὶ τὸν
πρὸς τὴν ἐργασίαν ἐπιτήδειον τούτοις σίδηρον
τροφήν τε διαρκεῖν εἰς πολλὰς ἡμέρας δυναμένην,
σὺν ἐκείνοις ἅπασι καθίησιν αὐτὸν εἴς τινα τῶν
27 ἀφανῶν ὑπονόμων. καὶ μέχρι μὲν ἦν τὸ παλαιὸν
ὄρυγμα, προυχώρουν δι᾽ αὐτοῦ, τῆς στερεᾶς δὲ
γῆς ὑπαντώσης ταύτην ὑπενόμευον, ἐλπίδι τοῦ
πορρωτέρω δυνήσεσθαι προελθόντες ἐν ἀσφαλεῖ
28 ποιησάμενοι τὴν ἀνάδυσιν ἀποσώζεσθαι. ψευδῆ
δὲ τὴν ἐλπίδα διήλεγχεν ἡ πεῖρα τῶν ἔργων·
ὀλίγον τε γὰρ μόλις προύβαινον οἱ μεταλλεύοντες,
ἥ τε τροφὴ καίτοι ταμιευομένοις ἔμελλεν ἐπιλεί-
29 ψειν.¹ τότε δὴ τοίνυν, ὡς δι᾽ ἐκπλήξεως ἀπατῆσαι
τοὺς Ῥωμαίους δυνησόμενος, λευκοὺς ἐνδιδύσκει
χιτωνίσκους καὶ πορφυρᾶν ἐμπερονησάμενος
χλανίδα² κατ᾽ αὐτὸν ἐκεῖνον τὸν τόπον, ἐν ᾧ τὸ
30 ἱερὸν ἦν πρόσθεν, ἐκ τῆς γῆς ἀνεφάνη. τὸ μὲν
οὖν πρῶτον τοῖς ἰδοῦσι θάμβος προσέπεσε καὶ
κατὰ χώραν ἔμενον, ἔπειτα δ᾽ ἐγγυτέρω προσ-
31 ελθόντες ὅστις ἐστὶν ἤροντο. καὶ τοῦτο μὲν οὐκ
ἐδήλου Σίμων αὐτοῖς, καλεῖν δὲ τὸν ἡγεμόνα
προσέταττεν. καὶ ταχέως πρὸς αὐτὸν δραμόντων
ἧκεν Τερέντιος Ῥοῦφος· οὗτος γὰρ ἄρχων τῆς
στρατιᾶς κατελέλειπτο· πυθόμενός τε παρ᾽ αὐτοῦ
πᾶσαν τὴν ἀλήθειαν τὸν μὲν ἐφύλαττε δεδεμένον,
Καίσαρι δ᾽ ὅπως εἴη συνειλημμένος ἐδήλου.

in combat. Here, too, Titus learnt of the capture of
Simon, son of Gioras, which was effected as follows.

(2) This Simon during the siege of Jerusalem had
occupied the upper town; but when the Roman army
entered within the walls and were sacking the whole
city, he, accompanied by his most faithful friends,
along with some stone-cutters, bringing the tools
required for their craft, and provisions sufficient for
many days, let himself down with all his party into
one of the secret passages. So far as the old excava-
tion extended, they followed it; but when solid earth
met them, they began mining, hoping to be able
to proceed further, emerge in safety, and so escape.
But experience of the task proved this hope delusive;
for the miners advanced slowly and with difficulty,
and the provisions, though husbanded, were nearly
exhausted. Thereupon, Simon, imagining that he
could cheat the Romans by creating a scare, dressed
himself in white tunics and buckling over them a
purple mantle arose out of the ground at the very
spot whereon the temple formerly stood. The
spectators were at first aghast and remained motionless; but afterwards they approached nearer and
inquired who he was. This Simon declined to tell
them, but bade them summon the general. Accordingly, they promptly ran to fetch him, and Terentius
Rufus, who had been left in command of the force,
appeared. He, after hearing from Simon the whole
truth, kept him in chains and informed Caesar of the

---

¹ C: ἀπολείψειν the rest.
² χλαμύδα L Zon.: "chlamide" Lat.

32 Σίμωνα μὲν οὖν εἰς δίκην τῆς κατὰ τῶν πολιτῶν
ὠμότητος, ὧν πικρῶς αὐτὸς ἐτυράννησεν, ὑπὸ
33 τοῖς μάλιστα μισοῦσι πολεμίοις ἐποίησεν ὁ θεός,
οὐ βίᾳ γενόμενον αὐτοῖς ὑποχείριον, ἀλλ' αὐτὸν
ἑκουσίως εἰς τὴν τιμωρίαν παραβαλόντα, δι' ὃ[1]
πολλοὺς αὐτὸς ὠμῶς ἀπέκτεινε ψευδεῖς αἰτίας
34 ἐπιφέρων τῆς πρὸς Ῥωμαίους μεταβολῆς. οὐδὲ
γὰρ διαφεύγει πονηρία θεοῦ χόλον, οὐδὲ ἀσθενὴς
ἡ δίκη, χρόνῳ δὲ μέτεισι τοὺς εἰς αὐτὴν παρα-
νομήσαντας καὶ χείρω τὴν τιμωρίαν ἐπιφέρει τοῖς
πονηροῖς, ὅτε[2] καὶ προσεδόκησαν αὐτῆς ἀπηλλάχθαι
μὴ παραυτίκα κολασθέντες. ἔγνω τοῦτο καὶ
35 Σίμων εἰς τὰς Ῥωμαίων ὀργὰς ἐμπεσών. ἡ δ'
ἐκείνου γῆθεν ἄνοδος πολὺ καὶ τῶν ἄλλων στασιαστῶν πλῆθος ὑπ' ἐκείνας τὰς ἡμέρας ἐν τοῖς
36 ὑπονόμοις φωραθῆναι παρεσκεύασε. Καίσαρι δ'
εἰς τὴν παράλιον ἐπανήκοντι[3] Καισάρειαν Σίμων
προσήχθη δεδεμένος· κἀκεῖνον μὲν εἰς ὃν ἐπιτελεῖν
ἐν Ῥώμῃ παρεσκευάζετο θρίαμβον προσέταξε
φυλάττειν.

37 (iii. 1) Διατρίβων δ' αὐτόθι τὴν τἀδελφοῦ γενέθλιον ἡμέραν ἐπιφανῶς ἑώρταζε, πολὺ καὶ τῆς
τῶν Ἰουδαίων κολάσεως εἰς τὴν ἐκείνου τιμὴν
38 ἀνατιθείς. ὁ γὰρ ἀριθμὸς τῶν ἔν τε ταῖς πρὸς
τὰ θηρία μάχαις ἔν τε ταῖς ἀλληλοκτονίαις ἀναιρου-
μένων καὶ τῶν καταπιμπραμένων[4] πεντακοσίους
ἐπὶ τοῖς δισχιλίοις ὑπερέβαλε. πάντα μέντοι
Ῥωμαίοις ἐδόκει ταῦτα μυρίοις αὐτῶν ἀπ-

---

[1] *ed. pr.* (*cf.* Lat. "propterea quod"): δι' ὃν or δι' ὧν
MSS.   [2] After Lat. Niese: ὅτι MSS.
[3] A: ἐπανελθόντι MVR: παρελθόντι LC.
[4] καὶ τῶν καταπιμπραμένων in the MSS. stands after μάχαις:
transposed by Niese.

514

manner of his capture. Thus was Simon, in retribution for his cruelty to his fellow-citizens, whom he had mercilessly tyrannized, delivered by God into the hands of his deadliest enemies; not subjected to them by force, but spontaneously exposing himself to punishment—an act for which he had put many to a cruel death on false charges of defection to the Romans. For villainy escapes not the wrath of God, nor is Justice weak, but in due time she tracks down those who have transgressed against her and inflicts upon the sinners a chastisement the more severe, when they imagined themselves quit of it because they were not punished immediately.[a] This Simon learnt when he fell into the hands of the indignant Romans. His emergence from the ground led, moreover, to the discovery during those days of a large number of the other rebels in the subterranean passages. On the return of Caesar to Caesarea-on-sea Simon was brought to him in chains, and he ordered the prisoner to be kept for the triumph which he was preparing to celebrate in Rome.

(iii. 1) During his stay at Caesarea, Titus celebrated his brother's birthday [b] with great splendour, reserving in his honour for this festival [c] much of the punishment of his Jewish captives. For the number of those destroyed in contests with wild beasts or with one another or in the flames exceeded two thousand five hundred. Yet to the Romans, notwithstanding the myriad forms in which their victims

Titus celebrates family birthdays. October A.D. 70.

---

[a] Cf. Horace, Odes iii. 2. 31 f. "raro antecedentem scelestum | deseruit pede Poena claudo."

[b] Domitian was now eighteen, born 24th October, A.D. 52.

[c] Or "dedicating to his honour," but the verb (like the verbal adj. ἀναθετέον) doubtless connotes "postpone."

39 ὀλλυμένων τρόποις ἐλάττων κόλασις εἶναι. μετὰ
τοῦτο Καῖσαρ εἰς Βηρυτὸν ἧκεν· ἡ δ' ἐστὶν ἐν
τῇ Φοινίκῃ πόλις Ῥωμαίων ἄποικος· κἀνταῦθα
χρονιωτέραν ἐποιήσατο τὴν ἐπιδημίαν πλείονι
χρώμενος τῇ λαμπρότητι περὶ τὴν τοῦ πατρὸς
ἡμέραν γενέθλιον ἔν τε ταῖς τῶν θεωριῶν πολυ-
τελείαις καὶ κατὰ τὴν ἄλλην ἐπίνοιαν τῶν [ἄλλων][1]
40 ἀναλωμάτων. τὸ δὲ τῶν αἰχμαλώτων πλῆθος
τὸν αὐτὸν τρόπον ὡς πρόσθεν ἀπώλλυτο.

41 (2) Γενέσθαι δὲ συνέβη περὶ τὸν καιρὸν τοῦτον
καὶ τοῖς ἐν Ἀντιοχείᾳ τῶν Ἰουδαίων ὑπο-
λειπομένοις ἐγκλήματα καὶ κίνδυνον ὀλέθρου, τῆς
πόλεως ἐπ' αὐτοὺς τῶν Ἀντιοχέων ἐκταραχθείσης
διά τε τὰς ἐν τῷ παρόντι διαβολὰς αὐτοῖς ἐπενεχ-
θείσας καὶ διὰ τὰ προϋπηργμένα[2] χρόνῳ πρόσθεν
42 οὐ πολλῷ, περὶ ὧν ἀναγκαῖόν ἐστι διὰ συντόμων
προειπεῖν, ἵνα καὶ τῶν μετὰ ταῦτα πραχθέντων
εὐπαρακολούθητον ποιήσωμαι τὴν διήγησιν.

43 (3) Τὸ γὰρ Ἰουδαίων γένος πολὺ μὲν κατὰ
πᾶσαν τὴν οἰκουμένην παρέσπαρται τοῖς ἐπιχωρίοις, πλεῖστον δὲ τῇ Συρίᾳ κατὰ τὴν γειτνίασιν
ἀναμεμιγμένον ἐξαιρέτως[3] ἐπὶ τῆς Ἀντιοχείας
ἦν πολὺ διὰ τὸ τῆς πόλεως μέγεθος· μάλιστα δ'
αὐτοῖς ἀδεᾶ τὴν ἐκεῖ κατοίκησιν οἱ μετ' Ἀντίοχον
44 βασιλεῖς παρέσχον. Ἀντίοχος μὲν γὰρ ὁ κληθεὶς
Ἐπιφανὴς Ἱεροσόλυμα πορθήσας τὸν νεὼν ἐσύ-
λησεν, οἱ δὲ μετ' αὐτὸν τὴν βασιλείαν παραλαβόντες
τῶν ἀναθημάτων ὅσα χαλκᾶ πεποίητο πάντα τοῖς

[1] Bracketed by Niese: the Lat. rather suggests the
omission of ἄλλην.
[2] LC (cf. §§ 56, 269): ὑπηργμένα the rest.
[3] + δὲ (δ' C) AVRC.

perished, all this seemed too light a penalty. After
this Caesar passed to Berytus,[a] a city of Phoenicia
and a Roman colony. Here he made a longer sojourn, displaying still greater magnificence on the
occasion of his father's birthday,[b] both in the November.
costliness of the spectacles and in the ingenuity of
the various other items of expenditure. Multitudes
of captives perished in the same manner as before.

(2) It happened, moreover, about this time that The Jews
the remnant of the Jews at Antioch were incriminated of Antioch in peril.
and in danger of extermination, the Antiochene
community having been greatly excited against
them in consequence not only of the false accusations
now laid to their charge, but also of certain incidents
which had taken place not long before. Of these a
brief account must first be given, in order to render my
narrative of the subsequent events more intelligible.

(3) The Jewish race, densely interspersed among Their
the native populations of every portion of the world, previous
is particularly numerous in Syria, where inter- history.
mingling is due to the proximity of the two countries.
But it was at Antioch that they specially congregated,
partly owing to the greatness of that city, but mainly
because the successors of King Antiochus[c] had enabled them to live there in security. For, although
Antiochus surnamed Epiphanes[d] sacked Jerusalem
and plundered the temple,[e] his successors on the
throne restored to the Jews of Antioch all such votive

---

[a] *Beirut.*
[b] Vespasian was now sixty-one, born 17th November,
A.D. 9.
[c] Antiochus I Soter (reigned 280–261 B.C.) is apparently
meant.
[d] Antiochus IV Epiphanes (175–164 B.C.).
[e] *c.* 170 B.C., *B.* i. 31 f.

517

ἐπ᾽ Ἀντιοχείας Ἰουδαίοις ἀπέδοσαν εἰς τὴν
συναγωγὴν αὐτῶν ἀναθέντες, καὶ συνεχώρησαν
αὐτοῖς ἐξ ἴσου τῆς πόλεως τοῖς Ἕλλησι μετέχειν.
45 τὸν αὐτὸν δὲ τρόπον καὶ τῶν μετὰ ταῦτα βασιλέων αὐτοῖς προσφερομένων εἴς τε πλῆθος ἐπ-
έδωκαν καὶ τῇ κατασκευῇ καὶ τῇ πολυτελείᾳ τῶν
ἀναθημάτων τὸ ἱερὸν ἐξελάμπρυναν, ἀεί τε προσ-
αγόμενοι ταῖς θρησκείαις πολὺ πλῆθος Ἑλλήνων,
κἀκείνους τρόπῳ τινὶ μοῖραν αὐτῶν πεποίηντο.
46 καθ᾽ ὃν δὲ καιρὸν ὁ πόλεμος ἀνακεκήρυκτο,
νεωστὶ δ᾽ εἰς τὴν Συρίαν Οὐεσπασιανὸς κατα-
47 πεπλεύκει, τὸ δὲ κατὰ τῶν Ἰουδαίων παρὰ πᾶσιν
ἤκμαζε μῖσος, τότε δή τις Ἀντίοχος εἷς ἐξ αὐτῶν
τὰ μάλιστα διὰ τὸν πατέρα τιμώμενος, ἦν γὰρ
ἄρχων τῶν ἐπ᾽ Ἀντιοχείας Ἰουδαίων, τοῦ δήμου
τῶν Ἀντιοχέων ἐκκλησιάζοντος εἰς τὸ θέατρον
παρελθὼν τόν τε πατέρα τὸν αὑτοῦ καὶ τοὺς
ἄλλους ἐνεδείκνυτο, κατηγορῶν ὅτι νυκτὶ μιᾷ
καταπρῆσαι τὴν πόλιν ἅπασαν διεγνώκεισαν, καὶ
παρεδίδου ξένους Ἰουδαίους τινὰς ὡς κεκοινω-
48 νηκότας τῶν βεβουλευμένων. ταῦτα [δ᾽][1] ἀκούων
ὁ δῆμος τὴν ὀργὴν οὐ κατεῖχεν, ἀλλ᾽ ἐπὶ μὲν
τοὺς παραδοθέντας πῦρ εὐθὺς ἐκέλευον κομίζειν,
καὶ παραχρῆμα πάντες ἐπὶ τοῦ θεάτρου κατ-
49 εφλέγησαν, ἐπὶ δὲ τὸ πλῆθος ὥρμητο τῶν Ἰουδαίων
ἐν τῷ τάχιον ἐκείνους τιμωρίᾳ περιβαλεῖν τὴν
50 αὐτῶν πατρίδα σώζειν νομίζοντες. Ἀντίοχος δὲ

[1] om. PM.

---

[a] According to *Ap.* ii. 39 these rights were granted to the

offerings as were made of brass, to be laid up in their synagogue, and, moreover, granted them citizen rights on an equality with the Greeks.[a] Continuing to receive similar treatment from later monarchs, the Jewish colony grew in numbers, and their richly designed and costly offerings formed a splendid ornament to the temple.[b] Moreover, they were constantly attracting to their religious ceremonies multitudes of Greeks, and these they had in some measure incorporated with themselves. Now just at the time when war had been declared and Vespasian had recently landed in Syria, and when hatred of the Jews was everywhere at its height, a certain Antiochus, one of their own number and highly respected for the sake of his father, who was chief magistrate of the Jews in Antioch, entered the theatre [c] during an assembly of the people and denounced his own father and the other Jews, accusing them of a design to burn the whole city to the ground in one night; he also delivered up some foreign Jews as accomplices to the plot. On hearing this, the people, in uncontrollable fury, ordered the men who had been delivered up to be instantly consigned to the flames, and all were forthwith burnt to death in the theatre. They then rushed for the Jewish masses, believing the salvation of their native place to be dependent on their prompt chastisement.

Antiochus the renegade accuses the Antiochene Jews of incendiarism.

Jews of Antioch by Seleucus I Nicator, founder of the city and of the Seleucid dynasty (died 280 B.C.).

[b] Jews recognized but one "temple," at Jerusalem, and that must surely be intended; Whiston and Traill render "their temple," meaning apparently the "synagogue" mentioned above.

[c] The theatre was frequently used as a meeting-place for the ecclesia in Hellenic cities; cf. the scene in the theatre at Ephesus, Acts xix. 29.

519

προσεπέτεινε τὴν ὀργήν, περὶ μὲν τῆς αὑτοῦ
μεταβολῆς καὶ τοῦ μεμισηκέναι τὰ τῶν Ἰουδαίων
ἔθη τεκμήριον ἐμπαρέχειν¹ οἰόμενος τὸ ἐπιθύειν
51 ὥσπερ νόμος ἐστὶ τοῖς Ἕλλησιν· ἐκέλευε δὲ καὶ
τοὺς ἄλλους τὸ αὐτὸ ποιεῖν ἀναγκάζειν· φανεροὺς
γὰρ γενήσεσθαι τῷ μὴ θέλειν τοὺς ἐπιβεβου-
λευκότας. χρωμένων δὲ τῇ πείρᾳ τῶν Ἀντιοχέων
ὀλίγοι μὲν ὑπέμειναν, οἱ δὲ μὴ βουληθέντες
52 ἀνῃρέθησαν. Ἀντίοχος δὲ στρατιώτας παρὰ τοῦ
Ῥωμαίων ἡγεμόνος λαβὼν χαλεπὸς ἐφειστήκει
τοῖς αὑτοῦ πολίταις, ἀργεῖν τὴν ἑβδόμην οὐκ
ἐπιτρέπων, ἀλλὰ βιαζόμενος πάντα πράττειν ὅσα
53 δὴ καὶ ταῖς ἄλλαις ἡμέραις. οὕτως τε τὴν
ἀνάγκην ἰσχυρὰν ἐποίησεν, ὡς μὴ μόνον ἐπ᾽
Ἀντιοχείας καταλυθῆναι τὴν ἑβδομάδα ἀργεῖν²
ἡμέραν, ἀλλ᾽ ἐκεῖθεν ἀρξαμένου τοῦ πράγματος κἂν³
ταῖς ἄλλαις πόλεσιν ὁμοίως βραχύν τινα χρόνον.
54 (4) Τοιούτων δὴ τοῖς ἐπὶ τῆς⁴ Ἀντιοχείας
Ἰουδαίοις τῶν κατ᾽ ἐκεῖνον τὸν καιρὸν κακῶν
γεγενημένων δευτέρα πάλιν συμφορὰ προσέπεσε,
περὶ ἧς ἐπιχειρήσαντες ἀφηγεῖσθαι καὶ ταῦτα
55 διεξήλθομεν. ἐπεὶ γὰρ συνέβη καταπρησθῆναι
τὴν τετράγωνον ἀγορὰν ἀρχεῖά τε καὶ γραμματο-
φυλάκιον⁵ καὶ τὰς βασιλικάς, μόλις τε τὸ πῦρ
ἐκωλύθη μετὰ πολλῆς βίας ἐπὶ πᾶσαν τὴν πόλιν
περιφερόμενον, ταύτην Ἀντίοχος τὴν πρᾶξιν Ἰου-
56 δαίων κατηγόρει. καὶ τοὺς Ἀντιοχεῖς, εἰ καὶ
μὴ πρότερον εἶχον πρὸς αὐτοὺς ἀπεχθῶς, τάχιστ᾽
ἂν⁶ τῇ διαβολῇ παρὰ τὴν ἐκ τοῦ συμβεβηκότος
ταραχὴν ὑπαχθέντας πολὺ μᾶλλον ἐκ τῶν προ-
ϋπηργμένων τοῖς ὑπ᾽ αὐτοῦ λεγομένοις πιστεύειν

¹ VRC: μὲν παρέχειν PA: παρέχειν ML.
520

Antiochus further inflamed their fury; for, thinking to furnish proof of his conversion and of his detestation of Jewish customs by sacrificing after the manner of the Greeks, he recommended that the rest should be compelled to do the same, as the conspirators would thus be exposed by their refusal. This test being applied by the Antiochenes, a few submitted and the recalcitrants were massacred. Antiochus, having next procured the aid of troops from the Roman general, domineered with severity over his Jewish fellow-citizens, not permitting them to repose on the seventh day, but compelling them to do everything exactly as on other days ; and so strictly did he enforce obedience that not only at Antioch was the weekly day of rest abolished, but the example having been started there spread for a short time to the other cities as well.

(4) Such being the misfortunes which the Jews of Antioch had at that time experienced, a second calamity now befell them, in endeavouring to describe which I was led to narrate the previous history. For a fire having broken out, which burnt down the market-square, the magistrates' quarters, the record-office and the basilicae,[a] and the flames having with difficulty been prevented from spreading with raging violence over the whole city, Antiochus accused the Jews of the deed. The Antiochenes, even had they not been previously embittered against them, would, in the commotion produced by the accident, have readily been misled by the calumny; much more, after what had previously occurred, were they now

The great fire at Antioch laid to their charge.

---

[a] Law-courts and Exchange in one.

[2] LC : ἀργὴν the rest.   [3] C : καὶ the rest.
[4] ἐπὶ τῆς] ἐπ’ PA.   [5] χαρτοφυλάκιον L Zon.
[6] PAL¹ : τάχιστα the rest.

παρεσκεύασεν, ὡς μόνον οὐκ αὐτοὺς τὸ πῦρ
57 ἐνιέμενον ὑπὸ τῶν Ἰουδαίων ἑωρακότας, καὶ
καθάπερ ἐμμανεῖς γεγενημένοι μετὰ πολλοῦ τινος
οἴστρου πάντες ἐπὶ τοὺς διαβεβλημένους ὥρμηντο.
58 μόλις δ᾽ αὐτῶν ἐδυνήθη τὰς ὁρμὰς ἐπισχεῖν
Γναῖος[1] Κολλήγας τις πρεσβευτής, ἀξιῶν ἐπι-
τρέψαι Καίσαρι δηλωθῆναι περὶ τῶν γεγονότων·
59 τὸν γὰρ ἡγεμονεύοντα τῆς Συρίας Καισέννιον
Παῖτον[2] ἤδη μὲν Οὐεσπασιανὸς ἐξαπεστάλκει,
60 συνέβαινε δὲ παρεῖναι μηδέπω. ποιούμενος δ᾽
ἐπιμελῆ τὴν ἀναζήτησιν[3] ὁ Κολλήγας ἐξεῦρε τὴν
ἀλήθειαν, καὶ τῶν μὲν τὴν αἰτίαν ὑπ᾽ Ἀντιόχου
λαβόντων Ἰουδαίων οὐδεὶς οὐδ᾽ ἐκοινώνησεν,
61 ἅπαν δὲ τοὖργον ἔπραξαν ἄνθρωποί τινες ἀλιτήριοι
διὰ χρεῶν ἀνάγκας νομίζοντες, εἰ τὴν ἀγορὰν
καὶ τὰ δημόσια καταπρήσειαν γράμματα, τῆς
62 ἀπαιτήσεως ἀπαλλαγὴν ἕξειν. Ἰουδαῖοι μὲν οὖν
ἐπὶ μετεώροις ταῖς αἰτίαις τὸ μέλλον ἔτι καραδοκοῦντες ἐν φόβοις χαλεποῖς ἀπεσάλευον.

63 (iv. 1) Τίτος δὲ Καῖσαρ τῆς περὶ τοῦ πατρὸς
ἀγγελίας αὐτῷ κομισθείσης, ὅτι πάσαις μὲν
ποθεινὸς ταῖς κατὰ τὴν Ἰταλίαν πόλεσιν ἐπῆλθεν,
μάλιστα δ᾽ ἡ Ῥώμη[4] μετὰ πολλῆς αὐτὸν ἐδέξατο
προθυμίας καὶ λαμπρότητος, εἰς πολλὴν χαρὰν
καὶ θυμηδίαν ἐτράπετο, τῶν περὶ αὐτοῦ φροντίδων
64 ὡς ἥδιστον ἦν ἀπηλλαγμένος. Οὐεσπασιανὸν γὰρ
ἔτι μὲν καὶ μακρὰν ἀπόντα πάντες οἱ κατὰ τὴν
Ἰταλίαν ἄνθρωποι ταῖς γνώμαις περιεῖπον ὡς
ἥκοντα, τὴν προσδοκίαν ἐκ τοῦ πάνυ θέλειν

---

[1] Bekker: νέος or νέος ὢν mss.: Ναῖος Niese (cf. A. xix.
166).   [2] Hudson: Πέτον mss.
[3] P: ζήτησιν the rest.   [4] Ῥωμαίων M.

inclined to believe the statements of Antiochus, and to imagine that they had all but seen with their own eyes the Jews setting fire to the town. And so, like maniacs, in a wild frenzy they all rushed upon the accused. With great difficulty Gnaeus Collega,[a] the deputy-governor, succeeded in restraining their fury, requesting permission to lay the facts before Caesar ; for as it happened, the governor of Syria, Caesennius Paetus,[b] already sent out by Vespasian, had not yet arrived. By careful investigation Collega then discovered the truth. Not one of the Jews incriminated by Antiochus had any part in the affair, the whole being the work of some scoundrels, who, under the pressure of debts, imagined that if they burnt the market-place and the public records they would be rid of all demands. The Jews, with these charges hanging over them and still anxiously awaiting the issue, were thus in troubled waters and in grave alarm.

(iv. 1) Meanwhile, Titus Caesar, having received news of the eagerness with which all the Italian cities had greeted his father's approach, and that Rome in particular had given him an enthusiastic and splendid reception, experienced heart-felt joy and satisfaction at this most agreeable relief from anxiety on his behalf. For even while Vespasian was still far off, all the Italians were paying respect to him in their hearts as if he were already come, mistaking, in their keen desire, their expectation of him for his actual *Enthusiastic reception of Vespasian in Rome.*

---

[a] Gn. Pompeius Collega, consul in A.D. 93 (Tac. *Agr.* 44).

[b] C. Caesennius Paetus, consul in 61, disgraced himself in a campaign against the Parthians in 63 and was deprived by Nero of his command ; as governor of Syria he made an inglorious attack on the innocent Antiochus, king of Commagene, described below, §§ 219 ff.

ἄφιξιν αὐτοῦ νομίζοντες καὶ πάσης ἀνάγκης
65 ἐλευθέραν τὴν πρὸς αὐτὸν ἔχοντες εὔνοιαν. τῇ
τε γὰρ βουλῇ κατὰ μνήμην τῶν γεγενημένων
ἐν ταῖς τῶν ἡγεμόνων μεταβολαῖς συμφορῶν
εὐκταῖον ἦν ἀπολαβεῖν ἡγεμόνα γήρως σεμνότητι
καὶ πράξεων ἀκμῇ πολεμικῶν κεκοσμημένον, ᾧ
τὴν ὑπεροχὴν πρὸς μόνην ἠπίσταντο τὴν τῶν
66 ἀρχομένων σωτηρίαν ἐσομένην. καὶ μὴν ὁ δῆμος
ὑπὸ τῶν ἐμφυλίων κακῶν τετρυχωμένος ἔτι
μᾶλλον ἐλθεῖν αὐτὸν ἔσπευδε, τότε δὴ βεβαίως
μὲν ἀπαλλαγήσεσθαι τῶν συμφορῶν ὑπολαμβάνων,
ἀπολήψεσθαι δὲ τὴν ἄδειαν μετὰ τῆς εὐετηρίας
67 πεπιστευκώς. ἐξαιρέτως δὲ τὸ στρατιωτικὸν εἰς
αὐτὸν ἀφεώρα· μάλιστα γὰρ οὗτοι τῶν κατωρθω-
μένων αὐτῷ πολέμων ἐγίνωσκον τὸ μέγεθος, τῆς
ἀπειρίας δὲ τῶν ἄλλων ἡγεμόνων καὶ τῆς ἀνανδρίας πεπειραμένοι πολλῆς μὲν αἰσχύνης αὐτοὺς
ἐπεθύμουν ἀπηλλάχθαι, τὸν μόνον δὲ καὶ σῴζειν
αὐτοὺς καὶ κοσμεῖν δυνάμενον ἀπολαβεῖν ηὔχοντο.
68 τοιαύτης δ' εὐνοίας ἐξ ἁπάντων ὑπαρχούσης τοῖς
μὲν κατὰ τὰς ἀξιώσεις προὔχουσι τῶν ἀνδρῶν
οὐκέτ' ἀνεκτὸν ἦν ἀναμένειν, ἀλλὰ πορρωτάτω
69 τῆς Ῥώμης αὐτῷ προεντυχεῖν ἔσπευδον. οὐ μὴν
οὐδὲ τῶν ἄλλων τις ἠνείχετο τῆς ἐντεύξεως τὴν
ἀναβολήν, ἀλλ' οὕτως ἐξεχέοντο πάντες ἀθρόοι
καὶ πᾶσιν εὐπορώτερον καὶ ῥᾷον ἐδόκει τοῦ
μένειν τὸ ἀπιέναι, ὡς καὶ τὴν πόλιν αὐτὴν τότε
πρῶτον ἐν ἑαυτῇ λαβεῖν ὀλιγανθρωπίας αἴσθησιν
ἤδειαν[1]· ἦσαν γὰρ ἐλάττους τῶν ἀπιόντων οἱ
70 μένοντες. ἐπεὶ δὲ προσιὼν ἠγγέλλετο, καὶ τὴν
ἡμερότητα τῆς ἐντεύξεως αὐτοῦ τὴν πρὸς ἑκάστους
ἐδήλουν οἱ προελθόντες,[2] ἅπαν ἤδη τὸ λοιπὸν

arrival. and exhibiting an affection for him wholly free from constraint. For to the Senate, mindful of the calamities undergone in the changes of their rulers,[a] nothing was more desirable than to gain once more an emperor adorned with the gravity of years and the finest fame for military achievements, whose exaltation they were assured would make only for the welfare of his subjects. The people, too, exhausted by civil disorders, were still more eager for his coming, expecting now at last to obtain permanent release from their miseries, and confident that security and prosperity would again be theirs. But above all the army had their eyes on him ; for they knew best the magnitude of the wars that he had won, and, having had proof of the inexperience and cowardice of the other emperors, longed to be rid of such deep disgrace and prayed that they might be granted him who alone could both bring them salvation and add lustre to their arms. Amidst such feelings of universal goodwill, those of higher rank, impatient of awaiting him, hastened to a great distance from Rome to be the first to greet him. Nor, indeed, could any of the rest endure the delay of meeting, but all poured forth in such crowds—for to all it seemed simpler and easier to go than to remain—that the very city then for the first time experienced with satisfaction a paucity of inhabitants; for those who went outnumbered those who remained. But when he was reported to be approaching and those who had gone ahead were telling of the affability of his reception of each party, the whole re-

[a] A.D. 68-69 was the year of the four emperors—Nero, Galba, Otho, Vitellius.

---

[1] Hudson after Lat. iucundam : ἰδίαν MSS.

[2] L Lat. : προσελθόντες the rest.

πλῆθος ἅμα γυναιξὶ καὶ παισὶν ἐπὶ ταῖς παρόδοις
71 ἐξεδέχετο, καὶ καθ' οὓς γένοιτο παριὼν οὗτοι
πρὸς τὴν ἡδονὴν τῆς θέας καὶ τὸ μειλίχιον αὐτοῦ
τῆς ὄψεως παντοίας ἠφίεσαν φωνάς, τὸν εὐεργέτην
καὶ σωτῆρα καὶ μόνον ἄξιον ἡγεμόνα τῆς Ῥώμης
ἀνακαλοῦντες· ἅπασα δ' ἡ πόλις ὡς νεὼς ἦν
72 στεφανωμάτων καὶ θυμιαμάτων ἀνάπλεως. μόλις
δ' ὑπὸ πλήθους τῶν περὶ αὐτὸν ἱσταμένων δυνη-
θεὶς εἰς τὸ βασίλειον ἐλθεῖν, αὐτὸς μὲν τοῖς ἔνδον
θεοῖς θυσίας τῆς ἀφίξεως χαριστηρίους ἐπετέλει,
73 τρέπεται¹ δὲ τὰ πλήθη πρὸς εὐωχίαν καὶ κατὰ
φυλὰς καὶ γένη καὶ γειτονίας ποιούμενοι τὰς
ἑστιάσεις ηὔχοντο τῷ θεῷ σπένδοντες αὐτόν τ'
ἐπὶ πλεῖστον χρόνον Οὐεσπασιανὸν ἐπιμεῖναι τῇ
Ῥωμαίων ἡγεμονίᾳ, καὶ παισὶν αὐτοῦ καὶ τοῖς ἐξ
ἐκείνων ἀεὶ γινομένοις φυλαχθῆναι τὸ κράτος
74 ἀνανταγώνιστον. ἡ μὲν οὖν Ῥωμαίων πόλις
οὕτως Οὐεσπασιανὸν ἐκδεξαμένη προθύμως εὐθὺς
εἰς πολλὴν εὐδαιμονίαν ἐπεδίδου.
75   (2) Πρὸ δὲ τούτων τῶν χρόνων, ἐν οἷς Οὐεσπασιανὸς μὲν περὶ Ἀλεξάνδρειαν ἦν, Τίτος δὲ
τῇ τῶν Ἱεροσολύμων προσήδρευε πολιορκίᾳ,
76 πολὺ μέρος Γερμανῶν ἐκινήθη πρὸς ἀπόστασιν, οἷς
καὶ Γαλατῶν οἱ πλησίον² συμφρονήσαντες κοινῇ
μεγάλας ἐλπίδας αὐτοῖς συνέθεσαν ὡς καὶ τῆς
77 Ῥωμαίων ἀπαλλαξόμενοι δεσποτείας. ἐπῆρε δὲ

---

¹ προτρέπεται PAM.   ² πλεῖστοι PAM¹.

ᵃ The story of this revolt is narrated at length by Tacitus,
Hist. iv. 12-37, 54-79, v. 14-26 (where the *History* breaks off).
The German leader, Julius Civilis, at the head of the Batavians,

maining population, with wives and children, were by now waiting at the road-sides to receive him ; and each group as he passed, in their delight at the spectacle and moved by the blandness of his appearance, gave vent to all manner of cries, hailing him as "benefactor," "saviour," and "only worthy emperor of Rome." The whole city, moreover, was filled, like a temple, with garlands and incense. Having reached the palace, though with difficulty, owing to the multitude that thronged around him, he offered sacrifices of thanksgiving for his arrival to the household gods. The crowds then betook themselves to festivity and, keeping feast by tribes and families and neighbourhoods, with libations prayed God that Vespasian might himself long be spared to the Roman empire, and that the sovereignty might be preserved unchallenged for his sons and their descendants throughout successive generations. And, indeed, the city of Rome, after this cordial reception of Vespasian, rapidly advanced to great prosperity.

(2) However, before this period, while Vespasian was at Alexandria and Titus occupied with the siege of Jerusalem, a large portion of the Germans had been incited to revolt ; and the neighbouring Gauls, sharing their aspirations, conceived, in partnership with them, high hopes of release from Roman domination.[a] The Germans were instigated to

A revolt of Germans and Gauls

who occupied the Delta of the Rhine, began by playing for Vespasian, but after the defeat of Vitellius (October 69 A.D.) ended by playing for himself. His Gallic associate, Julius Classicus, a distinguished nobleman of the Treveri, aspired to set up an *imperium Galliarum*. "The Batavians and the Gauls had a common interest in their hostility to Rome, and so far they co-operated ; but Civilis had nothing to do with the *imperium Galliarum* " (Bury).

τοὺς Γερμανοὺς ἅψασθαι τῆς ἀποστάσεως καὶ
τὸν πόλεμον ἐξενεγκεῖν πρώτη μὲν ἡ φύσις οὖσα
λογισμῶν ἔρημος ἀγαθῶν καὶ μετὰ μικρᾶς ἐλπίδος
78 ἑτοίμως ῥιψοκίνδυνος· ἔπειτα δὲ καὶ μῖσος τὸ
πρὸς τοὺς κρατοῦντας, ἐπεὶ μόνοις ἴσασι Ῥωμαίοις τὸ γένος αὐτῶν δουλεύειν βεβιασμένον.
οὐ μὴν ἀλλὰ μάλιστά γε πάντων ὁ καιρὸς αὐτοῖς
79 θάρσος ἐνεποίησεν· ὁρῶντες γὰρ τὴν Ῥωμαίων
ἀρχὴν ταῖς συνεχέσι τῶν αὐτοκρατόρων ἀλλαγαῖς
ἐν ἑαυτῇ τεταραγμένην, πᾶν τε μέρος τῆς ὑπ᾽
αὐτοῖς οἰκουμένης πυνθανόμενοι μετέωρον εἶναι
καὶ κραδαίνεσθαι, τοῦτον σφίσιν αὐτοῖς ἄριστον
ὑπὸ τῆς ἐκείνων κακοπραγίας καὶ στάσεως καιρὸν
80 ᾠήθησαν παραδεδόσθαι. ἐνῆγον δὲ τὸ βούλευμα
καὶ ταύταις αὐτοὺς ταῖς ἐλπίσιν ἐτύφουν Κλασσικός
τις καὶ Κιουίλιος[1] τῶν παρ᾽ αὐτοῖς [ὄντες][2]
81 ἡγεμόνων, οἳ δῆλον μὲν ὡς ἐκ μακροῦ ταύτης
ἐφίεντο τῆς νεωτεροποιίας, ὑπὸ τοῦ καιροῦ δὲ
θαρσῆσαι προαχθέντες τὴν αὐτῶν γνώμην ἐξ-
έφηναν· ἔμελλον δὲ προθύμως διακειμένοις τὴν
82 πεῖραν τοῖς πλήθεσι προσφέρειν. πολλοῦ δὲ μέρους
ἤδη τῶν Γερμανῶν τὴν ἀποστασίαν ἀνωμολογη-
κότος καὶ τῶν ἄλλων οὐκ ἄνδιχα φρονησάντων,
ὥσπερ ἐκ δαιμονίου προνοίας Οὐεσπασιανὸς πέμ-

---

[1] Gelenius : Οὐίτιλλος mss.   [2] om. P.

attempt this insurrection and to declare war, in
the first place, by their natural disposition, which is
devoid of sound judgement and ready to rush into
danger with but slight hope of success [a]; secondly,
by hatred of their conquerors, knowing that none
but the Romans have reduced their race to servitude.
But what most of all inspired them with confidence
was this golden opportunity. For seeing the Roman
empire internally disordered through the continuous
change of its masters, and hearing that every quarter
of the world beneath their sway was seething and
quivering with excitement, they thought that an
excellent opportunity was here presented to themselves by their enemy's disasters and dissensions.[b]
The scheme was fostered and the nation inflated
with these crazy expectations by a certain Classicus
and Civilis, leading men among them, who had
notoriously long been meditating this rebellion, and
who were now emboldened by the occasion to
disclose their plans and were to test the mettle of
those masses so eager for rebellion. A large
section of the Germans was, accordingly, already
committed to the revolt, and their views had met
with no opposition from the rest, when Vespasian,
as if by the guidance of providence, dispatched

[a] *Cf.* the description of Tacitus : " si civitas, in qua orti
sunt, longa pace et otio torpeat, plerique nobilium adoles-
centium petunt ultro eas nationes, quae tum bellum aliquod
gerunt, quia et ingrata genti quies, et facilius inter ancipitia
clarescunt," *Germ.* 14.
[b] Tac. *Hist.* iv. 54, adds a further reason for the enemy's
elation : " Galli sustulerant animos, eandem ubique exer-
cituum nostrorum fortunam rati . . . sed nihil aeque quam
incendium Capitolii, ut finem imperio adesse crederent,
inpulerat."

πει γράμματα Πετιλίῳ[1] Κερεαλίῳ τὸ[2] πρότερον
ἡγεμόνι Γερμανίας γενομένῳ, τὴν ὕπατον διδοὺς
τιμὴν καὶ κελεύων ἄρξοντα Βρεττανίας ἀπιέναι.
83 πορευόμενος οὖν ἐκεῖνος ὅποι προσετέτακτο καὶ
τὰ περὶ τὴν ἀπόστασιν τῶν Γερμανῶν πυθόμενος,
ἤδη συνειλεγμένοις αὐτοῖς ἐπιπεσὼν καὶ παραταξάμενος πολύ τε πλῆθος αὐτῶν ἀναιρεῖ κατὰ
τὴν μάχην καὶ τῆς ἀνοίας παυσαμένους ἠνάγκασε
84 σωφρονεῖν. ἔμελλον δὲ κἀκείνου μὴ θᾶττον εἰς
τοὺς τόπους παραβαλόντος δίκην οὐκ εἰς μακρὰν
85 ὑφέξειν· ἡνίκα γὰρ πρῶτον ἡ τῆς ἀποστάσεως
αὐτῶν ἀγγελία τῇ Ῥώμῃ προσέπεσε, Δομετιανὸς
Καῖσαρ πυθόμενος οὐχ ὡς ἂν ἕτερος ἐν τούτῳ
τῆς ἡλικίας, νέος γὰρ ἦν ἔτι παντάπασιν, τηλικοῦτον ἄρασθαι μέγεθος πραγμάτων ὤκνησεν,
86 ἔχων δὲ πατρόθεν ἔμφυτον τὴν ἀνδραγαθίαν καὶ
τελειοτέραν τὴν ἄσκησιν τῆς ἡλικίας πεποιημένος
87 ἐπὶ τοὺς βαρβάρους εὐθὺς ἤλαυνεν. οἱ δὲ πρὸς
τὴν φήμην τῆς ἐφόδου καταπεσόντες ἐπ' αὐτῷ
σφᾶς αὐτοὺς ἐποιήσαντο μέγα[3] τοῦ φόβου κέρδος
εὑράμενοι τὸ χωρὶς συμφορῶν ὑπὸ τὸν αὐτὸν
88 πάλιν ζυγὸν ὑπαχθῆναι. πᾶσιν οὖν ἐπιθεὶς τοῖς
περὶ τὴν Γαλατίαν τάξιν τὴν προσήκουσαν Δο-
μετιανός, ὡς μηδ' αὖθις ἄν ποτε ῥᾳδίως ἔτι τἀκεῖ
ταραχθῆναι, λαμπρὸς καὶ περίβλεπτος ἐπὶ κρείτ-

---

[1] Lat. : Βεντιδίῳ mss.   [2] PM : τῷ the rest.
[3] M : μετὰ the rest.

---

[a] Q. Petilius Cerealis, a near relative of Vespasian, and an
energetic but rash commander, had been defeated in A.D. 61
by the Britons under Boadicea. Espousing Vespasian's
claim to the Empire in 69, he suffered another defeat beneath

letters to Petilius Cerealius,[a] previously in command in Germany, conferring upon him consular dignity and instructing him to set out to take over the governorship of Britain.[b] He, while proceeding accordingly to his appointed sphere, heard of the revolt of the Germans, fell upon them just when their forces were united, and, having in a pitched battle slain masses of them, forced them to abandon their folly and learn prudence. But, even had Cerealius not so promptly visited the spot, they were doomed ere long to suffer chastisement. For as soon as the news of their rebellion reached Rome, Domitian Caesar, on hearing of it, hesitated not, as another at his age might have done—for he was still a mere stripling—to shoulder such a burden of responsibility. Inheriting by nature his father's prowess and blessed with a training beyond his years, he forthwith marched off against the barbarians. Their hearts failing them at the rumour of his approach, they threw themselves on his mercy, finding it a highly advantageous relief from their terror to be again reduced under the same yoke without experiencing disaster. Domitian having therefore duly settled all affairs in Gaul, so as to prevent any disorder in future from lightly recurring in that quarter, returned to Rome, with brilliant honours

is crushed by Cerealius

and Domitian.

the walls of Rome. His success in crushing the German and Gallic revolt was, according to Tacitus, not so rapid and unchequered as it is here represented by Josephus. Sent as consular legate, c. A.D. 71-72, to the government of Britain, he was successful in defeating the Brigantes and called out the talents of Agricola. (Tac. *Agr.* 8. 17.)

[b] Tacitus does not mention the previous command in Germany or the instruction given at this juncture to proceed to Britain.

τοσι μὲν τῆς ἡλικίας, πρέπουσι δὲ τῷ πατρὶ
κατορθώμασιν εἰς τὴν Ῥώμην ἀνέζευξε.

89 (3) Τῇ δὲ προειρημένῃ Γερμανῶν ἀποστάσει
κατὰ τὰς αὐτὰς ἡμέρας καὶ Σκυθικὸν τόλμημα
90 πρὸς Ῥωμαίους συνέδραμεν. οἱ γὰρ καλούμενοι
Σκυθῶν Σαρμάται, πολὺ πλῆθος ὄντες, ἄδηλοι
μὲν τὸν Ἴστρον ἐπεραιώθησαν εἰς τὴν ἐπιτάδε,
πολλῇ δὲ βίᾳ καὶ χαλεποὶ διὰ τὸ παντάπασιν
ἀνέλπιστον τῆς ἐφόδου προσπεσόντες πολλοὺς
μὲν τῶν ἐπὶ τῆς φρουρᾶς Ῥωμαίων ἀναιροῦσι,
91 καὶ τὸν πρεσβευτὴν τὸν ὑπατικὸν Φοντήιον[1]
Ἀγρίππαν ὑπαντιάσαντα [καὶ][2] καρτερῶς μαχό-
μενον κτείνουσι, τὴν δ' ὑποκειμένην χώραν
ἅπασαν κατέτρεχον ἄγοντες καὶ φέροντες ὅτῳ
92 περιπέσοιεν. Οὐεσπασιανὸς δὲ τὰ γεγενημένα καὶ
τὴν πόρθησιν τῆς Μυσίας πυθόμενος Ῥούβριον[3]
Γάλλον ἐκπέμπει δίκην ἐπιθήσοντα τοῖς Σαρμάταις.
93 ὑφ' οὗ πολλοὶ μὲν αὐτῶν ἐν ταῖς μάχαις ἀπέθανον,
τὸ δὲ περισωθὲν μετὰ δέους εἰς τὴν οἰκείαν
94 διέφυγεν. τοῦτο[4] δὲ τῷ πολέμῳ τέλος ἐπιθεὶς
ὁ στρατηγὸς καὶ τῆς εἰς τὸ μέλλον ἀσφαλείας
προυνόησε· πλείοσι γὰρ καὶ μείζοσι φυλακαῖς

---

[1] *ed. pr.*: Φροντήιον mss. : Pompeium Lat.
[2] om. VRC.
[3] Lat. : Γούβριον mss.   [4] P: τούτῳ the rest.

---

[a] Josephus, the client of the Flavians, clearly exaggerates
the share of Domitian in this campaign. Tacitus, *Hist.* iv.
85 f. gives a different story. The victory was won when
Domitian, with Mucianus, reached Lugdunum ; " unde
creditur Domitianus occultis ad Cerialem nuntiis fidem eius
temptavisse, an praesenti sibi exercitum imperiumque

and universally admired for achievements surpassing his age and befitting his father.[a]

(3) Simultaneously with the above mentioned revolt of the Germans a daring Scythian outbreak against the Romans took place.[b] For the Scythian people called Sarmatians, a very numerous tribe, stealthily crossed the Ister[c] to its hither bank, and, falling upon the Romans with great violence, the more formidable because their attack was utterly unexpected, slew large numbers of the Roman guards, and among them the consular legate, Fonteius Agrippa,[d] who advanced to meet them and died fighting gallantly; they then overran all the territory to the south, harrying and plundering whatever fell in their way. Vespasian, on hearing of what had taken place and of the devastation of Moesia, dispatched Rubrius Gallus[e] to punish the Sarmatians. By him multitudes of them were slain in the ensuing battles, and the survivors fled in terror to their own country. The general, having thus brought the war to a conclusion, further took precautions for future security by posting more numerous and

Simultaneous invasion of Moesia by the Sarmatians.

traditurus foret." Slighted by the older officers, Domitian withdrew into seclusion.

[b] Josephus seems to be the sole authority for the events described in this section. Tacitus, *Hist.* iv. 54, merely alludes to a rumour of such an invasion as one of the incitements to the Gauls to join Civilis in revolt : " vulgato rumore a Sarmatis Dacisque Moesica ac Pannonica hiberna circumsederi ; paria de Britannis fingebantur."

[c] The *Danube.*

[d] Proconsular governor of the province of Asia in A.D. 69, he had been recalled in 70 to take command of Moesia (Tac. *Hist.* iii. 46).

[e] The part taken by him in the war of Otho against Vitellius and in subsequent events is mentioned by Tacitus, *Hist.* ii. 51, 99.

τὸν τόπον[1] διέλαβεν, ὡς εἶναι τοῖς βαρβάροις τὴν
95 διάβασιν τελέως ἀδύνατον. ὁ μὲν οὖν περὶ τὴν
Μυσίαν πόλεμος ταχεῖαν οὕτως ἔλαβε τὴν κρίσιν.
96 (v. 1) Τίτος δὲ Καῖσαρ χρόνον μέν τινα δι-
έτριβεν ἐν Βηρυτῷ, καθὰ προειρήκαμεν, ἐκεῖθεν
δ᾽ ἀναζεύξας καὶ δι᾽ ὧν ᾔει πόλεων τῆς Συρίας
ἐν πάσαις θεωρίας τε συντελῶν πολυτελεῖς καὶ
τῶν Ἰουδαίων τοὺς αἰχμαλώτους[2] εἰς ἐπίδειξιν
τῆς ἑαυτῶν ἀπωλείας ἀποχρώμενος, θεᾶται κατὰ
97 τὴν πορείαν ποταμοῦ φύσιν ἀξίαν ἱστορηθῆναι. ῥεῖ
μὲν γὰρ μέσος Ἀρκέας τῆς Ἀγρίππα βασιλείας
καὶ Ῥαφαναίας, ἔχει δὲ θαυμαστὴν ἰδιότητα·
98 πολὺς γὰρ ὤν, ὅτε ῥεῖ, καὶ κατὰ τὴν φορὰν οὐ
σχολαῖος, ἔπειτα δὲ πᾶς ἐκ τῶν πηγῶν ἐπιλείπων
ἐξ ἡμερῶν ἀριθμὸν ξηρὸν παραδίδωσιν ὁρᾶν τὸν
99 τόπον· εἶθ᾽ ὥσπερ οὐδεμιᾶς γενομένης μεταβολῆς
ὅμοιος κατὰ τὴν ἑβδόμην ἐκδίδωσι, καὶ ταύτην
ἀεὶ τὴν τάξιν ἀκριβῶς τετήρηται διαφυλάττων·
ὅθεν δὴ καὶ Σαββατικὸν αὐτὸν κεκλήκασιν ἀπὸ
τῆς ἱερᾶς τῶν Ἰουδαίων ἑβδόμης οὕτως ὀνομά-
σαντες.
100 (2) Ὁ δὲ τῶν Ἀντιοχέων δῆμος ἐπεὶ πλησίον
ὄντα Τίτον ἐπυνθάνοντο, μένειν μὲν ἐντὸς τειχῶν
ὑπὸ χαρᾶς οὐχ ὑπέμενον, ἔσπευδον δ᾽ ἐπὶ τὴν

---

[1] πόταμον Destinon.
[2] τοὺς αἰχμαλώτους P (cf. v. 36): τοῖς αἰχμαλώτοις the rest.

---

[a] § 39. [b] Beirut.
[c] Arka, at the northern extremity of the Lebanon range,
N.E. of Tripolis ("Ἄρκην τὴν ἐν τῷ Λιβάνῳ A. i. 138); " the
Arkite " appears already in Gen. x. 17.
[d] Part of the additional territory conferred by Vespasian
upon Agrippa II in reward for his loyalty during the war;
not mentioned as part of his realm in B. iii. 56 f., probably

stronger garrisons throughout the district, so as to render the passage of the river totally impossible to the barbarians. The war in Moesia was thus speedily decided.

(v. 1) Titus Caesar, as we have already mentioned,[a] stayed for some time at Berytus.[b] Departing thence, he exhibited costly spectacles in all the cities of Syria through which he passed, making his Jewish captives serve to display their own destruction. In the course of his march he saw a river, the nature of which deserves record. It runs between Arcea,[c] a town within Agrippa's realm,[d] and Raphanea,[e] and has an astonishing peculiarity. For, when it flows, it is a copious stream with a current far from sluggish ; then all at once its sources fail and for the space of six days it presents the spectacle of a dry bed ; again, as though no change had occurred, it pours forth on the seventh day just as before. And it has always been observed to keep strictly to this order ; whence they have called it the Sabbatical river, so naming it after the sacred seventh day of the Jews.[f]

(2) The people of Antioch, on hearing that Titus was at hand, through joy could not bear to remain within their walls, but hastened to meet him and

<table>
<tr><td></td><td>Titus visits the "Sabbatical" river.</td></tr>
<tr><td></td><td>Titus at Antioch refuses the local petition to expel the Jews.</td></tr>
</table>

because Josephus there confines himself to regions with Jewish residents, Schürer, G.J.V. (ed. 3 and 4) i. 594 f.

[e] § 18.

[f] It is curious that the Jewish historian represents the river as a sabbath-breaker, working on one day in seven ; while the pagan Pliny makes it strictly sabbatarian : " in Iudea rivus sabbatis omnibus siccatur " N.H. xxxi. 11. The missionary, Dr. W. M. Thomson, claims to have identified this river in 1840 with the Neba el Fuarr " now quiescent two days and active on a part of the third." For the explanation of these intermitting fountains as " merely the draining of subterranean reservoirs of water, on the principle of the siphon " see his The Land and the Book 264 f.

101 ὑπάντησιν· καὶ τριάκοντα σταδίων ἐπὶ πλέον
προῆλθον οὐκ ἄνδρες μόνον ἀλλὰ καὶ γυναικῶν
102 πλῆθος ἅμα παισὶ τῆς πόλεως ἐκχεόμενοι. κά-
πειδήπερ ἐθεάσαντο προσιόντα, παρὰ τὴν ὁδὸν
ἑκατέρωθεν καταστάντες τάς τε δεξιὰς προύτεινον
προσαγορεύοντες καὶ παντοίοις ἐπιφημίσμασι
103 χρώμενοι συνυπέστρεφον· συνεχὴς δ' ἦν αὐτῶν
παρὰ πάσας ἅμα τὰς εὐφημίας δέησις ἐκβαλεῖν
104 τῆς πόλεως τοὺς Ἰουδαίους. Τίτος μὲν οὖν
οὐδὲν ἐνέδωκεν πρὸς ταύτην τὴν δέησιν, ἀλλ'
ἡσυχῇ τῶν λεγομένων ἐπήκουεν· ἐπ' ἀδήλῳ δὲ
τῷ τί φρονεῖ καὶ τί ποιήσει πολὺς καὶ χαλεπὸς
105 τοῖς Ἰουδαίοις ὁ φόβος ἦν· οὐδὲ γὰρ ὑπέμεινεν
ἐν Ἀντιοχείᾳ Τίτος, ἀλλ' εὐθὺς ἐπὶ τὸ Ζεῦγμα
τὸ κατὰ τὸν Εὐφράτην συνέτεινε τὴν πορείαν,
ἔνθα δὴ καὶ παρὰ τοῦ Πάρθων βασιλέως Βολογέσου
πρὸς αὐτὸν ἧκον στέφανον χρυσοῦν ἐπὶ τῇ κατὰ
106 τῶν Ἰουδαίων νίκῃ κομίζοντες. ὃν δεξάμενος
εἱστία τοὺς βασιλικούς, κἀκεῖθεν εἰς τὴν Ἀντιό-
107 χειαν ἐπανέρχεται. τῆς δὲ βουλῆς καὶ τοῦ δήμου
τῶν Ἀντιοχέων πολλὰς ποιησαμένων δεήσεις
ἐλθεῖν εἰς τὸ θέατρον αὐτόν, ἐν ᾧ πᾶν τὸ πλῆθος
ἠθροισμένον ἐξεδέχετο, φιλανθρώπως ὑπήκουσε.
108 πάλιν δ' αὐτῶν σφόδρα λιπαρῶς ἐγκειμένων καὶ
συνεχῶς δεομένων ἐξελάσαι τῆς πόλεως τοὺς
Ἰουδαίους, εὔστοχον ἐποιήσατο τὴν ἀπόκρισιν,
109 εἰπών " ἀλλ' ἥ γε πατρὶς αὐτῶν, εἰς ἣν ἐκβαλεῖν
ἐχρῆν ὄντας Ἰουδαίους, ἀνῄρηται, καὶ δέξαιτ'
110 ἂν οὐδεὶς αὐτοὺς ἔτι τόπος." ἐπὶ δευτέραν οὖν
Ἀντιοχεῖς τρέπονται δέησιν τῆς προτέρας ἀπο-
στάντες· τὰς γὰρ χαλκᾶς ἠξίουν δέλτους ἀνελεῖν
αὐτόν, ἐν αἷς γέγραπται τὰ δικαιώματα τῶν

advanced to a distance of over thirty furlongs, not only men, but a crowd of women and children also, streaming out from the city. And when they beheld him approaching, they lined the road on either side and greeted him with extended arms, and invoking all manner of blessings upon him returned in his train; but all their acclamations were accompanied by a running petition to expel the Jews from the town. Titus, unmoved by this petition, listened in silence to what was said; but the Jews, uncertain as to his opinion and intentions, were kept in deep and distressing alarm. For Titus, making no stay at Antioch, at once pushed on to Zeugma [a] on the Euphrates, where a deputation from Bologeses,[b] king of Parthia, waited upon him, bringing him a golden crown in recognition of his victory over the Jews. Having accepted this and provided a banquet for the king's messengers, he returned thence to Antioch. The senate and people of that city having earnestly besought him to visit their theatre, where the whole population was assembled to receive him, he graciously assented. Once more they persistently pressed and continuously entreated him to expel the Jews from the city, to which he pertinently replied : " But their own country to which, as Jews, they ought in that case to be banished, has been destroyed, and no other place would now receive them." So relinquishing their first request the Antiochenes turned to a second, petitioning him to remove the brazen tablets on which were inscribed the privileges

[a] On the right bank of the upper Euphrates, in the region of Samosata ; it took its name from its bridge of boats.
[b] Vologeses I (= Arsaces XXIII) ; cf. §§ 237, 242.

111 Ἰουδαίων. οὐ μὴν οὐδὲ τοῦτο Τίτος ἐπένευσεν
αὐτοῖς, ἀλλ' ἐάσας πάντα κατὰ χώραν τοῖς ἐπ'
Ἀντιοχείας Ἰουδαίοις ὡς πρότερον εἶχον εἰς
112 Αἴγυπτον ἀπηλλάττετο. καὶ κατὰ τὴν πορείαν
τοῖς Ἱεροσολύμοις προσελθὼν καὶ τὴν λυπρὰν
ἐρημίαν βλεπομένην ἀντιτιθεὶς τῇ ποτε τῆς
πόλεως λαμπρότητι, καὶ τὸ μέγεθος τῶν ἐρ-
ρηγμένων κατασκευασμάτων καὶ τὸ πάλαι κάλλος
εἰς μνήμην βαλλόμενος, ᾤκτειρε τῆς πόλεως
113 τὸν ὄλεθρον, οὐχ ὥσπερ [ἄλλος]¹ ἄν τις αὐχῶν
ὅτι τηλικαύτην οὖσαν καὶ τοσαύτην εἷλε κατὰ
κράτος, ἀλλὰ πολλάκις ἐπαρώμενος τοῖς αἰτίοις
τῆς ἀποστάσεως ὑπάρξασι καὶ ταύτην ἐπὶ τῇ
πόλει τὴν τιμωρίαν γενέσθαι παρασκευάσασιν·
οὕτως ἔκδηλος ἦν οὐκ ἂν θελήσας ἐκ τῆς συμφορᾶς τῶν κολασθέντων γενέσθαι τῆς ἀρετῆς
114 τὴν ἐπιφάνειαν. τοῦ δὲ πολλοῦ πλούτου τῆς
πόλεως ἔτι κἂν τοῖς ἐρειπίοις οὐκ ὀλίγον μέρος
115 ἀνηυρίσκετο· τὰ μὲν γὰρ πολλὰ ἀνέσκαπτον οἱ
Ῥωμαῖοι, τὰ πλείω δ' ἐκ μηνύσεως τῶν αἰχμαλώτων ἀνηροῦντο,² χρυσόν τε καὶ ἄργυρον καὶ
τῆς ἄλλης τὰ τιμιώτατα κατασκευῆς, ἅπερ οἱ
κεκτημένοι πρὸς τὰς ἀδήλους τοῦ πολέμου τύχας
κατὰ γῆς ἀποτεθησαυρίκεσαν.

116   (3) Τίτος δὲ τὴν προκειμένην ποιούμενος πορείαν
ἐπ' Αἰγύπτου³ καὶ τὴν ἔρημον ᾗ τάχιστα διανύσας
117 ἧκεν εἰς Ἀλεξάνδρειαν, καὶ πλεῖν ἐπὶ τῆς Ἰταλίας
διεγνωκὼς δυοῖν αὐτῷ ταγμάτων συνηκολουθηκό-
των ἑκάτερον ὅθενπερ ἀφῖκτο πάλιν ἀπέστειλεν,
εἰς μὲν τὴν Μυσίαν τὸ πέμπτον, εἰς Παννονίαν
118 δὲ τὸ πεντεκαιδέκατον. τῶν αἰχμαλώτων δὲ
τοὺς μὲν ἡγεμόνας Σίμωνα καὶ Ἰωάννην, τὸν δ'⁴

of the Jews. But this, too, Titus refused, and, leaving the status of the Jews of Antioch exactly as it was before, he set out for Egypt. On his way he visited Jerusalem, and contrasting the sorry scene of desolation before his eyes with the former splendour of the city, and calling to mind the grandeur of its ruined buildings and their pristine beauty, he commiserated its destruction ; not boasting, as another might have done, of having carried so glorious and great a city by storm, but heaping curses upon the criminal authors of the revolt, who had brought this chastisement upon it : so plainly did he show that he could never have wished that the calamities attending their punishment should enhance his own deserts. Of the vast wealth of the city no small portion was still being discovered among the ruins. Much of this the Romans dug up, but the greater part they became possessed of through the information of the prisoners, gold and silver and other most precious articles, which the owners in view of the uncertain fortunes of war had stored underground. *He revisits Jerusalem*

(3) Titus, now proceeding on his projected march to Egypt, traversed the desert with all possible dispatch and reached Alexandria. Here, having determined to sail for Italy, he dismissed to their respective former stations the two legions which had accompanied him,[a] the fifth to Moesia, the fifteenth to Pannonia. Of the prisoners, the leaders, Simon and John, together with seven hundred of the rank *en route for Egypt.*

[a] § 19.

---

[1] om. PA.
[2] ἀνηύρισκον PAM : auferebant Lat.
[3] Niese : Αἴγυπτον MSS.   [4] Niese : τ' (or τε) MSS.

ἄλλον ἀριθμὸν ἑπτακοσίους ἄνδρας ἐπιλέξας μεγέθει τε καὶ κάλλει σωμάτων, ὑπερβάλλοντας,
προσέταξεν εἰς τὴν Ἰταλίαν αὐτίκα μάλα κομί-
ζεσθαι, βουλόμενος αὐτοὺς ἐν τῷ θριάμβῳ παρ-
119 αγαγεῖν. τοῦ πλοῦ δ᾽ αὐτῷ κατὰ νοῦν ἀνυσθέντος
ὁμοίως μὲν ἡ Ῥώμη περὶ τὴν ὑποδοχὴν εἶχε καὶ
τὰς ὑπαντήσεις ὥσπερ ἐπὶ τοῦ πατρός, λαμπρότερον δ᾽ ἦν Τίτῳ καὶ αὐτὸς ὁ πατὴρ ὑπαντῶν
120 καὶ δεχόμενος. τῷ δὲ πλήθει τῶν πολιτῶν
δαιμόνιόν τινα τὴν χαρὰν παρεῖχε τὸ βλέπειν
121 αὐτοὺς ἤδη τοὺς τρεῖς ἐν ταὐτῷ γεγονότας. οὐ
πολλῶν δ᾽ ἡμερῶν διελθουσῶν ἕνα καὶ κοινὸν
ἔγνωσαν τὸν ἐπὶ τοῖς κατορθωμένοις ποιήσασθαι
θρίαμβον, καίπερ ἑκατέρῳ τῆς βουλῆς ἴδιον ψηφι-
122 σαμένης. προδιασαφηθείσης δὲ τῆς ἡμέρας ἐφ᾽
ἧς ἔμελλεν ἡ πομπὴ γενήσεσθαι τῶν ἐπινικίων,
οὐδεὶς οἴκοι καταλέλειπτο τῆς ἀμέτρου πληθύος
ἐν τῇ πόλει, πάντες δ᾽ ὅπη καὶ στῆναι μόνον ἦν
οἷόν ⟨τε⟩[1] προεληλυθότες τοὺς τόπους κατειλή-
φεσαν, ὅσον τοῖς ὀφθησομένοις μόνον εἰς πάροδον
ἀναγκαίαν καταλιπόντες.
123 (4) Τοῦ δὲ στρατιωτικοῦ παντὸς ἔτι νύκτωρ
κατὰ λόχους καὶ τάξεις ὑπὸ τοῖς ἡγεμόσι δι-
εξωδευκότος καὶ περὶ θύρας ὄντος οὐ τῶν ἄνω
βασιλείων ἀλλὰ πλησίον τοῦ τῆς Ἴσιδος ἱεροῦ,
ἐκεῖ γὰρ ἀνεπαύοντο τῆς νυκτὸς ἐκείνης οἱ
124 αὐτοκράτορες, περὶ αὐτὴν ἀρχομένην ἤδη τὴν
ἕω πρόιασιν Οὐεσπασιανὸς καὶ Τίτος δάφνη μὲν
ἐστεφανωμένοι, πορφυρᾶς δ᾽ ἐσθῆτας πατρίους

[1] ins. Herwerden.

and file, whom he had selected as remarkable for their stature and beauty, he ordered to be instantly conveyed to Italy, wishing to produce them at the triumph. After a voyage as favourable as he could His arrival have desired, Rome gave him such a reception and welcome as it had given to his father;[a] but with the added lustre that Titus was met and received by his father himself. The crowd of citizens was thus afforded an ecstasy of joy by the sight of the three princes[b] now united. Before many days had elapsed they decided to celebrate their achievements by one triumph in common, though the senate had decreed a separate triumph to each. Previous notice having been given of the day on which the pageant of victory would take place, not a soul among that countless host in the city was left at home : all issued forth and occupied every position where it was but possible to stand, leaving only room for the necessary passage of those upon whom they were to gaze.

(4) The military, while night still reigned, had all The marched out in companies and divisions, under their morning commanders, and been drawn up, not round the triumph. doors of the upper palace,[c] but near the temple of Isis[d] ; for there the emperors[e] reposed that night. At the break of dawn, Vespasian and Titus issued forth, crowned with laurel and clad in the traditional

[a] §§ 63 ff.
[b] Including Domitian.
[c] On the Palatine hill.
[d] The temple of Isis and Serapis, in the Campus Martius, near the present Collegio Romano ; destroyed by fire in A.D. 80, along with most of the buildings on the Campus Martius.
[e] Or rather *imperatores* in the sense of victorious generals.

ἀμπεχόμενοι, καὶ παρίασιν εἰς τοὺς Ὀκταουίας
125 περιπάτους· ἐνταῦθα γὰρ ἥ τε βουλὴ καὶ τὰ τέλη
τῶν ἀρχόντων οἵ τε ἀπὸ τῶν τιμημάτων ἱππεῖς
126 τὴν ἄφιξιν αὐτῶν ἀνέμενον. πεποίητο δὲ βῆμα
πρὸ τῶν στοῶν, δίφρων αὐτοῖς ἐλεφαντίνων ἐπ’
αὐτοῦ κειμένων, ἐφ’ οὓς παρελθόντες ἐκαθέσθησαν,
καὶ τὸ στρατιωτικὸν εὐθέως ἐπευφήμει πολλὰς
αὐτοῖς τῆς ἀρετῆς μαρτυρίας ἀποδιδόντες ἅπαντες·
κἀκεῖνοι χωρὶς ὅπλων ἦσαν [ἐν]¹ ἐσθῆσιν² σηρικαῖς
127 ἐστεφανωμένοι δάφναις. δεξάμενος δ’ αὐτῶν τὴν
εὐφημίαν Οὐεσπασιανὸς ἔτι βουλομένων λέγειν
128 τὸ τῆς σιγῆς ἐποιήσατο σύμβολον, καὶ πολλῆς
ἐκ πάντων ἡσυχίας γενομένης ἀναστὰς καὶ τῷ
περιβλήματι τὸ πλέον τῆς κεφαλῆς μέρος ἐπι-
καλυψάμενος³ εὐχὰς ἐποιήσατο τὰς νενομισμένας·
129 ὁμοίως δὲ καὶ Τίτος ηὔξατο. μετὰ δὲ τὰς εὐχὰς
εἰς κοινὸν ἅπασιν Οὐεσπασιανὸς βραχέα διαλεχθείς,
τοὺς μὲν στρατιώτας ἀπέλυσεν ἐπὶ τὸ νενο-
μισμένον ἄριστον αὐτοῖς ὑπὸ τῶν αὐτοκρατόρων
130 εὐτρεπίζεσθαι, πρὸς δὲ τὴν πύλην αὐτὸς ἀνεχώρει
τὴν ἀπὸ τοῦ πέμπεσθαι δι’ αὐτῆς αἰεὶ τοὺς
θριάμβους τῆς προσηγορίας ἀπ’ αὐτῶν τετευχυῖαν.
131 ἐνταῦθα τροφῆς [τε]⁴ προαπογεύονται καὶ τὰς
θριαμβικὰς ἐσθῆτας ἀμφιασάμενοι τοῖς τε παρ-
ιδρυμένοις τῇ πύλῃ θύσαντες θεοῖς ἔπεμπον τὸν

---

¹ C: om. the rest.   ² Niese: ἐσθήσεσιν mss.
³ Hudson: ἀποκαλυψάμενος mss.
⁴ C Lat.: om. the rest.

purple robes, and proceeded to the Octavian walks [a] ; for here the senate and the chief magistrates and those of equestrian rank were awaiting their coming. A tribunal had been erected in front of the porticoes, with chairs of ivory placed for them upon it ; to these they mounted and took their seats. Instantly acclamations rose from the troops, all bearing ample testimony to their valour : the princes were unarmed, in silk-robes and crowned with bays. Vespasian, having acknowledged their acclamations, which they wished to prolong, made the signal for silence ; then amidst profound and universal stillness he rose and, covering most of his head with his mantle, recited the customary prayers, Titus also praying in like manner. After the prayers, Vespasian, having briefly addressed the assembled company, dismissed the soldiers to the customary breakfast provided for them by the emperors, and himself withdrew to the gate which, in consequence of the triumphal processions always passing through it has thence derived its name.[b] Here the princes first partook of refreshment, and then, having donned their triumphal robes and sacrificed to the gods whose statues stood beside the gate, they sent the

[a] The *Porticus* (or *Opera Porticus*) *Octaviae*, originally built by Metellus in 146 B.C., rebuilt by Augustus and named after his sister ; the portico enclosed two temples and a group of other buildings, destroyed in the fire of Titus. It lay to the W. of the Capitol near the Theatrum Marcelli.

[b] The *Porta Triumphalis*, between the Capitol and the Tiber.

θρίαμβον διὰ τῶν θεάτρων διεξελαύνοντες, ὅπως
εἴη τοῖς πλήθεσιν ἡ θέα ῥᾴων.

132 (5) Ἀμήχανον δὲ κατὰ τὴν ἀξίαν εἰπεῖν τῶν
θεαμάτων ἐκείνων τὸ πλῆθος καὶ τὴν μεγαλο-
πρέπειαν ἐν ἅπασιν οἷς ἄν τις ἐπινοήσειεν ἢ
τεχνῶν ἔργοις ἢ πλούτου μέρεσιν ἢ φύσεως

133 σπανιότησιν· σχεδὸν γὰρ ὅσα τοῖς πώποτ' ἀνθρώποις εὐδαιμονήσασιν ἐκτήθη κατὰ μέρος ἄλλα
παρ' ἄλλοις θαυμαστὰ καὶ πολυτελῆ, ταῦτ' ἐπὶ
τῆς ἡμέρας ἐκείνης ἀθρόα τῆς Ῥωμαίων ἡγεμονίας

134 ἔδειξε τὸ μέγεθος. ἀργύρου γὰρ καὶ χρυσοῦ καὶ
ἐλέφαντος ἐν παντοίαις ἰδέαις κατασκευασμάτων
ἦν ὁρᾶν οὐχ ὥσπερ ἐν πομπῇ κομιζόμενον πλῆθος,
ἀλλ' ὡς ἂν εἴποι τις ῥέοντα ποταμόν, καὶ τὰ
μὲν ἐκ πορφύρας ὑφάσματα τῆς σπανιωτάτης
φερόμενα, τὰ δ' εἰς ἀκριβῆ ζωγραφίαν πεποικιλ-

135 μένα τῇ Βαβυλωνίων τέχνῃ· λίθοι τε διαφανεῖς,
οἱ μὲν χρυσοῖς ἐμπεπλεγμένοι στεφάνοις, οἱ δὲ
κατ' ἄλλας ποιήσεις, τοσοῦτοι παρηνέχθησαν,
ὥστε μαθεῖν ὅτι μάτην εἶναί τι τούτων σπάνιον

136 ὑπειλήφαμεν. ἐφέρετο δὲ καὶ θεῶν ἀγάλματα
τῶν παρ' αὐτοῖς μεγέθεσι θαυμαστὰ καὶ κατὰ τὴν
τέχνην οὐ παρέργως πεποιημένα, καὶ τούτων
οὐδὲν ὅ τι μὴ τῆς ὕλης τῆς πολυτελοῦς, ζῴων
τε πολλαὶ φύσεις παρήγοντο κόσμον οἰκεῖον

137 ἁπάντων περικειμένων. ἦν δὲ καὶ τὸ κομίζον
ἕκαστα τούτων πλῆθος ἀνθρώπων ἁλουργαῖς ἐσθῆσι
καὶ διαχρύσοις κεκοσμημένον, οἵ τ' εἰς αὐτὸ τὸ
πομπεύειν διακριθέντες ἐξαίρετον εἶχον καὶ κατα-

___

[a] The triumphs as a rule passed southwards from the
Porta Triumphalis " through the Forum Boarium into the

pageant on its way, driving off through the theatres, in order to give the crowds an easier view.[a]

(5) It is impossible adequately to describe the multitude of those spectacles and their magnificence under every conceivable aspect, whether in works of art or diversity of riches or natural rarities; for almost all the objects which men who have ever been blessed by fortune have acquired one by one—the wonderful and precious productions of various nations—by their collective exhibition on that day displayed the majesty of the Roman empire. Silver and gold and ivory in masses, wrought into all manner of forms, might be seen, not as if carried in procession, but flowing, so to speak, like a river; here were tapestries borne along, some of the rarest purple, others embroidered by Babylonian art with perfect portraiture; transparent gems, some set in golden crowns, some in other fashions, swept by in such profusion as to correct our erroneous supposition that any of them was rare. Then, too, there were carried images of their [b] gods, of marvellous size and no mean craftsmanship, and of these not one but was of some rich material. Beasts of many species were led along all caparisoned with appropriate trappings. The numerous attendants conducting each group of animals were decked in garments of true purple dye, interwoven with gold; while those selected to take

The triumphal procession.

Circus, and thence by the Vicus Tuscus into the Forum, and along the Via Sacra up to the Temple of Jupiter Capitolinus " (Burn, *Rome*, 46). In this instance the triumph apparently began with a detour northwards through the three theatres on the Campus Martius, viz., those of Marcellus, Balbus, and Pompey.

[b] Roman; Josephus is writing for the Greek-speaking world at large.

πληκτικὴν περὶ αὐτοὺς τοῦ κόσμου τὴν πολυ-
138 τέλειαν. ἐπὶ τούτοις οὐδὲ τὸν αἰχμάλωτον ἦν
ἰδεῖν ὄχλον ἀκόσμητον, ἀλλ' ἡ τῶν ἐσθήτων
ποικιλία καὶ τὸ κάλλος αὐτοῖς[1] τὴν ἀπὸ τῆς
κακώσεως τῶν σωμάτων ἀηδίαν ἔκλεπτε τῆς
139 ὄψεως. θαῦμα δ' ἐν τοῖς μάλιστα παρεῖχεν ἡ
τῶν φερομένων πηγμάτων κατασκευή· καὶ γὰρ
διὰ μέγεθος ἦν δεῖσαι τῷ βεβαίῳ τῆς φορᾶς
140 ἀπιστήσαντα, τριώροφα γὰρ αὐτῶν πολλὰ καὶ
τετρώροφα πεποίητο, καὶ τῇ πολυτελείᾳ τῇ περὶ
141 τὴν κατασκευὴν ἦν ἡσθῆναι μετ' ἐκπλήξεως. καὶ
γὰρ ὑφάσματα πολλοῖς διάχρυσα περιβέβλητο,
καὶ χρυσὸς καὶ ἐλέφας οὐκ ἀποίητος πᾶσι περι-
142 επεπήγει. διὰ πολλῶν δὲ μιμημάτων ὁ πόλεμος
ἄλλος εἰς ἄλλα μεμερισμένος ἐναργεστάτην ὄψιν
143 αὐτοῦ παρεῖχεν· ἦν γὰρ ὁρᾶν χώραν μὲν εὐδαίμονα
δῃουμένην, ὅλας δὲ φάλαγγας κτεινομένας πολεμίων, καὶ τοὺς μὲν φεύγοντας τοὺς δ' εἰς αἰχμαλωσίαν ἀγομένους, τείχη δ' ὑπερβάλλοντα μεγέθει
μηχαναῖς ἐρειπόμενα καὶ φρουρίων ἁλισκομένας
ὀχυρότητας καὶ πόλεων πολυανθρώπους περιβόλους
144 κατ' ἄκρας ἐχομένους, καὶ στρατιὰν ἔνδον τειχῶν
εἰσχεομένην, καὶ πάντα φόνου πλήθοντα[2] τόπον,
καὶ τῶν ἀδυνάτων χεῖρας ἀνταίρειν ἱκεσίας, πῦρ
τε ἐνιέμενον ἱεροῖς καὶ κατασκαφὰς οἴκων ἐπὶ
145 τοῖς δεσπόταις, καὶ μετὰ πολλὴν ἐρημίαν καὶ
κατήφειαν ποταμοὺς ῥέοντας οὐκ ἐπὶ γῆν γεωρ-
γουμένην, οὐδὲ ποτὸν[3] ἀνθρώποις ἢ βοσκήμασιν

---

[1] Destinon: αὐτῆς mss.
[2] πληθύοντα or πληθύνοντα inferior mss.
[3] πατητὴν Destinon: Niese suspects a lacuna after
βοσκήμασιν.

546

part in the pageant itself had about them choice
ornaments of amazing richness. Moreover, even
among the mob of captives, none was to be seen
unadorned, the variety and beauty of their dresses
concealing from view any unsightliness arising from
bodily disfigurement.[a]

But nothing in the procession excited so much
astonishment as the structure of the moving stages[b];
indeed, their massiveness afforded ground for alarm
and misgiving as to their stability, many of them
being three or four stories high, while the magnificence of the fabric was a source at once of delight
and amazement. For many were enveloped in
tapestries interwoven with gold, and all had a frame-
work of gold and wrought ivory. The war was shown
by numerous representations, in separate sections,
affording a very vivid picture of its episodes. Here
was to be seen a prosperous country devastated, there
whole battalions of the enemy slaughtered ; here a
party in flight, there others led into captivity ; walls
of surpassing compass demolished by engines, strong
fortresses overpowered, cities with well-manned
defences completely mastered and an army pouring
within the ramparts, an area all deluged with blood,
the hands of those incapable of resistance raised in
supplication, temples set on fire, houses pulled down
over their owners' heads, and, after general desolation and woe, rivers flowing, not over a cultivated
land, nor supplying drink to man and beast, but

The
pictorial
stages
(*pegmata*).

---

[a] From wounds or the like ; they had been selected for
their handsome figures, § 118.

[b] Greek πῆγμα, transliterated in Lat. *pegma*, Juv. *Sat.* iv.
122 ; translated in Low Lat. *pagina*, whence English *pageant*,
originally meaning " a movable scaffold, such as was used
in the representation of the old mysteries " (Skeat).

ἀλλὰ διὰ τῆς ἔτι πανταχόθεν[1] φλεγομένης· ταῦτα
γὰρ Ἰουδαῖοι πεισομένους αὐτοὺς τῷ πολέμῳ
146 παρέδοσαν. ἡ τέχνη δὲ καὶ τῶν κατασκευασμάτων
ἡ μεγαλουργία τοῖς οὐκ ἰδοῦσι γινόμενα τότ'
147 ἐδείκνυεν ὡς παροῦσι. τέτακτο δ' ἐφ' ἑκάστῳ
τῶν πηγμάτων ὁ τῆς ἁλισκομένης πόλεως στρατηγὸς ὃν τρόπον ἐλήφθη, πολλαὶ δὲ καὶ νῆες
148 εἵποντο. λάφυρα δὲ τὰ μὲν ἄλλα χύδην ἐφέρετο,
διέπρεπε δὲ πάντων τὰ ἐγκαταληφθέντα[2] τῷ ἐν
Ἱεροσολύμοις ἱερῷ, χρυσῆ τε τράπεζα τὴν ὁλκὴν
πολυτάλαντος καὶ λυχνία χρυσῆ μὲν ὁμοίως
πεποιημένη, τὸ δ' ἔργον ἐξήλλακτο τῆς κατὰ τὴν
149 ἡμετέραν χρῆσιν συνηθείας. ὁ μὲν γὰρ μέσος ἦν
κίων ἐκ τῆς βάσεως πεπηγώς, λεπτοὶ δ' ἀπ'
αὐτοῦ μεμήκυντο καυλίσκοι τριαίνης σχήματι
παραπλησίαν τὴν θέσιν ἔχοντες, λύχνον ἕκαστος
αὐτῶν ἐπ' ἄκρον κεχαλκευμένος· ἑπτὰ δ' ἦσαν
οὗτοι τῆς παρὰ τοῖς Ἰουδαίοις ἑβδομάδος τὴν
150 τιμὴν ἐμφανίζοντες. ὅ τε νόμος ὁ τῶν Ἰουδαίων
ἐπὶ τούτοις ἐφέρετο τῶν λαφύρων τελευταῖος.
151 ἐπὶ τούτοις παρῆεσαν πολλοὶ Νίκης ἀγάλματα
κομίζοντες· ἐξ ἐλέφαντος δ' ἦν πάντων καὶ χρυσοῦ
152 ἡ κατασκευή. μεθ' ἃ Οὐεσπασιανὸς ἤλαυνε πρῶτος καὶ Τίτος εἵπετο, Δομετιανὸς δὲ παρίππευεν,
αὐτός τε διαπρεπῶς κεκοσμημένος καὶ τὸν ἵππον
παρέχων θέας ἄξιον.
153 (6) Ἦν δὲ τῆς πομπῆς τὸ τέλος ἐπὶ τὸν νεὼ[3]

---

[1] ἔτι πανταχ. MLVR: ἐπιπανταχόθεν PAC.
[2] ed. pr.: καταληφθέντα mss.
[3] τὸν νεὼ AL: τῷ νεῷ P: τὸν νεὼν the rest.

---

[a] Commemorating the naval action on the lake of Tiberias
(B. iii. 522 ff. with note on 531).

across a country still on every side in flames   For
to such sufferings were the Jews.destined when they
plunged into the war ; and the art and magnificent
workmanship of these structures now portrayed the
incidents to those who had not witnessed them, as
though they were happening before their eyes.   On
each of the stages was stationed the general of one
of the captured cities in the attitude in which he was
taken.   A number of ships also followed.[a]

The spoils in general were borne in promiscuous The spoils
from the
Temple.
heaps ; but conspicuous above all stood out those
captured in the temple at Jerusalem.[b]   These consisted of a golden table,[c] many talents in weight, and
a lampstand,[d] likewise made of gold, but constructed
on a different pattern from those which we use in
ordinary life.   Affixed to a pedestal was a central
shaft, from which there extended slender branches,
arranged trident-fashion, a wrought lamp being
attached to the extremity of each branch ; of these
there were seven, indicating the honour paid to that
number among the Jews.   After these, and last of
all the spoils, was carried a copy of the Jewish Law.
Then followed a large party carrying images of
victory, all made of ivory and gold.   Behind them
drove Vespasian, followed by Titus ; while Domitian
rode beside them, in magnificent apparel and mounted
on a steed that was itself a sight.

(6) The triumphal procession ended at the temple Execution
of Simon.

[b] The Jewish spoils—table of shew-bread, incense-cups,
and trumpets—as borne in the procession still figure on the
inner side of the Arch of Titus above the Forum in Rome.

[c] The table of shew-bread.

[d] Or " candlestick " as it is commonly, but erroneously,
called.

τοῦ Καπετωλίου Διός, ἐφ᾿ ὃν ἐλθόντες ἔστησαν·
ἦν γὰρ παλαιὸν πάτριον περιμένειν, μέχρις ἂν
τὸν τοῦ στρατηγοῦ τῶν πολεμίων θάνατον ἀπ-
154 αγγείλῃ τις. Σίμων οὗτος ἦν ὁ Γιώρα, τότε πε-
πομπευκὼς ἐν τοῖς αἰχμαλώτοις, βρόχῳ δὲ περι-
βληθεὶς εἰς τὸν ἐπὶ τῆς ἀγορᾶς ἐσύρετο τόπον
αἰκιζομένων αὐτὸν ἅμα τῶν ἀγόντων· νόμος δ᾿
ἐστὶ Ῥωμαίοις ἐκεῖ κτείνειν τοὺς ἐπὶ κακουργίᾳ
155 θάνατον κατεγνωσμένους. ἐπεὶ δ᾿ ἀπηγγέλθη τέλος
ἔχων καὶ πάντες εὐφήμησαν, ἤρχοντο τῶν θυσιῶν,
ἃς ἐπὶ ταῖς νομιζομέναις καλλιερήσαντες εὐχαῖς
156 ἀπῄεσαν εἰς τὸ βασίλειον. καὶ τοὺς μὲν αὐτοὶ
πρὸς εὐωχίαν ὑπεδέχοντο, τοῖς δ᾿ ἄλλοις ἅπασιν
εὐτρεπεῖς[1] κατὰ τὸ οἰκεῖον αἱ τῆς ἑστιάσεως ἦσαν
157 παρασκευαί. ταύτην γὰρ τὴν ἡμέραν ἡ Ῥωμαίων
πόλις ἑώρταζεν ἐπινίκιον μὲν τῆς κατὰ τῶν
πολεμίων στρατείας, πέρας δὲ τῶν ἐμφυλίων
κακῶν, ἀρχὴν δὲ τῶν ὑπὲρ τῆς εὐδαιμονίας
ἐλπίδων.

158 (7) Μετὰ δὲ τοὺς θριάμβους καὶ τὴν βεβαιοτάτην
τῆς Ῥωμαίων ἡγεμονίας κατάστασιν Οὐεσπασιανὸς
ἔγνω τέμενος Εἰρήνης κατασκευάσαι· ταχὺ δὲ
δὴ μάλα καὶ πάσης ἀνθρωπίνης κρεῖττον ἐπινοίας
159 ἐτετελείωτο. τῇ γὰρ ἐκ τοῦ πλούτου χορηγίᾳ
δαιμονίῳ χρησάμενος, ἔτι καὶ τοῖς ἔκπαλαι
κατωρθωμένοις γραφῆς τε καὶ πλαστικῆς ἔργοις
160 αὐτὸ κατεκόσμησεν· πάντα γὰρ εἰς ἐκεῖνον τὸν

---

[1] Niese from Lat. (instructi): εὐπρεπεῖς MSS.

---

[a] The Mamertine prison at the N.E. end of the Forum.
[b] Or (with the other reading) " handsome provision had
been made."

of Jupiter Capitolinus, on reaching which they halted; for it was a time-honoured custom to wait there until the execution of the enemy's general was announced. This was Simon, son of Gioras, who had just figured in the pageant among the prisoners, and then, with a halter thrown over him and scourged meanwhile by his conductors, had been haled to the spot abutting on the Forum, where Roman law requires that malefactors condemned to death should be executed.[a] After the announcement that Simon was no more and the shouts of universal applause which greeted it, the princes began the sacrifices, which having been duly offered with the customary prayers, they withdrew to the palace. Some they entertained at a feast at their own table : for all the rest provision had already been made[b] for banquets in their several homes. For the city of Rome kept festival that day for her victory in the campaign against her enemies, for the termination of her civil dissensions, and for her dawning hopes of felicity.

(7) The triumphal ceremonies being concluded and the empire of the Romans established on the firmest foundation, Vespasian decided to erect a temple of Peace.[c] This was very speedily completed and in a style surpassing all human conception. For, besides having prodigious resources of wealth on which to draw he also embellished it with ancient masterpieces of painting and sculpture ; indeed, into that shrine were accumulated and stored all objects for

Erection of the Templum Pacis, A.D. 75.

[c] The date of dedication, the sixth year of Vespasian's reign (A.D. 75), is known from Dion Cassius lxvi. 15. The temple, surrounded by a forum, lay to the S.E. of the Forum Romanum, between the Via Sacra and the Carinae. Pliny and Herodian testify to its magnificence (Burn, *Rome*, 140).

νεὼ συνήχθη καὶ κατετέθη, δι' ὧν τὴν θέαν
ἄνθρωποι πρότερον περὶ πᾶσαν ἐπλανῶντο τὴν
οἰκουμένην, ἕως ἄλλο παρ' ἄλλοις ἦν κείμενον
161 ἰδεῖν ποθοῦντες. ἀνέθηκε δ' ἐνταῦθα καὶ τὰ ἐκ
τοῦ ἱεροῦ τῶν Ἰουδαίων χρυσᾶ κατασκευάσματα
162 σεμνυνόμενος· ἐπ' αὐτοῖς. τὸν δὲ νόμον αὐτῶν
καὶ τὰ πορφυρᾶ τοῦ σηκοῦ καταπετάσματα
προσέταξεν ἐν τοῖς βασιλείοις ἀποθεμένους φυλάττειν.

163 (vi. 1) Εἰς δὲ τὴν Ἰουδαίαν πρεσβευτὴς Λου-
κίλιος[1] Βάσσος ἐκπεμφθεὶς καὶ τὴν στρατηγίαν[2]
παρὰ Κερεαλίου Οὐετιλιανοῦ παραλαβὼν τὸ μὲν
ἐν τῷ Ἡρωδείῳ φρούριον προσηγάγετο μετὰ
164 τῶν ἐχόντων, μετὰ ταῦτα δὲ πᾶν ὅσον ἦν στρατιωτικὸν συναγαγών, πολὺ δ' ἦν κατὰ μέρη
διῃρημένον, καὶ τῶν ταγμάτων τὸ δέκατον, ἔγνω
στρατεύειν ἐπὶ Μαχαιροῦντα· πάνυ γὰρ ἦν ἀναγκαῖον ἐξαιρεθῆναι τὸ φρούριον, μὴ διὰ τὴν ὀχυρότητα πολλοὺς εἰς ἀποστασίαν ἐπαγάγηται.
165 καὶ γὰρ τοῖς κατέχουσι βεβαίαν ἐλπίδα σωτηρίας
καὶ τοῖς ἐπιοῦσιν ὄκνον καὶ δέος ἡ τοῦ χωρίου
166 φύσις ἦν παρασχεῖν ἱκανωτάτη. αὐτὸ μὲν γὰρ
τὸ τετειχισμένον πετρώδης ὄχθος ἐστὶν εἰς μήκιστον ὕψος ἐγηγερμένος, ὡς εἶναι καὶ διὰ τοῦτο
δυσχείρωτος, μεμηχάνηται δ' ὑπὸ τῆς φύσεως
167 εἶναι μηδὲ προσιτός· φάραγξιν γὰρ πάντοθεν
ἀσύνοπτον ἐχούσαις τὸ βάθος περιτετάφρευται,
μήτε περαθῆναι ῥᾳδίως δυναμέναις καὶ χωσθῆναι
168 παντάπασιν ἀμηχάνοις. ἡ μὲν γὰρ ἀπὸ τῆς

---

[1] Lat., *ed. pr.*: Λούκιος mss.
[2] PAL Lat.: στρατιὰν the rest.

the sight of which men had once wandered over the
whole world, eager to see them severally while they
lay in various countries. Here, too, he laid up the
vessels of gold from the temple of the Jews, on which
he prided himself; but their Law and the purple
hangings of the sanctuary he ordered to be deposited
and kept in the palace.

(vi. 1) Meanwhile, Lucilius Bassus had been
dispatched to Judaea as legate, and, taking over the
command from Cerealius Vetilianus,[a] had reduced
the fortress of Herodium[b] with its garrison to surrender. He next concentrated all the numerous
scattered detachments of troops, including the
tenth legion, having determined to march against
Machaerus.[c] This fortress it was absolutely necessary to eradicate, lest its strength should induce
many to revolt; since the nature of the place was
specially adapted to inspire its occupants with high
hopes of security and to deter and alarm its assailants.
For the site that is fortified is itself a rocky eminence,
rising to so great a height that on that account alone
its reduction would be difficult; while nature had
further contrived to render it inaccessible. For it is
intrenched on all sides within ravines of a depth
baffling to the eye, not easy to traverse and utterly
impossible to bank up. The valley which hems it in

Lucilius
Bassus, sent
to Judaea,
marches on
MACHAERUS.

Description
of the
fortress.

---

[a] Sextus Vettulenus Cerialis (as he is named in an inscription) was commander of the fifth legion during the war,
B. iii. 310, etc., and after it was left by Titus in command of
the army of occupation, *i.e.* the tenth legion with other units
(§ 5).
[b] Herod's fortress and burial place, 60 stades due S. of
Jerusalem.
[c] E. of the Dead Sea, near its northern end.

ἑσπέρας περιτέμνουσα παρατείνει σταδίους ἑξήκοντα, πέρας αὑτῆς τὴν Ἀσφαλτῖτιν ποιουμένη
λίμνην· κατὰ τοῦτο δέ πη καὶ αὐτὸς ὁ Μαχαιροῦς
τὴν ὑψηλοτάτην ἔχει κορυφὴν ὑπερανίσχουσαν·
169 αἱ δ' ἀπὸ τῆς ἄρκτου καὶ μεσημβρίας φάραγγες
μεγέθει μὲν ἀπολείπονται τῆς προειρημένης,
170 ὁμοίως δ' εἰσὶν ἀμήχανοι πρὸς ἐπιχείρησιν. τῆς
δὲ πρὸς ἀνατολὴν φάραγγος τὸ μὲν βάθος οὐκ
ἔλαττον ἑκατὸν εὑρίσκεται πήχεων, τέρμα δὲ
γίνεται πρὸς ὄρος ἀπαντικρὺ κείμενον Μαχαιροῦντος.

171 (2) Ταύτην τοῦ τόπου κατιδὼν τὴν φύσιν
βασιλεὺς Ἰουδαίων Ἀλέξανδρος πρῶτος ἐπ' αὐτοῦ
τειχίζει φρούριον, ὃ μετὰ ταῦτα Γαβίνιος Ἀριστο-
172 βούλῳ πολεμῶν καθεῖλεν. Ἡρώδῃ δὲ βασι-
λεύοντι παντὸς ἔδοξε μᾶλλον ἐπιμελείας ἄξιον
εἶναι καὶ κατασκευῆς ὀχυρωτάτης, μάλιστα καὶ
διὰ τὴν τῶν Ἀράβων γειτνίασιν· κεῖται γὰρ ἐν
ἐπικαίρῳ πρὸς τὴν ἐκείνων γῆν ἀποβλέπον.
173 μέγαν μὲν οὖν τόπον τείχεσιν καὶ πύργοις περι-
βαλὼν πόλιν ἐνταῦθα κατῴκισεν, ἐξ ἧς ἄνοδος
174 εἰς αὐτὴν ἔφερε τὴν ἀκρώρειαν. οὐ μὴν ἀλλὰ
καὶ περὶ αὐτὴν ἄνω τὴν κορυφὴν τεῖχος ἐδείματο
καὶ πύργους ἐπὶ ταῖς γωνίαις ἕκαστον[1] ἑξήκοντα
175 πηχῶν ἀνέστησεν. μέσον δὲ τοῦ περιβόλου βασίλειον ᾠκοδομήσατο μεγέθει τε καὶ κάλλει τῶν
176 οἰκήσεων πολυτελές, πολλὰς δὲ καὶ δεξαμενὰς
εἰς ὑποδοχὴν ὕδατος καὶ χορηγίαν ἄφθονον ἐν
τοῖς ἐπιτηδειοτάτοις τῶν τόπων κατεσκεύασεν,
ὥσπερ πρὸς τὴν φύσιν ἁμιλληθείς, ἵν' αὐτὸς τὸ
κατ' ἐκείνην τοῦ τόπου δυσάλωτον ὑπερβάληται

[1] R: ἑκατὸν the rest.

on the west extends to sixty furlongs, ending at the lake Asphaltitis[a]; and somewhere in this direction Machaerus itself reaches its highest commanding peak. The ravines on the north and south, though less extensive than this, are equally impracticable for purposes of attack. That on the east is found to be no less than a hundred cubits in depth and is terminated by a mountain facing Machaerus.

(2) Noting these natural advantages of the site, Alexander,[b] king of the Jews, was the first to crown it with a fortress, which was subsequently demolished by Gabinius[c] in his war with Aristobulus. But Herod, on becoming king, regarded the place as supremely deserving of attention and of the strongest fortification, more especially from its proximity to Arabia, conveniently situated, as it was, with regard to that country, which it faces. He accordingly enclosed an extensive area with ramparts and towers and founded a city there, from which an ascent led up to the ridge itself. Furthermore, on the top, surrounding the actual crest, he built a wall, erecting towers at the corners, each sixty cubits high. In the centre of the enclosure he built a palace with magnificently spacious and beautiful apartments; he further provided numerous cisterns at the most convenient spots to receive the rain-water and furnish an abundant supply, as if he were vying with nature and endeavouring by these artificial defences to surpass the well-nigh impregnable strength which

Its history

Herod's buildings.

---

[a] The Dead Sea.   [b] Alexander Jannaeus, 104–78 B.C.
[c] *Legatus* of Pompey in the war with Aristobulus (*B.* i. 140) and from 57–55 B.C. proconsular governor of Syria (*B.* i. 160 ff.).

177 ταῖς χειροποιήτοις ὀχυρώσεσιν· ἔτι γὰρ καὶ
βελῶν πλῆθος καὶ μηχανημάτων ἐγκατέθετο καὶ
πᾶν ἐπενόησεν ἑτοιμάσασθαι τὸ παρασχεῖν δυνάμενον τοῖς ἐνοικοῦσιν μηκίστης πολιορκίας καταφρόνησιν.
178 (3) Ἐπεφύκει δ' ἐν τοῖς βασιλείοις πήγανον
ἄξιον τοῦ μεγέθους θαυμάσαι· συκῆς γὰρ οὐδεμιᾶς
179 ὕψους καὶ πάχους ἐλείπετο. λόγος δ' ἦν ἀπὸ
τῶν Ἡρώδου χρόνων αὐτὸ διαρκέσαι, κἂν ἐπὶ
πλεῖστον ἴσως ἔμεινεν, ἐξεκόπη δ' ὑπὸ τῶν
180 παραλαβόντων τὸν τόπον Ἰουδαίων. τῆς φάραγγος
δὲ τῆς κατὰ τὴν ἄρκτον περιεχούσης τὴν πόλιν
Βαάρας ὀνομάζεταί τις τόπος, ⟨ὃς⟩[1] φύει ῥίζαν
181 ὁμωνύμως λεγομένην αὐτῷ. αὕτη φλογὶ μὲν τὴν
χροίαν ἔοικε, περὶ δὲ τὰς ἑσπέρας σέλας ἀπ-
αστράπτουσα τοῖς ἐπιοῦσι καὶ βουλομένοις λαβεῖν
αὐτὴν οὐκ ἔστιν εὐχείρωτος, ἀλλ' ὑποφεύγει
καὶ οὐ πρότερον ἵσταται, πρὶν ἄν τις οὖρον
γυναικὸς ἢ τὸ ἔμμηνον αἷμα χέῃ κατ' αὐτῆς.
182 οὐ μὴν ἀλλὰ καὶ τότε τοῖς ἁψαμένοις πρόδηλός
ἐστι θάνατος, εἰ μὴ τύχοι τις αὐτὴν ἐκείνην
ἐπενεγκάμενος τὴν ῥίζαν ἐκ τῆς χειρὸς ἀπηρτη-
183 μένην. ἁλίσκεται δὲ καὶ καθ' ἕτερον τρόπον
ἀκινδύνως, ὅς ἐστι τοιόσδε· κύκλῳ πᾶσαν αὐτὴν
περιορύσσουσιν, ὡς εἶναι τὸ κρυπτόμενον τῆς
184 ῥίζης βραχύτατον. εἶτ' ἐξ αὐτῆς ἀποδοῦσι κύνα,
κἀκείνου τῷ δήσαντι συνακολουθεῖν ὁρμήσαντος,
ἡ μὲν ἀνασπᾶται ῥᾳδίως, θνήσκει δ' εὐθὺς ὁ

[1] ins. Destinon.

---

[a] Mentioned as a small garden herb in Luke xi. 42.
Ruta graveolens is still cultivated in Palestine, while *ruta*
556

she had bestowed upon the site. For, moreover, he stocked it with abundance of weapons and engines, and studied to make every preparation to enable its inmates to defy the longest siege.

(3) Within the palace once grew a plant of rue,[a] of an amazing size ; indeed, in height and thickness no fig-tree surpassed it. Tradition said that it had lasted from the times of Herod ; and it would probably have continued for ages, had it not been cut down by the Jews, who took possession of the place. In the ravine [b] which encloses the town on the north, there is a place called Baaras,[c] which produces a root bearing the same name. Flame-coloured and towards evening emitting a brilliant light, it eludes the grasp of persons who approach with the intention of plucking it, as it shrinks up and can only be made to stand still by pouring upon it certain secretions of the human body.[d] Yet even then to touch it is fatal, unless one succeeds in carrying off the root itself,[e] suspended from the hand. Another innocuous mode of capturing it is as follows. They dig all round it, leaving but a minute portion of the root covered ; they then tie a dog to it, and the animal rushing to follow the person who tied him easily pulls it up, but instantly dies—a vicarious

bracteosa is a common wild plant (Tristram quoted in *Encycl. Bibl. s.v.*).

[b] The *Wady Zerka*, running down to the Dead Sea (probably = Nahaliel of the wilderness wanderings, Numb. xxi. 19).

[c] The warm springs (see below) of " Baaru " are mentioned by Jerome (" iuxta Baaru in Arabia, ubi aquas calidas sponte humus effert ") and elsewhere, Schürer, *G.J.V.* i. 414.

[d] *Cf. B.* iv. 480.

[e] Meaning doubtful: perhaps " unless one happens *to bring with one* the self-same root."

κύων ὥσπερ ἀντιδοθεὶς τοῦ μέλλοντος τὴν βοτάνην
ἀναιρήσεσθαι· φόβος γὰρ οὐδεὶς τοῖς μετὰ ταῦτα
185 λαμβάνουσιν. ἔστι δὲ μετὰ τοσούτων κινδύνων
διὰ μίαν ἰσχὺν περισπούδαστος· τὰ γὰρ καλούμενα
δαιμόνια, ταῦτα δὲ πονηρῶν ἐστιν ἀνθρώπων
πνεύματα τοῖς ζῶσιν εἰσδυόμενα καὶ κτείνοντα
τοὺς βοηθείας μὴ τυγχάνοντας, αὕτη ταχέως
ἐξελαύνει, κἂν προσενεχθῇ μόνον τοῖς νοσοῦσι.
186 ῥέουσι δὲ καὶ θερμῶν ὑδάτων πηγαὶ κατὰ τὸν
τόπον, πολὺ τὴν γεῦσιν ἀλλήλων διαφέρουσαι·
πικραὶ μὲν γὰρ αὐτῶν τινές εἰσιν, αἱ δὲ γλυκύτητος
187 οὐδὲν ἀπολείπουσαι. πολλαὶ δὲ καὶ ψυχρῶν ὑδάτων ἀναδόσεις οὐ μόνον ἐν τῷ χθαμαλωτέρῳ τὰς
188 πηγὰς παραλλήλους ἔχουσαι,[1] ἀλλ᾿ ὡς ἂν καὶ
μᾶλλόν τις θαυμάσειε, σπήλαιον γάρ τι πλησίον
ὁρᾶται κοιλότητι μὲν οὐ βαθύ, τῇ πέτρᾳ δὲ
189 προυχούσῃ σκεπόμενον· ταύτης ἄνωθεν ὡσανεὶ
μαστοὶ δύο ἀνέχουσιν, ἀλλήλων ὀλίγῳ διεστῶτες,
καὶ ψυχροτάτην μὲν ἅτερος πηγήν, ἅτερος δὲ
θερμοτάτην ἐκδίδωσιν, αἳ μισγόμεναι ποιοῦσι
λουτρὸν ἥδιστον παιώνιόν τε νοσημάτων, πολλῷ
δὲ μάλιστα νεύρων ἄκεσιν. ἔχει δ᾿ ὁ τόπος καὶ
θείου καὶ στυπτηρίας μέταλλα.
190 (4) Βάσσος δὲ[2] περισκεψάμενος τὸ χωρίον ἔγνω
ποιεῖσθαι τὴν πρόσοδον χωννὺς τὴν φάραγγα τὴν
πρὸς ταῖς ἀνατολαῖς καὶ τῶν ἔργων εἴχετο,
σπουδὴν ποιούμενος ᾗ τάχος ἐξᾶραι τὸ χῶμα
καὶ δι᾿ αὐτοῦ ῥᾳδίαν ποιῆσαι τὴν πολιορκίαν.
191 οἱ δ᾿ ἔνδον ἀπειλημμένοι τῶν Ἰουδαίων αὐτοὶ
καθ᾿ ἑαυτοὺς ἀπὸ τῶν ξένων διακριθέντες ἐκείνους
μὲν ἠνάγκασαν, ὄχλον ἄλλως εἶναι νομίζοντες,
ἐν τῇ κάτω πόλει παραμένειν καὶ τοὺς κινδύνους

victim, as it were, for him who intended to remove
the plant, since after this none need fear to handle it.
With all these attendant risks, it possesses one virtue
for which it is prized ; for the so-called demons—in
other words, the spirits of wicked men which enter
the living and kill them unless aid is forthcoming—
are promptly expelled by this root, if merely applied
to the patients.   In this same region flow hot springs,
in taste widely differing from each other, some being
bitter, while others have no lack of sweetness. Many
springs of cold water also gush up, nor are these
confined to the low-lying ground where all are in
a line [a] ; but—what is still more remarkable—hard
by may be seen a cave, of no great depth and screened
by a projecting rock, above which protrude, as it were,
two breasts, a little distance apart, one yielding
extremely cold water, and the other extremely hot.
These when mixed provide a most delightful bath,
possessing general medicinal properties, but particularly restorative to the sinews. There are also
sulphur and alum mines in the district.

(4) Bassus, after reconnoitring the place on all
sides, decided to approach it by filling up the eastern
ravine ; to this task he now applied himself, labouring to raise with all speed the embankment which
was to facilitate the siege. The Jewish party shut
up within now separated themselves from their alien
colleagues and, regarding the latter as a mere rabble,
compelled them to remain in the lower town and to

Siege of Machaerus.

---

[a] Or " on one level."

[1] PM : ἔχουσιν the rest.   [2] +πάντη C.

192 προεκδέχεσθαι, τὸ δ' ἄνω φρούριον αὐτοὶ κατα-
λαβόντες εἶχον καὶ διὰ τὴν ἰσχὺν τῆς ὀχυρότητος
καὶ προνοίᾳ τῆς σωτηρίας αὐτῶν· τεύξεσθαι γὰρ
ἀφέσεως ὑπελάμβανον, εἰ τὸ χωρίον Ῥωμαίοις
193 ἐγχειρίσειαν. πείρᾳ δὲ πρότερον ἐβούλοντο τὰς
ὑπὲρ τοῦ διαφεύξεσθαι τὴν πολιορκίαν ἐλπίδας
ἐλέγξαι. διὰ τοῦτο καὶ προθύμως ἐποιοῦντο τὰς
ἐξόδους ἀνὰ πᾶσαν ἡμέραν, καὶ τοῖς χοῦσι[1]
συμπλεκόμενοι πολλοὶ μὲν ἔθνησκον, πολλοὺς δὲ
194 τῶν Ῥωμαίων ἀνήρουν. ἀεὶ δὲ τοῦ[2] κρατεῖν ὁ
καιρὸς ἐβράβευεν ἑκατέροις τὸ πλέον, τοῖς μὲν
Ἰουδαίοις, εἰ πρὸς ἀφυλακτοτέρους προσπέσοιεν,
τοῖς δ' ἐπὶ τῶν χωμάτων προϊδομένοις, εἰ τὴν
195 ἐκδρομὴν αὐτῶν δέχοιντο πεφραγμένως. ἀλλ' οὐκ
ἐν τούτοις ἔμελλεν γενήσεσθαι τὸ πέρας τῆς
πολιορκίας, ἔργον δέ τι πραχθὲν ἐκ συντυχίας
παράλογον τῆς παραδόσεως τοῦ φρουρίου τὴν
196 ἀνάγκην ἐπέστησε τοῖς Ἰουδαίοις. ἦν ἐν τοῖς
πολιορκουμένοις νεανίας τολμῆσαί τε θρασὺς καὶ
197 κατὰ χεῖρα δραστήριος, Ἐλεάζαρος ὄνομα· γε-
γόνει δ' οὗτος ἐν ταῖς ἐκδρομαῖς ἐπιφανής, τοὺς
πολλοὺς ἐξιέναι καὶ κωλύειν τὴν χῶσιν παρακαλῶν
καὶ κατὰ τὰς μάχας πολλὰ καὶ δεινὰ τοὺς Ῥωμαίους διατιθείς, τοῖς δὲ σὺν αὐτῷ τολμῶσιν
ἐπεκτρέχειν ῥαδίαν μὲν τὴν προσβολὴν τιθέμενος,
ἀκίνδυνον δὲ παρέχων τὴν ἀναχώρησιν τῷ τελευ-
198 ταῖος ἀπιέναι. καὶ δή ποτε τῆς μάχης διακρι-
θείσης καὶ γεγονυίας ἀμφοτέρων ἀναχωρήσεως
αὐτός, ἅτε δὴ περιφρονῶν καὶ νομίζων οὐκ ἂν
ἔτι τῶν πολεμίων οὐδένα τότε μάχης ἄρξειν,
μείνας τῶν πυλῶν ἔξω τοῖς ἐπὶ τοῦ τείχους
διελάλει καὶ πᾶς πρὸς ἐκείνοις τὴν διάνοιαν ἦν.

bear the first brunt; while they themselves seized
and held the fortress above, both on account of the
strength of its defences and with an eye to their own
safety, conceiving that they could obtain pardon,
were they to surrender the fort to the Romans.
However, they wished first to put to the test their
hopes of escaping a blockade; accordingly, they
daily made spirited sallies and engaged in close
combat with those at work on the mound, losing
many of their own men, but killing many of the
Romans. It was, however, invariably the opportunity which, in the main decided the victory in
favour of either side: of the Jews if they fell upon
their enemy when off his usual guard, of those on the
mounds if they foresaw and met their sally in a
posture of defence. It was not, however, these
encounters which were destined to end the siege,
but a casual and surprising incident constrained the
Jews to surrender the fortress. Among the besieged
was a youth of daring enterprise and strenuous energy
named Eleazar. He had distinguished himself in the
sallies by stimulating most of his comrades to come
out and check the progress of the earthworks, and
in the engagements by frequently making fearful
havoc of the Romans; besides easing the attack for
all who ventured out with him and covering their
retreat by being the last to withdraw. Now on one
occasion, when the battle was over and both parties
had retired, he, disdainfully assuming that none of
the enemy would now resume the fight, remained
outside the gates conversing with his comrades on
the wall and devoting his whole attention to them

The capture
of Eleazar

---

¹ Destinon: τυχοῦσι MSS. ² τὸ Niese with P.

199 ὁρᾷ δὲ τὸν καιρὸν τοῦ Ῥωμαϊκοῦ τις στρατοπέδου
Ῥοῦφος γένος Αἰγύπτιος, καὶ μηδενὸς ἂν προσ-
δοκήσαντος ἐξαίφνης ἐπιδραμὼν σὺν αὐτοῖς ἀράμενος αὐτὸν τοῖς ὅπλοις, ἕως κατεῖχε τοὺς ἀπὸ
τῶν τειχῶν ἰδόντας ἔκπληξις, φθάνει τὸν ἄνδρα
200 μεταθεὶς[1] πρὸς τὸ Ῥωμαίων στρατόπεδον. τοῦ
δὲ στρατηγοῦ κελεύσαντος γυμνὸν διαλαβεῖν αὐτὸν
καὶ καταστήσαντας εἰς τὸ φανερώτατον τοῖς
ἐκ τῆς πόλεως ἀποβλέπουσι μάστιξιν αἰκίζεσθαι,
σφόδρα τοὺς Ἰουδαίους τὸ περὶ τὸν νεανίαν
πάθος συνέχεεν, ἀθρόα τε ἡ πόλις ἀνώμωξε, καὶ
θρῆνος ἦν μείζων ἢ καθ' ἑνὸς ἀνδρὸς συμφοράν.
201 τοῦτο συνιδὼν ὁ Βάσσος κατὰ τῶν πολεμίων
ἀρχὴν ἐποιήσατο στρατηγήματος, καὶ βουληθεὶς
αὐτῶν ἐπιτεῖναι τὸ περιαλγές, ἵνα βιασθῶσιν ἀντὶ
τῆς σωτηρίας τἀνδρὸς ποιήσασθαι τοῦ φρουρίου
202 παράδοσιν, τῆς ἐλπίδος οὐ διήμαρτεν. ὁ μὲν
γὰρ προσέταξε καταπηγνύναι σταυρὸν ὡς αὐτίκα
κρεμῶν τὸν Ἐλεάζαρον, τοῖς δ' ἀπὸ τοῦ φρουρίου
τοῦτο θεασαμένοις ὀδύνη τε πλείων προσέπεσε,
καὶ διωλύγιον ἀνώμωζον οὐκ ἀνασχετὸν εἶναι
203 τὸ πάθος βοῶντες. ἐνταῦθα δὴ τοίνυν Ἐλεάζαρος
ἱκέτευεν αὐτοὺς μήτ' αὐτὸν περιδεῖν ὑπομείναντα
θανάτων τὸν οἴκτιστον καὶ σφίσιν αὐτοῖς τὴν
σωτηρίαν παρασχεῖν τῇ Ῥωμαίων εἴξαντας ἰσχύϊ
204 καὶ τύχῃ μετὰ πάντας ἤδη κεχειρωμένους. οἱ
δὲ καὶ πρὸς τοὺς ἐκείνου λόγους κατακλώμενοι
καὶ πολλῶν ἔνδον ὑπὲρ αὐτοῦ δεομένων, ἦν γὰρ
ἐκ μεγάλης καὶ σφόδρα πολυανθρώπου συγγενείας,
205 παρὰ τὴν αὐτῶν φύσιν εἰς οἶκτον ἐνέδωκαν, καί
τινας ἐξαποστείλαντες κατὰ τάχος διελέγοντο
ποιεῖσθαι τὴν παράδοσιν τοῦ φρουρίου ἀξιοῦντες,

Thereupon, spying his opportunity, a soldier in the
Roman ranks named Rufus, a native of Egypt, made
a sudden dash upon him, such as none could have
expected, lifted him up, armour and all, while the
spectators on the wall were paralysed with astonishment, and succeeded in transporting the fellow to the
Roman camp. The general having ordered him to
be stripped and carried to the spot most exposed to
the view of the onlookers in the city and there
severely scourged, the Jews were profoundly affected
by the lad's fate, and the whole town burst into such
wailing and lamentation as the misfortune of a mere
individual seemed hardly to justify. Observing this, _{leads to the surrender of}
Bassus proceeded to practise a ruse upon the enemy, _{the fort.}
desiring so to intensify their distress as to compel
them to purchase the man's life by the surrender of
the fort ; and in this hope he was not disappointed.
For he ordered a cross to be erected, as though
intending to have Eleazar instantly suspended ; at
which sight those in the fortress were seized with
deeper dismay and with piercing shrieks exclaimed
that the tragedy was intolerable. At this juncture,
moreover, Eleazar besought them not to leave him
to undergo the most pitiable of deaths, but to consult
their own safety by yielding to the might and fortune
of the Romans, now that all others had been subdued. Overcome by his appeals, which were backed
by many interceders within—for he came of a distinguished and extremely numerous family—they
yielded to a compassion contrary to their nature and
hastily dispatched a deputation to discuss the sur-

---

[1] μετατιθεὶς PA.

ἵν᾽ ἀδεεῖς ἀπαλλάττωνται κομισάμενοι τὸν Ἐλεά-
206 ζαρον. δεξαμένων δὲ τῶν Ῥωμαίων καὶ τοῦ
στρατηγοῦ ταῦτα, τὸ πλῆθος τῶν ἐν τῇ κάτω
πόλει τὴν γεγενημένην ἰδίᾳ τοῖς Ἰουδαίοις πυ-
θόμενοι σύμβασιν αὐτοὶ κατὰ νύκτα λαθόντες
207 ἔγνωσαν ἀποδρᾶναι. τὰς πύλας δ᾽ αὐτῶν ἀνοιξάν-
των παρὰ τῶν τὴν ὁμολογίαν πεποιημένων πρὸς
τὸν Βάσσον ἧκεν μήνυσις, εἴτ᾽ οὖν τῆς σωτηρίας
αὐτοῖς φθονησάντων εἴτε [καὶ]¹ διὰ δέος, μὴ τὴν
αἰτίαν αὐτοὶ λάβωσι τῆς ἐκείνων ἀποδράσεως.
208 οἱ μὲν οὖν ἀνδρειότατοι τῶν ἐξιόντων ἔφθασαν
διεκπαίσασθαι καὶ διαφυγεῖν, τῶν δ᾽ ἔνδον κατα-
λειφθέντων ἄνδρες μὲν ἀνῃρέθησαν ἐπὶ τοῖς χιλίοις
ἑπτακόσιοι, γύναια δὲ καὶ παῖδες ἠνδραποδίσθη-
209 σαν. τὰς δὲ πρὸς τοὺς παραδόντας τὸ φρούριον
ὁμολογίας οἰόμενος δεῖν ὁ Βάσσος διαφυλάττειν
αὐτούς τ᾽ ἀφίησιν καὶ τὸν Ἐλεάζαρον ἀπέδωκε.
210   (5) Ταῦτα δὲ διοικησάμενος ἠπείγετο τὴν στρατιὰν ἄγων ἐπὶ τὸν προσαγορευόμενον Ἰάρδην
δρυμόν· πολλοὶ γὰρ εἰς αὐτὸν ἠγγέλθησαν ἠθροῖσθαι
τῶν κατὰ τὰς πολιορκίας πρότερον ἔκ τε Ἱερο-
211 σολύμων καὶ Μαχαιροῦντος ἀποδράντων. ἐλθὼν
οὖν ἐπὶ τὸν τόπον καὶ γνοὺς τὴν ἀγγελίαν οὐκ
ἐψευσμένην πρῶτον μὲν τοῖς ἱππεῦσιν ἅπαν
κυκλοῦται τὸ χωρίον, ὅπως τοῖς διεκπαίεσθαι
τολμῶσιν τῶν Ἰουδαίων ἄπορος ἡ φυγὴ γίνηται
διὰ τοὺς ἱππέας· τοὺς δὲ πεζοὺς ἐκέλευσεν δενδρο-
212 τομεῖν τὴν ὕλην, εἰς ἣν καταπεφεύγεσαν. καθ-
ίστανται δὲ διὰ τοῦτο πρὸς ἀνάγκην οἱ Ἰουδαῖοι
τοῦ δρᾶν τι γενναῖον, ὡς ἐκ παραβόλου² ἀγωνί-

¹ MLC: om. the rest.

render of the fortress, stipulating for permission to depart in safety, taking Eleazar with them. The Romans and their general having accepted these conditions, the people in the town below, hearing of the separate compact that had been made by the Jews, determined on their part to make off secretly by night. But no sooner had they opened the gates than information was given to Bassus by those who had made the treaty with him; whether grudging them their lives, or maybe from fear of being held answerable for their flight. The most courageous of the fugitives, however, contrived to cut their way through and escape; of those left in the town, the men, numbering seventeen hundred, were slain, the women and children were enslaved. Bassus, holding himself bound to observe his agreement with those who had surrendered the fortress, let them depart and restored Eleazar.

(5) Having settled affairs here, Bassus pushed on with his troops to the forest called Jardes,[a] it being reported that many who had previously fled from Jerusalem and Machaerus during the respective sieges had congregated in this quarter. On reaching the spot and finding the report correct, he began by surrounding the whole place with his cavalry, to prevent the escape of any Jews attempting to break through; he then ordered the infantry to fell the trees among which the fugitives had taken cover. The Jews were thus reduced to the necessity of attempting some gallant feat, in the hope that by a desperate struggle they might possibly escape; and

Battle of the forest of Jardes.

---

[a] Unidentified.

² text doubtful: τοῦ παραβόλως A²: παραλόγου P.

σασθαι τάχα ἂν καὶ διαφυγόντες, ἀθρόοι δὲ[1] καὶ
μετὰ βοῆς ἄξαντες ἐνέπιπτον τοῖς κεκυκλωμένοις.

213 οἱ δ' αὐτοὺς ἐδέχοντο καρτερῶς, καὶ πολλῇ τῶν
μὲν ἀπονοίᾳ τῶν δὲ φιλονεικίᾳ χρωμένων χρόνος
μὲν οὐκ ὀλίγος διὰ τοῦτο τῇ μάχῃ προύβη, τέλος
δ' αὐτῆς οὐχ ὅμοιον ἀπέβη τοῖς ἀγωνισαμένοις.

214 Ῥωμαίων μὲν γὰρ δώδεκα τοὺς πάντας συνέβη
πεσεῖν ὀλίγους τε τρωθῆναι, [τῶν][2] Ἰουδαίων δὲ
ἐκ τῆς μάχης ταύτης οὐδεὶς διέφυγεν, ἀλλ' ὄντες

215 οὐκ ἐλάττους τρισχιλίων πάντες ἀπέθανον, καὶ ὁ
στρατηγὸς αὐτῶν Ἰούδας ὁ τοῦ Ἀρεῖ παῖς, περὶ
οὗ πρότερον εἰρήκαμεν ὅτι τάξεως ἡγούμενός
τινος ἐν τῇ πολιορκίᾳ τῶν Ἱεροσολύμων κατά
τινας διαδὺς τῶν ὑπονόμων ἔλαθεν ἀποδράς.

216 (6) Περὶ δὲ τὸν αὐτὸν καιρὸν ἐπέστειλε Καῖσαρ
Βάσσῳ καὶ Λαβερίῳ[3] Μαξίμῳ, οὗτος δ' ἦν
ἐπίτροπος, κελεύων πᾶσαν γῆν ἀποδόσθαι τῶν

217 Ἰουδαίων. οὐ γὰρ κατῴκισεν ἐκεῖ πόλιν ἰδίαν
αὑτῷ[4] τὴν χώραν φυλάττων, ὀκτακοσίοις δὲ
μόνοις ἀπὸ τῆς στρατιᾶς διαφειμένοις χωρίον
ἔδωκεν εἰς κατοίκησιν, ὃ καλεῖται μὲν Ἀμμαοῦς,
ἀπέχει δὲ τῶν Ἱεροσολύμων σταδίους τριάκοντα.

218 φόρον δὲ τοῖς ὁπουδηποτοῦν οὖσιν Ἰουδαίοις
ἐπέβαλεν, δύο δραχμὰς ἕκαστον κελεύσας ἀνὰ
πᾶν ἔτος εἰς τὸ Καπετώλιον φέρειν, ὥσπερ
πρότερον εἰς τὸν ἐν Ἱεροσολύμοις νεὼν συνετέλουν.

---

[1] τε Niese.   [2] om. P.
[3] Lat. : Λιβερίῳ or Λεβερίῳ mss.
[4] Dindorf: αὐτῷ L Lat. : αὐτῶν the rest.

---

[a] One of the leaders of the Zealots, who distinguished himself during the siege, B. vi. 92; his escape from Jerusalem
has not been previously mentioned.

so, in a mass and with a shout, they dashed out and fell upon their surrounding foes. These met them stubbornly, and so, with prodigious efforts of despair on the one side and emulation on the other, the contest was long protracted; but the issue was widely different for the combatants. For the Romans lost in all but twelve dead and a few wounded, while of the Jews not a man emerged from that battle: all, to the number of no less than three thousand, perished. Among the slain was their general Judas, son of Ari, whom we have previously mentioned [a] as in command of a company at the siege of Jerusalem, whence he secretly escaped through some of the underground passages.

(6) About the same time Caesar sent instructions to Bassus and Laberius Maximus,[b] the procurator, to farm out [c] all Jewish territory. For he founded no city there, reserving the country as his private property, except that he did assign to eight hundred veterans discharged from the army a place for habitation called Emmaus,[d] distant thirty furlongs from Jerusalem. On all Jews, wheresoever resident, he imposed a poll-tax of two drachms,[e] to be paid annually into the Capitol as formerly contributed by

Jewish territory sold and tax imposed on all Jews.

---

[b] L. Laberius Maximus, mentioned in inscriptions.

[c] So or "lease" (" verpachten "), not " sell," Schürer, *G.J.V.* i. 640, in reply to Mommsen.

[d] Probably to be identified both with the modern *Kulonieh* (Colonia), some four miles N.W. of Jerusalem, and with the Emmaus of the N.T., though St. Luke (xxiv. 13) doubles the distance to 60 furlongs. See the full discussion in Schürer, *G.J.V.* i. 640 ff.

[e] So Dion Cassius lxvi. 7 καὶ ἀπ' ἐκείνου δίδραχμον ἐτάχθη, τοὺς τὰ πάτρια αὐτῶν ἔθη περιστέλλοντας τῷ Καπιτωλίῳ Διῒ κατ' ἔτος ἀποφέρειν.

καὶ τὰ μὲν Ἰουδαίων τότε τοιαύτην εἶχε κατάστασιν.

219 (vii. 1) Ἤδη δ' ἔτος τέταρτον Οὐεσπασιανοῦ
διέποντος τὴν ἡγεμονίαν συνέβη τὸν βασιλέα τῆς
Κομμαγηνῆς Ἀντίοχον μεγάλαις συμφοραῖς παν-
220 οικεσίᾳ περιπεσεῖν ἀπὸ τοιαύτης αἰτίας. Και-
σέννιος Παῖτος,[1] ὁ τῆς Συρίας ἡγεμὼν τότε
καθεστηκώς, εἴτ' οὖν ἀληθεύων εἴτε καὶ διὰ τὴν
πρὸς Ἀντίοχον ἔχθραν, οὐ σφόδρα γὰρ τὸ σαφὲς
ἠλέγχθη, γράμματα πρὸς Καίσαρα διεπέμψατο,
221 λέγων τὸν Ἀντίοχον μετὰ τοῦ παιδὸς Ἐπιφανοῦς
διεγνωκέναι Ῥωμαίων ἀφίστασθαι, συνθήκας πρὸς
222 τὸν βασιλέα τῶν Πάρθων πεποιημένον· δεῖν οὖν
προκαταλαβεῖν αὐτούς, μὴ φθάσαντες τῶν πραγμάτων [ἄρξασθαι][2] πᾶσαν τὴν Ῥωμαίων ἀρχὴν
223 πολέμῳ συνταράξωσιν. ἔμελλε δὲ[3] Καῖσαρ τοιού-
του μηνύματος αὐτῷ προσπεσόντος μὴ περιορᾶν·
καὶ γὰρ ἡ γειτνίασις τῶν βασιλέων ἐποίει τὸ
224 πρᾶγμα μείζονος ἄξιον προνοίας· τὰ γὰρ Σαμόσατα, τῆς Κομμαγηνῆς μεγίστη πόλις, κεῖται
παρὰ τὸν Εὐφράτην, ὥστ' εἶναι τοῖς Πάρθοις,
εἴ τι τοιοῦτον διενενόηντο, ῥᾴστην μὲν τὴν διάβασιν,
225 βεβαίαν δὲ τὴν ὑποδοχήν. πιστευθεὶς οὖν ὁ
Παῖτος καὶ λαβὼν ἐξουσίαν πράττειν ἃ δοκεῖ
συμφέρειν οὐκ ἐμέλλησεν, ἐξαίφνης δὲ τῶν περὶ
τὸν Ἀντίοχον οὐδὲν προσδοκώντων εἰς τὴν
Κομμαγηνὴν ἐνέβαλεν, τῶν μὲν ταγμάτων ἄγων
τὸ ἕκτον καὶ πρὸς τούτῳ λόχους καί τινας ἴλας
226 ἱππέων· συνεμάχουν δὲ καὶ βασιλεῖς αὐτῷ τῆς

---

[1] Hudson: Κεσσένιος (or Κεσέννιος) Πέτος mss. and so (Πέτος)
below.

[2] om. PAM : ἅψασθαι Herwerden.   [3] om. P.

them to the temple at Jerusalem.[a] Such was the
position of Jewish affairs at this date.

(vii. 1) But while Vespasian was now for the fourth
year holding imperial sway, Antiochus, king of Commagene,[b] became involved, with all his family, in
serious disasters, which arose as follows. Caesennius
Paetus,[c] then governor of Syria (whether speaking
sincerely or out of enmity to Antiochus, was never
clearly ascertained) sent letters to Caesar stating
that Antiochus with his son Epiphanes had determined to revolt from Rome and was in league with
the king of Parthia ; it, therefore, behoved Caesar
to forestall them, lest they should be beforehand
in creating trouble and convulse the whole Roman
empire with war. Such a report, thus conveyed to
him, Caesar could not afford to overlook, seeing that
the proximity of these princes to each other made
the matter deserving of special precaution. For
Samosata, the chief city of Commagene, lying on the
Euphrates, would afford the Parthians, if they harboured any such designs, a most easy passage and
an assured reception. Paetus being, accordingly,
accredited and empowered to act as he thought fit,
did not hesitate, but suddenly, while Antiochus and
his friends were expecting nothing of the sort, invaded Commagene, at the head of the sixth legion,
supplemented by some cohorts and a few squadrons
of horse ; he had the further support of two sove-

Marginal notes:
Misfortunes of Antiochus, king of Commagene, a victim of slander.
A.D. 72-3.

Paetus invades his territory.

---

[a] The temple tax, originally a third of a shekel (Neh. x. 32),
afterwards half a shekel (Ex. xxx. 13), = 2 Tyrian drachms,
was paid by all Jews of twenty years old and upwards. *Cf.*
Matt. xvii. 24, Jos. *A.* xviii. 312.
[b] In N. Syria. [c] § 59 note.

μὲν Χαλκιδικῆς λεγομένης Ἀριστόβουλος, τῆς
227 Ἐμέσης δὲ καλουμένης Σόαιμος. ἦν δ' αὐτοῖς
τὰ περὶ τὴν εἰσβολὴν ἀνανταγώνιστα· τῶν γὰρ
κατὰ τὴν χώραν οὐδεὶς ἤθελε χεῖρας ἀνταίρειν.
228 Ἀντίοχος δὲ τῆς ἀγγελίας ἀδοκήτως προσπεσού-
σης πολέμου μὲν οὐδ' ἐπίνοιαν πρὸς Ῥωμαίους
ἔσπασεν, ἔγνω δὲ πᾶσαν τὴν βασιλείαν ὡς εἶχεν
ἐπὶ ὀχήματος¹ καταλιπὼν μετὰ γυναικὸς καὶ
τέκνων ὑπεξελθεῖν, οὕτως ἂν οἰόμενος καθαρὸν
Ῥωμαίοις αὐτὸν ἀποδεῖξαι τῆς ἐπενηνεγμένης
229 αἰτίας. καὶ προελθὼν ἀπὸ τῆς πόλεως ἑκατὸν
σταδίους πρὸς τοῖς εἴκοσιν εἰς τὸ πεδίον ἐν αὐτῷ
καταυλίζεται.
230 (2) Παῖτος δ' ἐπὶ μὲν τὰ Σαμόσατα τοὺς
καταληψομένους ἀποστέλλει καὶ δι' ἐκείνων εἶχε
τὴν πόλιν, αὐτὸς δὲ μετὰ τῆς ἄλλης δυνάμεως
231 ἐπ' Ἀντίοχον ἐποιεῖτο τὴν ὁρμήν. οὐ μὴν ὁ
βασιλεὺς οὐδ' ὑπὸ τῆς ἀνάγκης προήχθη πρᾶξαί
τι πρὸς Ῥωμαίους πολεμικόν, ἀλλὰ τὴν αὐτοῦ
232 τύχην ὀδυρόμενος ὅ τι δέοι παθεῖν ὑπέμενε· νέοις
δὲ καὶ πολέμων ἐμπείροις καὶ ῥώμῃ σωμάτων
διαφέρουσιν οὐ ῥᾴδιον ἦν τοῖς παισὶν αὐτοῦ τὴν
συμφορὰν ἀμαχεὶ καρτερεῖν· τρέπονται οὖν πρὸς
233 ἀλκὴν Ἐπιφανής τε καὶ Καλλίνικος. σφοδρᾶς
δὲ τῆς μάχης καὶ παρ' ὅλην τὴν ἡμέραν γενομένης
αὐτοὶ τὴν ἀνδρείαν διαπρεπῆ παρέσχον καὶ μηδὲν
ἐλαττωθείσῃ τῇ σφετέρᾳ δυνάμει ἑσπέρᾳ² διελύ-
234 θησαν. Ἀντιόχῳ δ' οὐδ' ἐπὶ τῇ μάχῃ τοῦτον

¹ conj. Naber: σχήματος mss.
² om. Lat.: ἅμ' ἑσπέρᾳ Destinon.

ᵃ The district of either (1) Chalcis (*'Anjar*) in the Lebanon
range, or (2) another Chalcis further N. in Syria. Herod, the
570

reigns, Aristobulus of the region named Chalcidice,[a] and Soemus of Emesa,[b] as the other principality is called. Their invasion was unopposed, not a man throughout the country wishing to lift a hand against them. Antiochus, confronted with the unexpected tidings, never entertained a moment's thought of a war with Rome, but decided to quit the realm, leaving everything as it was, and to abscond in a chariot with his wife and children, hoping thus to clear himself in the eyes of the Romans of the charge under which he lay. Proceeding, accordingly, from the capital one hundred and twenty furlongs into the plain, he there encamped.

Flight of Antiochus.

(2) Paetus sent a detachment to occupy Samosata, and through them held the town, while he with the rest of his force hastened in pursuit of Antiochus. Even in these straits, however, the king could not be induced to take any hostile action against the Romans, but lamenting his lot was content to submit to whatever suffering might be in store for him. His sons, on the contrary, with the advantages of youth, military experience, and unusual physical strength, could not lightly brook this calamity without a struggle; Epiphanes[c] and Callinicus, accordingly, had resort to arms. In the fierce contest which ensued, lasting the whole day, the princes displayed conspicuous gallantry, and their troops had sustained no diminution of strength when night parted the combatants. Yet, even after such an issue of the conflict,

grandson of Herod the Great, was king of Chalcis in Lebanon and had a son Aristobulus, who may be the sovereign here mentioned. See Schürer, *G.J.V.* i. 724.

[b] *Homs.*

[c] He has appeared before in a foolhardy venture beneath the walls of Jerusalem, v. 460 ff.

κεχωρηκυίᾳ τὸν τρόπον μένειν ἀνεκτὸν ἐδόκει,
λαβὼν δὲ τὴν γυναῖκα καὶ τὰς θυγατέρας μετ'
ἐκείνων ἐποιεῖτο τὴν φυγὴν εἰς Κιλικίαν, καὶ
τοῦτο πράξας τὰ φρονήματα τῶν οἰκείων στρα-
235 τιωτῶν κατέκλασεν· ὡς γὰρ κατεγνωσμένης ὑπ'
αὐτοῦ τῆς βασιλείας ἀπέστησαν καὶ πρὸς τοὺς
Ῥωμαίους μετεβάλοντο, καὶ πάντων πρόδηλος
236 ἦν ἀπόγνωσις. πρὶν οὖν τελέως ἐρημωθῆναι τῶν
συμμάχων τοῖς περὶ τὸν Ἐπιφανῆ σώζειν αὐτοὺς
ἐκ τῶν πολεμίων ἦν ἀναγκαῖον, καὶ γίνονται δέκα
σύμπαντες ἱππεῖς οἱ μετ' αὐτῶν τὸν Εὐφράτην
237 διαβαλόντες,[1] ἔνθεν ἤδη μετ' ἀδείας πρὸς τὸν βασιλέα τῶν Πάρθων Βολογέσην κομισθέντες οὐχ ὡς
φυγάδες ὑπερηφανήθησαν, ἀλλ' ὡς ἔτι τὴν παλαιὰν
ἔχοντες εὐδαιμονίαν πάσης τιμῆς ἠξιώθησαν.
238   (3) Ἀντιόχῳ δ' εἰς Ταρσὸν ἀφιγμένῳ τῆς
Κιλικίας ἑκατοντάρχην Παῖτος ἐπιπέμψας δεδε-
239 μένον αὐτὸν εἰς Ῥώμην ἀπέστειλεν. Οὐεσπασιανὸς δ' οὕτως οὐχ ὑπέμεινεν πρὸς αὐτὸν ἀναχ-
θῆναι τὸν βασιλέα, τῆς παλαιᾶς ἀξιῶν φιλίας
μᾶλλον αἰδῶ λαβεῖν ἢ. διὰ τὴν τοῦ πολέμου
240 πρόφασιν ἀπαραίτητον ὀργὴν διαφυλάττειν· κελεύει
δὴ καθ' ὁδὸν ἔτ' ὄντος αὐτοῦ τῶν δεσμῶν ἀφαιρεθῆναι καὶ παρέντα τὴν εἰς [τὴν][2] Ῥώμην ἄφιξιν
τὸ νῦν ἐν Λακεδαίμονι διάγειν, δίδωσί τε μεγάλας
αὐτῷ προσόδους χρημάτων, ὅπως μὴ μόνον
ἄφθονον ἀλλὰ καὶ βασιλικὴν ἔχοι [τὴν][3] δίαιταν.
241 ταῦτα τοῖς περὶ τὸν Ἐπιφανῆ πυθομένοις, πρότερον σφόδρα περὶ τοῦ πατρὸς δεδιόσιν, ἀνείθησαν
αἱ ψυχαὶ μεγάλης καὶ δυσδιαθέτου φροντίδος.

---

[1] Holwerda: διαλαβόντες most mss.: διαβάντες LC.
[2] om. ML.   [3] om. PAML.

Antiochus could not bring himself to remain, but accompanied by his wife and daughters fled to Cilicia, thereby breaking the spirits of his own troops ; for, regarding him as having pronounced sentence on his realm, they mutinied and went over to the Romans, and despair was manifest in all faces. Epiphanes and his followers were consequently forced to seek safety from the enemy in flight, before they were entirely deserted by their allies. Ten horsemen, in fact, were all that crossed the Euphrates with the two brothers ; thence they proceeded unmolested to Bologeses,[a] king of Parthia, by whom they were treated not with disdain, as fugitives, but with every mark of respect, as though still enjoying their ancient prosperity.

(3) Antiochus, on reaching Tarsus in Cilicia, was arrested by a centurion, sent after him by Paetus, who dispatched his prisoner in chains to Rome. Vespasian, however, could not suffer the king to be brought up to him thus, thinking it more fitting to respect an ancient friendship than, on the pretext of war, to cherish inexorable wrath. He accordingly gave orders, while he was still on the road, that he should be released from his chains, abandon his journey to Rome, and remain for the present in Lacedaemon ; he, moreover, assigned him a revenue sufficient to maintain not merely an ample but a regal establishment. On hearing of this, Epiphanes and Callinicus, hitherto in serious alarm on their father's account, were relieved from their grave and disturbing anxiety. They had hopes, moreover, of

His reconciliation with Vespasian.

---

[a] § 105.

242 ἐλπὶς δὲ καὶ αὐτοῖς τῶν παρὰ Καίσαρος διαλλαγῶν
ἐγένετο Βολογέσου περὶ αὐτῶν ἐπιστείλαντος· οὐδὲ
γὰρ εὐδαιμονοῦντες ὑπέμενον ἔξω τῆς Ῥωμαίων
243 ζῆν ἡγεμονίας. δόντος δὲ Καίσαρος ἡμέρως
αὐτοῖς τὴν ἄδειαν εἰς Ῥώμην παρεγένοντο, τοῦ τε
πατρὸς ὡς αὐτοὺς ἐκ τῆς Λακεδαίμονος εὐθὺς ἐλ-
θόντος πάσης ἀξιούμενοι τιμῆς κατέμενον ἐνταῦθα.
244 (4) Τὸ δὲ τῶν Ἀλανῶν ἔθνος ὅτι μέν εἰσι
Σκύθαι περὶ τὸν Τάναϊν καὶ τὴν Μαιῶτιν λίμνην
245 κατοικοῦντες, πρότερόν που δεδηλώκαμεν, κατὰ
τούτους δὲ τοὺς χρόνους διανοηθέντες εἰς τὴν
Μηδίαν καὶ προσωτέρω ταύτης ἔτι καθ᾽ ἁρπαγὴν
ἐμβαλεῖν τῷ βασιλεῖ τῶν Ὑρκανῶν διαλέγονται·
τῆς παρόδου γὰρ οὗτος δεσπότης ἐστίν, ἣν ὁ
βασιλεὺς Ἀλέξανδρος πύλαις σιδηραῖς κλειστὴν
246 ἐποίησε. κἀκείνου τὴν εἴσοδον αὐτοῖς παρασχόντος ἀθρόοι καὶ μηδὲν προϋποπτεύσασι τοῖς
Μήδοις ἐπιπεσόντες χώραν πολυάνθρωπον καὶ
παντοίων ἄναμεστον βοσκημάτων διήρπαζον
247 μηδενὸς αὐτοῖς τολμῶντος ἀντίστασθαι. καὶ γὰρ
ὁ βασιλεύων τῆς χώρας Πάκορος ὑπὸ δέους εἰς
τὰς δυσχωρίας ἀναφεύγων τῶν μὲν ἄλλων ἁπάντων
παρακεχωρήκει, μόλις δὲ παρ᾽ αὐτῶν ἐρρύσατο
τήν τε γυναῖκα καὶ τὰς παλλακὰς αἰχμαλώτους
248 γενομένας ἑκατὸν δοὺς τάλαντα. μετὰ πολλῆς
οὖν ῥαστώνης ἀμαχεὶ ποιούμενοι τὰς ἁρπαγὰς
μέχρι τῆς Ἀρμενίας προῆλθον πάντα λεηλατοῦντες.

---

[a] This is the first mention of them in the *War*; the allusion
to a previous remark has possibly been carelessly taken over
by Josephus from the source from which this section,
irrelevant to Jewish history, has been derived.

[b] The *Don*.   [c] *Sea of Azov*.   [d] S. of the Caspian.

[e] The "Caspian Gates" was the name given to a mountain

their own reconciliation with Caesar, through the representations which Bologeses had addressed to him on their behalf; for, however favourable their lot, the thought of living outside the Roman empire was intolerable. Caesar having then graciously granted them safe conduct, they came to Rome, where they were promptly joined by their father from Lacedaemon; and there they took up their abode, treated with every mark of honour.

(4) The Alani—a race of Scythians, as we have somewhere previously remarked,[a] inhabiting the banks of the river Tanais [b] and the lake Maeotis [c]— contemplating at this period a predatory incursion into Media and beyond, entered into negotiations with the king of the Hyrcanians,[d] who was master of the pass which king Alexander had closed with iron gates.[e] Being granted admission by him, masses of them fell upon the Medes, who suspected nothing, and plundered a populous country, filled with all manner of live-stock, none venturing to oppose them. For Pacorus,[f] the monarch of the country, had fled in terror up into his fastnesses, abandoning all his possessions, and having with difficulty recovered from them his wife and concubines, who had been taken prisoners, by a ransom of a hundred talents. Pursuing, therefore, their raids with perfect ease and unresisted, they advanced as far as Armenia, laying

Invasion of Media by the Alani, a Scythian tribe.

pass, or series of difficult passes, in the Taurus range S. of the Caspian Sea (Grote, *Hist. of Greece*, ed. 4, x. 127 f.). Arrian (iii. 20) describes how Alexander the Great, in pursuit of Darius, failed to overtake him before he reached this point, but says nothing about the "iron gates" mentioned by Josephus.

[f] Brother of Vologeses I, king of Parthia, mentioned above, § 237.

249 Τιριδάτης δ' αὐτῆς ἐβασίλευεν, ὃς ὑπαντιάσας
αὐτοῖς καὶ ποιησάμενος μάχην παρὰ μικρὸν ἦλθεν
250 ἐπ' αὐτῆς ζωὸς ἁλῶναι τῆς παρατάξεως· βρόχον
γὰρ αὐτῷ περιβαλών τις πόρρωθεν[1] ἔμελλεν
ἐπισπάσειν, εἰ μὴ τῷ ξίφει θᾶττον ἐκεῖνος τὸν
251 τόνον κόψας ἔφθη διαφυγεῖν. οἱ δὲ καὶ διὰ τὴν
μάχην ἔτι μᾶλλον ἀγριωθέντες τὴν μὲν χώραν
ἐλυμήναντο, πολὺ δὲ πλῆθος ἀνθρώπων καὶ τῆς
ἄλλης λείας ἄγοντες ἐξ ἀμφοῖν τῶν βασιλειῶν
πάλιν εἰς τὴν οἰκείαν ἀνεκομίσθησαν.

252 (viii. 1) Ἐπὶ δὲ τῆς Ἰουδαίας Βάσσου τελευτήσαντος Φλάυιος Σίλβας διαδέχεται τὴν ἡγεμονίαν, καὶ τὴν μὲν ἄλλην ὁρῶν ἅπασαν τῷ
πολέμῳ κεχειρωμένην, ἓν δὲ μόνον ἔτι φρούριον
ἀφεστηκός, ἐστράτευσεν ἐπὶ τοῦτο πᾶσαν τὴν
ἐν τοῖς τόποις δύναμιν συναγαγών· καλεῖται δὲ
253 τὸ φρούριον Μασάδα. προεστήκει δὲ τῶν κατειληφότων αὐτὸ σικαρίων δυνατὸς ἀνὴρ Ἐλεάζαρος,
ἀπόγονος Ἰούδα τοῦ πείσαντος Ἰουδαίους οὐκ
ὀλίγους, ὡς πρότερον δεδηλώκαμεν, μὴ ποιεῖσθαι
τὰς ἀπογραφάς, ὅτε Κυρίνιος τιμητὴς εἰς τὴν
254 Ἰουδαίαν ἐπέμφθη. τότε γὰρ οἱ σικάριοι συν-
έστησαν ἐπὶ τοὺς ὑπακούειν Ῥωμαίων θέλοντας
καὶ πάντα τρόπον ὡς πολεμίοις προσεφέροντο,
τὰς μὲν κτήσεις ἁρπάζοντες καὶ περιελαύνοντες,
255 ταῖς δ' οἰκήσεσιν αὐτῶν πῦρ ἐνιέντες· οὐδὲν γὰρ
ἀλλοφύλων αὐτοὺς ἔφασκον διαφέρειν, οὕτως
ἀγεννῶς τὴν περιμάχητον Ἰουδαίοις ἐλευθερίαν

----

[1] om. PA.

----

[a] Another brother of Vologeses I.   [b] § 162.
[c] L. Flavius Silva Nonius Bassus (the full name given in
an inscription) was consul in A.D. 81.

everything waste. Tiridates,[a] the king of that country, who met them and gave them battle, narrowly escaped being taken alive in the engagement ; for a noose was thrown round him by a distant enemy who would have dragged him off, had he not instantly cut the rope with his sword and succeeded in escaping. The Alani, whose savagery was increased by this opposition, made havoc of the country, and, carrying off masses of the population and booty of all kinds from both kingdoms, returned once more to their own land.

(viii. 1) In Judaea, meanwhile, Bassus[b] had died and been succeeded in the governorship by Flavius Silva,[c] who, seeing the whole country now subjugated by the Roman arms, with the exception of one fortress still in revolt, concentrated all forces in the district and marched against it. This fortress was called Masada[d] ; and the Sicarii who had occupied it had at their head a man of influence named Eleazar. He was a descendant[e] of the Judas who, as we have previously stated,[f] induced multitudes of Jews to refuse to enroll themselves, when Quirinius was sent as censor to Judaea. For in those days the Sicarii clubbed together against those who consented to submit to Rome and in every way treated them as enemies, plundering their property, rounding up their cattle, and setting fire to their habitations ; protesting that such persons were no other than aliens, who so ignobly sacrificed the hard-won[g]

Flavius Silva attacks the last Jewish fortress of MASADA *held by the Sicarii under Eleazar, A.D. 73 (probably).* *Crimes of the Sicarii.*

[d] *Sebbeh,* above the W. coast of the Dead Sea, near its lower end, S. of En Gedi. The Roman siege-works are said to be still clearly recognizable.

[e] Son of Jairus (*B.* ii. 447) and apparently grandson of Judas.   [f] *B.* ii. 118, *cf.* 433.

[g] Or " highly prized," " to be fought for."

προεμένους καὶ δουλείαν αἱρεῖσθαι τὴν ὑπὸ Ῥω-
256 μαίοις ἀνομολογηκότας. ἦν δ' ἄρα τοῦτο πρόφασις εἰς παρακάλυμμα τῆς ὠμότητος καὶ τῆς
πλεονεξίας ὑπ' αὐτῶν λεγόμενον· σαφὲς δὲ διὰ
257 τῶν ἔργων ἐποίησαν. οἱ μὲν γὰρ αὐτοῖς τῆς
ἀποστάσεως ἐκοινώνησαν καὶ τοῦ πρὸς Ῥωμαίους
συνήραντο πολέμου,[1] καὶ παρ' ἐκείνων δὲ τολμή-
258 ματα χείρω πρὸς αὐτοὺς ἐγένετο, κἀπὶ τῷ ψεύ-
δεσθαι πάλιν[2] τὴν πρόφασιν ἐξελεγχόμενοι μᾶλλον
ἐκάκουν τοὺς τὴν πονηρίαν αὐτῶν διὰ τῆς δικαιο-
259 λογίας ὀνειδίζοντας. ἐγένετο γάρ πως ὁ χρόνος
ἐκεῖνος παντοδαπῆς ἐν τοῖς Ἰουδαίοις πονηρίας
πολύφορος, ὡς μηδὲν κακίας ἔργον ἄπρακτον
καταλιπεῖν, μηδ' εἴ τις ἐπινοίᾳ[3] διαπλάττειν
ἐθελήσειεν, ἔχειν ἄν τι καινότερον ἐξευρεῖν.
260 οὕτως ἰδίᾳ τε καὶ κοινῇ πάντες ἐνόσησαν, καὶ
πρὸς ὑπερβάλλειν[4] ἀλλήλους ἔν τε ταῖς πρὸς θεὸν
ἀσεβείαις καὶ ταῖς εἰς τοὺς πλησίον ἀδικίαις
ἐφιλονείκησαν, οἱ μὲν δυνατοὶ τὰ πλήθη κακοῦντες,
οἱ πολλοὶ δὲ τοὺς δυνατοὺς ἀπολλύναι σπεύδοντες·
261 ἦν γὰρ ἐκείνοις μὲν ἐπιθυμία τοῦ τυραννεῖν, τοῖς
δὲ τοῦ βιάζεσθαι καὶ τὰ τῶν εὐπόρων διαρπάζειν.
262 πρῶτοι μὲν οὖν οἱ σικάριοι τῆς παρανομίας καὶ
τῆς πρὸς τοὺς συγγενεῖς ἦρξαν ὠμότητος, μήτε
λόγον ἄρρητον εἰς ὕβριν μήτ' ἔργον ἀπείρατον[5]
εἰς ὄλεθρον τῶν ἐπιβουλευθέντων παραλιπόντες.
263 ἀλλὰ καὶ τούτους Ἰωάννης ἀπέδειξεν αὐτοῦ

---

[1] Niese here suspects a lacuna.
[2] pridem (=πάλαι) Lat.
[3] τι ἐπινοίᾳ PA[1]: τις ἐπινοίᾳ the rest.
[4] Niese προσυπερβάλλειν with P: for adverbial πρός cf.
A. xix. 110 (καὶ πρὸς ἔρις αὐτοῖς ἦν).
[5] Dindorf: ἀπείραστον MSS.

liberty of the Jews and admitted their preference for the Roman yoke. Yet, after all, this was but a pretext, put forward by them as a cloak for their cruelty and avarice, as was made plain by their actions. For the people did join with them in the revolt and take their part in the war with Rome, only, however, to suffer at their hands still worse atrocities ; and when they were again convicted of falsehood in this pretext, they only oppressed the more those who in righteous self-defence reproached them with their villainy.

Indeed,[a] that period had, somehow, become so prolific of crime of every description amongst the Jews, that no deed of iniquity was left unperpetrated, nor, had man's wit been exercised to devise it, could he have discovered any novel form of vice. So universal was the contagion, both in private and in public life, such the emulation, moreover, to outdo each other in acts of impiety towards God and of injustice towards their neighbours ; those in power oppressing the masses, and the masses eager to destroy the powerful. These were bent on tyranny, those on violence and plundering the property of the wealthy. The Sicarii were the first to set the example of this lawlessness and cruelty to their kinsmen, leaving no word unspoken to insult, no deed untried to ruin, the victims of their conspiracy. Yet even they were shown by John to be more moderate than

Other Jewish criminals.

John of Gischala.

[a] The mention of Masada, the last stronghold of the rebels, and of their chief, leads to this digression (§ 274) on the general iniquities of other insurgents and their leaders.

579

μετριωτέρους· οὐ γὰρ μόνον ἀνῄρει πάντας ὅσοι
τὰ δίκαια καὶ συμφέροντα συνεβούλευον, καθάπερ
ἐχθίστοις μάλιστα δὴ τῶν πολιτῶν τοῖς τοιούτοις
προσφερόμενος, ἀλλὰ καὶ κοινῇ τὴν πατρίδα
μυρίων ἐνέπλησε κακῶν, οἷα πράξειν ἔμελλεν
ἀνθρώπους[1] ἤδη καὶ τὸν θεὸν ἀσεβεῖν τετολμηκώς·
264 τράπεζάν τε γὰρ ἄθεσμον παρετίθετο καὶ τὴν
νενομισμένην καὶ πάτριον ἐξεδιῄτησεν ἁγνείαν,
ἵν' ᾖ μηκέτι θαυμαστόν, εἰ τὴν πρὸς ἀνθρώπους
ἡμερότητα καὶ κοινωνίαν οὐκ ἐτήρησεν ὁ τῆς πρὸς
265 θεὸν εὐσεβείας οὕτω καταμανείς. πάλιν τοίνυν
ὁ Γιώρα Σίμων τί κακὸν οὐκ ἔδρασεν; ἢ ποίας
ὕβρεως ἐλευθέρων ἀπέσχετο[2] σωμάτων οἳ τοῦτον
266 ἀνέδειξαν τύραννον; ποία δ' αὐτοὺς φιλία, ποία
δὲ συγγένεια πρὸς τοὺς ἐφ' ἑκάστης ἡμέρας
φόνους οὐχὶ θρασυτέρους ἐποίησε; τὸ μὲν γὰρ
τοὺς ἀλλοτρίους κακῶς ποιεῖν ἀγεννοὺς ἔργον
πονηρίας[3] ὑπελάμβανον, λαμπρὰν δὲ φέρειν ἐπίδειξιν ἡγοῦντο τὴν ἐν τοῖς οἰκειοτάτοις ὠμότητα.
267 παρημιλλήσατο δὲ καὶ τὴν τούτων ἀπόνοιαν ἡ
τῶν Ἰδουμαίων [μανία][4]· ἐκεῖνοι γὰρ οἱ μιαρώτατοι
τοὺς ἀρχιερέας κατασφάξαντες, ὅπως μηδὲ μέρος
τι[5] τῆς πρὸς τὸν θεὸν εὐσεβείας διαφυλάττηται,
πᾶν ὅσον ἦν λείψανον ἔτι πολιτικοῦ σχήματος
268 ἐξέκοψαν, καὶ τὴν τελευτάτην εἰσήγαγον διὰ
πάντων ἀνομίαν, ἐν ᾗ τὸ τῶν ζηλωτῶν κληθέντων
γένος ἤκμασεν, οἳ τὴν προσηγορίαν τοῖς ἔργοις
269 ἐπηλήθευσαν· πᾶν γὰρ κακίας ἔργον ἐξεμιμήσαντο,
μηδ' εἴ τι πρότερον προϋπάρχον ἡ μνήμη παρα-

---

[1] Exc. : ἄνθρωπος mss.

himself. For not only did he put to death all who
proposed just and salutary measures, treating such
persons as his bitterest enemies among all the citizens,
but he also in his public capacity loaded his country
with evils innumerable, such as one might expect
would be inflicted upon men by one who had already
dared to practise impiety even towards God. For
he had unlawful food served at his table and
abandoned the established rules of purity of our
forefathers; so that it could no longer excite surprise, that one guilty of such mad impiety towards
God failed to observe towards men the offices of
gentleness and charity. Again, there was Simon, Simon ben
son of Gioras: what crime did not he commit? Or Giora.
what outrage did he refrain from inflicting upon the
persons of those very freemen who had created him
a despot?[a] What ties of friendship or of kindred but
rendered these men more audacious in their daily
murders? For to do injury to a foreigner they considered an act of petty malice, but thought they cut
a splendid figure by maltreating their nearest
relations. Yet even their infatuation was outdone The
by the madness of the Idumaeans. For those most Idumaeans.
abominable wretches, after butchering the chief
priests,[b] so that no particle of religious worship might
continue, proceeded to extirpate whatever relics were
left of our civil polity, introducing into every de-
partment perfect lawlessness. In this the so-called The Zealots.
Zealots excelled, a class which justified their name
by their actions; for they copied every deed of ill,
nor was there any previous villainy recorded in

[a] B. iv. 574 ff. [b] iv. 314 ff.

---

[2] ἀπέσχοντο M.   [3] Exc.: + εἶναι MSS.
[4] om. VRC Lat.   [5] VRC Lat.: ἔτι the rest.

270 δέδωκεν αὐτοὶ παραλιπόντες ἀζήλωτον. καίτοι
τὴν προσηγορίαν αὐτοῖς ἀπὸ τῶν ἐπ' ἀγαθῷ
ζηλουμένων ἐπέθεσαν, ἢ κατειρωνευόμενοι τῶν
ἀδικουμένων διὰ τὴν αὐτῶν θηριώδη φύσιν ἢ τὰ
271 μέγιστα τῶν κακῶν ἀγαθὰ νομίζοντες. τοιγαροῦν
προσῆκον ἔκαστοι τὸ τέλος εὕροντο, τοῦ θεοῦ τὴν
ἀξίαν ἐπὶ πᾶσιν αὐτοῖς τιμωρίαν βραβεύσαντος·
272 ὅσας γὰρ ἀνθρώπου δύναται φύσις κολάσεις
ὑπομεῖναι, πᾶσαι κατέσκηψαν εἰς αὐτοὺς μέχρι
καὶ τῆς ἐσχάτης τοῦ βίου τελευτῆς, ἣν ὑπέμειναν
273 ἐν πολυτρόποις αἰκίαις ἀποθανόντες. οὐ μὴν ἀλλὰ
φαίη τις ἂν αὐτοὺς ἐλάττω παθεῖν ὧν ἔδρασαν·
274 τὸ γὰρ δικαίως ἐπ' αὐτῶν οὐ προσῆν. τοὺς δὲ
ταῖς ἐκείνων ὠμότησι περιπεσόντας οὐ τοῦ
παρόντος ἂν εἴη καιροῦ κατὰ τὴν ἀξίαν ὀδύρεσθαι·
πάλιν οὖν ἐπάνειμι πρὸς τὸ καταλειπόμενον μέρος
τῆς διηγήσεως.

275 (2) Ἐπὶ γὰρ τὸν Ἐλεάζαρον καὶ τοὺς κατ-
έχοντας σὺν αὐτῷ τὴν Μασάδαν σικαρίους ὁ τῶν
Ῥωμαίων στρατηγὸς ἧκε τὰς δυνάμεις ἄγων,
καὶ τῆς μὲν χώρας ἁπάσης εὐθὺς ἐκράτει φρουρὰς
ἐν τοῖς ἐπικαιροτάτοις αὐτῆς μέρεσιν ἐγκατα-
276 στήσας, τεῖχος δὲ περιέβαλε κύκλῳ περὶ πᾶν τὸ
φρούριον, ὅπως μηδενὶ τῶν πολιορκουμένων ᾖ
ῥᾴδιον διαφυγεῖν, καὶ διανέμει τοὺς φυλάξοντας.
277 αὐτὸς δὲ καταστρατοπεδεύει τόπον ὡς μὲν πρὸς
τὴν πολιορκίαν ἐπιτηδειότατον ἐκλαβών, καθ' ὃν
αἱ τοῦ φρουρίου πέτραι τῷ πλησίον ὄρει συνήγγιζον,
ἄλλως δὲ πρὸς ἀφθονίαν τῶν ἐπιτηδείων δύσκολον·
278 οὐ γὰρ ἡ τροφὴ μόνον πόρρωθεν ἐκομίζετο καὶ
σὺν μεγάλῃ ταλαιπωρίᾳ τῶν ἐπὶ τοῦτο τεταγμένων
Ἰουδαίων, ἀλλὰ καὶ τὸ ποτὸν ἦν ἀγώγιμον [εἰς

history that they failed zealously to emulate. And yet they took their title from their professed zeal for virtue, either in mockery of those they wronged, so brutal was their nature, or reckoning the greatest of evils good. Accordingly these each found a fitting end, God awarding due retribution to them all. For every punishment that human nature is capable of enduring descended upon them, even to those last dying moments of life, endured by them amid the agonies of manifold torture.[a] And yet one may say that they suffered less than they inflicted; for no suffering could match their deserts. However, the present would not be the occasion to deplore, as they deserve, the victims of their barbarities; I will, therefore, resume the interrupted thread of the narrative.

(2) The Roman general advanced at the head of his forces against Eleazar and his band of Sicarii who held Masada, and, promptly making himself master of the whole district, established garrisons at the most suitable points, threw up a wall all round the fortress, to make it difficult for any of the besieged to escape, and posted sentinels to guard it. He himself encamped at a spot which he selected as most convenient for siege operations, where the rocks of the fortress abutted on the adjacent mountain, although ill situated for commissariat purposes. For not only were supplies conveyed from a distance, entailing hard labour for the Jews told off for this duty, but even water had to be brought into the

Silva's preparations for the siege.

---

[a] Cf. §§ 417 ff. for the tortures inflicted on the Sicarii with the object of inducing them to own Caesar as lord, and borne with a determination worthy of the early Christian martyrs; these fanatics at any rate died nobly.

τὸ στρατόπεδον]¹ τοῦ τόπου μηδεμίαν ἐγγὺς πηγὴν
279 ἀναδιδόντος. ταῦτ' οὖν προοικονομησάμενος ὁ
Σίλβας ἐπὶ τὴν πολιορκίαν ἐτράπετο πολλῆς ἐπι-
τεχνήσεως καὶ ταλαιπωρίας δεομένην διὰ τὴν ὀχυρότητα τοῦ φρουρίου τοιοῦδε τὴν φύσιν ὑπάρχοντος.
280 (3) Πέτραν· οὐκ ὀλίγην τῇ περιόδῳ καὶ μῆκος
ὑψηλὴν πανταχόθεν περιερρώγασι βαθεῖαι φάραγγες,² κάτωθεν ἐξ ἀοράτου τέρματος κρημνώδεις
καὶ πάσῃ βάσει ζώων ἀπρόσιτοι, πλὴν ὅσον κατὰ
δύο τόπους τῆς πέτρας εἰς ἄνοδον οὐκ εὐμαρῆ
281 παρεικούσης. ἔστι δὲ τῶν ὁδῶν ἡ μὲν ἀπὸ τῆς
Ἀσφαλτίτιδος λίμνης πρὸς ἥλιον ἀνίσχοντα, καὶ
πάλιν ἀπὸ τῆς δύσεως ᾗ ῥᾷον³ πορευθῆναι.
282 καλοῦσι δὲ τὴν ἑτέραν ὄφιν, τῇ στενότητι προσ-
εικάσαντες καὶ τοῖς συνεχέσιν ἑλιγμοῖς· κλᾶται
γὰρ περὶ τὰς τῶν κρημνῶν ἐξοχὰς καὶ πολλάκις
εἰς αὐτὴν ἀνατρέχουσα καὶ κατὰ μικρὸν αὖθις
283 ἐκμηκυνομένη μόλις ψαύει τοῦ πρόσω. δεῖ δὲ
παραλλὰξ τὸν δι' αὐτῆς βαδίζοντα τὸν ἕτερον
τῶν ποδῶν⁴ ἐρείδεσθαι. ἔστι δὲ πρόδηλος ὄλεθρος·
ἑκατέρωθεν γὰρ βάθος κρημνῶν ὑποκέχηνε τῇ
φοβερότητι πᾶσαν εὐτολμίαν ἐκπλῆξαι δυνάμενον.
284 διὰ τοιαύτης οὖν ἐλθόντι σταδίους τριάκοντα
κορυφὴ τὸ λοιπόν ἐστιν, οὐκ εἰς ὀξὺ τέρμα
συνηγμένη, ἀλλ' ὥστ' εἶναι κατ' ἄκρας ἐπίπεδον.
285 ἐπὶ ταύτῃ πρῶτον μὲν ὁ ἀρχιερεὺς ᾠκοδομήσατο
φρούριον Ἰωνάθης καὶ προσηγόρευσε Μασάδαν,
ὕστερον δ' Ἡρώδῃ τῷ βασιλεῖ διὰ πολλῆς ἐγένετο
286 σπουδῆς ἡ τοῦ χωρίου κατασκευή. τεῖχός τε γὰρ

¹ om. P.   ² +καὶ P Lat.
      ³ ἡ ῥᾷων Niese (ed. min.) after VR.
                  ⁴ τοῖν ποδοῖν C.

584

camp, there being no spring in the neighbourhood. Having completed these preliminary arrangements, Silva turned his attention to the siege, which demanded great skill and severe exertion, owing to the strength of the fortress, the nature of which was as follows.

(3) A rock of no slight circumference and lofty The rock of from end to end is abruptly terminated on every side Masada by deep ravines, the precipices rising sheer from an invisible base and being inaccessible to the foot of any living creature, save in two places where the rock permits of no easy ascent. Of these tracks one leads from the Lake Asphaltitis *a* on the east,*b* the other, by which the approach is easier, from the west. The former they call the snake, seeing a resemblance to that reptile in its narrowness and continual windings ; for its course is broken in skirting the jutting crags and, returning frequently upon itself and gradually lengthening out again, it makes painful headway. One traversing this route must firmly plant each foot alternately. Destruction faces him ; for on either side yawn chasms so terrific as to daunt the hardiest. After following this perilous track for thirty furlongs, one reaches the summit, which, instead of tapering to a sharp peak, expands into a plain. On this plateau the high priest Jonathan *c* first erected a fortress and called it Masada; the subsequent planning of the place engaged the serious attention of King Herod. For and Herod's fortress upon it.

a The *Dead Sea.*

b Literally " towards the sun-rising," a phrase found in Herodotus (iii. 98).

c Brother of Judas Maccabaeus and his successor as Jewish leader, 161–143 B.C., *B.* i. 48 f.

ἤγειρε περὶ πάντα τὸν κύκλον τῆς κορυφῆς ἑπτὰ
σταδίων ὄντα, λευκοῦ μὲν λίθου πεποιημένον,
ὕψος δὲ δώδεκα καὶ πλάτος ὀκτὼ πήχεις ἔχον,
287 τριάκοντα δ' αὐτῷ καὶ ἑπτὰ πύργοι πεντηκοντα-
πήχεις ἀνειστήκεσαν, ἐξ ὧν ἦν εἰς οἰκήματα
διελθεῖν περὶ πᾶν τὸ τεῖχος ἔνδον ᾠκοδομημένα.
288 τὴν γὰρ κορυφὴν πίονα καὶ πεδίου παντὸς οὖσαν
μαλακωτέραν ἀνῆκεν εἰς γεωργίαν ὁ βασιλεύς,
ἵν' εἴ ποτε τῆς ἔξωθεν τροφῆς ἀπορία γένοιτο,
μηδὲ ταύτῃ κάμοιεν οἱ τὴν αὐτῶν σωτηρίαν τῷ
289 φρουρίῳ πεπιστευκότες. καὶ βασίλειον δὲ κατεσκεύασεν ἐν αὐτῷ κατὰ τὴν ἀπὸ τῆς ἑσπέρας
ἀνάβασιν, ὑποκάτω μὲν τῶν τῆς ἄκρας τειχῶν,
πρὸς δὲ τὴν ἄρκτον ἐκκλῖνον.¹ τοῦ δὲ βασιλείου
τὸ τεῖχος ἦν ὕψει μέγα καὶ καρτερόν, πύργους
290 ἔχον ἑξηκονταπήχεις ἐγγωνίους τέτταρας. ἥ τε
τῶν οἰκημάτων ἔνδον καὶ στοῶν καὶ βαλανείων
κατασκευὴ παντοία καὶ πολυτελὴς ἦν, κιόνων
μὲν ἁπανταχοῦ μονολίθων ὑφεστηκότων, τοίχων
δὲ καὶ τῶν ἐν τοῖς οἰκήμασιν ἐδάφων λίθου
291 στρώσει πεποικιλμένων. πρὸς ἕκαστον δὲ τῶν
οἰκουμένων τόπων ἄνω τε καὶ περὶ τὸ βασίλειον
καὶ πρὸ τοῦ τείχους πολλοὺς καὶ μεγάλους
ἐτετμήκει λάκκους ἐν ταῖς πέτραις φυλακτῆρας
ὑδάτων, μηχανώμενος εἶναι χορηγίαν ὅση τῷ²
292 ἐκ πηγῶν ἐστι χρωμένοις. ὀρυκτὴ δ' ὁδὸς ἐκ
τοῦ βασιλείου πρὸς ἄκραν τὴν κορυφὴν ἀνέφερε
τοῖς ἔξωθεν ἀφανής. οὐ μὴν οὐδὲ ταῖς φανεραῖς
293 ὁδοῖς ἦν οἷόν τε χρήσασθαι ῥᾳδίως πολεμίους· ἡ
μὲν γὰρ ἑῴα διὰ τὴν φύσιν, ὡς προείπαμεν, ἐστὶν
ἄβατος, τὴν δ' ἀπὸ τῆς ἑσπέρας μεγάλῳ κατὰ τὸ
στενότατον πύργῳ διετείχισεν, ἀπέχοντι τῆς ἄκρας

first he enclosed the entire summit, a circuit measuring seven furlongs, with a wall of white stone, twelve cubits high and eight broad ; on it stood thirty-seven towers, fifty cubits high, from which access was obtained to apartments constructed round the whole interior of the wall. For the actual top, being of rich soil and softer than any plain, was given up by the king to cultivation ; in order that, should there ever be a dearth of provisions from outside, those who had committed their lives to the protection of the fortress might not suffer from it. There, too, he built a palace on the western slope, beneath the ramparts on the crest and inclining towards the north. The palace wall was strong and of great height, and had four towers, sixty cubits high, at the corners. The fittings of the interior—apartments, colonnades, and baths—were of manifold variety and sumptuous ; columns, each formed of a single block, supporting the building throughout, and the walls and floors of the apartments being laid with variegated stones. Moreover, at each spot used for habitation, both on the summit and about the palace, as also before the wall, he had cut out in the rock numerous large tanks, as reservoirs for water, thus procuring a supply as ample as where springs are available. A sunk road led up from the palace to the summit of the hill, imperceptible from without. But even of the open approaches it was not easy for an enemy to make use ; for the eastern track, as we have previously stated,[a] is from its nature impracticable, while that on the west Herod barred at its narrowest point by a great tower,

---

[a] §§ 281-3.

[1] P (ἐκκλίνων) A : ἐγκλίνον the rest.
[2] Niese : τῶν mss.

πήχεων οὐκ ἔλαττον διάστημα χιλίων, ὃν οὔτε
παρελθεῖν δυνατὸν ἦν οὔτε ῥᾴδιον ἑλεῖν· δυσέξοδος
δὲ καὶ τοῖς μετὰ ἀδείας βαδίζουσιν ἐπεποίητο.
294 οὕτως μὲν οὖν πρὸς τὰς τῶν πολεμίων ἐφόδους
φύσει τε καὶ χειροποιήτως τὸ φρούριον ὠχύρωτο.

295 (4) Τῶν δ' ἔνδον ἀποκειμένων παρασκευῶν ἔτι
μᾶλλον ἄν τις ἐθαύμασε τὴν λαμπρότητα καὶ τὴν
296 διαμονήν· σῖτός τε γὰρ ἀπέκειτο πολὺς καὶ πολὺν
χρόνον ἀρκεῖν ἱκανώτατος οἶνός τε πολὺς ἦν καὶ
ἔλαιον, ἔτι δὲ παντοῖος ὀσπρίων καρπὸς καὶ
297 φοίνικες ἐσεσώρευντο. πάντα δ' εὗρεν ὁ Ἐλεάζαρος τοῦ φρουρίου μετὰ τῶν σικαρίων ἐγκρατὴς
δόλῳ γενόμενος ἀκμαῖα καὶ μηδὲν τῶν νεωστὶ
κειμένων ἀποδέοντα· καίτοι σχεδὸν ἀπὸ τῆς
παρασκευῆς εἰς τὴν ὑπὸ Ῥωμαίοις ἅλωσιν ἑκατὸν
ἦν χρόνος ἐτῶν· ἀλλὰ καὶ Ῥωμαῖοι τοὺς περι-
298 λειφθέντας τῶν καρπῶν εὗρον ἀδιαφθόρους. αἴτιον
δ' οὐκ ἂν ἁμάρτοι τις ὑπολαμβάνων εἶναι τὸν
ἀέρα τῆς διαμονῆς, ὕψει τῶν[1] περὶ τὴν ἄκραν
πάσης ὄντα γεώδους καὶ θολερᾶς ἀμιγῆ κράσεως.
299 εὑρέθη δὲ καὶ παντοίων πλῆθος ὅπλων ὑπὸ τοῦ
βασιλέως ἀποτεθησαυρισμένον,[2] ὡς ἀνδράσιν ἀρκεῖν μυρίοις, ἀργός τε σίδηρος καὶ χαλκὸς ἔτι
δὲ καὶ μόλιβος, ἅτε δὴ τῆς παρασκευῆς ἐπὶ
300 μεγάλαις αἰτίαις γενομένης· λέγεται γὰρ αὐτῷ
τὸν Ἡρώδην τοῦτο τὸ φρούριον εἰς ὑποφυγὴν
ἑτοιμάζειν διπλοῦν ὑφορώμενον κίνδυνον, τὸν μὲν
παρὰ τοῦ πλήθους τῶν Ἰουδαίων, μὴ καταλύσαντες
ἐκεῖνον τοὺς πρὸ αὐτοῦ βασιλέας ἐπὶ τὴν ἀρχὴν
καταγάγωσι, τὸν μείζω δὲ καὶ χαλεπώτερον ἐκ

---

[1] τῷ Niese with A².
[2] C Lat.: -ισμένων the rest.

distant no less than a thousand cubits from the crest. This tower it was neither possible to pass nor easy to capture; exit being rendered difficult even for passengers who had no cause for alarm. So strongly had this fortress been intrenched against an enemy's attack, both by nature and the hand of man.

(4) But the stores laid up within would have excited still more amazement, alike for their lavish splendour and their durability. For here had been stored a mass of corn, amply sufficient to last for years, abundance of wine and oil, besides every variety of pulse and piles of dates. All these Eleazar, when he with his Sicarii became through treachery master of the fortress,[a] found in perfect condition and no whit inferior to goods recently laid in; although from the date of storage to the capture of the place by the Romans well-nigh a century had elapsed.[b] Indeed, the Romans found what remained of the fruits undecayed. It would not be erroneous to attribute such durability to the atmosphere, which at the altitude of the citadel is untainted by all earth-born and foul alloy. There was also found a mass of arms of every description, hoarded up by the king and sufficient for ten thousand men, besides unwrought iron, brass, and lead; these preparations having, in fact, been made for grave reasons. For it is said that Herod furnished this fortress as a refuge for himself, suspecting a twofold danger: peril on the one hand from the Jewish people, lest they should depose him and restore their former dynasty to power; the greater and more serious from Cleopatra,

Herod's stores found in perfect condition.

The fortress stocked as a refuge for himself.

[a] *B.* ii. 408, *cf.* 433.
[b] If the fortress was stocked in Cleopatra's lifetime (§ 300), upward of a century had elapsed, from before 31 B.C. to A.D. 73.

301 τῆς βασιλευούσης Αἰγύπτου Κλεοπάτρας. αὕτη
γὰρ τὴν αὑτῆς γνώμην οὐκ ἐπεῖχεν, ἀλλὰ πολλάκις
Ἀντωνίῳ λόγους προσέφερε, τὸν μὲν Ἡρώδην
ἀνελεῖν ἀξιοῦσα, χαρίσασθαι δ' αὐτῇ τὴν βα-
302 σιλείαν τῶν Ἰουδαίων δεομένη. καὶ μᾶλλον ἄν
τις ἐθαύμασεν ὅτι μηδέπω τοῖς προστάγμασιν
Ἀντώνιος ὑπακηκόει, κακῶς ὑπὸ τοῦ πρὸς αὐτὴν
ἔρωτος δεδουλωμένος, οὐχ ὅτι περὶ τοῦ μὴ
303 χαρίσασθαι προσεδόκησεν. διὰ τοιούτους μὲν φόβους Ἡρώδης Μασάδαν κατεσκευασμένος ἔμελλε
Ῥωμαίοις ἀπολείψειν ἔργον τοῦ πρὸς Ἰουδαίους
πολέμου τελευταῖον.

304 (5) Ἐπεὶ γὰρ ἔξωθεν ἤδη περιτετειχίκει πάντα
τὸν τόπον ὁ τῶν Ῥωμαίων, ὡς προείπαμεν,
ἡγεμὼν καὶ τοῦ μή τινα ἀποδρᾶναι πρόνοιαν
ἐπεποίητο τὴν ἀκριβεστάτην, ἐνεχείρει τῇ πολιορκίᾳ μόνον εὑρὼν ἕνα τόπον ἐπιβολὴν χωμάτων
305 δέξασθαι δυνάμενον. μετὰ γὰρ τὸν διατειχίζοντα
πύργον τὴν ἀπὸ τῆς δύσεως ὁδὸν ἄγουσαν εἴς
τε τὸ βασίλειον καὶ τὴν ἀκρώρειαν ἦν τις ἐξοχὴ
πέτρας εὐμεγέθης τῷ πλάτει καὶ πολὺ προ-
κύπτουσα, τοῦ δ' ὕψους τῆς Μασάδας τριακοσίους
πήχεις ὑποκάτω· Λευκὴν δ' αὐτὴν ὠνόμαζον.
306 ἐπὶ ταύτην οὖν ἀναβὰς καὶ κατασχὼν αὐτὴν ὁ
Σίλβας ἐκέλευε τὸν στρατὸν χοῦν ἐπιφέρειν.
τῶν δὲ προθύμως καὶ μετὰ πολλῆς χειρὸς ἐργα-
ζομένων στερεὸν εἰς διακοσίους πήχεις ὑψώθη
307 τὸ χῶμα. οὐ μὴν οὔτε βέβαιον οὔτ' αὐτάρκες
ἐδόκει τοῦτο τὸ μέτρον εἶναι τοῖς μηχανήμασιν
εἰς ἐπιβάθραν, ἀλλ' ἐπ' αὐτοῦ βῆμα λίθων μεγάλων
συνηρμοσμένων ἐποιήθη πεντήκοντα πήχεων εὖρός
308 τε καὶ ὕψος. ἦν δὲ τῶν ἄλλων τε μηχανημάτων
590

queen of Egypt. For she never concealed her intention, but was constantly importuning Antony, urging him to slay Herod, and praying him to confer on her the throne of Judaea.[a] And, far from expecting him to refuse to gratify her, one might rather be surprised that Antony should never have obeyed her behests, basely enslaved as he was by his passion for her. It was such fears that drove Herod to fortify Masada, which he was destined to leave to the Romans as a final task in their war with the Jews.

(5) The Roman general, having now completed his wall surrounding the whole exterior of the place, as we have already related,[b] and taken the strictest precautions that none should escape, applied himself to the siege. He had discovered only one spot capable of supporting earthworks. For in rear of the tower which barred the road leading from the west to the palace and the ridge, was a projection of rock, of considerable breadth and jutting far out, but still three hundred cubits below the elevation of Masada; it was called Leuce.[c] Silva, having accordingly ascended and occupied this eminence, ordered his troops to throw up an embankment. Working with a will and a multitude of hands, they raised a solid bank to the height of two hundred cubits. This, however, being still considered of insufficient stability and extent as an emplacement for the engines, on top of it was constructed a platform of great stones fitted closely together, fifty cubits broad and as many high. The engines in general were similarly constructed to those first

The siege.

----

[a] Cf. B. i. 359 f. (c. 34 B.C.).
[b] §§ 275 f.
[c] " White (cliff)."

ἡ κατασκευὴ παραπλησία τοῖς ὑπὸ μὲν Οὐεσπασιανοῦ πρότερον, μετὰ ταῦτα δ' ὑπὸ Τίτου πρὸς
309 τὰς πολιορκίας ἐπινοηθεῖσι, καὶ πύργος ἑξη-
κοντάπηχυς συνετελέσθη σιδήρῳ καταπεφραγ-
μένος ἅπας, ἐξ οὗ πολλοῖς ὀξυβελέσι καὶ πετροβόλοις βάλλοντες οἱ Ῥωμαῖοι τοὺς ἀπὸ τοῦ
τείχους μαχομένους ταχέως ἀνέστειλαν καὶ προ-
310 κύπτειν ἐκώλυσαν. ἐν ταὐτῷ δὲ καὶ κριὸν ὁ
Σίλβας μέγαν κατασκευασάμενος, συνεχεῖς κελεύσας ποιεῖσθαι τῷ τείχει τὰς ἐμβολὰς μόλις μὲν
311 ἀλλ' οὖν ἀναρρήξας τι μέρος[1] κατήρειψε. φθάνουσι
δ' οἱ σικάριοι ταχέως ἔνδοθεν οἰκοδομησάμενοι
τεῖχος ἕτερον, ὃ μηδ' ὑπὸ τῶν μηχανημάτων
ἔμελλεν ὅμοιόν τι πείσεσθαι· μαλακὸν γὰρ αὐτὸ
καὶ τὴν σφοδρότητα τῆς ἐμβολῆς ὑπεκλύειν
312 δυνάμενον τοιῷδε τρόπῳ κατεσκεύασαν. δοκοὺς
μεγάλας ἐπὶ μῆκος προσεχεῖς ἀλλήλαις κατὰ τὴν
τομὴν συνέθεσαν. δύο δ' ἦσαν τούτων στίχοι
παράλληλοι, τοσοῦτον διεστῶτες ὅσον εἶναι πλάτος
τείχους, καὶ μέσον ἀμφοῖν τὸν χοῦν ἐνεφόρουν.
313 ὅπως δὲ μηδ' ὑψουμένου τοῦ χώματος ἡ γῆ
διαχέοιτο, πάλιν ἑτέραις δοκοῖς ἐπικαρσίαις τὰς
314 κατὰ μῆκος κειμένας διέδεον. ἦν οὖν ἐκείνοις
μὲν οἰκοδομία τὸ ἔργον παραπλήσιον, τῶν μηχανημάτων δ' αἱ πληγαὶ φερόμεναι πρὸς εἶκον[2] ἐξελύοντο
καὶ τῷ σάλῳ συνιζάνον ἐποίουν αὐτὸ στεριφώτερον.
315 τοῦτο συνιδὼν ὁ Σίλβας πυρὶ μᾶλλον αἱρήσειν
ἐνόμιζεν τὸ τεῖχος, καὶ τοῖς στρατιώταις προσ-
έταττε λαμπάδας αἰθομένας ἀθρόους ἐσακοντίζειν.
316 τὸ δ' οἷα δὴ ξύλων τὸ πλέον πεποιημένον ταχὺ
τοῦ πυρὸς ἀντελάβετο καὶ τῇ χαυνότητι πυρωθὲν

---

[1] PA : + αὐτοῦ the rest.

devised by Vespasian and afterwards by Titus for their siege operations; in addition[a] a sixty-cubit tower was constructed entirely cased in iron, from which the Romans by volleys of missiles from numerous quick-firers and *ballistae* quickly beat off the defenders on the ramparts and prevented them from showing themselves. Simultaneously, Silva, having further provided himself with a great battering-ram, ordered it to be directed without intermission against the wall, and having, though with difficulty, succeeded in effecting a breach, brought it down in ruins. The Sicarii, however, had already hastily built up another wall inside, which was not likely to meet with a similar fate from the engines; for it was pliable and calculated to break the force of the impact, having been constructed as follows. Great beams were laid lengthwise and contiguous and joined at the extremities; of these there were two parallel rows a wall's breadth apart, and the intermediate space was filled with earth. Further, to prevent the soil from dispersing as the mound rose, they clamped, by other transverse beams, those laid longitudinally. The work thus presented to the enemy the appearance of masonry, but the blows of the engines were weakened, battering upon a yielding material which, as it settled down under the concussion, they merely served to solidify. Observing this, Silva, thinking it easier to destroy this wall by fire, ordered his soldiers to hurl at it showers of burning torches. Being mainly made of wood, it quickly caught fire, and, from its hollow nature becoming ignited right through

The wall is breached and the defenders second wooden wall

is destroyed by fire.

---

[a] Vespasian had constructed three similar towers at Jotapata, but not more than 50 feet high, *B.* iii. 284.

2 πρὸς εἴκον Hudson : προσεικὸς MSS.

317 διὰ βάθους φλόγα πολλὴν ἐξεπύρσευσεν. ἀρχο-
μένου μὲν οὖν ἔτι τοῦ πυρὸς βορρᾶς ἐμπνέων
τοῖς Ῥωμαίοις φοβερὸς ἦν· ἄνωθεν γὰρ ἀποστρέφων
ἐπ᾽ ἐκείνους ἤλαυνε τὴν φλόγα, καὶ σχεδὸν ἤδη
τῶν μηχανημάτων ὡς συμφλεγησομένων ἀπ-
318 έγνωσαν[1]· ἔπειτα δ᾽ αἰφνίδιον νότος μεταβαλὼν
καθάπερ ἐκ δαιμονίου προνοίας καὶ πολὺς ἐναντίον
πνεύσας τῷ τείχει φέρων αὐτὴν προσέβαλε, καὶ
319 πᾶν ἤδη διὰ βάθους ἐφλέγετο. Ῥωμαῖοι μὲν
οὖν τῇ παρὰ τοῦ θεοῦ συμμαχίᾳ κεχρημένοι
χαίροντες εἰς τὸ στρατόπεδον ἀπηλλάττοντο, μεθ᾽
ἡμέραν ἐπιχειρεῖν τοῖς πολεμίοις διεγνωκότες,
καὶ τὰς φυλακὰς νύκτωρ ἐπιμελεστέρας ἐποιήσαντο, μή τινες αὐτῶν λάθωσιν ἀποδράντες.

320 (6) Οὐ μὴν οὔτ᾽ αὐτὸς Ἐλεάζαρος ἐν νῷ
δρασμὸν ἔλαβεν οὔτ᾽ ἄλλῳ τινὶ τοῦτο ποιεῖν
321 ἔμελλεν ἐπιτρέψειν. ὁρῶν δὲ τὸ μὲν τεῖχος ὑπὸ
τοῦ πυρὸς ἀναλούμενον, ἄλλον δ᾽ οὐδένα σωτηρίας
τρόπον οὐδ᾽ ἀλκῆς ἐπινοῶν, ἃ δὲ ἔμελλον Ῥωμαῖοι
δράσειν αὐτοὺς καὶ τέκνα καὶ γυναῖκας αὐτῶν,
εἰ κρατήσειαν, ὑπ᾽ ὀφθαλμοὺς αὑτῷ τιθέμενος,
322 θάνατον κατὰ πάντων ἐβουλεύσατο. καὶ τοῦτο
κρίνας ἐκ τῶν παρόντων ἄριστον, τοὺς ἀνδρω-
δεστάτους τῶν ἑταίρων συναγαγὼν τοιούτοις ἐπὶ
323 τὴν πρᾶξιν λόγοις παρεκάλει· "πάλαι διεγνω-
κότας ἡμᾶς, ἄνδρες ἀγαθοί, μήτε Ῥωμαίοις μήτ᾽
ἄλλῳ τινὶ δουλεύειν ἢ θεῷ, μόνος γὰρ οὗτος
ἀληθής ἐστι καὶ δίκαιος ἀνθρώπων δεσπότης,
ἥκει νῦν καιρὸς ἐπαληθεῦσαι κελεύων τὸ φρόνημα
324 τοῖς ἔργοις. πρὸς ὃν αὐτοὺς μὴ καταισχύνωμεν,

---

[1] ἀπεγνώκεσαν LVRC.

blazed up in a volume of flame. At the first outbreak of the fire, a north wind which blew in the
faces of the Romans caused them an alarm; for,
diverting the flame from above, it drove it against
them, and the fear that all their engines would be
burnt up had almost reduced them to despair. Then
suddenly the wind veering, as if by divine providence,[a]
to the south and blowing with full force in the opposite
direction, wafted and flung the flames against the
wall, which now through and through[b] was all ablaze.
The Romans, thus blessed by God's aid, returned
rejoicing to their camp, with the determination of
attacking the enemy on the morrow; and throughout
that night they kept stricter watch lest any of them
should secretly escape.

(6) However, neither did Eleazar himself con-
template flight, nor did he intend to permit any
other to do so. Seeing the wall consuming in the
flames, unable to devise any further means of
deliverance or gallant endeavour, and setting before
his eyes what the Romans, if victorious, would inflict
on them, their children and their wives, he deliberated
on the death of all. And, judging, as matters stood,
this course the best, he assembled the most doughty
of his comrades and incited them to the deed by such
words as these:

"Long since, my brave men, we determined
neither to serve the Romans nor any other save God,
for He alone is man's true and righteous Lord; and
now the time is come which bids us verify that
resolution by our actions. At this crisis let us not
disgrace ourselves; we who in the past refused to

Eleazar's first speech to the besieged recommending self-destruction.

---

[a] For similar providential aid *cf. B.* iv. 76 (at Gamala).
[b] Or "from top to bottom."

πρότερον μηδὲ δουλείαν ἀκίνδυνον ὑπομείναντες,
νυνὶ¹ δὲ μετὰ δουλείας ἑλόμενοι τιμωρίας ἀνηκέ-
στους, εἰ ζῶντες ὑπὸ Ῥωμαίοις ἐσόμεθα· πρῶτοί
τε γὰρ πάντων ἀπέστημεν καὶ πολεμοῦμεν αὐτοῖς
325 τελευταῖοι. νομίζω δὲ καὶ παρὰ θεοῦ ταύτην²
δεδόσθαι χάριν τοῦ δύνασθαι καλῶς καὶ ἐλευθέρως
ἀποθανεῖν, ὅπερ ἄλλοις οὐκ ἐγένετο παρ' ἐλπίδα
326 κρατηθεῖσιν. ἡμῖν δὲ πρόδηλος μέν ἐστιν ἡ
γενησομένη μεθ' ἡμέραν ἅλωσις, ἐλευθέρα δ' ἡ
τοῦ γενναίου θανάτου μετὰ τῶν φιλτάτων αἵρεσις.
οὔτε γὰρ τοῦτ' ἀποκωλύειν οἱ πολέμιοι δύνανται
πάντως εὐχόμενοι ζῶντας ἡμᾶς παραλαβεῖν, οὔθ'
327 ἡμεῖς ἐκείνους ἔτι νικᾶν μαχόμενοι. ἔδει μὲν
γὰρ εὐθὺς ἴσως ἐξ ἀρχῆς, ὅτε τῆς ἐλευθερίας
ἡμῖν ἀντιποιεῖσθαι θελήσασι πάντα καὶ παρ'
ἀλλήλων ἀπέβαινε χαλεπὰ καὶ παρὰ τῶν πολεμίων
χείρω, τῆς τοῦ θεοῦ γνώμης στοχάζεσθαι καὶ
γινώσκειν ὅτι τὸ πάλαι φίλον³ αὐτῷ φῦλον Ἰου-
328 δαίων⁴ κατέγνωστο· μένων γὰρ εὐμενὴς ἢ μετρίως
γοῦν [ἡμῖν]⁵ ἀπηχθημένος, οὐκ ἂν τοσούτων μὲν
ἀνθρώπων περιεῖδεν ὄλεθρον, προήκατο δὲ τὴν
ἱερωτάτην αὐτοῦ πόλιν πυρὶ καὶ κατασκαφαῖς
329 πολεμίων. ἡμεῖς δ' ἄρα καὶ μόνοι τοῦ παντὸς
Ἰουδαίων γένους ἠλπίσαμεν περιέσεσθαι τὴν ἐλευθερίαν φυλάξαντες, ὥσπερ ἀναμάρτητοι πρὸς τὸν
θεὸν γενόμενοι καὶ μηδεμιᾶς μετασχόντες παρα-
330 νομίας,⁶ οἳ καὶ τοὺς ἄλλους ἐδιδάξαμεν; τοιγαροῦν
ὁρᾶτε, πῶς ἡμᾶς ἐλέγχει μάταια προσδοκήσαντας
κρείττονα τῶν ἐλπίδων τὴν ἐν τοῖς δεινοῖς ἀνάγκην

---

¹ VRC (the form usual in speeches in Jos.): νῦν the rest.
² + ἡμῖν C Lat.   ³ φιλούμενον A.
⁴ + ἀπώλειαν L Lat.: + ἀπωλείᾳ C.   ⁵ om. P.

submit even to a slavery involving no peril, let us not
now, along with slavery, deliberately accept the
irreparable penalties awaiting us if we are to fall
alive into Roman hands. For as we were the first
of all to revolt, so are we the last in arms against
them. Moreover, I believe that it is God who has
granted us this favour, that we have it in our power
to die nobly and in freedom—a privilege denied to
others who have met with unexpected defeat. Our
fate at break of day is certain capture, but there is
still the free choice of a noble death with those we
hold most dear. For our enemies, fervently though
they pray to take us alive, can no more prevent this
than we can now hope to defeat them in battle.
Maybe, indeed, we ought from the very first—when,
having chosen to assert our liberty, we invariably
experienced such hard treatment from one another,
and still harder from our foes—we ought, I say, to
have read God's purpose and to have recognized that
the Jewish race, once beloved of Him, had been
doomed to perdition. For had he continued to be
gracious, or but lightly incensed, he would never
have overlooked such wholesale destruction or have
abandoned His most holy city to be burnt and razed
to the ground by our enemies. But did we forsooth
hope that we alone of all the Jewish nation would
survive and preserve our freedom, as persons guiltless
towards God and without a hand in crime—we who
had even been the instructors of the rest? Mark,
now, how He exposes the vanity of our expectations,
by visiting us with such dire distress as exceeds all

---

⁶ παρανομίας M : culpae Lat. : om. the rest.

331 ἐπαγαγών· οὐδὲ¹ γὰρ ἡ τοῦ φρουρίου φύσις
ἀνάλωτος οὖσα πρὸς σωτηρίαν ὠφέληκεν,² ἀλλὰ
καὶ τροφῆς ἀφθονίαν καὶ πλῆθος ὅπλων καὶ τὴν
ἄλλην ἔχοντες παρασκευὴν περιττεύουσαν ὑπ'
αὐτοῦ περιφανῶς τοῦ θεοῦ τὴν ἐλπίδα τῆς σωτηρίας
332 ἀφῃρήμεθα. τὸ γὰρ πῦρ εἰς τοὺς πολεμίους
φερόμενον οὐκ αὐτομάτως ἐπὶ τὸ κατασκευασθὲν
τεῖχος ὑφ' ἡμῶν ἀνέστρεψεν, ἀλλ' ἔστι ταῦτα
χόλος πολλῶν ἀδικημάτων, ἃ μανέντες εἰς τοὺς
333 ὁμοφύλους ἐτολμήσαμεν. ὑπὲρ ὧν μὴ τοῖς ἐχθίστοις Ῥωμαίοις δίκας ἀλλὰ τῷ θεῷ δι' ἡμῶν
αὐτῶν ὑπόσχωμεν· αὗται δ' εἰσὶν ἐκείνων μετριώ-
334 τεραι· θνησκέτωσαν γὰρ γυναῖκες ἀνύβριστοι καὶ
παῖδες δουλείας ἀπείρατοι, μετὰ δ' αὐτοὺς ἡμεῖς
εὐγενῆ χάριν ἀλλήλοις παράσχωμεν καλὸν ἐντάφιον
335 τὴν ἐλευθερίαν φυλάξαντες. πρότερον δὲ καὶ τὰ
χρήματα καὶ τὸ φρούριον πυρὶ διαφθείρωμεν·
λυπηθήσονται γὰρ Ῥωμαῖοι, σαφῶς οἶδα, μήτε
τῶν ἡμετέρων σωμάτων κρατήσαντες καὶ τοῦ
336 κέρδους ἁμαρτόντες. τὰς τροφὰς μόνας ἐάσωμεν·
αὗται γὰρ ἡμῖν τεθνηκόσι μαρτυρήσουσιν, ὅτι μὴ
κατ' ἔνδειαν ἐκρατήθημεν, ἀλλ' ὥσπερ ἐξ ἀρχῆς
διέγνωμεν, θάνατον ἑλόμενοι πρὸ δουλείας."
337 (7) Ταῦτα Ἐλεάζαρος ἔλεγεν. οὐ μὴν κατὰ
ταὐτὸ³ ταῖς γνώμαις προσέπιπτε τῶν παρόντων,
ἀλλ' οἱ μὲν ἔσπευδον ὑπακούειν καὶ μόνον οὐχ
ἡδονῆς ἐνεπίμπλαντο καλὸν εἶναι τὸν θάνατον
338 νομίζοντες, τοὺς δ' αὐτῶν μαλακωτέρους γυναικῶν
καὶ γενεᾶς οἶκτος εἰσῄει, πάντως δὲ καὶ τῆς

¹ Bekker: οὔτε mss.   ² ὠφέλησεν PAM.
³ Niese: κατ' αὐτὸ mss.

598

that we could anticipate. For not even the impregnable nature of this fortress has availed to save us ; nay, though ample provisions are ours, piles of arms, and a superabundance of every other requisite, yet we have been deprived, manifestly by God Himself, of all hope of deliverance. For it was not of their own accord that those flames which were driving against the enemy turned back upon the wall constructed by us ;[a] no, all this betokens wrath at the many wrongs which we madly dared to inflict upon our countrymen. The penalty for those crimes let us pay not to our bitterest foes, the Romans, but to God through the act of our own hands. It will be more tolerable than the other.[b] Let our wives thus die undishonoured, our children unacquainted with slavery ; and, when they are gone, let us render a generous service to each other, preserving our liberty as a noble winding-sheet. But first let us destroy our chattels and the fortress by fire ; for the Romans, well I know, will be grieved to lose at once our persons and the lucre. Our provisions only let us spare ; for they will testify, when we are dead, that it was not want which subdued us, but that, in keeping with our initial resolve, we preferred death to slavery."

(7) Thus spoke Eleazar ; but his words did not touch the hearts of all hearers alike. Some, indeed, were eager to respond and all but filled with delight at the thought of a death so noble ; but others, softer-hearted, were moved with compassion for their wives and families, and doubtless also by the vivid

His speech failing to have effect

---

[a] §§ 317 f.
[b] *Cf.* 2 Sam. xxiv. 14 " Let us fall now into the hand of the Lord," etc.

ἑαυτῶν προδήλου τελευτῆς, εἴς τε¹ ἀλλήλους
ἀποβλέποντες τοῖς δακρύοις τὸ μὴ βουλόμενον
339 τῆς γνώμης ἐσήμαινον. τούτους ἰδὼν Ἐλεάζαρος
ἀποδειλιῶντας καὶ πρὸς τὸ μέγεθος τοῦ βουλεύματος τὰς ψυχὰς ὑποκλωμένους ἔδεισε, μή ποτε
καὶ τοὺς ἐρρωμένως τῶν λόγων ἀκούσαντας
αὐτοὶ συνεκθηλύνωσι ποτνιώμενοι καὶ δακρύοντες.
340 οὔκουν ἀνῆκε τὴν παρακέλευσιν, ἀλλ' αὐτὸν
ἐπεγείρας καὶ πολλοῦ λήματος² πλήρης γενόμενος
λαμπροτέροις ἐνεχείρει λόγοις περὶ ψυχῆς ἀθα-
341 νασίας, μέγα τε σχετλιάσας καὶ τοῖς δακρύουσιν
ἀτενὲς ἐμβλέψας "ἦ πλεῖστον," εἶπεν, "ἐψεύσθην
νομίζων ἀνδράσιν ἀγαθοῖς τῶν ὑπὲρ τῆς ἐλευθερίας
ἀγώνων συναρεῖσθαι,³ ζῆν καλῶς ἢ τεθνάναι
342 διεγνωκόσιν. ὑμεῖς δ' ἦτε τῶν τυχόντων οὐδὲν
εἰς ἀρετὴν οὐδ' εὐτολμίαν διαφέροντες, οἵ γε καὶ
τὸν ἐπὶ μεγίστων ἀπαλλαγῇ κακῶν φοβεῖσθε
θάνατον, δέον ὑπὲρ τούτου μήτε μελλῆσαι μήτε
343 σύμβουλον ἀναμεῖναι. πάλαι γὰρ εὐθὺς ἀπὸ τῆς
πρώτης αἰσθήσεως παιδεύοντες ἡμᾶς οἱ πάτριοι
καὶ θεῖοι λόγοι διετέλουν, ἔργοις τε καὶ φρονήμασι
τῶν ἡμετέρων προγόνων αὐτοὺς βεβαιούντων,
ὅτι συμφορὰ τὸ ζῆν ἐστιν ἀνθρώποις, οὐχὶ θάνατος.
344 οὗτος μὲν γὰρ ἐλευθερίαν διδοὺς ψυχαῖς εἰς τὸν
οἰκεῖον καὶ καθαρὸν ἀφίησι τόπον ἀπαλλάσσεσθαι,
πάσης συμφορᾶς ἀπαθεῖς ἐσομένας, ἕως δ' εἰσὶν

---

¹ τε MC Lat.: om. the rest.
² Richter: λήμματος MSS.
³ Niese: συναιρεῖσθαι or συναίρεσθαι MSS.

---

^a This speech at the close of the war forms a sort of
counterpart to that of Agrippa before its outbreak (B. ii.

prospect of their own end, and their tears as they looked upon one another revealed their unwillingness of heart. Eleazar, seeing them flinching and their courage breaking down in face of so vast a scheme, feared that their whimpers and tears might unman even those who had listened to his speech with fortitude. Far, therefore, from slackening in his exhortation, he roused himself and, fired with mighty fervour, essayed a higher flight of oratory on the immortality of the soul. Indignantly protesting and with eyes intently fixed on those in tears, he exclaimed : [a]

"Deeply, indeed, was I deceived in thinking that _he renews his appeal._ I should have brave men as associates in our struggles for freedom—men determined to live with honour or to die. But you, it seems, were no better than the common herd in valour or in courage, you who are afraid even of that death that will deliver you from the direst ills, when in such a cause you ought neither to hesitate an instant nor wait for a counsellor. For from of old, since the first dawn of intelligence,[b] we have been continually taught by those precepts, ancestral and divine—confirmed by the deeds and noble spirit of our forefathers—that life, not death, _"Life not death is_ is man's misfortune.[c] For it is death which gives _man's mis-_ liberty to the soul and permits it to depart to its own _fortune._ pure abode, there to be free from all calamity ; but

345–401). An acknowledgement of the nation's guilt must be put into the mouth of one of the leaders of the insurgents.
[b] _Cf. Ap._ ii. 178 "our thorough grounding in the laws from the first dawn of intelligence." But it is not so much the Hebrew Law as Greek poetry and philosophy which inspire what follows. It is interesting to compare the speech of Josephus at Jotapata on the crime of suicide, _B._ iii. 362 ff.
[c] _Cf._ § 358 with the parallel from Euripides.

ἐν σώματι θνητῷ δεδεμέναι καὶ τῶν τούτου κακῶν
συναναπίμπλανται, τἀληθέστατον εἰπεῖν, τεθνήκασι·
κοινωνία γὰρ θείῳ πρὸς θνητὸν ἀπρεπής ἐστι.
345 μέγα μὲν οὖν δύναται ψυχὴ καὶ σώματι συν-
δεδεμένη· ποιεῖ γὰρ αὐτῆς ὄργανον αἰσθανόμενον
ἀοράτως αὐτὸ κινοῦσα καὶ θνητῆς φύσεως περαι-
346 τέρω προάγουσα ταῖς πράξεσιν· οὐ μὴν ἀλλ’
ἐπειδὰν ἀπολυθεῖσα τοῦ καθέλκοντος αὐτὴν βάρους
ἐπὶ γῆν καὶ προσκρεμαμένου χῶρον ἀπολάβῃ
τὸν οἰκεῖον, τότε δὴ μακαρίας ἰσχύος καὶ πανταχόθεν ἀκωλύτου μετέχει δυνάμεως, ἀόρατος
μένουσα τοῖς ἀνθρωπίνοις ὄμμασιν ὥσπερ αὐτὸς
347 ὁ θεός· οὐδὲ γὰρ ἕως ἐστὶν ἐν σώματι θεωρεῖται·
πρόσεισι γὰρ ἀφανῶς καὶ μὴ βλεπομένη πάλιν
ἀπαλλάττεται, μίαν μὲν αὐτὴ φύσιν ἔχουσα τὴν
ἄφθαρτον, αἰτία δὲ σώματι γινομένη μεταβολῆς.
348 ὅτου γὰρ ἂν ψυχὴ προσψαύσῃ,[1] τοῦτο ζῇ καὶ
τέθηλεν, ὅτου δ’ ἂν ἀπαλλαγῇ μαρανθὲν ἀποθνήσκει·
349 τοσοῦτον αὐτῇ περίεστιν ἀθανασίας. ὕπνος δὲ
τεκμήριον ὑμῖν ἔστω τῶν λόγων ἐναργέστατον,
ἐν ᾧ ψυχαὶ τοῦ σώματος αὐτὰς μὴ περισπῶντος
ἡδίστην μὲν ἔχουσιν ἀνάπαυσιν ἐφ’ αὑτῶν γενό-
μεναι, θεῷ δ’ ὁμιλοῦσαι κατὰ συγγένειαν πάντη
μὲν ἐπιφοιτῶσι, πολλὰ δὲ τῶν ἐσομένων προ-
350 θεσπίζουσι. τί δὴ δεῖ δεδιέναι θάνατον τὴν ἐν
ὕπνῳ γινομένην ἀνάπαυσιν ἀγαπῶντας; πῶς δ’
οὐκ ἀνόητόν ἐστι τὴν ἐν τῷ ζῆν ἐλευθερίαν
351 διώκοντας τῆς ἀιδίου φθονεῖν αὑτοῖς; ἔδει μὲν
οὖν ἡμᾶς οἴκοθεν πεπαιδευμένους ἄλλοις εἶναι
παράδειγμα τῆς πρὸς θάνατον ἑτοιμότητος· οὐ

---

[1] P (a Sophoclean word like the phrase which follows):
προσάψηται the rest.

so long as it is imprisoned in a mortal body and tainted with all its miseries, it is, in sober truth, dead, for association with what is mortal ill befits that which is divine. True, the soul possesses great capacity, even while incarcerated in the body ; for it makes the latter its organ of perception, invisibly swaying it and directing it onward in its actions beyond the range of mortal nature. But it is not until, freed from the weight that drags it down to earth and clings about it, the soul is restored to its proper sphere, that it enjoys a blessed energy and a power untrammelled on every side, remaining, like God Himself, invisible to human eyes. For even while in the body it is withdrawn from view : unperceived it comes and unseen it again departs, itself of a nature one and incorruptible, but a cause of change to the body. For whatever the soul has touched lives and flourishes,[a] whatever it abandons withers and dies ; so abundant is her wealth of immortality.

"Let sleep furnish you with a most convincing proof of what I say—sleep, in which the soul, undistracted by the body, while enjoying in perfect independence the most delightful repose, holds converse with God by right of kinship, ranges the universe and foretells many things that are to come. Why then should we fear death who welcome the repose of sleep ? And is it not surely foolish, while pursuing liberty in this life, to grudge ourselves that which is eternal ? *The analogy of sleep.*

"We ought, indeed, blest with our home training, to afford others an example of readiness to die ; if, *The Indian example of self-immolation.*

---

[a] ζῇ καὶ τέθηλεν, after Soph. *Trach.* 235 καὶ ζῶντα καὶ θάλλοντα ; the same poet supplies the word for " touch," προσψαύειν.

μὴν ἀλλ' εἰ καὶ τῆς παρὰ τῶν ἀλλοφύλων δεόμεθα
πίστεως, βλέψωμεν εἰς Ἰνδοὺς τοὺς σοφίαν
352 ἀσκεῖν ὑπισχνουμένους. ἐκεῖνοί τε γὰρ ὄντες
ἄνδρες ἀγαθοὶ τὸν μὲν τοῦ ζῆν χρόνον ὥσπερ
ἀναγκαίαν τινὰ τῇ φύσει λειτουργίαν ἀκουσίως
353 ὑπομένουσι, σπεύδουσι δὲ τὰς ψυχὰς ἀπολῦσαι
τῶν σωμάτων, καὶ μηδενὸς αὐτοὺς ἐπείγοντος
κακοῦ μηδ' ἐξελαύνοντος πόθῳ τῆς ἀθανάτου
διαίτης προλέγουσι μὲν τοῖς ἄλλοις ὅτι μέλλουσιν
ἀπιέναι, καὶ ἔστιν ὁ κωλύσων οὐδείς, ἀλλὰ πάντες
αὐτοὺς εὐδαιμονίζοντες πρὸς τοὺς οἰκείους ἕκαστοι
354 διδόασιν ἐπιστολάς· οὕτως βεβαίαν καὶ ἀληθεστά-
την ταῖς ψυχαῖς τὴν μετ' ἀλλήλων εἶναι δίαιταν
355 πεπιστεύκασιν. οἱ δ' ἐπειδὰν ἐπακούσωσι τῶν
ἐντεταλμένων αὐτοῖς, πυρὶ τὸ σῶμα παραδόντες,
ὅπως δὴ καὶ καθαρωτάτην ἀποκρίνωσι τοῦ
356 σώματος τὴν ψυχήν, ὑμνούμενοι τελευτῶσιν· ῥᾷον
γὰρ ἐκείνους εἰς τὸν θάνατον οἱ φίλτατοι προ-
πέμπουσιν ἢ τῶν ἄλλων ἀνθρώπων ἕκαστοι τοὺς
πολίτας εἰς μηκίστην ἀποδημίαν, καὶ σφᾶς μὲν
αὐτοὺς δακρύουσιν, ἐκείνους δὲ μακαρίζουσιν ἤδη
357 τὴν ἀθάνατον τάξιν ἀπολαμβάνοντας. ἆρ' οὖν
οὐκ αἰδούμεθα χεῖρον Ἰνδῶν φρονοῦντες καὶ διὰ
τῆς αὑτῶν ἀτολμίας τοὺς πατρίους νόμους, οἳ
πᾶσιν ἀνθρώποις εἰς ζῆλον ἥκουσιν, αἰσχρῶς
358 ὑβρίζοντες; ἀλλ' εἴ γε καὶ τοὺς ἐναντίους ἐξ
ἀρχῆς λόγους ἐπαιδεύθημεν, ὡς ἄρα μέγιστον
ἀγαθὸν ἀνθρώποις ἐστὶ τὸ ζῆν συμφορὰ δ' ὁ
θάνατος, ὁ γοῦν καιρὸς ἡμᾶς παρακαλεῖ φέρειν

---

[a] Cf. the allusion in *Ap.* i. 179 to the Indian philosophers
from whom Aristotle, as there quoted, considers that the
Jews are descended.   [b] Or " letters."

however, we really need an assurance in this matter from alien nations, let us look at those Indians *a* who profess the practice of philosophy. They, brave men that they are, reluctantly endure the period of life, as some necessary service due to nature, but hasten to release their souls from their bodies; and though no calamity impels nor drives them from the scene, from sheer longing for the immortal state, they announce to their comrades that they are about to depart. Nor is there any who would hinder them : no, all felicitate them and each gives them commissions *b* to his *c* loved ones; so certain and absolutely sincere is their belief in the intercourse which souls hold with one another. Then, after listening to these behests, they commit their bodies to the fire, that so the soul may be parted from the body in the utmost purity, and expire amidst hymns of praise. Indeed, their dearest ones escort them to their death more readily than do the rest of mankind their fellow-citizens when starting on a very long journey ; for themselves they weep, but them they count happy as now regaining *d* immortal rank. Are we not, then, ashamed of being more mean-spirited than Indians, and of bringing, by our faint-heartedness, shameful reproach upon our country's laws, which are the envy of all mankind ?

"Yet, even had we from the first been schooled in the opposite doctrine and taught that man's highest blessing is life and that death is a calamity, *e* still the crisis is one that calls upon us to bear it with

"God has sentenced us to destruction.

c sc. " departed."

d Or " receiving."

e Probably here, as in § 343, there is a reminiscence of the Euripidean Τίς οἶδεν, εἰ τὸ ζῆν μέν ἐστι κατθανεῖν, | τὸ κατθανεῖν δὲ ζῆν κάτω νομίζεται; (Dindorf, Frag. 634).

εὐκαρδίως αὐτόν, θεοῦ γνώμῃ καὶ κατ' ἀνάγκας
359 τελευτήσοντας[1]· πάλαι γάρ, ὡς ἔοικε, κατὰ τοῦ
κοινοῦ παντὸς Ἰουδαίων γένους ταύτην ἔθετο
τὴν ψῆφον ὁ θεός, ὥσθ' ἡμᾶς τοῦ ζῆν ἀπηλλάχθαι
360 μὴ μέλλοντας αὐτῷ χρῆσθαι κατὰ τρόπον. μὴ
γὰρ αὐτοῖς ὑμῖν ἀνάπτετε τὰς αἰτίας μηδὲ χαρί-
ζεσθε τοῖς Ῥωμαίοις, ὅτι πάντας ἡμᾶς ὁ πρὸς
αὐτοὺς πόλεμος διέφθειρεν· οὐ γὰρ ἐκείνων ἰσχύϊ
ταῦτα συμβέβηκεν, ἀλλὰ κρείττων αἰτία γενομένη
361 τὸ δοκεῖν ἐκείνοις νικᾶν παρέσχηκε. ποίοις γὰρ
ὅπλοις Ῥωμαίων τεθνήκασιν οἱ Καισάρειαν Ἰου-
362 δαῖοι κατοικοῦντες; ἀλλ' οὐδὲ μελλήσαντας[2] αὐτοὺς ἐκείνων ἀφίστασθαι, μεταξὺ δὲ τὴν ἑβδόμην
ἑορτάζοντας τὸ πλῆθος τῶν Καισαρέων ἐπιδραμὸν
μηδὲ χεῖρας ἀνταίροντας ἅμα γυναιξὶ καὶ τέκνοις
κατέσφαξαν, οὐδ' αὐτοὺς Ῥωμαίους ἐντραπέντες,
οἳ μόνους ἡμᾶς ἡγοῦντο πολεμίους τοὺς ἀφ-
363 εστηκότας. ἀλλὰ φήσει τις ὅτι Καισαρεῦσιν ἦν
ἀεὶ διαφορὰ πρὸς τοὺς παρ' αὐτοῖς, καὶ τοῦ
καιροῦ λαβόμενοι τὸ παλαιὸν μῖσος ἀπεπλήρωσαν.
364 τί οὖν τοὺς ἐν Σκυθοπόλει φῶμεν; ἡμῖν γὰρ
ἐκεῖνοι διὰ τοὺς Ἕλληνας πολεμεῖν ἐτόλμησαν,
ἀλλ' οὐ μετὰ τῶν συγγενῶν ἡμῶν Ῥωμαίους
365 ἀμύνεσθαι. πολὺ τοίνυν ὤνησεν αὐτοὺς ἡ πρὸς
ἐκείνους εὔνοια καὶ πίστις· ὑπ' αὐτῶν μέντοι
πανοικεσίᾳ πικρῶς κατεφονεύθησαν ταύτην τῆς
366 συμμαχίας ἀπολαβόντες ἀμοιβήν· ἃ γὰρ ἐκείνους
ὑφ' ἡμῶν[3] ἐκώλυσαν, ταῦθ' ὑπέμειναν ὡς αὐτοὶ

---

[1] Lat. (morituros): τελευτήσαντας MSS.
[2] A² (adding ἴσμεν): μελλήσοντας the rest.
[3] +⟨παθεῖν⟩ Holwerda.

---

[a] B. ii. 457 (opening of the war, A.D. 66).

a stout heart, since it is by God's will and of necessity that we are to die. For long since, so it seems, God passed this decree against the whole Jewish race in common, that we must quit this life if we would not use it aright. Do not attach the blame to yourselves, nor the credit to the Romans, that this war with them has been the ruin of us all; for it was not their might that brought these things to pass, but the intervention of some more powerful cause has afforded them the semblance of victory.

"The Romans cannot claim the credit of victory."

"What Roman weapons, I ask, slew the Jews of Caesarea?[a] Nay, they had not even contemplated revolt from Rome, but were engaged in keeping their sabbath[b] festival, when the Caesarean rabble rushed upon them and massacred them, unresisting, with their wives and children, without even the slightest respect for the Romans, who regarded as enemies only us who had revolted. But I shall be told that the Caesareans had a standing quarrel with their Jewish residents and seized that opportunity to satisfy their ancient hate. What then shall we say of the Jews in Scythopolis,[c] who had the audacity to wage war on us in the cause of the Greeks, but refused to unite with us, their kinsmen, in resisting the Romans? Much benefit, to be sure, did they reap from their goodwill and loyalty to the men of Scythopolis! Ruthlessly butchered by them, they and all their families—that was the recompense that they received for their alliance; the fate from which they had saved their neighbours at our hands, that they endured, as though they had themselves desired to

"Consider the Jewish disasters for which they are not responsible."

---

[b] Greek "seventh day"; the massacre of the Roman garrison in Jerusalem and of the Jews of Caesarea took place simultaneously, on a sabbath, *B.* ii. 456 f.   [c] *B.* ii. 466 ff.

δρᾶσαι θελήσαντες. μακρὸν ἂν εἴη νῦν ἰδίᾳ περὶ
367 ἑκάστων λέγειν· ἴστε γὰρ ὅτι τῶν ἐν Συρίᾳ πόλεων
οὐκ ἔστιν ἥτις τοὺς παρ' αὐτῇ κατοικοῦντας
Ἰουδαίους οὐκ ἀνῄρηκεν, ἡμῖν πλέον ἢ 'Ρωμαίοις[1]
368 ὄντας πολεμίους· ὅπου γε Δαμασκηνοὶ μηδὲ
πρόφασιν εὔλογον πλάσαι δυνηθέντες φόνου μιαρω-
τάτου τὴν αὐτῶν πόλιν ἐνέπλησαν ὀκτακισχιλίους
πρὸς τοῖς μυρίοις Ἰουδαίους ἅμα γυναιξὶ καὶ
369 γενεαῖς ἀποσφάξαντες. τὸ δ' ἐν Αἰγύπτῳ πλῆθος
τῶν μετ' αἰκίας ἀνῃρημένων ἕξ που μυριάδας
ὑπερβάλλειν ἐπυνθανόμεθα. κἀκεῖνοι μὲν ἴσως
ἐπ' ἀλλοτρίας γῆς οὐδὲν ἀντίπαλον εὑράμενοι τοῖς
πολεμίοις οὕτως ἀπέθανον, τοῖς δ' ἐπὶ τῆς οἰκείας
τὸν πρὸς 'Ρωμαίους πόλεμον ἀραμένοις ἅπασι
τί[2] τῶν ἐλπίδα νίκης ἐχυρᾶς παρασχεῖν δυναμένων
370 οὐχ ὑπῆρξε; καὶ γὰρ ὅπλα καὶ τείχη καὶ φρουρίων
δυσάλωτοι κατασκευαὶ καὶ φρόνημα πρὸς τοὺς
ὑπὲρ τῆς ἐλευθερίας κινδύνους ἄτρεπτον[3] πάντας
371 πρὸς τὴν ἀπόστασιν ἐπέρρωσεν. ἀλλὰ ταῦτα
πρὸς βραχὺν χρόνον ἀρκέσαντα καὶ ταῖς ἐλπίσιν
ἡμᾶς ἐπάραντα μειζόνων ἀρχὴ κακῶν ἀνεφάνη[4]·
πάντα γὰρ ἧλω, καὶ πάντα τοῖς πολεμίοις ὑπέπεσεν,
ὥσπερ εἰς τὴν ἐκείνων εὐκλεεστέραν νίκην, οὐκ
εἰς τὴν τῶν παρασκευασαμένων σωτηρίαν εὐ-
372 τρεπισθέντα. καὶ τοὺς μὲν ἐν ταῖς μάχαις ἀπο-
θνήσκοντας εὐδαιμονίζειν προσῆκον· ἀμυνόμενοι
γὰρ καὶ τὴν ἐλευθερίαν οὐ προέμενοι τεθνήκασι·
τὸ δὲ πλῆθος τῶν ὑπὸ 'Ρωμαίοις γενομένων τίς
οὐκ ἂν ἐλεήσειε; τίς οὐκ ἂν ἐπειχθείη πρὸ τοῦ
373 ταὐτὰ παθεῖν ἐκείνοις ἀποθανεῖν; ὧν οἱ μὲν

---

[1] 'Ρωμαῖοι Lowth, Hudson, and Naber.
[2] Holwerda: τε mss.

inflict it. Time would fail me now to name each instance severally; for, as you know, there is not a city in Syria which has not slain its Jewish inhabitants, though more hostile to us than to the Romans.[a] Thus, the people of Damascus,[b] though unable even to invent a plausible pretext, deluged their city with the foulest slaughter, butchering eighteen thousand[c] Jews, with their wives and families. As for Egypt,[d] we were told that the number of those who there perished in tortures perhaps exceeded sixty thousand.

"Those Jews, maybe, perished as they did, because they were on alien soil, where they found themselves no match for their enemies. But consider all those who in their own territory embarked on war with Rome: what did they lack of all that could inspire them with hopes of assured success? Arms, ramparts, fortresses well nigh impregnable, a spirit undaunted by risks to be run in the cause of liberty— these encouraged all to revolt. Yet these availed but for a brief season, and after buoying us up with hopes proved the beginning of greater disasters. For all were taken, all succumbed to the enemy, as though furnished for his more glorious triumph, and not for the protection of those who provided them. Those men who fell in battle may fitly be felicitated, for they died defending, not betraying, liberty; but the multitudes in Roman hands who would not pity? Who would not rush to his death ere he shared their

[a] Possibly we should read "than were the Romans."

[b] B. ii. 559 ff.

[c] 10,500 according to B. ii. 561. Hegesippus in the present passage reads 8000.

[d] B. ii. 487 ff.

[3] ἄτρεστον VRC.   [4] ἐφάνη L.

στρεβλούμενοι καὶ πυρὶ καὶ μάστιξιν αἰκιζόμενοι
τεθνήκασιν, οἱ δ' ἀπὸ θηρίων ἡμίβρωτοι πρὸς
δευτέραν αὐτοῖς τροφὴν ζῶντες ἐφυλάχθησαν,
γέλωτα καὶ παίγνιον¹ τοῖς πολεμίοις παρασχόντες.
374 ἐκείνων μὲν οὖν ἀθλιωτάτους ὑποληπτέον τοὺς
ἔτι ζῶντας, οἳ πολλάκις εὐχόμενοι τὸν θάνατον
375 λαβεῖν οὐκ ἔχουσιν. ποῦ δ' ἡ μεγάλη πόλις, ἡ
τοῦ παντὸς Ἰουδαίων γένους μητρόπολις, ἡ
τοσούτοις μὲν ἐρυμνὴ τειχῶν περιβόλοις, τοσαῦτα
δ' αὑτῆς φρούρια καὶ μεγέθη πύργων προβεβλη-
μένη, μόλις δὲ χωροῦσα τὰς εἰς τὸν πόλεμον
παρασκευάς, τοσαύτας δὲ μυριάδας ἀνδρῶν ἔχουσα
376 τῶν ὑπὲρ αὐτῆς μαχομένων; ποῦ γέγονεν ἡμῖν
ἡ τὸν θεὸν ἔχειν οἰκιστὴν πεπιστευμένη; πρόρ-
ριζος ἐκ βάθρων ἀνήρπασται, καὶ μόνον αὐτῆς
μνημεῖον ἀπολείπεται τὸ τῶν ἀνῃρημένων² ἔτι
377 τοῖς λειψάνοις ἐποικοῦν. πρεσβῦται δὲ δύστηνοι
τῇ σποδῷ τοῦ τεμένους παρακάθηνται καὶ γυναῖκες
ὀλίγαι πρὸς ὕβριν αἰσχίστην ὑπὸ τῶν πολεμίων
378 τετηρημέναι. ταῦτα τίς ἐν νῷ βαλλόμενος ἡμῶν
καρτερήσει τὸν ἥλιον ὁρᾶν, κἂν δύνηται ζῆν
ἀκινδύνως; τίς οὕτω τῆς πατρίδος ἐχθρός, ἢ τίς
οὕτως ἄνανδρος καὶ φιλόψυχος, ὡς μὴ καὶ περὶ
379 τοῦ μέχρι νῦν ζῆσαι μετανοεῖν; ἀλλ' εἴθε πάντες
ἐτεθνήκειμεν πρὶν τὴν ἱερὰν ἐκείνην πόλιν χερσὶν
ἰδεῖν κατασκαπτομένην πολεμίων, πρὶν τὸν ναὸν
380 τὸν ἅγιον οὕτως ἀνοσίως ἐξορωρυγμένον. ἐπεὶ
δὲ ἡμᾶς οὐκ ἀγεννὴς ἐλπὶς ἐβουκόλησεν, ὡς τάχα
που δυνήσεσθαι τοὺς πολεμίους ὑπὲρ αὐτῆς

---

¹ PA : παιδιὰν the rest.
² ἀνῃρημένων PAL: ἀνῃρηκότων αὐτὴν στρατόπεδον the rest.

fate ? Of them some have perished on the rack or tortured by fire and scourge ; others, half-devoured by wild beasts, have been preserved alive to provide them with a second repast, after affording merriment and sport for their foes. But most miserable of all must be reckoned those still alive, who have often prayed for death and are denied the boon.

"And where now is that great city, the mother-city of the whole Jewish race, intrenched behind all those lines of ramparts, screened by all those forts and massive towers, that could scarce contain her munitions of war, and held all those myriads of defenders ? What has become of her that was believed to have God for her founder [a] ? Uprooted from her base she has been swept away, and the sole memorial of her remaining is that of the slain [b] still quartered in her ruins ! Hapless old men sit beside the ashes of the shrine and a few women, reserved by the enemy for basest outrage.

"Which of us, taking these things to heart, could bear to behold the sun, even could he live secure from peril ? Who such a foe to his country, so unmanly, so fond of life, as not to regret that he is still alive to-day ? Nay, I would that we had all been dead ere ever we saw that holy city razed by an enemy's hands, that sacred sanctuary so profanely uprooted ! But seeing that we have been beguiled by a not ignoble hope, that we might perchance find means of

[a] The rendering " inhabitant " in older translations is unwarranted ; οἰκιστής is a synonym for κτίστης in B. ii. 266.
[b] Text doubtful : if correct, μνημεῖον seems to be used in the double sense of " memorial " and tomb. But the reading of the other мss. " the camp of those that destroyed her " is perhaps right.

ἀμύνασθαι, φρούδη δὲ γέγονε νῦν καὶ μόνους
ἡμᾶς ἐπὶ τῆς ἀνάγκης καταλέλοιπεν, σπεύσωμεν
καλῶς ἀποθανεῖν, ἐλεήσωμεν ἡμᾶς αὐτοὺς καὶ
τὰ τέκνα καὶ τὰς γυναῖκας, ἕως ἡμῖν ἔξεστιν παρ'
381 ἡμῶν αὐτῶν λαβεῖν τὸν ἔλεον. ἐπὶ μὲν γὰρ
θάνατον ἐγεννήθημεν καὶ τοὺς ἐξ αὑτῶν ἐγεννή-
σαμεν, καὶ τοῦτον οὐδὲ τοῖς εὐδαιμονοῦσιν ἔστι
382 διαφυγεῖν· ὕβρις δὲ καὶ δουλεία καὶ τὸ βλέπειν
γυναῖκας εἰς αἰσχύνην ἀγομένας μετὰ τέκνων οὐκ
ἔστιν ἀνθρώποις κακὸν ἐκ φύσεως ἀναγκαῖον,
ἀλλὰ ταῦτα διὰ τὴν αὑτῶν δειλίαν ὑπομένουσιν
οἱ παρὸν πρὸ αὐτῶν ἀποθανεῖν μὴ θελήσαντες.
383 ἡμεῖς δ' ἐπ' ἀνδρείᾳ μέγα φρονοῦντες Ῥωμαίων
ἀπέστημεν καὶ τὰ τελευταῖα νῦν ἐπὶ σωτηρίᾳ
384 προκαλουμένων ἡμᾶς οὐχ ὑπηκούσαμεν. τίνι
τοίνυν οὐκ ἔστιν ὁ θυμὸς αὐτῶν πρόδηλος, εἰ
ζώντων ἡμῶν κρατήσουσιν; ἄθλιοι μὲν οἱ νέοι
τῆς ῥώμης τῶν σωμάτων εἰς πολλὰς αἰκίας
ἀρκέσοντες, ἄθλιοι δ' οἱ παρηβηκότες φέρειν τῆς
385 ἡλικίας τὰς συμφορὰς οὐ δυναμένης. ὄψεταί
τις γυναῖκα πρὸς βίαν ἀγομένην, φωνῆς ἐπακού-
σεται τέκνου πατέρα βοῶντος χεῖρας δεδεμένος;
386 ἀλλ' ἕως εἰσὶν ἐλεύθεραι καὶ ξίφος ἔχουσιν,
καλὴν ὑπουργίαν ὑπουργησάτωσαν· ἀδούλωτοι μὲν
ὑπὸ τῶν πολεμίων ἀποθάνωμεν, ἐλεύθεροι δὲ
μετὰ τέκνων καὶ γυναικῶν τοῦ ζῆν συνεξέλθωμεν.
387 ταῦθ' ἡμᾶς οἱ νόμοι κελεύουσι, ταῦθ' ἡμᾶς
γυναῖκες καὶ παῖδες ἱκετεύουσι· τούτων τὴν
ἀνάγκην θεὸς ἀπέσταλκε,[1] τούτων Ῥωμαῖοι τἀ-
ναντία θέλουσι, καὶ μή τις ἡμῶν πρὸ τῆς ἁλώσεως
388 ἀποθάνῃ δεδοίκασι. σπεύσωμεν οὖν ἀντὶ τῆς

---

[1] ἐκέλευσε C: ἐπέσταλκε should perhaps be read.

avenging her of her foes, and now that hope has vanished and left us alone in our distress, let us hasten to die honourably ; let us have pity on ourselves, our children and our wives, while it is still in our power to find pity from ourselves. For we were born for death, we and those whom we have begotten ; and this even the fortunate cannot escape. But outrage and servitude and the sight of our wives being led to shame with their children—these are no necessary evils imposed by nature on mankind, but befall, through their own cowardice, those who, having the chance of forestalling them by death, refuse to take it. But we, priding ourselves on our courage, revolted from the Romans, and now at the last, when they offered us our lives, we refused the offer.[a] Who then can fail to foresee their wrath if they take us alive ? Wretched will be the young whose vigorous frames can sustain many tortures, wretched the more advanced in years whose age is incapable of bearing such calamities. Is a man to see his wife led off to violation,[b] to hear the voice of his child crying ' Father ! ' when his own hands are bound ? No, while those hands are free and grasp the sword, let them render an honourable service. Unenslaved by the foe let us die, as free men with our children and wives let us quit this life together ! This our laws enjoin,[c] this our wives and children implore of us. The need for this is of God's sending,[d] the reverse of this is the Romans' desire, and their fear is lest a single one of us should die before capture. Haste

---

[a] vi. 350 f.   [b] Or " by violence."
[c] Rhetorical statement : the Law contains no such express injunction.
[d] Or perhaps " ordering."

JOSEPHUS

ἐλπιζομένης αὐτοῖς καθ᾽ ἡμῶν ἀπολαύσεως ἔκπληξιν τοῦ θανάτου καὶ θαῦμα τῆς τόλμης καταλιπεῖν.''

389 (ix. 1) Ἔτι βουλόμενον αὐτὸν παρακαλεῖν πάντες ὑπετέμνοντο καὶ πρὸς τὴν πρᾶξιν ἠπείγοντο,
ἀνεπισχέτου τινὸς ὁρμῆς πεπληρωμένοι, καὶ δαι-
μονῶντες ἀπῇεσαν ἄλλος πρὸ ἄλλου φθάσαι γλι-
χόμενος καὶ ταύτην ἐπίδειξιν εἶναι τῆς ἀνδρείας
καὶ τῆς εὐβουλίας νομίζοντες, τὸ μή τις ἐν ὑστάτοις γενόμενος ὀφθῆναι· τοσοῦτος αὐτοῖς γυναικῶν
καὶ παιδίων καὶ τῆς αὐτῶν σφαγῆς ἔρως ἐνέπεσεν.

390 καὶ μὴν οὐδ᾽ ὅπερ ἄν τις ᾠήθη τῇ πράξει προσ-
ιόντες ἠμβλύνθησαν, ἀλλ᾽ ἀτενῆ τὴν γνώμην δι-
εφύλαξαν οἵαν ἔσχον τῶν λόγων ἀκροώμενοι,
τοῦ μὲν οἰκείου καὶ φιλοστόργου πάθους ἅπασι
παραμένοντος, τοῦ λογισμοῦ δὲ ὡς τὰ κράτιστα

391 βεβουλευκότος τοῖς φιλτάτοις ἐπικρατοῦντος. ὁμοῦ
γὰρ ἠσπάζοντο γυναῖκας περιπτυσσόμενοι καὶ
τέκνα προσηγκαλίζοντο τοῖς ὑστάτοις φιλήμασιν

392 ἐμφυόμενοι καὶ δακρύοντες, ὁμοῦ δὲ καθάπερ
ἀλλοτρίαις χερσὶν ὑπουργούμενοι συνετέλουν τὸ
βούλευμα, τὴν ἐπίνοιαν ὧν πείσονται κακῶν ὑπὸ
τοῖς πολεμίοις γενόμενοι παραμύθιον τῆς ἐν τῷ

393 κτείνειν ἀνάγκης ἔχοντες. καὶ πέρας οὐδεὶς τηλι-
κούτου τολμήματος ἥττων εὑρέθη, πάντες δὲ διὰ
τῶν οἰκειοτάτων διεξῆλθον, ἄθλιοι τῆς ἀνάγκης,
οἷς αὐτοχειρὶ γυναῖκας τὰς αὐτῶν καὶ τέκνα

394 κτεῖναι κακῶν ἔδοξεν εἶναι τὸ κουφότατον. οὔτε[1]
δὴ τοίνυν τὴν ἐπὶ τοῖς πεπραγμένοις ὀδύνην ἔτι
φέροντες καὶ τοὺς ἀνῃρημένους νομίζοντες ἀδικεῖν
εἰ καὶ βραχὺν αὐτοῖς ἔτι χρόνον ἐπιζήσουσι, ταχὺ

[1] Destinon with Lat.: οὗτοι mss.

614

we then to leave them, instead of their hoped-for
enjoyment at securing us, amazement at our death
and admiration of our fortitude."

(ix. 1) He would have pursued his exhortation but How the
was cut short by his hearers, who, overpowered by deed was
some uncontrollable impulse, were all in haste to do done.
the deed. Like men possessed they went their way,
each eager to outstrip his neighbour and deeming it
a signal proof of courage and sound judgement not to
be seen among the last : so ardent the passion that
had seized them to slaughter their wives, their little
ones and themselves. Nor, as might have been
expected, did their ardour cool when they approached
the task : inflexibly they held to the resolution, which
they had formed while listening to the address, and
though personal emotion and affection were alive in
all, reason which they knew had consulted best for
their loved ones, was paramount. For, while they
caressed and embraced their wives and took their
children in their arms, clinging in tears to those
parting kisses, at that same instant, as though served
by hands other than their own, they accomplished
their purpose, having the thought of the ills they
would endure under the enemy's hands to console
them for their constraint in killing them. And in
the end not one was found a truant in so daring a
deed : all carried through their task with their
dearest ones. Wretched victims of necessity, to whom
to slay with their own hands their own wives and
children seemed the lightest of evils ! Unable,
indeed, any longer to endure their anguish at what
they had done, and feeling that they wronged the
slain by surviving them if it were but for a moment,

615

μὲν τὴν κτῆσιν ἅπασαν εἰς ταὐτὸ σωρεύσαντες
395 πῦρ εἰς αὐτὴν ἐνέβαλον, κλήρῳ δ' ἐξ αὑτῶν
ἑλόμενοι δέκα τοὺς ἁπάντων σφαγεῖς ἐσομένους,
καὶ γυναικί τις αὐτὸν καὶ παισὶ κειμένοις παρα-
στρώσας καὶ τὰς χεῖρας περιβαλών, παρεῖχον
ἑτοίμους τὰς σφαγὰς τοῖς τὴν δύστηνον ὑπουργίαν
396 ἐκτελοῦσιν. οἱ δ' ἀτρέπτως[1] πάντας φονεύσαντες
τὸν αὐτὸν ἐπ' ἀλλήλοις τοῦ κλήρου νόμον ὥρισαν,
ἵν' ὁ λαχὼν τοὺς ἐννέα κτείνας ἑαυτὸν ἐπὶ πᾶσιν
ἀνέλῃ· πάντες οὕτως αὑτοῖς ἐθάρρουν μήτ' εἰς
τὸ δρᾶν μήτ' εἰς τὸ παθεῖν ἄλλος ἄλλου διαφέρειν.
397 καὶ τέλος οἱ μὲν τὰς σφαγὰς ὑπέθεσαν, ὁ δ' εἷς
καὶ τελευταῖος τὸ πλῆθος τῶν κειμένων περι-
αθρήσας, μή πού τις ἔτ' ἐν πολλῷ φόνῳ τῆς αὐτοῦ
λείπεται χειρὸς δεόμενος, ὡς ἔγνω πάντας ἀνῃρημένους, πῦρ μὲν πολὺ τοῖς βασιλείοις ἐνίησιν,
ἀθρόᾳ δὲ τῇ χειρὶ δι' αὑτοῦ πᾶν ἐλάσας τὸ ξίφος
398 πλησίον τῶν οἰκείων κατέπεσε. καὶ οἱ μὲν ἐτε-
θνήκεσαν ὑπειληφότες οὐδὲν ἔχον ψυχὴν ὑποχείριον
399 ἐξ αὑτῶν Ῥωμαίοις καταλιπεῖν, ἔλαθεν δὲ γυνὴ
πρεσβῦτις καὶ συγγενὴς ἑτέρα[2] τις Ἐλεαζάρου,
φρονήσει καὶ παιδείᾳ πλείστων γυναικῶν δια-
φέρουσα, καὶ πέντε παιδία τοῖς ὑπονόμοις, οἳ
ποτὸν ἦγον ὕδωρ διὰ γῆς,[3] ἐγκατακρυβῆναι[4] τῶν
400 ἄλλων πρὸς τῇ σφαγῇ τὰς διανοίας ἐχόντων, οἳ
τὸν ἀριθμὸν ἦσαν ἑξήκοντα πρὸς τοῖς ἐνακοσίοις
γυναικῶν ἅμα καὶ παίδων αὐτοῖς συναριθμουμένων.
401 καὶ τὸ πάθος ἐπράχθη πεντεκαιδεκάτῃ Ξανθικοῦ
μηνός.

---

[1] PA: ἀτρέστως the rest (cf. § 370).
[2] ἑταίρα ML (cf. § 404).   [3] trs. διὰ γῆς ὕδωρ A.
[4] abditi Lat. : ἐγκατακρυβεῖσαι Destinon.

616

they quickly piled together all the stores and set them on fire ; then, having chosen by lot ten of their number to dispatch the rest, they laid themselves down each beside his prostrate wife and children, and, flinging their arms around them, offered their throats in readiness for the executants of the melancholy office. These, having unswervingly slaughtered all, ordained the same rule of the lot for one another, that he on whom it fell should slay first the nine and then himself last of all ; such mutual confidence had they all that neither in acting nor in suffering would one differ from another. Finally, then, the nine bared their throats, and the last solitary survivor, after surveying the prostrate multitude, to see whether haply amid the shambles there were yet one left who needed his hand, and finding that all were slain, set the palace ablaze, and then collecting his strength drove his sword clean through his body and fell beside his family. They had died in the belief that they had left not a soul of them alive to fall into Roman hands ; but an old woman and another, a relative of Eleazar, superior in sagacity and training to most of her sex, with five children, escaped by concealing themselves in the subterranean aqueducts, while the rest were absorbed in the slaughter. The victims numbered nine hundred and sixty, including women and children ; and the tragedy occurred on the fifteenth of the month Xanthicus.

The seven survivors.

c. 2 May A.D. 73.[a]

---

[a] The day of the month follows the reckoning of Niese, the year that of Schürer, *G.J.V.* i. 639 f. ; Niese reckons the year as A.D. 72 (Schürer, *ibid.*).

402 (2) Οἱ δὲ Ῥωμαῖοι μάχην ἔτι προσδοκῶντες,
ὑπὸ τὴν ἔω διασκευασάμενοι καὶ τὰς ἀπὸ τῶν
χωμάτων ἐφόδους ταῖς ἐπιβάθραις γεφυρώσαντες
403 προσβολὴν ἐποιοῦντο. βλέποντες δ᾽ οὐδένα τῶν
πολεμίων, ἀλλὰ δεινὴν πανταχόθεν ἐρημίαν καὶ
πῦρ ἔνδον καὶ σιωπήν, ἀπόρως εἶχον τὸ γεγονὸς
συμβαλεῖν, καὶ τέλος ὡς εἰς ἄφεσιν βολῆς ἠλάλαξαν,
404 εἴ τινα τῶν ἔνδον προκαλέσαιντο. τῆς δὲ βοῆς
αἴσθησις γίνεται τοῖς γυναίοις, κἀκ τῶν ὑπονόμων
ἀναδῦσαι τὸ πραχθὲν ὡς εἶχε πρὸς τοὺς Ῥωμαίους
ἐμήνυον, πάντα τῆς ἑτέρας¹ ὡς ἐλέχθη τε καὶ τίνα
405 τρόπον ἐπράχθη σαφῶς ἐκδιηγουμένης. οὐ μὴν
ῥᾳδίως αὐτῇ προσεῖχον τῷ μεγέθει τοῦ τολμήματος
ἀπιστοῦντες, ἐπεχείρουν τε τὸ πῦρ σβεννύναι
καὶ ταχέως ὁδὸν δι᾽ αὐτοῦ τεμόντες τῶν βασιλείων
406 ἐντὸς ἐγένοντο. καὶ τῷ πλήθει τῶν πεφονευμένων ἐπιτυχόντες οὐχ ὡς ἐπὶ πολεμίοις ἥσθησαν,
τὴν δὲ γενναιότητα τοῦ βουλεύματος καὶ τὴν ἐν
τοσούτοις ἄτρεπτον ἐπὶ τῶν ἔργων ἐθαύμασαν
τοῦ θανάτου καταφρόνησιν.

407 (x. 1) Τοιαύτης δὲ τῆς ἁλώσεως γενομένης
ἐπὶ μὲν τοῦ φρουρίου καταλείπει φυλακὴν ὁ
στρατηγός, αὐτὸς δὲ μετὰ τῆς δυνάμεως ἀπῆλθεν
408 εἰς Καισάρειαν. οὐδὲ γὰρ ὑπελείπετό τις τῶν
κατὰ τὴν χώραν πολεμίων, ἀλλ᾽ ἤδη πᾶσα διὰ
μακροῦ τοῦ πολέμου κατέστραπτο πολλοῖς καὶ
τῶν ἀπωτάτω κατοικούντων αἴσθησιν καὶ κίνδυνον
409 ταραχῆς παρασχόντος. ἔτι δὲ καὶ περὶ Ἀλεξάνδρειαν τὴν ἐν Αἰγύπτῳ μετὰ ταῦτα συνέβη
410 πολλοὺς Ἰουδαίων ἀποθανεῖν· τοῖς γὰρ ἐκ τῆς
στάσεως τῶν σικαρίων ἐκεῖ διαφυγεῖν δυνηθεῖσιν
οὐκ ἀπέχρη τὸ σώζεσθαι, πάλιν δὲ καινοτέροις
618

(2) The Romans, expecting further opposition, Entry of
the
Romans.
were by daybreak under arms and, having with
gangways formed bridges of approach from the
earthworks, advanced to the assault. Seeing none
of the enemy but on all sides an awful solitude, and
flames within and silence, they were at a loss to
conjecture what had happened. At length, as if for
a signal to shoot, they shouted, to call forth haply
any of those within. The shout was heard by the
women-folk, who, emerging from the caverns, informed the Romans how matters stood, one of the
two [a] lucidly reporting both the speech and how the
deed was done. But it was with difficulty that they
listened to her, incredulous of such amazing fortitude; meanwhile they endeavoured to extinguish
the flames and soon cutting a passage through them
entered the palace. Here encountering the mass of
slain, instead of exulting as over enemies, they
admired the nobility of their resolve and the contempt of death displayed by so many in carrying it,
unwavering, into execution.

(x. 1) The fortress being thus taken, the general All Judaea
subdued.
left a garrison on the spot and himself departed with
his army to Caesarea. For not an enemy remained
throughout the country, the whole having now been
subdued by this protracted war, which had been felt
by many even in the remotest parts, exposing them
to risk of disorder. Moreover, at Alexandria in Fate of
Sicarii
refugees
in Egypt.
Egypt, after this date many Jews met with destruc-
tion. For certain of the faction of the Sicarii who
had succeeded in fleeing to that country, not content

---

[a] Eleazar's relative, § 399.

---

[1] ἐταλπας ML.

ἐνεχείρουν πράγμασι καὶ πολλοὺς τῶν ὑποδεξα-
μένων ἔπειθον τῆς ἐλευθερίας ἀντιποιεῖσθαι, καὶ
Ῥωμαίους μὲν μηδὲν κρείττους αὑτῶν ὑπολαμ-
411 βάνειν, θεὸν δὲ μόνον ἡγεῖσθαι δεσπότην. ἐπεὶ
δ' αὐτοῖς τῶν οὐκ ἀφανῶν τινες Ἰουδαίων ἀντ-
έβαινον, τοὺς μὲν ἀπέσφαξαν, τοῖς δ' ἄλλοις
ἐνέκειντο πρὸς τὴν ἀπόστασιν παρακαλοῦντες.
412 ὁρῶντες δ' αὐτῶν τὴν ἀπόνοιαν οἱ πρωτεύοντες
τῆς γερουσίας οὐκέτ' ἀσφαλὲς αὐτοῖς ἐνόμιζον
περιορᾶν, ἀλλὰ πάντας ἀθροίσαντες εἰς ἐκκλησίαν
τοὺς Ἰουδαίους ἤλεγχον τὴν ἀπόνοιαν τῶν σικαρίων, πάντων αἰτίους ἀποφαίνοντες ἐκείνους τῶν
413 κακῶν· καὶ νῦν ἔφασαν αὐτούς, ἐπείπερ οὐδὲ
πεφευγότες τῆς σωτηρίας ἐλπίδα βεβαίαν ἔχουσιν,
γνωσθέντας γὰρ ὑπὸ Ῥωμαίων εὐθὺς ἀπολεῖσθαι,
τῆς αὐτοῖς προσηκούσης συμφορᾶς ἀναπιμπλάναι
τοὺς μηδενὸς τῶν ἁμαρτημάτων μετασχόντας.
414 φυλάξασθαι τοίνυν τὸν ἐξ αὐτῶν ὄλεθρον τὸ
πλῆθος παρεκάλουν καὶ περὶ αὐτῶν πρὸς Ῥωμαίους
415 ἀπολογήσασθαι τῇ τούτων παραδόσει. συνιδόντες[1]
τοῦ κινδύνου τὸ μέγεθος ἐπείσθησαν τοῖς λεγομένοις, καὶ μετὰ πολλῆς ὁρμῆς ἐπὶ τοὺς σικαρίους.
416 ᾄξαντες συνήρπαζον αὐτούς. τῶν δ' ἑξακόσιοι
μὲν εὐθὺς ἑάλωσαν, ὅσοι δ' εἰς τὴν Αἴγυπτον
καὶ τὰς ἐκεῖ Θήβας διέφυγον, οὐκ εἰς μακρὰν
417 συλληφθέντες ἐπανήχθησαν. ἐφ' ὧν οὐκ ἔστιν
ὃς οὐ τὴν καρτερίαν καὶ τὴν εἴτ' ἀπόνοιαν εἴτε
τῆς γνώμης ἰσχὺν χρὴ λέγειν οὐ κατεπλάγη·
418 πάσης γὰρ ἐπ' αὐτοὺς βασάνου καὶ λύμης τῶν

---

[1] + οὖν M *ed. pr.*: + δὲ L: οἱ δὲ συνιδόντες C.

---

[a] It appears from Philo (*In Flaccum*, 10, § 74 Cohn) that

620

with their escape, again embarked on revolutionary schemes, and sought to induce many of their hosts to assert their independence, to look upon the Romans as no better than themselves and to esteem God alone as their lord. Meeting with opposition from certain Jews of rank, they murdered these; the rest they continued to press with solicitations to revolt. Observing their infatuation, the leaders of the council of elders,[a] thinking it no longer safe for them to overlook their proceedings, convened a general assembly of the Jews and exposed the madness of the Sicarii, proving them to have been responsible for all their troubles. " And now," they said, " these men, finding that even their flight has brought them no sure hope of safety—for if recognized by the Romans they would instantly be put to death—are seeking to involve in the calamity which is their due persons wholly innocent of their crimes." They, accordingly, advised the assembly to beware of the ruin with which they were menaced by these men and, by delivering them up, to make their peace with the Romans. Realizing the gravity of the danger, the people complied with this advice, and rushed furiously upon the Sicarii to seize them. Six hundred of them were caught on the spot; and all who escaped into Egypt and the Egyptian Thebes were ere long arrested and brought back. Nor was there a person who was not amazed at the endurance and—call it which you will—desperation or strength of purpose, displayed by these victims. For under every form of torture and laceration of body, devised

Their refusal under persecution to own Caesar as lord.

from the time of Augustus the single ἐθνάρχης at Alexandria was superseded by a γερουσία, over which a certain number of ἄρχοντες presided, Schürer, *G.J.V.* iii. 41.

σωμάτων ἐπινοηθείσης ἐφ᾽ ἓν τοῦτο μόνον, ὅπως
αὐτῶν Καίσαρα δεσπότην ὁμολογήσωσιν, οὐδεὶς
ἐνέδωκεν οὐδ᾽ ἐμέλλησεν εἰπεῖν, ἀλλὰ πάντες
ὑπερτέραν τῆς ἀνάγκης τὴν αὐτῶν γνώμην διεφύ-
λαξαν, ὥσπερ ἀναισθήτοις σώμασι χαιρούσῃ μόνον
οὐχὶ τῇ ψυχῇ τὰς βασάνους καὶ τὸ πῦρ δεχόμενοι.
419 μάλιστα δ᾽ ἡ τῶν παίδων ἡλικία τοὺς θεωμένους
ἐξέπληξεν· οὐδὲ γὰρ ἐκείνων τις ἐξενικήθη Καίσαρα
δεσπότην ἐξονομάσαι. τοσοῦτον ἄρα τῆς τῶν
σωμάτων ἀσθενείας ἡ τῆς τόλμης ἰσχὺς ἐπεκράτει.

420 (2) Λοῦπος¹ τότε διῴκει τὴν Ἀλεξάνδρειαν
καὶ περὶ τοῦ κινήματος τούτου Καίσαρι κατὰ
421 τάχος ἐπέστειλεν. ὁ δὲ τῶν Ἰουδαίων τὴν
ἀκατάπαυστον ὑφορώμενος νεωτεροποιίαν καὶ δείσας, μὴ πάλιν εἰς ἓν ἀθρόοι συλλεγῶσι καί τινας
αὐτοῖς συνεπισπάσωνται, προσέταξε τῷ Λούπῳ
τὸν ἐν τῇ Ὀνίου καλουμένῃ² νεὼν καθελεῖν τῶν
422 Ἰουδαίων. ἣ³ δ᾽ ἐστὶν ἐν Αἰγύπτῳ καὶ διὰ
τοιαύτην αἰτίαν ᾠκίσθη τε καὶ τὴν ἐπίκλησιν
423 ἔλαβεν· Ὀνίας Σίμωνος υἱός, εἷς τῶν ἐν Ἱεροσολύμοις ἀρχιερέων, φεύγων Ἀντίοχον τὸν Συρίας
βασιλέα πολεμοῦντα τοῖς Ἰουδαίοις ἧκεν εἰς
Ἀλεξάνδρειαν, καὶ δεξαμένου Πτολεμαίου φιλοφρόνως αὐτὸν διὰ τὴν πρὸς Ἀντίοχον ἀπέχθειαν
ἔφη σύμμαχον αὐτῷ ποιήσειν τὸ τῶν Ἰουδαίων
ἔθνος, εἰ πεισθείη τοῖς ὑπ᾽ αὐτοῦ λεγομένοις.
424 ποιήσειν δὲ τὰ δυνατὰ τοῦ βασιλέως ὁμολογή-

---

¹ Λοῦππος in some mss. here and below.
² Hudson with Lat.: καλούμενον mss.   ³ ὁ PMC.

ᵃ Unidentified ; M. Rutilius Lupus (probably of the same
family) was the Roman governor of Egypt at the outbreak of
the later Jewish war under Trajan, A.D. 116.

for the sole object of making them acknowledge Caesar as lord, not one submitted nor was brought to the verge of utterance ; but all kept their resolve, triumphant over constraint, meeting the tortures and the fire with bodies that seemed insensible of pain and souls that wellnigh exulted in it. But most of all were the spectators struck by the children of tender age, not one of whom could be prevailed upon to call Caesar lord. So far did the strength of courage rise superior to the weakness of their frames.

(2) Lupus [a] was then in control at Alexandria, and without delay reported this commotion to Caesar. The emperor, suspicious of the interminable tendency of the Jews to revolution, and fearing that they might again collect together in force and draw others away with them, ordered Lupus to demolish the Jewish temple in the so-called district of Onias.[b] This is a region in Egypt which was colonized and given this name under the following circumstances. Onias, son of Simon, and one of the chief priests at Jerusalem, fleeing from Antiochus,[c] king of Syria, then at war with the Jews, came to Alexandria, and being graciously received by Ptolemy,[d] owing to that monarch's hatred of Antiochus, told him that he would make the Jewish nation his ally if he would accede to his proposal. The king having promised to do what

Demolition of Jewish temple of Onias in Egypt.

Story of its origin.

---

[b] This temple is often mentioned in Josephus : *B.* i. 33, *A.* xii. 387 f., xiii. 62 ff., 285, xx. 236 f. Leontopolis, its site (*A.* xiii. 70), has been identified as *Tell-el-Yehudiyyeh*, N.E. of Memphis at the southern end of the Delta ; excavations have laid bare the remains of the Jewish temple (Flinders Petrie, *Hyksos and Israelite cities*, quoted by G. B. Gray on Isa. xix. 19).

[c] Antiochus Epiphanes.

[d] Ptolemy Philometor, 182-146 B.C.

623

σαντος ἠξίωσεν ἐπιτρέπειν αὐτῷ νεών τε που
τῆς Αἰγύπτου κατασκευάσασθαι καὶ τοῖς πατρίοις
425 ἔθεσι θεραπεύειν τὸν θεόν· οὕτως γὰρ Ἀντιόχῳ
μὲν ἔτι μᾶλλον ἐκπολεμώσεσθαι τοὺς Ἰουδαίους
τὸν ἐν Ἱεροσολύμοις νεών πεπορθηκότι, πρὸς
αὐτὸν δ' εὐνοϊκωτέρως ἕξειν καὶ πολλοὺς ἐπ'
ἀδείᾳ τῆς εὐσεβείας ἐπ' αὐτὸν συλλεγήσεσθαι.
426 (3) Πεισθεὶς Πτολεμαῖος τοῖς λεγομένοις δίδωσιν
αὐτῷ χώραν ἑκατὸν ἐπὶ τοῖς ὀγδοήκοντα σταδίους[1]
ἀπέχουσαν Μέμφεως· νομὸς δ' οὗτος Ἡλιοπολίτης[2]
427 καλεῖται. φρούριον ἔνθα κατασκευασάμενος Ὀνίας
τὸν μὲν ναὸν οὐχ ὅμοιον ᾠκοδόμησε τῷ ἐν Ἱεροσολύμοις, ἀλλὰ πύργῳ παραπλήσιον λίθων με-
428 γάλων εἰς ἑξήκοντα πήχεις ἀνεστηκότα· τοῦ
βωμοῦ δὲ τὴν κατασκευὴν πρὸς τὸν οἰκεῖον[3]
ἐξεμιμήσατο καὶ τοῖς ἀναθήμασιν ὁμοίως ἐκό-
σμησεν, χωρὶς τῆς περὶ τὴν λυχνίαν κατασκευῆς·
429 οὐ γὰρ ἐποίησε λυχνίαν, αὐτὸν δὲ χαλκευσάμενος
λύχνον χρυσοῦν ἐπιφαίνοντα σέλας χρυσῆς ἁλύσεως
430 ἐξεκρέμασε. τὸ δὲ τέμενος πᾶν ὀπτῇ πλίνθῳ
περιτετείχιστο πύλας ἔχον λιθίνας. ἀνῆκε δὲ
καὶ χώραν πολλὴν ὁ βασιλεὺς εἰς χρημάτων
πρόσοδον, ὅπως εἴη καὶ τοῖς ἱερεῦσιν ἀφθονία
431 καὶ τῷ θεῷ πολλὰ τὰ πρὸς τὴν εὐσέβειαν. οὐ
μὴν Ὀνίας ἐξ ὑγιοῦς γνώμης ταῦτα ἔπραττεν,
ἀλλ' ἦν αὐτῷ φιλονεικία πρὸς τοὺς ἐν τοῖς
Ἱεροσολύμοις Ἰουδαίους ὀργὴν τῆς φυγῆς ἀπο-

---

[1] L: σταδίοις C: σταδίων the rest.
[2] Dindorf: Ἡλιουπολίτης mss.   [3] οἴκοι MVRC.

---

[a] Josephus here corrects his previous statement that the
temple of Onias resembled that at Jerusalem, *B.* i. 33 (so *A.*

624

was in his power, he asked permission to build a
temple somewhere in Egypt and to worship God after
the manner of his fathers ; for, he added, the Jews
would thus be still more embittered against Antiochus,
who had sacked their temple at Jerusalem, and more
amicably disposed towards himself, and many would
flock to him for the sake of religious toleration.

(3) Induced by this statement, Ptolemy gave him
a tract, a hundred and eighty furlongs distant from
Memphis, in the so-called nome of Heliopolis.   Here
Onias erected a fortress and built his temple (which
was not like *a* that in Jerusalem, but resembled a
tower) of huge stones and sixty cubits in altitude.
The altar, however, he designed on the model of that
in the home country, and adorned the building with
similar offerings, the fashion of the lampstand *b*
excepted ; for, instead of making a stand, he had a
lamp wrought of gold which shed a brilliant light
and was suspended by a golden chain.   The sacred
precincts were wholly surrounded by a wall of baked
brick, the doorways being of stone.   The king, moreover, assigned him an extensive territory as a source
of revenue, to yield both abundance for the priests
and large provision for the service of God.   In all
this, however, Onias was not actuated by honest
motives ; his aim was rather to rival the Jews at
Jerusalem, against whom he harboured resentment

xii. 388, xiii. 63, xx. 236).   Probably, as Dr. Eisler suggests,
correspondence took place between the Emperor and the
governors Lupus and Paulinus (§§ 433 ff.) concerning the
demolition of the temple ; from this correspondence Josephus
learned the particulars here given.   The close of Book vii of
the *War* appears to be a later appendix.

b For a description of the Jerusalem lampstand or
"candlestick" see §§ 148 f.

μνημονεύοντι, καὶ τοῦτο τὸ ἱερὸν ἐνόμιζε κατασκευάσας εἰς αὐτὸ περισπάσειν ἀπ' ἐκείνων τὸ
432 πλῆθος. ἐγεγόνει δέ τις καὶ παλαιὰ πρόρρησις
ἔτεσί που πρόσθεν ἑξακοσίοις· Ἡσαΐας ὄνομα
τῷ προαγορεύσαντι τοῦδε τοῦ ναοῦ τὴν ἐν Αἰγύπτῳ
γενησομένην ὑπ' ἀνδρὸς Ἰουδαίου κατασκευήν.
τὸ μὲν οὖν ἱερὸν οὕτως ἐπεποίητο.

433 (4) Λοῦπος δ' ὁ τῆς Ἀλεξανδρείας ἡγεμὼν τὰ
παρὰ Καίσαρος λαβὼν γράμματα καὶ παραγενό-
μενος εἰς τὸ ἱερὸν καί τινα τῶν ἀναθημάτων
434 ἐκφορήσας τὸν ναὸν ἀπέκλεισε. Λούπου δὲ μετὰ
βραχὺ τελευτήσαντος Παυλῖνος διαδεξάμενος τὴν
ἡγεμονίαν οὔτε τῶν ἀναθημάτων οὐδὲν κατέλιπε,[1]
πολλὰ γὰρ διηπείλησε τοῖς ἱερεῦσιν εἰ μὴ πάντα
προκομίσειαν, οὔτε προσιέναι τῷ τεμένει τοὺς
435 θρησκεύειν βουλομένους ἀφῆκεν,[2] ἀλλ' ἀποκλείσας
τὰς πύλας ἀπρόσιτον αὐτὸ παντελῶς ἐποίησεν,
ὡς μηδ' ἴχνος ἔτι τῆς εἰς τὸν θεὸν θεραπείας ἐν
436 τῷ τόπῳ καταλιπεῖν. χρόνος ἦν εἰς τὴν ἀπό-
κλεισιν τοῦ ναοῦ γεγονὼς ἀπὸ τῆς κατασκευῆς
ἔτη τρία καὶ τεσσαράκοντα καὶ τριακόσια.

437 (xi. 1) Ἥψατο δὲ καὶ τῶν περὶ Κυρήνην
πόλεων ἡ τῶν σικαρίων ἀπόνοια καθάπερ νόσος.

---

[1] C: κατελείπετο (-λίπετο R) the rest.   [2] ἐφῆκεν Niese.

---

[a] The period of Isaiah's prophecies was actually c. 740–
700 B.C., some 800 years before this time.
[b] The reference is to Isa. xix. 18 f., and in particular to the
words (partially quoted in A. xiii. 68) " In that day shall there
be an altar to the Lord in the midst of the land of Egypt."
The passage is regarded by modern critics as a late insertion
in Isaiah ; by some even so late as to be *vaticinium post
eventum*, the city in *v.* 18, whose name is variously given in
different texts as " city of righteousness," " of destruction,"

for his exile, and he hoped by erecting this temple to attract the multitude away from them to it. There had, moreover, been an ancient prediction made some six hundred years before [a] by one named Esaias, who had foretold the erection of this temple in Egypt by a man of Jewish birth.[b] Such, then, was the origin of this temple.

(4) Lupus, the governor of Alexandria, on receipt of Caesar's letter, repaired to the temple and, having carried off some of the votive offerings, shut up the building. Lupus dying soon after, Paulinus, his c. A.D. 73. successor in office, completely stripped the place of its treasures, threatening the priests with severe penalties if they failed to produce them all, prohibited would-be worshippers from approaching the precincts, and, closing the gates, debarred all access, so as to leave thenceforth no vestige of divine worship on the spot. The duration of the temple from its erection to its closure was three hundred and forty-three years.[c]

(xi. 1) The madness of the Sicarii further attacked, Further like a disease, the cities around Cyrene. Jonathan, sedition of
Sicarii in
Cyrene.

or " of the sun," being taken as a reference to Leontopolis. See G. B. Gray, *Internat. Crit. Comm., in loc.*

[c] The first figure is probably corrupt ; 243 years, *i.e. c.* 170 B.C.–A.D. 73, would be approximately correct. Dr. Eisler, however, in a forthcoming work, has an ingenious explanation of the figure in the text. "By one of those errors in calculation, not rare and easily intelligible in this author, Josephus imagined that the duration of the Onias temple . . . was a period of 343 ($= 7 \times 7 \times 7$) years or seven jubilees. . . . This mystical number indicates that J. saw in the destruction of the *two* Jewish temples, at Heliopolis and in Jerusalem, God's judgement upon the impious transgression of the deuteronomic law (of the single sanctuary). . . . Some idea similar to that of the seventy year-weeks of Daniel may have been in his mind."

627

438 διαπεσὼν¹ γὰρ εἰς αὐτὴν Ἰωνάθης, πονηρότατος
ἄνθρωπος καὶ τὴν τέχνην ὑφάντης, οὐκ ὀλίγους
τῶν ἀπόρων ἀνέπεισε προσέχειν αὐτῷ καὶ προήγαγεν εἰς τὴν ἔρημον σημεῖα καὶ φάσματα δείξειν
439 ὑπισχνούμενος. καὶ τοὺς μὲν ἄλλους ἐλάνθανε
ταῦτα διαπραττόμενος καὶ φενακίζων, οἱ δὲ τοῖς
ἀξιώμασι προύχοντες τῶν ἐπὶ τῆς Κυρήνης
Ἰουδαίων τὴν ἔξοδον αὐτοῦ καὶ παρασκευὴν τῷ
τῆς πενταπόλεως Λιβύης ἡγεμόνι Κατύλλῳ προσ-
440 αγγέλλουσιν. ὁ δ' ἱππέας τε καὶ πεζοὺς ἀποστείλας ῥᾳδίως ἐκράτησεν ἀνόπλων, καὶ τὸ μὲν
πλέον ἐν χερσὶν ἀπώλετο, τινὲς δὲ καὶ ζωγρη-
441 θέντες ἀνήχθησαν πρὸς τὸν Κάτυλλον. ὁ δ'
ἡγεμὼν τοῦ βουλεύματος Ἰωνάθης τότε μὲν
διέφυγε, πολλῆς δὲ καὶ λίαν ἐπιμελοῦς ἀνὰ
πᾶσαν τὴν χώραν ζητήσεως γενομένης ἥλω, καὶ
πρὸς τὸν ἡγεμόνα ἀναχθεὶς αὐτῷ μὲν ἐμηχανᾶτο
τῆς τιμωρίας ἀπαλλαγήν, τῷ Κατύλλῳ δ' ἔδωκεν
442 ἀφορμὴν ἀδικημάτων. ὁ μὲν γὰρ τοὺς πλουσιω-
τάτους τῶν Ἰουδαίων ἔλεγε καταψευδόμενος διδα-
σκάλους αὐτῷ τοῦ βουλεύματος γεγονέναι, (2)
443 προθύμως δὲ τὰς διαβολὰς ἐκεῖνος ἐξεδέχετο
καὶ τῷ πράγματι πολὺν ὄγκον περιετίθει μεγάλα
προστραγῳδῶν, ἵνα δόξειε καὐτὸς Ἰουδαϊκόν
444 τινα πόλεμον κατωρθωκέναι. τὸ δὲ δὴ τούτου
χαλεπώτερον, πρὸς γὰρ τῷ πιστεύειν ῥᾳδίως ἔτι
καὶ διδάσκαλος ἦν τῶν σικαρίων τῆς ψευδολογίας·
445 κελεύσας γοῦν αὐτὸν ὀνομάσαι τινὰ τῶν Ἰουδαίων
Ἀλέξανδρον, ᾧ πάλαι προσκεκρουκὼς φανερὸν
ἐξενηνόχει τὸ μῖσος, τήν τε γυναῖκα τὴν ἐκείνου
[Βερενίκην ταῖς αἰτίαις]² συμπλέξας,³ τούτους μὲν
πρῶτον ἀνεῖλεν, ἐπὶ δ' αὐτοῖς ἅπαντας τοὺς

an arrant scoundrel, by trade a weaver, having taken
refuge in that town, won the ear of not a few of the
indigent class, and led them forth into the desert,
promising them a display of signs and apparitions.
His knavish proceedings escaped detection in general;
but the men of rank among the Jews of Cyrene
reported his exodus and preparations to Catullus, the
governor of the Libyan Pentapolis. Catullus, having
dispatched a body of horse and foot, easily overpowered the unarmed crowd, the greater number of
whom perished in the encounter, a few being taken
prisoners and brought up to Catullus. Jonathan, the
originator of the plot, escaped at the time, but after
a prolonged and extremely diligent search throughout the country was caught. On being brought
before the governor, he contrived to elude punishment himself, while affording Catullus a handle for
injustice, by falsely asserting that he had received
his instructions in the scheme from the wealthiest of
the Jews.

(2) These calumnies were readily entertained by
Catullus, who invested the affair with serious importance, pompously exaggerating it, in order that
he too might be thought to have won a Jewish war.
But—what was far worse—not only did he show this
easy credulity, but he actually prompted the Sicarii
in falsehood. Thus he instructed Jonathan to name
one Alexander, a Jew, with whom he had formerly
quarrelled and was now at open enmity, further
implicating his wife Berenice in the allegations.
These were his first victims. After them he slew all

Criminal
action of
Catullus,
the Roman
governor
in Libya.

---
¹ διεκπεσών Zon.
² om. Βερενίκην P Exc.: om. ταῖς αἰτίαις PA.
³ συνεμπλέξας VC.

629

JOSEPHUS

εὐπορίᾳ χρημάτων διαφέροντας ὁμοῦ τρισχιλίους[1]
446 ἐφόνευσεν ἄνδρας· καὶ ταῦτα πράττειν ἐνόμιζεν
ἀσφαλῶς, ὅτι τὰς οὐσίας αὐτῶν εἰς τὰς τοῦ
Καίσαρος προσόδους ἀνελάμβανεν.

447 (3) Ὅπως δὲ μηδὲ ἀλλαχοῦ τινες τῶν Ἰουδαίων
ἐλέγξωσιν αὐτοῦ τὴν ἀδικίαν, πορρωτέρω τὸ
ψεῦδος ἐξέτεινε καὶ πείθει τὸν Ἰωνάθην καί τινας
τῶν ἅμ' ἐκείνῳ συνειλημμένων νεωτερισμοῦ κα-
τηγορίαν ἐπιφέρειν τοῖς ἐν Ἀλεξανδρείᾳ τε καὶ
448 Ῥώμῃ τῶν Ἰουδαίων δοκιμωτάτοις. τούτων εἷς
τῶν ἐξ ἐπιβουλῆς αἰτιαθέντων ἦν Ἰώσηπος ὁ
449 ταῦτα συγγραψάμενος. οὐ μὴν κατ' ἐλπίδα τῷ
Κατύλλῳ τὸ σκευώρημα προεχώρησεν· ἧκε μὲν
γὰρ εἰς τὴν Ῥώμην τοὺς περὶ τὸν Ἰωνάθην
ἄγων δεδεμένους καὶ πέρας ᾤετο τῆς ἐξετάσεως
εἶναι τὴν ἐπ' αὐτοῦ καὶ δι' αὐτοῦ γενομένην
450 ψευδολογίαν. Οὐεσπασιανὸς δὲ τὸ πρᾶγμα ὑπο-
πτεύσας ἀναζητεῖ τὴν ἀλήθειαν καὶ γνοὺς ἄδικον
τὴν αἰτίαν τοῖς ἀνδράσιν ἐπενηνεγμένην τοὺς μὲν
ἀφίησι τῶν ἐγκλημάτων Τίτου σπουδάσαντος,
δίκην δ' ἐπέθηκεν Ἰωνάθῃ τὴν προσήκουσαν·
ζῶν γὰρ κατεκαύθη πρότερον αἰκισθείς.

451 (4) Κατύλλῳ δὲ τότε μὲν ὑπῆρξε διὰ τὴν
πρᾳότητα τῶν αὐτοκρατόρων μηδὲν πλεῖον ὑπομεῖναι καταγνώσεως, οὐκ εἰς μακρὰν δὲ νόσῳ
καταληφθεὶς πολυτρόπῳ καὶ δυσιάτῳ χαλεπῶς
ἀπήλλαττεν, οὐ τὸ σῶμα μόνον κολαζόμενος, ἀλλ'
452 ἦν ἡ τῆς ψυχῆς αὐτῷ νόσος βαρυτέρα. δείμασι
γὰρ ἐξεταράττετο καὶ συνεχῶς ἐβόα βλέπειν
εἴδωλα τῶν ὑπ' αὐτοῦ πεφονευμένων ἐφεστηκότα,

[1] τρισχιλίους] τι χιλίους P.

630

the well-to-do Jews, three thousand persons in all ; a step which he thought that he could safely take, as he confiscated their property to the imperial exchequer.

(3) Moreover, to prevent any Jews elsewhere from exposing his iniquity, he extended his lies further afield, and prevailed on Jonathan and some others who had been arrested along with him to bring a charge of sedition against the most reputable Jews both in Alexandria and Rome. Among those thus insidiously incriminated was Josephus, the author of this history.[a] The upshot, however, of the scheme did not answer to Catullus's expectations. For he came to Rome, bringing Jonathan and his associates in chains, in the belief that the false accusations brought up before him and at his instance would be the end of the inquiry. But Vespasian, having his suspicions of the affair, investigated the facts ; and discovering that the charge preferred against these men was unjust, on the intercession of Titus he acquitted them, and inflicted on Jonathan the punishment that he had deserved. He was first tortured and then burnt alive.

Josephus incriminated.

(4) Catullus, on that occasion, owing to the lenity of the emperors, suffered nothing worse than a reprimand ; but not long after he was attacked by a complicated and incurable disease and came to a miserable end, not only chastised in body, but yet more deeply deranged in mind. For he was haunted by terrors and was continually crying out that he saw the ghosts of his murdered victims standing at

Divine retribution on Catullus.

---

[a] Josephus alludes to this again in his autobiography (*Vita* §§ 424 f.) : " Jonathan . . . asserted that I had provided him with arms and money."

καὶ κατέχειν αὐτὸν οὐ δυνάμενος ἐξήλλετο τῆς
εὐνῆς ὡς βασάνων αὐτῷ καὶ πυρὸς προσφερομένων.
453 τοῦ δὲ κακοῦ πολλὴν ἀεὶ τὴν ἐπίδοσιν λαμβάνοντος
καὶ τῶν ἐντέρων αὐτῷ κατὰ διάβρωσιν ἐκπεσόντων,
οὕτως ἀπέθανεν, οὐδενὸς ἧττον ἑτέρου τῆς προνοίας τοῦ θεοῦ τεκμήριον γενόμενος, ὅτι τοῖς
πονηροῖς δίκην ἐπιτίθησιν.

454   (5) Ἐνταῦθα τῆς ἱστορίας ἡμῖν τὸ πέρας ἐστίν,
ἣν ἐπηγγειλάμεθα μετὰ πάσης ἀκριβείας παραδώσειν τοῖς βουλομένοις μαθεῖν, τίνα τρόπον
οὗτος ὁ πόλεμος Ῥωμαίοις πρὸς Ἰουδαίους
455 ἐπολεμήθη. καὶ πῶς μὲν ἡρμήνευται, τοῖς ἀνα-
γνωσομένοις κρίνειν ἀπολελείφθω, περὶ τῆς ἀληθείας
δὲ οὐκ ἂν ὀκνήσαιμι θαρρῶν λέγειν, ὅτι μόνης
ταύτης παρὰ πᾶσαν τὴν ἀναγραφὴν ἐστοχασάμην.

his side ; and, unable to restrain himself, he would leap from his bed as if torture and fire were being applied to him. His malady ever growing rapidly worse, his bowels ulcerated and fell out ; and so he died, affording a demonstration, no less striking than any, how God in his providence inflicts punishment on the wicked.

(5) Here we close the history, which we promised Epilogue. to relate with perfect accuracy for the information of those who wish to learn how this war was waged by the Romans against the Jews. Of its style [a] my readers must be left to judge ; but, as concerning truth, I would not hesitate boldly to assert that, throughout the entire narrative, this has been my single aim.

[a] Or possibly "How it has been rendered" (into Greek); cf. the allusion to the Aramaic original in B. i. 3 (where, however, the verb used is μεταβαλών).

APPENDIX

THE PRINCIPAL ADDITIONAL PASSAGES IN
THE SLAVONIC VERSION

THE first nineteen of these passages are translated from
the German rendering of the Slavonic version produced by
the late Dr. Berendts and Dr. Grass, *Flavius Josephus vom
Jüdischen Kriege, Buch i-iv, nach der slavischen Über-
setzung*, Dorpat, Teil i, 1924–1926, Teil ii, 1927 ; the last
three passages from Dr. Berendts' translation in *Texte und
Untersuchungen*, Neue Folge, vol. xiv, 1906. The history
of these passages is obscure. They include some obvious
Christian interpolations [a] ; on the other hand, the Slavonic
version, in which they are found, has been thought by
some scholars to have preserved, at least in part, the
author's original draft of the *Jewish War*. The reader is
referred to a forthcoming work of Dr. Robert Eisler, " The
Messiah Jesus and John the Baptist, as described in the
unpublished ' Capture of Jerusalem ' of Flavius Josephus
and the Christian sources," of which an English edition
will shortly be published by Messrs. Methuen, and an
American edition by Lincoln MacVeagh (The Dial Press).
The writer is greatly indebted to Dr. Eisler for assistance
in the preparation of this Appendix. Notes which he has
kindly supplied are indicated by the initials R. E.

(1) HEROD'S DREAM

[i. 328, inserted after προσημαίνουσιν.]

(But when Herod was in Antioch, he saw a dream which

[a] Supposed interpolations, according to Dr. Eisler's critical
edition of the text, are placed in square brackets in the
following translation.

revealed to him in advance his brother's death.) Now the dream was on this wise. There were four [a] ears of corn: the first was dry through frost, but the second stood upright, while wolves fell upon the third and cut (it) down and dragged it behind them. But the interpretation of it was on this wise. The first ear was Phasael, whom poisoning had dried up; the second ear was himself, inasmuch as he was [b] unscathed; while the third was his brother Joseph, whom warriors cut down and dragged away without burial. And his soul was stirred within him; at once terror seized him, and he went forth from the bed-chamber about midnight like one possessed. For the soul, which had understood sooner than the spirit, [c] was afraid. (And forthwith there came to him the melancholy tidings.)

(2) A DISCUSSION OF JEWISH PRIESTS: "HEROD IS NOT THE MESSIAH"

[Replacing i. 364-370 (middle) in the Greek.]

But Herod spent little (time) in Jerusalem, and marched against the Arabs. At that [d] time the priests mourned and grieved one to another in secret. They durst not (do so openly for fear of) [e] Herod and his friends.

For (one Jonathan) [f] spake: "The law bids us have no foreigner for king. [g] Yet we wait for the Anointed, the meek one, [h] of David's line. But of Herod we know that he is an Arabian, [i] uncircumcised. The Anointed will be

[a] So the text; but no further mention is made of the fourth.

[b] Lit. "is." According to Dr. Eisler, the present tense shows that the source was written while Herod the Great was still alive.   [c] Or "mind" (*Geist*).   [d] Lit. "the."

[e] An apparent lacuna: words supplied by Berendts-Grass.

[f] The name, which has fallen out, is supplied from the sequel.   [g] Deut. xvii. 15.   [h] Zech. ix. 9.

[i] According to *B.J.* i. 123 he was an Idumaean; his friend Nicolas of Damascus represented him as belonging to one of the first Jewish families that returned from Babylon, *Ant.* xiv. 9; Christians called him a Philistine.

called meek, but this (is) he who has filled our whole land with blood. Under the Anointed it was ordained for the lame to walk, and the blind to see,[a] (and) the poor to become rich.[b] But under this man the hale have become lame, the seeing are blinded, the rich have become beggars. What is this? or how? Have the prophets lied? The prophets have written that there shall not want a ruler from Judah, until he come unto whom it[c] is given up; for him do the Gentiles hope.[d] But is this man the hope for the Gentiles? For we hate his misdeeds. Will the Gentiles perchance set their hopes on him? Woe unto us, because God has forsaken us, and we are forgotten of him![e] And he will give us over to desolation and to destruction. Not as under Nebuchadnezzar and Antiochus (is it). For then were the prophets teachers also of the people, and they made promises concerning the captivity and concerning the return. And now—neither is there any whom one could ask, nor any with whom one could find comfort."

But Ananus the priest answered and spake to them: "I know all books.[f] When Herod fought beneath the city wall,[g] I had never a thought that God would permit him to rule over us. But now I understand that our desolation is nigh. And bethink you of the prophecy of Daniel; for he writes[h] that after the return[i] the city of Jerusalem shall stand for seventy weeks of years, which are 490 years, and after these years shall it be desolate." And when they had counted the years, (they) were thirty years

[a] Is. xxxv. 5 f.

[b] Cf. Is. lxi. 1 (" to preach good tidings unto the poor ").

[c] sc. the rulership.

[d] Gen. xlix. 10 : " The sceptre shall not depart from Judah . . . until Shiloh come ; and unto him shall the obedience of the peoples be." Shiloh is interpreted above, as in the Targum, to mean " he whose it is."

[e] Cf. Is. xlix. 14, " Zion said, Jehovah hath forsaken me and the Lord hath forgotten me."

[f] i.e., of Scripture or of the Messianic Scriptures.

[g] Lit., " before the city," when besieging Antigonus in Jerusalem in 37 B.C., B.J. i. 343 ff.

[h] Dan. ix. 24 ff.   [i] Of the exiles from Babylon.

and four.[a] But Jonathan answered and spake : " The numbers of the years are even as we have said. But the Holy of Holies,[b] where is he ? For this Herod he (sc. the prophet) cannot call the Holy one[c]—(him) the bloodthirsty and impure."

But one of them, by name Levi, wishing to outwit them, spake to them what he got[d] with his tongue, not out of the books, but in fable. They, however, being learned in the Scriptures, began to search for the time when the Holy one would come ; but the speeches of Levi they execrated, saying, " Soup[e] is in thy mouth, but a bone in thy head," wherefore also they said to him that he had breakfasted all night and that his head was heavy with shame, as it were a bone. But he, overcome with shame, fled to Herod and informed him of the speeches of the priests which they had spoken against him. But Herod sent by night and slew them all, without the knowledge of the people, lest they should be roused ; and he appointed others.

(And when it was morning the whole land quaked, etc., as in § 370 Greek text.)

[a] This seems to mean that they reckoned that there were 34 more years still to run of the 490, within which, according to Daniel ix. 24, the Messiah was to appear. Berendts takes it to mean "Herod has 34 years to reign"; i.e., from his capture of Jerusalem in 37 B.C. to his death in 4 B.C. (cf. B.J. i. 665 ; Ant. xvii. 191). But we are not told that the priests were also prophets ; this debate, moreover, is represented as taking place in the year of Herod's Arab campaign (32 B.C.), not in that of his accession (37 B.C.). Herod was evidently dead when this chapter was written.

[b] Dan. ix. 24, " Seventy weeks are decreed . . . to anoint a Holy of Holies." [The "Holy of Holies" is the last Messianic high-priest, cf. 1 Chron. xxiii. 13: "Aaron was set aside for a holy one of holies " (literal trans. of MT.). R. E.]

[c] [The "Holy one " of God (Mark i. 24, Luke iv. 34, Jo. vi. 69) is again the Messianic high-priest. R. E.]

[d] German festbekam, [for Greek ἐπηξεν. R.E.]

[e] Dr. R. Eisler would read " putty," thinking that the Greek reading underlying the Slavonic has arisen through confusion of maraq, " soup " and marqah, " putty."

SLAVONIC "ADDITIONS"

(3) Antipater's[a] Comparison of Himself to
Heracles fighting the Hydra

[Replacing the sentence in i. 588, " Then there were these
hydra heads, the sons of Aristobulus and Alexander, shooting
up."]

But there are growing up against me and against my
children the heads of the hydra (?). Just as Heracles
sought to cut off the hundred heads of that beast with the
sword, and, when he had not (yet) reached the last head,
the heads again grew up, until he called Iolaus to his aid ;
(and as,) while Heracles hewed, Iolaus burnt out with a
fire-brand the places that appeared through the gash, and
thereby the growth of the heads of that beast was stayed
—even so have I cut off Aristobulus and Alexander, but
have gained no profit therefrom. For there are those who
(stand) in their place, their sons, but I have no Iolaus to
help me. And I know not how I should fulfil my desire.

(4) First Invective against the Romans (or
Latins)

[Replacing i. 601-605.]

But Antipater, knowing nothing of these things, amused
himself in Rome. And he lived just as becomes a king's
son, alike in the magnificence of his surroundings, attend-
ance and dress, and in munificence. Accordingly he gave
large presents to the Roman authorities, and induced them
to write in praise of himself to Herod.

And after receiving the presents, the [Italians, who are
called] Latins wrote such praise of Antipater, as cannot be
expressed, saying : " This man alone is thy defender and
guardian and shield and deliverer from thy shameful sons.
Had it not been for him, thy two first reprobate sons would
have killed thee. And those two who are now here study-

[a] Not " Herod's," as in Berendts-Grass (List of Contents).

APPENDIX

ing philosophy clamour loudly against thee, reviling and representing thee as a monster."

For such are the Latins : they run to accept presents and break their oath for the sake of presents. And they see no sin in calumny, saying, "With words have we spoken, but we have not killed (anyone) ourselves," since the accursed wretches think that he is a murderer, who kills with the hand, but that calumny and denunciation and instigation against one's neighbour are not murder. Had they known the law of God, they would have been shown long since what a murderer is.[a] But they are aliens, and our doctrine[a] touches them not. Therefore did they lie against the two sons of Herod, who were then being educated in Rome, Archelaus (and) Philip, and wrote so that he should kill them.

But Herod, having fortified himself[b] against external things, and in consequence of the first painful inquiries, attached no credit to the Roman letters.

(5) Second Invective against the Romans

[In i. 610, in place of the words παραχρῆμα μὲν ἔσπευδεν.]

(And during the time when he[c] was in Cilicia, he received his father's letter, of which we have spoken.) And he was highly delighted, and prepared a sumptuous dinner for his travelling companions and for the Romans, who through flattery had received from him three hundred talents.[d]

[a] [Allusions to the rabbinic doctrine ('Arakin 15 b, Jer. Peah i. 16 a, etc.) that "calumny is threefold killing." It kills (in the end) the calumniator, the calumniated, and him who believes the calumny. R. E.]

[b] Lit. "his mind" (seinen Sinn).

[c] i.e., Antipater, on his homeward journey from Rome to Palestine.

[d] The Greek text in § 605 states that "his returns showed an expenditure of 200 talents" in Rome. The Slavonic omits that statement, but the 300 talents here mentioned may possibly have some connexion with that other sum.

SLAVONIC "ADDITIONS"

For they are insatiable in receiving ; but if anyone gives them more to-day, to-morrow they want (still) more. And as the sea cannot be filled, nor hell satisfied, nor woman's passion, even so are the Romans insatiable in receiving ; in truth they are Solomon's leeches,[a] people who give their body and their soul for a reward.[b] Yet they are ready also to give up their limbs [c] and their brothers and children,[d] the former in that (by training) they convert boldness (and) fury into valour,[e] but the others in that they are covetous of gold, like ravens on a corpse. Many also for some trifle are prepared to surrender their (military) clothing, their cities, as also their generals.[f] We shall describe them in the sequel, but now we (will) relate the matter in hand.

(When Antipater came to Celenderis, etc.)

[a] An allusion to the Proverbs of Solomon xxx. 15 f., " The leech hath two daughters, Give, give. There are three things that are never satisfied . . . Sheol, and the barren womb, the earth that is not satisfied with water. . . ." " Woman's passion " above (vice " the barren womb ") follows the LXX text (ἔρως γυναικός, xxiv. 51).

[b] [An allusion to the gladiatorial profession. Cf. Petronius 117 "tamquam legitimi gladiatores domino corpora animasque addicimus." R. E.]

[c] [An allusion to the auctorati, freeborn Romans entering the arena as gladiators for the sake of lucre. Cf. Tacitus, Ann. xiv. 14. R. E.]

[d] [An allusion to Romans selling their sons to the lanista, to be trained as gladiators. R. E.]

[e] die einen, indem sie durch (Zucht) Keckheit (und) Tollheit in Mannhaftigkeit verwandeln. [Cf. B.J. iv. 1. 6, § 45 τὸ . . . τῆς ὁρμῆς μανιῶδες ἐμπειρίᾳ . . . κατορθοῦμεν. He means the lanistae, the trainers of the gladiators' schools. R. E.]

[f] [The text has " and their clothing " at the end, but this makes a bad anticlimax. Dr. Eisler transposes the words and explains them as referring to deserters bartering away their outfit for civilian clothes and a little money.]

APPENDIX

(6) Moralizing on Divine Providence as exemplified in Abraham

[Following upon the trial and condemnation of Antipater, in place of i. 641-644.]

Therefore is it fitting to marvel at Divine Providence, how it requites evil for evil, but good for good. And it is impossible for man to hide from [a] His Almighty right hand, either for the just or for the unjust; but more still does His mighty [b] eye look upon the just. And indeed Abraham, the forefather of our race, was led out of his land, because he had offended his brother in the division of their territories [c]; and whereby he sinned, even thereby he received also his punishment. And again for his obedience [d] He gave him the promised land.[e]

(7) Appeal of the Rabbis Judas and Matthias quoting Previous Examples of Heroism

[i. 650 : this fuller address in *oratio recta* replaces that in *oratio obliqua* in the Greek ; the introduction also contains some additional words.]

For Herod had at that time erected a golden eagle over the great gate of the temple, in honour of the emperor ;

[a] " before."

[b] *hochherrliches* : cf. θεοῦ μέγας ὀφθαλμός, *B.J.* i. 84 and 378, where it is mentioned in conjunction with His right hand (οὐ διαφεύξονται τὸν μέγαν ὀφθαλμὸν αὐτοῦ καὶ τὴν ἀνίκητον δεξιάν).

[c] [An allusion to an otherwise unknown legend about Abraham depriving his brother Haran of his fair share of the land and consequently losing his own. According to Yacut ii. 231 the city of Haran was named after this brother of Abraham. In *Ant.* i. 7. 1 Josephus says that Abraham had to leave Mesopotamia, τῶν Μεσοποταμιτῶν στασιασάντων πρὸς αὐτόν. He does not wish to tell the Gentiles that it was a quarrel between Abraham and his brother Haran which drove him out of the country. R. E.]

[d] Gen. xii. 4.

[e] [This he shares fairly with Haran's son Lot. R. E.]

and he called it the golden-winged eagle.[a] This the two (doctors) exhorted the people to cut down, saying : "Easy is it to die for the law of (our) fathers ; for immortal glory will follow those who die thus,[b] while for their souls there awaits eternal joy. But those who die in unmanliness, loving the body, not desiring a manly death, but finding their end in sickness, these are inglorious, and will suffer unending torments in the underworld.[c] Forward, ye Jewish men ! Now is the time to play the man. We will show what reverence we have for the law of Moses, in order that our people may not be put to shame, in order that we may not offend our lawgiver. For an example of heroism we have Eleazar [d] first, and the seven brethren,[e] the Maccabees, and their mother, who acted manfully. For Antiochus,[f] who had defeated and captured our country and domineered over us, was defeated by those seven striplings and by the aged teacher [g] and by the grey-haired woman. We, too, will show ourselves like them, that we may not appear weaker than the woman. But should we also be tortured for our zeal for God, then will our garland be yet better wreathed. But should they even kill us, then will our souls, after quitting the(ir) dark abode, pass over to (our) forefathers, where Abraham (is) and those (descended) from him."

(8) HEROD'S SINS AND PUNISHMENT

[Replacing the last clause in i. 656, "His condition led diviners to pronounce his maladies a judgement on him for his treatment of the professors."]

For the eye of God looked invisibly upon his sins. He

[a] The words " in honour . . . eagle " are not in the Greek.
[b] Or " there " (da).
[c] Cf. B.J. vi. 46 ff., where, however, Titus speaks only of the "obliteration in subterranean night " and " oblivion " of those dying on a sick-bed, not of " unending torments."
[d] 2 Macc. vi. 18 ff.   [e] 2 Macc. vii.   [f] Epiphanes.
[g] 2 Macc. vi. 18, "Eleazar, one of the principal scribes . . . well stricken in years."

643

had indeed defiled his dominion with bloodshed and with
illicit intercourse with foreign women.[a] And because he
had made others childless, therefore killed he also his
children with his (own) hands ; [b] and because he spared not
his body in wantonness, therefore contracted he so foul a
disease.

(9) [" JOHN THE FORERUNNER "] [c]

[Inserted between ii. 110 and iii.]

Now at that time there walked among the Jews a man
in wondrous garb, for he had put animals' hair upon his
body wherever it was not covered by his (own) hair ; and in
countenance he was like a savage. He came to the Jews
and summoned [d] them to freedom, saying : " God hath
sent me to show you the way of the Law, whereby ye may
free yourselves from many masters ; and there shall be no
mortal ruling over you, but only the Highest [e] who hath
sent me." And when the people heard that, they were
glad ; [and there went after him all Judaea and the (region)
around Jerusalem.] [f] And he did nothing else to them,
save that he dipped them into the stream of the Jordan
and let (them) go, admonishing them to desist from evil
works ; (for) so would they be given a king who would

[a] Or " with other men's wives."

[b] Cf. (6) above, for the punishment fitting the crime.

[c] This title, clearly of Christian origin, appears in the
Slavonic MSS. : the text, here and in the later passage (11),
mentions no name and speaks of " the savage."

[d] Lit. " enticed."

[e] I have not found any parallel use of ὁ ὕψιστος in
Josephus : ἀρχιερεὺς θεοῦ ὑψίστου occurs in an edict of
Augustus, Ant. xvi. 163.

[f] Cf. Matt. iii. 5, " Then went out unto him (i.e. John)
Jerusalem and all Judaea and all the region round about
Jordan "; Mk. i. 5, " And there went out unto him all the
country of Judaea and all they of Jerusalem." [The sentence
—evidently a· Christian interpolation—is not to be found
in the Rumanian version of Josephus, Cod. Gaster No. 89.
R. E.]

set them free and subject all (the) insubordinate, but he himself would be subject to no one—(he) of whom we speak. Some mocked, but others put faith (in him).

And when he was brought to Archelaus *a* and the doctors of the Law had assembled, they asked him who he was and where he had been until then. And he answered and spake : " I am a man *b* and hither *c* the spirit of God hath called me, and I live on cane and roots and fruits of the tree.*d* " But when they threatened to torture him if he did not desist from these words and deeds, he spake nevertheless : " It is meet rather for *you* to desist from your shameful works and to submit to the Lord your God."

And Simon, of Essene extraction,*e* a scribe, arose in wrath and spake : " We read the divine books every day ; but thou, but now come forth from the wood like a wild beast, dost thou dare to teach us and to seduce the multitudes with thy cursed speeches ? " And he rushed (upon him) to rend his body. But he spake in reproach to them : " I will not disclose to you the secret that is among you,*f* because ye desired it not. Therefore has unspeakable misfortune come upon you and through your own doing." And after he had thus spoken, he went forth to the other side of the Jordan ; and since no man durst hinder him, he did what (he had done) before.

---

a Ethnarch, 4 B.C.–A.D. 6, a date much earlier than that assigned to John's ministry in the New Testament.

b For " a man " (Dr. Eisler would render " Enosh ") one MS. reads " pure."

c For " hither " other MSS. read " because."

d Slavonic " wood-shavings." Dr. Eisler adopts a suggestion of Wohleb that there has been a confusion in the *Greek* exemplar of the Slavonic between καρπῶν "fruits," and κάρφων (ξυλίνων) " shavings."

e Cf. Ἐσσαῖος . . . γένος, B.J. i. 78.

f [The secret of the βασιλεία ἐντὸς ὑμῶν, Luke xvii. 21. Cf. τὰ μυστήρια τῆς βασιλείας, Matt. xiii. 11. R. E.]

APPENDIX

(10) THE NOVICE'S OATH ON ADMISSION TO THE ESSENE ORDER

[This shows some enlargement on the Greek text in ii. 138 f. The additional matter and altered phraseology are printed in italics. After " his character is tested for two years " the Slavonic continues :—]

And if he is not suitable, they dismiss him from their community ; if he appears worthy, they enrol him in (their) society. And before *they enrol him, they bind him by tremendous oaths, and he standing before the doors,* pledges himself with tremendous oaths, *invoking the living God and calling to witness His almighty right hand* [a] *and the Spirit of God, the incomprehensible,* [b] *and the Seraphim and Cherubim, who have insight into all, and the whole heavenly host,* that he will be pious, etc.

(11) " THE WILD MAN " (JOHN), HEROD PHILIP'S DREAM AND THE SECOND MARRIAGE OF HERODIAS

[After ii. 168.]

Philip, during his government, saw a dream, to wit that an eagle plucked out both his eyes ; and he called all his wise men together. When some explained the dream in this manner and others in that, there came to him suddenly, without being called, that man of whom we have previously written,[c] that he went about in animals' hair and cleansed the people in the waters of the Jordan. And he spake : " Hear the word of the Lord—the dream that thou hast seen. The eagle is thy venality, for that bird is violent and rapacious. And this sin will take away thine eyes,

---

[a] *Cf.* (6) above. p. 642 n. *b.*
[b] *den nicht zu fassen den* (= perhaps ἀκατάληπτον).
[c] (9) above.

which are thy dominion and thy wife." [a] And when he had thus spoken, Philip expired before evening, and his dominion was given to Agrippa.[b]

And his wife [Herodias][c] was taken by Herod [d] his brother. Because of her all law-abiding people [e] abhorred him, but durst not accuse (him) to his face. But only this man, whom we called a savage, came to him in wrath and spake: " Forasmuch as thou hast taken thy brother's wife, thou transgressor of the law, even as thy brother has died a merciless death, so wilt thou too be cut off by the heavenly sickle. For the divine decree will not be silenced, but will destroy thee through evil afflictions in other lands ; [f] because thou dost not raise up seed unto thy brother, but gratifiest (thy) fleshly lusts and committest adultery, seeing

[a] [The Rumanian Josephus has another explanation of the dream : "The dream that thou hast seen, heralds thy death ; for the eagle is a bird of prey and has destroyed thine eyes." The object of the alteration is to avoid the stricture on Philip's venality, just as in *Ant.* xviii. 106 f., where Philip is called a mild and just ruler, the correction is intended to please his relative, Josephus's patron, Agrippa II. R. E.]

[b] Philip the Tetrarch died in A.D. 33-34, *Ant.* xviii. 106 ; Agrippa I was appointed king by Caligula on his accession some three years later (A.D. 37).

[c] According to Dr. Eisler a Christian gloss derived from the Gospel narrative (Mark vi. 17, Matt. xiv. 3). The first husband of Herodias was not Philip the tetrarch, as here represented, but a half-brother of Antipas, who is called by Josephus (*Ant.* xviii. 136) simply " Herod," though he may have borne the second name, Philip ; according to the same passage of *Ant.*, the second marriage of Herodias took place in the lifetime of her first husband. [The name Herodias is not found after the words " his wife " in the Rumanian Josephus or in the Hebrew or in the Arabic text of Josippon, although the story runs in all three versions exactly as in the Russian. R. E.]

[d] Herod Antipas.

[e] *Gesetzesleute.*

[f] Antipas was banished by Caligula to Lugdunum in Gaul in A.D. 39, *Ant.* xviii. 252, *cf. B.J.* ii. 183 (" to Spain ").

APPENDIX

that he has left four children." [a] But Herod, when he heard (that), was wroth and commanded that they should beat him and drive him out. But he incessantly accused Herod, wherever he found him, until he (Herod) grew furious, and gave orders to slay him.

Now his nature was marvellous and his ways not human. For even as a fleshless spirit, so lived he. His mouth knew no bread, nor even at the passover feast did he taste of unleavened bread, saying : " In remembrance of God, who redeemed the people from bondage, is (this) given to eat, and for the flight (only), since the journey was in haste." [b] But wine and strong drink he would not so much as allow to be brought nigh him ; and every beast he abhorred (for food) ; and every injustice he exposed ; and fruits of the trees [c] served him for (his) needs.

(12) The Ministry, Trial and Crucifixion of " The Wonder-worker " (Jesus)

[Between ii. 174 and 175.]

At that time there appeared a man, if it is permissible to call him a man.[d] His nature [and form] were [e] human, but his appearance (was something) more than (that) of a man ; [notwithstanding [f] his works were divine]. He worked miracles wonderful and mighty. [Therefore it is impossible for me to call him a man ;] but again, if I look

---

[a] *i.e.*, it was not a case of a Levirate marriage in accordance with the Law, Deut. xxv. 5 ff. The statement about these " four children " conflicts with *Ant.* xviii. 136 f., according to which Herodias by her first marriage had one daughter, Salome, and Philip the Tetrarch died childless.

[b] *Cf.* Ex. xii. 11 " ye shall eat it in haste."

[c] Slavonic " wood-shavings " ; see p. 645, note *d*.

[d] *Cf.* the opening of the disputed passage in *Ant.* xviii. 63 Γίνεται δὲ κατὰ τοῦτον τὸν χρόνον Ἰησοῦς σοφὸς ἀνήρ, εἴγε ἄνδρα αὐτὸν λέγειν χρή.

[e] The Russian has the singular ("was"), which suggests that the words "and form" are a later addition.

[f] Or " at least " (*doch*).

648

at the nature which he shared with all,[a] I will not call him an angel. And everything whatsoever he wrought through an invisible power, he wrought by word and command. Some said of him, " Our first lawgiver is risen from the dead [b] and hath performed [c] many healings and arts," while others thought that he was sent from God. Howbeit in many things he disobeyed the Law and kept not the Sabbath according to (our) fathers' customs. Yet, on the other hand, he did nothing shameful ; nor (did he do anything) with aid of hands,[d] but by word alone did he provide [e] everything.

And many of the multitude followed after him and hearkened to his teaching ; and many souls were in commotion, thinking that thereby the Jewish tribes might free themselves from Roman hands. Now it was his custom in general to sojourn over against the city upon the Mount of Olives ; [f] and there, too, he bestowed his healings upon the people.

And there assembled unto him of ministers[g] one hundred and fifty, and a multitude of the people. Now when they saw his power, that he accomplished whatsoever he would by (a) word,[h] and when they had made known to him their will, that he should enter into the city and cut down the Roman troops and Pilate and rule over us,[i] †the disdained us not†.[j]

---

[a] *die allgemeine Natur*, doubtless representing a Greek τὴν κοινὴν φύσιν : cf. *B.J.* iii. 369 τῆς κοινῆς ἀπάντων ζῴων φύσεως.

[b] *Cf.* Mark vi. 14 f., Luke ix. 7 f., where it is conjectured that Jesus may be " one of the old prophets " ; but the identification with Moses in this passage is unparalleled.

[c] *erwiesen.*

[d] Lit. " nor hand-acts."   [e] Or " prepare " (*bereitete*).

[f] The Galilaean ministry is ignored.

[g] [Russ. *sluga* = ὑπηρέται.   R. E.]

[h] *Cf.* the spurious epistle of Tiberius to Pilate, λόγῳ μόνῳ τὰς ἰάσεις ἐπετέλει, ed. M. R. James, *Texts and Studies*, v. p. 79.

[i] One Slavonic MS. has " them."

[j] Text doubtful : one MS. has " but he heeded not."

APPENDIX

And when thereafter knowledge of it came to the Jewish leaders, they assembled together with the high-priest and spake : " We are powerless and (too) weak *a* to withstand the Romans. Seeing, moreover, that the bow is bent, we will go and communicate to Pilate what we have heard, and we shall be clear of trouble, lest he hear (it) from others, and we be robbed of our substance and ourselves slaughtered and our children scattered." And they went and communicated (it) to Pilate. And he sent and had many of the multitude slain. And he had that Wonder-worker brought up, and after instituting an inquiry concerning him, he pronounced judgement : " He is [a benefactor, not] a malefactor, [nor] a rebel, [nor] covetous of kingship.*b* " [And he let him go ; for he had healed his dying wife.*c*]

[And he went to his wonted place and did his wonted works. And when more people again assembled round him, he glorified himself through his actions more than all. The teachers of the Law were overcome with envy, and gave thirty talents to Pilate,*d* in order that he should put him to death. And he took (it) and gave them liberty to execute their will themselves.] And they laid hands on him and crucified him †contrary† *e* to the law of (their) fathers.

---

a *Cf.* the use of ἀσθενής with inf. = " too weak " in *e.g.* Jos. *Ant.* x. 215, xiv. 317.

b [Russ. *czarizadeč*, an otherwise unknown word, probably a literal translation of φίλαρχος. R. E.]

c [This sentence is missing in the Rumanian version. The legend occurs first in the mediaeval *Vita beatae Mariae et Salvatoris rhytmica*, which quotes among its many sources Josephus—evidently an interpolated copy. R. E.]

d The bribery of Pilate is mentioned in the spurious epistle of Tiberius above mentioned (δῶρα ὑπὲρ τοῦ θανάτου αὐτοῦ ἔλαβες).

e [Russ. *čres*. Not the usual preposition employed by the translator in this sense. In I. § 209 he translates παρά in παρὰ τὸν Ἰουδαίων νόμον by *krome*. The Rumanian Josephus has the genuine reading " according to the law of the emperors." Josephus spoke of the *supplicium more maiorum* of the Romans. R. E.]

SLAVONIC "ADDITIONS"

(13) THE FOLLOWERS OF "THE WONDER-WORKER"
(THE EARLY CHRISTIANS)

[Replacing ii. 221 f. (= Herodian family history). The first paragraph below roughly corresponds to ii. 219 f., which is here presented in a condensed and altered form.]

But before the completion of the work he him-
self [a] died at Caesarea after reigning three years. *Since*
he had no son [b] Claudius again sent his officers to those
kingdoms, Cuspius Fadus and Tiberius Alexander, both
of whom kept the people in peace, by not allowing any
departure in anything from the pure laws.

Cf. ii. 219

Cf. ii. 220

But if anyone deviated from the word of the Law, information was laid before the teachers of the Law ; whereupon they punished and banished him or sent (him) to Caesar.

And since in the time of those (rulers) many followers of the Wonder-worker afore-mentioned had appeared and spoken to the people of their Master, (saying) that he was alive, although he was [c] dead, and " He will free you from your bondage," many of the multitude hearkened to the(ir) preaching and took heed to their injunctions—[not on account of their reputation] ; for they were of the humbler sort, some mere shoemakers, others sandal-makers, others artisans. [But wonderful were the signs [d] which they worked, in truth what they would.]

---

[a] Agrippa I.

[b] The Greek, in the parallel passage, has " He left issue . . . three daughters . . . and one son Agrippa. As the last was a minor," etc. This son, Agrippa II, was the close friend of Josephus, and the ignorance shown in the words italicized above is indeed surprising, if Josephus can be held to have written them. Berendts attaches these words to the preceding sentence, but the sense requires the division of sentences given above : *cf.* the Greek. [It is possible that " grown-up," " of age " ($\check{\epsilon}\phi\eta\beta\sigma$ or the like) has dropped out. R. E.]

[c] Perhaps " had been."

[d] *Cf.* the N.T. use of $\sigma\eta\mu\epsilon\hat{\imath}\alpha$ for " miracles."

651

APPENDIX

But when these noble procurators saw the falling away
of the people, they determined, together with the scribes,
to seize (them) [and put (them) to death], for fear lest
the little might (not) be little, if it ended in the great.
[But they shrank back and were in terror at the signs,[a]
saying, " Not through medicines [b] do such wonders come
to pass; but if they do not proceed from the counsel of
God, then will they quickly be exposed." [c]   And they gave
them liberty to go where they would.[d]   But afterwards,
being prevailed on (?) [e] by them], they sent them away,
some to Caesar, others to Antioch to be tried, others (they
exiled) to distant lands.

Cf. ii. 223 (But Claudius removed the two officers (and) sent
Cumanus, etc.)

(14) Speech of Josephus to his Galilaean Troops

[The first paragraph, on the training of the troops, and the
second, being the first portion of the speech, correspond
roughly to ii. 576-582, but are sufficiently different to bear
quotation.   The remainder of the speech has no parallel in
the Greek.   The speech, as is usual in the Slavonic version,
is in *oratio recta*.]

And he collected forces, a hundred thousand young men,
armed them, and taught them the art of war, knowing that
the Roman army was victorious not through weapons
only, but rather through discipline and incessant training.
And he set over them captains of ten and of hundreds and
of thousands, and over these *a commander-in-chief*.[f]   And

---

[a] *i.e.*, miracles.
[b] [Russ. *otrawlenijemi* = διὰ φαρμακείας. R. E.]
[c] *Cf.* the words of Gamaliel in Acts v. 38 f.
[d] Or " to do as they would."   [e] *veranlasst* (?).
[f] In the Greek " over these, generals in command of
more extensive divisions." [Josephus betrayed by the use
of this word—which is altered in the later Greek text—that
he himself was *not* the commander-in-chief of the Galilean
forces, but only some kind of commissary of the Galilean
revolutionary synhedrion accompanying the troops. R. E.]
652

he taught them the trumpet-call and the advance and the retreat and how to reinforce a defeated division, and fortitude of soul, to endure wounds and not to fear death.

And he said to them, " If you thirst for victory, renounce the usual malpractices, theft and robbery and rapine. And do not defraud your kinsmen ; regard it not as an advantage to injure others. For war can be better conducted, if the warriors have a good conscience [a] and their souls are aware that they have kept themselves pure from every crime. (But) if they are condemned by their evil deeds, then will God be their enemy, and the foreigners (will) have an easy victory.

" [b] But do you have regard for one another. Put away wrath (and) anger.[c] But if any of those in lower station misconducts himself,[d] do not be quickly provoked against them, nor resort to blows, but let them stand with meekness before the officers, correct some of (their faults) and forgive the rest.[e] But if (your) subordinates do aught amiss, refrain from punishment with the hand : punish with a threatening tongue. Castigation by bitter words is enough for the knave. If, on the other hand, you look into everything and inflict corresponding penalties, either, not tolerating the blows, they will desert to your enemies and become an addition to their strength and (another) enemy for you, or they will grow inured to the blows and

---

[a] = Slav. *s'wĕstj*, conj. Berendts : мss. *wĕstj* = " name."

[b] Here begins the new matter.

[c] This, together with the context before and after, has a superficial resemblance to S. Paul's Epistle to the Ephesians iv. 26-32, " Be ye angry and sin not. . . . Let him that stole steal no more. . . . *Let all . . . wrath and anger . . . be put away . . .* and be ye kind one to another, tenderhearted, forgiving each other." [But " be ye angry and sin not " comes from Ps. iv. 4 and the numerous rabbinical parallels collected by Strack-Billerbeck, *Komm. z. N.T. aus Talm. u. Midr.* vol. iii. (Munich, 1926), pp. 602 ff., show that Josephus uses the commonplaces of moralizing rhetoric. R. E.]   [d] *sich verfehlt.*

[e] *weiset das eine zurecht, das andere aber vergebet.*

APPENDIX

careless of your affairs, doing (yet) more wrong and injury."

(15) THE TRICK BY WHICH JOSEPHUS SAVED HIS LIFE AT JOTAPATA

[In place of iii. 387-391 we read :]

And he, commending his salvation to God the Protector,[a] said, " Since it is well pleasing to God that we should die, let us be killed in turn.[b] Let him whose turn comes last [c] be killed by the second." And when he had thus spoken, *he counted the numbers with cunning, and thereby misled them all.[d]* And they were all killed, one by another, except one ; and, anxious not to stain his right hand with the blood of a fellow-countryman, he besought this one, and they both went out alive.

(16) AN ABOMINATION (OF DESOLATION) IN THE HOLY PLACE

[Added at the end of iv. 157—the passage describing the scandalous election by lot of a high-priest]

(But all (the) priests, when they beheld from a distance how the divine Law was dishonoured, wept and bitterly groaned, because they [e] had degraded [f] and trodden under

[a] *dem Versorger* = Gr. τῷ κηδεμόνι.

[b] *der Reihe nach.*

[c] *Auf welchen das Ende der Reihe fallen wird, i.e.* apparently he who draws the lowest numbered lot, though the lots are not here mentioned.

[d] The Greek has " He, however (*should one say by fortune, or by the providence of God ?*) was left alone with one other."

[e] The Zealots.

[f] *vernichtet* : the Greek has the phrase τὴν τῶν ἱερῶν τιμῶν κατάλυσιν.

foot the priestly consecration) and had set at naught the covenant of God, and because every pernicious and shameful deed had grown up[a] among them. And (they thought that) the desolation of the city would ensue and prophecy would cease, if abomination were to be found in the holy place.[b]

(17) The Words of the Zealots over the Bodies of Ananus and Jesus

[Replacing iv. 316, which runs in the Greek text, " And, standing over their dead bodies, they scoffed at Ananus for his patronage of the people, and at Jesus for the address which he had delivered from the wall."]

And, standing over their dead bodies, they insulted them, saying over Ananus, " In truth thou art a friend of Jerusalem and art worthy of the honour with which thou art honoured." And over Jesus they said, " Very eloquent art thou and wise, and much trouble didst thou give thyself, when speaking from the battlements. But now rest ! " [c]

(18) The Zealots disregarded the Warnings of Scripture and the Lessons of History

[Replacing and amplifying iv. 407.]

So also (was it) in Jerusalem. Because the metropolis was beset with riot and robbers, therefore also did the(se)

---

[a] *herangereift* = " come to maturity."
[b] These last words seem to betray the influence on the Russian translator of the familiar passage Matt. xxiv. 15, " when ye see the abomination of desolation . . . standing *in the holy place* " (both Greek texts of Dan. ix. 27 have ἐπὶ τὸ ἱερόν). But the references to the " covenant " and the cessation of prophecy come directly from Daniel (ix. 27 " make a firm covenant," 24 " seal up . . . prophecy ").
[c] For a short speech in *oratio recta* in similar circumstances *cf.* the Greek text of iv. 343 (slightly amplified in the Slavonic).

miscreants, who had found a favourable opportunity for their lust, fulfil their will and follow evil ways,[a] recognizing neither the Law of God, nor David's instruction [b] nor Solomon's,[c] nor the threatenings of the prophets, nor the words of the holy men who in word and writing have pronounced glory and praise for the virtuous, but for the reprobate ignominy and disgrace and pain, in order that those who give ear to them may be zealous and uplifted to what is good, but may abhor the wicked and turn away their face from their works. But these men have cast the instructions of those (saints) behind them as a heavy burden, they have walked after the pleasure of their heart, not calling to mind what they [d] have endured, neither Nebuchadnez(z)ar (and) the captivity, nor what Antiochus laid upon them, nor yet the bondage in Egypt, nor yet the divine deliverance.

(19) Ruse of Vitellius at the Battle of Bedriacum [e]

[After iv. 547.]

Cf. iv. 547   (On the first day Otho was victor, but on the second Vitellius.) For he had during the night strewn (the ground with) three-pronged irons.[f] And in the morning after they had drawn up in order of battle, when Vitellius feigned flight, Otho pursued after them with his troops. And they reached the place on which the irons were strewn. Then were the horses lamed, and it was impossible

  [a] *gingen auf unredlichen Wegen* = " went on foul ways " : the Greek has εἰς τὴν ἐρημίαν ἀφίσταντο " made off into the wilderness."   [b] In the Psalms.
  [c] In Proverbs.   [d] *i.e.*, their nation.
  [e] None of the classical authors who describe the battle— Dio Cassius, Plutarch, Suetonius, Tacitus—mentions this incident. Vitellius himself was not on the scene : his generals were in command.
  [f] *dreigehörnte Eisen.* [The ⋆-shaped contrivance commonly called "caltraps" is meant. It was still used in the last war for similar purposes. R. E.]

either for the horses or for the men to extricate themselves.
And the soldiers of Vitellius, who had turned back, slew
all who lay (there). (But Otho saw what had befallen *Cf.* iv. 548
(and) killed himself.)

(20) THE INSCRIPTION IN THE TEMPLE CONCERNING JESUS

[Inserted in v. 195, after the mention of the *stelae* warning
foreigners not to pass the barrier to the inner court.]

(And in it [a] there stood equal [b] pillars [c] and upon them *Cf.* v. 194
titles in Greek and Latin and Jewish [d] characters, giving
warning of the law of purification, (to wit) that no foreigner
should enter within ; for it [e] was called the inner sanctuary, *Cf.* v. 195
being approached by fourteen steps and the upper area
being built in quadrangular form.)

And above these titles was hung a fourth title in the
same characters, announcing that Jesus (the) king did not
reign, (but was) crucified [by the Jews], because he pro-
phesied the destruction of the city and the devastation
of the temple.

(21) THE RENT VEIL OF THE TEMPLE AND THE RESURRECTION

[After v. 214. Clearly a Christian interpolation, or, in
Dr. Eisler's opinion, two distinct interpolations, the first and
last paragraphs, printed in italics, being the work of an
earlier hand, the middle paragraph—which is not found in

[a] *i.e.*, the stone balustrade.
[b] The Greek text has ἐξ ἴσου διαστήματος " at equal
intervals."
[c] [Russ. *stolpi*. He means square pillars, built of rect-
angular blocks with the inscription inscribed on the front
side of the stones. One of them was found by Clermont-
Ganneau and is now in the Tschinili Kiosk Museum in
Constantinople. R. E.]
[d] The Gr. text does not contain the words " and Jewish."
[e] The inner portion.

APPENDIX

the Rumanian version, Cod. Gaster No. 89—that of a much later hand.   See Dr. Eisler's forthcoming work, *The Messiah Jesus*.]

This curtain [a] was before this generation entire, because the people were pious ; but now it was grievous to see, for it was suddenly rent from the top to the bottom,[b] when they through bribery delivered to death the benefactor of men and him who from his actions was no man.

And of many other fearful signs might one tell, which happened then.[c]   And it is said that he, after being killed and after being laid in the grave, was not found.   Some indeed profess that he had risen, others that he was stolen away by his friends.[d]   But for my part I know not which speak more correctly.   For one that is dead cannot rise of himself, though he may do so with the help of the prayer of another righteous man, unless he be an angel or another of the heavenly powers, or (unless) God himself appears as a man and accomplishes what he will, and walks with men and falls and lies down and rises again, as pleases his will.   But others said that it was not possible to steal him away, because they set watchmen around his tomb,[e] thirty Romans and a thousand Jews.[f]

SUCH (*IS THE STORY TOLD*) OF THAT CURTAIN.   *There are also (objections) against this reason for its rending.*

(22) INTERPRETATIONS OF THE ORACLE OF THE WORLD-RULER

[Replacing vi. 313.]

Some understood that this meant Herod,[g] others the crucified Wonder-worker Jesus, others again Vespasian.

[a] *Katapetasma.*   [b] Matt. xxvii. 51, Mark xv. 38.
[c] Matt. xxvii. 51 ff.   [d] Matt. xxvii. 64, xxviii. 13-15.
[e] Matt xxvii. 64 ff.
[f] These numbers come from some apocryphal source.   In the spurious *Acts of Pilate* Pilate assigns 500 soldiers to the Jews to watch the tomb (Tischendorf, *Evangelia Apocrypha*, 1853, pp. 293 f.).   [g] *Cf.* passage (2) above.

OMISSIONS IN THE SLAVONIC VERSION
(BOOKS I-IV)

The following complete sections have no equivalent in the Slavonic. The deficiency in some cases may be due to the translator, who curtailed a text which he failed to understand. But some instances, discussed in detail in Dr. Eisler's book, suggest that he may have had before him a Greek exemplar shorter than the printed text. The list (which is confined to the four books for which a translation of the Slavonic is available) may therefore have its use.

Book I.—§§ 1-30 (Proem), 115, 164-168 (in part), 178, 179 (περὶ ὧν . . . λέγειν) and 180, 182 (ending περὶ ὧν . . . ἐροῦμεν), 189-194, 223 (mid.)-224, 228, 231 f., 238 (mid.)-240, 256-260, 272, 274-276, 280 and 281 (part), 305-309, 334, 362 (most)-369 (for substitute see above, p. 636), 375, 386, 403 (end)-407 (part), 408 (end)-414 (mid.), 420 (end)-421, 576 f., 603-605 (for substitute see p. 639), 641-644.

Book II.—§§ 15-19, 21, 40-66, 178-180, 182, 213, 217, 221 f., 233, 242, 257, 260, 268, 271-283, 323, 354, 366 (end)-367, 376-378, 386 (end)-387, 388 (end)-389, 407, 410 (mid.)-412 (mid.), 423 and 424 (part), 428 (end)-429, 431-434, 439 (mid.)-450 (mid.), 465 (end)-478, 513 (end)-514, 519 (end)-521, 531 (end)-532, 536, 542, 556 (mid.)-557, 558 (end)-562, 564 f:, 571 f., 573 (mid.)-575, 588 (mid.)-589, 603, 622-625, 629-631, 645 (end)-646, 650, 652 f. (most).

Book III.—§§ 17 (mid.)-19 (mid.), 21 f., 44 (45-71 lacuna in Slavonic ms.), 87 f., 114, 117, 125, 127, 140, 146-148 (mid.), 149, 152 (mid.)-153, 156, 159 f., 164, 168, 177, 179 f., 182-185, 190-192, 195 f., 198, 217 f., 226, 237-239

659

APPENDIX

(mid.), 244-245 (mid.), 247-248 (mid.), 250, 258-270, most of 272-283, 296 f., most of 299-304, 306, 311, 316, most of 330-332, 380, 395-397, 413, 415, 418-421, most of 423-426, 429-431, 440, 442, 444, 460, 464 f., 467, 479 f., 489, 514, 521, most of 522-531.

Book IV.—§§ 54-62, 82, 86, 100, 105, most of 107-111, 119, 129, 150-152, 161, 179-180 (mid.), 184 f., 188, 194-199, 200 (end)-201, 209-213, 222 f., 237, 263 f., 266, most of 274-281, 291-298 (mid.), 302-304, 307 f., 310 f., 328-330, 347, 349-352, 354-356, 363 f., 374, 392, 401, 424, 426-427 (mid.), 430, 432, 466, 475, 485, 496, 507-508 (mid.), 519, 549, 554, 558, 609-615, 621, 627, 630 f.

INDEXES TO
THE JEWISH WARS

INDEXES TO VOLS. II AND III

INDEX I. GENERAL

For the body of the work references are to the books of the *Jewish War* (Roman figures); and to the sections shown in the left margin of the Greek text and in the headline of the English text (Arabic figures); for the Introduction and Appendix reference is made to the pages.

GENERAL INDEX

225, 242-247; makes Herod king of the Jews, 281-285; near Athens, 309; besieges Samosata, 321 f.; in Egypt, 327; enslaved by Cleopatra, 359 ff.; defeated at Actium, 386; his death, 396; urged by Cleopatra to kill Herod, vii. 301

Anuath Borceaus, iii. 51

Apamea, i. 216, 218 f., 362; ii. 479

Apellaeus, month of, iv. 654

Apheku, tower of, ii. 513

Aphthia, iv. 155

Apionem, Contra, Introd. xv, xix, xxvii

Apollonia, i. 166

Aqueduct, Pilate's, ii. 175

Arabia, i. 6, 89, 267, 274, 276, 286; iii. 47; v. 160

Arabia Felix, ii. 385

Arabs, Herod's war against, i. 365-385, 388; as Roman mercenaries, ii. 69 f., 76; Arab archers at Jotapata, iii. 168, 211, 262; their cruelty and avarice, v. 551, 556; *et passim*

Aramaic edition of the *Jewish War*, Introd. ix-xi; i. 3 n.

Arbela, i. 305

Archelaus, king of Cappadocia, i. 446 f., 456, 499-512, 513, 516-518, 523, 530, 538, 559, 561; ii. 114

Archelaus, son of Herod by Malthace, Introd. xxiii; i. 562; educated at Rome, 602; as Herod's heir, i. 646, 664, 668 ff.; his accession, ii. 1 ff.; claims confirmation of title in Rome, 14 ff.; accused by Antipater, 26; defended by Nicolas, 34; made ethnarch, 94; deposed, 111 ff.; App. 640, 645

Archelaus, son of Magaddatus, a deserter, vi. 229-231

Archives and Archive office, burnt, ii. 427; vi. 354

Aretas (III), king of Arabia and Coele-Syria, i. 103; befriends Hyrcanus II and is defeated by Aristobulus, i. 124-131; attacked by Scaurus, 159

Aretas (IV), king of Arabia, i. 574; ii. 66

Arethusa, i. 156

Argarizin, i. 63

Aristeus, of Emmaus, v. 532

Aristobulus I, son of Hyrcanus, i. 64, 65; first Jewish post-exilic king, 70; murders Antigonus, 72-77; his illness and death, 81-84

Aristobulus II, son of Alexandra, i. 109, 114; revolt of, 117; fights Hyrcanus, 120; becomes king, 122; plot against, 124-127; appeals to Pompey, 132; war with Pompey, 133-154; taken prisoner to Rome, 157; escapes from Rome, 171; sent back by army of Gabinius, 172; sent back to Rome, 173; set at liberty by Caesar, 183; his death, 184; v. 396, 398; vii. 171

Aristobulus=Jonathan, brother of Mariamme, murdered by Herod, i. 437 n.

Aristobulus, son of Herod by Mariamme, his education and marriage, i. 445 ff.; his prolonged quarrel with his father, i. 445 ff., 467, 478, 496, 516, 519, etc.; put to death, 551; App. 639; his family, i. 552, 557, 565; ii. 222

Aristobulus, son of preceding, brother of Agrippa I, i. 552; ii. 221

Aristobulus, son of Herod, king of Chalcis, ii. 221; made king of lesser Armenia, 252; vii. 226 (?)

Arius, Roman centurion, ii. 63, 71

Ark, recovery of, from Philistines, v. 384

Armenia, i. 116, 127; vii. 18, 248; greater Armenia, ii. 222; lesser Armenia, ii. 252

Arous, Samaritan village, ii. 69

Arpha, iii. 57

Artabazes, son of Tigranes, i. 363

Artemisius, month of, ii. 284, 315; iii. 142; v. 302, 466; vi. 296

Artorius, vi. 188

Asamon, ii. 511

Asamonaeus, i. 36. See Hasmonaeans

Ascalon, i. 185, 187, 422; ii. 98, 460, 477; attacked by the Jews, iii. 9, 12, 23; iv. 663

Asochaeus (=Shishak), vi. 436

664

GENERAL INDEX

GENERAL INDEX

Cleitus, ii. 642 ff.

Cleopatra, mother of Ptolemy Lathyrus, i. 86

Cleopatra (Selene), daughter of Ptolemy Physcon, i. 116

Cleopatra, wife of Antony, i. 243; entertains Herod, 277; plots against Herod and covets Judaea, 359-363, 365, 367, 389-391, 440; her death, 396 f.; Herod's fear of, vii. 300 ff.

Cleopatra of Jerusalem, wife of Herod, i. 562

Clermont-Ganneau, M., v. 194; App. 657

Coele-Syria, i. 103, 155, 213, 225 n., 366

Colchians, ii. 366

Collega, Gn. Pompeius, vii. 58, 60

Commagene, v. 461; vii. 219, 224 f.

Commentaries, of Vespasian and Titus, Introd. xx - xxii, xxiv, xxvii; of Julius Caesar, Introd. xxi

Coponius, ii. 117

Coptus, iv. 608

Corbonas, the sacred treasure, ii. 175

Corcyra, vii. 72

Coreae (Corea), i. 134; iv. 449

Corinth, Isthmus of, iii. 540 n.

Corinthian bronze, gate of, v. 201

Corinthus, an Arab, i. 576 f.

Cos, i. 423, 532

Costobar, husband of Salome, i. 486

Costobar, relative of Agrippa II, ii. 418, 556

Crassus, governor of Syria, his death in Parthia, i. 179 f.

Cremona, iv. 634, 642

Crete, ii. 103

Crucifixion, of Jewish prisoners, v. 449 ff.; of Jesus, App. 650

Cumanus, procurator of Judaea, banished by Claudius, ii. 223-245

Cuthaeans, i. 63

Cydasa, iv. 104 f.

Cypros, mother of Herod the Great, i. 181

Cypros, wife of Agrippa I, ii. 220

Cypros, fortress of, i. 407, 417; ii. 484

Cyprus, i. 86 n.; ii. 108

Cyrene, vi. 114; sedition of *sicarii* in, vii. 437, 439

Cyrenians, ii. 381

Cyrus, i. 70 n.; v. 389; vi. 270

DABARITTHA, ii. 595

Dacians, ii. 369

Daesius, month of, iii. 282, 306, 315; iv. 449, 550

Dagon, god of Philistines, v. 384

Dagon, fortress near Jericho, i. 56

Dalaeus, vi. 280

Dalmatia, ii. 369 f.

Damascus, i. 103, 115, 127, 129, 131, 212, 236, 362, 398, 399, 422; massacre of Jews in, ii. 559 ff., vii. 368

Daniel, prophecy of, App. 637

Daphne, (1) near Antioch, i. 243, 328; (2) source of Jordan, iv. 3

Darius, son of Hystaspes, i. 476

Darius, cavalry commander, ii. 421

David, king, i. 61; v. 137, 143; vi. 439 f.

David, Psalter of, App. 656

Dead Sea. See Asphaltitis

Decapolis, iii. 446

Deinaeus, ii. 235

Dellius, i. 290

Delta, of Nile, i. 191

Delta, a quarter of Alexandria, ii. 495

Demetrius I, i. 38 n.

Demetrius III, surnamed the Unready, i. 92-95, 99

Demetrius, commander of Gamala, i. 105

Demetrius of Gadara, freedman of Pompey, i. 155

Demosthenes, Introd. xvi, xviii

Destiny or Fate personified (τὸ χρεών), i. 233, 275; v. 355, 514, 572; vi. 49, 314. See also Fate

Dicaearchia (Puteoli), ii. 104

Didius, i. 392

Diogenes, put to death by Pharisees, i. 113

Dion Cassius, Introd. xxvii

Diophantus, i. 529

Diospolis, i. (132†), 366

Dium, i. 132

Dius, month of, ii. 555

Dolesus, iv. 416

Domitian, iv. 646, 649; acting ruler, 654; marches against the Ger-

667

GENERAL INDEX

GENERAL INDEX

GENERAL INDEX

Jotape, ii. 221

Juba, king of Libya, ii. 115

Jucundus, two cavalry commanders named, (1) i. 527 ; (2) ii. 291

Jucundus, Aemilius, ii. 544

Judaea, i. 22, 32, 37, 41, 49, 51, 61, 98, 103, 105, 127, 129, 134, 138, 157, 160, 174, 180, 183, 199, 201, 225, 231, 240, 249, 288, 291, 309, 323, 362, 364 f., 371, 445, 499, 513, 604, 606, 659, 660 ; ii. 16, 43, 65, 85, 90, 96, 116, 169, 184, 186, 202, 247, 252, 265 ; iii. 1 ; description of, 48-58, 143, 409 ; iv. 406-409, 473, 545, 550, 657 ; v. 41 ; vi. 7, 238 ; vii. 163, 252 f.

Judas Maccabaeus, i. 37 ; makes alliance with Romans, 38 ; recovers the temple, 39 ; in the battle of the elephants, 41 f. ; defeat of, 45 ; his death, 47

Judas, of Galilee, founder of the Zealots, ii. 118, 433 ; vii. 253

Judas (or Judes), son of Ari, Zealot, vi. 92 ; vii. 215

Judas, son of Ezechias, brigand, ii. 56

Judas, son of Jonathan, ii. 451, 628

Judas, son of Merton, vi. 92

Judas, son of Sepphoraeus, i. 648 ; App. 642 f.

Judas, the Essene, prophesies murder of Antigonus, i. 78 ff.

Judes, son of Chelcias, v. 6

Judes, son of Judes (or of Judas), v. 534

Judes, son of Mareotes, vi. 148 (perh. = Judas son of Merton, above)

Julia, daughter of Augustus, ii. 25, 168 n.

Julia, wife of Augustus, ii. 167 f. [= Livia, i. 566, 641]

Julianus, Marcus Antonius, procurator of Judaea, vi. 238

Julianus, a centurion, vi. 81-91

Julias (Bethsaida, on Lake of Gennesareth), ii. 168 ; iii. 57, 515 ; iv. 454

Julias (Betharamatha, or Livias, in Peraea), ii. 168, 252 ; iv. 438

Jupiter Capitolinus, temple of, vii. 153

Justus, of Tiberias, Introd. xx f., xxvii

KEDASA, ii. 459 ; perh. = Cydasa, iv. 104

Kedron, v. 70, 147, 252, 254, 303, 504 ; vi. 192

LABERIUS MAXIMUS, vii. 216

Lacedaemon, vii. 240 ; Lacedaemonians, i. 425, 513 ; ii. 359 (381)

lanistae, App. 640 n.

Laodicea, i. 231, 422

Laqueur, R., Introd. vii, x, xxii, xxvi, xxix, xxxi

Lathyrus. See Ptolemy

Latins, invective against, App. 639 f.

Law of Moses, App. 643 ; the way of the Law, App. 644

Lawgiver, the first, App. 649

Lazarus, v. 567

Lebanon (Libanus), i. 185, 188, 329 ; iii. 57 ; v. 36

Leeches, Solomon's, App. 641

Lepidus, Larcius, vi. 237

Leuce, cliff, vii. 305

Levi, father of John of Gischala, ii. 575, 585 ; iv. 85

Levi, attendant of Josephus, ii. 642

Levi, priest, App. 638

Levias, iv. 141

Libanus, Mt. See Lebanon

Liberalius, centurion, vi. 262

Libya, ii. 115 f., 363, 494 ; iii. 107 ; iv. 608 ; vii. 439

Lictor's fasces, ii. 365 n.

Life, the, or *Vita*, Introd. xix ff., xxvi. See Julia

Livia, the Empress, i. 566, 641. See Julia

Lollius, i. 127

Longinus, tribune, ii. 544

Longinus, Roman trooper, v. 312

Longus, his gallantry, vi. 186 f.

Lous, the month of, ii. 430 ; vi. 220, 250, 374

Lot, App. 642 n.

Lucian, Introd. xvi n.

Lucius, Roman soldier, vi. 188 f.

Lucullus, i. 116

Lugdunum, App. 647 n.

Lupus, governor of Egypt, vii. 420 f., 433 f.

675

GENERAL INDEX

GENERAL INDEX

GENERAL INDEX

679

GENERAL INDEX

GENERAL INDEX

GENERAL INDEX

683

GENERAL INDEX

INDEX II. BIBLICAL PASSAGES

QUOTED IN THE NOTES

References are to Books and Sections; and to pages of the Appendix.

INDEX OF BIBLICAL PASSAGES